THE MAINSTREAM OF
CIVILIZATION

Fifth Edition SINCE 1660

Stanley Chodorow
University of California, San Diego

MacGregor Knox
University of Rochester

Conrad Schirokauer
The City College of The City University of New York

Joseph R. Strayer

Hans W. Gatzke

THE MAINSTREAM OF
CIVILIZATION

SINCE 1660

Fifth Edition

HBJ **Harcourt Brace Jovanovich, Publishers**
San Diego   New York   Chicago   Austin   Washington, D.C.
London   Sydney   Tokyo   Toronto

The Mainstream of Civilization   Since 1660
Fifth Edition

ISBN: 0-15-551581-0

Library of Congress Catalog Card Number: 88-82140

Printed in the United States of America

Preface

Writing a history of civilization is an almost foolhardy enterprise. But it is easier to do if you have done it before, as the authors of the first four editions of this history, Joseph R. Strayer and Hans W. Gatzke, noted dryly in their preface to the previous edition. We, their successors, had not done it before. But we did have the robust framework that the original authors left to us. We have done our best to preserve that framework while adding, in our rewriting, many things of our own.

Following the "mainstream of civilization" requires a gradual shift of geographic focus from the Mediterranean to Europe, and ultimately to the entire globe. It demands descriptions of the major civilizations east and south of Europe, from Byzantium and Islam to India, China, and Japan. And as the mainstream flows toward the present, the need to understand that present dictates an ever more detailed analysis and narrative. We have sought in that narrative to combine clarity with at least some of the complexity revealed in the historical evidence. We have attempted to convey to readers the texture and flavor of past civilizations and the astonishing variety of human possibilities and accomplishments. We have emphasized the interrelationships of all spheres of life, from politics and warfare to economics, art, scholarship, and religion. We have suggested at least some of the differing ways in which contemporaries and historians have understood the past. Above all, we have tried to explain that past, to explain historical change. Why and how have states, institutions, and ideas risen, flourished, and crumbled into dust? Why did events happen as they did, and not otherwise?

Writing history is a contentious business. That is one of its attractions. As our narrative moves toward the present it inevitably touches on issues that arouse passionate debate, and not only among historians. We have tried to address those issues honestly, as we see them. We hope and trust that what we have written will provoke readers to further exploration, discussion, and—yes—even debate. The human past is too intriguing and too weighted with consequences for the present to leave exclusively to academic professionals. It is and should be the common property of all literate individuals.

This book inevitably draws heavily upon the publications, contributions, and advice of other scholars. Our format precludes detailed references to our sources, but we have sought wherever possible to hint at our major debts in the "suggestions for further reading" that follow each chapter. We owe special thanks to Conrad Schirokauer, City College of the City University of New York, for his contribution of Chapters 6 and 15. For their perceptive comments and criticisms, we thank

Stanley Engerman, University of Rochester; Benton H. Fatherree, Hinds Junior College, Raymond Campus; William B. Hauser, University of Rochester; Tina Isaacs; Brenda Meehan-Waters, University of Rochester; Williamson Murray, Ohio State University; Thomas X. F. Noble, University of Virginia, Charlottesville; David S. Sefton, Eastern Kentucky University; Robert Westbrook, University of Rochester; Mary Young, University of Rochester; and Perez Zagorin, University of Rochester. All have helped to make this book better, but they bear no responsibility for sins of omission or commission and errors of fact or judgment, which belong to the authors alone.

Finally, we owe a very great debt to the late Hans W. Gatzke. Despite the increasingly debilitating effects of a tragic illness, he oversaw with tact and consideration the transition from one "team" of authors to the next. He set an ambitious goal for the new team: a major revision and recasting of the book. He shaped the plan for that revision, and suggested a number of the new themes that we have attempted to emphasize. He read many of the rewritten chapters with warm encouragement and a critical eye. To his memory, and to that of the late Joseph R. Strayer, we thankfully dedicate this fifth edition.

Stanley Chodorow / MacGregor Knox

A Note on the Paperbound Editions

*T*his volume is one of a number of variant printings of the Fifth Edition of *The Mainstream of Civilization.* It is not a revised or condensed text. Many users of the Fourth Edition found the various paperbound versions of that edition useful because the variant printings made it possible for them to fit the text into their own patterns of teaching and scheduling. In the Fifth Edition, the publishers have continued the practice of preparing separate paperbound volumes. Users may choose the volume that best corresponds to the chronological period covered by their courses. The variants are:

1. A two-volume edition

    The first volume, *To 1715* (Chapters 1 through 21), starts with the beginnings of Western civilization in the ancient Middle East and continues to the end of the Middle Ages. The second volume, *Since 1660* (Chapters 20 through 36), begins with the seventeenth century and carries the account forward to the present day.

2. A two-volume edition

    The first volume, *To 1500* (Chapters 1 through 15), starts with the beginnings of Western civilization in the ancient Middle East and continues to the end of the Middle Ages. The second volume, *Since 1500* (Chapters 16 through 36), after a Prologue that summarizes events to the year 1500, begins with the Renaissance and carries the account forward to the present day.

In all the variant printings, the pagination, index (except for *To 1500*, which has its own index), illustrations, maps, and other related materials from the one-volume version are retained. The difference between the one-volume and the other versions of this book is a difference only in form.

Contents

List of Maps

Introduction

History as Foresight and Memory

History is the story of the human past. It is also the only available introduction to the human future. The first critically thinking historian, Thucydides the Athenian, implied as much in introducing his history of the great war between the two rival Greek cities of Athens and Sparta in the fifth century B.C. Thucydides addressed his history to those "who want to understand clearly the events which happened in the past and which (human nature being what it is) will, at some time or other and in much the same ways, be repeated in the future." He added that his book was "not a piece of writing designed to meet the taste of an immediate public, but was done to last for ever."

No modern historian would dare make the latter claim. "For ever" is a length of time beyond human grasp, and the mass-market tastes of the immediate public now have a weight that Thucydides the aristocrat would have roundly condemned. But Thucydides' book, the most penetrating historical work of the ancient world, has nevertheless survived for 2,400 years, and has probably enjoyed more readers in the last three centuries than in its entire previous existence. And Thucydides' perception that human affairs follow patterns visible to the trained eye has remained the fundamental argument for studying history.

The future is by definition unknowable and unpredictable; events are unique, and never repeat themselves precisely. But they often follow patterns. Individuals are unique, and are free to make their own history. That freedom gives the unfolding of history its element of suspense. But individuals also band together to create societies. Those societies have structures—languages, religions, intellectual traditions, artistic styles, and political, social, economic, and military institutions—that constrain individuals in the ways they can make history, that limit the range of thoughts and actions open to them. Those historical structures operate in consistent ways that the mind can analyze. Historical situations separated by centuries and continents have similarities, and sometimes develop according to a similar logic. Historical analogies—the comparison between one set of historical structures or events and another—are powerful if treacherous tools for probing future possibilities.

Historical analysis faces inevitable limitations. Evidence about the past is always incomplete. Politics, warfare, religion, philosophy, and art have left more traces than has everyday life. The leisured few loom far larger in the surviving sources than the experiences and aspirations of the sweat-soaked many. Men appear more frequently than women. Societies with writing have left far more behind them than those without. Twentieth century technology—aerial photography, radiocarbon dating, precise chemical analysis, meticulous archaeological technique—has disclosed much about voiceless societies and groups, and has broadened our knowledge even of societies that left extensive literatures. Textual analysis and source criticism—close scrutiny of the style, content, context, purposes, and reliability of surviving texts—have deepened our understanding of the written sources. The fragmentary nature of the evidence transmitted from the past nevertheless limits the historian's ability to see clearly and to draw valid conclusions. And in the nineteenth and twentieth centuries, the written record has swollen exponentially with the coming of mass literacy and the creation of immense bureaucracies. Too much evidence rather than too little is the affliction of the historian of the recent past.

Worse, the historian's own values inevitably color and sometimes drastically distort both the selection of evidence and the analysis of ideas and events. The past is the indispensable key to the present, but the present can also crush the past. Crusading religions and combative secular ideologies such as nationalism or Marxism-Leninism tend to alter history to fit preconceived dogma. Traumatic experiences such as wars, revolutions, or economic catastrophes tend to impel the historian to seek escape in a largely imaginary and far more pleasant past, or to rewrite the recent past as a one-way street leading with deterministic inevitability to the cataclysmic present. And historians, although their calling should lead them to take the long view, sometimes fall victim to passing fads. The historian's only defenses against ideological distortion and trendiness are the search for detachment and the passionate commitment to the verifiable evidence that has distinguished the best historical writing from Thucydides onward.

For history, if painstakingly and honestly written, offers to those who pursue it a sense of the probabilities, of the range of outcomes inherent in a given historical situation. Historical knowledge can teach us how the world works.

But it is also indispensable in a second way. History is memory. Historical knowledge is self-knowledge. It tells us how our world, our own society, and we as individuals got to where we are. Memory can give pleasure, but is also decisive in our lives. For the individual, memory is the essential component of identity. For society, the "collective memory" or knowledge of the society's past and shared values is equally indispensable. It is part of the glue that binds society together. When a society suffers collective amnesia, when it loses its historical consciousness, the values formed through that society's history inevitably erode. That decay undermines the society's political, social, and intellectual cohesion, and may threaten its survival.

In the empires, city-states, monarchies, and tribal polities of the past and in the single-party dictatorships of the present, religion, custom, political indoctrination, and force have usually sufficed to maintain cohesion. But our own civilization has over the last three centuries evolved a historically unique concept: laws that guarantee the rights of the ruled against the rulers, the rights of individuals against the state. Those laws have provided an unprecedented measure of freedom for individuals to worship as they please, to follow their economic interests, to pursue private happiness. The victories of rights against the state in the seventeenth and eighteenth centuries and of representative democratic government in the nineteenth century marked an immense leap forward in human freedom and economic dynamism. But that freedom has also carried with it the possibility that its heirs might one day lose it, through forgetfulness of the sacrifices and struggles that had secured it and through ignorance of its historical uniqueness and potential fragility. Historical knowledge can guard against that outcome as no other knowledge can.

History as the History of Civilization

If our present comes from our past, what is the shape of that past? The readers of this book, by the fact that they read the English language, are heirs to a tradition that stretches back to the first millennium B.C., to the Greeks on the one hand and to the Hebrew authors of the Old Testament on the other. That *civilization*—a term coined in the eighteenth century and derived from the Roman word for city, *civitas*—is the civilization of the West, the civilization of Europe.

Civilization above all means cities, a human institution less than 10,000 years old. Cities require a highly developed peasant agriculture to feed them, architects and laborers to erect them, artisans to people them, bureaucrats to organize and tax them, soldiers to defend them, rulers to rule them, and religious or communal myths and customs to engender loyalty to the existing order. Cities mean a degree of social stratification, of differences between the high and the low, unknown in the hunter-gatherer or cattle-herding nomad societies that preceded them. Cities mean *literacy, organization,* and *specialization* of work. And the degree of literacy, organization, and specialization affects the density of population a given civilization can support and the character and attainments of that civilization. The Greek city-states were capable of efforts and achievements far surpassing those of the Scythian nomads to the north and of the ramshackle Persian empire to the east.

Cities have meant the intensified development of religion, philosophy, technology, art, and literature. The great religions, from those of ancient Egypt and Mesopotamia through Hinduism and Buddhism to Christianity and Islam, were urban creations presiding over urban civilizations—even though Islam achieved its early successes through the swords of desert warrior nomads. Philosophy, the quest for the principles and realities underlying human knowledge and existence, was an offshoot of religion that first arose in the Greek cities and in the urban civilizations of China and India. Technological advance, from improvements in tools and weapons to the building of fortifications, roads, and aqueducts, was a precondition and consequence of the rise of cities. Highly developed art, from architecture and sculpture to ceramics and painting, has been the mark of urban civilizations. And writing, invented for the tax accounting of the bureaucrats and the records of the city priesthoods, eventually made possible the flowering of poetry, drama, history, and science.

Cities have meant common values that bind the inhabitants together, that induce them to accept the sacrifices—often without immediate or apparent compensating benefits—which specialization and organization impose. Those values can derive from a variety of sources. The great religions, the modern ideologies that claim to grasp the meaning and destination of history, the cult of the nation-state, and the sense of duty toward the community that is the "civic religion" of democracies have all provided the myths and values needed to sustain urban civilization. Those myths and values have in turn been related to the type of civilizaton they spring from and support.

Finally, cities have meant conflict as well as achievement. Hunter-gatherers and nomads raid their neighbors for booty, women, slaves, and cattle. All adult males are by definition warriors. But in urban civilizations, specialization of work extends to warfare, to the creation of hereditary warrior castes or of standing armies and navies that in time of war command the entire resources of the state. Urban civilizations, by virtue of literacy, organization, and specialization, are capable of a violence far more systematic and long-lasting than that of their predecessors. Externally, that violence has resulted in the formation of *state systems,* of highly competitive groups of rival states. In such systems, as the greatest of Greek philosophers, Plato, bitingly remarked, "What most people call peace . . . is just a name; in fact there is by nature an everlasting undeclared war of all against all." And even within the city walls, fierce conflicts between rival groups among the ruling few or between the few and the downtrodden many have frequently broken the peace.

The history of civilization must thus seek to analyze the gradual increase of literacy, organization, and specialization over the last three millennia. Such a history must be a political history, for politics is the key to understanding the nature, growth, and collapse of *states*—the large-scale political units whose character, success, or failure has been a matter of life or death for the inhabitants of all known civilizations. A history of civilization must be an economic and social history, for economic and social relationships shape politics, and are in turn shaped by politics. A history of civilization must be a history of art, literature, and ideas—for art, literature, and ideas define and reflect the systems of shared beliefs without which no civilization is possible. Above all, a history of civilization must seek to analyze the interconnections of politics, economics, and ideas that determine the character, development, and fate of civilizations.

And as seen from the late twentieth century, the history of human civilization as a whole centers on the history of the West, the history of Europe. For Europe's civilization, although at first merely one of the world's major traditions, spread outward after 1492 to dominate the entire globe. That outcome was nevertheless not foreordained, for Europe started late The earliest civilizations arose as early as 3,000 B.C. in the great river valleys of Egypt, Mesopotamia, India, and China. The first recognizably Western civilization only appeared after 1,000 B.C. in the Greek city-states of Greece, Asia Minor, southern Italy, and Sicily. The Greeks borrowed much from their predecessors to the east and south, including the alphabet they took from their Phoenician rivals. But the Greeks were unique. In the space of little more than three centuries—the sixth through fourth centuries B.C.—they invented the Western traditions of philosophical, historical, and scientific inquiry. They created the concept of individual freedom. They laid the foundations of Western literature. They made Western civilization self-conscious, inquiring, and *historical*. And in the fourth century B.C., the immense conquests of Alexander of Macedon, heir to a half-barbarian kingdom on Greece's northern border, spread Greek civilization—and Greek-ruled cities named Alexandria—from Egypt to the borders of India.

The successors of Alexander, the Romans, dominated the entire Mediterranean basin for five centuries. In art and literature they borrowed much from the Greeks. In law, statecraft, and military organization they were bold and ruthless innovators who solved brilliantly the problem that had perplexed the Greeks: how to create large-scale and long-lasting political units that ruled over citizens and noncitizens alike. The only contemporary civilization that rivalled the brilliance of Rome and the extent of Rome's power was China, which experienced a merciless unification in the same centuries as the Roman conquest of the Mediterranean.

Roman legions, Roman roads, Roman cities, and Roman laws civilized Europe as far east as the great river barriers of the Rhine and the Danube and as far north as the wild borders of Scotland. Rome provided the political order within which a new religion, which blended the Hebrew traditions of the Old Testament with the philosophical conceptions of the Greeks, could spread and prosper. In the fourth century A.D., that new religion, Christianity, became the official religion of the empire. By that point Rome was near collapse. Interrelated and mutually reinforcing pressures from within and without brought the empire down: bloody civil wars, brigandage and piracy, economic decay, plague epidemics, loss of intellectual self-confidence and social cohesion, and vastly increased barbarian pressure on the Rhine-Danube frontier.

In the fifth century A.D., Rome fell to waves of invaders, as the pitiless Huns on their shaggy steppe ponies drove the warlike Germanic tribes across Rome's crumbling borders. The western half of the empire collapsed. The unity of the Mediterranean basin was gone. A Greek-speaking remnant of the empire centered on Byzantium survived in the east for another thousand years, but had small influence on developments in the west. In the seventh and eighth centuries A.D., the Arabian tribes, under the green banner of their new religion, Islam, conquered the eastern Mediterranean and swept across northern Africa to Spain. Those conquests further divided Rome's inland sea—between the heirs of Greece, Rome, and Jerusalem and the heirs of the prophet Mohammed. The *ancient world*, the Greco-Roman civilization of the Mediterranean basin, had ceased to exist.

The new *medieval* civilization that eventually arose in western Europe after the eighth century was thus thrown back on its own resources. It saved only a fragment of its Roman inheritance, as Rome had been only a part of the ancient world. And the new rulers of western Europe, the Germanic peoples, had never been part of that world. They only gradually assimilated the fragments of Latin literature and Roman law that Rome had left behind. They were slow to blend with the Latin peoples they had conquered. They and their subjects were equally slow to absorb Christianity. But the fusion over some six centuries of those disparate ethnic and intellectual elements ultimately produced a distinctive European civilization.

Once its fundamental character was set, medieval Europe developed rapidly. It eagerly received lost Greek texts, decimal numbers, and algebra from its neighbors, the more highly developed Arabs and Byzantines. Many of its basic institutions and ideas, such as universities and representative assemblies, originated in the twelfth and thirteenth centuries. Its centers were in the north, in the triangle bounded by the formerly Roman cities of Paris [*Lutetia Parisiorum*], Cologne [*Colonia*] and London [*Londinium*], and in north Italian cities such as Florence, Bologna, and Padua. Its periphery, from Sicily, Spain, and Ireland to Scandinavia, Poland, and Bohemia, developed more slowly. And beyond that periphery Western influence almost ceased. Byzantium remained apart: Greek in language, despotic in politics, and Orthodox rather than Catholic in religion. Byzantium's influence dominated the southern and eastern Slavic peoples that had moved into eastern Europe as the Germanic peoples moved west. Byzantium likewise inspired the embryonic Russian state, until Mongol conquerors subjugated Moscow and Kiev in the thirteenth century and forced them to face eastward for more than 200 years.

South and east of Byzantium lay the civilizations of Islam, which began to close themselves to new ideas just as Europe was beginning its ascent. Still further east lay the great civilizations of India, China, and Japan. Each had characteristic values—religious in India, scholarly and bureaucratic in China, military and bureaucratic in Japan. All three had on occasion borrowed from their neighbors, but they nevertheless tended toward self-absorption and the perfection of existing modes of thought rather than the acquisition of new knowledge. India suffered Moslem conquest, constant wars, and crushing taxation. China after the sixteenth century showed little interest in exploration or seaborne trade. Japan, which had borrowed much from China, fiercely walled itself off after 1600. And after pioneering efforts—gunpowder, rockets, firearms, crucible steel, iron smelting with coke—none of the eastern civilizations developed a tradition of scientific inquiry and technological innovation rivaling that of the West.

By the fifteenth century, medieval Europe had begun to break out of its original mold, and out of its narrow and rain-sodden peninsula off the Eurasian landmass. Since the twelfth century, Europeans had shown an insatiable scholarly curiosity about distant lands, and a thirst for trade and booty. Europeans had given evidence of a precocious fascination with machinery—from clocks and windmills to ships and cannon—rarely seen to the south and east. European scholars had begun to lay the groundwork for the seventeenth-century scientific revolution that immeasurably increased humanity's mastery over nature, and transformed its view of its place in the universe.

In the last decade of the fifteenth century, Europeans leapt across the globe—the Spaniards to the New World in 1492 and the Portuguese around Africa to India in 1498. Europe's new seaborne empires—the empires of the *early modern* age of Western expansion—soon dominated the fringes of Africa and Asia, and conquered three newly discovered continents: North America, South America, and Australia.

Then came two further revolutions within Europe itself. The collapse of the French monarchy in 1788–89 opened 25 years of revolution and war that spread the democratic ideas of the French revolutionaries and the notion of nationalism—the political religion of the nation-state—eastward across Europe. Simultaneously, an industrial revolution that transformed humanity's power over nature and over its own existence began in Britain. Those twin revolutions—of mass politics and nationalism, and of engine-powered machines and economic freedoms—have been the driving forces of the *modern* era in which we still live. They transformed Europe and the world. For the first time in history, one civilization brought all others into increasingly direct contact with it, and forced its rivals to emulate it or go under.

Those rivals ultimately maintained or reasserted their independence—within the framework of the worldwide state system that Europe established—by adopting Western ideas and techniques. The world has not become one; mortal rivalries between states, religions, ideologies, and cultures continue to rend it. But for good or ill, a recognizably Western global civilization has taken shape, bound together by an accelerating revolution of science and technology, an ever-expanding world market, and a thickening web of mass communications. That is the present which a history of civilization must seek to explain.

THE MAINSTREAM OF
CIVILIZATION

Fifth Edition SINCE 1660

20
Absolutism and Constitutionalism, 1660–1715

*T*he last half of the seventeenth century was the age of France. Its population of roughly 18 million in 1650 dwarfed the 7.5 million of Spain and the roughly 5 million of England. Its economy and its bureaucratic-military machine were the largest in Europe, and much of Europe imitated its culture.

But French power had limits. Internally, high taxation, government regulation of the economy, religious persecution, and oppressive censorship stunted economic growth. Externally, Louis XIV's attempts to dominate western Europe welded together a series of coalitions against France. In the two great worldwide conflicts of 1689–97 and 1701–14, England, the Dutch United Provinces, and Habsburg Austria compelled even the magnificent "Sun King" of France to recognize the law of relations between states: the law of the balance of power.

Other powers declined with giddying rapidity, or stagnated. Sweden, outclassed militarily and demographically, ceased to be a great power. The Ottoman Turk state mounted its last great threat to western Europe, and then began the decline that by the late eighteenth century made it the "sick man" of the state system. The internal anarchy and external decline of Poland that led to its disappearance from the map between 1772 and 1795 became visible. Spain declined further. The Dutch reached their economic and demographic limits, and settled down to enjoy their riches.

Winners also emerged. The Habsburgs at last defeated the Turks for good, and consolidated their own hereditary possessions into a state more centralized than anything before it in south-central Europe. England took from the Dutch the mastery of the outer seas, as the Dutch had taken it from Portugal. Russia, a backward power until now outside the European system, suffered the first of the barbaric "revolutions from above" that ultimately made it a military giant. And the uncouth electorate of Brandenburg, a poor and obscure state on the eastern fringes of Germany, began its momentous rise to great power status.

Opposite: Louis XIV, by Hyacinthe Rigaud (1701).

559

THE FRANCE OF LOUIS XIV

Louis XIV, the "Sun King" (r. 1643–1715), was the living symbol of French military, political, and cultural domination. He was born in 1638 and took power decisively into his own hands the day after Mazarin's death in 1661. He died at the age of 77 and left the throne to his great-grandson. By temperament and training he incarnated divine-right monarchy—the notion that hereditary monarchy was the only divinely approved form of government, that kings answered to God alone for their conduct, and that subjects owed absolute obedience to their king as the direct representative of God on earth. His education was sketchy, and he had little imagination and no sense of humor. But he possessed the qualities indispensable for personal rule—willingness to work relentlessly, a commanding presence, and an imperious will.

Louis may not have said the famous words often ascribed to him—"I am the state." But he practiced them. He sought to personify the concept of sovereignty. He took a deep interest in the elaborate etiquette and ceremonial of his court, for it dramatized his supremacy over the nobility. He also conducted the business of the state in per-

The Sun King's emblem.

Bishop Bossuet on Absolutism

Jacques Bénigne Bossuet was tutor to Louis XIV's son in the 1670s, and the most zealous and prominent theorist of the king's absolutism.

The royal power is absolute. With the aim of making this truth hateful and insufferable, many writers have tried to confound absolute government and arbitrary government. But no two things could be more unlike. . . . The Prince need render an account of his acts to no one. . . . Without this absolute authority the king could neither do good nor repress evil. . . . God is infinite, God is all. The prince, as prince, is not regarded as a private person: he is a public personage, all the state is in him; the will of all the people is included in his. As all perfection and all strength are united in God, so all the power of individuals is united in the person of the prince. What grandeur that a single man should embody so much! . . .

From Jacques Bénigne Bossuet, "Politics Drawn from the Very Words of Scripture," in *Readings in European History*, ed. by James Harvey Robinson (Boston: Ginn, 1906), Vol. II, pp. 275–76.

son, as his own "first minister," from Mazarin's death in 1661 to his own in 1715. That required a dedication uncommon in monarchs, but Louis XIV set his preferred pastimes of hunting and womanizing aside when the state demanded it. "If you let yourself be carried away by your passions," he once remarked, "don't do it in business hours."

The administrative machine that served Louis XIV culminated in a three to five member "High Council" (*Conseil d'en Haut*) of great ministers that met almost daily under the king. Professional "secretaries" at the head of bureaucracies then executed the decisions taken in council. In the provinces, the *intendants* received ever more power as the direct representatives of the central government for justice, finance, and general administration.

Three great ministers of middle class origin, Jean-Baptiste Colbert, Michel Le Tellier, and his son, the Marquis de Louvois, directed this machine under the king's close supervision. Colbert, cold, gloomy, and fanatically precise, served as Controller General of Finance. He reduced waste, attempted to streamline the tax system, and gave France its first serious attempt at an annual budget of income and expenditure. He sought to force France's economic growth by punitive tariffs against the Dutch, state-supported industrial projects, and colonial enterprises. He doubled the king's net income between 1661 and 1671. Le Tellier and Louvois, as ministers of war, then spent the proceeds.

The old French monarchy had imposed its authority through its law courts. It had also frequently consulted provincial assemblies or the Estates General of France. The new monarchy that Richelieu had founded and Louis XIV perfected imposed its authority and its taxes by decree. Louis XIV checked the pretensions of the *parlements*, deliberately neglected to summon the Estates General, and crushed with military force and mass hangings the many attempts at tax rebellion in

Louis XIV on the Duties of a King

In the 1660s and 1670s, Louis XIV and his staff prepared notes to instruct his son in the art of ruling.

I have often wondered how it could be that love for work being a quality so necessary to sovereigns should yet be one that is so rarely found in them. Most princes, because they have a great many servants and subjects, do not feel obligated to go to any trouble and do not consider that if they have an infinite number of people working under their orders, there are infinitely more who rely on their conduct and that it takes a great deal of watching and a great deal of work merely to insure that those who act do only what they should and that those who rely tolerate only what they must. The deference and the respect that we receive from our subjects are not a free gift from them but payment for the justice and the protection that they expect to receive from us. Just as they must honor us, we must protect and defend them, and our debts toward them are even more binding than theirs to us, for indeed, if one of them lacks the skill or the willingness to execute our orders, a thousand others come in a crowd to fill his post, whereas the position of a sovereign can be properly filled only by the sovereign himself.

. . . of all the functions of sovereignty, the one that a prince must guard most jealously is the handling of finances. It is the most delicate of all because it is the one that is most capable of seducing the one who performs it, and which makes it easiest for him to spread corruption. The prince alone should have sovereign direction over it because he alone has no fortune to establish but that of the state.

From Louis XIV, *Memoirs for the Instruction of the Dauphin*, ed. by Paul Sonnino (New York: Free Press, 1970), pp. 63–64.

The medal on the left (1661) celebrates the young Louis' purported accessibility to his subjects. The one on the right (1685) extols the new discipline and professionalism of his armies.

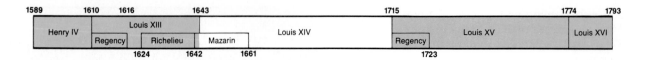

the provinces. Above all, the king completed Richelieu's work of destroying the political power of the French nobility.

The Domestication of the Nobility

The Fronde had forced Louis XIV to flee Paris three times, and had left him fiercely determined, above all else, to break the turbulent nobility to the monarchy's service. His principal weapons were three. First, he denied the nobility its traditional share in the power of the state, while sharply curtailing independent noble power in the provinces. He chose his ministers almost exclusively from commoners, rotated provincial governors to prevent collusion with the local nobility, and treated *parlements* and provincial assemblies with contempt. Second, he cheapened the status of the nobility by deliberately increasing its numbers; the title of Marquis soon became almost a joke. Finally, he required the high nobility, upon pain of harassment, to serve him at court.

That service was bound up with Louis XIV's deliberate display of himself as the symbol of the state. In 1683 he moved court and government from the Louvre in central Paris to Versailles, 15 miles away. There he made his home in the formal gardens and ornate chateau that he had built on marshland, at great cost in lives and treasure. There he also felt safe; Versailles was the first French royal residence completely without fortifications.

Louis moved with impassive dignity through the innumerable court gatherings in the mirrored halls of Versailles. Years of self-conscious practice in kingship gave him a public façade—cool, courteous, impersonal, imperturbable—that fitted perfectly the artificiality of

the small world of the court, as far removed from reality as Versailles itself was physically removed from the bustle of Paris. In that atmosphere, a ball seemed as important as a battle, and holding the basin for the king's morning ablutions became a task as coveted as the command of armies. Instead of competing in the provinces for political power against the monarchy, nobles squandered their fortunes and exhausted their energies in jockeying for social prestige under the king's vigilant eye.

He left the nobility one additional outlet—war. Military service harnessed the nobility's inborn aggressiveness to the purposes of the state. But that service also had a political cost. It created a noble "war party" at court that encouraged the king's own megalomania.

The Destruction of the Huguenots

Beside the nobility, only religious forces and groups stood as potential challenges to Louis XIV's absolutism. The king clashed with several popes who challenged his "Gallican" claim to control the Church in France. But those quarrels never led to a break with Rome, for in doctrine Louis XIV was strictly orthodox. And after 1680 he became increasingly concerned about the fate of his own soul. When his queen, Maria Theresa, died in 1683, he gave up all mistresses except the pious Madame de Maintenon, whom he secretly married. The king's growing piety naturally expressed itself politically. The wars of religion were over, but in the late seventeenth century religion and affairs of state remained tightly intertwined.

Louis XIV enthusiastically persecuted the Jansenists, an austere group of Catholic "puritans" who emphasized the teachings of St. Augustine on original sin, the depravity of man, and the need for divine grace. Louis, whose confessors were Jesuits, thought the Jansenists impertinent in their disapproval of his numerous mistresses, and subversive, for the pope had condemned them. In 1710–12 Louis razed their principal monastic center to the ground.

But it was the Huguenots, one of the most loyal and industrious groups in France, who felt the full force of Louis XIV's religious enthusiasm. Two religions under one prince was indeed, by seventeenth-century standards, a strange anomaly. And the French clergy had long insisted that the continued existence of Protestantism in France was an insult to the king's dignity and authority. After 1679 Louis apparently embraced the idea of atoning for his own numerous sins of the flesh—and his tacit alliance with the Ottoman Turks against Catholic Habsburg Austria—by crushing heresy in France.

He began by gradually tightening his interpretation of the Edict of Nantes, by which Henry IV had granted toleration to the Huguenots and ended France's religious civil wars in 1598. Louis proceeded by forced conversions of Protestants, the destruction of Protestant chapels, and the quartering of royal troops on Protestant families. In 1685 he took the final step. At the urging of his Jesuit advisers, he announced that since all heretics had reconverted to Catholicism, the Edict of Nantes no longer served any purpose and was therefore revoked. The state closed all remaining Protestant churches and schools, and the Church baptized all Protestant children as Catholics. Louis enforced the Revocation with imprisonment, torture, and condemnation to the galleys. Many Huguenots continued to practice their faith in secret. Perhaps 200,000, over a fifth of the Protestant population of France, fled to England, the Dutch Netherlands, Brandenburg, and the New World. Their industry and skill

contributed mightily to the rapid economic growth of their new homes.

The Revocation of the Edict of Nantes was an act of religious intolerance that rivalled the Spanish expulsion of the *moriscos* in 1609–14, the Habsburg ravaging of Bohemia after the battle of the White Mountain in 1620, or the systematic impoverishment and degradation of the Catholics of Ireland by English conquerors from

The palace of Versailles (1686), with the king arriving by carriage.

Cartoon of 1686 showing a royal dragoon, as "missionary," forcibly converting a Huguenot "heretic" to Catholicism.

Elizabeth I to Cromwell and his successors. But in those cases, unlike that of France, ethnic hatred had compounded religious savagery. The revocation of the Edict of Nantes was unique in the seventeenth century—a large-scale act of barbarism that was *purely* religious in origin. It was the last such act in western Europe until Germany's attempt to exterminate the European Jews between 1941 and 1944.

Literature and Fashion: The Primacy of France

To dramatize his conception of kingship, Louis chose as his emblem the sun god, Apollo. The symbol of the sun, on whose rays all earthly life depends, became the theme of the architecture and sculpture of the new palace at Versailles. The "Sun King" patronized and presided over an "Augustan Age" of French culture. As befitted such a patron, the prevailing taste was classical. It emphasized form, order, balance, and proportion—the presumed ideals of reasonable individuals throughout history.

Pierre Corneille (1606–84) was the father of French classical tragedy. In 1636 he wrote *Le Cid*, the first of a series of powerful dramas that glorified willpower and the quest for perfection. Corneille was still active when Louis began his personal rule, but the dramatist's brilliant younger contemporary, Jean Racine (1639–99) soon eclipsed him. Racine wrote more realistically than Corneille about human beings in the grip of violent and sometimes coarse passions. He brought French tragedy to its highest point of perfection between 1667 and 1677. Then he underwent a religious conversion that caused him to renounce drama as immoral.

Some of the audience for the tragedies of Corneille and Racine had little respect for the comic playwright Molière (1622–73), but his biting satirical dramas became an unsurpassable model for future French dramatists. From 1659 to his death in 1673 he was

Caricature of Molière as an actor.

the idol of aristocratic audiences at Versailles. All three playwrights concentrated on portraying types, not individuals—the hero, the man of honor violently in love, the miser, the hypocrite—embodiments of human passions and foibles that belonged to all times and places. Partly as a result, French classical drama of the age of Louis XIV was easily exportable. French literary standards influenced cultivated Europeans everywhere, although French literary creativity flagged in the later years of Louis XIV's reign, as religious persecution, religious and political censorship, and economic exhaustion intensified.

In the other arts, and in social conventions, France likewise swayed the rest of Europe, although Louis XIV's growing religious intolerance and military aggressiveness prompted resistance to French culture, especially in Protestant republics such as the Dutch United Provinces, where middle-class art and manners flourished. French fashions in dress nevertheless spread across Spain, Italy, and much of Germany. The masters of the ponderous French baroque style, which ruled the design and decoration of Versailles, replaced the Italians as the arbiters of European architecture. The French language became the language of diplomacy and polite conversation, and the French court became the model for countless smaller courts throughout Catholic Europe. As Florence had been the center of the Italian Renaissance, and Spain of the Counter-Reformation, so France in the late seventeenth century was the center of European politics, diplomacy, and culture.

France's Bid for European Domination

Richelieu and Mazarin had begun the process of creating a large and dependable standing army to replace the disorderly semi-mercenary, semi-feudal military system of the previous century. Louis and his formidable ministers of war, Le Tellier and Louvois, completed

Engraving of a performance of Molière's last play, *Le Malade imaginaire* (1673). Molière died on stage on the fourth night of the performance.

that task. The ministers subordinated the aristocratic officer corps and the provincial private armies to royal authority, developed a supply system that functioned, standardized the organization of infantry and artillery, and followed the example of Gustavus Adolphus in giving the troops uniforms. The Seigneur de Vauban, the father of modern military engineering, invented the first effective bayonet and perfected the science of building—and smashing—fortifications in the age of gunpowder. Above all, Le Tellier and Louvois provided their master with numbers. By the 1660s Louis possessed by far the largest and best-equipped army in Europe: 100,000 men in peace and up to 400,000 in war, numbers not seen in the West since the fall of Rome.

This unprecedented power inevitably brought the temptation to use it. War aroused the enthusiasm of the nobility and kept it occupied in ways that did not threaten the state. War exercised and justified the enormous and costly standing army. Above all, successful war enhanced the glory of the monarch, a glory that was Louis XIV's constant concern. War might per-

The Conquests of Louis XIV   1661–1715

France before 1668

Acquisitions by the Treaty of Aix-la-Chapelle, 1668

Acquisitions by the Treaty of Nimwegen, 1678

Acquisitions by the Treaty of Utrecht, 1713

Louis XIV entering Strasbourg, September 1681. Note the fortifications in the style of Vauban.

Officer and musketeer of the French Guard (late seventeenth century).

haps make him the arbiter not only of France but of Europe as well.

Louis XIV's first two wars (1667–68, 1672–79) were relatively limited in aim. The decline of Spain and the collapse of the Holy Roman Empire left a power vacuum on France's eastern borders; Louis therefore sought to annex the Spanish Netherlands (later Belgium), Franche-Comté, and parts of western Germany and to reduce the Dutch to commercial and territorial vassalage. In each of the two wars, alliances that at different times included the United Provinces, Sweden, and the Habsburg monarchy checked him after initial French victories. The Dutch held off his first onslaught in 1672 by opening their dikes and flooding their countryside. England simultaneously attacked the Dutch by sea, but withdrew from the war in 1674. By 1678 Louis had gained only Franche-Comté and a few border fortresses in Flanders.

Thereafter, Louis briefly chose legal chicanery over musketry. He established French courts called Chambers of Reunion to "reunite" to France all lands on France's borders that had in

the past been dependencies of French territories. That gave Louis control of the independent Protestant republic of Strasbourg in 1681, much to the indignation of the inhabitants and of Protestants throughout Europe. The Revocation of the Edict of Nantes in 1685 provided further evidence of the Sun King's arrogance.

In 1686 the Habsburg Emperor, Spain, Sweden, and several German states formed the defensive League of Augsburg. Habsburg victories in Hungary over the Turks, who were allied with Louis, shifted the balance in the West against France. Louis replied with the most senseless atrocity since the Thirty Years' War—his armies systematically devastated the Palatinate in 1688 simply to cow his enemies. That act instead helped weld his opponents together. And French distraction in Germany allowed William of Orange, ruler of the Dutch Netherlands and Louis XIV's most implacable enemy, to claim the English throne in 1688–89. England and the Dutch, the two greatest economic powers of the age, then joined the League of Augsburg and closed the circle around over-mighty France.

The participants' newly acquired worldwide interests made this war the first world war, waged in India, the Caribbean, and North America as well as in Europe. After ten years of fighting, France agreed to the Peace of Ryswick in 1697. Louis retained the gains made before 1678, but had to renounce nearly all conquests after that date except Strasbourg. England emerged from the war stronger than it had been in 1689, and France weaker.

The War of the Spanish Succession, 1701–14

The Peace of Ryswick brought only four years' respite. Louis had made peace in the hope of gaining a greater prize than any for which he had yet contended—the Spanish Empire. Charles II of Spain, bizarre end-product of generations of syphilitic degeneration and Habsburg inbreeding, and last of the Spanish Habsburg line that had ruled since 1516, was losing a 30-year struggle against numerous diseases. By 1697 he was close to death and had no direct heir. That raised an issue of vital importance to all Europe: would the Spanish Empire fall to Emperor Leopold I of the Austrian Habsburg line, pass to the French Bourbon dynasty (for Louis XIV was both the son and the widower of Spanish Habsburg princesses), or suffer dismemberment among its rivals?

England and the Dutch had obvious economic and strategic interests in preventing France from grasping Spain's colonial trade or the Spanish Netherlands. Louis seemed willing to compromise and twice concluded secret treaties that partitioned the Spanish dominions with the English and Dutch. But when news of the second treaty reached Madrid, the dying Charles II lost his temper. He refused to see parts of his Catholic empire pass to Protestant powers; instead, he made a will that left all his dominions to a grandson of Louis XIV. After the death of Charles II in 1699, Spain proclaimed that grandson King Philip V of Spain.

Louis XIV tore up the secret partition treaties, recognized the will of Charles II, and sent French troops to claim the Spanish Netherlands. In 1701 William of Orange formed yet another coalition against France, the Grand Alliance of the Hague. England, Holland, and Emperor Leopold I of Austria bound themselves to fight until they had ended the threat of Bourbon control of Spain and of the Spanish colonies. Louis had made his last and most far-reaching bid for the domination of Europe. But this time his enemies were as unyielding and powerful as he was, and they forced him to fight for France's life.

Warfare had by now become thoroughly professional. In the long wars since 1618, innovators such as Gustavus Adolphus, Maurice of Orange, Le Tellier, and Louvois had replaced noble amateurism and independent military entrepreneurship with professional officers corps that bore the "king's commission." Ragged bands of freebooters yielded to disciplined ranks, rigidly drilled in the new fire tactics. The combination of musket and bayonet united fire and shock in one weapon, and drove out the clumsy combinations of pikemen and musketeers that had ruled the battlefield since the Spanish victory at Pavia in 1525. Commanders learned to coordinate infantry, the new mobile artillery, and cavalry. Sieges, thanks to Vauban, became a scientific exercise; the precise orchestration of artillery fire and trench digging permitted the battering of breaches in the strongest fortifications and their seizure by infantry assault.

In the new world war of 1701–14, the French soon found themselves outdone. Two commanders of genius led the Allied armies—England's John Churchill, first Duke of Marlborough, and the great Habsburg general and scourge of the Turks, Prince Eugene of Savoy. Marlborough's diplomacy held the ramshackle coalition together while his generalship smashed the great armies of Louis XIV in four battles of unprecedented slaughter that cost France up to 80,000 casualties—Blenheim (1704), Ramillies (1706), Oudenarde (1708), and Malplaquet (1709). England trounced the French at sea and seized Gibraltar, from which it thereafter dominated the western Mediterranean. An allied army even invaded Spain and several times took Madrid.

Louis XIV, with France exhausted militarily and in the grip of famine, sued for peace in 1709–10 on almost any terms. The Allies thereupon demanded that he send French troops to help expel his own grandson from Madrid. That was too great a humiliation; Louis XIV refused, and appealed with success to his subjects. Famine and economic crisis filled the French armies with new recruits, who preferred the risks of the battlefield to the certainty of starvation. A xenophobic reaction in Spain, and French generalship, helped drive the English and

Austrian invaders out. In 1710 the English war party, the Whigs, gave way to the Tories, and a war-weary England recalled Marlborough. In 1712, at Denain, the French severed Prince Eugene of Savoy's communications and forced him to retreat. It was the Allies' turn to seek peace.

The Peace of Utrecht, 1713–14

In theory, the Peace of Utrecht of 1713 and other treaties of 1714 that ended the war of the Spanish Succession gave France the prize that Louis had sought since 1701. Louis's grandson remained on the throne of Spain as Philip V—but only on condition that no subsequent Bourbon should unite the crowns of Spain and France. And Louis gave up all conquests east of the Rhine and his bid for the Spanish Netherlands and for Spain's colonial trade. France survived as the greatest single power, but the war had drained it of money and blood, and had made Louis XIV's government bankrupt and hated. When the great king died at last in 1715, France's common people reputedly "openly returned thanks to God."

England was the chief victor. It emerged from the war with the dominance of the seas that it held until the twentieth century. From France it took Newfoundland, Acadia (modern New Brunswick and Nova Scotia), and the Hudson's Bay Territory. It kept Gibraltar and Minorca, seized from Spain, and received the *Asiento*—the lucrative privilege of supplying African slaves to the Spanish colonies that provided an opening for large-scale smuggling of other goods.

The Austrian Habsburgs gained the Spanish Netherlands (which now became the Austrian Netherlands), and replaced Spain as the dominant power in Italy through the acquisition of Milan, Naples, and Sicily. Two new smaller powers, Brandenburg-Prussia and the Duchy of Savoy, increased their territories and prestige; they had chosen the winning side. The Dutch achieved their minimum war aim—

they kept the Scheldt River closed, thus blocking the trade of Antwerp, the chief port of the Austrian Netherlands. But the long strain of fighting France for almost half a century had demoralized them. They could no longer compete at sea with England and soon slipped from the ranks of the great powers.

The Peace of Utrecht ended the first bid for European hegemony since the days of Philip II of Spain. Louis XIV's attempt to gain for France the domination of western Europe and the wider world had summoned up, through the workings of the balance of power, the coalition that had checked France. War had prevented the universal domination of one power. The European state system had survived a challenge to its very existence.

ENGLAND: THE EMERGENCE OF PARLIAMENTARY MONARCHY

While Louis XIV consolidated absolute monarchy in France, the English created a constitutional monarchy controlled by Parliament. The restoration of king, Parliament, and Anglican Church in 1660 had established an equilibrium between Crown and Parliament. But that balance had remained unstable. Who was to exercise sovereignty, the king or the gentry and merchants of Parliament? What was the religious settlement to be, and who was to make it? Who was to control foreign policy? These three questions had dominated the preceding 40 years of turmoil and civil war. They still awaited answers.

Charles II and the "Cavalier Parliament"

Charles II (r. 1660–85), utterly unlike his too stubborn father, was witty, attractive, worldly, a king of hearty sexual appetites and shrewd political sense. He had lived long in exile in France, and took his cousin Louis XIV

The House of Commons, on the Great Seal of England (1651).

as his model. Charles was resolved not to risk exile or execution in the manner of his father. He instead hoped to restore England to Catholicism and to establish a French-style absolute monarchy through dissimulation, manipulation, and compromise. That ambition Charles II pursued through 25 years of court intrigue, party politics, and secret diplomacy that kept both Parliaments and ministers guessing about the king's intentions.

The "Cavalier Parliament" of 1661–79 held a commanding position at the beginning of the reign. It was the preserve of the gentry and of the aristocracy, now partly restored to its ancient influence in both local and national government. Both groups were for the moment strongly royalist and determined to stamp out all remaining political and religious radicalism. But they also had no intention of allowing the Crown to be financially independent of Parliament.

In place of the old idea that "the king should live of his own," Parliament now granted Charles a regular income from customs and excise duties. But it was not enough to meet even the ordinary expenses of government, let alone the expenses of Charles's wild doings at court or of his numerous mistresses and illegitimate children. And foreign war was unthinkable unless Parliament approved the objectives and voted money. Charles therefore allowed Parliament, under the leadership of his father's adviser, Edward Hyde, Earl of Clarendon, to have its way for a time.

Parliament thus dictated the religious settlement. The Cavalier Parliament was as strongly pro-Anglican as it was pro-royalist. Between 1661 and 1665 it passed statutes known inaccurately as the "Clarendon Code"—Clarendon himself favored toleration—that excluded from local government Puritans who "dissented" from the established Church and purged Puritan ministers from the Anglican clergy. Later legislation barred dissenters from Parliament, from service in the army or

navy, and from the universities at Oxford or Cambridge.

Puritanism and social radicalism appeared to be intertwined. The Cavalier Parliament was therefore determined to stamp out the first and discourage the second. But while the Clarendon Code lowered the social status of dissenters and narrowed their opportunities, it did not greatly decrease their number. Presbyterians, Congregationalists, Baptists, and Quakers formed persistent and numerous religious minorities that bitterly opposed both Anglicanism and Catholicism. Charles himself sought toleration as a first step to restoring Catholicism. In 1672 he issued a "Declaration of Indulgence" that suspended the operation of the Code against both Puritans and Catholics, and appeared to assert—in the manner of Charles I—that royal prerogative could thwart acts of Parliament. Parliament forced him to withdraw the Declaration, and imposed on him a Test Act that excluded non-Anglicans from civil and military office. To the Anglican gentry of Parliament, Puritans remained radicals and Catholics traitors.

Foreign Policy: The French Alliance

Two natural calamities, a fierce outbreak of bubonic plague that killed 60,000 of the 450,000 inhabitants of London in 1665 and a fire that destroyed much of the city in 1666, contributed to widespread unrest. Public opinion blamed the fire on an alleged Catholic plot. Uneasiness increased as king and Parliament drifted apart over foreign policy. In 1665 Parliament forced Charles into a commercial war with the Dutch, but denied him the money needed to win. When swift victories did not follow, Parliament unfairly held Clarendon responsible, and exiled him.

After Louis XIV began his attack on the Spanish Netherlands in 1667, English opinion began to see the military power of Catholic France as more threatening than the commercial ri-

Charles II, the "Merry Monarch."

London's catastrophic great
fire of 1666.

valry of the Protestant Dutch. But
Charles held to his connection with
Louis, and in 1670 Charles allied England with France against the Dutch
through the notorious secret Treaty of
Dover. In the Treaty, Louis XIV offered
money and French troops if Charles
were to declare himself a Catholic and
reconvert England to Catholicism.

Charles was probably unsure of how
far down that road he meant to travel.
He did acquire both a pro-French foreign policy and a French mistress who
reported to Louis XIV's ambassador.
English forces also attacked the Dutch
along with the French in 1672. Between
1675 and 1681 he concluded with Louis
four additional secret agreements in
which he undertook to thwart Parliament's anti-French moves in return for
more French money. The existence of
this close understanding with Louis
inevitably leaked out and created fear
of French domination and a return to
Catholicism. The landed classes represented in Parliament were increasingly
suspicious of Charles II and prone to
panic.

Whigs and Tories:
The Origins of Party Politics

In 1678 these accumulated fears exploded in the lurid "Popish Plot." A
disreputable former Anglican clergy-

man named Titus Oates concocted a
story about a Jesuit plot to kill the king,
to place his Catholic brother James,
Duke of York, on the throne with
French help, and to massacre England's Protestants. Parliament described it as "a damnable and hellish
plot, for assassinating and murdering
the king and rooting out and destroying the Protestant religion." A new
civil war seemed about to break out.

The Earl of Shaftesbury, a great
landowner who had fought for Parliament in the Civil War, rallied a "Country Party" that campaigned fiercely to
exclude James from the succession to
the throne. In response, an Anglican
and royalist "Court Party" assembled,
although at first without much enthusiasm, to support Charles II and his
brother. The Court party denigrated
the Shaftesbury group as "Whigs," a
name hitherto applied to Scottish Presbyterian rebels. The Whigs in turn baptized their antagonists "Tories," a kind
of Irish Catholic brigand.

The Whigs controlled the three brief
Parliaments that followed the dissolution of the Cavalier Parliament in 1679.
Shaftesbury and his associates merrily
pressed the execution of some 35 Catholics for alleged complicity in the imaginary "Popish Plot." But the Whig
leaders overplayed their hand. Opinion swung back toward the king, and it
was soon the turn of the Whigs to suffer. By 1681 Shaftesbury had fled
abroad, the inventors of the Popish
Plot were disgraced or executed, and
Charles II was stronger than any monarch since the early days of James I.
Until his death in 1685 Charles ruled
without Parliament, with his brother
James by his side and with the subsidies of Louis XIV filling his coffers.

These difficult years were nevertheless momentous for the West's tradition of political liberty. This struggle
between the king and factions of the
gentry in Parliament created the ancestors of modern political parties—
groups organized for the purpose of
electioneering and of controlling government through a representative as-

sembly. Whigs and Tories were in part the descendants of the Parliamentarians and Royalists of the 1640s. But the great crisis of the 1680s, instead of civil war, produced the system of Parliamentary rule that England later passed on to its colonies and indirectly to the West as a whole.

The "Glorious Revolution" of 1688

James, Duke of York, succeeded his brother Charles II in 1685 as James II (r. 1685–88). He was a bigoted convert to Catholicism who lacked Charles's shrewdness and flexibility. Within three years he had infuriated almost every political and religious group of importance in England, and had provoked the revolution that Charles II had succeeded in avoiding.

Early successes made him overconfident. He introduced Catholics into the high command of both army and navy, and camped a standing army a few miles from London. He surrounded himself with Catholic advisers and attacked Anglican control of the universities. He claimed the power to suspend or dispense with acts of Parliament. In a vain attempt to win the support of Puritans as well as Catholics, he issued a Declaration of Indulgence along the lines of his brother's—thus further alienating the Anglican establishment. By revoking borough charters and browbeating sheriffs, he tried to ensure the election of a Parliament favorable to his policies. These measures, along with the example of Louis XIV's revocation of the Edict of Nantes in 1685, terrified England's Protestants.

The event that triggered James II's downfall was a happy one—the unexpected birth in June 1688 of a son to his Catholic queen. Until then, Protestants had consoled themselves with the thought that James II's two elder daughters by another marriage, Mary and Anne, were Protestants, and would succeed James. Now the existence of a Catholic male heir prolonged the Catholic threat indefinitely into the future. But unlike the events of 1641,

the intense political tension of 1688 did not produce civil war. This time the king had no "king's party." He had alienated Anglicans and dissenters, Tories and Whigs, aristocracy and commoners. The result was instead a bloodless "revolution," a rapid and fundamental political change that established the limited or parliamentary monarchy that has persisted to the present.

The agent of James II's downfall was William of Orange, *stadholder* and hero of the Dutch Republic, the man who had opened the dikes to halt the French invasion in 1672. In 1677, in pursuit of allies against France, he had married James II's eldest daughter, Mary, and had thus acquired a claim to the English throne. In June 1688 a group of prominent Englishmen, both Whigs and Tories, invited William to cross the English Channel and save the Protestant cause in England. That November William landed a Dutch army on the southern coast and marched slowly toward London. The countryside rose against James II, and William tactfully allowed the friendless king to flee to France. An improvised Parliament declared that James had abdicated the throne by flight and invited William and Mary to become joint sovereigns on condition that they accept a "Bill of Rights" that severely limited royal power.

This bloodless "Glorious Revolution" established at last the sovereignty of Parliament, which had made a king and could regulate the succession to the throne. William was strong-willed, but his priorities were continental and Dutch—the forging of an ever more powerful coalition against Louis XIV. He therefore grudgingly accepted Parliament's conditions. The "Jacobite" supporters of James II and his son invaded Ireland in 1690 and staged two bloody rebellions in the Scottish Highlands in 1715 and 1745, but all such attempts at a second Restoration failed. Parliament had won.

The Bill of Rights emphatically barred the king from suspending acts

James II, who swiftly alienated even traditional supporters of the monarchy (engraved after a painting by Kneller, 1688).

The speaker of the House of Lords offers William and Mary the English crown (from a contemporary engraving).

John Locke (1632–1704), champion of "natural rights" and government by consent.

of Parliament or interfering with the courts. It furnished a base for the steady expansion of civil liberties in the generation after 1688. Parliament established religious toleration and freedom from arbitrary arrest. Censorship of the press quietly withered. The king had to summon Parliament annually, for he could neither pay nor control his armed forces without parliamentary consent. Regular meetings of Parliament in turn strengthened the parties and made the king dependent on their support. The monarch vetoed a parliamentary bill for the last time in 1707.

Hobbes Answered: John Locke and the Theory of Limited Government

The English Civil War and Glorious Revolution followed the Dutch revolt against Spain as the second of the Western revolutions that ended absolute monarchy and ultimately led to democratic representative government. The weight of tradition demanded that English leaders in 1641–49 and 1688–89 deny that their acts were revolutionary. Parliament chopped off the head of one king and replaced another in the name of the *traditional* "liberties of England." But that half-fiction was unsatisfactory.

John Locke (1632–1704), a friend of the Earl of Shaftesbury who had founded the Whig party, provided a theoretical foundation for what Parliament had done and for the subsequent evolution of representative government. Locke probably wrote most of *Of Civil Government: Two Treatises* while in political exile in Holland in 1683–89, but it emerged from the presses in 1690 as a belated rationale for the acts of Parliament during the Glorious Revolution. In it he at last answered Thomas Hobbes's justification of absolute sovereignty with a convincing theory of limited government.

Locke attacked the divine-right theory of monarchy and challenged Hobbes's claim that the only alternative to anarchy was absolute authority. Locke's first principle was that all individuals possess a natural right to "life, liberty, and property." That notion was revolutionary in his age of entrenched privilege. It remains revolutionary in our own, in which dictatorships rule most of humanity. From this premise of "natural rights," and from a more optimistic view of human nature than that of Hobbes, Locke derived the rest of his system. Like Hobbes and many predecessors and contemporaries, Locke argued that government was a contract in which humanity exchanged the anarchy of the "state of nature" for the security that government provided. But Locke's insistence that rights were "natural" and prior to all government allowed him—unlike Hobbes—to limit the authority of government. The source of sovereignty, thanks to the natural rights of the governed, was the governed themselves: "The people alone can appoint the form of the commonwealth." It therefore followed, for Locke, that a government acting without the consent of the governed thereby dissolved the contract and gave the subject a right to resistance or revolution.

Locke also provided a principle for the ordering of government. Fearing the concentration of power, he proposed a strict separation of powers that would allow the elected representatives of the people to check a tyrannical executive. Above all, he relentlessly emphasized property as the foundation of all freedom and the purpose of government itself: "The great and chief end. . . . of men's uniting into commonwealths and putting themselves under government is the preservation of their property." Some twentieth-century commentators have denigrated what they describe as Locke's doctrine of "possessive individualism," his equation of property and liberty—but have failed to offer concrete examples of societies that enjoy liberty without property.

In the eighteenth century, Locke's ideas were a powerful rationale for a society based on wealth rather than inherited privilege and for a new kind of government, limited in its powers. Inalienable natural rights, government by consent, right of revolution, and the sanctity of property seemed increasingly "self-evident" to Englishmen after 1688, and ultimately to the American colonists in 1776.

The Emergence of the Cabinet System

At the level of practice rather than that of theory, factional struggles in Parliament replaced struggles between king and Parliament after 1688. The Glorious Revolution made gentry and merchants the real masters of both central and local government in England. Generally speaking, aristocratic landowners, bankers, merchants, and most dissenters were Whigs, while the smaller gentry, the Anglican parish clergy, and some great lords were Tories. But parties were still loosely organized, and small cliques often held the balance of power.

Given the fluidity of parliamentary alignments and the monarchy's residual powers, it took over a century for a smoothly operating system of constitu-

Locke on Government by Consent   1690

Compare with "Bishop Bossuet on Absolutism," page 560.

Men being, as has been said, by nature all free, equal, and independent, no one can be put out of this estate and subjected to the political power of another without his own consent, which is done by agreeing with other men, to join and unite into a community for their comfortable, safe, and peaceful living, one amongst another, in a secure enjoyment of their properties, and a greater security against any that are not of it. . . . When any number of men have so consented to make one community or government, they are thereby presently incorporated, and make one body politic, wherein the majority have the right to act and conclude the rest. . . . Absolute, arbitrary power, or governing without settled standing laws, can neither of them consist with the ends of society and government, which men would not quit the freedom of the state of Nature for, and tie themselves up under, were it not to preserve their lives, liberties, and fortunes, and by stated rules of right and property to secure their peace and quiet.

From John Locke, *Of Civil Government: Two Treatises* (New York: Everyman's Library, 1924), pp. 164–65, 186.

Medal of Queen Anne (1702–14).

Anti-Catholic woodcuts showing the "prodigious cruelties" of religious warfare in Ireland (1689).

tional government to emerge by the slow accretion of precedent. The ultimate answer was the "cabinet system"—government by a committee of leaders of the majority party in Parliament, acting under the leadership of a "prime minister" and acknowledging primary responsibility to Parliament rather than to the crown for their actions.

During the reigns of William and Mary (1689–1702) and of Mary's sister, Queen Anne (1702–14), the foundations of that system emerged, although parliamentary leaders had as yet no sense of their goal and monarchs still considered ministers responsible to themselves rather than to Parliament. The old privy council had long been too unwieldy for effective action. Instead, a "cabinet council" or inner circle of important ministers had developed under Charles II. The members of this "cabinet" slowly discovered that efficiency demanded that they settle major issues among themselves and then present a united front to the monarch. And within the cabinet a leader, the "prime minister," inevitably emerged.

In order to gain Parliament's indispensable support in war or peace, both William and Anne occasionally found it advisable to choose their ministers from the majority party. By Queen Anne's death in 1714 it had become evident that the real government of England was slowly falling into the hands of a cabinet of ministers who controlled a parliamentary majority, often by bribery, but felt themselves ultimately responsible to the political interests of that landed and moneyed majority.

The Religious Settlement

The Glorious Revolution also produced an unprecedented measure of religious toleration. The fanaticism unleashed in the Civil War had given religious intolerance a bad name, and both Anglicans and Puritans were now more afraid of Catholic France than of one another.

Puritans had supported Anglicans against the Catholic, James II, but King William, thanks to the Dutch Republic's unique tradition of toleration, now insisted on a religious truce. The result was the "Toleration Act" of 1689, which allowed dissenters to worship as they pleased and to educate their clergy and laity in schools of their own. Most of the existing anti-Catholic statutes, along with the acts excluding dissenters from civil and military offices remained in effect, but after 1689 their enforcement lacked rigor.

The Act of Settlement of 1701 provided that the sovereign should always be an Anglican Protestant and finally quieted fear that a Catholic might succeed to the throne. The act also settled the succession, in case James II's two daughters should die without children, on the descendants of that daughter of James I who had married the ill-fated Frederick V of the Palatinate before the Thirty Years' War. That succession brought the Elector of Hanover to the throne in 1714, when Queen Anne died without direct heirs, and the Stuart dynasty ended.

Ireland and Scotland: Repression and Union

Civil War and Glorious Revolution also indirectly furthered the unification of the British Isles. England, Ireland, and Scotland all had the same king from James I's succession in 1603, but union went no further than the common crown. The two smaller kingdoms, especially Ireland, suffered greatly during the seventeenth century from involvement in England's religious and political struggles.

The native Irish were Catholic; Protestant England therefore despised them and feared them as potential allies of Catholic Spain and France. To cope with that strategic threat, James I had settled Protestant colonists in the northeastern province of Ulster. But the Ulster Protestants were Presbyterians and soon became anti-Stuart, while the Catholic Irish were generally loyal to the Stuart dynasty. In 1641 the Catholics had revolted. Cromwell crushed them with fire and terror in 1649, and massacred the Catholic garrisons at Drogheda and Wexford (". . . being in the heat of action, I forbade them to spare any that were in arms in the town."). In 1690, James II landed in Ireland with French troops and Catholic support, but William of Orange routed him at the Battle of the Boyne. The much-celebrated anniversary of that Protestant victory remains to the present day a source of sectarian bloodshed in Ulster. After the Boyne, English and Irish Protestant landlords systematically persecuted the Catholic Irish and their religion, while reserving both economic and political power for themselves.

The Scots, who had given England a king in 1603, had somewhat better fortune. Scotland had a sixth of England's population, but its Protestantism, its long tradition of parliamentarism, its military power, and its poverty—which made it unrewarding as prey—allowed it to make a satisfactory bargain. Scottish resistance to the imposition of Anglicanism had triggered the crisis that ultimately led to Civil War in 1642. Nevertheless, much of Scotland, especially the Highlands inhabited by the turbulent and ruthless Catholic clansmen, remained strongly attached to the native Stuart dynasty. From 1650 to 1745, the clans provided a base for risings in support of the Stuarts. The Scots parliament accepted the Revolution of 1688, but refused the Act of Settlement of 1701. It threatened to choose a separate king of its own—possibly the exiled pretender James II—if James II's last daughter, Anne, died without producing an heir.

That frightened London into serious negotiation. In 1707 the Whig government and the Scots agreed to an Act of Union that eliminated the risk that Scotland might choose a separate monarch, and created the kingdom of "Great Britain." Scotland retained its own laws and its Presbyterian state religion, but surrendered its separate parliament in return for representation in London and full participation in the dynamic English economy. The loss of political independence and the coming of a money economy even to the wild Highlands caused disgruntlement, especially among the clans. But the Act of Union was successful, unlike England's difficult relationships with Ireland or with the colonies in America. Scottish merchants and administrators helped build the British empire. Scottish philosophers, economists, and historians contributed mightily to the widening of human knowledge in the eighteenth century known as the Enlightenment (see pp. 601–11).

The Growth of British Power

A final consequence of the Revolution, after parliamentary government, religious toleration, and the settlement with Scotland, was to unite crown and Parliament on foreign policy and to turn the energies of the next generations from domestic conflict to foreign war. Given England's fear of Catholicism, William of Orange had no difficulty bringing his new kingdom into the Grand Alliance against Louis XIV, who had given refuge to James II. Parliamentary monarchy soon demonstrated that it was more deadly to its enemies than Stuart absolutism. The government of William and his successors was able to raise money, the sinew of war, in ways that only the Dutch could match.

In 1694 William's Whig ministers created a Bank of England to mobilize England's growing commercial and financial power against France. Within a few days of its founding, the Bank had raised over a million pounds of investors' money, and it promptly lent the money to the government at 8 percent interest. The resulting permanent national debt was a revolutionary instrument. It financed the defeat of Louis XIV and provided the foundation for the subsequent commercial and maritime supremacy of Britain. Throughout the next century British wealth, trans-

The Economic and Social
Division of Europe

muted into ships of the line, gave the island kingdom a striking power out of all proportion to its size and population. The Peace of Utrecht of 1713 gave British sea power, the guarantor of British trade, a position without serious rivals. That heralded the elimination of France as a colonial competitor and Britain's domination of the world outside Europe.

CENTRAL AND EASTERN EUROPE, 1648–1721

An imaginary line running north from the Adriatic Sea to the Elbe River that flows into the North Sea divided the economy of early modern Europe into two sharply defined halves. West of that line, the towns and their trade were increasingly dominant. The majority of the population still lived on the land, but most peasants were free workers and many of them small landowners. Most serfs had become agricultural wage laborers in and after the crisis of the Black Death. Most nobles had become landlords who hired labor for wages, or simply lived on rents from tenants. Though still a minority, the urban middle classes were increasingly influential.

East of the line, in Hungary, Bohemia, Poland, Prussia, and Russia lay a land of lord and peasant. Towns were small, poor, and weak. Landed estates were larger and the landed nobility far more powerful politically than in western Europe. And in the sixteenth and seventeenth centuries, noble power was still growing. Grain prices rose with the price revolution of the sixteenth century, while the growth of the trading networks centered on Antwerp and Amsterdam offered export markets. That situation provided an economic rationale for the imposition of a "second serfdom" in eastern Europe. The nobles, now enmeshed in a money economy, sought to lower labor costs by binding their peasants to the land and imposing on them two to five days a week of compulsory labor. The profits earned on exports in turn further increased the nobles' power. And in the political sphere, the states of eastern Europe encouraged and promoted noble domination. Either the state was the nobility, as in Hungary or Poland, or it made a tacit bargain that delivered the peasants to the nobility in return for noble service to the state, as in Brandenburg-Prussia and Russia.

As in western Europe, states were machines for power. They had to be, for the flat plains of central and eastern Europe offered no "natural frontiers" to check the invader. A state could only remain a state so long as it had an army. But the revolution in military technique since gunpowder had become widespread in the fifteenth century had so raised the costs of armies that only stongly centralized states with relentless tax systems could afford them. Few such states existed in central and eastern Europe in the seventeenth century. Most eastern rulers faced the same obstacles to centralized government that western rulers had faced two centuries or more before—a powerful landed nobility, a church that owned large portions of the land, a middle class too small to bear the weight of heavy taxation, a desperately poor agrarian economy, a limited commerce,

The crown of the Holy Roman Empire of the German Nation, used from 961 to 1792.

infant industries, and a peasantry tied to the land and thus incapable of meeting the need of new industries for labor.

The Holy Roman Empire

The one large political organization that bridged eastern and western Europe was the Holy Roman Empire. But the Thirty Years' War had left it a political fiction. A Habsburg remained emperor and a Diet or deliberative assembly met "perpetually" at Regensburg after 1663, but the Empire had no common army, administration, taxes, laws, calendar, or tariffs. It included perhaps 1,800 political units and petty rulers, including free cities, free imperial knights, ecclesiastical principalities, counties, margravates, duchies, and the kingdom of Bohemia. The Peace of Westphalia had recognized the full sovereignty of the 300 or so larger units within the Empire and had accorded France and Sweden the right to take part in the Diet's deliberations. This Empire, as Voltaire (see p. 603) remarked in the mid-eighteenth century, was "neither Holy, nor Roman, nor an Empire."

The ruling families of a few large states—Bavaria, Saxony, Hanover, Brandenburg, and Austria—sought to expand their territories and prestige by war or marriage. Augustus the Strong of Saxony, in addition to fathering according to legend more than 300 children, secured election in 1696 as king of Poland. In 1701 the Elector of Brandenburg obtained the emperor's consent to style himself "king in Prussia." And in 1714 the Elector of Hanover became king of Britain. But only two great powers emerged from the wreck of the Holy Roman Empire—Austria and Brandenburg-Prussia.

The Habsburgs: Europe and Austria Defended

The attempt of Emperor Ferdinand II (r. 1619–37) to revive and strengthen the Empire under Habsburg control collapsed in the Thirty Years' War. The Habsburgs of Vienna thereafter turned to a policy that Ferdinand had also fostered. The Habsburgs sought to consolidate and expand their hereditary lands in Austria and the Danube Valley into a centralized monarchy that could hold its own against the states of western Europe. The chief architect of that policy was Emperor Leopold I (r. 1658–1705), with the help and occasional prodding of some capable civil servants and one remarkable general, Prince Eugene of Savoy.

Achieving the Habsburg objective required the reduction of Austria, Bohemia, and Hungary to a semblance of uniformity and obedience. In the Duchy of Austria and neighboring Tyrol, Leopold's lawyers established his ascendancy over the nobility. Bohemia was even less of an impediment. The Emperor Ferdinand II had smashed its native Czech nobility after the Battle of the White Mountain in 1620, and in 1627 had made the previously elective crown of Bohemia a hereditary possession of the Habsburg family. Hungary, on the fiercely contested border between the West and Islam, was different. Although the Habsburgs had usually been the elected monarchs there since early in the sixteenth century, the Ottoman Turks directly or indirectly ruled almost two thirds of the kingdom. The Hungarian nobility was turbulent, and the Hungarian Protestants were numerous and inclined to fear the Turks less than the Catholic Habsburgs.

But the Ottoman Empire was no longer the power that had taken Constantinople in 1453, smashed the Hungarians at Mohács in 1526, and sought Mediterranean mastery at Lepanto in 1571. The Ottomans failed to keep pace with the West in technology, above all in the technology of war. Their metallurgy, their cannon and handguns, remained those of the sixteenth century. Ottoman logistics and tactics likewise failed to match the growing professionalization that overtook war in the West during and after the Thirty

Emperor Leopold I (above) and Prince Eugene of Savoy (below), who ended the Ottoman Turk threat to central Europe.

Years' War. But Ottoman troops nevertheless remained fearsome in the attack and tenacious in defense. And after 1656, the Ottoman central government briefly revived under a vigorous line of grand viziers (first ministers to the Sultan), the Köprülü family. In the 1660s the Ottomans began a new thrust up the Danube Valley against their Habsburg antagonists. Louis XIV, intent on tipping the European balance in France's favor, allied himself with the Turks and with Hungarian rebels against Leopold I.

But Austria prevailed and acquired a prestige and a sense of mission that long endured. From July to September 1683 a Turkish army of more than 100,000 besieged Vienna after laying waste to everything in its path. Volunteers rushed to Austria's aid from all across the Continent. The greatest pope of the century, Innocent XI, proclaimed Europe's last crusade against Islam. A coalition army under the leadership of King John Sobieski of Poland descended from the heights outside Vienna upon the Turks and routed them. For the next 16 years, Austria and its allies fought their way laboriously back down the Danube Valley. In 1697, Prince Eugene of Savoy at last broke the Turkish army at the battle of Zenta, near the present Yugoslav-Hungarian border. Turkey ceased to be a threat and soon became a victim.

The resulting Peace of Carlowitz in 1699 gave the Habsburgs all of Hungary. The Emperor crushed the Hungarian Protestants and executed many of them for treason. The Hungarian nobility retained its serfs and many of its old privileges in return for recognizing the ultimate sovereignty of Vienna. But the Habsburgs imprudently left local administration to the nobility, and failed to create a uniform, centralized system of administration for all their possessions. Eugene's victories nevertheless established a strong state in the Danube Valley where none had existed before. The Treaties of Ryswick in 1697 and Carlowitz in 1699 thus marked the emergence of the two new great powers that had risen to check the overbearing ambition of Louis XIV—Britain and Austria. And by the end of the century, two further contenders for great power status had begun their ascent—Brandenburg-Prussia and Russia.

The Curious Rise of Brandenburg-Prussia

Prussia, the power that emerged from the obscure Electorate of Brandenburg, was the most improbable of all seventeenth- and eighteenth-century claimants to great power status. The Habsburgs and even the primitive Grand Duchy of Muscovy had extensive territorial bases. The Hohenzollern dynasty that created Prussia had been mere margraves—counts of a "mark," or frontier province—in Brandenburg since 1417. The one distinction of the small, sandy, and barren principality around Berlin was that after about 1230 it was one of the seven "electorates" of the Holy Roman Empire, states whose rulers—at least in theory—voted to elect the emperor.

In the early seventeenth century, by the accidents of dynastic inheritance, the Hohenzollern family acquired two further territories of importance—the Duchy of Cleves and some neighboring lands on the Rhine in 1614, and the Duchy of Prussia on the Baltic coast to the northeast in 1618. The total population of all Hohenzollern possessions was perhaps 1.5 million. The provinces lacked defensible boundaries, standing military forces, and a central administration other than the household of the Elector. Each of the provincial estates jealously guarded their inherited privileges. Nothing suggested that this chance agglomeration of provinces was capable of becoming a powerful state, especially since the Thirty Years' War had devastated Brandenburg. Berlin lost over half its population, and the Hohenzollern dominions as a whole probably lost almost one-third of their people, a loss that took 40 years to make up.

One man changed this situation. Frederick William of Hohenzollern, the Great Elector (r. 1640–88), was the first of the line of remarkable rulers that made Prussia. Born in 1620, he succeeded to power in 1640 after an education in Holland that had emphasized the latest in statecraft and technology. A devout Calvinist, he had learned toleration from the Dutch, and, in an age of fanaticism he respected the Lutheranism of his subjects. Above all, he learned from the helplessness of Brandenburg during the war. "A ruler is treated with no consideration if he does not have troops and means of his own," he advised his son in 1667. "It is these, Thank God! which have made me considerable since the time that I began to have them."

He inherited in 1640 a poorly equipped and mutinous army of 2,500 men. Before the end of the Thirty Years' War in 1648 his ceaseless efforts had increased it to 8,000 disciplined troops; by his death in 1688 he had a peacetime force of 30,000 which could expand to 40,000 in time of war. In the 48 years of his reign, the Great Elector built upon Brandenburg-Prussia's meager population the strongest military power in Germany, except for Austria's.

To accomplish that end, he needed money. Raising it required administrative centralization and the crushing of the provincial estates that largely controlled taxation. In Brandenburg he struck a bargain with the Estates in 1653 that provided him with a lump sum that he used to raise further troops. That force in turn allowed him to collect taxes without further votes by the Estates, which—like Louis XIV—he never summoned again. In Prussia, far to the east, the townsmen were more stubborn than in Brandenburg, and the hard-bitten nobility, the *Junkers* (from *Jungherr*, "young lord"), proved exceedingly unruly. The provincial opposition turned to Poland for support, but Frederick eventually crushed the resistance and executed its leaders. After campaigns against both Poland and Sweden, he also secured clear title to Prussia, which he had originally held as a fief from the King of Poland. Only Cleves and the western principalities defied Frederick with some success. There he was unable to introduce his most hated tax, the excise, despite nine separate attempts.

Despite some setbacks, Frederick set up a tax system under civil servants of his own choosing that extended to all his territories. He deprived the nobility of the power it had exercised through the Estates and pressed it into state service as officers in the new standing army. In return, he confirmed and strengthened Junker control over the serfs. Power, not the betterment of the lowly, was the Great Elector's objective.

But against the background of the Thirty Years' War, the creation of the standing army and the order it brought was nevertheless a contribution to the welfare of the population. Devastation by foreign armies was even worse than Junker oppression. With the relative peace that Frederick William brought, the population could tolerate heavier taxation and centralization. Frederick William's foreign policy was cautious. He sold his support to a succession of temporary allies in return for subsidies that helped pay for his army, while avoiding heavy fighting. The Swedes came close to Berlin in 1675, but he drove them off at the battle of Fehrbellin, a sign of Brandenburg-Prussia's rise and of Sweden's decline.

Frederick William likewise tailored economic and religious policy to the needs of the state. He helped revive and improve agriculture after 1648 and encouraged industry and commerce. He made Brandenburg a haven for religious refugees—Lutherans, Calvinists, and large numbers of Huguenots after Louis XIV revoked the Edict of Nantes in 1685. These immigrants, together with Dutch, Swiss, and other newcomers, brought new skills in agriculture and industry, helped increase the population, and added considerably to the strength of the state. He welcomed

Frederick William, the Great Elector, painted by his contemporary, Mathias Czwiczeic.

even the more radical Protestant sects and the Jews but drew the line at the Jesuits, whom he considered too intolerant.

The recognition in 1701 of the Great Elector's son as Frederick I, "King in Prussia" (that is, in the province of Prussia, outside the boundary of the Empire) symbolized the appearance of a new power in Europe. In 1720, at the end of the Great Northern War that paralleled in eastern Europe the War of the Spanish Succession, the Hohenzollerns gained Pomerania and the vital port of Stettin from Sweden.

Prussia, as the Hohenzollern lands became known, had in 80 years transformed itself from a chance agglomeration of feeble provinces into a state on the threshold of great power status. The coincidental weakness of its neighbors, rivals, or overlords—Sweden, Poland, Russia, and the Empire—gave it the opportunity. But this "Sparta of the North" rose primarily through its own efforts, through its army. All states in the fiercely competitive European system were machines for war, but Prussia devoted to its military relatively more of its population, resources, and energies than any other state. The army was the first institution common to all the Great Elector's lands, and its supporting bureaucracy was the model for Prussia's later organs of civil government. The nobility served the state in the army and bureaucracy, and came to identify itself with state and army to an extent without parallel elsewhere. That army, the army that conquered true great power status for Prussia in the coming wars of the mid-eighteenth century, *was* the Prussian state.

Russia: Revolution from Above

To the east of Prussia, Sweden, Poland, and the Ottoman Empire, no great power existed in the seventeenth century. The only contender was Muscovy, a state closer in constitution to the Ottoman Empire than to anything in Europe. As in the Ottoman Empire,

in India, and in China, the Muscovite tsar "owned" his territory and his subjects, who enjoyed no rights against the state. That was no accident. Muscovy acquired its statecraft from Byzantium, and above all from the Mongols, its overlords from around 1240 until 1480 (see pp. 377–79).

The rulers of Muscovy were fully conscious of their uniqueness. They derided the "limited" monarchs to the west as "men under contract" to their subjects. In a letter addressed to Queen Elizabeth I of England in 1570, Tsar Ivan the Terrible had mocked her as no true sovereign, but one who had "men who rule beside you, and not only men, but trading boors." In Russia, even nobles lacked rights—even property rights—against the state; Ivan broke the hereditary nobility or *boyars* by torture, massacre, and wholesale confiscation of land in the 1560s and 1570s. He largely replaced them with a new "service nobility" that owed abject obedience to the autocrat. Scornful xenophobia characterized Muscovy's external relations. The alternation of despotism and anarchy marked its internal politics.

Anarchy at first seemed Muscovy's lot after the unlamented death of Ivan the Terrible in 1584. The customary succession disputes, the "Time of Troubles," lasted until the accession in 1613 of the Romanov dynasty, which ruled Russia until 1917. Thereafter, religious strife compounded the weakness of the state. A reforming leader of the Orthodox Church, Patriarch Nikon, provoked a devastating schism in the 1660s by revising ritual and liturgy to bring them closer to the original Greek text of the Bible. That exasperated the traditionalist masses, to whom the Old Slavonic texts were sacrosanct. The Church split into a shallowly based state institution and fiercely independent sects of "Old Believers" who braved executions and exile for their faith. As many as 20,000 may have burned themselves to death in the belief that the end of the world was at hand.

Abroad, Russia fared poorly against Swedes, Poles, and Turks, and remained cut off from access to either Baltic or Black sea. English merchants made contact with Moscow in the 1550s by the icy route around Norway to the bleak port of Archangel on the White Sea, and German merchants were also active in the capital. But Russia's chief import, then and later, was the West's technology, especially its military technology. The Renaissance and Reformation reached only as far as Catholic Poland.

In 1689, a new monarch, Peter I (r. 1682–1725), seized power at the age of 17 in a palace coup. He was nearly seven feet tall, with inexhaustible energy and appetites, and a ferocious will. His insatiable curiosity led him to spend much time with the Dutch and Germans who lived in the "German Quarter" of Moscow. There he probably conceived the ambition of making Russia a great power by rapidly adopting western technology, civil and military institutions, and customs. The partial realization of that ambition ultimately earned for him the title of Peter the Great.

Peter at first allowed others to rule for him, but in 1695 he ventured a first campaign against the Turkish fortress of Azov, where the Don River enters the Black Sea. The attack failed, but in 1696, with the help of Swiss, Dutch and Habsburg experts, he built a fleet on the Don River, cut the fortress off from supplies and reinforcements, and stormed it. The lesson Peter I drew was that he needed additional western expertise to create a navy and to modernize his archaic army.

In 1696–97, thinly disguised as a private citizen, Peter visited Holland, England, Germany, and Austria. There he learned how societies centuries ahead of Russia built ships, made munitions, and conducted government and diplomacy. He worked in the shipyards, eagerly questioned everyone he met about western naval and military technology, and drank steadily through the night with his Russian companions. When he returned to Russia he brought with him over a thousand Western experts—seaman, gunners, shipwrights, engineers, mathematicians, surgeons.

An outburst of xenophobia at home cut short his European tour. The *strel'tsy*, a barbarous and undisciplined palace guard that he had thwarted in his seizure of power in 1689, remained a threat. In 1696, in league with the "Old Believers" and distrustful of Peter's increasingly obvious intention of introducing Western innovations, the *strel'tsy* marched on the Kremlin. Peter hastened back to Moscow to find that trusted aides had suppressed the revolt. He then made an example of the rebels that would long haunt even the memories of his countrymen, long accustomed to indiscriminate bloodshed. The tsar executed over a thousand *strel'tsy* to the accompaniment of torture on a scale not seen since Ivan the Terrible.

He also determined to use his autocratic sovereign power to "westernize" his subjects externally, by force if need be. In 1699–1700 he forbade the traditional long robes and the beards that his subjects wore in the belief that God was bearded and man was made in his image. The tsar himself took a hand in the shaving of his courtiers. He fought the resulting xenophobic and Orthodox reaction with brutal repression. He also ended the seclusion of women and instituted western-style social gatherings of both sexes at which polite conversation and ballroom dancing rather than strong drink were the chief entertainments. His will to transform Russia brooked no opposition; when his son and heir Alexis showed himself a slothful devotee of tradition, Peter I had him arrested, tortured, and put to death in 1618.

But Peter I's priorities were above all military. He sought first to imitate Western power, not Western civilization. Beginning in 1699, he set up a new army using German and other foreign experts as officers. An overwhelming defeat by the Swedes at

Contemporary cartoon of Peter cutting the beard of a Russian noble. Those who kept their beards had to pay a tax and carry a license (below).

| 1462 | | 1613 | | | | 1917 |

Grand Dukes of Moscow and First Tsars of Russia | House of Romanov

Peter I   Catherine II

1689   1725   1762   1796

Narva in 1700 only spurred him on; Russia had to either modernize its army, or perish. The tsar encouraged the vital iron industry of the Urals, set up cannon foundries, and created schools for gunnery, navigation, engineering, and officer training. By 1709, the year of his great victory over Charles XII of Sweden at Poltava, Russia had a modern army of over 100,000. By the end of Peter's reign in 1725 that army had swelled to 210,000 regulars and 100,000 auxiliaries that included the dreaded Cossack cavalry. The navy had grown from nothing to 24 ships of the line. Those were powerful forces indeed for a state with a population of only 8 million.

The army, the largest in eastern Europe, had the chance to achieve results, for Russia was at peace only one year in all of Peter's long reign. In the south it failed to hold Azov. Peter had to leave the Turks to his successors. But in the Great Northern War, the tsar seized

Peter the Great.

from Sweden the vital coastline on the Gulf of Finland. That gave him the "window on the sea," the direct contact with western Europe through the ice-free southern Baltic that was his primary geopolitical goal.

Peter's subjects, who bore the weight of his gigantic social engineering project, bought these military accomplishments dearly. The net effect of Peter's sometimes haphazard social and fiscal legislation was to divide a relatively complex society with a variety of subtle status gradations into two great classes—the "service nobility," and the more or less enserfed peasantry. A century after Peter I, a Russian intellectual could still quip bitterly that Russian society was divided into "slaves of the sovereign [the nobles], and slaves of the landlord [the serfs]; the former are called free only with regard to the latter."

Peter systematized the service nobility system he had inherited. All landowners owed service, and he decreed in 1714 the hated innovation of primogeniture, which forced noble younger sons off the land and into the army and navy. By instituting a fourteen-step "Table of Ranks" of 1722, Peter defined nobility in terms of one criterion alone, service. He made explicit what Louis XIV and the Great Elector could only implicitly practice—that service to the state, not birth, determined rank. In Russia, a lieutenant's commission now automatically brought noble status. That provided a career leading to ennoblement for the ambitious sons of commoners and helped divert them into state service and away from commerce and industry.

But it was the peasantry, not the nobility, that paid most for Peter's innovations. In return for its service, the nobility gained a freer hand than ever before in dealing with serfs. A new tax census classified all doubtful cases as serville, thus increasing the number of serfs. And the state demanded from the peasantry forced labor, military service, and taxes on an unprecedented scale. Supporting the new army required conscription, on the model of Sweden. After 1705 each 20 households had to furnish one recruit every year. The state provided the new military industries with serfs and convicts as labor, while a new head tax ("soul tax") tripled both state income and the tax burden. Forced labor and taxation, by one estimate, extorted from each household the equivalent of 125 to 187 days of labor each year. The ultimate result was depopulation, as peasants died of their privations or fled to the Don Cossacks to the southeast.

After 1709 Peter moved the seat of government from Moscow to a new city built on conquered territory on the Gulf of Finland: St. Petersburg, named for his patron saint. That change was the symbol of the tsar's aim of rivaling the West. The new city faced west, and its nearby naval base, Kronstadt ("royal city" *in German*) claimed the mastery of the Baltic. The methods that created the new capital, and its price, were also characteristic both of Peter's work and of that of later autocrats who sought to imitate him both in Russia and in other backward states. St. Petersburg rose in an unhealthy marshland at the mouth of the Neva River and was a deliberate break with the Moscow-centered past. Peter compelled nobles and merchants to settle and build there. Construction proceeded rapidly through annual forced labor drafts of 20,000 peasants. Many perished from disease and exposure.

This new capital, founded upon the bones of dead peasants, became the center of a new bureaucratic structure that the tsar built haphazardly over the primitive central administration he had inherited. The western conception of "the state," as distinct from the private staff of the sovereign, now made its entry into Russian history. Peter set up provincial administrations, supervisory boards to coordinate the bureaucracy, and a "senate," or central administrative body tasked with interpreting his orders. He also created an organ, the *Preobrazhenskii Prikaz*, to ferret out "political crime," from tax evasion, to criticism of the tsar, to coup attempts. The deliberate vagueness of its charter, its sweeping authority, and its ruthless suppression of individuals for their political opinions rather than their deeds made it the ancestor of the modern police state.

The new Russian state that Peter created thus dominated its society in a way unknown even in Brandenburg-Prussia, much less in western Europe. The state mastered the Orthodox Church, already weakened by the great schism. After 1700 Peter neglected to appoint a patriarch and made the Church a mere department of his bureaucracy. The state defined the nobil-

---

Peter the Great: The Bronze Horseman

The first and greatest modern Russian poet, Aleksandr Sergeyevich Pushkin (1799–1837), summed up Peter's place in Russian history in "The Bronze Horseman" (1833), named for the tsar's statue at St. Petersburg.

That square, the lions, and him—the one
Who, bronzen countenance upslanted
Into the dusk aloft, sat still,
The one by whose portentous will
The city by the sea was planted . . .
How awesome in the gloom he rides!
What thought upon his brow resides!
His charger with what fiery mettle,
His form with what dark strength endowed!
Where will you gallop, charger proud,
Where next your plunging hoofbeats settle?
Oh, Destiny's great potentate!
Was it not thus, a towering idol
Hard by the chasm, with iron bridle
You reared up Russia to her fate?

From Alexander Pushkin, *Collected Narrative and Lyrical Poetry*, trans. by Walter Arndt (Ann Arbor: Ardis Publishers, 1984), p. 437.

ity by its service, and by demanding residence at St. Petersburg reinforced an already existing pattern of absentee landlordism that weakened the grip of the nobility on rural society. The state stunted the towns, and ensured that the small and timorous middle classes that eventually emerged would be dependent on state employment and state contracts.

The state then ordered its subjects to develop a consciousness, a public opinion. Peter was the first Russian sovereign to speak of "the common good." He founded Russia's first newspaper. He recognized that rivalling the West ultimately required the voluntary collaboration of his subjects and the development of economic and intellectual initiative *from below*. But as his successors discovered, initiative from below was a deadly threat to the autocracy's own power. That tension, the result of the grafting of Western technology and military institutions onto non-Western social and political structures, was a pattern much seen later. Its consequence was a cycle of repression, "thaw," and further repression that has continued—despite the leap from tsarist to Communist autocracy in 1917—to the present.

But that ultimate consequence of Peter's work was far in the future when he died in 1725. What he left was a Russian great power, a military giant, irrevocably part of the European state system. And his example created a tradition of dynamic autocracy, of brutal revolutions from above carried through by pitiless force, that later Russian rulers sought to emulate or surpass.

The Losers: Sweden and Poland

While Prussia grew and Russia transformed itself, their Swedish and Polish neighbors declined. Sweden had burst on Europe as a military power of first rank when Gustavus Adolphus had swept into Germany in 1630–31. The Baltic virtually became a Swedish lake, with Swedish imperial outposts that stretched from the Gulf of Finland to the North Sea. Copper, iron, and agriculture were Sweden's chief resources; superior cannon and muskets its chief military advantage. But Swedish power rested on shaky foundations. The country had a population of less than 2 million—not much larger than Brandenburg-Prussia or the Dutch Republic. The empire that Gustavus Adolphus had acquired was overextended; its enemies, from Russia and Poland to Prussia and Denmark, were hungry for revenge.

When young Charles XII (r. 1697–1718) came to the throne, a coalition of Russia, Poland, and Denmark pounced on his Baltic territories. But Charles proved a greater commander even than Gustavus Adolphus. He crushed the coalition's forces in a series of lightning campaigns. Then success intoxicated him. In 1708–09 he launched Sweden into a foolhardy attempt to smash Russia, and met devastating defeat at Poltava in the Ukraine. He subsequently escaped to Turkey, spent some years at the Ottoman court seeking allies, and died in the siege of an obscure Norwegian fortress in 1718. His meteoric career exhausted Sweden. In the peace settlements of 1719 to 1721 that ended this "Great Northern War," Hanover, Denmark, Prussia, and Russia divided Sweden's Baltic empire. Sweden retired for good into the ranks of the second-class powers.

Poland, an elective monarchy originally formed in 1386 through the union of the crowns of Poland and Lithuania, suffered a similar fate. Polish prosperity and culture had reached their peak in the sixteenth century. Roman Catholicism had linked Poland to western Europe and had conveyed the influence of the Renaissance, the Protestant revolt, and the Counter-Reformation. But by the beginning of the seventeenth century Poland's economic and political decline had begun.

In France, Prussia, and Russia the state tamed the nobility. In Poland the nobility gradually became the state, thanks to the elective character of the monarchy. Until the 1570s the Polish

The Baltic: A Swedish Lake   1621–1721

nobility had usually elected the legal heirs of their monarchs, but thereafter they chose candidates that appeared to favor their own interests. By 1700 the nobility had deprived the monarchy of most of its powers, although petty German princes still sought election to gain the prestige of a royal title.

Noble power had consequences. It sunk the peasants more deeply in serfdom than anywhere else in Europe. It checked the small and weak towns, prevented the rise of urban middle classes, and froze the Polish economy in rural backwardness. Above all, it concentrated political power in the Polish Diet, which now represented only the nobility, since representatives of the towns no longer dared attend.

The Diet's procedure, tailor-made to preserve noble domination, was notorious—one negative vote, the "liberum veto," could block any action. Moreover, the liberum veto allowed any member to "explode" a Diet session—to dissolve it and wipe out all legislation it had passed up to that moment. Of 57 Diets held in the century after 1652, all but nine "exploded," and in one case a member cast a veto simply to see what would happen. And if by some accident legislation did emerge from the Diet, no machinery existed to enforce it against the provincial assem-

Medals celebrating an abortive "Treaty of Eternal Peace" between Russia and Poland (1686). Left: King John Sobieski, Poland's last great king. Right: personifications of Poland and Russia.

blies of lesser nobles or the private estate jurisdictions of the landed magnates. John Sobieski (1674–96), a native Pole of high integrity, was the last great king. He saved Vienna from the Turks but failed to save Poland from its nobility. After him Poland declined into incoherence, and extinction at the hands of Austria, Russia, and Prussia between 1772 and 1795.

ABSOLUTISM, CONSTITUTIONALISM, AND THE BALANCE OF POWER

The half century from 1660 to 1715 was thus a period of dramatic change. Internally, absolute divine-right monarchy reached its height in the France of Louis XIV. Powers from Madrid to St. Petersburg attempted to imitate the French model. Nevertheless, a few smaller peoples such as the Swiss had rejected monarchy in favor of republican government. The Dutch "sea beggars" had even shown that a republic could compete in the great power arena. But it took England's Glorious Revolution and Marlborough's victories to demonstrate to Europe that even the very greatest powers could choose alternatives to absolute monarchy.

Externally, relations between states and the workings of the balance of power almost completely superseded the religious-ideological conflicts that had rent Europe before 1648. France's bid for mastery after 1672 provoked the rise of England and Austria as great powers. Two great empires of the sixteenth century, Spain and the Ottoman Turks, continued their decline. Two peoples of limited resources and numbers, the Dutch and the Swedes, briefly claimed great power status in the mid-seventeenth century, but lacked staying power. Two new powers appeared in eastern Europe to join the balance—military Prussia and semi-barbaric Russia. The rivalries of these states—Britain against France, France against Austria, Austria against Prussia, Austria and Russia against the Ottoman Empire—were the forces that moved European war and diplomacy after 1715.

Suggestions for Further Reading

Western Europe

J. Stoye, *Europe Unfolding, 1648–1688* (1969), and J. B. Wolf, *The Emergence of the Great Powers, 1685–1715* (1951), provide useful introductions, but see also W. Doyle, *The Old European Order, 1660–1800* (1978).

C. J. Friedrich and C. Blitzer, *The Age of Power* (1957), covers the general theme of this chapter. R. Hatton, *Europe in the Age of Louis XIV* (1969), is excellent on social history. P. Goubert, *Louis XIV and Twenty Million*

Frenchmen (1970), wittily relates the career of the king to the social history of France. See also J. B. Wolf, *Louis XIV* (1968), and W. H. Lewis, *The Splendid Century* (1954), an elegant account of the reign. On England, see especially C. Hill, *The Century of Revolution, 1603–* *1714* (1961). G. N. Clark, *The Later Stuarts, 1660–1714* (1934), is a fine synthesis. C. H. Wilson, *England's Apprenticeship, 1603–1763* (1965), covers England's emergence as a great power.

Eastern Europe

For the lands east of the Elbe, see especially S. H. Cross, *Slavic Civilization Through the Ages* (1948), and O. Halecki, *Borderlands of Western Civilization* (1952). On Germany, see H. Holborn, *A History of Modern Germany, 1648–1840* (1964). R. W. J. Evans, *The Making of the Habsburg Monarchy* (1979), and H. G. Koenigsberger, *The Habsburgs and Europe* (1971), are useful surveys. On Prussia, S. B. Fay and K. Epstein, *The Rise of* *Brandenburg-Prussia to 1786* (1937, 1964), is concise. See also F. Carsten, *The Origins of Prussia* (1954). B. H. Sumner, *Peter the Great and the Emergence of Russia* (1950), is a useful short account. For analysis, see especially R. Pipes, *Russia under the Old Regime* (1974), and J. Blum, *Lord and Peasant in Russia from the Ninth to the Nineteenth Century* (1961).

21
The Scientific Revolution and the Enlightenment

*U*ntil the seventeenth century the growth of knowledge about nature had been slow, fumbling, and discontinuous. Scholars had observed natural phenomena, had in many cases recorded them, and had sometimes derived useful generalizations from those observations. But "experiments" in the modern sense had been largely absent, and scientific inquiry was scarcely distinguishable from theological speculation.

That changed. By the eighteenth century, the age of rapidly broadening and deepening knowledge that became known as the Enlightenment, the West had accumulated a large body of empirically verifiable principles that allowed the prediction and manipulation of nature. That type of knowledge has continued to accumulate, with revolutionary effect. The ever-accelerating understanding of and mastery over nature, for good or ill, was the achievement of the West, the first civilization in history to make a clear distinction between science on the one hand and religion or magic on the other.

THE SCIENTIFIC REVOLUTION

A new method of inquiry, later called the "scientific method," emerged from the universities of Western Europe in the late thirteenth and fourteenth centuries, and achieved wide currency in western Europe after 1600. The new method was essentially a combination of two elements: careful observation and controlled experiment, and rational interpretation of the results of observation and experimentation, preferably using mathematics. That was the origin of modern science, an endeavor that a great twentieth-century mathematician-philosopher described as the "vehement and passionate interest in the relation of general principles to irreducible and stubborn facts."

The Medieval Universe

Precisely *why* the West took the lead in scientific speculation over the other great civilizations, China, Islam, and

India, remains unclear, although the early Western invention of complex devices such as clocks shows a similar precociousness. But even in the West, deep-rooted traditional assumptions about the nature of the universe long ruled. Medieval learning dictated that the universe was a finite sphere with the earth at the center. Between the center and the outermost limit, nine transparent spheres supposedly carried stars, planets, sun and moon in their daily revolutions about a motionless earth. The earth was the realm of change, decay, and original sin. The heavens were the realm of perfection and changelessness. Sun, moon, and heavenly bodies were perfectly spherical and moved in spherical tracks to the accompaniment of an ethereal "music of the spheres." The assumed dichotomy between heavenly perfection and earthly corruption demanded a sharp separation between the laws of heavenly and of earthly physics.

Even in the Middle Ages, not all scholars found this picture of the universe convincing. By the thirteenth and

Two of Galileo's telescopes.

The observatory of the Danish astronomer Tycho Brahe was the finest of the sixteenth century. Note the domes protecting the instruments.

fourteenth centuries a small but increasing number had begun to question it, including Franciscans, perhaps inspired by their founder's sensitive feeling for nature. The study of the Greco-Arabic scientific texts that had reached the West stimulated a group of scholars at Oxford and Paris to apply mathematical reasoning to problems of physics and astronomy, such as accelerated motion. Professors at the University of Padua continued these speculations in the fifteen and sixteenth centuries. At Padua, a center of medical training for three centuries, scholars vigorously debated the proper method of studying nature in the course of arguments about Aristotle. Medieval universities such as Oxford, Paris, and Padua kept interest in science alive and nurtured the first faint beginnings of the scientific revolution.

Most Europeans of 1500, however, did not question the Greek authorities, who had decreed that the normal state of everything in the universe was a state of rest. Aristotle had said that bodies moved only if a mover pushed or pulled them. Galen of Pergamum, in the second century A.D., had described

the anatomy of the human body so convincingly that doctors still saw it through his eyes. In that same century, the Greco-Egyptian astonomer Ptolemy had systematized a mathematical description of the observed irregularities of the movements of the planets so ingenious that European authorities saw no need to discard it until after 1500. Ptolemy assumed that all motion in the heavens was circular and proceeded at a constant rate. But since the observed pattern of actual planetary motion in the heavens was not precisely circular, Ptolemy had invented the "epicycle," an additional small circle in which the planet moved while traveling around the circumference of its larger "sphere" around the earth. He and his successors needed 80 epicycles to force the observed motion of the planets to fit the theory, but in the end Ptolemy's system explained what astronomers saw. Even more important, it permitted the prediction of lunar and planetary motion with some precision. At the close of the Middle Ages, few scholars saw much need to improve upon the observations and theories of the ancients.

The Background of Change

Nevertheless, forces in European society in the fourteenth, fifteenth, and sixteenth centuries prepared the way for a challenge to this orthodoxy. Artisans and craftsmen gradually adopted techniques more advanced than those of their medieval predecessors. The development of the glass industry and the invention of the lens at some point before 1300, to take but one example, gave the promise of vastly extending humanity's ability to observe natural processes. Breakthroughs in shipbuilding and navigation (see p. 497) permitted the voyages of discovery, which in turn stimulated interest in nature generally.

The Renaissance, with its emphasis on literature and art and its veneration for the wisdom of the ancients, was in some respects antiscientific. But the

Humanists were interested in Greek scientific texts as well as in Greek literature, and Renaissance patrons of the arts were also patrons of inventors and technicians. Humanistic study revealed that ancient scientific authorities had differed among themselves on key issues, just at the moment when the authority of Galen and Ptolemy was becoming shaky for other reasons. Anatomical studies by the great Renaissance artists and the increasing practice of dissection suggested that Galen had made mistakes. Growing skill in mathematics exposed the clumsiness of Ptolemy's explanations. By the opening years of the sixteenth century, conditions were ripe for a dramatic shift in the West's underlying assumptions about the universe.

1543: Vesalius and Copernicus

In 1543 two notable scientific works heralded the end of Medieval science. Andreas Vesalius, a Flemish anatomist at the University of Padua, published *On the Structure of the Human Body*, a marvelously careful description of human anatomy based on direct observation during dissection, and illustrated with graphic and accurate plates. Vesalius did not free himself completely from the authority of Galen, nor did his book offer much theoretical insight. But it was an influential example of the power of observation.

Even more powerful in its ultimate effect was the work of a Polish scholar, Mikolaj Kopérnik, better known as Copernicus. *On the Revolutions of the Heavenly Bodies* was a brilliant mathematical treatise that showed how to reduce Ptolemy's 80 epicycles to 34 by assuming that the earth turned on its axis once a day and moved around the sun once a year. Unlike Vesalius, Copernicus was not primarily an observer. During study at Padua in the early years of the century he had learned that some ancient authorities had held that the earth moved. That assumption made the motions of the moon and planets far simpler to ex-

plain mathematically than the accepted earth-centered theory. Copernicus, following the Medieval notion that "nature always acts in the simplest ways," eventually discarded Ptolemy on grounds of logic, rather than from observation. His ideas gradually spread.

In 1600, the Inquisition tried a former monk named Giordano Bruno as a heretic and burned him at the stake in Rome. He had published works arguing that the universe was not finite but infinite in extent, that numberless suns and planets like our own filled it, and that God was equally present in every planet or atom in the cosmos. He also maintained that the existence of the infinite made it impossible to arrive at absolute truth, or find limits to the extent of knowledge. Co-

Ptolemy's earth-centered and finite cosmos fit both available astronomical evidence and prevailing theological dogmas well enough to endure from the second century A.D. until the discoveries of Copernicus and Galileo.

Scientific revolutionaries of the seventeenth century: Francis Bacon (above) and René Descartes.

pernicus had inspired him, although Copernicus himself believed in the finite sphere of the fixed stars and the uniqueness of the earth. Despite the fires of the Inquisition, Bruno's intuition of the infinity of the universe ultimately prevailed. It was the beginning of modern cosmology.

The Purposes and Method of Science: Bacon and Descartes

Two major prophets of the early Scientific Revolution, Francis Bacon (1561–1626) and René Descartes (1596–1650) followed precursors such as Copernicus. Bacon, an English lawyer, statesman, and essayist, waged a vigorous scholarly battle against the deductive method of Medieval scholasticism, which began with premises usually taken on authority and deduced from them their logical consequences. That might help to organize truths already known, argued Bacon, but it could never discover new truths. Only inductive reasoning, starting from the direct observation of phenomena and developing from them principles that explained those observations, could produce new truths.

Bacon set a practical goal for science, the "domination" of humanity over nature. He pictured an imaginary future society of scientists whose end was to benefit mankind by conducting hundreds of experiments that discovered useful facts. Bacon failed to appreciate the importance of mathematical models in theoretical analysis, and he found Copernicus unconvincing. Although he praised experimentation, he performed almost no experiments and collected his data in the traditional way, from books. His writings nevertheless dramatized the importance of empirical research. The founding in 1662 of the Royal Society of London, the first scientific society in England, owed much to Bacon's inspiration. He was the remote ancestor of the great laboratories and team research projects of the twentieth century. His goal, the

mastery of nature through rational analysis, has—despite continuing criticism of its alleged arrogance—marked the West off from the other historic civilizations.

Descartes, a French mathematician and philosopher, was an even more important figure than Bacon, but he lacked Bacon's intuitive understanding of the need for observation. To Descartes, the excitement of science lay in mathematical analysis and theory. In a famous autobiographical account, he told how the literature and philosophy that he had studied as a youth had left him unsatisfied because he reached no *certain* conclusions. By contrast, the precision and certainty of mathematics aroused his enthusiasm. He set out to discover a mathematical "method of rightly conducting the reason and discovering truth in the sciences."

In November 1619, in a moment of intuition, he saw the exact correspondence between geometry and algebra—the truth that equations and curves on graphs were interchangeable. That intoxicating vision suggested to him a new way of grasping ultimate truth. If humanity systematically doubted all notions based on authority or custom and started with clear and precise ideas known to be true, it might deduce systematically the entire universe from a few simple principles, just as he had derived curves from equations.

Descartes was one of the first to believe that science could save humanity. His enthusiasm was infectious, and outran the knowledge available in the seventeenth century. He reduced the universe, including the human body, to a mathematically intelligible machine. Only the human intellect, he believed, resisted mathematical description. He therefore defined it as being outside the world of matter: mind comprehended the world but did not exist in it. His generalizations in astronomy, physics, and anatomy were often premature, and his passion for system building went far beyond his capacity to confirm generalizations by experiment. He did important work in optics, but that in no way confirmed his far-ranging theories.

Nevertheless, Descartes' enthusiasm for scientific "method," his belief that mathematics could describe all phenomena, and his insistence on systematic doubt of all earlier theorizing left a profound mark on the scientific thinking of three centuries that followed. Descartes made it easier for his successors to reject old ideas, and they gradually came to accept his belief that mathematics must be the language of science.

Experiment and Mathematics

Bacon and Descartes were too optimistic. Bacon thought that a generation of determined experimentation would establish a solid structure of knowledge about the universe. Descartes expected that a few basic mathematical axioms would soon lead, by deduction, to a universal science. He also believed in a universe far simpler than it now appears. One of Descartes' pupils even described the world as a gigantic piece of clockwork.

Meanwhile, experimentation and mathematics were developing steadily in the hands of a growing host of scientists. William Gilbert (1544–1603), court physician to Elizabeth I, coined the word "electricity" and deduced that the earth itself was a huge magnet. His *De magnete* (1600) remained the foremost work on magnetism until the early nineteenth century. William Harvey (1578–1627), who had studied at Padua, argued in a work published in 1628 that the blood must circulate from arteries to veins to heart, thence to the lungs, back to the heart and on once more to the arteries. He did this by estimating the amount of blood the heart pumped in a minute and arguing that it must go somewhere. Later in the century the new microscope revealed the tiny capillaries that actually connect arteries to veins.

Harvey Discovers the Circulation of the Blood

Since calculations and visual demonstrations have confirmed all my suppositions, to wit, that the blood is passed through the lungs and the heart by the pulsation of the ventricles, is forcibly ejected to all parts of the body, therein steals into the veins . . . flows back everywhere . . . from small veins into larger ones, and thence comes at last into the vena cava and to the auricle of the heart; all this too in such amounts that it cannot be supplied from the ingesta [food] and is also in greater bulk than would suffice for nutrition.

I am obliged to conclude that in all animals the blood is driven around a circuit with an unceasing, circular sort of motion, that this is an activity of the heart which it carries out by virtue of its pulsation, and that in sum it constitutes the sole cause for the heart's pulsatile movement.

From C. C. Gillispie, *The Edge of Objectivity* (Princeton, N.J.: Princeton University Press, 1960), p. 71.

Evangelista Torricelli (1608–47), Blaise Pascal, and others investigated the ancient proposition, long believed by most scholars, that "nature abhors a vacuum." They created vacuums in test tubes, invented the barometer, and discovered that the pressure of the atmosphere varies between sea level and mountain top. They proved inherited wisdom false, and their work showed a growing precision in observation and an increasing sophistication in controlling experiments and in quantifying their results.

Mathematics likewise rapidly advanced. The invention of decimals and of logarithms early in the century facilitated calculation. Pascal inaugurated the study of probability. At the end of the century Sir Isaac Newton and Baron Gottfried Wilhelm von Leibniz (1646–1716) crowned the work of many others by simultaneously but separately inventing the calculus, which provided the first mathematical method for describing accelerating or decelerating motion.

Kepler: The Foundations of Celestial Mechanics

It was in astronomy and physics that observational techniques and mathematical methods first united—producing results of a beauty and explanatory power that shattered for good all traditional notions of the place of science in human knowledge and of humanity in the universe.

The German astronomer Johannes Kepler (1571–1630) found discrepancies in Copernicus's theory troubling, although he nevertheless believed in it. He worked from the observations of his master, the Danish astronomer Tycho Brahe (1546–1601), which were far more accurate than those available to Copernicus. Brahe's data ultimately caused Kepler to discard reluctantly the universal belief, which Copernicus had not challenged, that heavenly bodies moved in circles.

Kepler concluded that the ellipse, whose properties geometricians had studied since the time of the Greeks, fitted Brahe's observations of Mars, the planet whose motion most contradicted the Ptolemaic and Copernican systems. The orbits of the planets, Kepler suggested, were elliptical, with the sun at one of the two foci of the ellipse. Further, he demonstrated that a line from the sun to a planet swept out equal areas of the ellipse in equal times and that the cube of the distance of each planet from the sun was proportional to the square of the time of its revolution. That was astounding proof of the intuition of Descartes and others that nature was in some mysterious sense mathematical. A geometrical figure, studied for centuries as an abstract form, "fit" the facts of nature. By implication, nature was perhaps itself a machine, intelligible to the careful observer equipped with mathematics.

The New Universe: Galileo

Kepler's work describing many of his findings appeared in 1609. During that same year a professor at Padua and Pisa, Galileo Galilei (1564–1642), turned on the heavens a newly invented instrument, the telescope. He soon published an account of what he saw. The changeless perfection and perfect sphericity of the heavenly bodies had dissolved before his gaze. He saw that the moon had craters and mountains, that spots moved on the sun, that rings encircled Saturn, and that Jupiter had four moons of its own. A bright new star—a supernova—had already appeared in 1572, and Brahe had noted it. In 1577 a new comet had cut a path through what should have been unchanging crystalline spheres. Now Galileo's telescope shattered forever the immutable, finite, spherical universe of the Middle Ages. Thoughtful scholars suspected that Bruno had been right. Humanity was looking out into infinite space, at a sparse population of stars like the sun that might themselves have solar systems.

The Medieval distinction between terrestrial and celestial physics was apparently dissolving. The moon and sun were not perfect globes and the stars were not changeless. Nor was the earth any longer the motionless center of the universe. The earth, like Mars and Jupiter, was a planet circling the sun against a backdrop of silent, infinite space. Perhaps the same forces and laws operated both on earth and in the heavens.

Such views soon attracted the wrath of the Church of the Counter-Reformation, which had denounced the Copernican theory in 1616. The Roman Inquisition condemned Galileo himself in 1632, threatened him with torture, and forced him to recant. The legend soon arose that after retracting his "heretical" view that the earth moved around the sun, he nevertheless muttered stubbornly under his breath *"Eppur si muove"*—"It *does* move." Nor could the Inquisition suppress Galileo's brilliantly written dialogues, which contributed mightily to the overthrow not only of Ptolemy in favor of Copernicus, but also of Aristotle in favor of a new physics.

The speculations of the fourteenth-century Franciscans inspired Galileo's physics, but he was far more thorough and accurate than they in developing mathematical formulas to describe motion. He worked out by experiment the law of falling bodies—the distance fallen increases as the square of the time fallen. He saw that projectiles followed parabolic paths that were the resultant of the two forces acting upon the projectile—the initial impetus that launched it and the downward pull of the earth. That insight was the beginning of modern ballistics, the scientific foundation of the new warfare.

Galileo also came close to formulating the key concept of modern mechanics, the law of inertia: that bodies tend to remain at rest or to continue in motion in straight lines unless outside forces act upon them. That deceptively simple proposition—so fundamentally different from Aristotle's conception of motion as the result of some mover's action—was the source of the law of gravitation. Galileo prepared the way, but it was a man born in the year Galileo died that made that decisive breakthrough.

The Synthesis of Celestial and Terrestrial Mechanics: Newton

Sir Isaac Newton (1642–1727), the greatest figure of the Scientific Revolution, was the man who married Kepler's astronomy to Galileo's mechanics, broke down all distinctions between celestial and terrestrial physics, and accomplished at least part of Descartes' dream of establishing a "universal science." A fundamental intuition came to Newton while he was still a student in his twenties at Cambridge University: the force that bends the moon into its orbit about the earth must be the same force that pulls an apple from its branch to the ground. A reciprocal force of attraction between every body in the universe must exist, and that force—although as yet inexplicable—must be calculable.

Newton's earliest calculations came close enough to mathematical proof to persuade him that the same force indeed operated on the moon and on the apple, and that this force varied "directly as the product of the masses" involved and "inversely as the square of the distance" separating those masses. For some time after formulating this "law" of gravitation in 1664–66 he seems to have lost interest. But twenty years later a friend, the astronomer Edmund Halley (who calculated the orbit of the famous comet) persuaded Newton to publish. Newton developed the necessary mathematics—the calculus—to prove his theory to his own satisfaction. He published his conclusions in 1687 in his *Philosophiae naturalis principia mathematica*, the "mathematical principles of natural philosophy." It was one of the most influential books in the history of human thought.

To scientists Newton's law of gravitation provided a simple and elegant explanation of a growing mass of data in astronomy and physics, and laid the foundations of future research in both sciences. Further, Newton improved on Bacon and Descartes by giving the scientific method its classic formulation in his fourth "Rule of Reasoning":

> In experimental philosophy [science] we are to look upon propositions collected by general induction from phenomena as accurately or very nearly true, notwithstanding any contrary hypotheses [theories] that may be imagined, till such time as other phenomena occur, by which they may either be made more accurate or liable to exceptions.

Newton's support of the experimental or inductive approach was aimed against the premature generalizing, the theoretical "system[s] . . . little better than a Romance," of Descartes and his followers. But Newton, unlike Bacon, was fully convinced of the necessity of mathematical theory. Newton combined at last both celestial and terres-

The greatest scientific revolutionary of all: Sir Isaac Newton, painted by Kneller.

Newton invented and built this first reflecting telescope.

trial physics on the one hand, and empirical observation and mathematical interpretation on the other.

The Newtonian Universe

News of Newton's work spread rapidly among laymen, thanks to popular scientific works that soon began pouring from the presses of London and Amsterdam. The new universe that Newton disclosed was far different from the comforting finite universe of the Middle Ages. Bodies moved through infinite space in response to predictable, universally operating forces. Mass, force, and motion were the key concepts, and mathematics made them intelligible.

The question "Why?" had obsessed the scholars of the Middle Ages, who had felt they understood a natural phenomenon once they had discovered its end or purpose. Seventeenth-century scientists limited themselves to asking "How?" The discovery of regular patterns in natural processes satisfied most of them. The world of Kepler, Galileo, and Newton was a vast machine, working according to laws expressible in mathematics, laws intelligible to anyone who followed the proper experimental and mathematical methods. The telescope continued to reveal an ever-larger portion of an apparently infinite cosmos. The new astronomy, after displacing the earth as the center of the universe, displaced the sun as well. The microscope, after the 1660s, began to reveal the wonders of the infinitely small foundations of life—bacteria, spermatozoa, cells, capillaries.

The question "Why?" nevertheless remained unanswered. What was the place of God and of humanity in this universe? That question did not become acute until the eighteenth century. No prominent seventeenth-century scientist thought that he was reading God out of the universe. Descartes considered himself a good Catholic and apparently did not see the theological dangers inherent in his sharp separation of the world of matter from the world of mind. Newton spent many of his later years absorbed in theological speculation and alchemy. The border between science and religion or magic was still fluid, and contradictions between faith and science were not clearly evident to most seventeenth-century scientists, or to their audience.

The French philosopher-scientist Blaise Pascal (1623–62), inventor of probability theory and of the first calculating machine, and contributor to fields as diverse as the calculus and the dynamics of gases and fluids, indeed attempted a synthesis between faith and the new sciences that were now revealing the infinitely great and the infinitesimally small. For Pascal, "the whole visible world [was] only an imperceptible atom in the ample bosom of nature," and the universe "an infinite sphere, the center of which is everywhere, the circumference nowhere." "The eternal silence of these infinite spaces frightens me," he confessed. Yet to examine a mite, "with its minute body and parts incomparably more minute, limbs with their joints, veins in the limbs, blood in the veins, humors in the blood, drops in the humors, vapors in the drops," was equally astonishing. "What is man in nature? A Nothing in comparison with the Infinite, an All in comparison with the Nothing, a mean between nothing and everything." Pascal related the new universe explicitly to Christianity, to Christ's sacrifice on the cross which made humanity, despite its apparent insignificance, the greatest presence in the universe beside God. Others soon saw less need to invoke Christianity.

By the later seventeenth century the hold of religious orthodoxy on Europe's intellectual elite was beginning to weaken. Religious authorities could no longer simply forbid scientific speculation or experiment. The burning or torture of "heretics" such as Giordano Bruno slowly went out of fashion, except in Spain. And scientists themselves began to demarcate their activities sharply from questions of faith. The charters of the many scientific societies and academies that sprang up throughout Europe during the century usually contained clauses forbidding purely theological or political discussion and establishing that the group would not investigate "ultimate" or "final" causes.

The earliest history of the Royal Society of London, published in 1667, suggests that scientific discussions offered a peculiar attraction to thoughtful individuals during and after a fanatically bitter religious and civil war such as the English Revolution. Science, which by definition dealt with the empirically verifiable, might thereby become politically and theologically neutral and benefit humanity in practical ways. Scientific truth gradually emerged as an alternative to theological truth. It was not entirely accidental that modern science arose as religious warfare went out of fashion, amid general revulsion at the devastation that fanaticism had wrought.

Nevertheless, Newton's new "world picture" did not explicitly contradict religious feeling. Some indeed found in the mechanistic universe a source of religious awe. Baruch or Benedict Spinoza (1632–77), an Amsterdam lens grinder and philosopher descended from the Jewish communities that Spain had expelled, concluded that the new universe of mass, force, and motion, operating in strict obedience to inexorable laws, *was* God. Spinoza saw no need to consider God as above, behind, or beyond nature, as a "free cause" apart from natural law. God was not "Creator" or "Redeemer," but a "God *or* Nature" that included all being and incarnated natural law: "God never can decree, nor ever would have decreed, anything but what is; God did not exist before his decrees, and would not exist without them." Humanity, like all else, was part of the natural order and thus of God, and wisdom consisted of contem-

plating that order with serenity and delight.

Both Jewish and Christian contemporaries considered Spinoza a dangerous atheistic radical, although he was the mildest, kindliest, and most optimistic of men. Most of his works emerged in print only after his death. Contemporaries pointed out that to claim that humanity was part of God made it difficult to explain evil. Later critics discerned in "Whatever is, is in God" a dangerous fatalism. But his notion of religion was destined to have great influence in the eighteenth century.

THE CULTURE OF THE BAROQUE

The age of the scientific revolution was also, especially in the Catholic areas of the Continent, the age of the "baroque" style in the visual arts. The baroque sprang up in the later sixteenth century, reached its climax about the middle of the seventeenth, and came to its end around the middle of the eighteenth. Eighteenth-century critics invented the term *baroque* (French for "odd" or "irregular"), after tastes had again changed, to stigmatize seventeenth-century art as a grotesque corruption of Renaissance styles. But by the late nineteenth century critics had come to consider the baroque a great achievement. More than most styles, it is difficult to define because it reflected the contrasts and contradictions of seventeenth-century culture as a whole— religious ecstasy and worldly sensuality, credulity and rationalism, violence and respect for order.

Baroque painters and sculptors portrayed voluptuous women in repose, heroes in battle, and saints in ecstasy with equal skill and zest. In general, the dominant notes of the baroque were tension and conflict, and a penchant for the grandiose and dramatic. Renaissance painters and writers had been interested in humanity itself. Ba-

The German high baroque: Vierzehnheiligen Church in Weiss, Bavaria.

trayed figures in a space bathed in and suffused with light. The greatest of Dutch painters, Rembrandt van Rijn (1606–69), spotlighted figures in the midst of darkened space, while others pictured them floating through apparently infinite voids. To baroque artists the supernatural was natural. The scientists' concern with mass, force, and motion paralleled the painters' and poets' concern with individuals caught in the tension between elemental forces. The typical hero of baroque literature, critics have suggested, is Satan in John Milton's *Paradise Lost* (1667), the only great epic poem in English. Swayed by colossal passions, Satan moves through vast three-dimensional spaces, and bends the forces of the universe to serve his implacable will to domination: "To reign is worth ambition though in hell:/Better to reign in hell than serve in heav'n." But God nevertheless frustrates Satan's designs in the end.

The most typical, although not usually the most beautiful products of baroque architecture were the great palaces: Versailles and the remodeled Louvre in France, Schönbrunn in Austria, or Blenheim, the regal residence in England that Marlborough received for his victories. The style of these buildings was fundamentally Renaissance-classical, but grander, more ornate, and above all larger, often to the point of excess. As with the many descendants of Versailles, the neo-classical official buildings of later centuries, excess served a political purpose. Sheer mass emphasized the power of the state. In this, as in much else, Louis XIV led the way. Even some baroque religious architecture, such as the massive elliptical colonnades that the great Giovanni Lorenzo Bernini (1598–1680) erected to frame St. Peter's in Rome, conveyed the majesty of God rather than his mercy.

The most original creation of the baroque were the operas that originated in Italy early in the seventeenth century. Drama set to music had existed in the West since the twelfth cen-

roque artists depicted the conflicts of humanity against the universe, of man against man, and of man within himself on a tragic and heroic scale.

Instructive parallels exist between the thought-worlds of the baroque artists and those of the seventeenth-century scientists. Galileo and Newton studied bodies or masses moving through space under the influence of conflicting forces such as gravitation and centrifugal force. To the great French dramatists of the age—Corneille, Racine, and Molière—the objects of study were typical human beings torn between conflicting passions, such as love and duty. Space intrigued baroque painters. The Dutch master Jan Vermeer (1632–75) portury. But the music had been essentially choral and polyphonic until around 1600, when a group of Florentine composers devised a *"dramma per musica"* (drama through music) in which the characters sang their parts as simple melodies without choral accompaniment. Opera immediately became, and has remained, a vast popular success. The grandiose and palatial stage settings, the dramatic conflicts of the action, and the emotional power of the music exactly suited the taste of the period. Italian composers led the way until the end of the seventeenth century—Claudio Monteverdi (1567–1643), Girolamo Frescobaldi (1583–1643), Alessandro Scarlatti (1660–1725), and the greatest master of Italian Baroque music, Antonio Vivaldi (1675–1741). But it was an Englishman, Henry Purcell (1658?–95), who wrote the most moving opera of the century, *Dido and Aeneas* (1687).

SEVENTEENTH-CENTURY THOUGHT ABOUT HUMANITY

While the outlook of the vast majority of the population of western Europe remained Medieval, the most adventurous minds of the seventeenth century developed notions about humanity that rested on Renaissance views but pressed beyond them. Their conceptions fall conveniently into three categories: individualism, relativism, and a rationalism tempered with empiricism.

Individualism

Radical thinkers of the seventeenth century took an increasingly individualist view of man in society. The most intense Christian piety of the period—whether it was the Catholic devotion preached by St. François de Sales, the stern conscience of the Puritans and Jansenists, or the warm inner conviction of the German Pietists—was highly individualistic. That trend was equally evident in political theory. The fashion was to start with the individual and then seek explanations of and justifications for the existence of societies and states.

Supporters of the divine-right theory of kingship remained numerous, but by mid-century the notion of an explicit or implicit "contract" between people and ruler was widespread. Hobbes and a few others that included Spinoza argued that this contract, once made, was irrevocable, and bound the ruled but not the ruler. Others, like the Parliamentarians in the English Civil War and John Locke in political philosophy, argued for a right of rebellion against rulers who broke the terms of the contract by acting against the general welfare.

The idea of a "social contract" soon took its place by the side of that of a "political contract." Society, according to social contract theorists, was itself the result of a voluntary agreement among individuals who had been absolutely independent in their original "state of nature." The two ideas mixed, somewhat confusedly, in Locke and later political philosophers. In both contracts, the individual with his rights and his "natural" independence logically came first; then came society or the state. The more radical thinkers of the seventeenth century thus came to think of society as an artificial organization of independent individuals that rested on the consent of those individuals. That was a radical break with the

Opera singers of the Baroque. Detail from an opera setting drawn by Ludovico Burnacinia, Vienna (1674).

Medieval conception of society as an organism or a "body" of which individuals were mere "members," each with an assigned place.

Relativism

The greatest thinkers of the Middle Ages were confident that the peoples of Christendom were God's chosen people, and that divine revelation gave humanity all necessary truths. But that self-assurance weakened during the sixteenth and seventeenth centuries, thanks to Humanism, to the voyages of discovery, and to the development of science.

Humanism had begun to reveal Greco-Roman civilization in historical perspective. Ancient literature, art, and historical writing brought alive a long dead society that offered numerous alternatives to the Medieval Christian system of belief. The Renaissance had first created the modern disciplines of history, archaeology, and philology. Seventeenth-century scholars broadened and deepened them. That steady development slowly impressed on thoughtful Europeans that other societies had existed in other times with values, beliefs, and institutions quite different from their own. That recognition was the origin of the concept of historical relativism, of the notion that value systems—including those of Christian Europe—were historical phenomena subject to change.

The age of discovery added to historical relativism a geographical counterpart. The discovery in America and Asia of other societies shattered European provincialism. The tribal hunter-gatherers of America and Africa, the urban civilizations of Aztecs and Incas, and the great empires of Asia with their advanced arts and amenities inspired study and reflection. Perhaps the "noble savages" of the New World were happier than the more cultured but "corrupted" Christians of Europe. Perhaps Persian sages and Chinese philosophers had something to teach Christians. Each society had different standards—was any value system grounded on anything more solid than custom? Doubts on these points affected increasing numbers of European thinkers in the seventeenth and eighteenth centuries. And scientific discovery likewise widened their vision of humanity's place in nature. European Christianity was not alone in time and space, and humanity itself might not be alone in the universe.

The work of Pierre Bayle (1647–1706), the great scholarly skeptic of the later seventeenth century, exemplifies the results of historical study, geographical exploration, and scientific discovery. Bayle was born a Huguenot, briefly converted to Catholicism, and then renounced all orthodox belief when his brother died in a French dungeon during an attempt at forced conversion. Bayle took up residence in the relatively tolerant Dutch Netherlands and devoted the latter part of his life to a crusade against superstition, religious intolerance, and dogma of all kinds. In 1697 he published a huge rambling book, the *Historical and Critical Dictionary*, which had enormous influence on eighteenth-century thought. Into the book he poured a relativism and skepticism acquired through extensive historical study, an amateur knowledge of science, and experience.

He defied convention by insisting that religion and political stability were not inseparable—atheists could be good citizens. He denounced religious conversions by force. He ridiculed astrology, a form of superstition even more current then than now. He derided tales of miracles. He distrusted all historical authorities, including the writers of the Old Testament, unless their account of events was inherently credible. An admirer of Descartes, his test of truth was "reason", and many scriptural accounts failed that rigorous test. Bayle was the most destructive critic of his generation. His war against traditional religion replaced, and in part derived from, the scarcely ended wars of religion.

Rationalism and Empiricism

The leading thinkers of the seventeenth century began a process that reached completion only in the eighteenth century by replacing the lost certainties of religious belief with a new object of worship—reason. It was the faculty that in theory distinguished humanity from the animal world. It was trustworthy; the triumphs of seventeenth-century science had proved that. An increasingly optimistic age concluded that reason gave humanity the *certain knowledge* of the world that religion no longer appeared to offer.

And reason provided a law, "natural law," to replace the foundation that religious belief now failed to provide for human knowledge. The idea of a law of nature that served as a standard of behavior for all humans at all times was not new. Greek philosophers such as Aristotle had enunciated a version of it, the Stoics had pressed it further, and Cicero had given the idea classic formulation: "There is in fact a true law— namely, right reason—which is in accordance with nature, applies to all men, and is unchangeable and eternal. By its commands this law summons men to the performance of their duties; by its prohibitions it restrains them from doing wrong."

St. Augustine had then Christianized that law by identifying it with the law of God. The Medieval scholastics had enthusiastically explicated it in the greatest detail as the basis of earthly law and morality. During the Renaissance and the Reformation, the rediscovery of Stoic texts and the work of Protestant scholars such as the father of modern international law, the Dutch jurist and diplomat Hugo Grotius (1583–1645), had secularized natural law once more, as a "law" inherent in the nature of humanity. Grotius, in *On the Law of War and Peace* (1625), attempted to find in natural law some basis for a "law of nations" that would transcend and moderate the religious fanaticisms of the Thirty Years' War. And the discovery of scientific "laws of nature" such as Kepler's laws of planetary motion further reinforced the belief that natural laws of human behavior must also exist. Success in proving mathematical and scientific laws inspired faith that reason could discern "natural law" in human affairs.

The most influential example of that faith was John Locke's claim that every individual in the "state of nature," before the existence of organized societies, possessed certain "natural rights," most notably life, liberty, and property. From that premise it followed, as proof followed axiom, that humanity had formed societies and set up governments mainly to preserve these rights. While Descartes had hoped to deduce the universe from a few central mathematical principles, Locke in his *Second Treatise of Government* (1690) assumed that he could deduce society and government from a few simple axioms about humanity and natural law.

An undercurrent of empiricism, of respect for the experience of the senses, nevertheless qualified that enthusiastic rationalism. Here as well, Locke led the way in his *Essay Concerning Human Understanding* (1690), which many readers hailed as the counterpart in the study of humanity to Newton's work on the forces of nature. Locke argued that all human ideas came from the experience of the senses. The mind at birth was a *tabula rasa*, a clean slate, on which experience gained through the senses gradually imprinted conceptions. No "innate ideas" exist, and contrary to Descartes, no axioms were self-evident. Outside forces, acting upon the mind, explained all human ideas.

That was the purest empiricism. Locke hoped that it would provide a weapon for destroying the superstitions and prejudices of the past. It proved destructive of much else, including some of Locke's own doctrines. Locke's theory of the mind did away with original sin, for experience might mold the *tabula rasa* of the mind to do good rather than evil. It did away equally with the revelation on which Christianity rested and with mathe-

The title page of John Locke's *Essay Concerning Human Understanding* (1690).

AN

ESSAY

CONCERNING

Humane Understanding.

In Four BOOKS.

Quam bellum est velle confiteri potius nescire quod nescias, quam ista effutientem nauseare, atque ipsum sibi displicere! Cic. de Natur. Deor. *l.* 1.

LONDON:

Printed for *Tho. Basset*, and sold by *Edw. Mory* at the Sign of the *Three Bibles* in St. *Paul's* Church-Yard. M DC XC.

matical axioms, for neither derived from the senses. Above all, it undermined Locke's own conception of "natural rights" that were innate and not based on experience.

The rationalism of Locke's natural-law theory of society clashed both with the empiricism of his theory of the mind and with the relativism in time and space that the Humanists and the great navigators had disclosed. The eighteenth century, the age known as the "Enlightenment," inherited this agonizing contradiction between rationalist faith in natural law and empiricist trust in sense-experience and in the evidence of comparative history.

THE ENLIGHTENMENT

The task that the leading thinkers of the eighteenth century set themselves was to popularize the methods and principles of seventeenth-century natural science and to apply these methods and principles to God, humanity, and society. Scientific discovery continued, but the most brilliant writers of the age concentrated their effort on applying the new scientific method to long-festering human ills—economic, social, political, and ecclesiastical. Their concern was less to discover new truth about nature than to apply the methods of natural science to the transformation of society.

The eighteenth century's own name for this movement was "the Enlightenment"—*les lumières* in French. The term suggested the dawn of a new age of reason and knowledge after a long dark night of ignorance, superstition, intolerance, and despotism of kings and priests. That new light was the light of science, as the great English poet Alexander Pope (1688–1744) elegantly proclaimed:

Nature and nature's law lay hid in night;
God said, "Let Newton be, " and all was light.

Correspondence, exchange of publications, and travel linked together a cultural movement that transcended state and religious boundaries. "Enlightened" writers and readers spanned Europe, from Russia to Spain, from Edinburgh to Naples, from the Philadelphia of Benjamin Franklin to the Virginia of Thomas Jefferson. But the center of the movement was indisputably Paris.

That was no accident. Most other countries were either too small or too backward to become major centers of "Enlightenment" thought and agitation. The major exception, England, had already fought its battles for religious toleration and political freedom. It had established after 1688 a freedom of thought and publication unprecedented elsewhere, even in the Dutch Netherlands. It had already had an Enlightenment or "pre-Enlightenment" through Hobbes, Locke, and many others. By 1715, the England of gentry and merchants was too successful, both internally and externally, to provide much nourishment for intellectual movements that fed on dissatisfaction with the existing order. Only the Scots, who delighted in stirring up their richer and duller neighbors to the south, were an exception. The philosopher and historian David Hume (1711–76) and the economist Adam Smith (1723–90) were major Enlightenment figures, and Edinburgh in the eighteenth century was one of the great European intellectual centers.

Three tendencies in French society united to make France the center of the Enlightenment. First, French government after the death of Louis XIV in 1715 became steadily more inept and ineffectual, both internally and in its wars and diplomacy (see pp. 624–25). Irresolution at home and defeat abroad sapped the prestige of the existing order and of the Church that upheld it. Second, the aristocracy began to take its revenge on the monarchy that had reduced it to the role of courtly lapdog. In the realm of ideas, that revenge consisted of the articulation and eager propagation of advanced and potentially subversive ideas. Finally, the gradually increasing wealth that commerce and industry produced inspired in the growing urban middle classes an increasing consciousness of their own worth and importance. That led to rising social tension between the privileged and the less privileged. That tension helped encourage an increasing body of literature that attacked the existing order at its weakest points: the obscurantism of the Church, the bureaucratic ineptitude of the noble-dominated royal administration, and the irresponsibility and arrogance of the nobility itself.

The weapons of the French Enlightenment writers were clarity, wit, and a deliberate ambiguity designed to ward off the wrath of officialdom. Government censors were often too slow-witted to catch hidden barbs aimed at Church or state, and after mid-century they often secretly agreed with the critics. Censorship stopped only the most blatantly subversive or obviously blasphemous attacks on the existing order, and after the 1750s it was almost powerless against the flood of social criticism and satire that poured from the presses. The source of that flood was Paris, the center of the intellectual life of continental Europe in the eighteenth century. There the greatest intellectual figures of the age met and conversed in the *salons* or weekly gatherings that intellectual women of the aristocracy had begun to organize. The inhabitants of this world of ideas, whether commoner or noble, shared a common feeling that they were leading a revolution of ideas without precedent in European history, a crusade to end the absurdities and barbarities of the old order.

The "Philosophes": Voltaire, Montesquieu, Diderot

London initially helped inspire Paris. The conventional date for the beginning of the Enlightenment as a movement was the visit to England in 1726–29 of a certain François Marie Arouet (1694–1778), better known by his penname, Voltaire. The French government had twice imprisoned Voltaire in the Bastille fortress in Paris for alleged or actual witticisms made at the expense of royal or noble personages; on the second occasion he had only achieved freedom by promising to leave for London. The man who came to personify the Enlightenment thus had good reason to hate the old regime.

In England he read Newton and Locke, and relished the relative freedom of English society in comparison with his own. After returning to France he published *Philosophical Letters on the English* (1733), which passed on to his readers in nonmathematical form Newton's main principles and popularized Locke's theories of human nature and limited government. Voltaire skillfully contrasted the rationality of Newton's method and the tolerant reasonableness of the English way of life with the arbitrary and capricious realities of Church, state, and society in France.

Voltaire's English letters set the tone of "enlightenment" propaganda in France for the next half-century. They were "philosophical" in the broad sense because they reflected on the

A gathering of *philosophes*, including Voltaire (center, with arm raised), Diderot (on Voltaire's left), and Condorcet (between them), from a contemporary engraving by Jean Huber.

facts of human existence and attempted to discover their meaning, and they searched for general principles useful to humanity as a whole. But the *philosophes*, as Voltaire and kindred spirits became known, had little use for metaphysics. They were less philosophers than popularizers, crusaders for the application of the best intellectual tools of the century to social problems. Voltaire was the greatest of them—the most prolific, the wittiest, the most readable, and perhaps the angriest. His preferred targets were bigotry, superstition, and despotism.

"*Écrasez l'infâme*," cried Voltaire in his innumerable letters, pamphlets, stories, and satires: crush that "infamous thing," the Church. In the famous entry on "Religion" in his *Philosophical Dictionary* (1764), he described a vision he claimed to have had of a desert filled with piles of bones of "Christians with their throats slit by one another in metaphysical disputes." He went on to report a "philosophical" conversation with the shades of Socrates and Jesus, who both deplored the spectacle he had just seen. And he attacked the religious intolerance of contemporary France as vigorously as the barbarism of the past. When he died in 1778, Voltaire was the most widely read author in Europe, the first writer to have made a fortune from the sale of his own writings. Paris buried him with a ceremony worthy of a king.

A second leading Enlightenment figure was the Baron Charles Louis de Secondat de Montesquieu (1689–1755), sometime president of the *parlement* of Bordeaux. Montesquieu attempted to create a "social science" by applying the methods of the natural sciences to the study of society. In his most famous work, *The Spirit of the Laws* (1748), he suggested that climate and other environmental factors helped determine forms of government, and he tried to discover what form of government best fitted a given set of environmental conditions. *The Spirit of the Laws* was not "scientific" by later standards, but it was the first serious attempt since the Greeks at tracing relationships between systems of government and the environment. In his popular *History of Civilization* (1756), Voltaire took over and elaborated Montesquieu's concepts.

Montesquieu, like Voltaire, found Locke's theory of limited government persuasive. As a French noble he wished to limit the perceived excesses of royal absolutism. He followed Locke in concluding that the ideal political form involved the separation and balancing of powers within government. That conclusion later had great influence on the authors of the American Constitution (see p. 644).

A third major figure of the French Enlightenment was Denis Diderot (1713–84), co-editor of the famous *Encyclopédie*, an immense encyclopedia designed to sum up the totality of human knowledge. Despite Jesuit protests and cuts by timorous printers, it appeared in 35 volumes between 1752 and 1780. Diderot was an enthusiast for science and saw the relationship between science and technology more clearly than most *philosophes*. The most remarkable feature of the *Encyclopédie* was the plates that show machinery

Voltaire on Superstition   1776

Almost everything that goes beyond the adoration of a Supreme Being and submission of the heart to his orders is superstition. One of the most dangerous is to believe that certain ceremonies entail the forgiveness of crimes. Do you believe that God will forget a murder you have committed if you bathe in a certain river, sacrifice a black sheep, or if someone says certain words over you? . . . Do better, miserable humans; have neither murders nor sacrifices of black sheep. . . .

Notice that the most superstitious ages have always been those of the most horrible crimes. . . . The superstitious man is ruled by fanatics and he becomes one himself. On the whole, the less superstition, the less fanaticism, and the less fanaticism, the fewer miseries.

From Voltaire, *Dictionnaire philosophique* (Paris: Editions de Cluny, n.d.; reproduction of the edition of 1776), Vol. III, pp. 218–25.

and industrial processes. But Diderot was no mere compiler; he was a confident prophet of the Enlightenment's this-worldly religion of humanity. The entries and content of the *Encyclopédie* reflected the interests and enthusiasms of Diderot and his fellow *philosophes*, and contained many of their most trenchant writings. The work was an immense success, and became the bible of the "enlightened" everywhere. Through it ran faith in humanity's reason, pride in its accomplishments, and sublime confidence in its future.

The Enlightenment Faith

No intellectual movement is successful unless it has followers as well as leaders. The Enlightenment, like the Renaissance, produced its full quota of earnest hacks and disreputable scribblers. It also enjoyed a public, vast by previous standards, of silent supporters. Twentieth-century scholarship has shown that the *Encyclopédie* enjoyed astonishing sales in tiny provincial towns. Periodicals, libraries, book societies, and literary and scientific discussion groups spread knowledge, social criticism, and scandalous gossip. The main ideas of the Enlightenment struck root all over Europe, and a new generation absorbed from them entirely new conceptions of human nature, society, and religion. Five words, each of which bore a heavy freight of meaning in the eighteenth century, sum up these ruling ideas: reason, nature, happiness, progress, and liberty.

The eighteenth century believed as passionately in reason as the seventeenth, but with a difference. The "reason" of Voltaire relied more upon experience and less on mathematics than that of Descartes. It was a weapon of skeptical inquiry based on observed facts—or on what Voltaire thought were facts—rather than a method of deduction from axioms. To the thinkers of the Enlightenment, reason was the alternative to superstition and prejudice. It was the only sure guide to the principles that governed humanity and

---

Historical Relativism in Montesquieu: The Effects of Climate and Geography

In Asia they have always had great empires; in Europe these could never exist. Asia has larger plains; it is cut out into much larger divisions by mountains and seas . . . and the rivers being not so large form more contrasted boundaries. Power in Asia, then, should be always despotic; for if their subjugation be not severe they would soon make a division inconsistent with the nature of the country.

In Europe natural divisions form many nations of moderate extent, in which ruling by laws is not incompatible with the maintenance of the state: on the contrary, it is so favorable to it that without this the state would fall into decay. It is this that has formed a genius for liberty that renders each part extremely difficult to be subdued and subjected to a foreign power. . . . Africa is in a climate like that of the south of Asia and is in the same servitude. . . .

Monarchy is more frequently found in fertile countries and a republican government in those which are not so, and this is sometimes a sufficient compensation for the inconveniences they suffer by the sterility of the land. Thus the barrenness of the soil of Attica established a democracy there.

From Charles de Secondat de Montesquieu, *The Spirit of the Laws* (Bohn Standard Library edition), Vol. I, Book XVII, Chs. 6, 7; Book XVIII, Ch. 1, pp. 289–91.

---

nature. Reason could discover the fundamental rationality of the universe, and it could also make human societies more rational. The *philosophes* were less interested in "pure" science than in applied science, less concerned with intellectual system-building than with specific reforms. They regarded "reason" as a pragmatic instrument, applicable equally to agriculture, government, social relations, astronomy, and physics.

Nature was a second favorite word of the Enlightenment. The precise meaning the *philosophes* attached to "nature" was not always clear, but to nearly all of them "nature" or "the natural" were the proper standards for measuring God and humanity. A thing "according to nature" was reasonable and therefore good. Voltaire and his contemporaries brought the idea of natural law to the peak of its prestige. One of them devised the following definition of natural law:

> The regular and constant order of facts by which God rules the universe; the order which his wisdom presents to the sense and reason of men, to serve them as an equal and common rule of conduct, and to guide them, without distinction of race or sect, towards perfection and happiness.

Order and law, then, ruled throughout the universe of the *philosophes*—laws of economics, of politics, and of morality as well as of physics and astronomy. Reason permitted the discovery of those laws. Humans might ignore or defy them, but did so at their peril. To the "enlightened," the road to happiness lay in conforming to nature and nature's laws. The enlightened elite of the eighteenth century looked on those who "broke" nature's laws in the same spirit as the clergy of the Middle Ages had regarded heretics who broke God's laws: they were rebels against the order of the universe.

Happiness in this world, not salvation and eternal rejoicing in the next, was the end the *philosophes* had in view. The Enlightenment, like the Scientific Revolution, was a secular movement. When Thomas Jefferson (see p. 642) cited "the pursuit of happiness" along with life and liberty as inalienable human rights, he was expressing a general sentiment of the age. Medieval Christianity's toleration of misery in this life in the expectation of compensation in the next angered the *philosophes*. They demanded the realization of Christian ideals here and now. They abominated cruelty, judicial torture, slavery, and the callous treatment of the insane. An enlightened Italian civil servant of the Habsburgs, Cesare Beccaria (1738–94), was the first to suggest that savage penalties do not necessarily prevent crime and to propose a theory of penology. And the philosophes were also cosmopolitan and even pacifist in temper. Voltaire penned some of the bitterest passages ever written about the "insanity" of war and the absurdity of blind patriotism.

Progress was an even more central constituent of the Enlightenment faith than happiness. The *philosophes* took the Christian idea of the spiritual progression of humanity from the Creation through the Incarnation to the Last Judgment, and secularized it. The progress of civilization, they believed, was now out of God's hands and in those of humanity, thanks to the discovery and use of nature's laws in government, economics, and technology. The *philosophes* were in general confident that both humanity and society were perfectible through human effort.

This was a major revolution in western thought. The Middle Ages could not have conceived of a progress that was purely secular and unrelated to God. Renaissance thinkers still felt themselves inferior to the heroic Greeks and Romans. But even before a symbolic literary battle between "ancients" and "moderns" that began in 1687, some thinkers had suggested that the "moderns" were as good as, and probably better than, the "ancients." By 1750 a French *philosophe*, economist, and civil servant, Anne-Robert-Jacques Turgot, could suggest that the essential element in history was humanity's slow struggle upward towards the crucial discovery of the scientific method. In 1794 the Marquis de Condorcet, a mathematician and aristocratic reformer under sentence of death during the French Revolution, wrote a *Sketch for a Historical Picture of the Progress of the Human Mind* that summed up all the optimism of his century. He saw "the strongest reasons for believing that nature has set no limit to the realization of our hopes" and foresaw "the abolition of inequality between nations, the progress of equality within nations, and the true perfection of humanity."

Progress, Condorcet concluded, was now "independent of any power that might wish to halt it" and "will never be reversed." The scientific method was irrevocably fixed in the human mind, and scientific knowledge of natural laws would continue to accumulate. Progress was thus accelerating and irreversible. The coming "perfection of mankind" was an intoxicating vision, a vision the majority of the enlightened shared, despite the abundance of historical evidence suggesting that civilizations declined as well as rose. How Condorcet reconciled his vision of progress with his own status as fugitive from the guillotine of the Revolution of "Liberty, Equality, Fraternity" is unclear.

Liberty, indeed, was yet another favorite word of the *philosophes*. They were acutely aware of the prevalence in France of arbitrary arrest and restrictions on speech, religion, trade, and employment. Looking at England through lightly rose-tinted glasses, they envied Englishmen their economic, political, and religious liberties. Their concern for liberty was potentially the most explosive tenet of their faith, but few considered that violence was necessary to secure it. Liberty, for the *philosophes*, was inseparable from reason. Reason would soon reveal the true natural laws governing all things, from trade, to government, to religion. The artificiality and corruption of the present would become evident to all. A "benevolent despotism," an enlightened philosopher-king, would lead humanity into a new golden age—or so Voltaire and many other *Encyclopédie* authors hoped. But what if despotism was by its very nature not benevolent?

The Enlightenment and Religion

The new ideas inevitably had religious consequences. To the "enlightened," religious fervor savored of the fanaticism of the wars of religion. The Enlightenment only prized enthusiasm for its new religion of reason, progress, and the "perfection of humanity." The fashionable form of belief common among the eighteenth century's educated elite came to be Deism, the belief in a God who is Creator but not Redeemer. The God of the Deists was a celestial watchmaker who had created the universe, wound it up, and then stepped aside to let it run according to natural law that he had laid down. God did not concern himself with humanity, or act in or through human history.

The essence of religion, for the Deist, was thus awe and reverence before the rationality and perfection of the universe—a feeling reflected in the beautiful hymns of Isaac Watts still heard in many Protestant churches. To a Deist such as Voltaire, talk of revelation, miracles, or the special intervention of God in the natural order was false. Dogma and ritual were "superstition", for humanity needed only reason to see God. The heart of natural religion was a morality common to all mankind. "Light is uniform for the star Sirius," Voltaire wrote, "and for us moral philosophy must be uniform."

Deism obviously tended to undermine orthodox Christianity and to substitute for it a rationalist belief in God as First Cause and in "natural law" as humanity's moral guide. A few *philosophes* such as Diderot went further and dared the censors by pushing beyond Deism to atheism. Baron Paul Henri d'Holbach (1723–89) was the complete "materialist," an ancestor of much nineteenth-century thought. His universe contained nothing but matter, humanity itself was a conglomeration of atoms, and natural law was the sole determinant of all events.

In the end, many Protestants found a compromise between Christian faith and the Enlightenment's rationalism, humanitarianism, and tolerance. The result was the nineteenth-century development of a liberal Protestantism. Others took the road of more intense piety. The cold rationality of Deism held no appeal for emotional natures, and only the educated could understand it. Hence the wide popularity of two warmly emotional Protestant movements, Pietism in Germany and Methodism in England and America.

Both emphasized the importance of the inner religious experience of individual "conversion." Pietism was a second and milder Protestant Reformation that challenged not the Pope, but the twin extremes of dogmatic orthodoxy and Deism that verged on unbelief. Individualist, tolerant, and indifferent to ceremonies, Pietism attracted followers among both Catholics and Protestants.

John Wesley (1703–91) was the leader of a somewhat parallel revival of a warm and personal Christian piety in England in the years following his conversion in 1738. When the Anglican clergy resisted his efforts, he took his message directly to the people. He addressed huge outdoor congregations and prayer meetings in remote chapels, taught his followers to sing their way to heaven with the hymns of his

brother Charles, and deluged the congregations he had established with streams of pamphlets from his printing presses. In the end, Anglican opposition forced Wesley to leave the established church and create a new denomination, Methodism, which took its name from the "methodical" piety of Wesley's followers that the orthodox had originally mocked. Methodism touched many thousands of Englishmen at home and in the colonies who found repellent the arid intellectualism that characterized much eighteenth-century Anglicanism. Methodism's wide following, its emphasis on other-worldly concerns, and its conspicuous loyalty to temporal authority in this world made it a more effective buttress of the social order than Anglicanism.

John Wesley preaching.

Economics, Society, and Politics

The *philosophes* were interested in social and political issues, but they were reformers, not revolutionaries. Their formula for reform was simply to discover by reason and experience the natural laws that should operate in any given situation and to clear away all supposedly artificial obstacles to their operation. The result, "reason" indicated, would be "progress" toward happiness and freedom.

That outlook encouraged the beginnings of the modern discipline of economics. In 1758 François Quesnay published his *Economic Survey*, which proposed the existence of natural economic "laws" and urged the end to all restrictions, such as government control of grain supplies and prices, that prevented those laws from operating. But Quesnay and French economists of his school were too much the products of France's predominantly agricultural society. They saw in agriculture the source of all wealth, and damned industry as "sterile" and commerce as parasitic. Adam Smith of Edinburgh saw more clearly. In *An Inquiry into the Nature and Causes of the Wealth of Nations* (1776), the first classic of modern economics, Smith extended the concept of "natural liberty" to commerce and industry.

He denounced all "mercantilist" practices, although he admitted that an age of warring states might make measures such as the Navigation Acts necessary for a time. In general, however, Smith maintained that state intervention interfered with the workings of the natural law of supply and demand and thus decreased rather than increased national wealth. The "invisible hand" of natural law, Smith argued, was a self-regulating mechanism that automatically maximized the wealth and freedom of any society that respected it. To tamper with it was both dangerous and self-defeating.

In political theory, similar lines of reasoning led to three distinct schools of thought. The first rested on the notion of "enlightened absolutism." The *philosophes*, children of their age, were no democrats. Voltaire thought government should be for the people, but by kings: "The people, stupid and barbarous, needs a yoke, a cattle prod, and hay." Most *philosophes* hoped for a mellowing of divine-right monarchy into a benevolent "enlightened" philosopher-kingship that would govern— perhaps with well-rewarded *philosophe* advice—according to natural law rather than royal caprice. A second, minority school believed that "reason" pointed in the direction of an English-style constitutional monarchy based on natural rights and on an explicit contract that bound the sovereign to respect his subjects' liberties. And a very few advanced a third theory, still too radical to be of much immediate influence: the theory of democratic government. That school's foremost prophet was the eccentric Jean-Jacques Rousseau (1712–78), author of *The Social Contract* (1762).

Rousseau: Prophet of Democracy and Despotism

Rousseau, a native of Geneva, appeared in Paris in 1742 after a wandering youth, came to know Diderot and other *philosophes* and for a time attempted to join them. But he was never easy in their company. He trusted reason, but relied even more on emotion. He trusted nature, but to him nature was the unspoiled simplicity of precivilized humanity, the "noble savage." After a sudden illumination experienced in 1749, he became convinced that humanity had lost more than it had gained by cultivating the arts and sciences. He lost all faith in progress. The seeming artificiality of Paris society increasingly irritated him, and he broke with his former friends. Voltaire thought him insane, and in his miserable later years Rousseau indeed suffered from delusions of persecution.

Rousseau was the greatest social critic of the Enlightenment. By temperament he was a shy and sensitive misfit who desperately wanted to belong. He knew himself to be "good," on the model of the "noble savage." He therefore blamed his unhappiness, his failure to fit in, on the alleged artificiality of existing society. That society of kings, aristocrats, and priests—he felt— had "corrupted" and humiliated him. Consequently he imagined an alternative, not as a program for revolution— although many readers took it as one— but as a critique of existing societies. In Rousseau's utopia, described in *The Social Contract*, free citizens associated by choice in a community of equals to govern themselves. By agreeing to form a community, they gave up all individual rights to the group. From their deliberations, a "general will" would inevitably emerge. Rousseau's belief in humanity's essential goodness precluded conflict or dissent within his ideal community. And once the "general will" emerged, all owed it absolute obedience.

Rousseau's ideal democracy was "direct democracy", the self-rule of a tightly knit community of active male citizens—for like most men of the Enlightenment, Rousseau considered it part of "the order of nature that woman obeys man." Perhaps Rousseau had in mind an idealized image of Ge-

The misfit as social critic: Jean-Jacques Rousseau.

neva as he wrote *The Social Contract*. In that city-state, citizens knew and trusted one another, and the minority normally accepted the majority's view with good grace, out of loyalty to the community. But it was Sparta, that least individualist and most austerely military of the Greek city-states, that recurred frequently in Rousseau's pages. It was his favorite model.

Perhaps Rousseau's knowledge of Sparta—of its relentless regimentation, its murderous *krypteia* or secret police, its ruthless enslavement of all surrounding cities—was imperfect. Perhaps, as modern scholarship has tended to assert, his proposals for a "progressive" education that would bring out the child's "natural" goodness and intellectual curiosity make Rousseau a prophet of individual freedom rather than Spartan uniformity. Perhaps his hostility to kings and aristocrats, indeed his temperamental aversion to all forms of authority, absolve him of responsibility for excesses committed after 1789 in the name of the "general will." But his theory of democracy was nevertheless a momentous illustration of the consequences—even the unintended consequences—of ideas.

Locke and Montesquieu had argued that the guarantee of political liberty was the separation of executive and legislative powers, since concentration of power threatened freedom. Their theory derived from an essential pessimism about human behavior, a long experience of human ambition and fallibility gained in the world of politics. Their theory of liberty was "negative"—liberty arose when institutional and legal checks limited the powers of government. That negative theory of liberty, of individual rights *against* government, was the foundation of modern representative democracies such as Britain and the United States.

Rousseau, an intellectual without worldly experience, took an entirely different view. For him humanity was "good" with the goodness of the noble savage. That goodness would express itself naturally in politics once the artificial restraints and corrupting influences of the old society fell away. Checks and balances, the separation of powers, the protection of specific rights would serve no purpose if "the people" governed itself. The "general will," by definition, could not will harm to itself! Rousseau's theory of liberty was "positive"—his liberty was the willing obedience to laws and decisions that the individual himself had helped to make. Rousseau's theory of liberty thus set no limit at all on what government could do if it expressed—*or claimed to express*—the general will. In a justly famous passage in *The Social Contract*, Rousseau even asserted that the community could force individuals to be free. That hard phrase was the precursor of an even harder reality after 1789.

Utopian visions like those of Rousseau, it later became clear, often originated among and appealed to intellectuals alienated from societies that in their view did not sufficiently appreci-

Rousseau: The Despotism of the General Will

The problem is to find a form of association . . . in which each, while uniting himself with all, may still obey himself alone, and remain as free as before. This is the fundamental problem of which the Social Contract provides the solution: . . . the total alienation of each associate, together with all his rights, to the whole community. . . . Each man, in giving himself to all, gives himself to nobody. . . . Each of us puts his person and all his power in common under the supreme direction of the general will, and, in our corporate capacity, we receive each member as an indivisible part of the whole. . . . In order that the social compact may not be an empty formula, it tacitly includes the undertaking, which alone can give force to the rest, that whoever refuses to obey the general will shall be compelled to do so by the whole body. This means nothing less than that he will be forced to be free.

From Jean Jacques Rousseau, *The Social Contract* (New York and London: Everyman's Library, 1913), Book I, Chs. 6 and 7, pp. 14–18.

ate them. Utopianism flourished best under autocracies—like that of the successors of Louis XIV—that pursued policies sufficiently repressive to generate hostility, but not repressive enough to crush it. And the utopian search for a society without conflict, of which Rousseau was the greatest forerunner and prophet, could even lead to an attack on representative democracies whose "negative freedoms" appeared to foster doubt, dissatisfaction, and disunity. Rousseau died in 1778, but only chronology bound him to the Enlightenment. His true home was the post-1789 world of revolution, nationalism, and Romanticism that he helped to shape.

ARTS AND LETTERS IN THE EIGHTEENTH CENTURY

The art and literature of the later seventeenth and early eighteenth centuries reflected the pervasive belief of Enlightenment scientists and philosophers in the rationality, intelligibility, and order of the universe. Rationalism blended easily with classicism. The regularity and harmony of Newton's universe seemed to accord both with the balance, proportion, rationality, and restraint for which classical Greek architecture and Greek and Roman writers had striven. The dictators of literary and artistic taste at the close of the seventeenth century were classicists. When *philosophes* such as Voltaire wrote dramas, they accepted classical standards as unquestioningly as had Corneille and Racine. The architects of the "Georgian" buildings of England and the beautifully proportioned Place de la Concorde in Paris accepted classical rules of balance and unity with equal zeal. Enthusiasm for classical antiquity reached its post-Renaissance climax after 1748, when Europe discovered the remains of the Roman city of Pompeii in startlingly well-preserved condition under the ashes and cinders from Mt. Vesuvius that had covered it in A.D. 79.

Jonathan Swift: social commentary through satire (portrait by Charles Jervas)

An Age of Prose

The "age of reason" was an age of prose. Essays, satirical tales, novels, letters, and histories were the characteristic literary forms of the eighteenth century. Authors bent their energies to description and narrative rather than to suggestion and imagination. The essays of Joseph Addison and Richard Steele, which began to appear in 1709, sketched a delightful picture of English rural society. Jonathan Swift's *Gulliver's Travels* (1726) and Voltaire's *Candide* (1759) offered biting social and philosophical commentary. As the century progressed, the novel emerged as the favorite form of literary expression; the most enjoyable example was perhaps Henry Fielding's *Tom Jones* (1749). Alongside fiction, philosophy, economics, and history prospered. The eighteenth century's greatest monument of historical scholarship was Edward Gibbon's history of *The Decline and Fall of the Roman Empire* (1776–88), which in a luminous style that will forever delight its readers, sardonically described the "triumph of barbarism and religion" over the greatest empire of the ancient world.

Painting, especially the portraits that now became exceedingly fashionable, well disclosed the elegant aristocratic flavor of eighteenth-century society. The delicate-featured and exquisitely groomed women who look coolly down on the observer, and the worldly, sometimes arrogant, faces of their husbands under their powdered wigs suggest the artificiality of aristocratic society, and sometimes the hardness of character of those who inhabited it. Opulent furniture and tableware, and the great town and country houses of nobles and wealthy merchants reflect the same aristocratic elegance.

But not all books and art served the enjoyment of the aristocracy. The first newspapers written for a wide audience of educated readers emerged in the eighteenth century. William Hogarth (1697–1764) made engravings of his satirical sketches of English society, and sold them by the thousands. Above all, novelists, dramatists, and musicians in London and Paris began to appeal to a middle-class audience. The Paris stage, with productions such as *The Barber of Seville* (1775) and *The Marriage of Figaro* (1784) of Pierre de Beaumarchais, turned a keen satirical edge against the aristocracy. The heroes and heroines of novels tended in-

Eighteenth-century art for the aristocracy: detail of a painting by Thomas Gainsborough (ca. 1748)

creasingly to imitate the middle-class origins of their audiences.

An Age of Music

But the greatest cultural achievement of the age was its music—above all German music. Two great Germans dominated the musical world of the early eighteenth century: Johann Sebastian Bach (1685–1750) and George Frederick Handel (1685–1759). Handel in his oratorios for chorus and instruments and Bach in his richly varied works for keyboard instruments, chamber groups, orchestras, and choruses, realized all the dramatic and emotive possibilities of the baroque style. As the century drew on, the orchestra, which had originated in the seventeenth century, expanded and took in new instruments, the pianoforte replaced the harpsichord, and music began to move from the aristocratic salon into the public hall.

Franz Joseph Haydn (1732–1809), who wrote both for chamber groups and for orchestras, developed the musical forms known as sonatas and symphonies. The other outstanding musical personality of the latter half of the century was Wolfgang Amadeus Mozart (1756–91), who was probably the most gifted musician in history. Born in Salzburg in Austria, he began his career as a child prodigy, lived only 35 years, and died in poverty. But within that short span he produced over 600 compositions that included unequalled masterpieces of invention and form— string quartets, sonatas, concertos, masses, symphonies, and operas such as *Le Nozze di Figaro* (The Marriage of Figaro, 1786), *Don Giovanni* (1787), and *Die Zauberflöte* (The Magic Flute, 1791).

THE LIMITS OF THE ENLIGHTENMENT

The Enlightenment was the creation of a small elite, although many of its essential ideas circulated widely and penetrated far down the social scale. It was largely confined to western Europe and the English-speaking world. And counter-currents soon arose to challenge the supremacy of reason in philosophy and of rational structure and classical balance in art.

Pietism, Methodism, and Rousseau's preference for emotion over reason were evidence of these currents. Even philosophers saw reason's limits. David Hume, who was along with Adam Smith the greatest figure of the Scottish Enlightenment, started from a close study of the great French skeptic Bayle. Hume ended by denying the possibility of certainty. Only the experience of the senses, unverifiable by any independent means, kept the mind informed about external reality. And for Hume, sense-experience was a sequence of disjointed impressions, upon which the mind—and the mind alone— imposed regularities, patterns, connections.

Hume's position, which has remained logically unassailable, cut at the root of the Enlightenment faith in the capacity of reason to discover laws in nature and human behavior. Hume did not doubt the validity of Newton's laws as a rule of thumb. What he denied was that anyone would ever be in a position to claim with certainty that Newton's laws applied to *all* times and in *all* places throughout the universe. Even observations that seemed to confirm those laws might not do so, for the evidence of the senses might be a snare. The sun *might* rise tomorrow; but then again it might not.

Hume was happy to concede that some kinds of knowledge were more certain than others. But he was the first philosopher to see the full depths of the predicament into which the collapse of the Medieval religious certainties had plunged humanity. In the philosopher's study, if not in practical affairs, certainty was unattainable. That was "the whimsical condition of mankind." The observer's point of view helped determine what the observer saw. Knowledge, like the human value-systems that varied

Wolfgang Amadeus Mozart

through historical time and geographic space, was relative.

Hume's skepticism did not yet shake an optimistic age that sought to replace God with Newton's clockwork universe. But a few farseeing individuals nevertheless understood what he had done. The greatest philosopher of the century, Immanuel Kant (1724–1804), took up Hume's challenge, although Kant never traveled more than a few miles from his native city of Königsberg in East Prussia. In his *Critique of Pure Reason* (1781), the most opaquely written of all the great works of Western thought, Kant saved scientific reason, at least in his own judgment, by limiting its domain to appearances, to the data of sense-experience.

The mechanical world of physics, Kant argued, *was* knowable with certainty, although only knowable to an observer equipped with concepts inherent to the mind, such as space and time. What was not knowable with certainty, for Kant, were the *true* natures of the "things-in-themselves" that humans perceived through their senses. Nor could reason deal with the domain of metaphysics and religion, the realm of things that transcended experience. Many thinkers saw in Kant's refutation of Hume a mere confirmation of the Scot's skepticism. Others reacted by taking Kant, who himself argued for the necessity of belief in God as one foundation of morality, as a point of departure for a renewed "leap into faith" in religion.

In literature, the slowly gathering revolt against the Enlightenment took the form of a celebration of emotion that defied classical notions of rationality and balance. French and English novelists cultivated extremes of sentimentality. Heroines suffered heartrending misfortune and mistreatment, while the author sought at every turn to arouse the reader's anger, pity, love, or terror. The most influential example was Samuel Richardson's 2,000-page tear-jerker, *Clarissa* (1748), which influenced Rousseau's *Nouvelle Héloise* (1761). The bizarre, grotesque, and fantastic returned to fashion. In both architecture and literature, critics began to revive the Gothic, despised since the Renaissance.

In Germany, which had never fallen totally under the sway of the French Enlightenment, a "Storm and Stress" (*Sturm und Drang*) movement in literature emphasized the great elemental emotions and denied the supremacy of reason. Johann Gottfried von Herder (1744–1803) conceived a philosophy of history that emphasized the uniqueness of each nation or race, the individuality of its genius, and the falsity of any view that denied that uniqueness in the name of universal reason. Johann Wolfgang von Goethe (1749–1832) published at the start of his long literary career *The Sorrows of Young Werther* (1774), a morbidly sentimental tale ending in suicide. The "Age of Reason" thus summoned up its opposite and successor—the age of Romanticism. The new age prized fierce emotion over harmony and equilibrium, and celebrated individual and national peculiarity over a cosmopolitan reason that embraced all humanity.

The Scientific Revolution and the Enlightenment were the most decisive break in the history of Western thought. The world picture of fifth-century Greece and of the Old and New Testaments, preserved through the Middle Ages and Renaissance, now gave way to a distinctively "modern" cast of mind. The world of Luther and Loyola, of Charles V and Philip II, was still organically related to the Middle Ages. The world of Newton and Locke, of Voltaire and Rousseau, was unmistakably our own.

Suggestions for Further Reading

The Scientific Revolution

M. Ashley, *The Golden Century* (1968), offers a fine survey of seventeenth-century social and cultural history. A. R. Hall, *The Scientific Revolution 1500–1800* (1966), is the best recent account. H. Butterfield, *The Origins of Modern Science 1300–1800* (1949), is highly readable, but C. Brinton, *The Shaping of the Modern Mind* (1953), covers a longer period. T. S. Kuhn, *The Copernican Revolution* (1957), describes the transformation of astronomical thought and offers an influential interpretation of how science advances. On the social background of scientific development, see D. Stimson, *Scientists and Amateurs: A History of the Royal Society* (1948). G. de Santillana, *The Crime of Galileo* (1955), elucidates the most famous case in the history of freedom of thought.

The Enlightenment

P. Hazard, *The European Mind: The Critical Years, 1680–1715* (1935, 1952), offers a still useful study of the transition from Scientific Revolution to Enlightenment. The most searching interpretation of the Enlightenment as a whole is E. Cassirer, *The Philosophy of the Enlightenment* (1932, 1951). C. Becker, *The Heavenly City of the Eighteenth Century Philosophers* (1932), attacks the Philosophes as doctrinaires, while P. Gay, *The Enlightenment: An Interpretation*, 2 vols. (1966–69), defends them. N. Hampson, *A Cultural History of the Enlightenment* (1969), is a useful introduction. C. R. Cragg, *Reason and Authority in the Eighteenth Century* (1964), and D. Mornet, *French Thought in the Eighteenth Century* (1929), deal with England and France respectively. R. S. Westfall, *Never at Rest: A Biography of Isaac Newton* (1981), discusses some of the leading intellectuals of the period, but see also T. Bestermann, *Voltaire* (1969), and J. N. Shklar, *Men and Citizens: A Study of Rousseau's Social Theory* (1969). L. Krieger, *Kings and Philosophers, 1689–1789* (1970), relates thought to politics. On specific topics, see M. F. Bukofzer, *Music in the Baroque Era* (1947); F. Fosca, *The Eighteenth Century* (1953) on painting; B. Semmel, *The Methodist Revolution* (1973); G. R. Craig, *The Church in the Age of Reason* (1961); and E. Fox-Genovese, "Women and the Enlightenment," in R. Bridenthal et al., *Becoming Visible: Women in European History* (1987).

22
The Twilight of the Old Regime, 1715–1789

The 75 years between the death of Louis XIV in 1715 and the outbreak of the French Revolution in 1789 were a period of relative stability, without religious wars or great rebellions, except for a desperate serf rising in distant Russia and the revolt of Britain's North American colonies in 1776. Monarchy remained the prevalent form of government, but divine-right monarchy evolved into "enlightened absolutism."

And monarchy, as in the seventeenth century, nevertheless rested on a compromise with the aristocracy. Even the republican or constitutional governments of the eighteenth century were aristocratic in tone. Whig aristocrats and merchants dominated the English Parliament. After the death of Louis XIV, French nobles of the sword and the robe prevailed in the royal councils, and reestablished the powers of the *parlement* law courts. Junkers commanded the armies of Prussia. Polish nobles made the Polish Diet a farce. The "service nobility" of Russia gradually emancipated itself from its duties to the state after the death of Peter the Great. And small oligarchies based on wealth ruled the Dutch Republic and the German "free cities" of the Holy Roman Empire.

Throughout Europe, the aristocracies of birth, office, and wealth reclaimed powers, rights, and privileges lost to the centralizing absolute monarchies of the seventeenth century. Only

monarchs or chief ministers of unusual ability succeeded in bending the revival of aristocratic influence to the purposes of the state. The undeclared war between monarch and aristocrat normally led to tacit compromise, an uneasy balance between centralization and decentralization, between absolute monarchy and aristocratic privilege. That balance was perhaps lacking in clarity and logic, but all remembered how fanatical adherence to principle had given birth to the bloody religious and civil wars of the previous two centuries. Elites that had the luxury of choice were therefore usually glad to accept the structure of society and government as they found it after 1715.

Abject poverty, injustice, and brutality remained widespread, but to the elite, the brilliant "civilization"—a word that first appeared in the 1750s—of the Paris salons or the London coffeehouses appeared to outweigh the tribulations of the poor. To those who looked back upon the devastation of the Thirty Years' War or the fanaticism of the "saints" of the English Revolution, social stability and political equilibrium were worth a high price in injustice. That eighteenth century equilibrium later seemed a lost golden age to the generation of aristocrats that witnessed 1789. A French noble spoke for his caste when he remarked that those who had not lived before the Revolution lacked all conception of the sweetness of life.

Opposite: Jeanne Antoinette Poisson, a witty and well-read daughter of a banker, received the title of Marquise de Pompadour after becoming mistress to Louis XV. She helped to ward off government and Church attempts to suppress or censor the *Encyclopédie*.

Frederick the Great of Prussia
inspects his troops (1778).

THE STATE SYSTEM

Equilibrium was likewise the rule in relations between states. The defeat of Louis XIV's bid for mastery had cost much blood and treasure. The great powers after 1715—France, Britain, Austria, Prussia, and Russia—agreed on few things, but they remained determined to prevent the dominance of a single state. Tacit "rules of the game" therefore evolved, for only issues of power divided these states. Unlike the two centuries that preceded it or the two that followed, no religious, national, or ideological quarrels rent the European state system in the eighteenth century. Chief of the "rules"

was "compensation"—the principle that if one state were fortunate or daring enough to acquire new territory, the other powers would receive compensating advantages, in order to preserve the power balance. "Compensation" often meant that small states suffered mutilation or suppression at the hands of the great. But the practice of compensation helped preserve the balance and sometimes preserved the peace.

Wars remained frequent, but were uniquely "limited" in both means and ends—although that happy situation was not always apparent to the relatively small numbers of professionals who fought, suffered, and died in them. Eighteenth-century war affected the civilian population far less than did war before 1715 and after 1789. Armies avoided pillaging, even on enemy territory. To allow the troops to forage gave them a chance to desert, and the devastation of territory that the state might later annex was bad business. Conscription fell out of fashion except in Russia, where most troops were serfs, and to a limited extent in Prussia. The troops, in the words of a British commander of a slightly later period, tended to be "the scum of the earth, enlisted for drink," or foreign mercenaries. Only esprit de corps, constant drill that made obedience in battle automatic, and a discipline based on flogging and hanging welded these forces together. The aim, in the view of Prussia's greatest king, was to make the troops more terrified of their own officers than of the enemy.

Warfare itself consisted of elaborate maneuver. Commanders normally avoided pitched battles, for trained troops were a precious investment. The 43,000 casualties at Malplaquet (1709) had shown all too well the vast slaughter that ensued when armies equipped with muskets blasted one another at ranges of 50 paces or less. Armies also moved slowly, for the axle-deep mud of Europe's roads did not allow swift movement of the artillery or of the thousands of wagons needed to transport food. In winter, war normally ceased. Campaigns usually centered around a single province or fortified strongpoint and ended indecisively. The ruling system of naval tactics had similar results. Fleets sailing in rigid battle lines blasted at one another from a distance. Engagements were rarely decisive, for commanders feared losing control of their fleets and shunned the bloody and confused close-range ship-to-ship duels that alone ensured annihilation of the enemy.

Limited objectives corresponded to these limitations of methods. The enemy of today might be the ally of tomorrow. Defeating any power too thoroughly might disturb the power balance and summon up unforeseeable complications. In these "cabinet wars"—decided in and directed from the royal cabinet or secretariat—statesmen and generals normally sought concrete political and economic objectives, not unconditional surrender or total destruction. Once a power attained its objectives or became convinced that they were unattainable, it concluded a truce or a peace. In spite of relentless competition—over prestige, land, population, colonies, and trade—the monarchs, bureaucrats, and aristocrats of the eighteenth century felt themselves part of a common civilization. The secret of the eighteenth-century equilibrium was the absence of the twin forces that drive inter-state conflicts to extremes—religious or ideological strife, and bids for universal domination by a single power.

Eighteenth-century statesmen were not unaware of the similarities between their system and Newton's picture of the universe—a stable order of perfectly balanced gravitational attraction and centrifugal repulsion in which every mass moved along predictable lines of force. Ministers took pride in their mastery of "political algebra," the exact calculation of the forces acting on state policy. Soldiers of a literary bent created elaborate geometrical systems to describe, on the model of siege warfare, the century's art of war. Only after mid-century did French theorists, such as Pierre de Bourcet and François de Guibert, begin the creation of a new strategy, operations, and tactics of movement, flexibility, surprise, and annihilation—the methods of the new revolutionary armies after 1792.

The eighteenth-century equilibrium remained precarious, a balance between dynamic forces. Wealth and trade increased steadily, for revolutions both in agriculture and industry were slowly beginning. Europe's economy and diplomacy were becoming global rather than continental; the struggle for empire reached toward the farthest corners of the earth. For the first time, battles fought in America,

The French nobility lampooned: *The Baron* (1785).

Europe in 1715

Africa, and Asia affected the balance of power in Europe. And in trying to maintain its position, each country accentuated its own particular sources of strength. Britain relied increasingly on naval power and commerce. Prussia depended on its army and bureaucracy. Russia intensified its reliance on serfdom. Austria compensated for weakness in Germany by increasing its power in southeastern Europe. France, the one power that refused to specialize, condemned itself to naval weakness, while its intellectual and cultural leadership masked, but did not remedy, its failure to overhaul its British rival in commerce and industry. Inept generalship and financial weakness even prevented France from profiting from its greatest strength before 1715 and after 1789, its land power.

Despite the appearance of equilibrium, powers still rose and fell, sometimes swiftly and decisively, as in the case of Poland. Intellectual and political change intersected with social and economic rivalries that culminated in the great upheavals after 1789. The years between 1715 and 1789, the twilight of the "old regime," fall conveniently into three periods of roughly a quarter-century each: (1) a generation of peace and relative prosperity from 1715 to 1740; (2) a period of worldwide warfare from 1740 to 1763; and (3) an interval of enlightened absolutism, aristocratic resurgence, and domestic unrest from 1763 to 1789.

PEACE AND PROSPERITY, 1715–40

Governments and peoples were thoroughly weary of war by the time the treaties of 1713–14 and 1719–21 restored peace to both western and eastern Europe. The age that followed was unheroic and happily corrupt, as postwar periods often are. But peace allowed the restoration of order and of law, and stimulated an enormous expansion of trade, particularly in western Europe.

Commerce and Industry

Seaborne commerce was the most conspicuous source of Europe's wealth during the eighteenth century. Thanks to the enterprise of their merchants and the technical skill of their mariners, the volume of foreign trade in Britain and France multiplied itself by five during the century. In the British case, colonial trade led the increase. Britain therefore needed and acquired a larger merchant marine than its rivals and the strongest navy in the world. In the French case, trade with other European states was the greatest source of increase. In both cases the accumulation of wealth in the hands of the upper classes was spectacular. For the first time the total wealth of Europe began to eclipse that of Asia. The two preceding centuries of exploration, conquest, and establishment of overseas trading networks now paid off handsomely. Sugar from the West Indies, wine from Portugal, and tobacco from Virginia might grace the tables of Liverpool merchants. Their wives might wear printed calico from India in summer and furs from Canada in winter. Their daughters might marry the heirs of aristocrats whose elegant and capacious Georgian houses were the visible evidence of the combined profits of land and mercantile investment.

The labor of slaves or serfs produced many of the commodities in which Europe's thriving trade dealt. The plantations of the West Indies serviced Europe's ever-increasing craving for sugar. That demand in turn created an almost insatiable demand for African slaves. Liverpool and London slave traders largely met that demand. The serfs who toiled without recompense for their landlords in the grain-producing regions of eastern Europe played a similar role in the economic order as the slaves of the West Indies. Some of the European economy still rested, as had the economy of the ancient world, on servile labor.

Despite the immense increase in overseas trade, the vast bulk of European commerce was within the European states themselves. And in all states except the Dutch Netherlands and perhaps Britain, agriculture still furnished most of the national product. Even Britain's vast foreign trade in the last third of the century only amounted to perhaps 10 percent of the growing British economy. And it was in Britain that the beginnings of revolutionary changes in industry became visible after mid-century (see pp. 681–87).

Boom and Bust: The Mississippi and South Sea Bubbles

European commercial capitalism, which had created the first joint-stock companies, stock exchanges, and state banks, continued to expand. The coming of peace in 1713–14 encouraged both financial speculation and wildcat commercial ventures. Those ventures in turn led in 1719 and 1720 to the first large-scale example of a typically modern phenomenon, a stock crash—or, as contemporaries described it, a "bubble."

Robert Walpole (left) dominating the House of Commons (engraving after a painting by Hogarth)

shoes") from the parliamentary opposition.

Under Walpole's ministry, Britain and its colonies prospered; the credit of the government remained high; the ruling aristocracy of landed and commercial wealth governed in its own interests, but far less repressively than did other European ruling classes. Voltaire, after his visit to England between 1726 and 1729, somewhat idealized English society and government. He neglected to mention to his French readers the ferocity of eighteenth-century English law toward crimes against property. In theory it imposed death by hanging for over 200 offenses, including on occasion the theft of items worth as little as 5 shillings. In practice, "transportation" to the colonies usually took the place of hanging, and English laws guaranteed equality and individual freedom to an extent unknown on the continent except perhaps in the Dutch Netherlands and Switzerland. But Walpole's golden age of the gentry did not last. In 1739 the London merchants and their spokesmen in Parliament forced him into a commercial war with Spain. Within three years his majority collapsed and he left office.

France: Louis XV and Cardinal Fleury

The peace that brought strength to Britain brought weakness to France. Louis XIV's great-grandson, Louis XV (r. 1715–74), became king at the age of five. The Duke of Orléans, the nephew of Louis XIV who governed as Regent during the new king's minority, secured his own power by concessions to the powerful elements in French society that the Sun King had kept leashed. Nobles reappeared as royal ministers. The *Parlement* of Paris boldly reasserted its ancient claim to register and enforce royal legislation—or not—as it saw fit. The French monarchy remained as absolute as ever in theory, but after Louis XIV it lacked the ruthless will needed to translate theory into practice. The

dissenters to hold public office. His policy of "salutary neglect" left the colonies to grow in population and wealth by their own efforts. Above all, he did his best to avoid war; he maintained until the 1730s the alliance with France that his predecessors had concluded in 1716–17 in order to safeguard Hanoverian possessions in Germany. Walpole's principal failure was domestic. He failed in 1733 to reform taxation by replacing customs duties, which encouraged smuggling, with excise taxes on tobacco and wines. The issue provoked a storm of irrational abuse ("No excise, no popery, no wooden consequent reinforcement of the privileges of the aristocracy exasperated the middle classes and in the long run condemned the royal government to financial ruin.

Cardinal Fleury, the leading minister from 1726 to 1743, arrested the decline for a time. But Fleury was no Richelieu. He came to power at the age of 73, and his policy, much like Walpole's, sought to avoid expensive wars and to conciliate rather than confront powerful domestic interests. Fleury dissociated himself from the courageous attempt of another minister to tax the nobility. He nevertheless stabilized the currency, encouraged trade, and had considerable success in damping down the continuing religious struggle between Jansenists and Jesuits. In foreign policy his overriding goal was to prevent the renewal of the coalitions against France that Louis XIV had inspired. Fleury therefore sought to cooperate with Walpole in making the Anglo-French alliance work.

When Fleury died in 1743 at the age of 90, Louis XV took Louis XIV as his model. Henceforth he sought to govern personally, without a first minister. But although Louis XV had inherited many of his great-grandfather's tastes— women and the hunt above all—he lacked the Sun King's relentless capacity for sustained work. The court frivolity with which Louis XIV had sought to corrupt the aristocracy had also corrupted the great king's successor. The consequence of the indolence of Louis XV, given the centralized administrative machine that the Sun King had left behind, was a fatal lack of coordination between the various branches of the bureaucracy and frequent paralysis. Louis XV did not govern himself, and from 1743 until his death in 1774 he largely prevented others from governing for him.

The aristocracy and the royal mistresses, of which the Marquise de Pompadour (1745–51) and Countess du Barry (1768–74) were the most conspicuous, inevitably filled the resulting power vacuum. Louis XV was not unaware of the declining health of the state: "After me, the deluge" was his most famous—and justly remembered— remark. But France, thanks to its size, its population, and a growth rate in trade and industry as rapid as Britain's, nevertheless remained potentially the most powerful nation in Europe.

Declining or Stagnant Powers

Elsewhere in Europe, with few exceptions, monarchical institutions likewise declined. In Spain a remarkable woman ruled: Elizabeth Farnese, the strong-willed Italian queen of that Philip V of Bourbon (r. 1700–46) whom Louis XIV had established on the throne. With the help of her husband's chief ministers, Elizabeth Farnese beat back the claims of the nobility, encouraged trade and industry, and reestablished Spain's diplomatic status as a great power. But Spanish society and government failed to respond to treatment. Centralization that robbed subjects of all initiative, a taxation more crushing than anything west of Russia, absurd guild regulations, a pitilessly intolerant Church that was the single largest social institution, an indolent nobility that amounted to 5 percent of the population, and a culturally rooted distaste for commerce and industry had bitten too deep. Spain failed to recover from depopulation, deforestation, and lethargy. Its economy, colonies, army, and navy stagnated, while other powers pressed onward.

Austria remained an imperfectly united empire that linked the three kingdoms of Austria, Bohemia, and

Habsburg domestic life, painted by Meytens: Empress Maria Theresa of Austria with her husband, Emperor Francis I, and their eleven children. The future Emperor Joseph II stands at right center.

the form of scraps of territory elsewhere; Spain received Naples and Sicily from Austria. Simultaneously, Austria and Russia fought the Ottoman Turks, whose decline accelerated as Europe's technological lead continued to grow.

Russia after Peter I failed to make its full weight felt for a generation. His succession law, enacted after his mortal quarrel with his son Alexei, gave the autocrat power to choose his own successor. That in effect made Russia until after 1800 an elective monarchy—and the Guards regiments and court nobles did the electing, with bayonets. Between 1725 and 1741, palace coups gave the crown successively to women or children who reigned but did not rule. From 1741 to 1762 Elizabeth, a daughter of Peter I, ruled firmly after seizing power with the help of the Guards and eliminating her opponents in the customary fashion—by torture, execution, deportation, and confiscation of land.

German and particularly Prussian influence predominated at court. As in France, the nobility freed itself from many of the restrictions that a great monarch had placed upon it. The Russian nobility extended the power over the serfs that Peter I had given it, while gradually escaping its corresponding obligation to serve the state. In Russia, as in Hungary and Prussia during the eighteenth century, the peasant thus sank ever deeper into serfdom, while the government made repeated concessions to the nobility. Until the accession of Elizabeth, and especially of Catherine the Great in 1762, Russia lacked strong rulers. But the feebleness of Peter I's immediate successors showed the full extent of his greatness. Despite weakness at the center, Russia retained the great power status the great tsar had won for it.

Prussia: Sergeant King, Undisciplined Son

Prussia, as usual, was an exception to a general trend, for its monarchy became more rather than less absolute. King

Hungary with two dependencies of entirely different cultures and traditions, northern Italy and the southern Netherlands. And the dynastic ties that bound together this bizarre assortment of territories were themselves open to challenge. The Habsburg Emperor Charles VI (r. 1711–40) had no son. He therefore spent almost 30 years in persuading both his provinces and the powers to accept a "Pragmatic Sanction" that established his daughter Maria Theresa as heir to his scattered lands. By his death in 1740 he had secured the agreement on paper of all concerned. But in the absence of a strong Habsburg army and central bureaucracy, treaties were a fragile defense against the greed of neighboring monarchs and the restlessness of the Hungarian nobility.

Farther to the east, the Polish and Ottoman empires continued their decline. France and Spain fought a desultory and trivial war against Austria and Russia over the succession to the Polish crown between 1733 and 1738. The Russian candidate for the throne won. The losers received "compensation" in

Frederick William I of Brandenburg-Prussia (r. 1713–40) was the most successful ruler of his generation. This strange, uncouth, and furious man, who smoked tobacco and drank beer in Gargantuan quantities, was the second of the three great Hohenzollerns that made the poor and backward territories of Brandenburg-Prussia into a great power.

Frederick William followed in the footsteps of the Great Elector, centralizing his administration in a board known as the General Directory, paring civil expenditures to the bone, and working his subordinates remorselessly. The purpose of this drill-sergeant king was to build the most formidable army in Europe. He echoed Richelieu in demanding absolute obedience to the state: "Salvation is from the Lord, but everything else is my business." After 1733, he militarized the peasantry by imposing a form of conscription, the "Canton System." Peasants in the ranks served Junker officers who were the brothers or cousins of the Junker landlords they labored for in civilian life. Frederick William doubled Prussia's peacetime standing army to 80,000, nearly equal to Austria's theoretical total of 100,000 men. But he was careful not to use his blue-coated and precisely drilled army , for he loved his "blue boys" too much to expend them in war.

His son Frederick II (r. 1740–86)—the third great Hohenzollern—thus inherited a treasury surplus, a ruthlessly efficient civil bureaucracy, and an army that was the fourth largest force on the continent and the most relentlessly trained. Frederick had initially impressed his father as a pathetic figure, unmilitary in habits and possessed of decadent tastes such as reading Voltaire and playing the flute. The irate father burned books, smashed flutes, and had Frederick beaten. When Frederick attempted to flee the country with a friend in 1730, the king had the friend beheaded before Frederick's eyes, threatened Frederick himself with death for "desertion," and set him to work in the provincial bureaucracy.

The experience rendered Frederick cold, dissimulating, and supremely cynical. But he also acquired a passion for administration and war, and a burning ambition to acquire glory and "establish his sovereignty like a rock of bronze." His opportunity came in 1740, the year in which his hated father and Charles VI of Habsburg both died.

THE WORLD WARS OF MID-CENTURY, 1740–63

Two great wars, the War of the Austrian Succession (1740–48) and the Seven Years' War (1756–63) punctuated the middle of the century. The wars were linked, and derived from two irreconcilable rivalries—Hohenzollern against Habsburg in central Europe, and Britain against France in North America, the West Indies, Africa, and India. Twice these separate conflicts became entangled, although the powers exchanged partners between the two wars. In the end, as established in the Peace of Paris of 1763, Britain and Prussia defeated France and Austria.

Father and son: Frederick William I in a characteristic pose, and the young Frederick II (below).

British Navy, Prussian Army

These wars demonstrated the superiority of the two greatest military institutions of the eighteenth century, the British navy and the Prussian army. Superiority in both cases rested on the unrivaled excellence of the officer corps. But behind the "wooden walls" of Britain's fleets or the ruler-straight ranks of Prussia's blue-coats stood two sharply different societies and political systems, each well adapted to the competitive environment they faced.

British sea power enjoyed many advantages. Britain was an island, safe from invasion by land and therefore able to pour into ships the men and money that continental rivals such as the Dutch or the French had to devote to armies. Maritime enterprise was both profitable and patriotic. Seafaring careers attracted enterprising younger sons of the nobility and gentry as well as yeomen and artisans. Britain's reservoir of experienced sailors was larger than that of France, its nearest rival, because the British by mid-century had the largest merchant marine in the world. Finally, the government and the

groups represented in Parliament recognized the paramount importance of trade and sea power. Despite occasional periods of neglect, Parliament supported naval construction and encouraged British shipping.

Britain's rival France had corresponding advantages—experienced sailors, a large merchant marine, warships superior in design even to the British, and colonial bases overseas. But France lacked secure access to the "strategic raw materials" of the day, the immense mast timbers and the turpentine and pine-tar of the Baltic. Above all, France had long land frontiers and a tradition of pushing those frontiers eastward. France inevitably gave its army priority, and exposed its navy to defeat. Like later continental challengers to the English-speaking sea powers, it lacked the resources to be *both* the greatest land power and the greatest sea power.

Nor did France prosper on land, for it ultimately faced a far more efficient power machine than itself: Prussia. The Prussian bureaucracy and fiscal system had emerged from institutions devised to support the army. The Junkers had

Maritime supremacy: the British Channel Fleet (1790).

acknowledged that their calling was to serve the king, in the army by preference, in the bureaucracy if necessary. Enterprising members of the small middle class established state-supported war industries or enlisted in the civil service. Serfs did labor service as civilians and military service as conscripts. The example of this army, with its harsh *"Kadavergehorsam"*—"corpse-obedience," the obedience that supposedly made the dead snap to attention—permeated Prussian society. In Britain, central government by Parliament, local government by amateurs, and freedom of opinion and commerce proved a formula for sea power. In Prussia, absolute monarchy, centralized professional administration, a disciplined aristocracy, state regulation of the economy, and automaton-like obedience produced the most effective land power for its size since Sparta.

The War of the Austrian Succession, 1740–48

In 1740 Maria Theresa (r. 1740–80), a beautiful, strong-willed, courageous, but inexperienced woman of 23, succeeded her father Charles VI in the Habsburg dominions, as established by the Pragmatic Sanction. That gave Frederick II of Prussia his opportunity. He had published an anonymous pamphlet against the supposed immorality of Machiavelli's political precepts, but he had learned the great Florentine's lessons well. In December 1740 he seized Silesia, Austria's rich province to the northeast of Bohemia. Possession of Silesia, with its million inhabitants, its linen industry, and its iron ore, would finally make Brandenburg-Prussia a great power.

Frederick's thrust caught Maria Theresa off guard, and the success of Frederick's shameless aggression encouraged Bavaria, Spain, and finally France to join in the attack, in violation of their Pragmatic Sanction pledges. But Hungary, which resented Habsburg rule, ironically proved Maria

Theresa's salvation. When she traveled to Budapest with her infant son and made an emotional appeal to the Hungarian Parliament, her bravery and tact inspired the Hungarian nobility to rise tumultuously to her support. An able minister, Count Haugwitz, centralized the Habsburg administration and reorganized the army during the wars that followed. Austria, a helpless victim in 1740, revived and become a formidable antagonist. But Frederick's armies fought brilliantly, and at Hohenfriedberg in 1745 he achieved Prussia's first great victory due above all to his own generalship. The combined pressure of France, Bavaria, and Prussia—shaky though their alliance was—proved too much for Maria Theresa. In 1748, at Aix-la-Chapelle, she consented to a peace treaty that left Silesia in Frederick's hands.

The Anglo-French overseas rivalry intersected with continental war. Britain went to war with Spain in 1739 over Spanish maltreatment of English merchants smuggling goods to the Spanish empire. That "war of Jenkins' Ear" (named after an unfortunate English trader), and French intervention in Germany in support of a Bavarian claimant to the office of Holy Roman Emperor, made conflict between France and Britain almost inevitable. France and Spain, thanks to their Bourbon family ties, normally cooperated closely after 1700, and France had developed a large economic stake in the Spanish colonies, which it supplied with most of their manufactured goods.

British and French interests also clashed in North America and India. The French military hold on Canada and Louisiana appeared to threaten the British colonies that stretched from Boston to Savannah. The fantastic rates of population growth of the British colonies on the eastern seaboard prompted a northward and westward expansion that appeared to threaten the French. In the West Indies both sides glowered at one another from their sugar-island strongholds. In India, where the Mughal empire had fallen into near-anarchy after the death in 1707 of the merciless Aurangzeb, its last strong ruler, the French and British East India companies sought to fill a power vacuum. From their respective bases at Pondicherry and Madras, each European power mobilized native rulers against the other. From Canada to the Carnatic Coast of India, France and Britain prepared for war, and British and French troops clashed in Germany as early as 1743.

In 1744 France declared war on Great Britain, and merged the continental and overseas wars. In 1745 a force of American colonial militia with British naval support boldly seized the key to Canada, the great fortress of Louisbourg on Cape Breton Island in the St. Lawrence estuary. In 1746 the French seized Madras. But the overseas conflict was indecisive because Britain failed to set clear objectives and establish priorities. The "Patriot" partisans of overseas war in Parliament denounced the continental commitment as "Hanoverianism," a pandering to the interests of George II, who led the British army in Germany to defend his possessions as Elector of Hanover against France. The French defeated the British in a hard-fought battle at Fontenoy in the Austrian Netherlands in 1745, while in 1747 the British navy twice annihilated French fleets escorting West Indies convoys. George II's son, "Butcher" Cumberland, savaged the Highland clans after his victory over the last pro-Stuart rising, which had broken out with French encouragement in 1745.

Neither side pressed its successes far, except in Scotland. The War of the Austrian Succession was a typical "limited" war. The Anglo-French duel ended in stalemate. The French surrendered Madras and the British government, much to the disgust of the American colonists, gave back Louisbourg. The French emerged from the war with increased prestige, an enlarged debt, and no concrete gains over either Britain or Austria. The British emerged with a clear sense of how to fight their next war with France.

The Overseas "War Before the War," 1749–55

The peace of Aix-la-Chapelle did not end the overseas conflict between Britain and France. Joseph Dupleix, France's greatest colonial adventurer, sought after 1748 to make the French East India Company a political as well as a commercial power in India. By securing allies among the warring native states that contended within the hollow shell of the Mughal empire, he hoped to increase his company's revenue and ultimately drive the British from India. The English East India Company reinforced its outposts. Clashes ensued in which the British largely prevailed, thanks to command of the sea and the brilliant leadership of Dupleix's great adversary, the legendary Robert Clive. In 1754 the company directors, fearing that Dupleix had overreached himself, recalled him to France. The ensuing truce merely postponed the struggle for mastery in south Asia that Dupleix had begun.

In America, open warfare did not break out until 1752. The French in Canada used the interval of peace to build a chain of forts from the St. Lawrence down the Ohio to the Mississippi to block the westward thrust of Britain's American colonists. London countered, reinforcing the colonies with ships and troops. Britain held the advantage; 1.2 million British subjects, including slaves, faced roughly 60,000 French. The French sought to even the odds by an alliance with Indian tribes whose interest in preventing British westward penetration ran parallel to that of France. French raids in turn provoked in 1754 an unsuccessful attempt, under the leadership of Lieutenant Colonel George Washington of the Virginia militia, to capture the vital French base at Fort Duquesne, on the site of modern Pittsburgh. In 1755, near the same spot, General George Braddock and a force of British regulars discovered that rigid European tactics were ill-suited to war in the woods. The "French and Indian War," the final round of the Anglo-French struggle for North America, had begun.

1701	1714	1740	1748	1756	1763	1789	1815
War of Spanish Succession	Walpole, Fleury, and Frederick William I	War of Austrian Succession	Diplomatic Revolution	Seven Years' War	Last Years of the Old Regime	Revolutionary Era	

The Climax of Old Regime Statecraft: The "Diplomatic Revolution" of 1756

Overseas struggle was merely one prelude to a second round of war in Europe. The other prelude was a "diplomatic revolution" by which the chief antagonists of the first general war of mid-century changed partners in preparation for the second. Britain had fought the War of the Austrian Succession in loose agreement with Austria, its traditional ally from the wars of 1689–97 and 1701–13. But London saw no British interest served in fighting simply to restore Silesia to Maria Theresa. Bourbon France had fought against its traditional Habsburg enemy in a still looser alliance with Prussia; Frederick distrusted Paris and twice deserted it to make truces with Austria. By 1748, all four major powers were disenchanted with their traditional allies.

The chief instigator of the ensuing "revolution" was Maria Theresa's chancellor, the wily Prince Wenzel Anton von Kaunitz. He began from the premise that the reconquest of Silesia—and the annihilation of Prussia—was the prerequisite for Austria's resurgence as a great power. That aim prompted Kaunitz to think the hitherto unthinkable. He sought to replace the ancient antagonism between Bourbon and Habsburg with a Franco-Austrian alliance, possibly with Russian support, against Prussia. Even the battlefield genius of Frederick II, Kaunitz was confident, would be helpless against the three strongest land powers in Europe.

Kaunitz sought with success to win over the Marquise de Pompadour, the current mistress of Louis XV. But the king remained reluctant—until Britain and Prussia unintentionally convinced him. London had long feared that its Austrian ally lacked the will and ability to help Britain defend Hanover against France, and the outbreak of Anglo-French hostilities overseas increased British anxieties. In 1755 London therefore sought Russian help in the usual British way; a subsidy treaty that exchanged British gold for allied troops. That treaty alarmed Frederick II, for it raised the specter of a large Russian army encamped on his eastern border. He therefore approached London, and in effect outbid Russia. By the treaty of Westminster of January 1756, Prussia itself agreed to defend Hanover, naturally in exchange for a British subsidy.

The spectacle of Prussia, France's ally, contracting a quasi-alliance with Britain, a power already in conflict with France from the Ohio to the Carnatic, finally aroused the wrath of Louis XV. Bourbon France made a defensive alliance with Habsburg Austria. Kaunitz also enlisted Russia, and planned war for 1757. Frederick II judged that his only chance was to strike first. The Austrians had hoped for such a blow, to weld Kaunitz's grand coalition together. Unfortunately for Kaunitz, Frederick II struck in August 1756, a year earlier than Vienna had anticipated. Unfortunately for Frederick, his aggression indeed did Kaunitz's work. It brought into play Austria's French alliance and created a grand coalition that almost destroyed Prussia.

The Seven Years' War, 1756–63

In the new war, the greatest worldwide conflict of the old regime, Britain thus fought for empire and Prussia for its life. After an inauspicious beginning, William Pitt became virtual prime minister of Britain. Pitt possessed a Roman nose, a talent for commanding oratory, and a clear sense of Britain's global objectives. Convinced of his own indispensability ("I am sure I can save this country, and nobody else can") he pushed his way into the cabinet in spite of the disfavor of George II. From 1757 to 1760, he tirelessly directed Brit-

View of the Taking of QUEBECK by the English Forces Commanded by Gen.ʳ Wolfe. Sep: 13. 1759.

Britain's command of the sea in action: Wolfe takes Québec, 1759.

ain's war and drove his subordinates to unprecedented exertions. In 1757, at Plassey near Calcutta, Robert Clive destroyed France's principal client, the Nawab of Bengal, and seized his rich province for Britain. That broke French power in India. Britain conquered France's chief slaving station at Gorée in Senegal and cut France's West Indian sugar islands off from their supplies of slaves and manufactured goods.

In the "year of miracles" of 1759, Pitt conquered for Britain the domination of the outer seas that it held with only brief interruptions until 1941. A brilliant young general, James Wolfe, led an amphibious expedition up the St. Lawrence River. Outside the walls of Québec city he defeated France at the cost of his own life, and ended the French empire in North America. British fleets captured the rich West Indies sugar island of Guadeloupe and drove the French fleet in a gale onto the lee shore of Quiberon Bay in western France. Command of the sea was the decisive ingredient in Britain's triumphs.

On the continent, Prussia survived only thanks to Frederick II and to his long-suffering troops, whom he drove toward the enemy with sarcastic wit: "You dogs, do you want to live for ever?" Prussia's "year of miracles" was 1757. At Rossbach in Saxony, Frederick with 21,000 troops decisively defeated a French army of 64,000 by attacking them in the flank. Having thus checked one of his three enemies, he hastened back to defend Silesia from Austrian invasion. A bare month after Rossbach he smashed an Austrian army of 80,000 at Leuthen with a mere 36,000 Prussian troops. A Prussian feint lured the Austrians into weakening their left, which Frederick then rolled up.

But these great victories produced no decisive strategic result. Frederick was the supreme artist of eighteenth-century warfare, but his instrument did not permit battles of annihilation. Pursuit, necessary to prevent a beaten enemy from reforming to fight again, was impossible with troops that deserted once out of sight of their officers. And Prussia's desperate position, exposed to the French from the west, the Austrians from the south, and the Russians from the east, prevented the great king from finishing off any one of his adversaries. The war dragged on; Russia made its weight felt, and in 1759 an Austro-Russian army heavily defeated Frederick at Kunersdorf in Silesia.

Frederick thought despairingly of abdication. But the divisions of his enemies saved him and Prussia. Kaunitz had not promised to France and Russia enough of the expected spoils to stimulate them to all-out effort. Austria understandably feared that Russian troops, once invited into central Europe, would not leave. France's naval and overseas campaigns had exhausted its treasury, and the disgrace of Rossbach had shattered the monarchy's already low reputation at home. Pitt's lavish subsidies to the armies of German princelings, along with token British forces, pinned the French down in bloody fighting in western Germany.

In 1760 Frederick temporarily lost Berlin and by the end of 1761 he appeared close to total defeat, as 300,000 allied troops penned him into a fortified camp in Silesia. His British ally abandoned him. George III (r. 1760–1820), who had succeeded his grandfather, wished to prove himself thoroughly English, unlike the first two Georges. He therefore withdrew from all involvement in German affairs and drove Pitt to resignation in October 1761. Lord Bute, George III's Scottish favorite, became chief minister and sought peace with France at almost any price, including the sacrifice of Prussia.

Then, on January 5, 1762, Elizabeth of Russia died. Her successor was the weak and eccentric Tsar Peter III, a German by birth and a fond admirer of Frederick the Great. He immediately withdrew Russia from the coalition. Only a crippled and sulking France now supported Vienna, and Maria Theresa and Kaunitz grudgingly abandoned their hopes of crushing the Prussian upstart. In February 1763, by the treaty of Hubertusburg, Austria and Prussia restored the boundaries of 1756. Prussia had successfully sustained its claim to Silesia and to great power status.

The Peace of Paris, 1763

The peace that emerged in January 1763 from the Anglo-French negotiations at Paris was overwhelmingly favorable to Great Britain. But contrary to Pitt's wishes it did not entirely eliminate France as an overseas rival. France received back most of the economic outposts it had lost—trading stations in India, Gorée in West Africa, rich sugar islands in the West Indies, the fishing rights off Canada, along with two tiny islands off Newfoundland, St. Pierre and Miquelon.

But in the long run only the continents counted. Trading posts could only flourish if they controlled a large hinterland. Sugar islands produced great wealth in a few square miles, but were incapable of defending themselves against a power, such as Britain, that controlled the sea. Failure at sea and the collapse of French land power in India and North America broke the

first French colonial empire for good. France agreed to maintain no further troops in India and to recognize Britain's native client rulers. France ceded to Britain all of Canada and of Louisiana east of the Mississippi, and Louisiana west of the Mississippi passed to Spain. Henceforth the British had no serious rivals in North America except the colonists they had planted there.

ENLIGHTENED ABSOLUTISM, 1763–89

In the quarter century that followed the Peace of Paris, the ancient institution of monarchy briefly seemed to take on new life. The major ideas of the Enlightenment—reason, natural law, happiness, progress, liberty—filtered through to the rulers. Some monarchs accepted the criticisms that *philosophes* had leveled at aristocratic and ecclesiastical privilege, unequal taxation, and the degraded condition of the peasantry and the urban lower classes. In addition, the great wars of mid-century strained the social fabric of most European states. The resurgence of the aristocracy forced monarchs to look to the middle classes for support. Only reform could restore order, revive trade, refill the treasuries of Europe's monarchs, and check the pretensions of the nobility. The fusion of new ideas and practical needs produced the phenomenon that contemporaries described as "enlightened absolutism."

The enlightened absolutist was naturally an ideal type that fitted few rulers of the later eighteenth century. George III of England made no pretense to "enlightenment," nor would his subjects have applauded if he had, for English loyalty to the post-1688 status quo ran deep. In his last years, Louis XV of France showed unexpected resolution and zeal, but during most of his reign he was enlightened in few senses of the word. A few minor monarchs such as Gustavus III of Sweden (r. 1771–92) and Charles III of Spain (r. 1759–88) had some claims to the title. But the three rulers that *philosophes* cited most often as enlightened absolutists were Catherine the Great of Russia, Frederick the Great of Prussia, and Joseph II of Austria.

The attack of the enlightened absolutists on irrational customs and vested interests, on aristocratic and Church power, on town and provincial privileges was not new. It was in most respects a continuation of the centralizing drive of the seventeenth-century monarchies. What had changed was the climate of opinion in which monarchs acted. The ideas of the Enlightenment, the practical example of Britain, and the victorious struggle for self-government of the British colonies in North America after 1776 stripped the doctrine of divine right of kings of its persuasiveness. Monarchs therefore had to appeal to their increasingly literate subjects with talk of following reason and of serving the public good. Frederick the Great described himself as "merely the first servant of the state." That state was not the people; their duty also was to serve the state—which the monarch personified. Monarchs might be "enlightened," but they sought to remain absolute. That monarchy felt compelled to justify itself by reference to the good of society was nevertheless a sign of fatal weakness.

Russia: Catherine the Great

Catherine II (r. 1762–96), the most remarkable woman ruler of the century, was no Russian. Princess of the German line of Anhalt-Zerbst, she married the eccentric crown prince Peter in 1745. A woman of high intelligence, masterful cunning, implacable will, and a warm heart, she maintained a succession of lovers with lavish gifts of lands and serfs; as the poet Pushkin later remarked, "many were called, and many chosen." In her youth, Catherine survived the snake-pit of the St. Petersburg court by making pretense of frivolity, while finding allies and a lover among the officers of the crucial Guards regiments. Her husband Peter,

after his accession as Peter III in 1762, alienated those same regiments by proposing to reform them along Prussian lines. He also appalled the pious by confiscating church lands. Six months after Peter's accession, Catherine seized power with the help of the Guards. Peter perished while under arrest, apparently at the hands of a relative of Grigori Orlov, Catherine's lover.

Catherine came to power with a genuine desire to improve the lot of her subjects. She read the works of *philosophes* such as Montesquieu and advanced thinkers such as Beccaria. She corresponded with Voltaire, persuaded Diderot to visit her court, and proclaimed publicly her adherence to the Enlightenment. But as autocrat she could not afford too much enlightenment. Survival required escape from the grip of the faction that had brought her to power and the elimination of all potential rivals for the throne. She therefore sought to widen her political base by conciliating the nobility as a whole. She confirmed the most important act of her husband's brief reign, his release of the nobility from any obligation to serve the state. She gave the nobility a monopoly on land ownership. She made promotion in the bureaucracy automatic, by seniority, a step that gravely weakened the effective power of her successors. In 1785 she granted the nobility a charter that conceded at last some rights against the state, some exemption from arbitrary arrest and the barbaric punishments customary in Muscovite law and practice. But since the autocrat could still revoke noble status at any moment, the rights Catherine's charter granted were as much a matter of form as of substance.

In 1767–68 she even summoned a Legislative Commission to codify Russia's laws. Every social group except serfs sent representatives, who assembled armed with statements of grievances. That was the autocracy's first open appeal to its subjects, its first at-

Determination: Catherine the Great, on a medal struck to commemorate her accession as empress of Russia.

tempt to give them a voice in government. It was also the last before the twentieth century, when the last tsar conceded under duress a sham parliament. Catherine dissolved the Commission before it could suggest laws; its passing marked the waning of her "enlightened" phase.

She nevertheless drew from it a sense of what her subjects, especially the nobility, wanted. What they wanted and Catherine conceded was the strengthening of serfdom. As early as 1765 she gave landlords the power to condemn serfs to forced labor without legal formalities. In 1767 she forbade serf complaints against landlords upon pain of penal servitude for life and flogging with the dreaded Russian whip—the knout. The knout, now that the nobility was no longer obliged to do state service that justified their holding of serfs, was soon needed, for the freeing of the nobility in turn raised expectations among the serfs. When Catherine disappointed those expectations, the greatest of all Russian peasant revolts convulsed the Volga region from 1773 to 1775 under the leadership of the Cossack Emelyan Pugachev, who claimed to be Peter III. The army ultimately massacred the insurgents and brought Pugachev in an iron cage to Moscow. There, in time-honored fashion, Catherine had him broken on the wheel, beheaded, dismembered, and burnt.

In the following years she sought to reorganize and strengthen local government to prevent further revolts, while extending the institution of serfdom to newly conquered provinces and to hitherto free categories of peasants. By the end of her reign, by one estimate, 34 million of the 36 million subjects of the Russian monarchy were serfs. By her encouragement of the nobility she furthered a process that never reached completion, the transformation of the service nobility into a Western-style aristocracy with rights against the state. In Russia, unlike western Europe, that process rested

upon the further enslavement of the peasantry, and left a dangerous legacy.

Conquest, not reform, made Catherine II "the Great" in her own lifetime. Peter the Great had broken a window to the west by driving the Swedes from the Baltic coast. Catherine pushed Russia's borders southward and westward against Poland and the Ottoman Empire. Poland was her first victim, for its borders at her accession were a mere 200 miles from Moscow. In 1763 Catherine secured the election to the Polish throne of a former lover, Stanislaus Poniatowski. Thereafter, Catherine and Frederick II of Prussia worked to block constitutional reforms that might revive the fortunes of the Polish state. In 1772 the two monarchs combined to carry out a First Partition of Poland. Frederick took West Prussia, and thus

Russia's Expansion in Europe   1462–1796

Maria Theresa on the First Partition of Poland

Frederick the Great, with his habitual cynicism, remarked that "Maria Theresa wept, but she kept on taking."

This unfortunate partition of Poland is costing me ten years of my life. . . . How many times have I refused to agree to it! But disaster after disaster heaped upon us by the Turks, misery, famine and pestilence at home, no hope of assistance from either France or England, and the prospect of being left isolated and threatened with war both by Prussia and Russia—it was all these considerations that finally forced me to accept that unhappy proposal which will remain a blot on my reign. God grant that I be not held responsible for it in the other world! I confess that I cannot keep from talking about this affair. I have taken it so to heart that it poisons and embitters all my days.

Excerpt from a letter to one of her diplomats, in *Readings in Western Civilization*, ed. by Paul L. Hughes and Robert F. Fries (Paterson, N.J.: Littlefield, Adams, 1960), p. 134.

secured a land bridge between Brandenburg and the province of Prussia. Catherine took a generous slice of northeastern Poland, with the pretext that Russian and Orthodox populations there were suffering under Polish rule. To preserve the balance of power the two monarchs thought it wise to offer the province of Galicia, northeast of Hungary, to Maria Theresa. That gift distressed the pious empress, but rea-

son of state triumphed over personal morality.

The first partition shocked the Poles into a patriotic revival that swept up even Poniatowski, who forgot that he owed his throne to Catherine. In 1791, after the outbreak of the French Revolution, Poland enacted a remarkable reform constitution that abolished the *liberum veto* and established a strong monarchy. Catherine gave a swift and ruthless answer. Early in 1792 she ceased a promising war against the Turks, rushed an army to Poland, and restored the old anarchy. In 1793, in partnership with Prussia alone, she carried out a Second Partition that reduced Poland to a narrow strip, wedged between Prussia, Russia, and Austria. The inhabitants of this rump-Poland, under the leadership of Thaddeus Kosciuszko, who had fought conspicuously in the American Revolution, rose against the partitioning powers. But Catherine's armies tracked down Kosciuszko and forced Poniatowski to abdicate. A third partition in 1795 wiped rump-Poland from the map by dividing it between Russia, Prussia, and Austria. In the three partitions, Catherine secured almost two-thirds of Poland's original territory. A Polish state did not reemerge until the simultaneous ruin of the three partitioning powers in 1917–18.

Catherine's successes against the crumbling Ottoman Empire were al-

The Partitions of Poland

most as decisive. In wars in 1768–74 and 1787–92, Catherine secured most of the northern shore of the Black Sea. By the Treaty of Kütchük Kainardji that ended the first war in 1774, Russia also received a vague right to protect Orthodox Christians in the Ottoman Empire, a right that later served as a perennial pretext for Russian intervention at Constantinople. Kütchük Kainardji marked the opening of the "Eastern Question"—the decay and partition of the Ottoman Empire—that bedeviled European diplomacy until its resolution by force in 1914–18. For the moment, the Ottoman Empire escaped the fate of Poland because of its size, its remoteness, and the mutual jealousies of its two European adversaries, Austria and Prussia. But at Catherine's death in 1796, little seemed to stand between Russian power and Constantinople, the gate to the Mediterranean.

Prussia: Frederick the Great

Frederick II of Prussia, who ruled until 1786, had better claims than Catherine to the title of "enlightened absolutist." The state he inherited, despite its military narrowness, was unlike the "half-German, half-Tartar" autocracy that fell to Catherine II. Prussia's enserfed peasants suffered under the Junkers but had far more rights than the serfs of Russia. Prussia possessed a middle class and was a recognizably Western society capable of accepting gradual reform.

Frederick burnished his reputation for enlightenment by inviting Voltaire to Potsdam. They eventually quarreled over the merits of Frederick's rather awful poetry, but agreed that the king's duty was to combat ignorance and superstition, to enhance the welfare of his subjects, and to promote religious toleration. The king welcomed all religious exiles, even Jesuits; only Jews remained hedged about with vexatious regulations. As a religious skeptic, Frederick found toleration easy.

In economic policy, he was the most determined "mercantilist" since Colbert. His state-directed enterprises sought to give Prussia self-sufficiency,

The Rise of Brandenburg-Prussia   1640–1795

above all in military supplies and equipment. He encouraged the new scientific agriculture that was slowly spreading from Holland. His policies induced 300,000 immigrants, including many skilled agricultural and industrial workers, to settle in Prussia. He also introduced Europe's first scheme for universal primary education, and thus founded a tradition that Prussia built on in the next century with startling effect. Finally, Frederick implemented a typical objective of enlightened absolutism by rationalizing Prussia's laws and court procedures.

Yet in many respects Frederick was less than "enlightened." He believed firmly in birth and privilege. The Junkers served him well as officers in the most important organ of the state, the army. In return for that service he trusted the nobility far more than had his father or the Great Elector. Frederick improved the lot of serfs on his own estates, but had little enthusiasm for emancipation. During his reign, noble estates expanded and the condition of the serfs worsened. His conception of society was static: nobles, townspeople, and peasants should remain at their respective posts. His preference for rigid caste lines over social mobility and for bureaucratic direction from above over unconstrained economic

initiative from below ultimately proved self-defeating.

Despite Frederick's enlightened pose, the discipline, efficiency, and ruthless centralization of the Prussian monarchy ultimately derived from a long Hohenzollern tradition entirely unrelated to the Enlightenment. The state that Frederick erected in wars between 1740 and 1763 and consolidated in peace from 1763 to 1786 was the most striking political achievement of his time. But without him, without a genius at the helm, it was doomed to stagnation thanks to his economic and social policies. Prussia's shattering military successes and the great king's monopoly of diplomacy, strategy, and tactics put the officer corps to sleep. The coming storms of the revolutionary era almost destroyed Prussia. It survived only thanks to the emergence of a "bureaucratic absolutism" in which the bureaucracy and army ran the state themselves, without much need of a monarch. That was Prussia's dangerous legacy to the German state that it ultimately created.

Austria: Joseph II

The monarch with the best claim to the title of enlightened absolutist was Joseph II of Austria (r. 1780–90). He professed contempt for the *philosophes* but was more devoted to the main tenets of the Enlightenment and to the welfare of his peoples than any of his fellow monarchs.

Frederick II's conquest of Silesia in 1740 prompted a drastic reorganization of the Habsburg Empire that enabled it to survive until 1918. Maria Theresa, during her long reign (1740–80), developed an imperial bureaucracy that controlled from Vienna all provinces of the empire except Hungary. In 1775 that machine imposed a tariff union on the empire, except for Hungary. It compelled the nobles to assume some of the burden of taxation. It limited the amount of labor they could extort from the peasantry and curbed the power of private noble courts over the serfs, for

Joseph II urging agricultural improvement on his peasants.

whom Maria Theresa did more than any other ruler of her time.

Her son Joseph, who became emperor and co-regent after the death of her husband in 1765, took an increasingly energetic part in her efforts at reform. But Joseph sought to move farther and faster than his mother. Until her death in 1780 he chafed under Maria Theresa's compromises, particularly over religion. During the ten years that Joseph II ruled, thousands of decrees poured from the imperial chancellery in Vienna. He proclaimed religious toleration for all Christians and Jews. He dissolved monasteries devoted solely to religious contemplation and gave their revenues to the hospitals that in the next century made Vienna the medical center of Europe. He applied to everyone in the Habsburg dominions, regardless of rank or nationality, a system of equal taxation in proportion to income. He imposed one language for official business, German, on all parts of the empire, including Belgium, Italy, and Hungary. Above all, Joseph II abolished serfdom. Early in his reign he issued a number of decrees that gave all serfs in the Habsburg dominions personal freedom—freedom to leave the land, to marry as they pleased, to choose whatever job they liked. That act of Joseph II was permanent, even though his successors repealed other decrees by which he sought to make those peasants who remained on the land into property owners, free of all forced labor obligations.

Through his policies of centralization and drastic reform, Joseph naturally made mortal enemies of the clergy, the landed nobility, non-German nationalities such as the Hungarians, and even peasants who failed to understand his intentions. In 1789, when revolution broke out in France, peasants in the Austrian Empire began to plunder and to murder landlords to gain the rights Joseph had held out to them. By 1790 both Belgium and Hungary were in revolt against his rule, and the Church was bitterly hostile.

Joseph II, the Enlightened Despot   1783

The following extracts illustrate the paradox of enlightened absolutism; only autocratic methods made reform conceivable.

I have not confined myself simply to issuing orders; I have expounded and explained them. With enlightenment I have sought to weaken and with arguments I have sought to overcome the abuses which had arisen out of prejudice and deeply rooted customs. I have sought to imbue every official of the state with the love I myself feel for the wellbeing of the whole. . . .

The good of the state can be understood only in general terms, only in terms of the greatest number. Similarly, all the provinces of the monarchy constitute one whole and therefore can have only one aim. It is necessary therefore that there should be an end to all the prejudices and all the jealousies between provinces [and] all races which have caused so much fruitless bickering. [Circular letter of Joseph II, 1783.]

But given Austria's structure and traditions, only the monarch could dictate unity and the end of "prejudices." The state needed a common language; Joseph II determined what it should be.

The German language is the universal tongue of my empire. I am the emperor of Germany. The states which I possess are provinces that form only one body—the state of which I am the head. If the kingdom of Hungary were the most important of my possessions, I would not hesitate to impose its language on the other countries. [Letter to a Hungarian noble, 1783.]

From T. C. W. Blanning, *Joseph II and Enlightened Despotism* (London: Longman Group, 1970), pp. 131–32, and Louis Léger, *Histoire de l'Autriche Hongrie* (Paris, 1879), p. 373.

Joseph lamented to his brother and successor Leopold that "I am the only one holding to the true course, and I am left to labor alone. . . . I am without any assistance whatsoever." Worn out, he died in 1790 after choosing a rueful epitaph: "Here lies Joseph II, who was unfortunate in everything that he undertook."

Joseph II, the "revolutionary Emperor," built a structure stronger than he knew. It survived both the revolutionary era and the coming nineteenth century. The crippling limitations under which Joseph labored stemmed above all from his position as a revolutionary without a party. His only supports were an unimaginative bureaucracy, a secret police that he had set up to combat opposition, and the Habsburg army. His brand of enlightened absolutism might have formed a bridge between divine-right monarchy and democratic politics. But his fate suggested that radical changes, at least on the Continent, demanded a broader base of popular support than he had been able to command.

BRITAIN, FRANCE, AND THE AMERICAN REVOLUTION, 1763–89

In France and British North America, revolution from below took the place of reform from above. Louis XV made a belated but vigorous attempt to quell internal opposition between 1770 and 1774. Thereafter the French monarchy drifted until its collapse after 1789 in the greatest of modern European revolutions. Overseas, the American colonists claimed their independence in the name of reason and natural rights. When Britain resisted, the colonists broke away by force.

France: Abortive Revolution from Above, 1770–74

The Seven Years' War severely strained both British and French government finances. Louis XV proposed to cope by making permanent a temporary war tax that fell on nobles and commoners alike and by levying a new tax on those who had bought judicial and administrative offices from the monarchy. Such measures, necessary if the monarchy hoped to avoid bankruptcy, raised a storm of opposition from nobility and middle classes alike. The *parlements*, narrow oligarchies of officeholders who had bought their positions, rationalized their privileges by borrowing from Locke. Any attack on their own tax exemption, they impudently proclaimed, violated the "fundamental

laws" of the kingdom and the "natural rights" of Frenchmen.

In 1770–71 Louis XV finally acted. His forceful ministers, the lawyer René de Maupeou for political affairs and the Abbé Joseph Marie Terray for finances, closed the *parlements*, exiled their most fractious members to distant villages, and reassessed taxes. Public opinion—except, significantly, for Voltaire—rose in outrage. But the king held fast and won. A new system of royal law courts replaced the *parlements*. Maupeou prepared to rationalize at last France's administration and finances. Then, in 1774, Louis XV caught smallpox and died. His son, Louis XVI (r. 1774–92), well-meaning and lamentably weak, was the monarchy's downfall. He dismissed Maupeou, acquiesced in the restoration of the *parlements*, and presided first over bankruptcy, then over revolution.

The Revolt of Britain's American Colonies

France's revolution did not begin until 1788–89, but events overseas furnished a powerful example. Britain's "salutary neglect" of its North American colonies did not survive the Seven Years' War. As in France, the financial strain of that conflict prompted a search for new revenues. Parliament in London naturally looked to its colonists. The colonies had in the past paid no taxes to Britain, but only customs duties that Parliament had imposed—but only loosely enforced—to channel colonial trade to Britain. The colonists' tax burden was thus a mere 4 percent of the average Englishman's. And while the colonists had done little fighting, London had paid dearly to defend them against the French, against France's Indian allies, and against the 1763 uprising of the Ottawa chief Pontiac. But unfortunately for the British government, its entirely reasonable efforts to raise revenue coincided with the elimination of French power in North America, which freed the colonists of their dependence on Britain. The result, thanks to the traditions of government that the colonies had acquired from England itself, was an explosion that shattered the British Empire.

"Salutary neglect" had permitted a political experiment possible in no other European colonial empire. The thirteen colonies, from quasi-theocratic Massachusetts, to anarchic Rhode Island, to Catholic Maryland, to Anglican Virginia, were in effect self-governing. The ministry in London appointed royal governors, but under the charters granted the colonies, the colonial legislatures, not Parliament, paid the governors' salaries and voted—or refused to vote—the revenues needed to carry on government. Elections to those legislatures were far more democratic than those for Parliament or for other European representative bodies. And the colonists took seriously John Locke's theory of limited government and the practice of England's "Glorious Revolution" of 1688. For them, the British Empire was a quasi-federal structure that rested on consent.

Parliament took a different view. In March 1765, it imposed a stamp tax on printed papers, including legal documents, commercial agreements, and newspapers. That tax, all too familiar to Europeans, aroused furious opposition in America among the most articulate and disputatious groups—lawyers, newspaper editors, and merchants. A congress of delegates from nine of the colonies urged "that no taxes be imposed on them but with their own consent." They claimed further that distance made it impossible in practical terms for Parliament to secure American "consent" to taxation. Parliament retreated. It repealed the Stamp Act in 1766 but at the same time declared that crown and Parliament had the right to tax the colonies if they so wished. In 1767 Parliament returned to the attack with an act that imposed duties on imports into the colonies of tea, paper, paint, lead, and glass. Unlike previous duties, its purpose was to raise revenue, not to regulate trade. The colonists replied with boycotts, and in 1770

Parliament withdrew all duties except those on tea.

Up to that point the colonists had shown little understanding of Britain's financial and military plight, and Parliament had shown little appreciation of the tradition that made the colonists doubt or fear its authority. But despite the death in 1770 of five Boston demonstrators at the hands of British troops (the so-called "Boston massacre"), the quarrel had not led to an irrevocable break. That changed after 1773, when Parliament replaced the East India Company's rule in India with a royal governor general. To compensate the Company for its lost independence, Parliament authorized it to sell its surplus tea directly to American retailers. That would presumably lower prices, increase sales, and thus increase British revenue from the tea duty.

A radical Massachusetts minority— not unconnected to the smuggling trade injured by the East India Company's tea imports—thereupon took action. A party of Bostonians thinly disguised as American Indians boarded three East Indiamen in Boston harbor in December 1773 and dumped thousands of pounds' worth of tea into the murky water. Parliament reacted to this "Boston Tea Party" with fury. In 1774 it closed the port of Boston, deprived the Massachusetts legislature of much of its power, and ordered the deportation of offenders for trial in England. That drove the other twelve colonies to rally behind Massachusetts out of fear that Parliament would likewise revoke or amend their charters.

Worse still, Parliament passed an otherwise statesmanlike measure, the Quebec Act of 1774, at a moment when it appeared to be a further attack on the English-speaking colonies. The act guaranteed the preservation of the French language and the Catholic religion in Canada, and defined Canada to include all territory north of the Ohio River and west of the Allegheny Mountains. It forbade American settlement beyond the mountains. That—and the Act's toleration for "Popery"—

Third of the Hanoverians: the unfortunate George III.

In April 1775, the British garrison at Boston sought to seize arms and gunpowder that the colonists had assembled at Concord. The Massachusetts militia met the redcoats on Lexington green and fired the shots "heard 'round the world." Although the redcoats reached their objective at Concord, American fire from behind houses and stone walls mercilessly harried them back to Boston. A Continental Congress assembled at Philadelphia and formally declared the colonies independent of king and Parliament on July 4, 1776. Its ringing words were Lockean to the very marrow:

> We hold these truths to be self-evident, that all Men are created equal, that they are endowed by their Creator with certain unalienable Rights, that among these are Life, Liberty and the Pursuit of Happiness. That to secure these rights, Governments are instituted among Men, deriving their just Powers from the Consent of the Governed. That whenever any Form of Government becomes destructive to those ends, it is the Right of the People to alter or to abolish it, and to institute new Government. . . .

That was a call to revolution in the Old World as well as in the New.

The American War of Independence

The ensuing War of Independence was a civil war in both colonies and mother country. The colonists had sympathizers in both England and Ireland. A Whig faction that included the founder of modern conservatism, Edmund Burke, in vain urged conciliation on George III and his inept prime minister, Lord North (1770–82). A group of "radicals," under the inspiration of a boisterous and debauched demagogue, John Wilkes, attacked the king's influence in Parliament, urged the publication of Parliamentary debates, and agitated for a democratization of parliamentary elections. Wilkes eventually made his peace with the king,

annoyed both rich and poor, land speculators and pioneers, in the English-speaking colonies.

The Quebec Act and the so-called "Intolerable Acts" against Massachusetts between them marked the point of no return. To George III and to a large majority of his English subjects, the American colonists had proved themselves childish and irresponsible rebels. To a majority of the colonials, Parliament was seeking to impose an unbearable tyranny, the kind of tyranny that they now argued it had been their main purpose to escape when they had originally emigrated. The government of George III succeeded in driving toward rebellion even sober, propertied men who feared unrestrained democracy as "the madness of the multitude." The colonists began to arm.

and the English radicals were too small a minority to carry much weight. But they nevertheless proclaimed the political faith of the Declaration of Independence, that government must rest on consent. Conversely, numerous "Tories" in the colonies, from Boston to the backwoods of North Carolina and Georgia, sympathized with or fought for the king. In the course of the war and its aftermath, some 80,000 fled or were driven out to Canada, and their lands confiscated.

The war itself pitted the disorganized colonial militias and the small Continental Army under George Washington against a succession of seaborne British task forces. The Americans' strengths were Washington's unique combination of daring and caution, the sluggish generalship of his British opponents, the smuggled muskets and powder that France supplied after 1776, and widespread popular support for the cause of independence. The British and their Hessian mercenary troops rarely commanded more than the ground under their own feet. Britain's assets were the battlefield professionalism of its troops and its command of the sea.

In October 1777, American forces cornered at Saratoga some 5,000 British troops that had descended from Canada. That victory, although it immediately followed Washington's loss of Philadelphia, ultimately decided the war. It induced Louis XVI and his ambitious foreign minister, the Comte de Vergennes, to intervene actively. French enthusiasts for American independence such as the Marquis de Lafayette had joined Washington well before France acted, but Vergennes, less idealistic than they, sought the humiliation of Britain. The French navy, improved since 1759, fought the British to a standstill in 1778 off Ushant, at the mouth of the Channel. Across the Atlantic it deprived Britain's forces of supplies and seaborne mobility until French defeat at the Battle of the Saintes (West Indies) in April 1782 restored Britain's naval supremacy.

That victory came too late for Britain in North America. At Yorktown in Virginia, a British force of 7,000, penned between the newly hostile sea and American and French troops, had surrendered on October 19, 1781. London, although it still occupied New York with 30,000 troops, recognized the futility of seeking to hold the colonists down by force. In the Treaty of Versailles of 1783, Britain conceded to the thirteen colonies their independence and all land east of the Mississippi, north of Florida, and south of the Great Lakes. France gained revenge for the loss of Canada, some colonial outposts, and immense new debts.

George Washington, victorious at the battle of Princeton (1777), by Charles Wilson Peale.

Yet independence did not settle the form of the new American state. During the war most colonies had summoned conventions and drafted written constitutions with bills of rights. Between 1777 and 1781 the Continental Congress had united the ex-colonies in a loose federal union under the Articles of Confederation. In July 1787 Congress enacted the Northwest Ordinance, a momentous document that extended the principles for which the colonists had fought to the still unsettled western territories. When these territories became populated, they would become not colonies or dependencies but "states," equal in status to the thirteen original members of the union.

But by 1787 it was clear that the Articles of Confederation failed to provide the necessary machinery for a common economic or foreign policy. The result was the summoning of a Constitutional Convention that hammered out, in secret proceedings at Philadelphia between May and September 1787, a new federal Constitution. That document, which began with a characteristic flourish ("We, the People of the United States . . ."), has endured. The Constitution and the Revolution that created it founded the longest continuous tradition of democratic politics in history.

The American Revolution in History

The American Revolution had profound effects on Europe and eventually on the world. America was not the first "new nation"; the Dutch United provinces that had defeated Spain had that honor. But it was the only "new nation" of the Enlightenment. Its revolution was entirely secular and its principles claimed universal applicability. It had proclaimed and acted on Locke's theories of natural equality, unalienable natural rights, government by consent, and the right to revolution. Its state and federal constitutions demonstrated Montesquieu's theory of the separation of powers. Its constitutional conventions showed that a people could create a new government in an orderly fashion by formal contract, and that liberty need not mean anarchy. Its example showed that small political units could federate into a larger union without recourse to centralized despotism. The American Revolution dramatized and propagated two of the West's principal political ideas—limited constitutional government and popular sovereignty or democracy. The latter, but not the former, was destined to play a decisive role in the coming revolution in France.

As the century that had opened with the wars of Louis XIV began to ebb, the movement of ideas and of politics was running strongly against the old regime. Aristocracy and enlightened absolutism were ceasing to command loyalty or even respect. The desire for equilibrium, whether social, international, or intellectual, no longer inspired the educated. Balance and order in both art and politics was giving way to the cultivation of emotion and the thirst for change. The American Revolution accelerated that movement. After 1789, the greatest of European revolutions provided emotion, change, and violence enough for all.

Suggestions for Further Reading

General

For overviews, see especially M. S. Anderson, *Europe in the Eighteenth Century* (1961); G. Rudé, *Europe in the Eighteenth Century* (1972); L. Krieger, *Kings and Philosophers, 1689–1789* (1970); and W. Doyle, *The Old European Order, 1660–1800* (1978). The relevant volumes of the *Rise of Modern Europe* series remain useful: P. Roberts, *The Quest for Security, 1715–1740* (1947); W. L. Dorn, *Competition for Empire, 1740–1763* (1940); and L. Gershoy, *From Despotism to Revolution, 1763–1789* (1944). O. H. Hufton, *The Poor of Eighteenth-Century France, 1750–1789* (1975), and L. Stone, *The Family, Sex and Marriage in England 1500–1800* (1977), are pioneering studies; A. Macfarlane, *Marriage and Love in England: Modes of Reproduction, 1300–1840* (1986), reaches conclusions radically different from those of Stone.

J. H. Parry, *Trade and Dominion: The European Overseas Empires in the Eighteenth Century* (1971); C. G. Robertson, *Chatham and the British Empire* (1948); and L. B. Wright, *The Atlantic Frontier: Colonial American Civilization, 1607–1763* (1947), provide useful discussions of overseas expansion. On economic and social change, see above all F. Braudel, *Civilization and Capitalism, 15th–18th Centuries* (1982).

The Major States

For discussions of developments within the major states, see especially J. Lough, *Introduction to Eighteenth-Century France* (1960); J. H. Plumb, *England in the Eighteenth Century* (1951); W. H. Bruford, *Germany in the Eighteenth Century* (1952); and H. Rosenberg, *Bureaucracy, Aristocracy, and Autocracy, the Prussian Experience, 1660–1815* (1958). For biographies of leading figures, see J. H. Plumb, *The First Four Georges* (1957); G. Ritter, *Frederick the Great* (trans. 1968); C. L. Morris,

Maria Theresa: The Last Conservative (1937); and G. S. Thomson, *Catherine the Great and the Expansion of Russia* (1950). On the American Revolution see especially E. S. Morgan, *The Birth of the Republic, 1763–1789* (1956); R. M. Calhoon, *Revolutionary America: An Interpretive Overview* (1976); and R. W. Tucker and D. C. Hendrickson, *The Fall of the First British Empire: Origins of the War of American Independence* (1982).

23
The French Revolution and Europe, 1789–1815

*T*he French Revolution, along with the industrial revolution that was simultaneously gathering force in Britain, changed the face of Europe and ultimately of the world. The Revolution was both political and social. Politically, it was a violent attack on the old order first in France and then in much of western Europe. The French monarchy, which traced its traditions to Charlemagne, collapsed. The French Republic's victorious wars with the monarchies of Europe created a belt of satellite republics from Holland to Italy. Socially, the Revolution swept away the clearly defined ranks of the old order. A new hierarchy, based in theory on wealth and talent rather than birth, took the place of the old regime's three-part division between nobles, clergy, and common people.

Above all, the Revolution changed the ways in which the peoples of western Europe looked at themselves. It created new words for new things. "Citizen," "revolutionary," "counter-revolutionary," "reaction," "guillotine," and the political concept of the nation-state joined the West's political vocabulary. The Revolution gave birth to nationalism and mass politics. It opened the modern age of mass-based democracy and mass-based despotism in which we still live.

UNDERLYING PRECONDITIONS FOR REVOLUTION

The collapse of the monarchy in 1788–89 came suddenly. Long-term forces in French society nevertheless prepared it—population growth, the expansion of the middle classes, and the rise of an informed public opinion equipped with advanced notions that were subversive of established authority. The eighteenth century had been one of dramatic rise in France's population, which increased by 40 percent, from 20 to 26 million, between 1700 and 1789. *La grande nation,* as the French called themselves, had a larger population than any other European state.

Rapid growth in numbers, then as now, meant youth. In 1789, 36 percent of France's population was under 20 years of age. That growth was precarious, for it rested on improvements in transport and distribution of food, not on major increases in agricultural productivity. A young and active population remained at the mercy of nature. Drought, storm, or grain blight produced serious shortages in 1770, 1774, 1778, 1782, 1784, and 1786. The years after 1770 were ones of increasingly violent fluctuations in agricultural out-

put and prices, while population increase depressed wages.

Expansion and diffusion of wealth nevertheless paralleled expansion of numbers. The size of the middle classes rose from perhaps 700,000 to 800,000 in 1700 to 2.3 million, or between 8 and 9 percent of the total population in 1789. The nobility at the apex of the pre-1789 society of orders remained essentially static over the century at between .5 and 1.5 percent of the population. Increasing numbers of wealthy commoners might hope to rise into the nobility, but only slowly, over several generations. Land ownership remained the chief source of wealth and badge of status, although nobles increasingly took an interest in trade and industry and the lines between noble and commoner were gradually blurring.

With the spread of wealth down the social ladder came the growth of a phe-

The Tennis Court Oath, by Jacques-Louis David, official painter to the Constituent Assembly and later to Napoleon. David did not complete this immense canvas, for most of those shown in it fell under suspicion during the Terror.

nomenon new in France, although already visible in England from the Civil War in the 1640s: literate public opinion. By 1789 perhaps 37 percent of France's people could read and write. The press grew from three semiofficial newspapers in 1700 to several hundred weeklies and dailies by 1789. Libraries and reading rooms sprang up even in the provinces. Nobles and commoners alike collaborated in spreading the ideas of the Enlightenment. The condemnation of ignorance, prejudice, and superstition by Voltaire and Diderot and the egalitarian creed of Rousseau reached a widening audience. The example of the American Revolution, carried back to France after 1783 by officers such as Lafayette, suggested that enlightened humanity could remodel institutions and society at will.

The new ideas divided nobility and middle classes alike. Only a small minority of either renounced loyalty to monarchy and Church in favor of Deism and a "republic of virtue." But the new ideas had consequences. They offered new myths, the perfectibility of man and of society and the primacy of the "general will," in place of the old certainties—original sin, redemption, and obedience to priests, nobles, and a God-ordained King.

FINANCIAL CRISIS AND NOBLE REVOLT

These long-term forces would have brought change. That they brought an explosion was the result of the coincidence of two short-term factors. The unusual incompetence of the royal government destroyed its authority just as the last and worst of a series of poor harvests encouraged peasants and urban crowds to revolt.

The crisis began as a financial and administrative one. War, sport of kings and aristocrats and vehicle for the aggrandizement of the state, had always imposed crushing burdens. Prosperity

after 1715 had freed France only gradually from the immense war debts that Louis XIV had left. The Seven Years' War of 1756–63 again brought heavy deficits. Then intervention in the American Revolution once more reduced France's finances to near-collapse.

Louis XVI, unlike his two immediate predecessors, kept no mistresses and lived a modest life, for a monarch. But he had neither the brains nor the ruthlessness needed to master events. Under his loose supervision, three ministers struggled against the approach of bankruptcy. Jacques Necker, a ponderous and supremely vain Swiss banker, coped during the American war by borrowing at ever higher rates while assuring King and public that the budget balanced.

With the end of war in 1783 came a reckoning. Louis XVI replaced Necker with Charles Alexandre de Calonne, whose ingenuity matched his poor judgment. By 1786 Calonne could borrow no more. He concluded that the only solution to the financial crisis was radical reform of what he described as "a Kingdom made up of lands with estates, lands without, lands with provincial assemblies, lands of mixed administration, a Kingdom where provinces are foreign one to another, where multifarious internal barriers separate and divide the subjects of the same sovereign, where certain areas are totally freed from burdens of which the others bear the full weight, where the richest class contributes least, where it is impossible to have either a constant rule or a common will . . . ."

Calonne proposed rationalization of France's ramshackle structure and the imposition of a single uniform land tax. It would strike the previously tax-exempt nobility and clergy that held between a third and a quarter of France's major source of wealth, the land. Since by custom the monarch needed some sort of approval for new taxes, Calonne in 1787 put the reforms to a hand-picked assembly of the very orders he proposed to tax.

When this Assembly of Notables predictably balked, Louis dismissed Calonne and replaced him with one of his fiercest critics, Loménie de Brienne, archbishop of Toulouse. Brienne in office attempted to cajole the Notables into accepting the reforms that he had himself denounced while in opposition. They refused. They demanded the convening of the Estates General of France, which had not met since 1614. Only that body, they now claimed, could approve new taxes. The nobility had opened the attack on the monarchy in the name of its own "historic privileges." It was the first of many groups to fish in troubled waters and be swept away.

Louis XVI sent the Notables home, and told the *parlement* of Paris, the judicial organ of the crown whose traditional task it was to register new laws, that the taxes were legal "because I wish it." Brienne's energetic minister of justice closed the *parlements*. Despite a petition from the dukes and peers of France, and riots in the provinces under the leadership of nobles and *parlement* lawyers, the King held firm. It looked briefly as if the government had won.

Then the bankers, friends of the still-ambitious Necker, refused to lend the money needed to operate. That blow brought the royal government to its knees. In August 1788 Louis XVI called the Estates General to meet in May 1789 and allowed Brienne to resign. The King then reappointed Necker, who brought with him fresh credit but no policy. The government had confessed incompetence and bankruptcy, and had appealed to its subjects for help. The Revolution had begun.

THE "THIRD ESTATE" AND THE MASSES

What sort of Revolution it would be was as yet undecided. The nobles and clergy who had defied their royal master expected to dominate the Estates

Caricature of the French peasant supporting the clergy and nobility, while doves and rabbits, protected by law for the sport of the nobility, eat the peasant's grain.

General. But the aristocratic agitation of spring and summer 1788, and still more the approach of the Estates General, drew into politics groups that had until now played no role.

The first of these was the middle classes. The reinstated *parlement* of Paris had decreed in September that voting in the Estates General be by order, following the 1614 precedent. That arrangement would place the commons, or Third Estate, who represented 98 percent of the population of France, in a permanent minority. Political clubs, in many cases led by nobles of advanced views, urged the "doubling" of the Third Estate, giving it twice its traditional number of representatives in order to equal the other two orders combined. The Abbé Emmanuel Sieyès, chief theorist of this movement, published in January 1789 the most famous pamphlet of the Revo-

Emmanuel Joseph Sieyea.

Theorist of the "Third Estate": the Abbé Sieyès.

lution: *What Is the Third Estate?* It began with three questions: "What is the Third Estate?—*everything*. What has it been until now in the political order?—*nothing*. What does it seek? *To be something*." Sieyès went on to demand the drafting of a constitution "which the nation alone has the right to do." That appeal to the *nation*, to popular sovereignty, meant the end of divine-right monarchy and ultimately of peace in Europe.

Initially the King encouraged the commons. At the end of December 1788 Necker proposed to checkmate the nobles by agreeing to double the Third Estate. The King concurred. Louis XVI's appeal to the privileged orders had begun the Revolution; his appeal to the Third Estate led to its breakthrough. But as the Estates General assembled at Versailles in May 1789, forces far more menacing to the established order than the lawyers, professional men, and bureaucrats of the Third Estate appeared on the scene—the peasantry and the urban lower classes. Their intervention converted a political struggle between elites, a conflict between the privileged and the merely rich or educated, into an upheaval that terrified nobles and Third Estate alike.

The motive force behind that upheaval was the traditional source of disorder in agricultural societies: hunger. The harvest of 1788, for the first time since the famine year of 1709, had been poor to disastrous throughout all of France. In Paris, the price of bread, the staple food of the population, rose by 60 percent between August 1788 and February 1789. Widespread distress in the countryside also decreased demand for manufactured goods. Production of textiles, France's major industry, dropped perhaps 50 percent. Urban workers lost their jobs just as food prices escalated.

The consequence was a rapid breakdown of order in the spring and summer of 1789, before the new harvest arrived. In the past, the government had coped with similar crises with price controls, emergency grain shipments, and judicious use of police and army. But now the royal administration was in a shambles and the example of the revolt of nobles and *parlements* emboldened the crowds.

In the cities, bread riots and other disturbances broke out with increasing frequency. In the countryside, the peasants ceased to pay taxes. They also ceased to pay the curious assortment of medieval obligations owed to landlords, local nobles, and the Church—money dues on land, the duty to use the nobles' flour mills, bakeries, wine presses or law courts, and tithes. These "seignorial dues," which a legal treatise of the day described as a "bizarre form of property," had been the chief grievance of the peasants against what now, at a stroke, became the "old regime."

The peasants burned tax records and registers of dues. Where they did not find the registers, they burned the castles of the nobles to make sure. In late July 1789 rumors swept the countryside that "the brigands," the "English gang" (shades of the Hundred Years' War), or "the aristocrats" were approaching to slaughter and pillage. This "Great Fear," symptom of social breakdown, was both cause and consequence of peasant violence against the privileged orders.

FROM ESTATES GENERAL TO OCTOBER DAYS

When the Estates General met on May 23, 1789, the royal government, ever indecisive, went back on the implicit alliance with the Third Estate it had sought in December 1788. The King refused to allow the commons to sit with the other two orders, and denied voting by head, which would have given the Third Estate a majority.

Under the leadership of Sieyès, the Third Estate therefore voted on June 17 to constitute itself as the "National Assembly"—a new authority, independent of the monarchy and implicitly claiming sovereignty. Liberal clergy and nobles joined the Third Estate. And when the King ordered the Assembly's meeting-hall closed on June 20, it met at a nearby indoor tennis court. In the first of many scenes of dramatic oratory that punctuated the Revolution, the representatives solemnly swore the "tennis court oath": not to disperse before they had given France a constitution.

The King, briefly resolute, replied on June 23 with a defense of "his" nobility and clergy and veiled threats to dissolve the Estates General. After he had left the hall, the leaders of the Third Estate exploded: "The nation in assembly does not take orders. . . . We will not move from our seats unless forced by bayonets." The resistance of the privileged orders crumbled. More and more joined the Assembly. It now officially took the title of Constituent Assembly and empowered a committee to write a constitution.

Paris Speaks: The Fall of the Bastille

Louis XVI, after wavering, swung again toward resistance. Royal troops, many of them Swiss and German regiments, concentrated around Paris. The King dismissed Necker. Counter-revolution seemed imminent. Then the removal of Necker set off an explosion in Paris that put the Constituent Assembly firmly in power. This city of 600,000, which dwarfed even the largest French provincial towns, was hungry. The urban crowds of shop owners, artisans, and housewives, with the backing of a rapidly growing ward organization independent of the royal authorities, attacked jails and barracks, seeking weapons. The police, a mere 2,000 backed by 3,500 troops, were powerless.

On July 14, 1789—coincidentally or not the day of the highest Paris bread prices in the entire eighteenth century—the crowd attacked the royal fortress at the center of Paris, the Bastille. With the assistance of royal troops who had mutinied, the crowd took the fortress and butchered its commander. With royal authority utterly destroyed and Paris in the hands of the insurgents, Louis XVI temporarily resigned himself to being a constitutional monarch.

The Fourth of August and the "Rights of Man"

The Constituent Assembly soon faced an emergency more serious than the menace of royal counter-revolution. By the end of July the revolt of the peasants, threatened not only noble prop-

The Bastille surrenders, July 14, 1789.

The Declaration of the Rights of Man and the Citizen   August 27, 1789

The representatives of the French people, constituted as a National Assembly, and considering that ignorance, forgetfulness, or contempt for the rights of man are the sole causes of public misfortunes and the degeneration of governments, have resolved to set forth in a solemn declaration the natural, inalienable, and sacred rights of man so that this declaration, constantly kept in mind by all members of society, may unceasingly recall to them their rights and duties. . . .

1. Men are born, and remain, free and equal in rights. Social distinctions can only be founded on usefulness to society.
2. The aim of every political bond is the preservation of the natural and inalienable rights of man. Those rights are liberty, property, security, and resistance to oppression.
3. The source of all sovereignty is in essence the nation. No body or individual can exercise authority that does not derive expressly from it. . . .
6. Law is the expression of the general will. All citizens have the right to contribute, personally or through their representatives, to its creation. It must be the same, whether it protects or punishes, for all. . . .

From *Archives parlamentaires de 1787 à 1860*, première série, (Paris: Librairie Administrative de Paul Dupont, 1877), Vol. 9, p. 236 (translation by M. Knox).

erty, but all forms of property in the countryside. Some members of the Assembly responded with calls for the restoration of order by force. Other more radical elements had begun to meet in a political club that later become known as the Jacobins. On the night of August 4, 1789, they took the Assembly by surprise. They induced the liberal—and landless—Vicomte de Noailles to propose the voluntary renunciation of noble and Church privileges.

In a frenzied meeting that lasted until two the next morning, the delegates renounced tithes, dues, the privileges of their orders, and the traditional rights of their towns and provinces. On sober second thought the Assembly decreed in the following days that some dues be paid off in installments. That hardly impressed the peasants, and seignorial dues were dead even before their final abolition without compensation in 1793. The old order, in law as well as fact, was gone. The Assembly achieved its object, and disorder in the countryside subsided for the moment.

At the end of August, in its second major act, the Constituent Assembly adopted a preamble to the new constitution—the "Declaration of the Rights of Man and the Citizen." The document owed something to the American Declaration of Independence, Constitution, and Bill of Rights. It proclaimed liberty, and equality of rights, in stark contrast to the legal and social distinctions between orders current across the continent. It led in 1791 to the emancipation of the Jews from the legal disabilities fastened upon them in the Middle Ages. Even women, whom most revolutionaries, with Rousseau, sought to confine to the role of wife and mother, began to demand equality through its principles. Olympe de Gouges, a woman writer in Paris, published in summer 1791 a widely discussed "Declaration of the Rights of Women."

But the Declaration's fundamental ideas were not those of Locke nor of the tradition of English common law that had molded the American Revolution. The Americans sought above all to prevent the executive or the national legislature, even if elected by the majority of the nation, from trampling upon individuals or upon local and state governments. The French, however, blithely assumed that the nation, once freed of "ignorance, forgetfulness, or contempt for the rights of man," would spontaneously express a General Will. That Will would in turn produce laws. Will and laws would by definition be incapable of oppression, except the presumably justified oppression of those whose actions or opinions violated their "duties" as citizens.

To these potentially dangerous notions the 1789 Declaration of the Rights of Man added an even more explosive element—the concept of the sovereign nation. In America, and even in a Britain that included Welsh and Scots, popular sovereignty meant little more than rule by elected representatives. In continental Europe, following the French example, it soon came to mean rule by one's own national or ethnic group. The political definition of the nation enshrined in the 1789 Declaration superseded the vague cultural notions of nationhood that had spread in the course of the eighteenth century with the increase in literacy.

This invention of 1789 later became known as national "self-determination" or "nationalism." It ultimately meant war of all against all, and war of unprecedented intensity. Monarchies might occasionally bow to custom, religion, or law, but the new nation-state recognized no law other than reason— its own reason. When its reason conflicted with that of others, force was the final arbiter. And the concept of nation made possible, for the first time in Europe, near-total mobilization. What other cultures had achieved with slave labor the French revolutionaries and their successors across Europe accomplished with the enthusiasm of free citizens.

The October Days

All this was still in the future in the late summer of 1789. The Constituent Assembly had partially pacified the peasantry, but it still faced revolutionary Paris. Its chief support was a middle-class militia, the National Guard, born in the disorders of July. The Guard, under the leadership of the "Hero of Two Worlds," the Marquis de Lafayette, was small guarantee against the increasingly politicized Paris crowd.

The grain harvest of 1789 was good, but had not yet reached the market. Supplies from the poor harvest of 1788

had run out. By late September Paris rang with cries of "When shall we have bread?" (as a pamphlet title put it). In this atmosphere, the arrival of a fresh regiment of royal troops at Versailles, greeted conspicuously by the unpopular queen, Marie Antoinette of Austria, set off a new explosion.

An armed crowd with 6,000 militant Paris housewives at its head marched on Versailles. They overwhelmed the royal guards and triumphantly brought king, queen, and crown prince ("the baker, the baker's wife, and the little baker's boy") back to Paris. Alongside the royal coach the crowd carried on pikes the heads of the guards killed defending their king. That was an inauspicious beginning for constitutional monarchy.

THE CONSTITUENT AND LEGISLATIVE ASSEMBLIES, 1789–91

With the royal family virtual prisoners in the Tuileries palace in Paris and the Constituent Assembly in undisputed control of government, the Revolution seemed to have won. What remained was to recast France's society and administration. A new hierarchy based on property replaced the old regime's decaying society of orders. The Constituent Assembly wiped from the map the old regime's quaint provincial and regional distinctions, and substituted 87 "departments" of roughly uniform size. Elected assemblies received control of local government, a brief reversal of the old regime's drive toward centralization. France's first constitution, adopted in September 1791, set up a single-chamber Legislative Assembly elected only by men wealthy enough to pay the equivalent of three days' wages in taxes. That was perhaps 15 percent of the total population. A further, steeper property qualification restricted eligibility for membership in the Legislative Assembly.

The new regime faced three problems to which it had no answer—the

Revolutionary propaganda: "Frenchwomen become free."

Playing cards of the Revolution: "Equality" and "Freedom of Religion" have taken the place of kings and queens.

financial crisis that had felled the old regime, the continuing agitation in Paris, and above all the refusal of the king to play the part assigned him. For the financial crisis, the nimble Marquis Charles Maurice de Talleyrand, bishop of Autun, found an expedient. The state would dissolve monasteries and nunneries, seize and sell off the Church lands, and in return give the parish clergy and bishops guaranteed salaries. The land expropriation went smoothly, but the July 1790 "Civil Constitution of the Clergy" aroused widespread resistance. Priests all over France refused to swear the required oath of loyalty to the state, and Rome soon backed them. The Revolution had gained a new and formidable adversary, and had opened a quarrel with the Church that divided France until the twentieth century.

Nor did the seizure of Church lands solve the financial crisis. The *assignats*, the new currency issued with land sale proceeds as backing, fuelled an inflation that guaranteed further urban unrest even when harvests were good. The lands themselves, sold off at scandalously low prices, enriched only their middle-class and peasant buyers. The main benefit to the revolutionary state of this massive transfer of property was indirect. Along with the sale after 1792 of the property of nobles who had fled abroad, it tied powerful middle-class and peasant groups to the Revolution.

The Constituent and Legislative Assemblies also failed to master Paris. The middle- and lower-middle classes there had by 1790–91 achieved a degree of politicization unthinkable under the old regime. The revolutionary ward organizations or *sections*, made up of fiercely radical butchers, bakers, innkeepers, and artisans, met frequently. The Paris municipal government, or *Commune*, was likewise soon in the hands of extremists. Around these organizations and around the frequent "Jacobin Club" meetings at the former Jacobin monastery there arose a unique revolutionary subculture. The *sansculottes*, literally those "without knee breeches," self-consciously repudiated the dress code of the old regime. Wearing trousers and red caps, carrying pikes and muskets, they addressed one another as "citizen" and demanded equality of wealth as well as of political rights. In this atmosphere, professional agitators and extremist journalists—Jacques Hébert, Georges Danton, Jean Paul Marat, and Camille Desmoulins—rubbed shoulders with international hangers-on of revolution such as the Prussian ex-baron and "orator of the human race," Anacharsis Clootz. With such leaders to spur it, revolutionary Paris was ready enough to turn its pikes and cannon even on the representatives of the nation, should it suspect them of betraying the Revolution.

Those representatives gave Paris occasion soon enough, for the conduct of the king soon rendered their moderation suspect. Louis XVI maintained secret contacts with monarchical elements in the Constituent Assembly, his many relatives who had fled abroad, and with Austria. In June 1791 he dashed for the nearest friendly border, Austrian Belgium. Hostile town authorities blocked the royal family's escape at Varennes, just short of safety. Once more France's king, queen, and crown prince returned to the Tuileries in humiliation.

The new constitution was thus practically useless even before its formal adoption in September 1791. The Constituent Assembly found itself with a monarch who had publicly demonstrated his disloyalty to revolutionary France. The king continued to appoint ministers and sanction legislation. But neither his throne nor his head were safe. Nor was the new Legislative Assembly, which replaced the Constituent Assembly in October 1791, well-suited to giving France stable government. Thanks to a proposal of Maximilien de Robespierre, the Jacobin provincial lawyer who had emerged as the most vocally high-principled of revolutionaries, the Constituent Assembly had voted to bar its members from running for the new Legislative Assembly. The measure did not encourage the self-denial and republican "virtue" it symbolized. Its main effect was to eliminate the modest store of parliamentary experience and political sense acquired since 1789.

Robespierre, "the Incorruptible."

WAR AND TERROR, 1792–94

Rather than govern, the Legislative Assembly went to war with all Europe. The dominant force in the new chamber proved to be a Jacobin group loosely associated with the commercial center of western France, Bordeaux. Collectively known as the "Gironde" after the name of Bordeaux's estuary, their leaders—Pierre Victurnien Vergniaud, Maximin Isnard, and Jacques Pierre Brissot—were above all brilliant orators. The Girondin recipe for leadership was simple—war.

In August 1791, after the king's flight to Varennes, the emperor of Austria and King of Prussia had proclaimed the intention of restoring Louis XVI to his rightful place in full control of France. This "Declaration of Pillnitz" was a deliberately empty threat, for emperor and king had made action dependent on cooperation from the rest of Europe. But along with the assembling of vengeful aristocratic

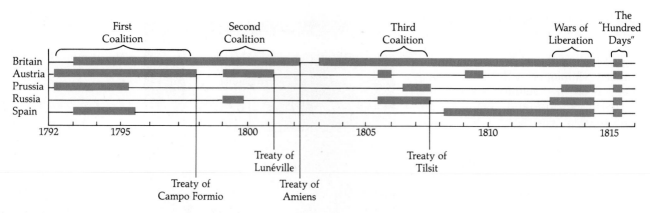

FIGURE 23-1   France at War with Europe, 1792–1815

émigrés in the German states along the Rhine, Austrian and Prussian hostility gave the French war party its opening. War, in Isnard's fervent words to the Assembly, was "indispensable for completing the revolution." At home it would consolidate Girondin power. Abroad, this "crusade for universal liberty," this war "of peoples against kings," would smash the old order in Europe as the Revolution had done in France.

Robespierre, almost alone, made a stand against war. The enemies of the Revolution, he insisted in debate with Brissot at the Jacobin Club, were within. King, court, and aristocrats wanted war to ensure French defeat. But Brissot's talk of easy victory over an immense conspiracy of "kings against peoples" carried the excitable Legislative Assembly. In April 1792 France declared on Austria a war that soon expanded to embrace all Europe. Except for a brief interval in 1802–03, war was to last until France's final defeat in 1814–15 (see Figure 23-1).

The Fall of the Monarchy: August–September 1792

The Gironde did not survive that long. The first act of the war galvanized Paris, and Paris destroyed the monarchy and ultimately the Gironde as well. The 1792 campaign began badly. Revolutionary indiscipline, lack of supplies, and the emigration of aristocratic officers crippled the army. The Prussian and Austrian armies advanced ponderously into eastern France. On July 25 the Prussian commander, the Duke of Brunswick, publicly proclaimed the intention of "delivering the King, the Queen, and the royal family from their captivity." That well-intentioned announcement seemed to revolutionary extremists the definitive proof that Louis XVI and his Austrian queen were conspiring with the enemy. The result was the "second revolution," the Paris insurrection of August 10, 1792.

That day far surpassed Bastille Day in violence. The king fled the Tuileries before the attacking crowd and revolutionary troops closed in. While his Swiss guards died at their posts, he placed himself and his family under the protection of the Legislative Assembly. That body, itself facing the pikes and cannon of the Paris wards, voted to "suspend" the king. A temporary executive council took charge until the election of a new legislature by universal male suffrage. The equality of "one man, one vote" thus came to France, and to Europe, for the first time. With it came equality of another kind. The guillotine, set up in a Paris square for the first time on August 13, extended the nobility's former privilege of decapitation to all.

The fall of the monarchy induced Lafayette, the commander of the army in Belgium, to defect to the Austrians; the Revolution had no more room for moderates. The Austro-Prussians

May 1789	June 1789		Oct. 1791		Sept. 1792		Oct. 1795
Estates General	National Constituent Assembly		Legislative Assembly (Constitutional Monarchy)		National Convention (Republic)		

seized the key border fortress of Verdun. In Paris, the fiery orator Danton urged the nation to rise: "Gentlemen, we need boldness [*de l'audace*], boldness, always boldness, and France is saved." On September 20, 1792, at the battle of Valmy, the revolutionary armies held, to the cry of *"Vive la Nation!"* The old regime's artillery, the best in Europe, persuaded the Prussians to withdraw.

Revolutionary Paris, without help from either Brissot or Robespierre, had again imposed its will on August 10. But it was not yet finished. Two hours after Danton's impassioned plea for boldness, the Paris *Commune* summoned its crowds to arm against Prussians and counter-revolutionaries. In this heated atmosphere, rumors flew of a supposed plot to let loose imprisoned aristocrats to slaughter the wives and children of patriots. Crowds attacked the Paris prisons. Brutal, sometimes drunken massacres disposed of between 1,100 and 1,400 aristocrats of all ages and both sexes, along with priests and other prisoners. Robespierre immediately justified these "September Massacres": "Do you want a Revolution without revolution?" He and his Jacobin associates now sought to turn the wrath of Paris against their Girondin rivals.

The Convention Executes the King

The new republic appeared to be the culmination of the Revolution. Within a year its partisans had remade even the calendar, making September 22, 1793, the first day of Year I and abolishing Sundays. The red, white, and blue tricolor of France replaced the Bourbon family's white with lilies. The *Marseillaise*, rousing and bloodthirsty marching song of a Marseilles battalion called to Paris during the August 10 rising, became the "national hymn."

The new assembly, the National Convention, was the most radical of the many legislative bodies of revolutionary France. For good reason. Public voting under the scrutiny of the revolutionary activists, not secret ballot, had been the preferred method of election. Only 10 percent of France's eligible population was brave enough or friendly enough to the Revolution to vote. Brissot and his Girondin companions returned, reelected in the provinces, and outnumbering Robespierre and his partisans.

But Robespierre took the initiative at home while the French armies, buoyed up by a fierce national pride, invaded Belgium and crossed the Rhine. In late November the revolutionaries discovered in the Tuileries a safe containing Louis XVI's secret correspondence with the émigrés. Robespierre and his terrifying young associate, Louis Antoine Saint-Just, demanded execution without trial: the king was guilty not merely of treason, but of being a king. The Convention nevertheless decided on a trial.

The affair desperately embarrassed the Gironde, which despite its hostility to the monarchy shrank from committing itself irrevocably by killing the king. The "mountain," Robespierre and the Jacobin extremists in the highest seats at the back of the Convention, carried the rest of the assembly with them. Louis XVI died by guillotine on January 21, 1793. Revolutionary France had executed a king who had ruled by divine right. It had eliminated what little chance still existed of internal and external peace. A week later, the Republic declared war on Great Britain and its ally Holland.

The Committee of Public Safety

Internal crisis and external defeat again combined to drive the Revolution to

Louis XVI in prison after the August 1792 insurrection, by Joseph Ducreux.

Queen Marie Antoinette resolutely faces the guillotine (sketched from life by David).

Portrait de Marie Antoinette

extremes. Paris food riots in February and March 1793 maintained pressure on the Convention. In March the imposition of conscription provoked the Catholic peasants of the Vendée, in the traditionalist far west of France, to revolt under royalist leadership. That guerrilla war dragged on for years and cost the young Republic dearly. The commander of the army in the low countries, Charles Dumouriez, lost decisively to the Austrians at Neerwinden, then defected. The supposedly oppressed peoples on France's borders proved remarkably reluctant to join the "crusade for universal liberty." The second city of France, Lyons, rose in May. In June and July much of the south, including Marseilles, followed. Royalists handed over to a British fleet the great Mediterranean naval base of Toulon.

The Convention proved equal to these challenges. In March it established a revolutionary court and "surveillance committees" to deal with dissent and counter-revolution. In April it created an executive, the Committee of Public Safety. To pacify Paris it temporarily imposed price controls (the "maximum") on grain and flour, and sent rapacious foraging parties into the countryside. Danton and Robespierre attacked the Gironde for alleged complicity with Dumouriez. The Convention, surrounded by the armed crowds of the Paris wards with 150 cannon, decreed the arrest of the Gironde for treason on June 2, 1793. In July, Robespierre and Saint-Just joined the Committee of Public Safety. France, for the first time since Louis XIV, had a government determined to rule.

The Committee included Lazare Carnot, the "organizer of victory" (for the army), Robert Lindet (for food supplies), Bertrand Barère de Vieuzac (for relations with the Convention), and the men of blood, Jean Nicolas Billaud-Varenne and Jean-Marie Collot d'Herbois (for repression). Ideological leadership rested with "the incorruptible" Robespierre and with Saint-Just. Responsible in theory to the Convention, in practice the great Committee ruled France alone for the next year. Its rule, which the revolutionary martyr Marat hailed as the "despotism of liberty," was more absolute than the old regime, and infinitely more effective.

Against the external enemy, the Committee ordered in August 1793 the mobilization of the entire population by the famed *levée en masse*. By 1794 850,000 men were under arms, far outnumbering the armies of the kings that France faced. Against the peasant guerrillas of the Vendée, the Committee sent General François Kellermann, victor over the Prussians at Valmy, with orders to deport noncombatants and seize crops and livestock. After the army retook Lyons, Collot d'Herbois and Fouché, emissaries of the Committee, killed thousands in reprisal for the revolt. The Convention changed the very name of France's second city to "Freed-City" (*Ville-Affranchie*). At Toulon an artillery major of Corsican extraction, Napoleon Bonaparte, found the key to driving the British fleet from the harbor, and retaking the town. His reward was promotion to brigadier general at age 23, for the Revolution

The Modern State Mobilizes its Citizens: The Levée en Masse

Barère to the Convention, August 23, 1793:

From this moment, until our enemies have been driven from the territory of the Republic, the entire French nation is permanently called to the colors. The young men will go into battle; married men will forge weapons and transport supplies; women will make tents and uniforms, and serve in the hospitals; children will make old cloth into bandages; old men will have themselves carried to the public squares to rouse the courage of the warriors and preach hatred of kings, and the unity of the Republic.

From *Archives parlementaires de 1787 à 1860*, première série (Paris: Librairie Administrative de Paul Dupont, 1907), Vol. 72, p. 674 (translation by M. Knox).

could not afford to neglect talent. By the end of 1793 the emergency in the south was over.

The Great Terror

Internally, the Committee and its lesser fellow, the Committee of General Security, moved to institutionalize terror. That instrument was too important to leave to the Paris agitators and crowds to which Convention and Committees owed their power. Committee and Convention damped down the activities of the Paris ward meetings, muzzled the press, and arrested some leading extremists in September 1793.

But the Committee's chief business was with those not extreme enough. "The gods," wrote the Robespierrist journalist Desmoulins, "are thirsty." Marie Antoinette, accused of treason and trumped-up charges of immorality, died bravely in October. The Gironde met the guillotine in November. Aristocrats, monarchist politicians, unsuccessful generals ("to encourage the others") followed. In the provinces, the traveling representatives of the Committees dispensed death to priests, aristocrats, and moderates by portable guillotine, firing squad, grapeshot, and "vertical deportation" (drowning). Perhaps 20,000 men and women perished in the Great Terror of 1793–94. Although that was a small number by the standards twentieth-century revolutions have set, the Terror left memories in France that long endured.

Elimination of the Gironde did not give Robespierre rest. The theories of the Enlightenment decreed that society, freed of the shackles of the old regime, would spontaneously express a General Will. Yet Robespierre recognized bitterly that revolutionary politics had failed to produce "one will, one." The fault therefore had to be that of surviving evil men—plotters, traitors, Parisian ward extremists, lukewarm Jacobins, and counter-revolutionaries. It was not simply war and internal threat that drove the revolu-

tionaries to shed ever more blood. It was their faith in the perfectibility of humanity and their claim to incarnate the General Will.

The leaders of the Paris crowd, Hébert and the *Enragés* or "wild men," were more radical socially than the Committee. They continued to agitate and tried to raise Paris in late March 1794. They failed and perished under the blade. Those more moderate than Robespierre—Danton, Desmoulins, and their allies in the center of the Convention—helped him against the Paris extremists. Then the moderate Jacobins began to plead for a relaxation of the Terror, for freedom of the press, and even for peace, for the spring of 1794 was a spring of French victories.

The Spirit of the Terror: Sayings of Saint-Just

This man [Louis XVI] must reign or die. . . . All kings are rebels and usurpers.
—To the Convention, November 1792.

The French people votes the liberty of the world.
—Draft constitution, April 1793.

The people and its enemies have nothing more in common except the sword. . . . *We must oppress tyrants.*
—To the Convention, October 1793.

Spare the aristocracy, and you will give yourselves fifty years of troubles. *Dare!* That one word summarizes the entire politics of our Revolution.
—To the Convention, February 1794.

There is something terrifying in the sacred love of one's country. It is so all-exclusive that it sacrifices everything, without pity, without fear, without regard for humanity, to the public interest. . . . You cannot make a republic with compromises, but only with ruthless severity, inflexible severity, toward those who have betrayed.
—To the Convention, for the Committee of Public Safety, demanding the heads of Danton and others, March 1794.

From Louis-Antoine de Saint-Just, *Pages Choisies* (Paris: Éditions du Point du Jour, 1947), pp. 121, 123, 162, 199, 206, 223; and Denis Roche, ed., *La liberté ou la mort* (Paris: Tchou, 1969), p. 49 (translation by M. Knox).

Here Lies All of France: cartoon of Robespierre executing the last Frenchman— the executioner.

Within a week of the decapitation of Hébert, the Committee arrested Danton and his group. Saint-Just, in the name of the Committees, accused them of treason before the Convention. They too died.

By these blows against Hébertists and Dantonists, the Committee created a wasteland around itself. The execution of the "wild men" destroyed its ties to the Paris wards. That of the Dantonists weakened the Committee's hold on the center of the Convention, the moderates from the provinces who held the parliamentary balance. The Committee now ruled by terror alone. The pace of arrests and executions increased rapidly. More than 1,400 perished in Paris alone in June and July 1794.

Thermidor

Victory sealed the fate of Robespierre, as defeat had that of the Gironde.

French troops, ever more experienced and more numerous, flooded once more across Belgium. The military emergency that had justified terror was over. Robespierre's associates began to think of their own survival. The relatively moderate Carnot and Barère joined with jealous members of the Committee of General Security. The bloodiest-handed of all, Collot d'Herbois and Billaud-Varenne, hoped the elimination of Robespierre would prove their ticket to respectability. The center of the Convention secretly offered support.

A Robespierre speech denouncing unspecified enemies induced the plotters to act before it was too late. On July 27, 1794—9 Thermidor by the revolutionary calendar—the plotters bodily prevented Robespierre from speaking to the Convention. Then, in command of the rostrum, they rushed through a decree for the arrest of the Robespierrists. The Paris wards, summoned to the rescue, understandably responded poorly; they too had suffered under the Committee's dictatorship. The next day, 10 Thermidor, Robespierre, Saint-Just, and company met the guillotine to which they had sent so many others. The Revolution had "iced over," Saint-Just wrote shortly before his arrest. The Robespierrists themselves, by their elimination of Hébert and the Paris ward agitators, had halted the seemingly unstoppable movement toward ever greater extremism. The Revolution was over, except for the endless war it had launched.

FROM CONVENTION TO DIRECTORY, 1794–99

The "reaction" of Thermidor, as it soon became known, produced a widespread sense of relief. French society, no longer cowed by terror and censorship, reasserted itself. The urban middle classes that had profited from the Revolution now sought to enjoy those profits in a frenetic round of banquets and dances. The *salons*, which educated women of the middle classes now led, reappeared. There ex-terrorists drank champagne with ex-aristocrats and with the new rich, land speculators and army contractors. The "gilded youth" of the better-off quarters of Paris equipped themselves with clubs and hunted Jacobins. In the provinces, a royalist "white terror" against republicans repeated the horrors of the terror of the Committees.

The relaxation of the price controls that the Robespierrists had imposed brought new Paris food riots in April and May 1795. But the Convention suppressed them and likewise crushed a revolt of royalist "gilded youth" in October. In the last case, young General Bonaparte mowed down the crowd with field artillery. Grapeshot, scientifically employed by loyal troops, made 1789-style urban insurrection obsolete.

What Thermidor failed to provide was a stable government responsive to the new society, ordered by wealth rather than rank, that emerged from the Revolution. The end of dictatorship by the executive meant increased danger of a restoration of the monarchy. The Convention nevertheless decreed a revolving membership for the Committee of Public Safety, and a reduction of its powers. In 1795, the Convention drafted and adopted yet another constitution, which remained in effect until the end of 1799. It divided power between a Directorate of five members and a legislature, the Five Hundred. Wealth once more became a prerequisite for voting.

The directors included Carnot, the Vicomte de Barras, and Jean-François Reubell, an Alsatian for whom France's "natural frontier" lay on the Rhine. Two thirds of the Five Hundred came by law from the outgoing Convention—the so-called "perpetuals." The Convention intended this measure as a guarantee against royalist agitation in the provinces. It helped achieve that object at the price of discrediting the new regime's claims to represent the nation.

The residual threat from Paris soon subsided. A poor harvest and an un-

precedentedly severe winter in 1795–96 reduced the poor to near-starvation. Survival, not revolt, became the chief concern of the remaining sans-culottes. The last major attempt to mobilize Paris was the so-called "Conspiracy of the Equals" in spring 1796. The "Equals," especially Gracchus Babeuf and the Italian revolutionary Filippo Buonarroti, confusedly advocated extreme egalitarianism and a primitive agrarian communism. Their plot failed utterly, but left an ideological legacy for the future.

It was the royalists who threatened the middle-class republic of 1795–99. But fortunately for the Directory, the young son of Louis XVI had died in prison in June 1795. His uncle, in exile, took the title of Louis XVIII and announced his intention of restoring the old regime in its entirety. That program inevitably alienated both the constitutional monarchists and the powerful middle-class and peasant groups that had profited from the Revolution. A royalist uprising in the west of France inadequately coordinated with a British and émigré landing at Quiberon ended in failure and massacre in 1795. Royalist deputies nevertheless did well enough in elections in 1797 and 1798 to force the Directors into a series of coups d'état and purges to maintain control of the Five Hundred.

Stability and representative government had been impossible under the Convention because of the strength of disloyal opposition and the exaggerated expectations of unity of ideologues such as Robespierre. It was likewise impossible under the Directory. By the end, in December 1799, the regime rested only on the army.

SON OF THE REVOLUTION: BONAPARTE

That army had in the hard years since 1792 acquired matchless military experience and prestige. The old regime had bequeathed it the most mobile and powerful artillery in Europe and the innovative tactical and strategic theories of Guibert and Bourcet. The war "of peoples against kings" unleashed the energies and loyalties needed to use those theories to the fullest. The result was a new kind of warfare.

Under the old regime, the eagerness of troops to desert and the inadequacy of the supply services had restricted the size and mobility of armies. No commander could easily control, feed, and move more than 70,000 men. But the new French armies, filled with nationalist fervor, deserted less and showed a fierce initiative on the battlefield. Their leaders could trust them to fight as skirmishers, tormenting with fire the rigid ranks of the old regime armies as the American revolutionaries had tormented the redcoats. The new

The Man of destiny: the young Napoleon, by David.

armies could march dispersed, in self-contained "divisions" of 8,000 to 10,000 infantry equipped with their own artillery for support. This style of movement helped prevent bottlenecks and allowed armies to feed themselves by looting the countryside through which they passed. The divisions, and still more the next largest units, the *army corps* of perhaps 30,000 men, offered unparalleled offensive and defensive power. Corps could and did hold against an entire enemy army—until other French corps arrived with crushing effect on the flank or rear of the enemy. Concentration of forces on the move, on the field of battle itself, replaced the old regime's rigid and time-consuming deployments. The new system of warfare, the ruthlessness of the French revolutionary commanders, and the numbers, fervor, and readiness for sacrifice of the French troops themselves overwhelmed their traditionalist opponents.

The supreme master of the new techniques, and ultimate beneficiary of the army's role as the Directory's sole support, was the young General Bonaparte. He rehabilitated himself from suspicions of terrorist and Jacobin sympathies by crushing the Paris crowd in October 1795. After a love match with the ex-mistress of the Director Barras, the fascinating Joséphine de Beauharnais, Bonaparte received command of the Army of Italy in the spring of 1796. He was 27 years old.

The Directory's chief war aim was to secure the west bank of the Rhine; Italy was a sideshow. Bonaparte made it the main theater. He began the fateful extension of French conquest far beyond the geographic "natural frontiers" supposedly sought by Louis XIV. In the brilliant campaign of 1796–97 he first crushed the Piedmontese allies of the Austrians, then the Austrians themselves. Increasingly independent of the Directory, he ruled and looted north Italy as he pleased. In 1797 the Austrians sued for peace. By the Treaty of Campo Formio they relinquished their claims to Belgium and to the north Italian plain. In compensation they received from Bonaparte and the Directory the cynical gift of the once-proud republic of Venice.

By late 1797 France dominated Europe from Holland to north Italy. Prussia, preoccupied with seizing its share of the third and final partition of Poland in 1794–95, made a separate peace with France in 1795. Only Britain, surrounded by its seas and fleet, now stood against revolutionary France. The First Coalition of the powers of Europe against Revolutionary France had collapsed.

The Revolution and Europe

For Bonaparte, the Revolution was "an idea that has found bayonets." France's ever-broadening rule indeed meant more than the rights of man. Intellectuals in lands as different as Britain and Germany initially greeted the revolution with delight. "Bliss was it in that dawn to be alive / And to be young was very heaven," the English poet William Wordsworth wrote of 1789. Others were less optimistic. As early as 1790 the passionate Anglo-Irish parliamentarian and political philosopher Edmund Burke prophesied, in his *Reflections on the Revolution in France*, that the uprooting of historic institutions would lead to the rule of "some popular general."

The common people on France's borders soon found that occupation by the republic's undisciplined armed hordes brought pillage and rape, the systematic exactions of French officialdom, and attacks on the Church. Even the "rights of man" offended against deeply held popular prejudices such as those against the Jews. The association of liberty and equality with French domination was ominous, because the counter-nationalisms that French ideas and French bayonets summoned up might eventually oppose democracy at home. For the moment, sporadic urban revolts and guerrilla struggles did no more than annoy the victorious Republic.

CANONNIER.

"Great battles are won by artillery," wrote Napoleon of his favorite weapon, pictured above.

A New French Empire in the Middle East?

Fearing both inactivity and premature involvement in the intrigues around the Directory, Bonaparte sought the leadership of a French expedition to Egypt in 1798. That dependency of the Ottoman Empire, the Directory thought, had potential as a French colony, as compensation for the lost empire of 1763. It might also threaten Britain's road to India.

These ambitions did not survive the destruction of the French fleet at the battle of the Nile in August 1798. Horatio Nelson, Britain's greatest naval leader, cut Bonaparte's naval communications and marooned him and his 40,000 troops. After a year of unrewarding campaigning against Egyptians, Turks, and British, Bonaparte slipped stealthily back to France in a frigate, and his discarded army ultimately surrendered to the British.

Strategically, that outcome was no surprise. French domination, then and later, ended at the high-tide mark. Culturally, however, the Egyptian expedition gave an immense impulse to Western historical and linguistic studies. Bonaparte, man of the Enlightenment, had taken with him to Egypt teams of experts to study the monuments and loot the artifacts of one of the oldest civilizations in continuous existence. In the booty the French swept up and the British later captured was a stone slab, found at Rosetta in the Nile delta and now in the British Museum in London. On it are three inscriptions of the same text: one in ancient Greek, one in phonetic Egyptian script, and one in hieroglyphics. The "Rosetta stone" provided the key with which a brilliant young scholar, Jean-François Champollion, deciphered hieroglyphics in 1821–22. That achievement opened the road to the reconstruction of three millennia of Egyptian history. The Egyptian expedition was not only symbolic of European colonial greed. It also demonstrated the West's voracious curiosity, which in the coming century blossomed into a series of new disciplines aimed at understanding other cultures—comparative history, philology and linguistics, anthropology, and sociology.

FROM FIRST CONSUL TO EMPEROR, 1799–1804

Bonaparte timed perfectly his arrival in France in October 1799. A Second Coalition against France had replaced the first. The Egyptian expedition had drawn Russia into the war, for Tsar Paul resented non-Russian attempts to bully the Turks. The Austrians also resumed fighting. A short but nasty Russian incursion into Switzerland and north Italy thoroughly alarmed French opinion. The Directory, internally split, was utterly discredited, and restoration of the monarchy threatened once more.

Sieyès, the propagandist of the Third Estate who had helped launch the Revolution, had only survived the Terror by being discreet. In May 1799 he reemerged to join the Directory. He sought now to stabilize the rule of the beneficiaries of the Revolution, the Third Estate, through one last coup d'état. For that he needed "a saber," a docile general. Bonaparte, whom Sieyès approached, was willing to consider the role with one difference: he would make this coup for himself.

And so, on November 9 and 10, 1799—18 Brumaire of the soon discarded revolutionary calendar—Bonaparte acted. With the help of his politician brother Lucien, of Sieyès, and of the bayonets of the army, he cowed the legislature and assumed power as "First Consul." Sieyès found himself shunted off into gilded retirement. Much of French opinion had hoped for and expected a monarch. Instead, France received a dictator.

To consolidate his rule, Bonaparte fell back on the technique of which he was the unparalleled master, battle. In the spring of 1800 he led a French army once more across the Alps and fell upon the Austrian rear. Close and bloody victory at Marengo, and General Jean-Victor Moreau's triumph at Hohenlinden on the German front compelled Austria to negotiate. The Second Coalition, as disunited as its predecessor, collapsed. By the Treaty of Lunéville (February 9, 1801), Austria conceded to France the Rhine frontier and dominance in Italy. Russia, following the dictates of the mad Tsar Paul, had already withdrawn from the war. Even Britain now consented to negotiate a grudging peace, the March 1802 Treaty of Amiens. Britain's mercantile elite was willing to attempt coexistence with the "Corsican tyrant," although continuing French control of Holland and Belgium was a threat to British security far greater than any conquest of Louis XIV.

Victory and peace allowed Napoleon, as he now began to style himself, to consolidate his hold on France. In the summer of 1802 he had himself proclaimed "First Consul for Life," and in December 1804, "Emperor of the French." The pope, with whom Napoleon had signed in 1801 a Concordat partly bridging the gap between France and the Church, officiated at the imperial coronation. But in an act contrary to custom that symbolized his will to power, Napoleon crowned himself.

Napoleon's rule meant more for France than the imposition of a new monarchy and a new aristocracy of generals and Bonaparte relatives. It completed the old regime's drive toward centralization, toward enlightened absolutism. The departments now received permanent administrators sent from Paris. These "prefects," almost all-powerful representatives of the central will in the provinces, long outlasted Napoleon. They still exist, although with recently diminished powers. This pattern of the modern, centralized, bureaucratic state was the most powerful legacy of the Revolution. It found ready imitators throughout continental Europe and, much later, in the "Third World."

Along with centralization came legal uniformity. Napoleon's second major internal innovation was his law code, eventually known as the Code Napoléon. It replaced the old regime's patchwork of customary and Roman law with a single national code. It proclaimed equality before the law, reverence for property, and the authority of the male head of the family. The Code, like the prefects, was a pattern much imitated. French bayonets imposed it in the ever larger areas annexed to France. Its example impelled satellites and even opponents to legal reforms. Eventually only England, with its constitution formed through the slow accretion of custom and precedent, remained unmoved.

THE CONQUEST OF EUROPE, 1803–07

Works of peace, although not uncongenial to Napoleon, did not for long contain his ambition. From late 1802 on he dispatched agents to the Middle East and prepared to stir up trouble for Britain in India. In Germany, after Lunéville, Napoleon acted as arbiter of a "princes' revolution" by which the larger territorial states gobbled up the ecclesiastical rulers. That display of French power offended Austria, which still held nominal overlordship over the now crippled Holy Roman Empire.

Britain, confident that a new coalition would soon form, resumed war in May 1803. Initially, London stood alone, and Napoleon concentrated 400,000 men of his newly reorganized *Grande Armée* on the Channel coasts. Southern England was virtually defenseless, at least by land. "If we can be the masters of the narrows for six hours, we shall be masters of the world," Napoleon wrote to one of his admirals. Neither six hours, nor the week actually needed were forthcoming. Napoleon had starved his navy of money, supplies, and equipment. Many of the technically skilled officers had emigrated, and revolutionary enthusiasm was little help at sea. The British blockade had prevented the French navy from acquiring the sea experience needed to mount an effective challenge. Napoleon waited with increasing impatience on winds, tides, and his ever-delaying admirals.

In the event, the campaign of 1805 was on land, in Germany. There Napoleon could bring his skill and France's

Napoleon'a claim to universal domination: the Emperor on his throne, by Ingres (1806).

power to bear. His coronation as emperor, with its overtones of a claim to the legacy of Charlemagne, had alarmed the Austrians. His crowning in May 1805 as "emperor" of the satellite kingdom of north Italy—where Charlemagne had also ruled—proved the final step that brought a new coalition into being. Austria and Russia now joined England. Irresolute Prussia, intent on absorbing the fat English-ruled German state of Hanover, remained neutral.

Napoleon broke camp at Boulogne and flung the *Grande Armée* into south Germany before Austrians and Russians could join forces. One Austrian army, under the inept General Karl Mack, found itself enveloped and forced to surrender at Ulm on October 20. But in the distant seas off Spain, the British navy the next day reversed Napoleon's run of luck. At Cape Trafalgar Nelson captured or sank over half the combined French-Spanish fleet. He paid for victory with his life, but ensured that Napoleon could never repeat the invasion threat of 1804. Trafalgar and the arrival of Russian armies in central Europe impelled Prussia slowly toward the coalition.

To extricate himself from an increasingly threatening situation, Napoleon characteristically chose battle. He lured the combined Austro-Prussian forces to attack him prematurely. On December 2, at Austerlitz north of Vienna, he faced 90,000 Austrians and Russians with 70,000 French. An Austro-Russian drive at Napoleon's flank led to weakness in their center. Napoleon saw his chance and sent a corps forward to break through and roll up the enemy line. The Austro-Russians lost 27,000 dead and prisoners to Napoleon's 8,000 casualties. Austria left the war. It was Napoleon's most brilliant victory.

The collapse of Austria left Napoleon master of the German states, which he had already helped restructure after Lunéville. Now, in July 1806, Napoleon imposed a second round of revolution from above. The Holy Roman Empire, now a decrepit relic,

died unlamented. Napoleon replaced it with a league of satellites, the Confederation of the Rhine. The remaining small states fell prey to their more powerful neighbors. The Germany of 1801 had had over 1,800 separate political units. By the end of 1806 fewer than 40 remained. Centralization was convenient for Napoleon's tax collectors, and for the Bonaparte relatives who received German states as gifts. But it also proved a mighty step toward the German nation-state that within a century came to dwarf and humiliate France.

Only Prussia, afraid that Napoleon would make peace with London and force it to disgorge Hanover, remained aloof from Napoleon's new German system. In October 1806, alone except for distant reassurances from St. Petersburg, Prussia went to war. Within a week Napoleon had launched the *Grande Armée* around the flank of the rigidly old-regime Prussian army. On October 14, 1806, converging French corps annihilated the Prussians at the twin battles of Jena and Auerstädt.

Within weeks Napoleon was in Potsdam, paying homage with his marshals at the tomb of Frederick the Great: "Hats off, gentlemen; if *he* were still alive, we would not be here." But unlike Austria the year before, Prussia did not quit at once. Europe's resistance to Napoleon's ever more explicit claim to universal domination was gradually stiffening. In cooperation with their Russian allies, the Prussians fought on in Poland. There, unlike the green lands of western Europe, the French found little to eat. The few roads were ice-covered bogs. The Russians appeared in force, and in the great slaughter at Eylau in February 1807 proved dogged if unimaginative opponents. The coming of summer helped the French maneuver. At Friedland in June Napoleon finally crushed the Russians with a victory he proclaimed "as decisive as Austerlitz, Marengo, and Jena."

Tsar Alexander, erratic grandson of the great Catherine and son of the

The imperial seal of Napoleon, "Emperor of the French, King of Italy, Protector of the Confederation of the Rhine."

madman Paul, whose removal by palace coup he had connived at in 1801, offered negotiations. The tsar met Napoleon on a raft moored in the river Niemen at Tilsit, and totally reversed Russian policy. Russia agreed to divide Europe—not for the last time—into western and eastern spheres of influence. Napoleon kept Germany, including Alexander's Prussian ally. To Russia fell Finland, Sweden, and Turkey. Alexander in return promised secretly to declare war on England and to cooperate with French efforts to close the continent to British trade.

Such a boycott, after the loss of much of the French navy at Trafalgar, was Napoleon's only weapon against Britain. In the "Berlin Decree," issued in November 1806, he had declared a "blockade" against British exports to the Continent. Bankruptcy, and revolts by factory workers thrown suddenly out of work, would in theory compel London to make peace. But this "Continental System" had leaks. Along the coastline that stretched from Spain to Russia, smugglers plied a roaring trade, with the connivance of corrupt French officials. And the British were lucky or skilled enough to avoid a total closing of their other markets. Until 1812 they avoided war with their most powerful seagoing neutral trading partner, the United States, despite bitter conflict over British searches and seizures of U.S. vessels. And in 1812–15, when the United States did go to war with Britain, Napoleon's break with Alexander once again opened Scandinavia and Russia to British exports.

FRANCE AND EUROPE, 1808–12

The manifest failure of the Continental System was only one sign that Napoleon's power had begun to wane after

Napoleonic Europe   1812

A Goya sketch of "The Disasters of War": a French dragoon contemplates Spaniards he has hanged.

Tilsit. More serious was growing resistance on the Continent. Revolutionary France had invented modern nationalism and through it had tapped unprecedented military power. Now others, in Prussia and even in Austria, began to follow its example. But the first check to Napoleon's power came from a country scarcely touched by the Enlightenment—Spain.

There, in 1808, a savage guerrilla war broke out against the French troops sent to impose Napoleon's brother Joseph on the throne of the Spanish Bourbons. In scenes fixed forever in historical memory by the genius of the Spanish painter Francisco Goya, the French shot, hanged and impaled the guerrillas, who in return hacked at the French with improvised weapons. Nobles, priests, and brigands led the masses, for the revolt was as much a reaction against the ideas the French brought as against the French themselves. Unaided, it might have petered out.

But Britain soon sent armies to Spain and Portugal. On the far periphery of

Europe, sea communications were more efficient than the appalling Spanish roads that linked the French to Paris. At Lisbon the Duke of Wellington, a skillful commander already proven in India, found a secure base. The "Spanish ulcer" resisted treatment by Napoleon in person in late 1808. Henceforth he left the matter to less competent subordinates, whom Wellington gradually wore down.

In Germany, the Tilsit settlement failed to extinguish the embers of a modern nationalism that eventually proved itself more terrifying than that of the French. Germany's sense of nationhood was at least as old as Luther's German Bible. The cultural revival of the late eighteenth century had given Germans a justified pride in their literature, which by the 1790s had begun to rival that of France. But it was French conquest that made German nationalism political. That origin gave it a peculiarly militant cast. And the imposition from without of the "rights of man and the citizen" and of the *Code Napoléon* helped make German nationalism potentially antidemocratic. In France, nationalism was subversive of the old regime. In Germany and further east it might serve to reinforce it.

That was certainly the lesson that Prussian soldiers and bureaucrats derived from defeat in 1806–07. King Frederick William III, his dominions halved after Tilsit, was even willing to appeal to his people in order to survive. He gave power to a cadre of unconventional civil servants and generals: Karl vom und zum Stein, Karl August von Hardenberg, August von Gneisenau, Gerhard von Scharnhorst. To defeat the French, Prussia needed what Hardenberg described as a "revolution in the good sense," an authoritarian "revolution from above." The reformers abolished serfdom, although dogged noble resistance prevented full implementation. They gave towns and cities limited self-government in order to engage the population in politics in support of the state. They abolished most of Frederick the Great's restrictions on freedom of commerce and industry and opened land ownership to non-nobles. Above all, they laid the basis for the imposition in 1814 of universal military service and the recruitment of non-noble officers. Their military-bureaucratic revolution from above sought to shore up enlightened absolutism with popular support. Its ultimate consequence was "bureaucratic absolutism," a power-state that bureaucrats and officers ruled under a thin veneer of royal authority.

For the moment the Prussian reformers could only hope that Napoleon would eventually falter. Austria, in April 1809, took Napoleon's Spanish defeats as a signal to renew the war. The Habsburgs incited the Tyrolese, whom Napoleon had detached from Austria, to a desperate guerrilla revolt. Dynastic Vienna appealed publicly to "the German nation." The old regime was learning new tricks. The Habsburg Archduke Charles, one of the most talented of Napoleon's opponents, fought him to a standstill at Aspern, near Vienna. Then Napoleon triumphed in a

Prussia Responds: Revolution from Above

Baron von Hardenberg to King Frederick William III, "On the Reorganization of the Prussian State," September 12, 1807:

The French Revolution, of which the present wars are the continuation, has given the French amid bloodshed and upheaval entirely new energies . . . . Neighbors and conquered have been carried away by the flood. All barriers created to dam it up have proved feeble. . . .

The illusion that we could withstand the Revolution most effectively by holding fast to the old . . . has itself resulted in the promotion and ever greater extension of the Revolution. The power of its principles is so great, they are so generally recognized and widely spread, that the state that fails to take them up voluntarily will either suffer destruction or be compelled from outside to accept them. . . .

Therefore, our goal, our guiding principle, is a revolution in the good sense, leading straight to the great purpose of the ennoblement of humanity through the wisdom of those in authority, rather than through a violent upheaval from below or without. Democratic principles in a monarchical government: that seems to me the form appropriate to the current spirit of the age. . . .

In other, but similar circumstances, although under an entirely different spirit of the age, Elector Frederick William the Great revolutionized . . . his state and laid the foundations for its later greatness.

From Georg Winter, ed., *Die Reorganisation des Preussischen Staates unter Stein und Hardenberg* (Leipzig: S. Hirzel, 1931), Vol. I, pp. 305–306 (translation by M. Knox).

gruelling two-day struggle at Wagram on July 5–6, 1809. Victory was becoming more difficult, as the rest of Europe began to imitate the revolution.

Austria, in the absence of Russian or Prussian support, eventually resolved on peace. Its new foreign minister, the devious Clemens von Metternich, bought Napoleon's good graces with the marriage offer of a Habsburg archduchess, Marie-Louise. Napoleon was happy to discard Joséphine and accept. Marriage alliance with the oldest major

The *Grande Armée's* flight across the icy Beresina River (late November 1812).

ruling house of Europe offered the Bonaparte dynasty much-needed legitimacy.

FROM MOSCOW TO SAINT HELENA, 1812–15

Napoleon's power still rested ultimately on force. With defeat in Russia in 1812, that force melted away. Until the end of 1811 Napoleon had expected that threats would hold Tsar Alexander to the Tilsit bargain. But Russian cooperation with the Continental System against Britain had always been weak, and Alexander had secretly approached Prussia and Austria with proposals for a new coalition. In the spring of 1812 Napoleon broke relations and launched what he himself described as "the most difficult enterprise I have ever attempted": the invasion of Russia.

The vanguard of the largest field army yet seen, over half a million men of whom 250,000 were French, crossed the Niemen in June 1812. The immense distances, the absence of roads, and

shortage of food and fodder devoured the *Grande Armée*. Russian resistance, compounded of equal parts courage, stubbornness, and vodka, stunned the French with its bitterness. As in Spain, guerrillas attacked French communications. Napoleon failed to bring the ever-retreating Russian armies to decisive battle. The immense slaughter at Borodino (almost 70,000 casualties) and the capture of Moscow in September 1812 were not victories. The Russian governor put the capital to the torch. Tsar Alexander, perhaps fearful of being deposed and strangled like his father should he show weakness, adamantly refused negotiation. After a month of indecision, Napoleon resolved upon a withdrawal for which he had made no preparations. The Russian winter and the pursuing Cossack cavalry did the rest. Perhaps 10,000 men out of the entire *Grande Armée* recrossed the Niemen in any condition to fight.

As Napoleon sprinted by coach for Paris to raise a new army, Germany turned against the French. Princes, literati, and middle classes united in an outpouring of national feeling. A mutinous Prussian general joined the advancing Russians with his army corps on New Years' Day 1813. The Prussian state soon followed. Austria too joined the new coalition after Metternich had in vain pressed Napoleon to settle for an empire confined to France and a European balance of power. Napoleon had replied that any such settlement would deprive him of the prestige needed to rule France itself. It was that iron law, and his own immense ambitions, that had impelled him toward universal empire.

Napoleon's utter refusal to compromise thus created the coalition that finally brought France down. By August 1813 the alliance was complete. Its forces caught and destroyed Napoleon's new and inexperienced army at Leipzig in October. The Allies had discovered how to defeat Napoleon by coordinating their movements, giving battle only when united, and defeating Napoleon's less talented subordinates separately before closing in on the Emperor himself.

With Germany gone and with Wellington advancing across the Pyrenees from Spain, Napoleon fought a desperately imaginative spring 1814 campaign north and east of Paris. He himself now suffered from a variety of ailments, his troops were green, his marshals weary, and his subjects desperate from never-ending war. But the Emperor proved as dangerous as ever on the battlefield.

The last coalition nevertheless held. Viscount Castlereagh, the British Foreign Secretary, welded the disparate allies—Britain, Austria, Russia, Prussia—together with the Treaty of Chaumont (March 9, 1814). That Quadruple Alliance pledged to fight on, to restore the balance of power, to confine France to its traditional boundaries, and to remain united for 20 years after war's end. The Allies drove toward Paris and ignored Napoleon's last bold attempt to cut their communications. Military defeat, the plotting of his ex-foreign minister, Talleyrand, and the

defection of key military figures finally brought Napoleon down. In early April 1814, he abdicated and received from the Allies the Tuscan island of Elba for his retirement.

Louis XVIII, his relatives, and their court returned to France in the baggage trains of the victorious allied armies. The restored Bourbons rapidly made themselves unloved. When Napoleon escaped from Elba and landed in southern France in March 1815, the army rallied to him. Joyous crowds carried the returned Emperor up the steps of the Tuileries.

The Allies were less delighted. Wellington and the Prussian commander, Blücher, rapidly concentrated in Belgium. Napoleon, intent on one last throw of the dice, advanced to meet them. After drubbing the Prussians at Ligny he attempted on June 18 to overwhelm Wellington at Waterloo before Blücher could join him. Wellington, as he freely if ungrammatically admitted, had been "never so near to being

Napoleon I: The Myth   1817

In spite of all the libels, I have no fear whatever about my fame. Posterity will do me justice. The truth will be known; and the good I have done will be compared with the faults I have committed. I am not uneasy as to the result. Had I succeeded, I would have died with the reputation of the greatest man that ever existed. As it is, although I have failed, I shall be considered as an extraordinary man: my elevation was unparalleled, because unaccompanied by crime. I have fought fifty pitched battles, almost all of which I have won. I have framed and carried into effect a code of laws that will bear my name to the most distant posterity. I raised myself from nothing to be the most powerful monarch in the world. Europe was at my feet. I have always been of opinion that the sovereignty lay in the people. In fact, the imperial government was a kind of republic. Called to the head of it by the voice of the nation, my maxim was, *la carrière est ouverte aux talents* [careers are open to talent] without distinction of birth or fortune. . . .

From *The Corsican*, ed. by R. M. Johnston (Boston: Houghton Mifflin, 1910), p. 492.

beat." Then the Imperial Guard recoiled from the thin red line of British infantry and the Prussians attacked Napoleon's flank. Napoleon's last "Hundred Days" in power and revolutionary France's career of conquest were over.

The Bourbons once more returned. Napoleon surrendered to the British, who shipped him to the desolate South Atlantic island of St. Helena. There he occupied himself until his death in 1821 with the construction of the Napoleonic myth: his empire built on force had been "a kind of republic," and he himself had been the champion of the national principle for other nations besides France.

The wars of the Republic and Empire had cost the *Grande Nation* perhaps 1.8 million lives. The rapid population growth of the eighteenth century subsided as the peasantry concentrated on enjoying and conserving. France henceforth lacked the will for a serious bid to overturn the balance of power. But war and Revolution had set loose and Napoleon had spread ideas and forces that victorious armies could not still. It had unleashed through the concept of the nation-state new energies within and new conflicts without. It had demonstrated to Europe that a society could discard its rulers and freely adopt new myths and institutions. It had established the pattern of the modern bureaucratic state. And it had shown that popular sovereignty unlimited by law might produce a "despotism of liberty" instead of democracy. These were powerful lessons for the future.

Suggestions for Further Reading

The French Revolution

The most balanced recent general history of the Revolution is F. Furet and D. Richet, *The French Revolution* (1970); for the "classic" French Marxist view, see G. Lefebvre, *The French Revolution* (1962–64), and A. Soboul, *The French Revolution: 1787–1799* (1971). C. Brinton, *A Decade of Revolution, 1789–1799* (1934), and A. Cobban, *A History of Modern France, Vol. I, 1715–1799* (1957), are fine introductory summaries. R. R. Palmer, *The World of the French Revolution* (1971), places the Revolution in its broader European context; E. J. Hobsbawm, *The Age of Revolution, 1789–1848* (1962), does the same, brilliantly, from a Marxist viewpoint. T. C. Blanning, *The Origins of the French Revolutionary Wars* (1986), is excellent on the Revolution's early foreign relations.

A good introduction to the fierce debate over whether the Revolution was a "class struggle" is the anthology of N. Hampson, *The Social History of the French Revolution* (1962). A. Cobban, *The Social Interpretation of the French Revolution* (1964), wittily attacks Lefebvre and Soboul. J. Talmon, *The Origins of Totalitarian Democracy* (1952), and F. Furet, *Interpreting the French Revolution* (trans. 1981), stress ideology rather than class as the Revolution's driving force. For the masses, see G. Rudé, *The Crowd in the French Revolution* (1959), and R. Cobb, *The Police and the People* (1970). On various phases of the Revolution, the following stand out: W. Doyle, *The Origin of the French Revolution* (1980); J. M. Thompson, *Robespierre and the French Revolution* (1953); R. R. Palmer, *Twelve Who Ruled* (1941); A. Soboul, *The Parisian Sans-Culottes and the French Revolution* (1964); C. Tilly, *The Vendée* (1964); M. Lyons, *France under the Directory* (1975); and A. Forrest, *The French Revolution and the Poor* (1981).

Napoleon

On Napoleon, G. Bruun, *Europe and the French Imperium, 1799–1814* (1938), is still serviceable. G. Lefebvre's two-volume *Napoléon* (trans. 1969), is masterful and comprehensive. P. Geyl, *Napoleon: For and Against* (1949), remains useful as a guide to early historical debate about the period. On Napoleon's domestic policy, see R. Holtman, *The Napoleonic Revolution* (1967); on foreign policy, S. T. Ross, *European Diplomatic History 1789–1815: France Against Europe* (1969). For Napoleon's relations with the two peripheral great powers that brought him down, see C. Oman, *Britain Against Napoleon* (1944), and A. Palmer, *Napoleon in Russia* (1967). D. Chandler, *The Campaigns of Napoleon* (1966), is a thorough recent treatment of Napoleon's wars, with good maps; for a contemporary's reflections on what those wars meant, see Carl von Clausewitz, *On War* (1976), ed. M. Howard and P. Paret.

24
The Demographic and Industrial Revolutions, 1750–1900

*W*hile the French Revolution convulsed Europe, other even more revolutionary forces had begun to transform the world. The coming of the machine, the substitution of mechanical precision and power for human skill and human or animal strength, was the greatest single change in humanity's existence since the agricultural revolution of the New Stone Age. In the late eighteenth century, one economy began for the first time in human history to generate an appreciable and ever-increasing surplus of food and goods. That economy was Britain's. Western Europe, the United States, and one non-European power, Japan, were soon to follow that lead.

Opposite: Iron and glass: the revolutionary Crystal Palace, site of Britain's Great Exhibition of 1851.

Steel for a new age: the Bessemer process.

This Western invention, the invention of widespread affluence and of sustained and self-sustaining economic growth, in turn made possible the continuation of an unprecedented growth of population that had begun before the coming of the machine—the demographic revolution. These two revolutions together provide the physical foundations of the societies in which we now live, societies orders of magnitude larger, richer, and more powerful than any before the nineteenth century. These twin revolutions provided both impetus and opportunity for the culmination of the Europeanization or "westernization" of the world begun in 1492. And the industrial revolution, the revolution of technology and science, shows signs of continued acceleration.

THE BIOLOGICAL AND ECONOMIC "OLD REGIME"

Before considering the origins of the demographic and industrial revolutions, it is worth describing the human and economic landscape they revolutionized. Before the eighteenth century, the lives of all except kings, large landowners, upper clergy, and small merchant and professional elites tended to be "nasty, brutish, and short." In most of western Europe agricultural technique was primitive and had changed relatively little from the

eleventh to the seventeenth centuries. Nobility, clergy, and warring states tended to eat up the small surpluses these economies generated after their inhabitants were fed. A precarious existence depended above all on two factors: favorable weather and the absence of disease. Drought or downpour, hail or frost—any vagary of the climate might spell famine and death. Plant or animal diseases might cause crop failures in isolated areas, or across the continent. By one count France had 13 general famines in the sixteenth century, 17 in the seventeenth, and 16 in the eighteenth century.

Human epidemics were even less forgiving than those of the plant and animal world. The Black Death of the fourteenth century remained a serious threat as late as the early 1700s. It struck Amsterdam each year between 1622 and 1628, killing perhaps 35,000. It struck Paris six times between 1612 and 1668, and London five times between 1593 and 1664–65. In greater London in 1664–65 it killed perhaps 60,000 out of a population of roughly 450,000. Columbus's discovery of America also contributed by introducing smallpox to the Indians and syphilis to the Europeans. The latter spread with fierce virulence from Spain across the Continent after 1493. A new form of tuberculosis, more dangerous than its predecessors, arrived in Europe from India in the eighteenth century. As late as 1831–32 the arrival of cholera from India produced a terrifying epidemic. And along with the great diseases came the lesser endemic ones. Smallpox infected perhaps 95 percent of the inhabitants of early modern Europe—and perhaps one in seven of those infected died. Malaria lessened life expectancy by perhaps a third. Before the eighteenth century it was endemic in marsh areas as far north as England. Typhus, typhoid fever, and a variety of no-longer identifiable but often fatal diseases were likewise widespread.

Death was thus ever-present under the "biological old regime." The death rate exceeded the birth rate—

population actually decreased—during famines and epidemics. Rapid temporary rises of the birth rate marked the recoveries from successive disasters, but infant mortality struck even more heavily than in the contemporary "Third World." In one prosperous French province in the seventeenth century infant deaths ran between 25 and 33 percent of all newborns in their first year. Only half of all newborns lived to the age of 20.

Accompanying the ever-presence of death was an overwhelming dreariness of life. Since the industrial revolution it has been fashionable to lament, on well-filled stomachs in the comfort of our well-heated houses, the purity and authenticity of "the world we have lost." But the inhabitants of pre-industrial Europe did not live in picturesque rural bliss. They fought a grim and often losing struggle for survival amid a squalid poverty without contemporary equivalent except in the "Third World."

The vast majority of Europe's inhabitants lived for and through backbreaking toil in fields and cottage workshops. Children worked with and for their parents from the moment they were capable. Those who did not work starved, and often enough those who did work starved. Agricultural work followed the tyranny of the seasons. There was too little work in winter, and too much and all at once at ploughing or harvest time, lest the crops spoil. Food had a desperate sameness. In the aftermath of the Black Death, population shortage and high wages had made meat a frequent food of the common people. But by the seventeenth century the population was again pressing against the limits of subsistence, and the vast majority of Europeans ate little but cereal. Wheat was the staple food, at least in Western Europe. Rye, barley, or oats—"in England a food for horses, in Scotland for men"— prevailed in outlying areas of the east and north. Rice was an exotic eastern import until the creation of broad malarial rice-fields in northern Italy after the fifteenth century. In the seventeenth and eighteenth centuries the New World crops, maize (corn) and potatoes, began to spread slowly but without changing the underlying pattern. The population ate peasant bread baked a few times a year and stored like bricks. Ergot fungus, which causes hallucinations and convulsions, often contaminated rye. Too exclusive a diet of corn meal mush (the Italian *polenta*) caused pellagra, a vitamin deficiency disease. Only the rich, and the small populations in the mountains and wastelands given over to sheep and cattle, ate much meat. As for shelter, the common people, until very late, lived in thatched hovels with dirt floors and one or two articles of furniture. In many cases the peasants shared the roof with their animals, as well as with bedbugs, fleas, and lice. Clothing was scarce, expensive, and rarely washed.

The monotony of isolation added to that of work, food, and lodging. Most peasants did not move beyond their native valleys. Peasant villages and even small towns were tight little societies riven with small hatreds and fiercely antagonistic toward outsiders. Only the rare journeys to local market towns or fairs, or the brief village religious festivals with their ritualized overeating and drunkenness, punctuated a bleak existence. Small wonder that the peasants of the French Alps summarized the height of happiness in such macabre terms as "happy as a dead'un." Misery seemed tolerable because it was familiar; no alternative had ever existed except for the small percentage of the population living above subsistence level.

The demographic and economic "old regime" began to give way to the new age in the course of the eighteenth century. The population of Europe had increased before, from 1100 to 1350. Then the Black Death had cut population by up to a third. Growth had resumed from 1450 to 1630, until the stagnation of the "seventeenth century crisis." Now, after 1750, Europe's population began to increase with an un-

FIGURE 24-1   World Population, 1000–2000

precedented and apparently uncheckable rapidity. The pattern was not unique. The populations of China and India, although statistics are sketchy, apparently grew at a similar rhythm, which clearly had a general cause (see Figure 24-1). The most likely source of the general upturn after 1750 is a change in weather patterns. After the "little ice age" in seventeenth and early eighteenth century, world climate appears to have warmed significantly. Agricultural production and thus nutrition improved. The death rate slowly declined and the birth rate rose. Population growth resumed at a rapid rate.

Two things that had little or no effect on the initial upturn of the population curve, despite the contrary impressions of contemporaries and historians, were modern medicine and sanitation and industrialization itself. Medicine and sanitation, with the possible exception of vaccination for smallpox, introduced in 1796, played little role before the 1850s, and then primarily in England,

the most advanced nation. The widespread draining of marshes, the removal of rotting refuse from villages and towns, the spread of soap and bathing, and the increasing commonness of cotton (and hence washable) underclothes probably cut the insect population of Europe. Malaria, transmitted by mosquitoes, and flea- and louse-borne plague and typhus did decrease. But the purpose of draining the marshes was to reclaim land for farming, and the other changes served comfort, not medicine. Conscious efforts against disease had to await the identification of causes and carriers of disease in the early and mid-nineteenth century.

As for industrialization, it affected Britain first, and primarily after 1760. The 1780s was the decisive decade in which British economic growth turned sharply upward. Industry, in other words, did not itself cause the demographic revolution. Nor does industry's existence or absence correlate neatly with population growth. Western Europe, which industrialized, grew 280 percent between 1680 and 1900 (71.9 million to 201.4 million), whereas China, which did not, grew at a roughly similar rate (150 million to 450 million). The peak growth rates of industrializing regions within Europe did outstrip most other areas. The presence of work encouraged both migration and earlier marriages that produced more children. England's population grew by a staggering 133 percent (from 4.93 million to 11.5 million) between 1680 and 1820, and 86 percent of that increase took place after 1760. But population also grew rapidly in nonindustrial areas. The population of England and Wales grew 48 percent between 1751 and 1801; that of Ireland, 75 percent.

Whatever its sources, the consequences of growth were startling. The total population of Europe to the Ural Mountains grew from perhaps 140 million in 1750 to 390 million in 1900. England and Russia, at opposite ends of the Continent and of the scale of social and economic development, led the way (see Figure 24-2). In Central Europe the populations of Germany and Austria-Hungary approximately doubled. Italy, thanks to massive emigration to the New World in the last quarter of the century, grew only 87 percent. France, whose career as *la grande nation* was over demographically as well as militarily, increased only 65 percent. And Ireland, the classic European example of the consequences of unchecked population growth unaccompanied by industrialization, suffered catastrophe. Population doubled in the seventeenth century, then more than doubled in the eighteenth century at the steepest rate in all Europe. That rise continued, from 5.25 million in 1800 to 8.5 million in 1845—of whom perhaps a quarter were unemployed. Then a potato blight and catastrophic famine in 1845–48 killed perhaps a million Irish, and flight to the New World cut population to around 4.5 million, where it thereafter remained.

What prevented further demographic catastrophes of the kind that afflicted Ireland, or China in the 1850s and 1860s, when perhaps 20 million

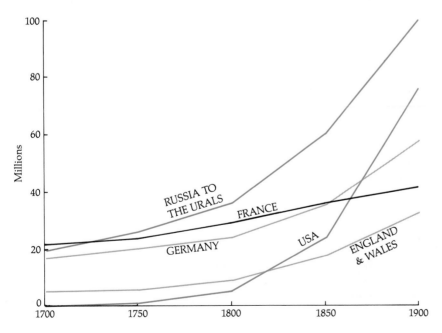

FIGURE 24-2   Population Increase by Country, 1700–1900

died in famines? As in Ireland and China, Europe's death rates gradually declined in the course of the century. Although birth rates also dropped, the spread between death and birth rate curves rapidly opened, and the population leapt upward. But unlike the outcome in Ireland and China, industrialization and medicine sustained Europe's increase. Only after the turn of the century did most of Europe pass through a "demographic transition" to a new pattern of lower birth rates. That transition was one symptom of the maturing of Europe's new industrial societies.

THE INDUSTRIAL REVOLUTION: CAUSES

The World Primacy of the West

Why did it happen? One way of addressing the question is to ask why it happened where it happened. First of all, why did it happen in the West? Second, why in Britain? Elimination offers a partial answer to the first question. Two other contenders, the Islamic World and China, might have led the way. They did not, although as we have seen, Islam had in the early Middle Ages provided the relatively backward West with lost Greek texts and irreplaceable concepts such as decimal numbers and algebra. In 1078 China briefly achieved a level of coal-smelted iron production (125,000 tons) that Britain did not match until 1796.

But the Islamic World and China shared negative characteristics. The savage waves of nomads from Central Asia hit them harder than Europe. The Jurchen nomads conquered China's major iron-producing provinces. The Mongols sacked Baghdad and ruled China as the Yuan dynasty. The Ottoman Turks overran and held the core lands of Islamic civilization. In China a second "conquest dynasty," the Manchus, had effects as disruptive as the Mongols.

Even more serious than invasion and foreign rule was a loss of impetus,

an intellectual turning inwards in those civilizations themselves. In the Islamic World, the phenomenon perhaps had doctrinal roots. "Islam" means "submission"—to the will of God. From the beginning, the religion's thrust toward a life totally devoted to God entailed potential hostility to nonreligious knowledge. In the tenth century, the "gates of independent judgment" about the Koran began to close. Futher speculation, either about theology or about the physical world became increasingly suspect, and slowed dramatically (see pp. 233–34). As for China, the Ming dynasty's great trading and war fleets of 1405–33 dominated the South China Sea and Indian Ocean, and were technologically superior to the Portuguese who followed less than 70 years later. But China's supremely confident ethnocentrism and the nomad land threat to its northern border turned it inwards for good.

Political disabilities multiplied the disadvantages of circumstances and culture. The Islamic World and China shared a similar form of government—centralized despotism. Caliphs, Ottoman sultans, and emperors of China in theory *owned* their territories and the inhabitants of those territories. Human inefficiency, frequent succession struggles, and the inevitable need to rely on elites, such as China's scholar-gentry, that might in time take on independent life, often tempered that absolute power in practice. But the claim to power remained total. All property in theory belonged to the ruler. He merely lent it to his subjects and could tax or reclaim it when he chose.

Europe—except for the Russian state (see pp. 580–84)—was different. After the assimilation or defeat of the Viking and Magyar raiders in the tenth century Europe suffered relatively little from outside invasion. Mongols and Turks only devastated fringe areas such as Muscovy, Hungary, and the Balkans. And far from relapsing into self-satisfaction, Europe developed that uniquely inquiring cast of mind already described in discussing the Renaissance and the seventeenth century scientific revolution. Theological speculation separated from inquiry about the physical world. Slowly and haltingly the West crossed the divide between magic and science. And after 1100 Europe's science and technology slowly overtook and surpassed those even of China. The Western obsession with clocks, with the mechanical measurement of time, was symbolic of far more—the application of rationality, calculation, and step-by-step empirical problem solving to broader and broader areas of human existence.

Politics also helped. Despite the efforts of popes and emperors, Europe remained divided into warring states and principalities. Charlemagne, Gregory VII, Charles V, Philip II, Louis XIV, and Napoleon all failed to establish universal empires. Europe also lacked the identification of government and religion seen in both Islam and China. The Investiture Conflict and the Protestant Reformation guaranteed that Caesar and God would remain distinct. That left space, however small at first, for freedom.

Finally, political diversity from very early allowed subordinate groups and small polities to claim *rights*, even against their rulers—a concept almost unimaginable elsewhere. From the security of their fortified walls, medieval towns could and did defy their overlords. The barons extorted the Great Charter from the English monarchy. The right of resistance to oppression became a stable principle of European political thought, and of no other. Relative freedom under laws, however limited in practice, persisted and widened over the centuries.

And its close connection to the free enjoyment of property allowed unprecedented latitude and security for economic activity. In western Europe, and in western Europe alone, great bankers such as the Medici or Fuggers could deal almost as equals with crowned heads. The straightjacket of the European mercantilist state was a small impediment to growth compared to the punitive taxation or confiscation that awaited Moslem or Chinese magnates whose economic success made them too conspicuous. Relative freedom from nomad devastation, the preeminence of curiosity and rationality, political pluralism and division between religious and secular power, and the concept of rights against the ruler were decisive in propelling Europe past its rivals.

The Primacy of Britain in Europe

Within Europe, Britain led the way after the seventeenth century. Even more than the rest of Europe, it enjoyed relative freedom from external threat. The last successful invasion had been that of 1066. Internal turmoil, from the Wars of the Roses to the Civil War of the 1640s and the anarchic Highland clan risings of 1715 and 1745, was superficial and short-lived compared to the great wars that rent the continent. And an inquiring cast of mind had long distinguished England, the land that had contributed more than any other to the scientific revolution. The Reformation and the ensuing breaking of the religious monopoly of the established church in the Civil War meant that religious restraints on freedom of speculation and the free flow of knowledge were conspicuous by their relative absence.

Finally, the nature of English politics and society made for English primacy over rivals such as France, just as the nature of European politics and society gave Europe the lead it had acquired by 1700. The remnants of English feudal institutions and land tenure had disappeared by the sixteenth century. England had ceased to have serfs or even a hereditary peasantry. After the mid-sixteenth century even mining rights, except in gold and silver, belonged to the landowner and not the monarch—a situation unique in Europe. When the Civil War of 1641–48 had pitted the crown against England's landowners organized in Parliament, the landowners had won, and had completed the process begun with the *Magna Carta*. Rights of property became absolute, conditional neither on service nor on claims of overlords, tenants, or Church. The purpose of government itself, as Locke had spelled it out in 1690, was simple: "The great and chief end . . . of men's uniting into commonwealths and putting themselves under government is the preservation of their property." That conception of property was far more absolute than that prevailing even in old-regime France, much less in lands east and south of France.

The consequence of England's history, by the eighteenth century, was thus a society with rights but without legally defined orders, a society enjoying social mobility undreamed of on the Continent. "All are accounted gentlemen in England who maintain themselves without manual labor," remarked a well-known eighteenth-century traveler's handbook. In this relatively "open aristocracy," wealth bought status with a speed and directness not visible in France. That was an immeasurable encouragement to the getting of wealth, and unlike its continental counterparts the British elite was relatively unembarrassed about how it acquired that wealth. In eighteenth-century Britain the barriers against nobles engaging in trade and industry that had begun to break down in old-regime France scarcely existed. At lower social levels, guild restrictions that still lived on the continent, especially in Germany, had likewise long crumbled.

British family structure and inheritance customs also fostered mobility and growth. Unlike France, where all children of the nobility inherited their parents' status, the younger sons of the great English families inherited neither land nor title. On the Continent, caste-bound younger sons had to make do with careers in church or army. In Britain younger sons went out into the world to earn money. These features made England into Europe's most dynamic society. It industrialized first because it alone was ready.

If the nature of English society explains why it industrialized, other factors help explain why it industrialized

when it did. First among them was the gradual but impressive growth of English agriculture, which between 1700 and 1800 increased its output per acre by 44 percent. New timetables for ploughing, new methods of field rotation with crops such as clover or turnips that returned nitrogen to the soil and supplied fodder, larger numbers of sheep and cattle eating that fodder and manuring the fields, selective breeding of livestock—all contributed to growth. The absence of a hereditary peasantry made it possible for landowners, whether "gentlemen" or merely prosperous farmers, to consolidate the medieval village common lands into "enclosed" fields, either by agreement with the villagers or by act of Parliament. Consolidation of holdings was virtually complete by the first decades of the nineteenth century. It made England a land of economically efficient large and medium farms, far different from the patchwork of open-field strips and peasant small-holdings still found in much of the Continent.

This "agricultural revolution" had three major consequences for British industrialization. Contrary to widespread opinion, enclosure apparently did not contribute by driving laborers off the land and into the new industrial labor force. The enclosed fields with their livestock and multiple crops required more rather than less labor than the old system. It was rural population increase, not enclosure, that filled the new industrial cities. But agriculture did help to keep that urban population fed, while enclosure freed land for industrial or mining development, and agricultural prosperity increased the market for industrial products.

But agriculture only provided a foundation for growth. Upon it and alongside it a rich commercial and industrial economy had arisen that already supplied a third of England's national product as early as 1700; by comparison, commerce and industry in France was at that date perhaps a fifth or less of the French economy. And England's commerce, unlike that of France, had already by 1700 created a

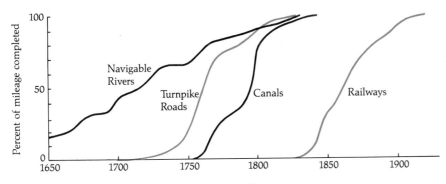

FIGURE 24-3　The Transport Revolution in Britain

From Eric Pawson, *The Early Industrial Revolution* (New York: Harper and Row, 1979), p. 153.

national market that matched goods with buyers. A cash economy centered on London reached to the far corners of the island, while barter, still prevalent in backward areas of France, was relatively rare. The internal customs barriers that bedeviled French merchants and the inter-state ones that cut eighteenth-century Germany into incoherent dwarf economies did not exist in England.

Even geography had favored the creation of a national market, for no part of Britain is more than 70 miles from the sea. Navigable rivers—the Thames, Severn, Tyne, Humber—improved with man-made banks and locks, made possible the economical transport of bulk cargoes such as coal, of which London already consumed 100,000 tons a year by the early seventeenth century. Beginning on a large scale in the 1760s, entrepreneurs promoted a massive expansion of canals and linked the major rivers into a national transport network. Similar private companies made British roads the best in Europe by the end of the eighteenth century (see Figure 24-3). Nor did the British market end with Britain itself. England's export trade, which grew sixfold during the eighteenth century, offered a further incentive for firms to expand production relentlessly.

England was thus already rich, and its people, along with those of Holland and the United States, enjoyed the world's highest standard of living in the late eighteenth century. That wealth, and the extent of England's national market, made it the only country in Europe that possessed the beginnings of a true mass market, a public capable of buying large quantities of inexpensive goods. The pull of that market at last brought into its own the West's love of gadgets and its willingness to search for practical results by trial and error. The pull of that market prompted the emergence of a cluster of technological innovations, swiftly spreading and mutually reinforcing, that propelled Britain into spectacular growth. For the first time in history, an economy expanded not primarily by increasing the input of labor but by replacing labor with machinery.

THE FIRST INDUSTRIAL REVOLUTION

The innovations of this "first industrial revolution" affected above all three key industries: cotton, coal, and iron. Cotton, the miracle fiber from India, the Middle East, and the slave economies of the Caribbean and American South, led the way. It was durable, lighter than linen, and easily washed, dyed, printed, or worked by machine. It also faced insatiable demand: As a London magazine put it in 1783, "every servant girl has her cotton gown and her cotton stockings."

A replica of Arkwright's water frame, patented in 1769.

In the 1730s the first of the major innovations, John Kay's flying shuttle, dramatically speeded up the weaving of cotton cloth. That created a bottleneck at the intermediate step of spinning the raw fibers into thread. By the 1750s the flying shuttle was in general use, and tinkerers and entrepreneurs bent to the task of mechanizing spinning. James Hargreaves's "spinning jenny" of 1765, Richard Arkwright's larger and more powerful "water frame," and Samuel Crompton's "mule," a hybrid with features from its two predecessors, filled the gap.

The new devices produced cotton thread in unprecedented quantities, and of a strength and fineness unattainable by hand spinning. A twelvefold leap upwards in cotton production and consumption between 1770 and 1800 in turn created further imbalances. The embryonic chemical industry found itself pressed for unprecedented quantities of soaps and bleaches to process textiles. And the flying shuttle of the home weavers

could no longer keep up with the output of thread. The answer was Arkwright's power-loom, invented in 1787. By 1833 one man with a 12-year-old boy as helper could produce as much as 20 hand-weavers. Annual production of cotton cloth skyrocketed from perhaps a million pounds a year in 1730 to 100 million in 1815.

That expansion created an entirely new institution, the factory. The grouping together of workers in large workshops was not new. It had existed in the ancient world and in Europe before the Industrial Revolution. But in all except the heaviest metal industries, such workshops had little or no competitive advantage over dispersed production. In 1770, the date of Arkwright's first large factory, the vast bulk of production still took place in home workshops under the "putting-out" system. The entrepreneur provided raw material to home workers (his subcontractors) and sold the finished product. Then the advent of power-driven machinery that was swifter, more efficient, and larger and more expensive than anything possible in the home or in small workshops compelled a concentration of industry into ever-larger units, into factories built around their machines and power sources. The "factory system" was an organizational and logistical leap comparable in magnitude to the technological advances that made it both necessary and possible.

The take-off of the cotton industry, with its pattern of new machines perpetually challenging entrepreneurs to further mechanize the slower phases of the production cycle, encouraged other industries as well. Coal and iron, the other two sectors of this first industrial revolution, felt the stimulus. Water power, which drove the early factories, was proving inadequate by the 1790s. Its force varied with the seasons and it compelled entrepreneurs to locate their factories only on suitable streams, often far from markets or sources of raw materials. The answer to that bottleneck was to tap an inanimate source

The Coming of Steam: A View from the Bottom   1818

When the spinning of cotton was in its infancy, and before those terrible machines for superseding the necessity of human labour, called steam engines came into use, there were a great number of what were then called *little masters;* men who with a small capital, could procure a few machines, and employ a few machines, and employ a few hands men and boys (say to twenty or thirty). . . . A few years however changed the face of things. Steam engines came into use, to purchase which, and to erect buildings sufficient to contain them and six or seven hundred hands, required a great capital. The engine power produced a more marketable (though not a better) article than the little masters could at the same price. The consequence was their ruin in a short time; and the overgrown capitalists triumphed in their fall.

Black Dwarf, September 30, 1818, pp. 623–24, quoted in Theodore Hamerow, *The Birth of a New Europe* (Chapel Hill: University of North Carolina Press, 1983), p. 13.

of power whose supply seemed almost infinite, coal.

The machine that turned the energy of coal into rotary motion to drive the new textile machines was the steam engine, the very symbol of the Industrial Revolution. Playthings such as the rotating kettle powered by a steam jet had existed since antiquity. But the first practical steam engine did not emerge until Thomas Savery's "fire engine" or steam-powered pump of 1698. Seven years later Thomas Newcomen, a blacksmith of Dartmouth in southern England, built the first true steam engine. It operated a crossbeam connected to a pump cylinder. Less than 1 percent of the energy released from its fuel did useful work, but that was enough. The machine was tireless and could be almost any size required. Its immediate use was to pump out and ventilate coal mines. It permitted a rapid expansion of coal production from ever-deeper seams, although its inefficiency prevented its use any distance from cheap coal.

Then, in the 1770s, James Watt invented an improved engine four times as efficient. This breakthrough created the "age of steam." The effectively unlimited coal deposits of northern England could henceforth power ever larger spinning and weaving machines. Watt's partner was appropriately immodest about their achievement: "I sell, Sir, what all the world desires to have—power."

Steam for pumping had permitted further expansion of coal production. Steam for industry in turn increased demand for coal. Steam power, coal, and the demands of war after 1793 between them revolutionized the iron industry. The English by 1740 had already consumed 10 or 11 pounds of iron per capita each year, far more than the French (although as late as the 1780s France's iron production was in absolute terms larger than Britain's). But English metallurgy soon came up against a seemingly unbreakable bottleneck in the need for fuel. The supply of wood to make charcoal for smelting

Watt's design drawing for his steam engine (1769).

iron ore into pig iron was limited. Coal, in its charred form, coke, normally contaminated the iron with impurities that rendered the finished product unusable.

After long experiment, Abraham Darby successfully smelted iron ore with coke (as the Chinese had before him) in 1709. But not until the 1750s did the technique become widespread. The triumph of coke metallurgy and further innovations such as the steam-powered forced-blast furnace and the preheated air blast drove British production of pig iron upward from 17,350 tons in 1740 to 2.7 million tons in 1852. That vast increase called forth further innovations elsewhere in the production cycle. The decisive breakthrough

The world's first cast-iron bridge, built in 1779 over the Severn River in England.

Iron ships: the huge *Great Eastern* (1858), built by Isambard Kingdom Brunel (1806–59), one of Britain's greatest engineers.

The opening of the world's first freight and passenger railway, the Stockton-Darlington Railway, on September 27, 1825.

in the processing of pig iron (from 2.5 to 5 percent carbon) into wrought iron (less than .1 percent carbon) came in the 1780s with Henry Cort's "puddling" and steam-powered rolling process. Crude standardized shapes such as iron beams, bars, and rails became possible for the first time. Britain's iron industry left France's in the dust.

As iron became ever cheaper, new sources of demand appeared. Weapons had traditionally been the largest single use of iron, and they remained so until after 1800. Royal Navy orders made the success of the Carron Company, Scotland's first major ironworks (1759), whose "carronade" or short naval cannon became synonymous with execution at short range. A new precision process for boring cannon from solid castings speeded production and made weapons more accurate. The steam engine's leaky cylinders also benefited from the new boring techniques. Iron beams began to appear in buildings and bridges in the 1770s, and the first practical fully iron-hulled ship emerged in 1815. Iron frames, rollers, gears, and pushrods replaced wood in the new generation of steam-powered textile machines, cutting vibration and permitting ever-higher operating speeds.

The culmination of the age of steam was of course the application of coal power to transport—the railroad and steamship, the first self-moving vehicles in world history. The first practical steamships were the creation of a French marquis, Claude Jouffroy d'Abbans, in the late 1770s and early 1780s. Americans and British developed the innovation further, and the first partially steam-powered Atlantic crossing came in 1819. The railroad was a combination of the steam engine with the rail-borne wagons used since the late sixteenth century in mines and quarries. In the late 1750s iron rails had begun to replace wood. Then, after 1800, a series of inventors sought to power a vehicle to run on those rails. In 1801–04 Richard Trevithick, developer of a high-pressure engine more efficient than Watt's, succeeded. After the mid-1820s the first railways began to spread across Britain and the United States.

Railroad and steamship drove forward the transport revolution begun with roads and canals. Railways immeasurably expanded the internal market, while the steamship widened the international one. Railway and steamship together provided the iron industry with demand that stretched it, as the consumer market had stretched the cotton industry. Each mile of railway track required three hundred tons of iron. By 1851, the year of the Great Exhibition at London that measured Britain's achievements against those of its European rivals, Britain had over 9,000 miles of track. Rails covered Britain like a web, linking mines, factories, ports, and cities of unprecedented size. The railroad was the last of the cluster of technologies of that first industrial revolution that made Britain the "workshop of the world."

THE SECOND INDUSTRIAL REVOLUTION: THE "FOLLOWERS"

By the time of the Great Exhibition, England had a commanding lead over its rivals. Its share of world industrial production had nevertheless already begun to drop, as others caught up (see Figure 24-4). In the next five decades

they closed the gap. New rivals beyond the seas, in America and ultimately in Japan (see pp. 778–80), rose to challenge both Britain and Europe.

These "followers" suffered from one major disadvantage. Their infant industries, especially in textiles, faced the competition of low-cost mass-produced British goods. But the followers were also the beneficiaries of Britain's pioneering. After Britain, industrialization would never again be an unforeseen and totally unplanned process. The followers had a model, and could study and seek to avoid some of that model's shortcomings. Second, followers could adopt technology already pioneered in Britain and save development costs. Finally, the industrialization of the followers roughly coincided with a new wave of innovations, the "second industrial revolution," that appeared between 1850 and 1880. The followers could enter the new industries of this second wave without the encumbrance of investment or labor force tied up in mature industries. In the new industries the followers could in some cases compete on even terms.

The new technologies were the four that propelled the industrial world into and through much of the twentieth century: steel, chemicals, electricity, and the internal combustion engine.

The factory: steam power and long rows of iron-framed machines. An English cotton mill in the early 1820s.

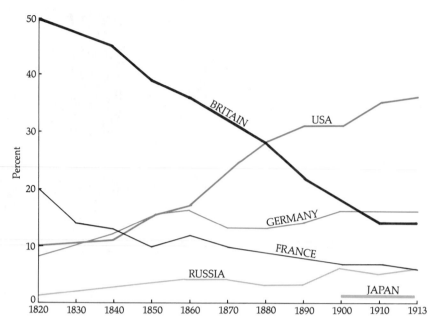

FIGURE 24-4   **Leader and Followers: Relative Shares of World Industrial Production**

Steel was initially the most important. An alloy of iron known since antiquity, steel contains between .1 and 2 percent carbon. It combines strength, hardness, and elasticity in unique proportions. It holds under stresses that snap brittle pig or cast iron (2.5 to 5 percent carbon) and spread wrought iron (less than .1 percent carbon) like butter.

Until the 1850s no process existed for making steel cheaply and in quantity. The oldest technique involved baking wrought iron bars at high temperature in a bed of carbon to diffuse it into the iron. Then a blacksmith laboriously reheated, folded, and hammered the iron bars into themselves by hand to distribute the carbon throughout the iron evenly. In the 1740s, along with the other metallurgical discoveries of the early Industrial Revolution, came a process, long known in China and South Asia, for making steel in small melting pots, or crucibles. After baking the wrought iron bars in carbon, the foundry masters melted them in crucibles, skimmed off impurities, and poured. The crucible process was small-scale and expensive, but it produced the hardest and most uniform steel yet made in appreciable quantities. And it made possible for the first time the casting of large steel objects such as drive shafts, railroad wheels or axles, and immense shell-firing cannon.

The new metallurgy: smelting iron with coke in Upper Silesia, 1841.

Then came two breakthroughs. In the 1850s Henry Bessemer, an armament designer, discovered that blowing air through a crucible filled with molten pig iron burned off the excess carbon rapidly and in the process generated the heat needed to keep the iron molten. The Bessemer converter eliminated the laborious intermediate steps required in earlier processes. Amid spectacular showers of sparks, it accomplished in ten or twenty minutes what had taken 24 hours and immense quantities of coal. The slightly later Siemens-Martin open-hearth furnace, which recirculated superheated combustion gases to create ever-higher temperatures, similarly made steel that was as cheap as wrought iron. That revolution made the age of steel, an age only now ending (see Figure 24-5).

In chemicals, another series of breakthroughs created entirely new industries. Until the mid-nineteenth century chemical production had mostly catered to the expanding textile industry's appetite for soaps and bleaches. Then, thanks to British and French laboratory work on organic chemicals derived from coal, came the synthetic dyes. There followed mineral oils, mineral oil derivatives, the anesthetic chloroform, nitrated high explosives and fertilizers, celluloid, cellulose fiber textiles such as rayon, and the first primitive plastics. Alfred Nobel, Swedish inventor of stabilized nitroglycerine, felt such remorse at the military uses of his product and the wealth he gained from it that he established the prizes—ironically including one for peace—that bear his name.

Electricity, the third key technology, came into its own in the 1800s. Its first practical use, the telegraph, dated from 1837–38. Undersea telegraph cable linked Britain and France by 1851 and spanned the Atlantic by 1866. The telegraph, Alexander Graham Bell's telephone (1876), and Guglielmo Marconi's radio (1897–1901) revolutionized communications. But electricity's most important use was as a source of power, after a series of inventions—

Rolling steel in a mill.

generators, alternators, transformers—from the 1860s to the 1880s. Electricity not only lighted the new industrial cities, replacing the coal gas lighting pioneered in Britain around 1800. Electricity also provided cheap, portable power in the factory, ultimately replac-

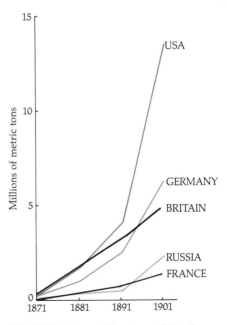

FIGURE 24-5   The Age of Steel

ing dangerous and breakdown-prone webs of transmission belts with compact, powerful electric motors.

Last came the internal combustion engine. By the mid-nineteenth century the limitations of steam were apparent. Steam engines were heavy. Their usual fuel, coal, was equally so, and required handling by legions of sweating stokers. Those characteristics made steam unsuitable for powering small vehicles. A German, Nicolaus Otto, provided the answer in 1876 with the first really practical internal combustion engine, which ran on coal gas. When converted to gasoline, it provided the motive power for the first automobiles in the 1890s, and for powered flight in 1903.

The technologies of the second industrial revolution encouraged changes in the techniques and organization of production. Cheap steel and the machine tool industry it greatly encouraged allowed the production for the first time of machines with interchangeable parts that required a minimum of filing and hand fitting during assembly. That innovation, despite the claims of Samuel Colt for his revolvers, remained more aspiration than reality until the 1870s. But after that, high-speed cutting steels, precision gauges, and a drive toward discipline and standardization in contentious matters such as screw threads made possible the mass production of ever more intricate machines.

Small arms were naturally the first application of interchangeable parts. By the 1850s a revolution in weaponry was underway. The flintlock musket, unreliable in rain and accurate to a mere hundred yards, had ruled the battlefield from the late seventeenth century to Waterloo. By 1850 the musket had given way to the Minié rifle with the all-weather mercury fulminate percussion cap. The new rifles fired heavy cylindrical bullets with hollow bases that expanded under pressure of the explosion to take the grooves of the rifle barrel. The resulting spin stabilized the bullet and made it lethal to a thousand yards.

Breech-loading arms, and weapons that did not have to be reloaded after each shot soon followed. Prussia's Dreyse and France's Chassepot breech-loading rifles offered a rate of fire five times higher than the muzzle-loading Minié. The first effective repeater was the revolver of the American, Samuel Colt. Brass cartridges replaced paper, making ammunition durable, waterproof, and quicker to load. Finally, in the 1880s came nitrated smokeless powder, the bolt-action magazine rifle, and the machine gun—a machine tool for killing. The latter was the creation of yet another American, Hiram Maxim, who succeeded in making a weapon that was truly automatic. The recoil from each shot reloaded and cocked the weapon, which was far lighter and more rapid-firing than its hand-cranked predecessors, the clumsy Gatling gun of the U.S. Civil War and the French *mitrailleuse* of 1870. Britain found the Maxim gun supremely useful in Africa, and made its inventor Sir Hiram Maxim.

The new techniques of mass production with interchangeable parts also found early application in the sewing machine. The American firm of Isaac Singer marketed this first domestic appliance on a worldwide scale after the 1850s. The same techniques, further rationalized, made possible in the twentieth century the production of automobiles on assembly lines. Mass production, in the proud words of the pioneer Henry Ford, was "the focusing upon a manufacturing system of the principle of power, accuracy, system, continuity, and speed."

The technology and organization of the second industrial revolution was different from that of the first. First, the new technologies required far greater amounts of capital than early textile innovators or even the eighteenth-century ironmasters had required. Until the coming of the railroads, entrepreneurs had tended to form closed partnerships that expanded primarily by ploughing back profits into the enterprise. The scale of the new industries placed family firms and partnerships at a disadvantage, except for a few giants such as the firm of Friedrich and Alfred Krupp, the "cannon kings" of the Ruhr. The solutions to this financial bottleneck, especially after midcentury, were the joint-stock company and large-scale bank loans to industry. Giant enterprises, bank financing, and close connections to the state became and remained conspicuous characteristics of German industry, and of those of many other followers. Britain, by contrast, resisted concentration and thus increasingly missed out on the economies of scale from which giant enterprises usually profit.

The second characteristic of the new technologies that aided the followers was a close connection to science. The inspired tinkerers that led the first industrial revolution shared the analytical, problem-solving, empirical cast of mind that had made the scientific revolution. But their discoveries had originated in workshop and forge, not in the laboratory. And their achievements were those of individual brilliance, not of teamwork. The new metallurgical, chemical, and electrical industries were different. From the beginning, the contribution of scientific theory to practice was great and ever-growing. Science-intensive industries in turn required ever larger numbers of scientists and trained technicians. The sheer size of the new enterprises required a group effort of management, scientists, and technicians.

In France, state institutions such as the *École Polytechnique* and lesser provincial institutes filled the gap in knowledge. But it was the reforming bureaucrats of Germany that triumphed in the new world of applied science and teamwork. Universal primary education and a widespread network of technical schools in many German states from the 1820s had no parallel on the continent, or anywhere else except perhaps the United States after mid-century. Britain, where primary education did not become compulsory until 1880 and where the elite

studied Latin and Greek but not chemistry, suffered accordingly. By 1872 the University of Munich alone had more graduate research chemists than all English universities combined. And German and American management proved remarkably skilled at the large-scale organization of research, development, and production.

The followers inevitably developed at different rates and achieved widely varying results. Belgium and France started first, in the 1820s. Belgium probably became the first society after Britain whose industry produced more by value than its agriculture. But it lacked the population and resources to be more than a minor industrial power. France was a potential rival to Britain, but it suffered from major constraints. Until the railway boom of the 1850s its communications were poor. Its large peasant sector acted as a drag on the rest of the economy, lessening demand. Above all, old habits of mind died hard. The French entrepreneur, with some exceptions, bowed to the social pressures of a society that despite Revolution and Terror remained less competitive and more hierarchical than Britain's. The French and even the Germans tended until quite late to see business as a zero-sum game in which victory came only at the expense of others—who also had their right to a "fair" living. Robber-baron success appeared antisocial. The French economy grew steadily, but industry's share of the national product did not surpass that of agriculture until 1909.

Germany and the United States took up the British challenge most fully. By the end of the century, thanks to the coal and iron of the Ruhr and to economic unity bloodily achieved in 1866–71 (see pp. 744–51), Germany had surpassed Britain. Pig iron output increased 20-fold between 1850 and 1870. Giants such as Krupps or the Borsig engineering works in Berlin dominated the production of locomotives, machinery, and engines of destruction. In chemicals, great firms such as AGFA, Höchst, and BASF captured 90 percent of the world market for synthetic dyes by 1900. AEG and Siemens, the electric giants, achieved positions in the world market that only their counterparts in the United States rivalled.

The economic development of the United States was if anything even more spectacular than Germany's. Growth rested on several factors. Land, once violently cleared of Indians, was "free." Vast mineral resources, from Appalachian coal to the Mesabi iron range to the gold of California, fuelled development. The highest birth rate in the West and the immigration of 30 million people between 1845 and 1914 provided enough labor to meet needs, but not so much to depress wages or to discourage the introduction of labor-saving machinery. Relatively high wages in turn promoted consumer demand.

Mechanization began in textile production, as in Britain, in the 1770s in the water-powered mills of New England. Eli Whitney's cotton gin (1793), which separated fibers from seeds quickly and cheaply, helped create a boom in the slave South. Cotton shipments to the mills of Massachusetts and Lancashire leapt upwards. By 1840 the United States had already passed Britain in steam engine horsepower. The Erie Canal, opened in 1825, cut across the Appalachians and connected the industry of the East with the grain of the Midwest. After 1830 railroads opened up sources of coal and iron and fed ever larger cities. Large farms and a relative shortage of labor encouraged a mechanization of agriculture on a scale undreamed of elsewhere. Cyrus McCormick's reaper (1831), the railroad, and the steamship allowed grain from the Great Plains to undersell European grain in European markets by the 1870s. Refrigeration, invented in the 1830s, made possible by the 1880s the mass distribution and export of meat. And in heavy industry, the United States created a Ruhr that stretched from Pittsburgh to Chicago

and outclassed all rivals. By 1914 the industrial output of the United States was almost 80 percent that of all Western Europe.

Last of the early followers came Italy, Russia, and Japan. Italy broke into rapid growth in the first decade of the new century, but its depressed agriculture and shortage of energy resources held it back until after 1945. Russia and Japan were the first cases of a phenomenon increasingly familiar later in the new century—the industrialization of societies that were either partially (Russia) or wholly (Japan) non-Western in politics and culture. Economic growth in both cases was spectacular. But political and cultural traditions did not always encourage the sober use of the unprecedented power that industrialization brought.

The second industrial revolution and the industrialization of the followers made a true world market. Before the French revolutionary wars Europe's mercantile world economy had shown some signs of the now familiar boom and bust pattern of the business cycle. The depression that followed the wars of the French Revolution had been unusually severe and widespread. By mid-century, transport and communications had begun to weld the world together. The California gold strike and an outbreak of railway fever fuelled an American, European, and world boom that broke in the first true world depression, the panic of 1857. Further growth culminated in a second collapse in 1873. That crash inaugurated a 20-year period of falling prices known misleadingly as the nineteenth century "great depression." The term is a misnomer because this was a period of unparalleled growth in output for the followers, especially Germany and the United States. Falling prices caused dislocation, especially in European agriculture. But they were a sign of health, a sign of the abundance that the mechanization of industry, agriculture, and transport made possible. And after

1896 a new boom lifted the world economy, with a brief interruption in 1907, until 1913.

THE INDUSTRIAL REVOLUTION: HUMAN AND SOCIAL CONSEQUENCES

The Industrial Revolution inevitably transformed or helped transform underlying features of all societies it touched—standard of living and life expectancy, the location and occupations of the population, the structure of the social hierarchy, and the character of the basic human unit, the family.

The Rise in Living Standards and Life Expectancy

England, along with Holland and the infant United States, had enjoyed the highest living standard before indus-

trialization. It preserved that lead throughout the nineteenth century except against the United States. Advance was nevertheless far from smooth; Britain, in particular, paid the price of pioneering. From the 1790s to the 1840s English real wages (wages adjusted for the cost of living) appear to have stagnated. The peak of the birth rate coincided with the triumph of the factories over domestic handicrafts. In addition, after the 1790s women and children made up an increasing proportion of the work force in factories and mines. Entrepreneurs could pay them less and dominate them more effectively than they could men. Factory work and the filth of the improvised industrial cities dragged life expectancy down below that of most rural areas.

In the realm of intangibles, the workers of the early Industrial Revolution also suffered. They exchanged the familiar if want-racked countryside or

The new industrial city, crowded and sooty. London by Gustav Doré.

small-town workshop for filthy slum streets and "dark satanic mills" enveloped in clouds of coal soot. The "Black Country" around Birmingham came by its name honestly. The workers exchanged the tyranny of the seasons and of crop blights for that of the tireless machine. Breaking the new industrial labor force to the discipline of the clock was one of the major challenges facing the early entrepreneurs. Workers long resisted the habit of regularity, of arriving for work on Mondays or arriving sober on Tuesdays. And the tyranny of the business cycle replaced that of nature. Overproduction or disruption of normal trade patterns could spell unemployment and massive distress for entire regions. The "cotton famine" that resulted from the U.S. Civil War (1861–65) caused near starvation in industrial Lancashire. In the new cities, overcrowding, poverty, and the sudden release from the traditional religious and social restraints of the tight rural community led to widespread illegitimacy, alcoholism, and prostitution.

But after 1840 conditions slowly improved. Between 1851 and 1878, British per capita real income increased by a startling 30 percent. Until 1900 it continued to rise at the unprecedented rate of between 17 and 25 percent per decade. And workers worked less; the average (estimated) workweek in British industry declined from almost 60 hours in the 1860s to around 53 hours in 1900. In Europe as a whole the estimated average workweek dropped from an appalling 84 hours in 1850 to 60 hours in 1910.

A dramatic increase in life expectancy reflected and paralleled the rise in real income. The crucial factor was a decline in infant mortality. The death rate of infants aged under one year dropped in England from 36 percent in 1751–60 to 11.7 percent in 1906–10. France's infant mortality after the turn of the twentieth century was slightly higher than Britain's, and Sweden's somewhat lower. Russia's remained at 25 percent as late as 1900–09. Adults

also lived longer. The drop in infant mortality and greater longevity together raised life expectancy in western Europe from below 40 years in 1840 to the mid-50s by 1900. That rapid change was unparalleled in human history.

What did this mean for the bulk of the population? For the first time, appreciable numbers of people began living significantly above subsistence level and consuming an ever-increasing variety of goods. Already in the 1780s English workers had come to expect tea, coffee, sugar, and inexpensive cottons. After 1850 workers paid an ever-decreasing proportion of their wages for food and lodging. They began to have money and time to spend on leisure and entertainment.

Industrialization naturally did not distribute its benefits equally. The elites had always lived better and longer than those at the bottom of the social pyramid. And industrialization opened the *relative* gap between rich and poor: the rich grew richer faster than the poor. The concentration of wealth therefore increased. The immense fortunes of the entrepreneurs generated envy in the increasingly politically conscious workers and fear in the landowning elites which had until now dominated society. That trend had political consequences.

Urbanization and Emigration

The new age also brought migrations unprecedented since the fall of the Roman Empire. Population growth dictated movement. The agricultural countryside simply could not support the increase in numbers after 1750. The growth of industry encouraged movement by providing jobs. After 1850 the revolution in transportation, the railroad and the steamship, made movement on an unprecedented scale possible. The result was urbanization and emigration.

Urbanization, the concentration of the population in cities, was most conspicuous in Britain, where the monster city, London, had long been the largest in western Europe. In 1800 it contained about 12 percent of Britain's total population (see Figure 24-6). By 1890 over 60 percent of the British lived in cities of over 10,000. German and Belgian figures were in the 30 percent range, and France's only 25 percent. Where sheep had grazed a generation or two before stood the largely unplanned cities of Manchester and Birmingham and the mine tailings and slag heaps of the Ruhr and the Pas-de-Calais. Not until after mid-century did the new cities gradually receive sewage systems, relatively clean water supplies, and housing that even remotely approximated the population's needs.

Emigration was the alternative to the cities. It tended to affect all countries with high rates of population increase, whether they led or followed industrially. Britain grew from 8.9 million in 1801 to 32.5 million in 1901, but nevertheless gave up millions of emigrants. Germany, between the "hungry forties" and the maturing of its industrial economy by 1900, gave up perhaps 5 million emigrants. France, with its stable peasant economy, low birth rate, and slow industrialization, showed a unique pattern of low emigration.

Predominantly agricultural countries also participated in this continent-wide migration. Ireland, after the famine, gave up roughly 3 million emigrants up to 1900. Scandinavian emigration peaked in the 1880s. Emigration from relatively backward areas such as Russia, Spain, and Italy continued to increase until World War I cut it short in 1914. Italy, with its overpopulated South and late industrialization, gave up an unprecedented 880,000 emigrants in 1913. The recipient of most of this great migration was the United States, which took 82 percent of all transatlantic emigration in 1866–70 and was still taking 61 percent in 1896–1900.

The combined effect of urbanization and emigration was to open up the old rural societies, as well as creating new social relations in the new cities and

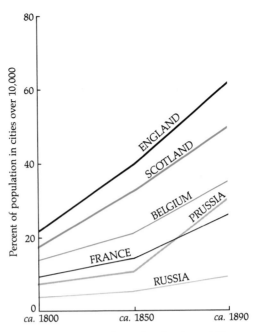

FIGURE 24-6   The Urbanization of Europe

the new lands across the oceans. Returnees from the cities and even from the New World (10 million people went back to Europe between 1886 and 1915) brought new ideas into the narrow agricultural communities from which they had escaped. Compulsory military service, which became almost universal after 1870, had similarly broadening effects. The knowledge that better or at least profoundly different patterns of life existed elsewhere was itself a powerful solvent of what remained of the old order.

Social Structure

The continent-wide transformation weakened old social groups and created new ones. The rapid rise of a new business elite undermined the social power of the nobility far more than the events of 1789 had done. In Britain the aristocracy controlled perhaps 20 percent of the national product in 1820. By 1850 that proportion had sunk to 10 percent. A decline in the role of agriculture paralleled that of the nobility, the elite that defined itself by ownership of

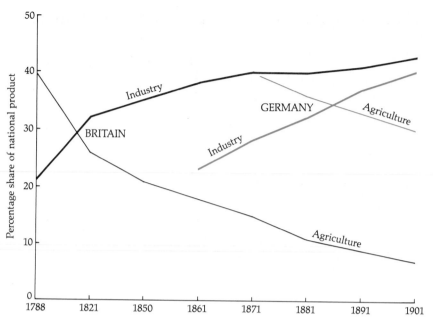

FIGURE 24-7   The Triumph of Industry over Agriculture: Germany and Britain

land. In the extreme case of Britain, decline was so precipitous that by 1901 less than 5 percent of the population actually worked in agriculture or fishing. France, as usual, resisted the trend. Simultaneously, the industrial population and the proportion of the national wealth that industry produced swiftly increased (see Figure 24-7). Industry's proportion of the national product passed agriculture before 1820 in Britain, around 1890 in Germany, and in the first decade of the new century in France.

In the new cities, the middle classes expanded rapidly. By the end of the century they made up a far larger proportion of the total population than ever before—from perhaps 20 percent in northwestern Europe to 5 percent in the south and east. The middle classes consisted first of all of the entrepreneurs, the driving force and chief beneficiaries of the new age of cotton, coal, and steam. Then came the professional middle classes, the ever-growing ranks of lawyers, doctors, higher bureaucrats, professors, and professional intellectuals. They lived not from entre-

preneurship but from intellectual work. The nineteenth century was theirs as no other century has been, for the nobility had lost its monopoly of power and the masses were as yet hesitant in pressing their claims.

Below the entrepreneurial and professional middle classes, new groups proliferated. Increasing specialization of work paralleled and influenced the increasing number of subtle gradations in the social hierarchy. The artisans and home handicraft workers, victims of the machine, dwindled. Only the continued existence of trades difficult to mechanize fully, such as clothing manufacture, guaranteed their continued existence. Alongside this "old lower middle class" of distressed artisans, there grew a "new lower middle class" of white collar workers in government or business bureaucracies. This group was as characteristic of the new age as the industrial workers below it.

The lower classes divided into numerous subcategories. Peasants and landless rural laborers stood at the bottom of the hierarchy in the country-

Women in the industrial work force: slitting pen nibs in a Birmingham factory (1851).

side. A large class of domestic servants made possible the leisured existence of the new middle classes. The industrial workers themselves were anything but uniform. They ranged from the "labor aristocracy," skilled iron and steel workers, machinists, and foremen, to unskilled or semiskilled workers at starvation wages. Below the working classes was an underclass of pickpockets, prostitutes, and beggars, sometimes organized into elaborate hierarchies, but often anarchic and always violent.

The lines between groups remained far more fluid than under the old society of orders on the Continent. Becoming an entrepreneur was relatively easy at first, at least in Britain, but class lines hardened as the century wore on. The amount of capital needed to enter industry increased dramatically with the advent of the steam engine and still more with the second industrial revolution. The new cities, unlike the old, were segregated by class. Workers had lived in attics and cellars, above and below the rich. In Manchester and Birmingham, the new rich instead retreated to villas in the countryside,

leaving the pestilential city centers to the poor. And the growth of an independent working-class culture and ideologies in response to the Industrial Revolution (see pp. 719–21) acted as a barrier to mobility. Those who did rise socially risked ostracism for "betraying their class."

From Traditional to Nuclear Family

Finally, the processes of industrialization and urbanization affected the very structure of the family and the role of women. Even before industrialization, the early modern family, with its extended kin networks and family ties based on subordination and respect, had begun to give way to the nuclear family of parents and children. The new nuclear family of parents and children, based at least in theory on love, may have existed in England since the late Middle Ages. It had in any case conquered the English middle classes by 1800. Family and workplace separated. The family became a private realm. The increasing fashion for romantic love as the chief rationale for marriage undermined the old role of the father as a monarch in miniature. Once children chose their own mates, patriarchal authority was under attack.

Similar developments, with a considerable lag, penetrated the urban areas of the Continent as well. First the upper middle classes adopted the new style, then the nobility. Finally it trickled down the social scale as the nineteenth century drew on. Increasing affluence, literacy, and longer lives encouraged the transition. Unlike the biological old regime, when plague or famine might at any moment strike down a spouse or child, affection was now a sounder emotional investment.

The new family structure hardly liberated women, but it did improve their status. The social conventions of romantic love ultimately sapped the Code Napoléon's attempts to bolster the power of the father, and eroded the all-dominance of the bewhiskered patriarchs of nineteenth-century Britain or Germany. A man could only with difficulty combine the roles of master, companion, and lover. And the separation of work from the home and the profusion of domestic servants meant that middle-class women had more leisure than before industrialization. A British male commentator noted in the 1850s that "the day is thrown idle on woman's hand. The thousand exciting events and under-takings that . . . stretch the faculties of man, are reckoned beyond her sphere." That leisure gave more and more educated women opportunity to reflect on their condition, and eventually to revolt against it.

By 1900, most of western Europe had passed through the fires of industrialization. Britain, Germany, and France had become industrial great powers. The United States had outstripped all rivals. Russia and Japan were beginning to overhaul Western Europe. Industrialization had transformed the ways of life of the peoples and classes it had touched. Some groups had lost; many more, despite the bitterness of the struggle, had won. And industrialization, along with that other revolution in France, had also helped transform the ideas and categories through which the West understood the world, and sought to change it.

Suggestions for Further Reading

The Pre-industrial World

On the world before industrialization, see the analysis of C. Cipolla, *Before the Industrial Revolution* (1975); for England, P. Laslett offers a quasi-nostalgic view in *The World We Have Lost* (1971). For the adventurous, F. Braudel, *Civilization and Capitalism, 15th–18th Centuries* (1982), provides an unparalleled guided tour of the pre-industrial world economy. C. McEvedy and F. Jones, *Atlas of World Population History* (1978), is first-rate.

Why the West, and Why Britain?

On the West's primacy and its causes, see especially D. Landes, *The Unbound Prometheus* (1972); E. L. Jones, *The European Miracle* (1981); W. O'Neill, *The Pursuit of Power* (1982); and N. Rosenberg and L. Birdzell, *How the West Grew Rich* (1986). For England's peculiarities, see the contrasting accounts of A. Macfarlane, *Marriage and Love in England* (1986), and L. Stone, *The Family,* *Sex, and Marriage in England 1500–1800* (1977), and the summary of recent demographic research in E. A. Wrigley, "The Growth of Population in Eighteenth-Century England," *Past and Present* (February, 1983), pp. 121–50. H. Perkin, *The Origins of Modern English Society 1780–1880* (1969), offers an excellent synthesis of the social causes of British industrialization.

The Industrial Revolution

On the interrelationship of technological change and economic growth, see above all D. Landes, *The Unbound Prometheus*. P. Deane, *The First Industrial Revolution* (1965), and E. Pawson, *The Early Industrial Revolution* (1979), are useful on Britain, as is T. S. Ashton, *The Industrial Revolution* (1970). On the industrialization of the followers, see T. Kemp, *Industrialization in Nineteenth-Century Europe* (1969), and C. Trebilcock, *The Industrialization of Continental Europe* (1981). B. Mitchell, *European Historical Statistics* (1981), is a useful source, and Paul Bairoch, "International Industrialization Levels from 1750 to 1980," *Journal of European Economic History* 2, no. 2, provides indispensable data on shifts in the economic balance of power. T. Hamerow, *The Birth of a New Europe* (1983), is a fine recent survey of the social and political consequences of industrialization.

25

The New Age: Theory and Practice

The twin revolutions in France and in the mills and iron foundries of Britain inevitably generated new ideas and profoundly modified old ones. The old certainties of religion, whether Catholic or Protestant, retained their validity for the great mass of the population of Europe throughout the nineteenth century. But religion gradually became central to fewer lives. Science appeared to undermine it. Urbanization and the decay of the traditional village community lessened its grip. In the realm of culture, a new movement, romanticism, fiercely attacked both the ideas and the style of the Enlightenment. In philosophy, two generations of Germans laid the foundations for much of nineteenth-century political thought. In politics, a "counter-Enlightenment" in some ways parallel to romanticism developed—conservatism, the ideology of opposition to revolutionary France and to all revolution. The antagonist of conservatism was the ill-assorted conglomerate of economic and political doctrines that goes by the name of liberalism. And beyond liberalism but related to it and locked in struggle with it came socialism, a ready-made political faith for the new industrial workers. Last of all, the French revolution's most powerful progeny, nationalism, spread eastward across Europe.

In the realm of practice, as opposed to theory, a variety of forces and tendencies modified European intellectual and social life. Literacy and increasing wealth brought into existence the phenomenon known as public opinion. Submerged social groups and categories, women and workers, began for the first time to make themselves heard.

THE FORCE OF IDEAS

Science and Scholarship

The nineteenth century opened new and unsuspected vistas. Mathematics, that abstruse discipline seemingly so remote from experience, equipped itself with the tools needed to inspire

Opposite: The climax of Chartism: rally at Kennington Common, London, April 1848.

700

Charles Darwin, father of modern biology and greatest scientific mind of the nineteenth century.

and describe the physical discoveries of the twentieth century. The creation of the first non-Euclidian geometry by a Russian, Nikolai Ivanovitch Lobachevsky (1793–1856) led to the invention of topology by Georg Friedrich Riemann (1826–66) of Göttingen. That, and the tensor calculus of Gregorio Ricci (1853–1925), in turn made possible the twentieth-century mathematics of space-time and gravity.

In physics, electricity and heat were the phenomena that nineteenth-century science explored most successfully. The discovery of electric current in 1786 led to Alessandro Volta's battery in 1799, to Hans Christian Oersted's discovery of a connection between magnetism and electricity of 1819, and to Michael Faraday's theory of electromagnetic induction of 1831. Ultimately James Clerk Maxwell, in his *Electricity and Magnetism* (1873) provided a mathematical synthesis suggesting that light was also an electromagnetic phenomenon. With electricity, advances in the laboratory created later technologies. The reverse occurred with the steam engine. It inspired Sadi Carnot, son of the Carnot of the Committee of Public Safety, to formulate in the 1820s generalizations that later physicists codified as the first and second laws of thermodynamics.

Chemistry's advance was even more spectacular than that of physics. John Dalton's sketch of an atomic theory in the first decade of the century opened the way for the study of chemical compounds and structures. The synthesis in 1828 of a compound found in nature, urea, opened the study of organic chemistry, the chemistry of carbon. By the 1860s, chemists had begun to explore the molecular structure of simple compounds such as benzene. In 1869 Dimitri Ivanovitch Mendeleev formulated a periodic law and table of elements that for the first time gave scientists a sketchy notion of some of the basic building blocks of the universe. It predicted the existence of elements as yet unknown; researchers using Mendeleev's theory isolated gallium (1871), scandium (1879), germanium (1886), and helium (1895).

But it was not until the end of the century that a series of breakthroughs on the boundary of chemistry and physics revolutionized science's picture of the world and placed the old Newtonian certainties in question. Wilhelm Roentgen's discovery of X rays (1895) soon led to the unearthing of radioactive elements that apparently emitted particles smaller than the atom. By the turn of the century the theoreticians Max Planck and Albert Einstein had begun to lay the foundations for a non-Newtonian physics that unified the universe of subatomic particles with that of space-time, and predicted the convertibility of matter into energy.

Biology, basically a creation of the nineteenth century, developed immediate practical uses after mid-century. The explorations of the world of bacteria by Louis Pasteur (1822–95) and Robert Koch (1843–1910) opened the door to an understanding of many diseases and aided Joseph Lister (1827–92) in the development of sterile surgical procedures.

But the greatest biological questions were theoretical. What caused the unparalleled diversity of life forms that eighteenth- and early nineteenth-century naturalists had classified? How had humanity originated? Studies in embryology in the 1820s implied that embryos, during their growth, might be recapitulating their species history, for bird embryos developed gill-slits. The study of fossils, still in its infancy, suggested change and development over immense periods of time. The discovery in 1856 of an apelike but large-brained skull at Neanderthal near the Ruhr implied that humanity might have nonhuman ancestors.

Geology, an entirely new science, appeared to offer corroboration. Charles Lyell's *Principles of Geology* (1830–33) provided the first satisfactory explanation of the Earth's physical features and their evolution. A variety of speculative thinkers suggested that life—and thus humanity as well—might also be the result of evolutionary processes. But the mechanism by which that evolution occurred was as yet a mystery. Jean Baptiste Lamarck, who invented the term "biology," proposed in 1809 that creatures acquired characteristics in response to changes in their environment and subsequently passed those characteristics to their offspring. That would account for diversity and change—if it were true.

It was Charles Darwin (1809–82) who most cogently suggested, after long investigations on the isolated Galápagos islands off Ecuador and elsewhere, that species evolved through a savage "struggle for life." Darwin announced that conclusion in 1858, after a fellow biologist, Alfred Russel Wallace (1823–1913), had sketched out a similar theory. The following year, Darwin published his path-breaking synthesis, *The Origin of Species by Means of Natural Selection, or the Preservation of Favored Races in the Struggle for Life*. Darwin argued, with a crushing weight of examples drawn from field research, that scarcity of food produced a fierce competition that killed off "unfit" variants of a given species before they could reproduce. "Sexual selection," or the triumph of the "fittest" males in competition for females further reinforced that mechanism. "Natural selection," working over immense spans of time, had produced the rich diversity visible in nature.

Darwin, although he recoiled from inevitable controversy with the religious establishment, ultimately extended his logic explicitly to humanity itself in *The Descent of Man* (1871): "Thus from the wars of nature, from famine and death, the most exalted object which we are capable of conceiving, namely the production of higher animals, directly follows." That claim, popularized in innumerable works by other "Darwinists," accomplished the most far-reaching revolution in the West's conception of itself since Copernicus had suggested that the Earth was not the motionless center of the universe. Darwin's explanation of humanity's place in the new world that science was uncovering made him the most widely influential scientific thinker of the century.

His theories also made him the father of modern biology. With a single powerful generalization he accounted for all the diversity of life. But Darwin's theory of evolution nevertheless had a major weakness: it accounted only for the change of *entire* species over time. Darwin could not provide a convincing physical cause for the all-important variations between *individuals* that drove those species changes. He fell back in part on Lamarck's untenable theory of the inheritance of acquired characteristics. Not until later did the long-neglected work of the Bohemian monk Gregor Mendel (1822–84), the father of genetics, provide the answer. In 1901 Hugo De Vries drew on Mendel's work to formulate a theory of genetic mutation by sudden random leaps. Subsequent experiments using the fast-multiplying fruit fly laid the groundwork of modern genetics, which explained individual variation and provided Darwin's basic insights with powerful support.

In the social sciences, the nineteenth century likewise opened a new age. The eccentric Auguste Comte (1798–1857) invented the word sociology, if not the discipline it describes. A revolution in sources, methods, and subjects transformed history—for better or worse—from a literary pastime into a scholarly profession. The German scholar Leopold von Ranke (1795–1886) laid down the doctrine that historians must first of all investigate and cross-check primary source materials, the evidence the historical actors themselves had left. Ranke's notion that the historian's duty was to reconstruct events "as they actually happened" was not new. Thucydides the Athenian had suggested something of the sort in his fifth-century B.C. history of the Peloponnesian War. But now, in the early nineteenth century, it was at last possible to attempt to translate that precept systematically into practice. In England, France, and Germany governments and private groups founded institutions such as London's Public Record Office for the collection and eventual publication of historical sources.

Vast multivolume national histories began to appear, monuments to the industry and learning of their authors, though, alas, not always readable. The Prussian professor of jurisprudence, Karl von Savigny (1779–1861) founded a historical school dedicated to explaining the evolution of law. He proclaimed the superiority of law grown by the slow accretion of precedent over the artificial law codes of the French.

Historical investigation even touched scripture. David Friedrich Strauss's *Life of Jesus* (1835) examined the Gospels as historical documents and expressed skepticism about their subject's divinity—and existence. The French intellectual Ernest Renan provoked outrage in the 1860s by describing Christ as "an incomparable man"; his biography of Christ was a popular success.

Finally, historians and philologists also began investigating the diversity of human languages and deriving general laws. A British scholar, Sir Henry Rawlinson, followed up Champollion's 1822 decipherment of hieroglyphics by reading Persian cuneiform inscriptions in 1835. German philologists studied shifts of consonants in numerous languages over many centuries, and deduced laws governing the evolution of languages. They demonstrated that the Indian language Sanskrit and most European languages shared a common Indo-European origin. That discovery helped open up the study of the prehistory of Europe and of South and Central Asia (see pp. 6–8).

Religion

Religious skepticism, as described in Chapter 21, had become commonplace among the educated in the course of the eighteenth century. The novelty of the nineteenth century was that detachment from religion began to spread among the masses. That was partly a consequence of politics. The American and French Revolutions, unlike the English Revolution of the 1640s, had been secular upheavals, and many French revolutionaries had been overtly anticlerical. Urbanization and its consequent social dislocation likewise sapped religion. In the improvised city of Birmingham in 1851 the churches could hold less than a third of the population. And many of the new industrial workers resented the churches' defense of the social status quo. Finally, the retreat from religion was in part a consequence of the same process of scientific advance that had inspired the deists and skeptics of the Enlightenment.

But the science of the nineteenth century appeared far more powerful, and less compatible with traditional religion, than that of the eighteenth century. Lyell's geology and Darwin's evolution placed in question the biblical account of creation. That above all affected Protestants (and to a lesser extent Jews), given the central place of the biblical texts in their beliefs. Darwin's work provoked a veritable "warfare of science and theology." The Archbishop of Canterbury, in a furious debate in 1860, sarcastically asked "Darwin's Bulldog," the biologist Thomas H. Huxley, which side of his family descended from apes. A minority of "fundamentalist" Protestants, especially strong in the United States, continued to assert the literal truth of the biblical account of creation. The majority, thanks to Protestantism's emphasis on the individual's freedom and direct relationship with God, made a variety of compromises between faith and reason.

Strong forces nevertheless counteracted the decline of religion. Women of the lower classes, submerged by custom and enforced illiteracy, tended to traditional piety. The rural masses held to their faith whether they remained at home or emigrated, as did so many Irish and Italians. Governments, whether of kings or liberals, continued to prize religion as a foundation for social order. Religion itself showed continued vitality and expansive force.

In England and the United States the nineteenth century was a time of intense religious ferment. The impetus of German Pietism and of its derivative, John Wesley's Methodism, were far from spent. Other Protestant sects expanded with equal rapidity. Waves of religious enthusiasm swept over South Wales, for instance, in 1807–09, 1828–30, 1839–48, 1854, and 1859. In America after 1800 a "Great Revival" moved westward with the frontier.

The politics of Wesley, the Pietists, and their offshoots tended to bolster the social order. In the words of the *Statutes of the Wesleyan Body* (1792), "the oracles of God" commanded obedience to the secular power. That attitude permeated English and American popular religion. Along with the early spread of democratic politics in those societies, it limited the appeal of the radical panaceas for the ills of *this* world so popular in continental Europe. And the spread of democracy helped the churches by providing a widely popular and easily defensible status quo.

European Catholicism was even more closely intertwined with the existing order than Protestantism, and after 1789 that order was under attack. Some advanced Catholic thinkers foresaw the need for the Church to distance itself from monarchy, lest the Church perish in monarchy's ruin. Félicité de Lamennais, a formerly ultraconservative French cleric, published *Words of a Believer* after the 1830 Paris revolution (see p. 730). It appealed for equality and democracy, and denounced "the passion to acquire and to possess." Rome damned Lamennais in two thundering encyclicals.

Pope Pius IX (r. 1846–78) appeared briefly as a champion of change. Then the revolutions of 1848 (see pp. 732–38) dissuaded him. His encyclical *Quanta cura* of 1864, with its appended *Syllabus*

errorum or "listing of errors," denounced the notion that "the Roman Pontiff can and ought to reconcile himself to and agree with progress, liberalism, and modern civilization." The reforming Pope Leo XIII (r. 1878–1903) reversed that uncompromising stance in a path-breaking encyclical of 1891 entitled *Rerum novarum* ("Of New Things"). The gradual de-christianization of the urban masses and the challenge of socialism had induced a rethinking. *Rerum novarum* was the charter of a new social and reforming Catholicism that condemned both capitalist greed and socialist denial of God. Leo XIII's successor, Pius X (r. 1903–14), reverted to rigid defense of received doctrine and purged the Church of "modernists" who sought to reconcile science with theology. But in the end it was Leo XIII's policy of adaptation to the new age that triumphed.

Romanticism

The notion of a new style, opposed to the rationalism and classicism of the Enlightenment (see pp. 612–13), emerged toward the end of the eighteenth century. The stormy young German writers of the "Sturm und Drang" movement of the 1780s, in particular, had defied convention and celebrated emotion. By 1800 German critics had coined the distinction between "classical" and "romantic." The term "romantic" has nevertheless escaped definition.

Some romantics, such as the great English poet George Gordon, Lord Byron (1788–1824), thought of themselves as revolutionaries: "I have simplified my politics into a detestation of all existing governments." The French poet, dramatist, and novelist Victor Hugo (1802–85) could write that "romanticism is liberalism in literature." Byron's friend Percy Bysshe Shelley (1792–1822) proclaimed that "poets are the unacknowledged legislators of the world." Heinrich Heine (1797–1856), the last major German romantic poet and the greatest German lyric poet of the century, was a life-long radical democrat. The French painter Eugène Delacroix (1798–1863) could paint, in *Liberty Leading the People* (1834), the quintessential romantic vision of the triumph of revolution (see p. 724).

Still other romantics, such as the English lyric poets William Blake (1757–1827) and William Wordsworth (1770–1850), outdid one another in their rejection of the "dark satanic mills" of the new age. In politics, Wordsworth's original enthusiam for the French Revolution gave way to bitter opposition even to modest Parliamentary reforms in England. Especially in Germany, romanticism turned increasingly into celebration of the Middle Ages, supposedly more authentic than the classical age, the Renaissance, or the alleged artificiality and frenchified rationalism of the detested eighteenth century. The eerie landscapes of Caspar David Friedrich (1774–1840), painted from imagination rather than life, well illustrate that preoccupation. In England, the medievalizing novels of Sir Walter Scott, the paintings of John Constable

and Joseph Turner, and the revival of Gothic as an architectural style embodied similar tendencies.

What the romantics, however diverse their politics and aesthetics, tended to share were four things. First, they rejected the eighteenth century's "classical" limitations on form and structure in art. In music, romantics from the unparalleled master of the symphony, Ludwig van Beethoven (1770–1827) to the dogmatic theorist and practitioner of "total opera," Richard Wagner (1813–83), gleefully disregarded inherited conventions of form, and of orchestra size and composition. Poets such as Wordsworth deliberately chose a poetic vocabulary closer to spoken English than to the measured couplets of predecessors such as Alexander Pope. Even continental drama discarded for good the restrictions on subject, time, and place that Aristotle's aesthetic theories had imposed.

Second, the romantics prized emotion, the stronger the better. That preoccupation led even former fellow travelers such as the great German poet

Cloister Graveyard in the Snow (1810), by Caspar David Friedrich.

Johann Wolfgang von Goethe (1749–1832) to conclude that "classic is that which is healthy, romantic that which is sick." The line between emotion and morbid self-preoccupation was narrow. But the romantic emphasis on the creative power of the individual's imagination was a liberating force. In combination with craftsmanship and self-discipline it could produce masterpieces.

Third, the romantics tended to celebrate nature. Their nature was not the manicured eighteenth-century ornamental garden, but the craggy uplands of Wordsworth's imagination:

> Once again
> Do I behold these steep and lofty cliffs
> That on a wild secluded scene impress
> Thoughts of more deep seclusion;
>   and connect
> The landscape with the quiet of the sky.

Rousseau, with his mystical *Reveries of a Solitary Wanderer* (1776–78) had shown the way. Nature, the "nature or God" of Spinoza, brought humanity—or at least skeptical intellectuals—closer to an otherwise unknowable God. The popularization of this "natural supernaturalism," as the English philosopher-historian Thomas Carlyle (1795–1881) called it, was one of the major legacies of romanticism.

Finally, the romantics both celebrated and embodied the cult of the solitary, youthful, misunderstood genius. The genius defied convention and perhaps suffered persecution for political radicalism, or like Byron, for sexual peccadillos. Like Shelley, the genius might be dead by 30; tuberculosis was as much the romantic disease as morbid introspection. The cult of the artist as misfit was in part an extension of romantic emphasis on imagination, on the creative powers of the individual. The collapse of aristocratic art patronage after 1789 may also have contributed, for the middle classes were not yet rich enough to step in. Age, respectability, and middle-class patrons nevertheless tamed those roman-

tics who survived. The movement did not outlast mid-century, but it broke Enlightenment formalism for good. Art was henceforth what the artist, the individual as towering genius, decreed it to be.

The Revolution in German Philosophy

Parallel to romanticism and not unrelated to it came an explosion of creativity in German philosophy. Misty speculation, including opposition to Newton's mathematically precise account of matter and motion, had long been a German specialty. Immanuel Kant (see p. 613) had sought to rescue reason from the skepticism of Enlightenment philosophers such as David Hume, who refused to accept as certain the evidence of the senses. Kant saved reason by limiting its domain. He postulated that the human mind was capable of limited knowledge of the world around it, but only on the basis of categories such as space and time, categories already built into the structure of the mind itself. Humanity could not perceive "things in themselves," things as they really were, except through those categories.

Kant's second main contribution was related to his theory of knowledge. Moral judgment was akin to the mind's inborn mechanism of perception, Kant argued. Morality was the result of a universal law found within ourselves. And for Kant, freedom was obedience to that law. The poet Heine rightly remarked that as a revolutionary, Kant put Robespierre in the shade. Kant's notion of morality, in particular, opened the way for individuals to discover moral standards for themselves. Kant was a loyal supporter of the Prussian state, but his doctrine struck at the root of any claim to authority that individuals chose not to accept.

Kant's theory of knowledge provoked his successors, especially Johann Gottlieb Fichte (1762–1814) and Georg Friedrich Wilhelm Hegel (1770–1831) to a decisive step. Fichte saw the implau-

Johann Wolfgang von Goethe, greatest of German poets, from a medal of 1829.

sibility of saying that things-in-themselves existed but that the mind could not know them. If the mind knew about them, they must exist. Rather than falling back into Enlightenment rationalism, Fichte and Hegel took a leap of faith even greater than Kant's. Both things-in-themselves and the mind must be part of a larger whole, a universal consciousness, an all-encompassing "world spirit" that was a descendant of Spinoza's "nature or God."

Hegel, the most influential philosopher of the century, proclaimed that history was the process of the self-realization of that world spirit. History thus had a goal. It also had a mechanism, the "dialectic," a step-by-step progress through a series of reversals or negations. It had already passed through three stages: the oriental, in which the despot alone was free; the ancient world, in which a few men in Greece and Rome had been free; and the Christian-Germanic civilization of northern Europe, which had at last recognized that humanity itself was or could be free.

In this process, this ever-upward striving toward the self-realization of the world spirit, the role of the individual was clear. Kant's self-determining individual must will an ever-closer identification with the world spirit. Hegel, as befitted a professor of philosophy at the University of Berlin, came to identify the world spirit with the Prussian power-state: "The State is the divine Idea as it exists on earth." Others took Kant's notion of self-determination and Hegel's goal-oriented theory of history, and put them to uses which their originators could hardly have foreseen.

Conservatism

Although Hegel inclined toward defense of the status quo, the doctrines that have acquired the name of conservatism had entirely different sources. First and most important was the Anglo-Irish Tory, Edmund Burke (1729–97). His inspired diatribe of 1790, *Reflections on the Revolution in France,* was uncannily prophetic. It still reads as if written in 1793–94, against the background of war and Terror. Burke denounced the doctrinaire logic of the French revolutionaries, whose "rage and frenzy will pull down more in half an hour than prudence, deliberation, and foresight can build in a hundred years." His model was the English constitution, that agglomeration of custom and precedent which over many centuries had created what freedom existed in Britain. Organic growth, not radical panaceas, was the only sound basis for a polity. Change was admissible, although "when I changed it should be to preserve." Even revolution, as in 1688 and 1776, might be permissible if it reasserted a historic tradition. But plans for change should not assume human perfectibility. They should postulate, on the basis of long sad experience, the "ignorance and fallibility of mankind."

Burke's commitment to individual liberty, which had led him to sympathize with the complaints of the American colonists, did not survive his translation into French and German. Burke militant, the Burke who wrote in 1796 that "it is with an *armed doctrine* that we are at war," was the Burke who inspired continental conservatives to create their own armed doctrines of counterrevolution. Joseph de Maistre (1754–1821), the most lively of the French conservative theorists, acknowledged Burke's influence. But his doctrine had little place for freedom: "All power, all discipline, are based on the executioner. He is at once the horror of human society and the tie that binds it together. . . . " In Germany, admirers of Burke invoked his name to support notions of a return to divine-right monarchy and medieval Christianity. That was not conservatism, but "reaction," an attempt to erase everything after 1789.

Liberalism

Conservatism or reaction was the faith of what became, from its place in the seating arrangements of the post-1815 French assemblies, the "Right." Liberalism was the creed of the "Left." Like most "isms," the term is exceedingly vague. It has so broadened in the twentieth century that it now conveys a mood rather than a body of ideas.

Nineteenth-century liberalism was narrower. It meant, first of all, a body of economic thought that preached *laissez-faire,* the removal of all artificial constraints on the market. In politics, nineteenth-century liberalism stood, more or less squarely, for individual freedom and for equality of opportunity if not of outcome. Political liberalism—like Locke, its founding father—identified liberty with property; that was the link between political and economic liberalism. Liberalism was an optimistic creed, uniting capitalism and individualism under the banner of "progress," that faith of the Enlightenment. Liberalism was the creed of the middle classes, to whom the explosive growth of industry and trade gave increasing self-confidence.

The "classical economists," of whom the three most conspicuous were Adam Smith (1723–90), Thomas Robert Malthus (1766–1834), and David Ricardo (1772–1823), asked many of the questions that still preoccupy economists. Smith and Ricardo in particular argued that the market alone could efficiently allocate resources. The "hidden hand" of supply and demand, by a self-operating law, would maximize the increase in wealth.

In his *Essay on the Principle of Population* (1798, revised 1803), Malthus explored the relationship between population and food. He concluded gloomily that "population, when unchecked, increases in a geometrical ratio. Subsistence only increases in an arithmetical ratio." Malthus's generalization that population—"when unchecked"—tends to outrun food made

nineteenth-century economics the "dismal science." It also provided Darwin with his principle of the "struggle for survival" in the face of inevitable scarcity.

But Malthus qualified his theory in an important way that escaped many later critics. A "preventive check" on population increase existed: the tendency in Europe and especially in Britain for men and women to marry late, and hence have fewer children than the biological maximum. Malthus theorized that "moral restraint" or a growing taste for consumer luxuries might induce individuals to procreate less. Eventually, such tendencies could lead to a shortage of labor, and "in the natural course of things" to a rise in wages. Malthus was a prophet of affluence as well as of doom.

His contemporary Ricardo had less foresight. In his *Principles of Political Economy and Taxation* (1817), the last great work of classical economics, Ricardo proclaimed what soon became known as the "iron law of wages." Since labor supply supposedly increased geometrically, wages would always remain just above starvation level. Raising wages above that level would merely encourage procreation. That would in turn increase the supply of labor until wages once more dropped. Generosity toward the workers was thus futile, even pernicious. Ricardo's misunderstanding of Malthus was highly convenient to the mill owners, hard men reared in a hard school. They enthusiastically embraced his doctrine. Economic science had shown conclusively, Ricardo's popularizers trumpeted, that poverty was inevitable and that efforts to avert it would produce ever more poverty.

Ricardo's other major contribution was to systematize a concept found in Adam Smith's work that had profound political implications. That was the "labor theory of value," the notion that the "value" of a manufactured article was proportional to the amount of labor required to make it. Ricardo used

Portrait medal of Adam Smith (1797).

Thomas Robert Malthus, pioneer of the study of population growth.

Jeremy Bentham contemplating "the greatest happiness of the greatest number."

John Stuart Mill, the conscience of nineteenth-century liberalism.

the theory to explain where profits came from. For him they were the difference between the cost of labor per article to the industrialist and the selling price of the article, after the deduction of the industrialist's overhead costs. Ricardo applauded profit; others could and did use his work to argue that profits were "surplus value" stolen from the workers.

The political ideas of nineteenth-century liberalism in part contradicted the "dismal science." The English philosopher and reformer Jeremy Bentham (1748–1832), the key figure in the transition from Enlightenment to nineteenth-century liberal thought, rejected the Lockean tradition of "natural rights." Instead, as befitted an age of machinery, Bentham postulated that "utility" must guide humanity. Bentham's utility dictated the search for "the greatest happiness of the greatest number," and he defined happiness merely as "pleasurable feelings and . . . freedom from pain." Translated into politics, that meant that the best government delivered the most pleasure and the least pain to the most people. "Utilitarianism" or "philosophic radicalism" legitimized democracy through utility rather than through natural rights. It also legitimized social engineering. "Utility," for Bentham, dictated the regimentation of the poor by their intellectual betters.

Bentham's most influential successor, John Stuart Mill (1806–73), drove Benthamite liberalism to one possible logical conclusion, and inevitably made himself unpopular. As a child prodigy, he had begun learning Greek at three under the supervision of his father James Mill, disciple of Bentham and a historian of India. As an adult, John Stuart Mill ran the examinations for the elite Indian Civil Service. His *On Liberty* (1859) proclaimed utility as "the ultimate appeal in all ethical questions." Government was suspect: "That government is best that governs least." Mill asserted that "the only purpose for which power can rightfully be exer-

cised over any member of a civilized community, against his will, is to prevent harm to others."

Mill, like Bentham, deduced that utility demanded democratic government. But what if that government, faced with the horrors of the contemporary factory system and with the plight of the poor, demanded limits on the economic freedom of the entrepreneur? Mill ultimately came to the conclusion that the state must intervene to protect children and improve living and working conditions. He also took up the domination of men over women. After raising the issue of votes for women in Parliament in 1867, he published *The Subjection of Women* (1869). The work largely derived from ideas that his wife, Harriet Taylor Mill, had already put forward. It scandalized middle-class opinion by insisting that women, too, should enjoy liberty. That demand followed from Mill's premises and from those of nineteenth-century liberalism generally. But few accepted that in the 1860s.

On the Continent, liberalism was more cautious than in Britain, as befitted the relative weakness of the middle classes until industrialization was well under way. In politics, constitutionalism before liberty was the preference of Benjamin Constant (1767–1830), France's answer to Bentham. Constant proclaimed liberty as "the object of all human association" but resisted extension of France's limited franchise. German liberals (see p. 739) tended to confuse national self-assertion with liberty. And in the realm of economics, French and German thinkers resisted the full force of *laissez-faire*, with its potential for dissolving all traditional social ties. Some German economists challenged liberal orthodoxy frontally. The influential Friedrich List (1789–1846) argued that industrialization in the face of British competition required a neo-mercantilist planned economy, protective tariffs, and state-supported railway construction.

Socialism

Despite its internal contradictions, economic and political liberalism was a thumping success as a secular religion of progress for the middle classes. Inevitably, it summoned up a counter-ideology, "socialism." The term, almost as indefinable as liberalism, implies concern for the good of society as a whole, in opposition to liberalism's focus on individual liberty, property, and profit. Socialism and its overlapping but more extreme companion, "communism," had a pedigree going back at least to the abortive Paris rising of Gracchus Babeuf and the "Equals" in 1796. But after 1815, as industrialization gathered force, it acquired new meaning.

Middle-class thinkers began to postulate an irrepressible enmity between workers and industrialists. Ricardo's economics, with its emphasis on inherent conflicts of interest between labor, capital, and landed wealth, provided tools for a radical attack on existing society. In England, a successful entrepreneur, Robert Owen (1771–1858), presented an alternative vision. Abolition of the profit motive and its replacement by "cooperation" would remake humanity, which in predictable Enlightenment fashion Owen saw as a product of its environment. Across the Channel, Charles Fourier (1772–1837) pressed similar notions, which included the foundation of "phalanxes," or self-sufficient model agrarian communities. Owen demonstrated the fallacy of Ricardo's "iron law" by raising wages and providing housing for the workers in his model factories at New Lanark, Scotland, while simultaneously increasing output and profits. His later attempt to found a utopia at New Harmony, Indiana, was less successful.

Robert Owen's vision of New Harmony, his utopian community in the Indiana wilderness.

Karl Marx, the bourgeois patriarch (right), with his wife, two daughters, and Friedrich Engels in the 1860s.

Marx the Determinist Philosopher of History

In the social production of their existence, men enter into definite, predetermined relationships that are independent of their will. Those relations of production correspond to a given stage of the development of material productive forces. The totality of those relations of production forms the economic structure of the society, the real base, upon which a juridical and political superstructure rises, and to which given forms of social consciousness correspond. The mode of production of material life conditions the social, political, and intellectual life process itself. It is not the consciousness of men that determines their existence, but rather the reverse: their social existence determines their consciousness.

From Karl Marx, preface to *A Contribution to the Critique of Political Economy* (1859), (translation by M. Knox).

A sterner prophet than Owen or Fourier was the French Count Henri de Saint-Simon (1760–1825). Although frequently classed with the "utopian" socialists Owen and Fourier, Saint-Simon was no enthusiast for model communities. He was the first to conceive of socialism as the outcome of an inexorable historical process affecting the whole of society. He prophesied that in the new society "rule over men" would give way to "the administration of things." His brave new world would be an earthly paradise in which *École Polytechnique* technocrats tamed nature for good with immense engineering projects. He was thus not only a father of socialism, but also the inspiration of the heroic age of French engineering that produced the Suez Canal (1869) and the first railroad tunnels through the Alps.

The theory that came to dominate European socialism, although it owed something to Saint-Simon, derived above all from a strange marriage between the misty realms of Hegelian philosophy and the apparent rigor of classical economics. Karl Marx (1818–83), a German Jew from the Prussian Rhineland, and Friedrich Engels, the scholarly son of a prosperous Rhineland industrialist, were its fathers. Marx became interested in philosophy while studying law at the University of Berlin, and gravitated to the "Left Hegelians." These followers of the recently dead Hegel had discovered that his dialectic, that process by which the world spirit constantly struggled for greater self-realization through successive negations, provided a basis for attacks on all existing ideas and institutions.

Following the example of Kant and Hegel, Marx set out to create a system. By 1844–46, he had arrived with Engels's help at a preliminary synthesis. Marx retained Hegel's dialectical mechanism and goal-oriented stage theory of history. But he replaced Hegel's mystical world spirit with humanity as a species. From another Left-Hegelian, the rigorous materialist Ludwig Feuerbach ("Man is what he eats"), Marx took the notion that humanity's essence was work. Human nature was to be a "free producer." But under capitalism, as Ricardo had seemingly demonstrated, humanity lost the product of its labor through the capitalist's appropriation of "surplus value." Under capitalism, Marx added, private property and specialization of work ("division of labor") had "alienated" humanity from its true nature as "free producer." Marx's theory was a sophisticated Hegelian version of the romantic and utopian socialist rejection of existing industrial society.

But for Marx, unlike his "utopian" predecessors, history would inexorably remedy the ills of past and present. Marx translated Hegel's dialectic of world spirit, of humanity's self-realization, into economics. Marx joked that he had stood Hegel "right side up," and discovered the "rational kernel within the mystical shell." Work, not the world spirit, powered history. Successive "modes of production," succeeding one another dialectically, created new modes of consciousness, new stages in the upward progress of the spirit. And instead of Hegel's oriental, ancient, and Germanic-Christian stages of history, Marx discerned a progression from ancient slave society, through "feudalism," to industrial capitalism, to communism.

For the dialectic expressed itself politically as the struggle between economic classes: "The history of all existing society is the history of class struggle." That struggle now pitted the new working class, the "proletariat" born of the industrial revolution, against the capitalist "bourgeoisie." That struggle, Marx confidently predicted, would end with "the victory of the proletariat," since capitalist industrialization created ever-larger numbers of ever more impoverished proletarians. And the proletariat's victory would bring the end of history—or rather of what Marx called "the prehistory of human society." For the proletariat, the class supposedly more al-

ienated than any other in history from humanity's essence as "free producer," had a historical mission. Victorious revolution would turn philosophy into reality: "The government of persons is replaced by the administration of things, and by the conduct of the processes of production. The state is not 'abolished.' *It withers away.*"

Marx had elaborated the main lines of his vision even before writing the fa-

Marx the Revolutionary Prophet

The history of all hitherto existing society is the history of class struggles.

Freeman and slave, patrician and plebeian, lord and serf, guildmaster and journeyman, in a word, oppressor and oppressed, stood in constant opposition to one another, carried on an uninterrupted, now hidden, now open fight, a fight that each time ended, either in a revolutionary re-constitution of society at large, or in the common ruin of the contending classes. . . .

The modern bourgeois society that has sprouted from the ruins of feudal society has not done away with class antagonisms. It has but established new classes, new conditions of oppression, new forms of struggle in place of the old ones.

Our epoch, the epoch of the bourgeoisie, possesses, however, this distinctive feature: it has simplified the class antagonisms: Society as a whole is more and more splitting up into two great hostile camps, into two great classes directly facing each other: Bourgeoisie and Proletariat. . . .

All previous historical movements were movements of minorities, or in the interests of minorities. The proletarian movement is the self-conscious, independent movement of the immense majority, in the interests of the immense majority. . . .

The advance of industry, whose involuntary promoter is the bourgeoisie, replaces the isolation of the laborers, due to competition, by their revolutionary combination, due to association. The development of Modern Industry, therefore, cuts from under its feet the very foundation on which the bourgeoisie produces and appropriates products. What the bourgeoisie, therefore, produces, above all, is its own grave-diggers. Its fall and the victory of the proletariat are equally inevitable.

From Karl Marx and Friedrich Engels, *The Communist Manifesto* (1848).

mous *Communist Manifesto* with which he and Engels sought unsuccessfully to influence the 1848 revolutions (see pp. 732–38). Marx spent the next 35 years as an exile in the center of world capitalism, London. There, drawing on the immense resources of the hospitable British Museum library, Marx fitted out his Hegelian framework with economic evidence that he believed proved its validity.

In *Capital,* the great unfinished work that began to appear in 1867 and set forth his system in its most elaborate form, Marx analyzed and damned the "capitalist mode of production." Its essence was greed: the capitalist was " . . . capital personified. His soul is the soul of capital." Capital was "dead labor, which, vampire-like, lives only by sucking living labor, and lives the more, the more labor it sucks." This demonic vision of capitalism had much in common with Marx's views on Judaism, as set forth in his notorious *On the Jewish Question* (1843). There, in pathological language, he had proclaimed that "money is the jealous God of Israel," and demanded an end to "the *empirical* essence of Judaism— huckstering."

Marx's system was at least four things: a philosophy of history, an economic theory, an analysis of society, and a call to revolution. The philosophy of history foundered on both logical and empirical grounds. Logically, no system can describe the "meaning" of history, as Marx or Hegel claimed to do. Neither the whole past nor the future is knowable. Statements about the meaning and destination of something in part unknowable are either guesses or professions of faith.

Empirically, most of Marx's professions of faith have fared badly, although he and Engels described them as "scientific." Capitalist industrialization has not produced societies polarized into ever-larger masses of ever more degraded proletarians and ever-smaller groups of ever-richer capitalists. Revolution has *not* come to the most advanced capitalist countries.

Capitalism has not collapsed. Instead, capitalist industrialization has led to relative affluence and to an ever-broadening number of social sub-categories (see pp. 695–97). In the most advanced countries it is the industrial proletariat, not the state, that has withered.

In addition, Marx's apparent assertion that economics determines all else has caused perplexity. If on the one hand the economic "base" strictly and directly determines the political-ideological "superstructure," much of recorded history is puzzling. Why did the "slave society" of antiquity produce such a startling variety of "superstructures," from the monarchies, aristocracies, tyrannies, oligarchies, and democracies of the Greeks to the Roman imperial order? How did the Catholic Church survive and why did its "superstructure" change so little from the "slave society" of Rome to the "late-capitalism" of the twentieth century? And if on the other hand, as Engels suggested in a famous escape clause, the "base" determines "the superstructure" only "in the last resort," what remains of Marx's grandiose system except the truism that economics interacts with other spheres of human activity?

Marx's economics have likewise proved an embarrassment. His prediction of an ever-falling rate of profit under capitalism ignored the "dialectical" driving force of science and technology. New technologies create industries that are vastly profitable until they grow to saturate their markets; then still newer technologies supersede them. Nor has Marx's labor theory of value, on which his critique of capitalist "exploitation" rests, aged well. It was as arbitrary and metaphysical as anything in Hegel. Marx was unable to measure "value" empirically, although he thought he could. Only prices are measurable, and they depend partly on factors—such as supply and demand— that have nothing to do with labor costs.

Marx's analysis of societies in terms of economic classes, although not original to him, has fared better. It filled a need for a short-hand to describe the distinctions between aristocrats, middle classes, and workers or peasants that actually existed in the European societies of his day. But despite Marx's claims to scientific rigor, he never defined class. The last chapter of volume III of *Capital*, where he attempted that task, breaks off unfinished. Marxist social analysis has thus suffered from a lack of clearly defined tools. Marx's prediction of increasing polarization between "proletariat" and "bourgeoisie," and the rigidity of his categories, have also made it difficult for later Marxists to classify white-collar workers, professionals, and their own class, the intellectuals.

Marx's call to revolution has proved to be the most powerful and durable part of his work. From the 1860s it made him the unchallenged intellectual leader of European and world socialism. But Marx's call to revolution has also labored under irreconcilable contradictions. His philosophy of history appeared to predict the almost automatic extinction of capitalism once economic conditions had ripened. That comforting thought might lead socialists to await the great day passively, a conclusion Marx and many later Marxists rejected. Marx left unresolved that tension between determinism and voluntarism, between the temptation to await the foreordained and the urge to force the pace of history.

Marx's occasional endorsement of revolutionary terror and of "dictatorship of the proletariat" also implicitly threatened his proclaimed goal of freedom. Marx celebrated Jacobin-style violence as midwife of history: under some circumstances there was "only one means to *curtail*, simplify and localize the bloody agony of the old society and the bloody birth-pangs of the new, only one means—the revolutionary terror." But he also recognized that humanity made its history not "as it please[d] . . . but under circumstances directly found, given, and transmitted from the past." Revolutionary terror would constitute part of the new society's "past," and might influence its future in directions other than liberation.

And what if the "dictatorship of the proletariat" refused to wither away? Marx doggedly refused to take that question seriously, even when his rival in the international socialist movement, the eccentric Russian aristocrat Mikhail Bakunin (1814–76), attacked him publicly. Bakunin's anarchist answer to oppression was improbable: smashing the state would return society to a state of nature in which humanity's essential goodness would at last prevail. But on the likely consequences of a transitional revolutionary dictatorship, Marx was the utopian and Bakunin the realist: "No dictatorship can have any other aim than to perpetuate itself."

Marx's vision conflicted in other ways with his goal of liberation. His claim to possess the truth about history encouraged a dangerous intolerance. If Marx, in Engels's famous words, was the Darwin of human society, if he had "discovered the fundamental law that determines the course and development of human history," then those who stood against Marx stood against history. Marx was not slow to point that out.

And as later critics have suggested, Marx's ideas contained implications for revolutionary regimes that went far beyond his advocacy of terror and temporary dictatorship. Since for Marx social antagonisms stemmed from class conflict, conflicts after the revolution were of necessity rooted in resistance by the old ruling classes. Anyone who disagreed with the new regime might thus become a legitimate target for further liberating violence. And if freedom meant social unity, as Marx—following thinkers as disparate as Rousseau and Hegel—assumed, then the more unity the more freedom. That notion could likewise easily lead to the elimination of all who failed to fit in. And if, as Marx argued, communism would enable humanity to control the conditions

Mikhail Bakunin, aristocrat and professional revolutionary.

Bakunin the Anarchist Foresees a Dictatorship over the Proletariat

In 1874–75 Marx copied into his notebooks long passages from *Statehood and Anarchy*, a work of his anarchist rival Mikhail Bakunin, and adorned them with furious comments (printed in brackets).

(Bakunin) . . . the so-called people's state will be nothing other than the quite despotic administration of the masses of the people by a new and very non-numerous aristocracy of real and supposed learned ones. The people is not learned, so it will be entirely freed from the cares of governing, wholly incorporated into the governed herd. A fine liberation! The Marxists sense this [!] contradiction and, realizing that the regime of the learned [*quelle reverie!*], the hardest, most offensive, and most contemptuous in the world will in fact be a dictatorship in spite of all the democratic forms, console themselves with the thought that the dictatorship will be temporary and short-lived.

(Marx commentary) [*Non, mon cher!* The *class domination* of the workers over the resisting strata of the old world must last until the economic foundations of the existence of classes are destroyed.]

(Bakunin). . . . They say that such a state yoke, a dictatorship, is a necessary transitional means for attaining the most complete popular liberation. So, to liberate the masses of the people they first have to be enslaved. Our polemic rests and is founded on this contradiction. They maintain that only a dictatorship, their own naturally, can create the people's will; we answer: no dictatorship can have any other aim than to perpetuate itself. . . .

From Robert C. Tucker, ed. *The Marx-Engels Reader*, 2nd ed. (New York: W. W. Norton, 1978), pp. 546–47.

diminished as the brutal conditions of early British industrialization gave way to rising real wages. Above all, Marx created a messianic faith in revolution. That faith arrived on the scene too late in the nineteenth century to preside over a genuine revolution. The twentieth century offered new opportunities.

Nationalism

From the beginning, socialism found itself in competition with an even more powerful ideological force: nationalism. The political notion of the nation-state, born in the French Revolution and spread in its wars, sowed deeper divisions than any between labor and capital. Nationalism, as it developed in nineteenth-century Europe, had four major components.

First was the political theory of the social contract and general will that the French Revolution had attempted to translate into political reality. When the nation of king and nobles gave way to the nation of freely associating citizens, nothing except the "general will" limited that nation's actions. Second came Kant's doctrine of the moral autonomy of the individual. When extended to nations, that autonomy, that "self-determination," likewise meant that nations need acknowledge no law they did not themselves choose. Third came Hegel's notion of the state as the moral force in a history that was proceeding through struggle toward a goal. Hegel was no German nationalist; he had hailed Napoleon as a historic individual whose conquests advanced the self-realization of the world spirit. But Hegel's deification of the Prussian state had nationalist uses.

The fourth and final component of European nationalism was the ethnic concept of the nation. That too was a German contribution. Johann Gottfried von Herder (1744–1803), a prominent exponent of *Sturm und Drang*, had worked out in the 1770s and 1780s a philosophy of history that provided a rationale for German resistance to the cultural domination of France. For

of its existence, then a regime that described itself as communist could do *anything it liked.* Nothing, no law either economic or moral need constrain it.

Marx's legacy was thus profoundly ambiguous. He made economics part of history. Economic forces, "modes of production," and social classes were henceforth objects of historical study alongside kings and battles. He offered a scathing critique of capitalism, although the credibility of that critique

Herder each nation, each *"Volk,"* was equally close to God. Each therefore had the duty to cultivate its own peculiarities: "Spew out the ugly slime of the Seine / Speak German, O you German!" Herder rejoiced in human diversity; like Hegel, he was no nationalist. But once again, his ideas had nationalist uses.

Successors such as Fichte were soon proclaiming the superiority of German. The French, Fichte wrote after French conquest in 1806, were Teutons who had frivolously abandoned their native tongue for a language derived from Latin. That had infected them with a "lack of seriousness." Herder and Fichte between them established language as a new test for nationhood. Language thus became a criterion for drawing or redrawing boundaries. It became what it had rarely been before: a matter of life and death.

In the decades after 1815, the French revolutionary conception of the general will, the notion of self-determination, the concept of the state as the moral force in history, and the ethnic-linguistic conception of the nation fused. The result was a unique invention, *a secular religion of the nation-state.* For the nationalist, individual freedom and self-fulfillment lay only in service to such a state. That peculiar belief distinguishes nationalism from patriotism, the instinctive loyalty to homeland, or from xenophobia, the traditional and unthinking hatred and contempt for foreigners. Patriotism and xenophobia have existed throughout history, but nationalism was an invention of the decades after 1789.

It soon spread eastward. Herder had provided a rationale for the study and cultivation of the language and culture of one's own *Volk.* In Germany the brothers Jakob and Wilhelm Grimm collected folk tales and Teutonic mythology, and explored the roots of the national language. Poles, Czechs, and Balkan nationalities followed their lead. Dictionaries and editions of medieval epic poems appeared, monuments to the peculiarities of each nation's his-

tory. Poets such as Sándor Petöfi (1822–49) in Hungary and Giacomo Leopardi (1798–1837) in Italy wrote verse celebrating the national spirit and demanding national liberation.

Politics followed poetry. Napoleon had attempted to mobilize Italians (1796), Hungarians (1809), and Poles (1812) in his wars against Austria and Russia. His defeat did not remove nationalism from politics. Italy, which remained under Austrian domination, gave the example. The conspiratorial sect of the *carbonari* ("charcoal burners") had originated in south Italy as a protest against French rule. After 1815, although lacking a discernible program, it served as a magnet both for police spies and for youth disaffected with the status quo. One such youth was Giuseppe Mazzini (1805–72), the greatest prophet of nineteenth-century nationalism.

Mazzini joined the *carbonari* in 1827 in his home town of Genoa and spent time in jail in 1830 for subversive activity. In exile in 1831 he founded a new type of conspiratorial organization: *Giovine Italia* or "young Italy." The movement had little practical success but its romantic emphasis on youthful fanaticism set a powerful example. Mazzini proclaimed liberty, but his liberty was the liberty of the individual to serve the national idea. Nationalist politics was a *"fede,"* a faith, a political religion.

Mazzini proclaimed the equality of all nationalities and their inevitable harmony once Europe became a "Europe of the Peoples." But he also insisted it was Italy's mission to provide "a new and more powerful Unity to all the nations of Europe." Italy had given Europe unity under Rome and under the Papacy. Now the "Third Rome," the "Rome of the Italian people," would fulfill that same universal mission. It would create a "third and still vaster Unity." That was no small claim, and it helped set a widely imitated pattern of nationalist megalomania. Nor did Mazzini address the decisive question. When the claims and "rights" of

The invention of national traditions: German peasant costume, as imagined by Ludwig Emil Grimm (1828).

Giuseppe Mazzini, prophet of the religion of the nation-state.

nationalities conflicted, who or what would decide?

FROM THEORY TO PRACTICE

Without a public capable of receiving them, ideas have little practical effect. In nineteenth-century Europe the gradual widening of literacy and of leisure created that public. States began systematically to take responsibility for their subjects' welfare and education. And submerged groups such as workers and women reacted to the new age with broadening demands for social and political rights.

The Role of the State

States traditionally have been machines for power, not welfare. Yet in the seventeenth and eighteenth centuries, the states of western Europe began to recognize that the prosperity and education of their inhabitants might increase that power (see pp. 633–40). Bureaucrats and enlightened absolutists began an expansion of the role of the state that ultimately created immense organizations supervising the education, health, and wealth of the citizenry. Power, necessary for survival, remained the state's ultimate purpose, but alongside it there gradually emerged the modern bureaucratic "welfare state."

The states of the nineteenth century, as befitted the age of *laissez-faire*, removed economic restraints that appeared to impede the creation of wealth. By the 1860s, the centralizing bureaucracies of the German states had overcome the fearful rear-guard action of small-town Germany, with its xenophobic guilds and restrictions on free competition. In Britain, a militant middle-class movement institutionalized *laissez-faire*. In 1846 Parliament abolished the grain tariffs or "Corn Laws" that the landed interests had imposed in the post-1815 slump. That step marked the political triumph of Britain's all-conquering industries over agriculture.

The state also intervened in the economy. Especially on the Continent, it took the lead in the creation of national markets and industrial economies. The obvious abuses of the factory system and the disastrous sanitary conditions in the new industrial cities also provoked outcry and government action. In Britain, legislation as early as 1802 had attempted to regulate working hours for apprentices. In 1819 Parliament passed the first of a series of Factory Acts, forbidding the work of children under nine and limiting the work of children over nine to twelve hours a day. An act of 1831 forbade night work by individuals under 21; an act restricting the work day to ten and a half hours passed in 1850. The first Factory Acts applied only to cotton mills but by the 1860s legislation covered most industries. Acts in 1841 and 1855 forbade the employment of women and children in mining. Parliament also sought to regulate city sanitation and standards for wholesome food and drink, beginning with the Public Health Act of 1848. France and Prussia passed similar laws. Despite a long record of poor enforcement and of collusion between factory inspectors and manufacturers, working and living conditions gradually improved.

In the face of British industrial competition, the continental states adopted various forms of protective tariffs. Prussia, in particular, made tariff policy an instrument of state power. Beginning in 1818, reforming Prussian bureaucrats aggressively pressed customs unions upon their smaller neighbors. In 1833, Prussia succeeded in creating a *Zollverein* or customs union that eventually covered all important German states except Austria. Prussia's bureaucracy and military also took the lead in the expansion of the railroad network. After mid-century, the army began gearing the railroads to its ever-faster mobilization system. Only the Russian state, in the period of its industrial "take-off" after 1880, surpassed the role of the Prussian state in economic development.

Prussia led in a second, absolutely decisive area: its school system pioneered mass literacy. That was a daring step. The value of widespread literacy in the eighteenth century was far from obvious, at least to the European upper classes. Catherine the Great neatly summarized their attitude in a letter reputedly sent to a subordinate: "We must not in any way provide instruction for the lower class of people. If they knew as much as you or I . . . they would no longer want to obey us. . . . " Even after 1800 members of the British Parliament could rail against the democratization of knowledge; it might render the lower orders "insolent to their superiors."

The Prussian bureaucracy, ruling over what a French intellectual in the 1830s described as the "classic country of barracks and schools," had no such qualms. Prussia, after 1819, became the first state in history to proclaim and begin to enforce universal school attendance. A literate subject was a more productive subject and a better soldier. France followed in 1833 by requiring villages and towns to maintain schools. The Habsburg monarchy followed in the 1860s. Britain, in the spirit of *laissez-faire*, neglected the issue, and paid dearly. It only established the principle of universal primary schooling in 1870 and only made it compulsory in 1880.

The coming of literacy worked yet another revolution. For most of human history, only very small elites had been able to read or write. At the beginning of the nineteenth century slightly over half of all adult males in England and France and perhaps one in three or four women could write their own names. A century later, literacy in the developed countries of western Europe was well over 95 percent of both men and women (see Figure 25-1). The industrial revolution made mass literacy possible, but it was the state that turned that potential into reality.

The inadequacies of the English school, 1856.

Workers

Mass literacy, among its many side effects, made the claims of the outsiders increasingly difficult to ignore. In politics, both workers and women participated in the revolutionary ferment that culminated in Europe-wide uprisings in 1848. In the workplace, workers by that point had long since begun to organize against the oppression they perceived. The introduction of machinery led to widespread artisan protest and machine breaking both in England and on the Continent. From 1811 to 1816 English rioters rose repeatedly to smash knitting machines and power looms in the name of a mythical "King Ludd." Agricultural workers imitated the "Luddites" in 1830–32 by smashing threshing machines and burning barns.

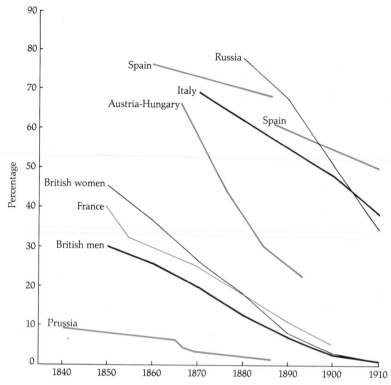

FIGURE 25-1   The Decline of Illiteracy

From Theodore S. Hamerow, *The Birth of a New Europe* (Chapel Hill: University of North Carolina Press, 1983), p. 169.

But incoherent protest and anarchic violence had little chance even against the decentralized British state. Workers explored other paths, beginning in the 1820s. With the Combination Acts of 1799 and 1800 Parliament had ended early attempts to organize rudimentary labor unions under the inspiration of the French Revolution. In 1824–25 Parliament relented and weakened the Acts, thanks to continued unrest and to the pleas of middle-class reformers for toleration of working-class "co-opera-tion." Strikes remained illegal but unions could now organize with rela-tive freedom. In 1829 Robert Owen presided over the founding of a "Soci-ety for Promoting Co-operative Knowl-edge" that in 1831 became the "Na-tional Union of the Working Classes," the first true British trade union.

The system of a national "general union" soon showed its limitations;

regional and craft loyalties were stronger than working-class solidarity. Nevertheless, the recurrent economic crises and the pressure of population growth meant continued unrest. In 1838 a leading workers' group, the London Working Men's Association, initiated a nationwide campaign of agi-tation for adoption by Parliament of universal male suffrage and other re-forms embodied in a "People's Char-ter." Chartist agitation, under the lead-ership of the fiery journalist and speaker Feargus O'Connor, continued sporadically for the next ten years but failed to move Parliament.

Chartism's internal rivalries and po-litical failure did not inhibit other working-class efforts. A National "As-sociation for the Protection of Labour" emerged in 1845 and by 1859 was able to persuade Parliament to authorize peaceful picketing. In 1868 a Trades Union Congress that represented over 100,000 workers met at Manchester. By 1875 British trade unions had won the right to strike and picket.

On the Continent working-class or-ganization inevitably lagged, given the gap in development between Britain and its followers and the relative unfa-miliarity of the notion of individual rights. Belgium prohibited labor unions until 1868. Revolutionary France had forbidden unions and strikes, and Napoleon's code had confirmed that ban in 1803. Socialist underground se-cret societies such as those of the agita-tor Auguste Blanqui and uprisings such as those of the impoverished silk workers of Lyon in 1831 and 1834 merely provoked savage repression. Not until after 1871 did the French working classes organize effectively. In Germany, revolutionary sects such as the tailor Wilhelm Weitling's "League of the Just" emerged a generation be-fore the creation of an organized Ger-man labor movement in the 1860s.

Despite rivalries between regions and crafts, home artisans and factory workers, skilled "labor aristocrats" and simple laborers, the European working classes were by the 1870s nevertheless well on their way to creating stable organizations through which to press their interests. In England the ideological glue that held them together was frequently the piety of the Protestant sects. On the Continent, most adopted orthodox Marxism under the guidance or inspiration of the "First International," the "International Working Men's Organization" that Marx and Engels helped found in 1864. Workers' organizations soon made increasingly effective demands for change, and gave birth to the first workers' political parties.

Women

The French and industrial revolutions made relative freedom for women possible, but did not produce it. As with workers, only struggle could do that. Olympe de Gouges had pointed out the inconsistency of proclaiming the Rights of Man while denying those rights to women. In her path-breaking *Vindication of the Rights of Women* (1792), the English writer Mary Wollstonecraft demanded equality, and freedom for women to best employ their talents. The romantic poet Shelley, son-in-law of Mary Wollstonecraft, put it succinctly in 1817: "Can man be free if woman be a slave?"

That question passed through three overlapping phases in the course of the nineteenth century: literary self-assertion, theoretical elaboration, and political action. First came literary self-assertion. Women intellectuals began to write with a frequency and eloquence that eventually won them grudging respect. Germaine de Staël, daughter of the banker Necker and France's leading woman writer until her death in 1817, took on Napoleon in print and had to take refuge in exile. Her novels *Corinne* (1804) and *Delphine* (1807) attacked conventional views of marriage and of woman's education. She also played a decisive role in explaining German romanticism to the rest of Europe. Napoleon had the first edition of her *De l'Allemagne* (1811) burned as "un-French."

The French romantic novelist and social critic George Sand (Amantine-Lucile-Aurore, Baroness Dudevant, 1804–76) was an adherent of Fourierist utopianism who scandalized French polite society by wearing men's suits and smoking in public. Fleeing a provincial marriage of convenience, Sand went to Paris and wrote some 80 popular novels. She supported herself and her two children on the proceeds, a virtually unprecedented achievement. She also advocated and practiced "free love," by which she and other Fourierists and Saint-Simonians meant cohabitation or marriage based on equality between the sexes and on sexual or emotional inclination rather than social convention. Sand, despite her deliberate unconventionality, was one of the prototypes of a phenomenon more common later in the century—the successful professional woman.

By mid-century, women authors were emerging whose achievements were unrivalled. Charlotte Brontë, in her novels *Jane Eyre* (1847) and *Shirley* (1849), presented strong women heroines in quest both of love and independence. Her sister Emily, before her death of tuberculosis, produced the violent and terrifying *Wuthering Heights* (1847), one of the greatest of English nineteenth-century novels.

By that point a growing theoretical literature by both men and women had begun to explore the question of woman's role. Their views fall into three rough categories: those who reaffirmed woman's traditional subordination to man, those who argued that women were equal but different, and those who insisted on an absolute legal and political equality that would allow women to be like men if they so chose.

The overwhelming mass of male opinion inevitably argued for woman's subordination. Many women still agreed. Woman's role was to obey, help, and comfort man the breadwinner, to bear and raise his children, and to preside over the home, a warm sanctuary in a cold and increasingly competitive new industrial world. That was the prescription of Sarah Stickney Ellis, an English writer of women's handbooks from the late 1830s on, and of numerous continental theorists from reactionaries such as De Maistre to liberals of all stripes.

The "equal but different" tradition was most prominent on the Continent. The title of a French tract of the 1830s sums up its message: *The Education of Mothers; or the Civilization of Mankind by Women.* Woman's first role was as mother. The mother's calling was to be the educator, the bearer of culture, the civilizer of the drunken, destructive, childlike male. As Jeanne Deroin (1805–94), the foremost French woman's advocate of mid-century, put it in the newspaper she published during the 1848 revolution, woman's "sublime humanitarian maternity" had the duty to "teach everyone how fraternity should be practiced." The world of politics and of relations between states should conform to the standards of the well-ordered home.

Nor should women seek to imitate men, insisted Louise Otto (1819–95), Deroin's foremost German counterpart. "True womanliness" was the goal. "Georgesandism" outraged Otto as much as it did any defender of the old order. Emancipation must not "[devalue] woman to become a caricature of a man." This tradition had appeal not only in Germany and France, but even in England and the United States. There it contributed not only to the assertion of women's rights but also to the temperance movement that gathered force as the nineteenth century drew on. And the notion of the mother as educator appealed to female eastern European nationalist theorists. It gave woman a decisive role in the national struggle. Man's vocation was to fight; woman's to transmit the *Volk* language and nationalize the minds of the young.

The third tradition that emerged in the course of the nineteenth century drew its ultimate inspiration from Locke. Men enjoyed autonomy and self-determination by natural right. To deny that same right to women was neither just nor civilized. Women must receive the same autonomy and education as men, even if that meant painful social readjustment. Wollstonecraft gave first expression to such views. John Stuart and Harriet Taylor Mill's *The Subjection of Women* (1869) provided the tradition's basic text. Its ideas were particularly influential in Britain and the United States, where they meshed with the Lockean political culture from which they derived.

Theorists of the "equal but different" tradition—and male supremacists—inevitably derided Mill for inciting women to what they described as antisocial self-indulgence. Ruthless individualism, the critics claimed, was no answer to the biological and social imperatives that governed women's conduct. Emancipation could not and must not mean emancipation from children, or from marriage, the fundamental building block of society. Women's biological role demanded special legal protection for the family, not the cold comfort of strict equality with men.

The issues at stake were so intractable and emotion-laden that the argument between the two schools has continued to the present. But regardless of theoretical differences, by the 1860s and 1870s a broadly based movement of women, primarily of the middle classes, had arisen both in Europe and in the United States. It increasingly turned to political action to secure women's rights (see pp. 800–801).

The new age of ideas after 1789 was thus both a continuation and a repudiation of the Enlightenment. Faith in "progress" and in the perfectibility of humanity swelled with the advance of science, the coming of steam-powered industry, and the spread of liberalism and socialism. Hitherto submerged groups found voices; states began to act as machines for welfare as well as for power. Yet strong countercurrents persisted. Conservatism or "reaction" inspired both nobles and intellectuals; the peasantry and many in the middle classes still held to traditional community and dynastic loyalties. Romanticism damned the new industrial age but also undermined the remains of the old order through its stormy cult of the individual. And nationalism, which many conservatives mistook for liberalism, soon revealed itself as the overriding political faith of the nineteenth and twentieth centuries, the force that transmuted "geographical expressions" into nation-states.

Suggestions for Further Reading

Science, Religion, and Culture

For overviews that place nineteenth-century thought in its political and social setting, see E. J. Hobsbawm, *The Age of Revolution, 1789–1848* (1962), and *The Age of Capital, 1848–1875* (1975). F. L. Baumer, *Modern European Thought: Continuity and Change in Ideas, 1600–1950* (1977), offers a useful general survey of the movement of ideas. For the fate of religion, see O. Chadwick, *The Secularization of the European Mind in the Nineteenth Century* (1975). On the impact of Darwin and geology, see especially W. Irvine, *Angels, Apes, and Victorians* (1955); J. C. Greene, *The Death of Adam* (1959); and C. C. Gillispie, *Genesis and Geology* (1951). For romanticism, see especially J. Barzun, *Classic, Romantic, and Modern* (1961); J. B. Halstead, ed., *Romanticism* (1965); J. Clay, *Romanticism* (1981); and M. le Bris, *Romantics and Romanticism* (1981). On German philosophy, see R. N. Stromberg, *European Intellectual History After 1789* (1981); R. Scruton, *From Descartes to Wittgenstein* (1981); K. Löwith, *From Hegel to Nietzsche* (1964); and G. D. O'Brien, *Hegel on Reason and History* (1975).

Social, Economic, and Political Thought

The best introduction to convervatism is still E. Burke, *Reflections on the Revolution in France*; K. Epstein, *The Genesis of German Conservatism* (1966), describes some of conservatism's continental ramifications. For liberalism, both economic and political, the classic texts are A. Smith, *The Wealth of Nations*; T. R. Malthus, *An Essay on Population*; and J. S. Mill, *Autobiography* and *On Liberty*. On Mill and his fellows, see especially J. Hamburger, *Intellectuals in Politics: John Stuart Mill and the Philosophic Radicals* (1965). G. Lichtheim, *The Origins of Socialism* (1969), and P. Singer, *Marx* (1980), offer concise introductions to socialism. K. Marx and F. Engels, *The Communist Manifesto,* and R. Tucker, ed. *The Marx-Engels Reader* (1972), provide a selection of the essential texts. L. Kolakovski, *Main Currents of Marxism*, Vol. 1 (1978), lucidly analyzes the intellectual development of Marx and Engels, explains their debts to earlier thinkers, dissects the weaknesses of their system, and suggests some of the potential consequences of their ideas—but see also D. Conway, *A Farewell to Marx* (1987). E. Kedourie, *Nationalism* (1966), is exemplary: one of the few intelligent books on a subject of overriding importance.

Consequences of the Industrial Revolution

For the intellectual and social impact of the industrial revolution, see especially the broadly conceived work of T. S. Hamerow, *The Birth of a New Europe* (1983). A. Briggs, *The Age of Improvement, 1783–1867* (1959), and E. P. Thompson, *The Making of the English Working Class* (1963), offer differing perspectives on English workers; L. Chevalier, *Working Classes and Dangerous Classes in Paris During the Nineteenth Century* (1971), and B. Moss, *The Origins of the French Labor Movement* (1976), cover France. R. Bridenthal et al., *Becoming Visible. Women in European History* (1987), offers a useful introduction to the changing status and aspirations of nineteenth-century women.

26
The Breakthrough of the Nation-State, 1815–1871

The defeat of revolutionary France ushered in a century of relative peace between European states. Four general wars and innumerable minor conflicts had punctuated the eighteenth century. Prussia and Russia had become great powers. Sweden had ceased to be one. Poland had ceased to be. But from 1815 to 1914 only three major conflicts—the Crimean War (1854–56) and the wars of Italian (1859–60) and German "unification" (1864, 1866, 1870–71)—affected even parts of Europe. And the nineteenth-century conflicts, unlike the world wars of 1701–14, 1740–48, 1756–63, and 1792–1815, were short and involved only some of the great powers.

The secret of this relative peace and stability was both ideological and structural. Fear of "the Revolution" had at last welded together the final coalition that brought Napoleon down. That fear inspired a settlement in 1814–15 that bound the powers together in a network of treaties and mutual obligations. Treaties, custom, and the consolidation of neutral buffer states separating the great powers made it harder than before for one power to challenge the rest. And fear of revolution, a fear that the three waves of unrest that convulsed Europe in 1820, 1830, and 1848 repeatedly reinforced, did not abate until after mid-century.

Then the collapse of the revolutionary myth in the failures of 1848 ushered in a brief era of almost unrestrained pursuit of state interest. And states pursued that interest under the banner of nationalism. The consequence was the breakthrough of the nation-state in central Europe: the creation of Italy in 1859–60 and of Prussia-Germany in 1866–71. Those "revolutions from above," especially the German one, destroyed the small and intermediate buffer states that had been a key restraining element in the 1814–15 settlement. Nevertheless, thanks to the weakness of the new Italian state and the temporary self-restraint of the German one, the main lines of the 1814–15 settlement survived the wars of mid-century. Only the rise after 1890 of a new challenge to the balance of power ended the "long peace" and inaugurated a new century of world wars.

UNDER THE SHADOW OF REVOLUTION: THE CONGRESS OF VIENNA AND AFTER

The victors over Napoleon faced two intertwined tasks—the restoration of a balance of power internationally and of internal stability to the wide areas of Europe that French arms had revolutionized. As Britain's foreign secretary, Castlereagh, put it, the victors needed to return Europe to "peaceful habits."

Opposite: The romantic vision of the 1830 Revolution: *Liberty Leading the People*, by Eugène Delacroix.

725

The Congress of Vienna: the official view, by Isabey.

The diplomats redrew the map of Europe in 1814–15 in ways that bore little relationship to the wishes of the populations concerned. Internally, the "reaction" that followed the restoration of many of Europe's ruling houses was undeniably oppressive. But by the standards set in later peace settlements, that of 1814–15 was both humane and durable.

Architects of the Vienna settlement: Castlereagh (left) and Metternich (right).

"Europe"—or rather the five great powers—met at Vienna in September 1814 to draw up the settlement. The four decisive figures in this first general European settlement since the Peace of Westphalia in 1648 were the neurotic Tsar Alexander of Russia, the wittily devious Talleyrand for Bourbon France, the bold and determined Castlereagh for Britain, and the self-infatuated host, Chancellor Prince Metternich for Austria. The indecisive Frederick William III of Prussia and his ministers cut lesser figures. Around the principals danced the nobility of Europe and its innumerable hangers-on, while Metternich's secret police rifled wastebaskets and boudoir drawers in search of diplomatic correspondence.

The two overriding issues were the settlement with France and the division of the spoils in central and eastern Europe. The allies initially tried to exclude Talleyrand from their deliberations. But the unpredictable tsar soon provoked a crisis that reversed the powers' roles. If France was the threat of yesterday, Alexander, with his insistence on entering Paris as a conqueror, might be that of tomorrow. His demand that the Congress confirm his control of most of Poland provoked alarm, since a Russia that close to central Europe would be an over-mighty neighbor. Even Alexander's promise to equip his Polish possessions with a constitution seemed a fig-leaf for the voracious expansionism of the Russian state. It was also ideologically unpleasing to Metternich, no lover of constitutions.

The tsar's ally Prussia acted in a manner only slightly less ominous for the future. The Prussian military reformers, intoxicated with their victory over Napoleon, now demanded the annexation of Saxony, whose king had changed sides too late in 1813. (In revolutionary times, as that expert at well-timed changes of allegiance, Talleyrand, remarked, treason was "a question of dates.") The upshot was deadlock. Prussia and Russia faced England and Austria, while the Prussian generals muttered of war. To redress the balance, Castlereagh and Metternich brought a willing Talleyrand into play. A brief triple alliance of the old enemies, France, Britain, and Austria, persuaded the Prussians and the tsar to back down.

France received back its historic borders and even pocketed some minor territorial gains. Russia gave up some Polish territory. Prussia kept some of Poland and secured only half of Saxony. It gained in compensation the ex-Napoleonic territories in northwestern Germany. Castlereagh placed a re-

luctant Prussia on the Rhine, in the front lines against a possible renewal of the French threat to the balance. England and Austria thus also unwittingly gave Prussia the immense coal and iron deposits of the Ruhr valley, with economic and political consequences immeasurably important for the future of Prussia, Germany, and Europe. The separation of the new Prussia into eastern and western halves generated additional pressure, if the Prussian power-state needed such pressure, for further expansion.

Europe in 1815

The Bourbons restored: Louis
XVIII of France.

Lesser issues at Vienna generated
less tension than the Poland-Saxony
deadlock. In principle—as proclaimed
by Talleyrand and Metternich—
"legitimacy" was to guide the settlement. That slogan was convenient for
Bourbon France and Habsburg Austria.
But it explains the actual shape of the
settlement less than the need for stability and balance that all concerned
deeply felt after almost 25 years of revolution and war.

The Bourbons indeed returned to
France, Spain, and eventually to Naples. The Pope reclaimed the Papal
States, stretching across central Italy.
Switzerland, released from its status as
satellite of revolutionary France, received a guarantee of perpetual independence and neutrality. But at British
insistence Holland received the ex-
Austrian territory of Belgium to
strengthen it as a barrier against
France. Piedmont-Sardinia likewise
and for the same reason received the
former republic of Genoa. Austria itself
kept Venetia and Lombardy.

In Germany expediency and the
quest for stability triumphed. The surviving princes, beneficiaries of the
princes' revolution of 1801–03 and of

Napoleon's redrawing of the map in
1806 and after, were poor examples of
"legitimacy." What emerged from the
deliberations of the German states at
the Congress was a loose league, a German "united nations" of 39 states and
mini-states, with an assembly sitting at
Frankfurt. Austria held the presidency
of this German Confederation with
Prussia as its sometimes reluctant second. The Confederation's two-fold
function was to give the awakening
German nation a political home now
that the Holy Roman Empire no longer
existed, and to serve as a defensive barrier against a resurgent France or an
over-mighty Russia. The Confederation's principal weaknesses were its
built-in split between Austria and Prussia and the egotism of the lesser
princes. Both conspired against the
greater unity that German nationalists
were already demanding.

The inconsiderate return of Napoleon in 1815 emphasized further the
need for continuing great power solidarity. France escaped after Waterloo
with the loss of some further small border territories and a cash indemnity.
The allies renewed the Quadruple Alliance for 20 years, thus confirming the
principle established at Vienna: the
great powers in concert would decide
all major international questions.

But reaffirmation of the balance of
power against France was the extent of
great-power agreement. The second
decisive issue that the powers faced in
recasting Europe, that of the nature of
the internal regimes of Europe's states,
brought the parting of the ways. The
symbol of the latent divergence between Britain and the three eastern
monarchies was Tsar Alexander's
treaty of the "Holy Alliance" of September 1815. This "piece of sublime
mysticism and nonsense," in
Castlereagh's scathing phrase, pledged
Russia, Austria, and Prussia to conduct
their policies in accordance with the
principles of the Christian religion.
Those principles, as interpreted by the
eastern monarchies, apparently included the suppression of liberalism

and revolution everywhere. The accession of most European states to the "Holy Alliance" diluted its already vague content and ensured that it had little practical effect, but the treaty gave its name to an era of obscurantism, arbitrary imprisonment, and muzzling of the press.

In Spain and Naples the restored Bourbons abolished the constitutions they had granted in 1812. Pope Pius VII reestablished his authority in the Papal States by again confining the Jews to ghettos, by reviving the Inquisition, and by abolishing the reforming law codes the French had brought. In Germany, Metternich struck effectively at freedom of expression. In 1819 a compliant Prussia and German Confederation adopted Metternich's repressive "Carlsbad Decrees," and suppressed liberal and nationalist agitation in Germany for a decade.

Even England passed through a brief but symptomatic repressive phase. The inevitable crisis of readjustment to a peacetime economy in 1815, combined with population growth, brought widespread poverty and unemployment. Unlike their counterparts on the Continent, middle-class radicals called not for revolution but for reform of the corrupt parliamentary voting system. The Tory (Conservative) government nevertheless replied with ill-considered force in 1819. Manchester constables routed a peaceful crowd of demonstrators with considerable loss of life in the so-called "Peterloo Massacre." Parliament passed the notorious "Six Acts" that made the expression of advanced opinions a crime. But neither Britain nor the continental monarchies had the bureaucratic machinery or propaganda techniques needed to remold their subjects' thought; that was reserved for the despotisms of the next century.

As for the "concert of Europe," for which the Quadruple Alliance had prescribed regular meetings, it soon broke up. At the conference of Aix-la-Chapelle (Aachen) in 1818 the great powers again welcomed France to their midst.

Cavalry disperses the crowd at the "Peterloo Massacre" (1819).

Then, in 1820, the first of a series of disturbances in southern Europe posed the question of intervention by the powers. A constitutionalist revolt against the Spanish Bourbons triggered disturbances in Naples, Piedmont, and Portugal. Castlereagh refused to attend the Congress of Troppau (1820) at which the three eastern monarchies declared their readiness to act. The ensuing congress of Laibach (1821), over British protests, authorized Austrian military intervention to restore the Bourbons in Naples and Sicily. Metternich dealt similarly with Piedmont. In October 1822, at Verona in north Italy, the last congress met to discuss intervention in Spain. Britain refused its consent, and withdrew: "Every nation for itself and God for us all," quipped George Canning, Castlereagh's successor.

British disapproval did not prevent a French army from crossing the Pyrenees to restore the Spanish Bourbons. Unlike 1808, no guerrilla resistance resulted. France was intervening for rather than against the Bourbons, the Church, and the landowning nobles. And the three eastern powers declined to follow Canning's dictum; the custom of consultation between great powers established at Vienna continued, though less formally than in the congress period.

If Britain's departure from Verona marked the effective end of the Quadruple Alliance, the Greek war of Independence (1821–29) soon crippled the "Holy Alliance" as well. The war was a major step in a process soon drearily familiar to European statesmen: the "Eastern Question," the breakup of the Ottoman Turk empire under the pressure of hostile great powers without and of nationalism within. Russia had humiliated the Turks in Catherine the Great's wars. The Serbs, under their chieftain "Black George," had set the example of national—or tribal—revolt against Constantinople in 1804. By 1817 the embryo of a Serb state had emerged, although under Turkish overlordship. The Greeks followed in 1821, by massacring all Turks in the Peloponnese—a massacre the Turks repaid with interest.

The Greek cause attracted support among western admirers of ancient Greece. Flamboyant figures such as the brilliant and dissolute English romantic poet Lord Byron flocked to Greece. Russia, always hostile to Turkey and now solicitous of its Slav "little brothers" under Turkish rule, broke with Metternich and lent aid to "the Revolution." A bizarre alignment of Britain and France with the Russia of Alexander's successor, the reactionary Tsar Nicholas I, annihilated the Turkish fleet at Navarino in 1827. In 1832 independent Greece received from Europe the quaint gift of a Bavarian prince as a ruler.

From 1830 Revolutions to 1840 Crisis

The second wave of revolutions, in 1830–32, was a more serious affair than the first. The breakdown of the "Holy Alliance" over Greece, the fading of the memory of revolutionary turmoil—but not of revolutionary achievements—contributed to its force. And far more than in 1820–21, nationalism drove events. Finally, as in 1789, Paris set the example that had been missing in 1820. Louis XVIII, who had acquiesced to a degree of constitutionalism after 1814, died in 1824. His successor, Charles X, considered himself king by divine right. He muzzled the press and defied the liberal majority in his Chamber of Deputies. The appointment of an ultramonarchist ministry in 1829 brought deadlock in the middle of a series of poor harvests.

When Charles X attempted in July 1830 to dissolve the Chamber and reduce the already small electorate to a mere 25,000 wealthy men, Paris responded with the well-tried methods of July 1789. Charles, amazingly unprepared to crush the revolt he had provoked, abdicated. Moderate liberals, with the help of that hardy perennial of Paris revolutions, the Marquis de Lafayette, took control. Their candidate, Louis Philippe of Orléans, son of a renegade cousin of Louis XVI who had helped unleash the revolution of 1789 and had taken the name "Philippe-Egalité," ascended the throne as first and last of the Orléans dynasty. The new "July monarchy" promised France an end to experiments in absolutism.

News of the Paris revolution swept across Europe and ignited further outbreaks. But these, with the exception of stirrings in Britain and the overthrow of a number of unpopular German princelings, were of a different pattern than events in France. In Belgium, north-central Italy, and above all in Poland, the 1830 revolutions were nationalist revolts against foreign domination. The Catholic and French- or Flemish-speaking Belgians assigned to Holland after 1815 increasingly chafed under Protestant Dutch rule. Their revolution succeeded because Britain, France, and Prussia restrained the Dutch from attempting reconquest. In 1839, the five great powers guaranteed Belgium the same perpetual independence and neutrality accorded Switzerland in 1815. In Italy, revolutionaries seeking a unified Italian state, and cooperating more effectively than in 1820–21, took over Modena, Parma, and much of the Papal States. Then Metternich's armies marched south once more and restored the "legitimate" rulers.

The most tragic of the events of 1830 occurred in Poland. There intellectuals and patriots rose against the relatively mild form of Russian rule experienced under Tsar Alexander's 1815 constitution. The Russian authorities initially showed the same unpreparedness and irresolution as Charles X and the Dutch, but they soon corrected their mistake. The Russian reconquest, aided by internal dissension among the Poles, brought mass executions and imprisonment, Russian military rule, and brutal though unsuccessful attempts to Russify the population. A generation of Polish intellectuals died or emigrated.

In Germany, minor disturbances led to the granting of constitutions in Saxony, Hanover, Brunswick, and

King Louis Philippe courts the public, in a contemporary cartoon.

Hesse-Kassel. In 1832, a nationalist mass movement staged a *Nationalfest* at Hambach near Frankfurt. A crowd of 30,000 heard speakers demand wider voting rights and a national state. Metternich replied with new Carlsbad-style decrees. Silence again descended in Germany.

Finally, the July Revolution of 1830 had repercussions even in Britain. The Conservative regime of the "Peterloo Massacre" had slowly mellowed. In 1829 the Duke of Wellington's cabinet tolerated Parliament's removal of long-standing discriminatory laws against Catholics. But the scandal of the parliamentary electoral system persisted. The absence of a mechanism for redistricting meant that the new industrial cities such as Birmingham and Manchester had no representation, while "pocket boroughs" and sleepy villages under the domination of one or two great landowners had seats in Parliament.

When the Conservatives balked at reform, elections in 1831 gave a majority to the opposition Whigs, or liberals. In 1832, after the House of Lords had tried and failed to block reform, the Reform Bill became law. It eliminated the worst abuses and extended the suf-

THE REFORM BILL.

The Reform Bill of 1832, dramatized in a contemporary cartoon. Pocket boroughs go into the "Reform Mill" and a triumphant Britannia emerges.

frage to one adult male in five, compared to one in twenty in Louis Philippe's France. Gradual reform, although fitful and grudgingly granted, helped Britain escape the continental cycle of bloody repression and bloodier revolution.

Internationally, the 1830 outbreaks restored the solidarity of the three eastern monarchies that the Greek war had broken. All three ruled Poles. Austria, Prussia, and Russia therefore met in 1833 at Münchengrätz in Bohemia. Under Metternich's guidance they arrived at agreements in the spirit of the "Holy Alliance" that lasted until 1848 and after. Russia and Austria pledged to resist jointly any threat to their Polish lands. They also bound themselves to oppose further changes in the status quo in Turkey and to act together if a change seemed unavoidable. This last agreement was a symptom of the continuing importance of the "Eastern Question," which was to drive Austria and Russia apart repeatedly until the final crisis of 1914.

After the close of the Greek affair, Russia had moved to assume the position of "protector" to and eventual heir of the ever-declining Ottoman Empire. A few months before Münchengrätz, Russia had landed troops at Constantinople to protect the Sultan from attack through Syria by his rebellious Egyptian vassal, the former Albanian bandit chieftain Mehemet Ali. Russian protectorate of Turkey inevitably aroused Britain, whose strategic interest in maintaining its Mediterranean route to India dictated keeping Russia locked in the Black Sea.

But not until Mehemet Ali's second war with Turkey in 1839–40 did the British have an opportunity to act. The boisterous Lord Palmerston, a fit successor to Castlereagh and Canning as foreign secretary, made full use of British power, now reaching its zenith relative to continental rivals. When Mehemet Ali's forces drove into Lebanon on their way to Constantinople, Palmerston orchestrated diplomatic cooperation between Britain, Austria

and Russia. At the scene, the Royal Navy bombarded Beirut and a landing force cut the Egyptians to shreds. Mehemet Ali subsided; the Turkish empire for the moment survived.

The only opposition came from Louis Philippe's France. Nostalgic for the Egyptian colony that Napoleon had failed to bequeath, France broke with its "liberal" partner, Britain, and in 1840 briefly challenged all of Europe. British naval supremacy and a sudden blaze of hostility to France across the Rhine brought Louis Philippe's ministers to their senses. As the crisis subsided, Britain took Russia's place as chief "protector" of Turkey. The Turkish Straits, by 1841 treaty between the great powers, were now closed to warships in time of peace: thus Russia was caged. If war came, Palmerston was confident Russia would remain so, for Turkey and Britain would be allies and Russia's Black Sea coasts would lie open to bombardment by the Royal Navy.

In Europe itself, the chief importance of the 1839–40 crisis was as warning for the future. The Germanies had reacted in kind to French bellicosity. Nationalist sentiment reached heights not touched at Hambach in 1832. "The Watch on the Rhine," a catchy anti-French tune, enjoyed fierce popularity. The marvelous Habsburg anthem of the great composer Haydn received new German-national words: "Germany, Germany, before everything, before everything in the world." The lack of moderation of *Deutschland über Alles* was symptomatic. Also symptomatic was Prussia's role in the crisis. As Germany's bulwark against France, the Prussian power-state gained a new German-national prestige.

THE END OF REVOLUTION, 1848–50

Fear of revolution, the chief inhibition of the status quo powers, still held German nationalism in check. Before the way was clear for the subversion of the international status quo, Europe had to pass in 1848–49 through a third and culminating round of the revolutions that had shaken it since 1815. The new upheavals combined features of 1789, 1820, and 1830.

The underlying structural preconditions for revolution in 1848 were similar to those of 1789 and 1830. Predominantly agrarian societies with rapidly expanding populations and relatively slow increases in productivity faced a food crisis. The population of most European states had increased by 30 to 40 percent in the 30 years from 1815 to 1845. Urban workers spent between 60 and 70 percent of their wages on food. And in the previous 50 years the working classes had come to depend disproportionately on one crop, an innovation from the Americas—the potato.

When a fungus rotted potato crops from 1845 to 1847 and grain blights also struck most of Europe, the result was unrest from Ireland to Poland. Agricultural collapse, as in 1788–89, also gen-

erated a downturn in commerce and industry; food prices and unemployment rose simultaneously in the cities, with grim consequences. Grain prices peaked in early 1847 and declined thereafter, but the business slump, and unemployment, continued (see Figure 26-1). And this temporary crisis sharpened the impact of a deeper structural change: the creeping introduction of machinery had begun by 1848 to impoverish or drive from business many of the artisans who formed the majority of the urban population. These conditions, in combination with the political myth of the Great Revolution of 1789, produced a chain reaction in the spring of 1848: western and central Europe's last revolutions from below.

But 1848 was also not 1789. The essential differences that made the transnational movement of 1848–49 far wider but immeasurably shallower than 1789 were four. First, the example of the Terror of 1792–94 deterred the

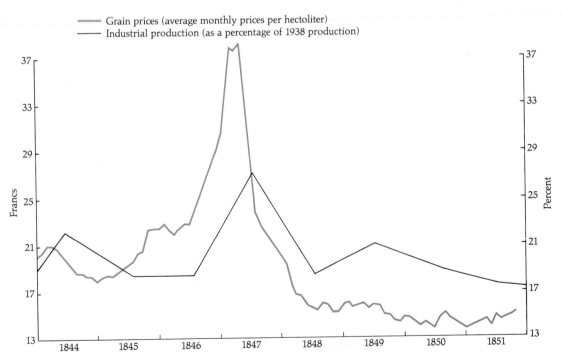

FIGURE 26-1   France: Economic Forces and Revolution, 1848

From Maurice Agulhon, *1848 ou l'apprentissage de la République* (Paris: Éditions du Seuil, 1973), pp. 100–01.

moderate liberals who led most of the revolutions from pushing too hard against the old order. One seasoned observer and participant in the events (Alexis de Tocqueville, whose *Democracy in America* is among the two or three greatest nineteenth-century works on politics) put it well: "We sought . . . to warm ourselves with the passions of our fathers, without quite managing it; we imitated their gestures and poses as we had seen them on the stage, since we could not imitate their enthusiasm or feel their rage."

Second, this absence of fanatical leadership from above found a counterpart below, at least in the countryside. The peasants of central Europe sacked a few manor houses and attacked Jewish moneylenders. But the old order in the countryside did not totally break down, as it had in the Great Fear of 1789. The ingredient that had helped convert noble and urban revolt into the destruction of the old order was largely absent in 1848.

In France the peasants had profited from 1789 and were now indifferent or hostile to Parisian radicalism. In Germany and Austria both monarchical bureaucrats and liberals moved swiftly to bribe the peasants into passivity. Officials and parliamentarians rather than revolutionaries abolished most remaining vestiges of service obligations to landowners. In Austrian Poland, in one of the earliest incidents in the wave of unrest that preceded 1848, the authorities had even crushed a nationalist rising by inciting non-Polish peasants to massacre their Polish landlords.

The revolutions of 1848 were thus essentially urban, except where, as in Hungary, the rural upper classes helped lead a national insurrection. And the revolutions came above all from two groups: the intellectuals and the aritisans. The former generally hated the old regime for its failure, as they saw it, to recognize their talents. Hunger or fear of hunger moved the artisans. The intellectuals demanded political or national rights; the artisans

economic ones. The intellectuals for the most part called for free competition, for industry, for "progress." The artisans aspired to return to the cozy world of guild restrictions, or, as a minimum, to a job guaranteed by the state. The intellectuals feared "the mob." The artisans in turn soon recognized how little the intellectuals offered them. This mutual hostility of the two principal revolutionary forces (forces briefly allied in 1793–94 under Robespierre) was the third major reason for the collapse of the 1848 revolutions.

The fourth and most important difference between 1848–49 and 1789–94 was the absence of war, which had spread the revolution of 1789 across Europe while necessitating and justifying radicalization at home. In 1848 the moderate liberals riding the wave of Parisian radicalism soon showed unexpected caution. The new French foreign minister, the poet Alphonse de Lamartine, took a sober line in the face of radical demands for yet another crusade of peoples against kings: "We love Poland, we love Italy, we love all oppressed peoples, but we love France above all else. . . ." Middle classes and peasantry, beneficiaries of 1789, had lost all desire to export revolution. France once again became a republic, but remained a status quo power. Further east, German radicals and even moderate liberals yearned for a great war—but the Prussian monarchy refused to oblige. And without a great revolutionary war to throw central and eastern Europe into the melting pot, the old order was bound to recover.

1848–49: From Outbreak to Collapse

The year of revolutions opened with a Sicilian uprising against the Bourbons of Naples: an antitax revolt, mixed with brigandage and Sicilian particularism. It was the overthrow of the king of the French, Louis Philippe of Orléans, on February 22–24, 1848, that roused Europe. The opposition to Louis Philippe staged banquets featuring speeches in favor of wider voting rights. When the government banned further banquets, the result was the now-customary explosion of violence. After fighting that produced fewer than 400 dead, Louis Philippe fled for London. Lamartine and other moderate republicans proclaimed the second French republic.

News traveled rapidly. On March 13, crowd violence in Vienna led to panic at the Habsburg court, which dismissed Metternich. The symbol of the reactionary Holy Alliance departed ignominiously for exile—in liberal London. Metternich's replacement with a cabinet of indecisive bureaucrats was the signal for further revolutionary outbreaks. The city of Milan, in an action justly famous as the first mass example of Italian nationalism, revolted against Austria. In five days of bitter fighting in March, the Milanese, armed with a few muskets and with pikes from La Scala opera house, harried the Austrian garrison. Field Marshal Joseph Radetzky, veteran of the wars against Napoleon, withdrew in defeat. The Hungarians, the principal subject nation of the Habsburgs after the Germans, demanded and received the right to domestic self-government. To the north, news of Metternich's fall unleashed street demonstrations in Berlin and other German cities. In Berlin, after his troops fired on the crowd on March 18, the eccentric King Frederick William IV panicked and virtually surrendered. Military Prussia received a ministry of moderate liberals and a constitution.

The revolution seemed to have swept all before it. Only the two great powers at the opposite ends of Europe and of the scale of political, social, and economic development were exempt: Britain and Russia. In Russia only the nobility was as yet politically conscious. In Britain the Chartist League's agitation for universal manhood suffrage never passed beyond the stage of decorous mass meetings.

But even in Paris, Vienna, and Berlin appearances were deceptive, for the armies remained intact. France unex-

The Vienna crowd mounts the barricades, March 1848.

pectedly took the lead in reining in the revolution. In April 1848 the new republic held the first free elections under universal manhood suffrage of any major European power. The results were a stinging repudiation of revolutionary Paris. Peasants and provincial middle classes voted for moderates and monarchists.

The new national assembly, faithfully representing the views of the majority of the electorate, soon began to dismantle the most striking gain the Paris crowd had achieved in the February revolution: the "national workshops" that gave the unemployed work at government expense. The unemployed and the revolutionary artisans of Paris understandably reacted. Without political leadership, without coordination, but with the tenacity of despair, they rose on June 22. The army and the paramilitary National Guard, under Eugène Cavaignac, a

The adventurer: Napoleon III.

republican general who had learned his trade in colonial Algeria, fought back pitilessly. Perhaps 5,000 died in the "June Days"; at least 3,000 were insurgents shot after resistance had ceased.

The republic, with its moderate-monarchist chamber, then faced the future without a monarch. Bourbons and Orléans had in turn proved themselves unsuitable. As in 1799, a Bonaparte stepped in to fill the vacuum. In December 1848 the votes of moderates and peasantry bore the dissolute and eccentric nephew of the great Napoleon, Louis Napoleon Bonaparte, into office as president of the republic. Revolutionary universal suffrage had proved remarkably conservative in practice.

The example France had given in the June days found a parallel in central Europe. Prince Alfred Windischgrätz, commander of the Habsburg forces in the Czech lands, crushed a quasi-insurrection in Prague in mid-June and dispersed the Slav Congress that had met to call for Czech rights. A man "equally devoid of fear or pity," he hit upon the simple expedient of withdrawing his troops from the rebellious city and bombarding it into submission with artillery.

In Italy, the Habsburgs also recovered rapidly. Charles Albert of Piedmont-Sardinia followed up the victorious insurrection of the Milanese by declaring war on Austria. Italy, he proclaimed grandly, would "do it itself": Piedmont alone would defeat Austria and seize north Italy. But his poorly led army ran afoul of the canny Radetzky at the battle of Custoza in July. Charles Albert's attempt to reverse that verdict the next spring led to a second defeat at Novara and his own abdication; his principal legacy was the constitution he had grudgingly granted in March 1848. Further south, the visionary Mazzini and the greatest soldier of Italy's wars of independence, Giuseppe Garibaldi, led an epic defense of the Roman republic that radical democrats had proclaimed in February 1849. French troops that Louis Napoleon sent—in a

bid for French Catholic support—ultimately prevailed.

Victory at Prague and Custoza emboldened the Habsburg court. The addled young emperor Ferdinand ultimately abdicated in favor of his military-minded nephew Francis Joseph. Revolutionary Vienna received the Windischgrätz treatment. By late fall 1848 only Hungary, against which the Habsburgs had mobilized smaller nationalities such as the Croats, still asserted autonomy. In April 1849, after victories over invading Habsburg armies, Hungary's most radical leader, the fiery Lajos Kossuth, proclaimed Hungarian independence within "historic" borders that included large numbers of Slavs and Rumanians. Revolutionary greater Hungary proved more than a match for the Habsburgs and their Croat and Rumanian allies. But Russia, fearing that Austria's collapse would mean revolution throughout central Europe and confident by now that France would not launch a war over Poland, intervened massively. By August 1849 Russian arms had bloodily restored Hungary to Habsburg control.

Far to the north, in Germany, the revolution fared no better. In the spring of 1848 leading liberals such as Max von Gagern of Hesse-Darmstadt urged on Frederick William IV of Prussia a revolutionary German-national war against Russia. Restoring Poland was to be the pretext, German unity and German domination of central Europe the real goal. But Frederick William, irresolute in many things, was firm on monarchical solidarity. He angrily rejected German liberalism's war: "By God, I shall not draw the sword against Russia."

The movement of German intellectuals that culminated in an all-German Parliament at Frankfurt in May 1848 therefore faced an insoluble dilemma. The war that nationalists yearned for to achieve unity required the cooperation of the very dynasties and princely armies that stood in the way of unity. The Frankfurt Parliament of lawyers and professors did succeed in launch-

Nationalities of the Habsburg Empire

ing a brief war against Denmark in April 1848, after the disputed but overwhelmingly German-speaking border duchies of Schleswig and Holstein had revolted from Denmark. But the Prussian troops who did most of the fighting stopped on Frederick William IV's orders when the king found he faced British, French, and above all Russian disapproval. A brief renewal of the war in 1849 ended similarly.

In Prussia itself the army and bureaucracy took heart after Windischgrätz's reduction of Vienna. Frederick William appointed a general as prime minister in November 1848. Then the king closed parliament and imposed a conservative constitution to

match the new face of his government. In spring 1849 Prussian troops moved south to crush short-lived democratic republics in Saxony, the Bavarian Palatinate, and Baden. The revolutionaries who had overthrown the grand duke of Baden fought with particular tenacity against a Prussian army under Frederick William IV's brother and eventual successor William. William in turn had a number of captured revolutionary leaders shot.

The end of revolution did not restore stability immediately to Germany. Frederick William had refused the crown of a united Germany that the moribund Frankfurt Parliament had offered him in April 1849. But his disdain for this "crown smelling of the gutter" did not prevent him from aspiring to a similar offer from his fellow-princes. Embarrassment in Hungary might yet induce Vienna to accept Prussian domination of Germany. By summer 1849 Frederick William had recruited most German princes for his "Prussian Union." Then Austria moved to reconstitute the German Confederation of 1815. Both powers appealed to Russia. In November 1850 a standoff nearly led to war when Austria and the Confederation challenged Prussia's control of the vital military roads across Hesse that linked the Prussian Rhineland to Berlin. Austrian and Prussian patrols traded shots for the first time since 1778. Prussia mobilized. Russia, seeking to restore the pre-1848 status quo and unenthusiastic about the emergence of a powerful

united Germany, backed Austria. Some Prussian generals were confident of victory but Frederick William was no more willing to fight Russia than he had been in 1848. By the treaty of Olmütz (November 29, 1850) Prussia agreed to dismantle the Prussian Union and to demobilize. After long negotiation, Berlin also consented to restore the German Confederation of 1815. That agreement, which Prussian chauvinists denounced as the "humiliation of Olmütz," put off the struggle for mastery in central Europe for a generation.

From Revolution to Nationalism

The failure of revolution in 1848 meant the end of an era dominated by the example of 1789. The old pattern of periodic agricultural crises, urban and rural revolt, middle-class radical leadership, and government irresolution and ineptitude had shown its limitation—at least in the absence of a continent-wide war. Railroads henceforth brought cheap food to urban markets and industrialization supplied work for impoverished and displaced ex-artisans. Middle-class intellectuals feared the masses they claimed to lead more than the old order they aspired to overthrow. And after the first shocks of March 1848, governments had swiftly recovered their resolve. The brilliant generalship of Radetzky and the successful brutality of Cavaignac, Windischgrätz, and Prince William of Prussia showed that the triumph of "the Revolution" was far from inevitable. Governments even began to imitate Britain in co-opting the lower orders.

The freedom from fear of revolution that Europe's statesmen now enjoyed liberated them from some pre-1848 restraints on vigorous pursuit of state power interests. The year 1848 also changed the definition of those interests by revealing the full power of the revolution's child, nationalism. From the Turkish Balkans to Schleswig-Holstein, awakened nationalities clamored for self-determination. History

The balance of power, by the French artist and caricaturist Honoré Daumier.

and reason, their nationalist intellectuals claimed, gave them "historic rights."

Under the old dynastic order, nationality and language had only sometimes been a matter of life or death. Now they became the single most powerful source of bloodshed. For each nationality defined "history" and "reason" according to its own convenience, and the mixed settlement pattern of central Europe ensured that right conflicted with right. The only remedy, as Kossuth had explained to the Serbs in 1849, was naked force: "The sword shall decide between us." That sword, the sword of nationalism, was to cleave first Europe and then the world.

In 1848—and this too was a portent for the future—the most powerful of European nationalisms showed its hand. The Frankfurt Parliament was short on deeds and long on deliberation, but it had one indisputable merit. Its discussions registered faithfully in cold print the aims of the German national movement. The Parliament debated the claims of the Poles in Posen, the activities of the Slav Congress in Prague, the rights of the Danes of Schleswig. Voices of moderation stood little chance in the face of calls for "healthy national egotism," of exhortations to resist "the attempts of the puny little nationalities to set up housekeeping in our midst, and like parasites to destroy our own existence," and of proclamations that Germany's final mission was to wrest world mastery from Britain. The unanswered long-term question was whether Europe could tolerate such a Germany.

THE MAKING OF ITALY AND GERMANY

In the aftermath of the year of revolutions, the "Holy Alliance" alignment that had maintained stability since 1815 appeared restored. Russia had underwritten Austria's survival and had shepherded Frederick William IV back

> # German Nationalism Speaks: Voices from the Frankfurt Parliament
>
> To want to resurrect Poland merely because its downfall fills with justified regret, I call moronic sentimentality. . . . Our right is none other than the right of the stronger, the right of conquest. . . . The German conquests in Poland were a necessity of nature. The law of history is not the same as that in the law books. History knows only the laws of nature, one of which tells us that a people does not gain the right to political independence through mere existence, but only through having the power to assert itself as a state among other states.
> —*Wilhelm Jordan (Berlin), a member of the center-left, in the debate on Posen, July 25, 1848.*
>
> . . . but it is our aim to found a giant empire [*Reich*] of 70 million, and if possible of 80 or 100 million, and plant the standard of Arminius [a famous Germanic chieftain who had smashed three Roman legions in A.D. 9] in that *Reich*, to stand there armed against east and west, against the Slavic and Latin peoples, to wrest mastery of the seas from the English, and to become the most powerful nation [*Volk*] on this earth—*that* is Germany's future! With that prospect in view, petty debates over the drafting of our constitution, all petty debates, [must] retreat into the background. . . .
> —*Count Friedrich Deym, a liberal Austrian noble, in the debate of October 27, 1848.*
>
> *Stenographischer Bericht über die Verhandlungen der deutschen constituirenden Nationalversammlung zu Frankfurt am Main* (Leipzig: Teubner, 1848–49), Vol. 2, pp. 1144–46; Vol. 4, p. 2882 (translation by M. Knox).

into the conservative fold. But restoration swiftly proved an illusion.

Napoleon Tilts the Balance, 1852–56

The chief agent of upheaval, for the last time in Europe's modern history, was France—or rather a Bonaparte. Louis Napoleon, political speculator and gang leader of the conspirators who had helped him to power, had none of the attributes of his great uncle. What he did have was a messianic belief, derived from a naive reading of his uncle's cynical propaganda, in the virtues of national self-determination. Even before taking power, he had conceived vague schemes for the reorganization

A CONSULTATION ABOUT THE STATE OF TURKEY.

A Consultation about the State of Turkey, a mid-nineteenth-century cartoon. The "Sick Man of Europe" (Turkey) is threatened by Death (Russia), while the physicians (France and England) hold their consultation.

Nicholas miscalculated both London's willingness to see Turkey bullied and the influence of a new factor in international politics, British public opinion. The Turks, confident of French and British support, refused Russia's demands.

Russia thereupon occupied the Turkish principalities at the mouth of the Danube, threatening Austria as well as Turkey. Britain and France ordered their fleets to Constantinople to overawe the tsar. That move encouraged the Ottoman Sultan, in October 1853, to declare war on Russia. In November, Russia's annihilation of the Turkish fleet at Sinope in the Black Sea (the "Sinope Massacre") galvanized the British public, which abhorred Russia after its intervention in Hungary.

When Russia refused to evacuate the Danubian principalities, Britain and France declared war. Britain fought to humble Russia and keep it from further encroachments on Turkey that would threaten British communications to India. Napoleon III fought to stir up trouble in Europe. Neither ran serious risks, for neither shared a border with Russia. For Austria it was otherwise; geography dictated that if it fought Russia it would fight for life itself. Austria therefore remained on the fence. It mobilized to urge Russia out of the principalities, but made no move. That fact, and the neutrality of Prussia and the lesser German states, prevented general war.

Instead, once the Russians evacuated the principalities in August 1854, Britain and France no longer had an objective. Russian "aggression" against Turkey had ceased. But bloodless victory did not lead to peace. The ebullient Palmerston spurred the cabinet and an inflamed British public demanded action. The allies pressed on in an attempt to destroy Russian power to threaten Turkey in the future. An allied amphibious expedition landed in the Crimea to attack Russia's principal Black Sea naval base, Sebastopol.

Predictably, given bitter Russian resistance and the immense logistical ef-

of Europe along lines far different than those of 1815. After the inevitable coup d'état in December 1851, he proclaimed himself Napoleon III, Emperor of the French, and began searching for a way to throw Europe's borders into the melting pot.

Given the newly restored stability in central Europe and Russian backing for Austria in Italy, the "Eastern Question" seemed to offer the best opportunities. Napoleon III might there acquire the Napoleonic prestige needed to consolidate his rule at home, and compel Russia to give up its role as guarantor of Austria. In 1851–52 Napoleon III challenged Russian claims to a protectorate over the Christian holy sites in the Ottoman Empire, which included Palestine. French battleship diplomacy at Constantinople provoked Tsar Nicholas to send an uncouth representative of his own to bully the Sultan. But fort of maintaining large forces by sea, the expedition was a fiasco. It required 18 months of bloody fighting to take Sebastopol. The new industrial fire-power was already beginning to make movement on the battlefield difficult. The Crimean War cost at least three quarters of a million dead, of which 80 percent died of cholera, dysentery, or typhus.

The war's main consequence was the disruption of the European state system, a disruption that ultimately permitted the wars that created Italian and German nation-states in 1859–60 and 1866–71. Russia indeed suffered a decisive check. It lost the right to have a Black Sea fleet, as Britain desired. But the war had other consequences London had neither bargained on nor greatly welcomed. Under Nicholas I's successor, Tsar Alexander II, Russia turned inward for a generation. Russian power no longer threatened Turkey. It also no longer upheld Austria. Indeed, Russia now sought revenge for the Austrian "ingratitude" that had repaid Russia's aid in Hungary in 1849 with a tilt toward the western powers in 1853–56.

France was the chief beneficiary of this breakdown of the conservative alignment. Napoleon III presided imperially over the 1856 Paris peace conference. Much to the disgust of the British, he was soon intriguing for a bargain with Russia that would help him to redraw the map of Europe. In this new situation, other statesmen also stirred.

The Making of Italy, 1858–60

In the last stages of the Crimean War, the "Italian Question" had reemerged from the limbo into which Radetzky's victories had thrust it in 1848–49. Piedmont had sent 15,000 troops to the Crimea to gain favor with Britain and France. Charles Albert's successor, the erratic Victor Emmanuel II, had wanted to fight at all costs to restore the prestige tarnished at Custoza and Novara. His liberal prime minister, Count

Britain in the Crimea: bewhiskered officers of the 8th Hussars.

Camillo di Cavour, had imposed war on his cabinet colleagues rather than risk a royal coup against the constitution and war under a ministry of conservatives. Cavour thus gained access to the Paris conference, at which he proceeded to embarrass the Austrians by criticizing their support of corrupt regimes in the Papal States and Bourbon Naples.

Dictatorial in temper but an admirer of the British parliament, Cavour was an unparalleled master of political improvisation, a "Piedmontese Machiavelli." His chief weakness was his tendency, striking even in the age of the duplicitous and vacillating Napoleon III, to flagrant untruths that diminished his credibility: "If we did for ourselves what we are doing for Italy, we should be real scoundrels." His goal was to expand Piedmont, not to create an Italian nation-state. He also labored under severe constraints. National revolution, if encouraged too much, might yet turn into barbaric peasant revolt. And only north Italy appeared suitable for annexation to Piedmont. The South

The makers of Italy: Count Camillo di Cavour (left) and Giuseppe Garibaldi (right).

was a world centuries behind Lombardy and Piedmont; great landowners and gangs—*mafia, n'drangheta,* and *camorra*—dominated a downtrodden peasantry under the theoretical sovereignty of pope and Bourbons. Above all, Cavour faced the unbroken power of Austria. The lesson of 1848–49 was that Italy could *not* do it itself.

Not all Italians agreed. Mazzini held to his vision of an Italy created through spontaneous uprising from below by the—nonexistent—nationalist masses. An Italian National Society came into being in 1857 with a more practical goal: support for a renewed Piedmontese bid for expansion. Garibaldi, revealed in 1848–49 as a great military talent, awaited his chance. The creation of an Italian state was ultimately the product both of a "royal war" of Cavour, king, and Napoleon III, and of pressure from below from Mazzini's ideas and Garibaldi's freebooters.

Initially everything depended on Napoleon III. In January 1858 the explosion of an Italian revolutionary's bomb outside the Paris Opera reminded Napoleon that he had yet to do "something for Italy." He soon approached Cavour. The two met in secret at Plombières near the Piedmontese border in July 1858 and agreed

on a program. A French-Piedmontese war against Austria would seize Lombardy, Venetia, Parma, and Modena for Piedmont. In return for committing 200,000 troops, Napoleon would receive Savoy, an Italian satellite state, and the domestic prestige of a Napoleonic Italian campaign. The Pope would lose territory but become head of an Italian confederation of states. To Cavour, Napoleon III allotted the task of provoking Austria into war without himself appearing the aggressor, and of providing 100,000 troops.

To present this Franco-Piedmontese war of conquest to international opinion as justified self-defense required all of Cavour's ingenuity. At the end, in April 1859, Austrian recklessness saved him. Vienna's bullying ultimatum demanding that Piedmont demobilize destroyed what little was left of Austria's international backing. England, despite misgivings about Napoleon III, stood aside; the aftermath of the 1857 Indian mutiny (see pp. 759–60) had absorbed most of Britain's limited land power. Russia watched Austria's humiliation with satisfaction. Only Prussia, Austria's other rival, offered aid. But its price was the reversal of Olmütz: Prussian supremacy in north Germany.

The Making of Italy   1859–70

The war itself was swift, for Napoleon III and Cavour had isolated their opponent. The Piedmontese army only scraped together 50,000 men instead of the 100,000 Cavour had blithely promised, but this time it faced no Radetzky. Piedmont fought a creditable holding action until the French arrived, partly by rail. In two bloody battles of June 1859 at Magenta and Solferino the French drove the Austrians back with furious charges against Minié rifle fire. Fortunately for the French, the Austrians were remarkably poor shots.

Then Napoleon III, appalled at a carnage for which he lacked his uncle's strong stomach, incensed at the meagerness of his allies' contribution, disquieted by signs that Cavour coveted central as well as north Italy, and unnerved at a Prussian threat on the Rhine, called a halt. By the July armistice of Villafranca with Emperor Francis Joseph, Napoleon III abandoned Cavour to his own devices. Piedmont would receive only Lombardy. Cavour, when he heard that Victor Emmanuel II had agreed without consulting him, resigned in chagrin. He seemed to have lost.

But Cavour had proved his indispensability, and Victor Emmanuel II recalled him in January 1860. Cavour soon engineered the annexation of Tuscany, Romagna, Parma, and Modena to enlarged Piedmont. Rigged plebiscites, a favorite Napoleonic device, seemingly confirmed the unanimity of national sentiment. Napoleon III, outwitted in his attempt to confine Piedmont to the north Italian plain, now demanded his price: Savoy, which was French-speaking, and the city of Nice, which was not. Cavour acquiesced, to the fury of Piedmontese public opinion. Garibaldi bitterly resented the cession of Nice, his home town, but he soon had his revenge. Despite Cavour's half-hearted attempts to stop them, Garibaldi and a volunteer "thousand" left Genoa for Sicily in early May 1860. Against Cavour's expectations and hopes, Garibaldi's ill-equipped troops routed the Bourbon army, raised the Sicilian peasantry, crossed to the mainland, and took Naples.

The epic campaign of "the Thousand" made Italy. To derail the social revolutionary elements of Garibaldi's program and to rescue the prestige of Piedmont, Cavour and Victor Emmanuel II had to act. The Piedmontese army invaded the Papal States and moved on Naples. Garibaldi, a monarchist at heart unlike the fiercely republican Mazzini, yielded his conquests to the new Kingdom of Italy. He received scant thanks from Cavour or from the Piedmontese army.

Italy was complete except for Venetia, which the new state received in 1866, Rome, which it took in 1870, and Trento and Trieste, which it did not conquer until 1918. As a colleague and rival of Cavour put it, the process of "making Italians" remained. Cavour's representatives in the South soon made themselves more hated than the Bourbons. The brutal imposition of Piedmont's French-style prefects, military conscription, and high taxes on the southerners triggered a guerrilla war that lasted over five years and cost more dead than the wars of 1848–49 and 1859–60. Italy's *Risorgimento*, its political unification, had come so swiftly and had joined areas so different in culture and traditions that "making Italians" required generations. Cavour, perhaps fortunately for his reputation, died of malaria and inept doctors in mid-1861. Time alone would tell if the foundations of the Italy that he and Garibaldi had created were sound.

"Mad Junker" and maker of Prussia-Germany: Otto von Bismarck.

The Struggle for Mastery in Germany, 1862–66

Austria's isolation had made a united Italy possible. That same isolation was the precondition for a far greater revolution in the state system than the birth of Italy, "least of the great powers." That revolution was the creation of a Prusso-German nation-state.

The Prussian military monarchy at first seemed an unlikely ally for the German nationalism it had spurned in 1848. But German unity, if it came at all, clearly had to come through one of the two German great powers, Prussia and Austria. And by the early 1860s Prussia possessed advantages Austria could not match. First, except for its Polish provinces, it was wholly German. Second, its Ruhr Valley coal and iron and its leadership since the 1830s of a German Customs Union, the *Zollverein*, had already made it the economic nucleus of any conceivable German nation-state. Third, its role as military bulwark against France and if need be Russia gave even its dynastic military establishment a certain national aura. Fourth, that military establishment soon proved that it had learned from Jena and Auerstädt. In its technique if not in its politics, the Prussian army was by 1860 the most innovative armed force in the world. Finally, after September 1862 Prussia had a leader as indispensable as Cavour— Otto von Bismarck.

Bismarck was a Pomeranian Junker by birth ("I am a Junker and I mean to profit by it") but his deep understanding of historical forces and political tactics far surpassed the blinkered outlook of his caste. He combined apparently genuine Pietist religious convictions with a total absence of political scruple. But like Cavour and unlike their successors in both countries, Bismarck recognized limits. Politics was "the art of the possible." Statesmen could exploit great historical forces but not stand against them: "the stream carries you, but cannot be ruled" ran his favorite Latin tag. Bismarck's political technique—like that of the great Napoleon in warfare—was to aim at a range of alternative goals and to be prepared to achieve them by a variety of means, always leaving for himself a fall-back position in the event of failure. When Bismarck gambled on war it was only after exploring and ruling out less risky alternatives and after reducing incalculable dangers as far as possible. And once war had achieved his ends, he became as fierce a defender of the new status quo as he had been an opponent of the old.

Bismarck, like Cavour, did not set out to found a nation-state. His early career as fiery opponent of liberalism and nationalism in the Prussian Chamber in 1848 had branded him, in words that Frederick William IV had perhaps meant as a compliment, as a "red reactionary, smells of blood." But Bismarck's appointment as Prussian ambassador to the German Confederation in 1851 led to a slow change in his outlook. He came to recognize two things— that Austria's claim to leadership of the Confederation was incompatible with Prussia's dignity and security, and that Prussia's natural ally in the struggle for mastery in Germany was German nationalism. Monarchical solidarity abroad and unbending conservatism at home were contrary to Prussia's interests as a state: "Prussia's mission is to extend itself." Prussia must not tie its trim frigate to the "moth-eaten Austrian galleon." In 1859 he had urged Berlin to "let Austria get thoroughly bogged down in its war with France and then break out southwards with our entire army, taking our border posts in our knapsacks and planting them either on [the Swiss border] or wherever the Protestant religion ceases to predominate. . . ."

Berlin ignored that shocking advice. What catapulted Bismarck into power as prime minister and foreign minister in September 1862 was not his ruthlessly unconventional approach to foreign affairs. It was rather the ever-deepening deadlock between the Prussian Chamber and the new king, William I, who had succeeded his incapacitated brother Frederick William IV as regent in 1858 and as king in 1861. The military-minded new king sought to more than double the strength of the army's line units to half a million men and to reduce correspondingly the role of the reserves, which had middle-class officers. The reorganization and the accompanying increase of compulsory military service from two years to three would drastically increase the weight of the army within Prussian society. It would also dramatically increase Prus-

Bismarck Takes Office: "Iron and Blood"   1862

Germany looks not to Prussia's liberalism, but to its power; Bavaria, Württemberg, Baden may indulge in liberalism, but Prussia's role is not for them. Prussia must concentrate its power and hold it concentrated for the favorable moment that we have already several times missed. Prussia's borders as drawn in the Vienna treaties do not favor a healthy state existence; the great questions of our time are not decided through speeches and majority votes—that was the great error of 1848 and 1849—but through iron and blood.

—*Bismarck, to the Prussian Chamber's budget committee, September 27, 1862.*

From *Bismarck: Die gesammelten Werke* (Berlin: Otto Stollberg Verlag, 1928), Vol. 10, p. 140 (translation by M. Knox).

sia's external striking power. But the liberal majority in the Prussian Chamber repeatedly blocked funding of these plans. William, determined to have his way on grounds both of military efficiency and of monarchical authority, morosely contemplated the English precedent, the struggle between crown and parliament in the 1640s. In this impasse the king turned to Bismarck as the one man steadfast enough to dominate the Chamber and see the king's will done.

Bismarck immediately sought to defuse the constitutional conflict by playing the card of German nationalism. In a speech that was half challenge and half enticement, he announced that "iron and blood" would settle the German question. The liberals professed to be shocked. Bismarck's first bid for liberal cooperation had failed, although some of them had long called for "a great genius or mighty tyrant . . . capable of decisive action."

The "iron and blood" speech also appalled the king. But Bismarck put the issue to him in military terms: he could fight for his throne or tamely surrender. The fight involved muzzling the press, disciplining liberal sympathizers

The new model Prussian army, 1861.

in the bureaucracy, and spending money that the Chamber had not appropriated on an army reorganization that it opposed. To the Chamber Bismarck impudently proclaimed his "loophole theory" of the constitution: when king and parliament disagreed, the king's latent powers entitled him to act for the general welfare. The conflict deepened. New elections returned the latest in a series of ever larger liberal majorities. Thanks to the "three-class" Prussian election law, which weighted votes by wealth, those majorities represented only middle-class opinion. But Bismarck's fellow Junkers would not yet let him play the masses against the liberals.

Foreign policy ultimately offered a way around the impasse, as Bismarck had hoped. A new Polish revolt, even more tragic than that of 1830, convulsed Russian Poland in 1863. Russian repression of the Poles alienated Napoleon III, whose alignment with Russia had underwritten the Italian war. Now each of the European great powers were isolated from one another—except Prussia, which maintained its "line to St. Petersburg." In this open situation, Bismarck soon found a cause that would allow him to undermine the status quo while professing conservative intentions acceptable to Russia and Austria. In 1863 the Danish monarchy moved to incorporate Schleswig, with its minority of Danes and majority of Germans, into Denmark. That step was a flagrant breach of the 1852 Treaty of London that had ended the first two rounds of German-Danish fighting in 1848–49 and had confirmed the continued membership of the Duchies of Schleswig and Holstein in the German Confederation. In January 1864 Bismarck therefore secured an alliance with Vienna to restore the status quo, if need be by force. He himself secretly aspired to annex the Duchies to Prussia as the first step toward Prussia's long-sought hegemony in north Germany.

The Danish war of 1864 was swift and decisive, and British protests to Berlin and Vienna were half-hearted.

Britain had tilted too close to the Confederacy in the U.S. Civil War, and found itself by 1864 facing the eventual prospect of a million battle-hardened Union Veterans on Canada's indefensible borders. It had no troops to spare to rescue Denmark. When the Danes foolishly rejected Bismarck's offer of a compromise, the Prussians stormed the key Danish position at Düppel in April 1864. In August, in the face of a Prussian amphibious threat to Copenhagen, the Danes ceded both Schleswig and Holstein unconditionally to Prussia and Austria.

That triumph demonstrated the power of the newly reorganized Prussian army, and lessened domestic pressure on Bismarck. Influential liberal publications soon came around to the view that Prussian state interest and German nationalism ran parallel: Prussia should annex the Duchies. Bismarck himself settled for a policy of gradual encroachment upon his Austrian partner. He would "try all roads, the most dangerous road, last." If Austria would concede Prussia the Duchies and the mastery of north Germany, Prussia would perhaps underwrite Austria's survival. If Austria proved obstinate, force would decide.

The Austrians professed themselves shocked at Bismarck's suggestions of virtual Prussian annexation of their joint property, the Duchies. Vienna had joined Bismarck's Danish war in hopes of a conservative partnership to cement the status quo in central Europe. Too late it discovered that its partner had other ideas. But Bismarck was not ready for war in 1865, although the newly victorious chief of the general staff, Helmuth von Moltke, was confident. Prussian and Austrian leaders met at Bad Gastein in August and "papered over the cracks." Prussia would administer Schleswig, Austria Holstein, and the partners would reject the claims of the German-national candidate to rule the Duchies, the Duke of Augustenburg.

The Gastein agreement lasted only a few months. Vienna was dimly aware that it could only preserve its position in the German Confederation with the support of the lesser states. It therefore broke the Gastein agreement and courted Augustenburg, the candidate of those states and of non-Prussian liberal opinion. Bismarck, on holiday at Biarritz, sounded out Napoleon III in October 1865; the Emperor did not object to Prussian expansion. He presumably expected a long and indecisive Austro-Prussian war that would give France numerous opportunities to intervene and demand its price. By February 1866 Bismarck was sure of his course. He put Austria's violations of the Gastein agreement to a Prussian crown council. William I, convinced of Austrian disloyalty, agreed that Prussia must prepare for war. The issue was simple: who was to be master in Germany.

Yet Bismarck still had to secure allies, and overcome William I's lingering scruples. Italy was happy to sign a three-month offensive alliance in April, thus performing the essential function of tying down large Austrian forces in Venetia. Bismarck, the conservative statesman, also conspired with Hungarian revolutionaries, justifying himself with a favorite quotation from Vergil: "If I cannot prevail on heaven, I shall mobilize hell." And he again appealed to German nationalism. Prussia promised to Germany after victory a parliament elected under universal manhood suffrage.

Securing allies was easy compared to the frustrations of managing the king's conscience: "I have brought the horse to the ditch; he must jump!" Then, as in 1859, Austria rescued its enemies with an ill-timed gesture that appeared provocative. Vienna's slow and cumbersome mobilization system meant that it could not wait if hostilities seemed inevitable. And Austrian mobilization, along with warnings from conservative aides against a "second Olmütz," finally induced William I to jump. On June 7, 1866, Prussian troops attacked the Austrians in Holstein and began to concentrate on the

---

Bismarck Demands War   February 1866

The Minister President spoke . . . [to the Prussian crown council] in the following terms: Prussia is the only workable political unit that has emerged from the ruins of the old German *Reich* [the Holy Roman Empire], and that is why Prussia had been called to lead Germany. Austria in its envy has always resisted the natural and entirely justified efforts of Prussia toward that goal; it has refused to concede to Prussia the leadership of Germany that it is incapable of exercising itself. . . . Austria has granted Prussia neither the influence due it in Germany, nor the secure position in the [Schleswig-Holstein] duchies necessary to both Prussia and Germany, nor the fruits of [Prussia's] victories. . . . It would be a humiliation, if Prussia now withdrew. Any such humiliation must be avoided at all costs. But in that case a break with Austria is probable. We must therefore discuss and decide the question of whether Prussia should pull back in fright from this obstacle—a break and possible war with Austria. . . . The whole historic development of German affairs and the hostile attitude of Austria drive us toward war. It would be an error to seek to avoid it now. . . .

From the Prussian crown council minutes, February 28, 1866, in *Die auswärtige Politik Preussens 1858–1871* (Berlin: G. Stalling, 1939), Vol. 6, pp. 611ff (translation by M. Knox).

---

borders of Bohemia.

The "Seven Weeks' War" was a startling demonstration of Prussia's efficiency and might. Moltke used telegraph and railroad, proven in the U.S. Civil War (see pp. 770–74), effectively for the first time in a European war. Three Prussian armies detrained on the Bohemian border and converged with unexpected speed on the Austrian forces east of Prague. On July 3, 1866, two of the Prussian armies attacked the Austrian positions at Königgrätz (Sadowa). The firepower of the Dreyse breechloading rifle shocked the Austrians: it fired five rounds a minute to the Austrian Miníe's one and a half. And unlike troops using muzzle-loaders, the Prussians could reload and fire while lying down. The Austrians held with counterattacks and heavy artillery fire. Then, in mid-afternoon, the third Prussian army under Crown Prince Frederick arrived on the Austrian

The Making of Germany   1866–71

flank, and decided the fate of Germany. The Austrians lost 25,000 dead and wounded and 20,000 prisoners.

Bismarck stepped in to check the enthusiasm of king and generals for a push on Vienna. Further fighting would only provoke French intervention, without serving any useful purpose. Bismarck insisted that Protestant Prussia could not successfully absorb the Catholic German populations that the total destruction of the Habsburg Empire would deliver to it. The king and Moltke yielded grudgingly. By the treaties of Nikolsburg and Prague (July–August 1866) Austria renounced any role in north Germany, acquiesced in Prussia's absorption of Schleswig-Holstein, Hanover, Hesse-Cassel, and Frankfurt, and agreed to the dissolution of the German Confederation of 1815 and the creation in its place of a North German Confederation under Prussia. To avoid French intervention Bismarck left nominal independence to defeated Baden, Württemberg,

and Bavaria. But he fastened upon them military alliances that in wartime made their armies mere appendages of Prussia's.

Domestically, the war of 1866 ended the Prussian constitutional conflict. Elections, held on the day of Königgrätz, returned a conservative majority. Victory intoxicated the remaining liberals, who gladly accepted Bismarck's promises that he would in future respect the Chamber's budget rights. With the liberals as allies, Bismarck now molded the North German Confederation, the pattern for the German nation-state. He personally supervised the drafting of the new constitution. It played off a universal male suffrage *Reichstag* or lower house against representatives of the princes in the upper house. Bismarck, as Prussian prime minister and foreign minister and as chancellor of the new Confederation, held the balance. Prussia had conquered Germany, and Bismarck Prussia.

The Struggle for Mastery in Europe, 1867–71

Yet the North German Confederation was not the Germany of the dreams of the German national movement. Bismarck himself, while no nationalist, aspired from the beginning to draw the south German states into his greater Prussia. Unfortunately the economic attraction of the Prussian *Zollverein*, of a unified national market with uniform tariffs, weights, measures, and law codes, was not enough to overcome south German particularism. "Württemberg wants to remain Württemberg as long as it has the power," said that state's chief minister—a sentiment heartily echoed in Bavaria and even Baden.

Bismarck therefore once more fell back on foreign policy to drive domestic affairs. Napoleon III offered the occasion. Disgruntled at his 1866 miscalculation, smarting over the 1867 defeat of his hare-brained scheme for an empire in Mexico (see p. 764), and under increasing pressure from a liberal public opinion he had helped create by loosening his control of press and politics in the early 1860s, Napoleon III too sought a foreign victory. An initial public clash in early 1867 over a French plan to buy Luxemburg from its ruler, the king of Holland, ended in humiliation for Napoleon. Both France and Prussia came to consider war inevitable as soon as frantic French military reforms were complete.

War came in 1870. The candidacy of a junior member of the Prussian royal house for the vacant throne of Spain offered the occasion. Bismarck had pressed the plan in secret, as one more small diplomatic blow against France, but he could not have known from the beginning that it would lead to war. When the candidacy prematurely became public, the French ambassador visited William I at the summer watering place of Ems, and impertinently demanded that Prussia renounce the candidacy "forever." William I, miffed, cut the interview short. When Bismarck received the foreign office tele-gram describing the interview, he asked Moltke if the army was ready. The chief of the general staff replied that the sooner war came, the greater Prussia's relative strength. Bismarck then edited the "Ems telegram" for release to the press. The edited version implied that William I had curtly refused the French demand and had ruled out further negotiation, thus handing France a major diplomatic humiliation.

In Paris, Napoleon III's ministers and supporters reacted as Bismarck had expected. Hysterical at the visible loss since 1866 of France's leading role in Europe, they clamored "To Berlin!" France declared war on July 19, 1870, without allies. Austria had no stomach for a rematch. Italy wisely chose to remain neutral, despite the childlike enthusiasm of Victor Emmanuel II for war, any war. Russia's only thought was to free itself of the degrading Black Sea naval disarmament imposed after the Crimean War. Britain watched impotently.

Moltke's mobilization timetables once again delivered three superlatively equipped Prussian and south German armies, now totalling 380,000 men, to their railheads. The French muddled about in tragic disorder. They now had a better breechloading rifle than the Germans, the Chassepot, and a secret weapon, the *mitrailleuse*, a primitive machine gun. But the cast-steel artillery of Krupp outclassed anything the French could field, and French logistics were chaotic.

The Germans drove across the border and pushed the French back in a series of punishing battles. At Gravelotte-St. Privat, on August 18, the elite Prussian Guard corps attacked uphill across open ground. The Chassepots of the French killed or wounded 8,000 Prussians, mostly in the space of 20 minutes. Fortunately for the Germans, the ineptly led French then fell back on the fortified city of Metz. Leaving a force to screen the city, the German armies pressed on to squash Napoleon III's reserve army against the Belgian border. Desperate breakout attempts by French cavalry failed in a hail of Prussian rifle fire. The French charges were magnificent, but no longer war; the armies of Europe were beginning to discover that firepower killed. On September 2, 1870, Napoleon III surrendered his army at Sedan.

Unlike Königgrätz in 1866, Sedan did not end the war. This last of Bismarck's wars was no "cabinet war" but rather the first of three Franco-German national wars that tore Europe apart and destroyed its world position. Paris, besieged, resisted under increasingly radical leadership. A French republic based on Tours and then on Bordeaux raised new armies in the style of 1793. Guerrillas, including the intrepid Garibaldi, harried Prussian patrols and rail lines. The Prussians replied by summarily executing civilians and burning farms and villages. Those brutal measures the normally humane Bismarck, after the third bottle of looted champagne, heartily approved.

Finally, after much death, destruction, and bitterness, the French agreed to an armistice in January and signed a peace treaty at Frankfurt on May 10,

1871. The war had cost perhaps 190,000 lives. Bismarck exacted an indemnity equivalent to a billion dollars, and annexed Alsace-Lorraine, whose inhabitants mostly spoke indeterminate dialects but considered themselves French. That least moderate of his peace settlements was the consequence of the nationalist furor Bismarck had helped stir up—to compel the south German states to put their weight behind the war effort and to acquiesce in greater unity. And Bismarck achieved that last objective even before the end of war with France. With bribes from the funds of the dispossessed house of Hanover, Bismarck overcame the scruples of the king of Bavaria, the last and most powerful holdout. On January 18, 1871, in Louis XIV's Hall of Mirrors in the Versailles palace, Bismarck had William I proclaimed German Emperor, or *Kaiser*.

Bismarck had said in 1866 that "If there is to be revolution, we would rather make it than suffer it." He had made it. His "revolution from above" had produced a German national state that dwarfed its neighbors militarily

Europe in 1871

and was soon to do so economically. Internally, Bismarck had struck a compromise with middle class national liberalism, a compromise that preserved Junker power far into the twentieth century. What he deliberately did not do was to fulfill all aims of the German national movement.

Except for the annexation of Alsace-Lorraine, Bismarck had struck compromises with the defeated. He had accepted limits. He had left the Catholic Austrian Germans outside his Protestant-dominated "lesser Germany." The unsatiated aspiration of many German nationalists for a "greater Germany" spanning the continent from Schleswig to Trieste and from Strasbourg to Riga might yet undo Bismarck's work.

Western and central Europe had traveled a long road since 1815. Revolution, the legacy of 1789, was played out. A final despairing outbreak, the "Paris Commune" of March–May 1871, succumbed to the troops of the French republic soon after France's peace with Germany. The republic shot 20,000 insurgents and deported another 10,000 to a tropical death in French Guyana. The myths and realities of the new nation-state— flag-bedecked ceremonies, conscription, elections, compulsory schooling, bureaucracies, and railroads—filled the place of revolution. The power of the nation-state held great potential for good, for the prosperity and freedom of its populations, but also for evil.

Suggestions for Further Reading

General

A brilliant introducton to the period up to 1848 is E. J. Hobsbawm, *The Age of Revolution, 1789–1848* (1962). For more detail, see F. A. Artz, *Reaction and Revolution, 1814–1832* (1934); W. L. Langer, *Political and Social Upheaval, 1832–1852* (1969); and J. Droz, *Europe between Revolutions, 1815–1848* (1968). For the various powers, see especially A. Briggs, *The Making of Modern England* (1959); A. Cobban, *A History of Modern France*, Vol. II (1957); T. S. Hamerow, *Restoration, Revolution, Reaction: Economics and Politics in Germany, 1815–1871* (1958); A. J. P. Taylor, *The Habsburg Monarchy, 1809–1918* (1948); and the sardonic and brilliant R. Pipes, *Russia under the Old Regime* (1975).

Europe to 1848

On international politics before 1848, H. Nicolson, *The Congress of Vienna: A study in Allied Unity, 1812–1822* (1946), and H. G. Schenk, *The Aftermath of the Napoleonic Wars* (1947), remain serviceable. The most successful overviews of 1848–49 are P. Robertson, *Revolutions of 1848: A Social History* (1952), and P. Stearns, *1848: The Revolutionary Tide in Europe* (1974). T. S. Hamerow, *Restoration, Revolution, Reaction* (1958), is outstanding on Germany. L. Namier, *1848: The Revolution of the Intellectuals* (1964), stresses the emergence of savagely competing nationalisms; see also, in general, E. Kedourie, *Nationalism* (1960).

Europe after 1848

The best survey of the post-1848 period is again E. J. Hobsbawm, *The Age of Capital, 1848–1875* (1975). A. J. P. Taylor's brilliant *The Struggle for Mastery in Europe, 1848–1918* (1954), is still the best synthesis of nineteenth-century international politics. M. S. Anderson, *The Eastern Question* (1966), expertly chronicles the decay of the Ottoman Empire and its consequences. On the Crimean War and after, see both W. E. Mosse, *The Rise and Fall of the Crimean System, 1855–1871* (1967), and P. W. Schroeder, *Austria, Great Britain, and the Crimean War* (1979). For France after 1848, see J. M. Thompson, *Louis Napoleon and the Second Empire* (1955). D. Mack Smith, *Cavour and Garibaldi, 1860: A Study in Political Conflict* (1954), *Victor Emmanuel, Cavour, and the Risorgimento* (1971), and *Cavour* (1985), are excellent on the creation of the Italian state. On Bismarck's revolution from above, see especially O. Pflanze, *Bismarck and the Development of Germany: The Period of Unification 1815–1871* (1963), and L. Gall, *Bismarck* (1986); T. S. Hamerow, *The Social Foundations of German Unification, 1858–1871* (1969), supplies the domestic background. On the military events, D. E. Showalter, *Railroads and Rifles: Soldiers, Technology, and the Unification of Germany* (1975); G. Craig, *The Battle of Königgrätz* (1965); and M. Howard, *The Franco-Prussian War* (1961), are excellent. H. Strachan, *European Armies and the Conduct of War* (1983), provides a useful overview.

27
Europe and the World in the Nineteenth Century

*I*n the wider world, the nineteenth century was the century of Britain. Its unchallengeable superiority at sea after Trafalgar (1805) ensured that the peace outside Europe would be a *pax Britannica*. Its growing industrial might and demographic prowess led to an expansion, virtually constant throughout the century, of the area under the British flag. By 1900 the British Empire ruled 23 percent of the world's land surface and 20 percent of its population. It was Britain that for the first time in history united most of humanity in a world market that pulsed with the erratic rhythms of the business cycle. The force of that market, more than anything else, drove to its culmination the Western conquest of the world begun in 1492.

But Britain's effortless superiority in the first decades after 1815 did not last.

Its economic lead slackened as the "followers" industrialized, with political consequences in the wider world. By the 1840s and 1850s American power was beginning to make its weight felt in North America and the Caribbean. As early as the 1850s America's maritime reach touched Japan. Northern victory in the U.S. Civil War meant that Britain faced an industrial giant which it could not match in the long run. And by the 1880s European rivals were appearing in strength in Africa and East Asia: France in West Africa, Indochina and China; Germany in Africa; and Russia in north China. By the end of the century a non-European power, Japan, had risen to dominate northeast Asia. That force was a sign of the impermanence of the garish empires British and Europeans had patched together. For along with the world

The impact of Western technology on the wider world. The East India Company's steamer *Nemesis* annihilates a Chinese fleet, 1841.

market, along with gunboats, Maxim guns, rum, and Bibles, the Europeans brought nationalism to the wider world.

THE BRITISH WORLD EMPIRE

The 1815 Settlement outside Europe

Britain had consolidated its first empire in the Seven Years' War. The loss of the American Colonies and the inconclusive war of 1812, embarrassing to both parties, had given the British "official mind" a sharp lesson in the limitations of British power in North America. But elsewhere Britain was unchallenged. Wars in India after 1798 confirmed the verdict of Plassey (1757): Britain was paramount on the subcontinent.

That immense land empire in South Asia provided both the troops and the commercial and strategic motives for further British acquisitions throughout the century. By 1815 the requirements of Imperial communications with India appeared secure. Britain held or had recently acquired title to a chain of bases controlling the decisive routes to India: Gibraltar and Malta, Ascension and St. Helena in the distant South Atlantic, and the Cape of Good Hope, Mauritius, and Ceylon seized from French and Dutch. Singapore, commanding the straits between the Indian Ocean and the China Seas, followed in 1819.

British naval supremacy had far-reaching effects. It largely ended piracy, from the Caribbean to the seas off Borneo. It also gradually curtailed the African slave trade. Britain had con-

The British Empire in the Nineteenth Century

trolled half of that trade by 1800, but had outlawed it by act of Parliament in 1807, thanks to the pressure of crusaders such as the redoubtable William Wilberforce (1759–1833). The United States, despite vociferous objections from its slave states, had followed suit the next year. Castlereagh had secured from the assembled powers at Vienna a declaration condemning the trade. In the ensuing decades, British diplomacy secured the agreement of holdouts such as France, Spain, and Portugal (1820). The frigates of the Royal Navy enforced the ban with increasing success. That did not end the vast forced migration to the new world of perhaps 11.7 million Africans, of whom 1.9 million died on the crossing; only the closing of the slave markets in New Orleans, Havana, and Brazil could do that. But it was a start. And Britain was the first major power in human history to abolish the institution of slavery it-

self, in 1833. For the moment, most others declined to imitate that example.

The Dynamics of British Expansion

Britain soon pressed on beyond the acquisitions of 1815. The forces behind that expansion came not from the corridors of power in London but from the mills and foundries of the Midlands and North, the slums of Birmingham and Liverpool, and the crumbling peasant societies of Scotland and Ireland. Britain imported raw materials and food, especially after the repeal of the Corn Laws in 1846, from the corners of the globe. It exported both goods and people. First came the adventurers, in search of booty or high-profit trade, and the missionaries, intent on imposing Christianity and "progress" on "the heathen." Then came the trading companies with systematic plans for development. To

Singapore, one of Britain's far-flung outposts, in 1830.

states that were capable of aspiring to follow the West's lead—the Ottoman Empire, Egypt, and some societies in Latin America—bankers happily extended credit. Finally, in areas where "white" settlement appeared promising, increasing numbers of emigrants set up societies that replicated the British and North American pattern.

The motive forces behind imperial expansion, economics and demography, remained virtually constant over the century except for a gradual decline in the rates of population increase and of economic growth. What changed, and what accounts for the changes in the forms that expansion took, was the available means. Western expansion had always faced constraints of distance and natural obstacles, disease, the resistance of native societies, and the unwillingness of European governments and peoples to make major sacrifices for empire. These constraints had not prevented the conquest of most of the new world. But between them they had limited European penetration before 1815 to the maritime fringes of Asia and Africa. On the Asian mainland only India had succumbed, after drawing the British in through its constant internecine strife and rich commerce.

After 1815 the means available to the Europeans and particularly to the British changed dramatically, thanks to the Industrial Revolution. First came steam. From the mid-sixteenth century, European sailing ships with their heavy weight of cannon had outmaneuvered and outfought Arab dhows and Chinese junks on the high seas. But inshore, square-riggers were clumsy and vulnerable to grounding or shifting winds. They could not move up narrow winding rivers against the current, and towing by human strength in the form of ships's boats was pathetically inefficient. European naval power thus ended at the high water mark except where the prize ashore was worth landing a substantial ground force.

Steam opened up the Asian and African coastal waters, and at last allowed European trade and power to penetrate the interior with little effort. The British East India Company gave the first demonstration of the potential of a steam-powered "river war" in its 1824–26 conflict with India's eastern neighbor, the kingdom of Burma. The Com-

Sir William Wilberforce, whose crusade against slavery led to its abolition throughout the British Empire in 1833.

pany's three shallow-draft steam craft carried the war as far as 500 miles up the Irrawaddy River, towing sailing ships, bombarding forts, destroying or capturing Burmese war boats. The British acquired large areas of the Burmese borderlands in the first of three wars that ultimately ended in 1885 with the total conquest of Burma.

Iron-hulled steam vessels were the next step. They demonstrated their worth in the 1839–42 "First Opium War" between Britain and China. River steamers such as the *Nemesis*, built for the East India Company in 1839, forced their way past the antiquated Chinese forts barring the way to Canton. Chinese defenses and war-junks had been adequate against wooden-hulled sailing ships that were unable to maneuver on rivers. Against iron-hulled steamboats they were powerless. The war ended when British steamers penetrated the Yangtze River and cut the Grand Canal, which supplied Beijing (Peking) with rice. Steam played a decisive role, albeit without open conflict, in Commodore Matthew Perry's opening of Japan in 1853–54. And in Indochina the French likewise made good use of river steamers in their conquests in the 1870s and 1880s.

The second of the major innovations that made British and European expansion possible was quinine. Of all the major tropical diseases—dysentery, yellow fever, dengue, and the numerous nameless fevers—the African falciparum strain of malaria is the most

"Whatever happens we have got / The Maxim Gun, and they have not," wrote the British satirist Hilaire Belloc (1870–1953) of this essential tool of empire.

consistently lethal. A few lucky and intrepid individuals, such as the Scottish East India surgeon Mungo Park, who explored the river Niger in the 1790s, managed to survive it. But the first attempt to navigate the Niger by steam, in 1832, ended with the death of 40 of 49 whites on the expedition. British garrisons on the Gold Coast between 1817 and 1836 lost 66 percent of their strength each year.

The antimalarial properties of the bark of a South American tree, the chinchona, had long been known or suspected. But not until 1820 did two French chemists isolate the alkaloid, quinine, that produced the effect. By the 1830s production of quinine in quantity had begun; experience soon suggested that it served best when taken regularly as a preventive. In 1854 a Niger expedition returned without casualties. The way for trade far in the interior and ultimately for the extension of European power into all of sub-Saharan Africa lay open.

The final change that permitted the British and European conquest of the world was the revolution in weaponry. The percussion cap in the 1820s and the revolver in the 1840s gave Europeans advantages over Indians or Chinese armed with flintlocks or matchlocks. But the chief advantage of the Europeans, as it had been for 200 years, was their logistical organization, trained leadership, and cohesion under fire. The bayonet remained as important as fire from the one-round-per-minute musket. Skilled enemies with European muskets, such as the Algerians or Afghans who resisted the French and British in the 1830s and 1840s, could turn colonial conquest into an expensive, long-drawn-out, and exceedingly grim business—or block it altogether. The greatest European advantage in weaponry was artillery, which was hard to transport except by river and small help against guerrillas.

Then came the Minié ball, which made the percussion cap rifle a deadly long-range weapon, and breechloaders such as the Sharps, Dreyse, and Chassepot. By the 1880s the box-magazine breech-loading rifle and the Maxim gun gave even small European forces, unless led with gross ineptitude, the ability to destroy native armies many times their size. In the climactic 1898 battle against the forces of the *Mahdi*, the Islamic prophet who had raised the Sudan against the unbeliever, the British lost 48 men. The *Mahdi*'s armies lost 11,000. The Maxim gun made possible a brief age of military tourism.

Demographic and economic forces drove expansion, and the revolutions in transport, tropical medicine, and weaponry made it far easier and cheaper than before. And British expansion was anything but a carefully planned process, obedient to the dictates of London. The government from the beginning held to the utilitarian principle that the best government governed least. Until the 1860s those who made British policy were supremely confident in the benefits of free trade to the world as well as to Britain. Palmerston had summed up that credo in a parliamentary speech in 1842, the year of the British victory that opened China. Commerce would lead "civilization with the one hand and peace with the other"; it would render mankind "happier, wiser, better." Free trade, one of its spokesmen announced in 1846, would make "foreign nations . . . valuable Colonies to us, without imposing on us the responsibility of governing them." The British formula, as two later historians have described it, was "informal empire"—"trade with informal control if possible; trade with rule when necessary."

Increasingly as the century drew on, trade with rule seemed more and more necessary, despite the laments of a central bureaucracy bent on sparing the taxpayers. Trade might make humanity "better"—more like the British—but not in the short term. Trade, and the inevitable missionaries and settlers (where appropriate), invariably required the protection of the flag. Trade required enforceable contracts and security for money and goods. Trade frequently conflicted with the customs, laws, or policies of those upon which it impinged, from the tribal empires of Africa to the long-established states of China and Japan. Trade and the loans that came with it in Latin America, the Ottoman Empire, and Egypt in many cases destroyed the authority of those who accepted it.

Trade, loans, missionaries, and settlers thus generated a variety of unstable mixtures of resistance and collaboration in the native societies affected. The interaction between the outward thrust of Britain and its imitators and the resistance or lack of it in non-Western societies was the mechanism that created the British Empire and completed the Western domination of the world.

Resistance took many forms. Tribes from the Afghans northwest of India to the Kaffirs and Zulus of Africa raided British possessions on the innumerable turbulent frontiers of empire. Religious or proto-nationalist groups—the Mahdists of the Sudan, the Egyptian army, and the Boer farmers of South Africa—rose against the British or against rulers who collaborated with them. And states such as China and Japan adamantly refused to open their markets or provide security for the persons and property of British merchants. Resistance or defiance normally called forth a British response. Typically, London or its agents on the spot intervened militarily to protect what they perceived as existing British interests. The security of India's borders, of the China trade, of the Suez Canal or Cape of Good Hope demanded increasingly strenuous action. That mechanism explains the patchwork character of expansion. Britain did not obey a grand design; it responded when action appeared unavoidable.

Collaboration, the converse of resistance, also helped govern the timing, extent, and ultimate demise of British and Western dominance. One corollary to London's belief in free trade and an absolute minimum of government intervention was the imperative need for willing native auxiliaries. Princes and tribal rulers, native troops, and Western-educated natives might all serve as more or less willing collaborators with Britain's informal empire. The collaborators found themselves caught between two worlds: the British world market and their own societies. If the market pressed too rapidly and disruptively against the native economy, institutions, or religious and cultural traditions, collaborators might fumble and collapse in the face of antiforeign revolt. That presented Britain with unenviable choices: to get out, or to go in at great and continuing expense and rule directly. And the establishment and maintenance of direct rule itself required continuing collaboration from the conquered. When that collaboration faltered or ceased, the European empires ultimately deflated like pricked balloons.

The "White" Colonies

The ideal collaborators were of course the colonists of Canada, Australia, New Zealand, and South Africa. The societies they created, with the exception of those of the French Canadians and Dutch-descended Boer farmers that London acquired in 1763 and 1814, were replicas of Britain. Britain's demographic expansion drove them. The satellite economies of Australia, New Zealand, and eventually Canada in turn contributed wool, grain, meat, and markets to British economic expansion. Along with the United States and Argentina, they also took the majority of Britain's immense overseas investments.

London, after its sad experience with the thirteen American colonies, did its best to defuse discontent by conceding self-government as soon as possible. Canada, the most populous and turbulent, came first. Conquest in the Seven Years' War and the subsequent immigration of large numbers of American loyalists after 1775–83 had disquieted the deeply rooted Catholic society of Norman peasants that France had planted in Québec. An effort, in the Constitutional Act of 1791, to give each of the two nationalities its own province failed to quiet unrest.

In 1837 the suppression of a Québecquois rising and a revolt in the English-speaking province of Upper Canada (now Ontario) required British troops. In the aftermath, the Earl of Durham, one of the authors of Britain's 1832 Reform Bill, became governor-general of the colonies. He recommended representative self-government of a unified province in which English-speakers would swamp the French. London adopted his recommendations in the 1840s, but the French-English conflict inevitably persisted. By the time of the U.S. Civil War, the need of a strong central government to promote internal cohesion, defense, and railway development was obvious. In 1867, after long negotiation between Canadian leaders, Parliament in London passed the British North America Act. Québec once again received its own administration, within the "Dominion of Canada," a federation that included the maritime provinces. Britain happily conceded to the colonials the management of their own affairs, including defense against rebellion and Indian raids.

The invention of the status of self-governing "Dominion" was decisive for Australia and New Zealand. The various territories of Australia, which had served from 1788 as a dumping ground for English convicts, received representative self-government in 1851–55. By then free immigrants far outnumbered the descendants of those deported to Botany Bay. In 1901 London was happy to concede Dominion status to the Commonwealth of Australia, a continent spanned by railroads and rich in wool, grain, and gold. The independence of New Zealand was a slower process, largely because of a series of exceedingly unpleasant land wars with the native Maoris, a fierce and tenacious Polynesian warrior people. The land-hungry settlers refused to dispense with London's protection before British troops broke Maori resistance. Self-government nevertheless

1756	1763		Great Mutiny 1857	Indian Independence 1947
Seven Years' War		British East India Company Control (Mughals keep imperial title)	Direct Rule by British Government	

came in 1876 and Commonwealth status in 1907.

The Indian Empire

In India the British, alone of the colonial powers, took steps in the nineteenth century to prepare the way for the ultimate independence of the non-European peoples they had conquered. The process was neither swift nor peaceful. To protect and extend its trade the East India Company had succeeded the Mughal emperors as paramount power on the subcontinent. That thrust culminated in the Third Mahratta War of 1817–18; the Company broke for good the power of the warrior Hindu states, the Mahratta confederacy. By that point the Company itself had ceased to be a private entity with a monopoly on India's trade. As early as 1773 the crown had taken for itself the power to appoint a governor-general. In 1784 London had asserted control of the Company's political activities. In 1833 the Company lost its trading function entirely; henceforth its only mission was to govern India through the elite Indian Civil Service.

The end of the Company trade monopoly and the extension of British direct rule intensified pressure on the native societies of the subcontinent. The Company had been content to leave Indian social and religious custom undistrubed except for ill-considered attempts to rationalize the tax structure and introduce Western notions of property law in place of the old relationships between peasant community and overlord. Once the Company lost its monopoly, the way was open for the ever-intensifying penetration of independent British merchants and missionaries. Pressure in Parliament and in the British press for the reform of Indian society mounted.

By the 1830s the reformers had won. A sense of mission impelled these disciples of Bentham: India was theirs in trust, to Westernize and prepare for self-government at some point in the far distant future. The great British historian Thomas Babington Macaulay, one of the reformers, spelled out the goal: to create "a class of persons Indian in colour and blood, but English in tastes, opinions, and intellects." And Karl Marx, from the depths of the British Museum library, celebrated in 1853 newspaper articles the creation in India of "a fresh class . . . endowed with the requirements for government and imbued with European science." Britain's mission, he triumphantly announced, was "the annihilation of the old Asiatic society, and the laying of the material foundations of Western society in Asia." Old Company hands had misgivings about this revolution from above and about the blind self-confidence that drove it. "Englishmen are as great fanatics in politics as Mohommedans in religion. They suppose that no country can be saved without English institutions," fumed a former governor of Madras.

The reform effort culminated with the 1848–56 administration of governor-general Lord Dalhousie, the very personification of utilitarian enterprise and "progress." Dalhousie introduced the telegraph, built the famous Grand Trunk Road across northern India, and planned the railways that by 1905 were the longest and best in Asia, with 33,000 miles of track. His irrigation canals made vast areas of northern India fertile.

In politics, a field less tractable than engineering, Dalhousie's messianic faith in the benefits of Western civilization made him an annexationist. He completed the conquest of the Sikhs of the Punjab, seized Sind in the west and lower Burma in the east, and gradually

A scene from the Great Mutiny, 1857: British firepower and discipline defeats the sepoys at Cawnpore.

annexed those Indian states under Company protection whose thrones fell vacant. British rule now brought ever-increasing missionary activity, equality before the law that disrupted these societies of rigidly demarcated castes, and interference with Hindu religious customs such as *sati*, the ritual burning of widows on their husbands' funeral pyres.

By 1857, the strain upon native society had grown intolerable. Over wide areas of northern India the population, from lord to peasant, had become convinced that Britain's ultimate purpose was to abolish Indian society and religion, whether Hindu or Moslem. The occasion but not the cause of the ensuing explosion was the foolish introduction into the Company's Indian army of Minié rifles that took paper cartridges waterproofed with tallow. Loading required biting the cartridge open. And when rumors, later confirmed, flew that the manufacturers had used tallow made from a blend of pig and cow fat, the *sepoys* or native soldiers faced an appalling dilemma. The cow was sacred to Hinduism, the pig forbidden to Moslems. The troops could bite the cartridge and suffer loss of caste if Hindu or defilement if Moslem. Or they could betray their deeply felt oath to the army.

Many chose mutiny, and rose against the British with the support of much of the population of the dusty plains around Delhi. Native leaders harked back to the proud days of Mahrattas and Mughals, and sought to drive the British from India. The *sepoys* committed numerous atrocities against British prisoners, women, and children. The British, isolated and fearful amid an immense and largely hostile population, fought a pitiless race war. They celebrated the reconquest of Delhi by lashing *sepoy* prisoners across gun barrels and blasting them to shreds. London dissolved the Company, drastically reorganized its Indian army, made India a possession of the crown, and publicly disclaimed any intention of tampering with its subjects' religions.

The Great Mutiny of 1857–58 was a shock not only to the British rulers of India, but to British imperial self-confidence. It drove home the obvious: non-Western societies did not automatically take to Western values. It revealed that the reformers' "fresh class" of English-educated collaborators lacked roots in the Indian population. The English henceforth proceeded with greater caution and infinitely lower expectations. Stability not social revolution became their goal. Creeping annexation ceased. The Indian subject princes, who for the most part had remained loyal, preserved their possessions into the twentieth century. Britain henceforth confined its activities primarily to administration, engineering, and the defense of India's borders.

Nevertheless, the reformers succeeded in the long term. The Great Mutiny was the last sizable traditional Indian revolt. English-educated Indians took an increasing role in the junior ranks of the administration, in the new English-speaking law courts, and in the creation of textile, coal, and steel industries. By the 1880s a modern Indian public opinion, both Hindu and Moslem, had come into being. The foundation, with help from British liberals, of the Indian Congress party in 1885 marked the birth of the force that ultimately succeeded the British. The Indians that Britain had educated in turn invented Indian nationalism.

Britain in Africa

Except for the Cape Colony and a few fever-ridden trading stations on the west coast, Britain in 1815 had little use for Africa. That changed. The penetration of British palm-oil traders, missionaries, and antislavery reformers, especially after mid-century, brought increasing clashes with indigenous forces. In West Africa, the warlike Ashanti kingdom in the hinterland of the Gold Coast was the main barrier. A punitive expedition in 1874 checked its power, but final annexation did not ensue until 1896. In East Africa, British attempts to put down the slave trade destroyed the authority of Britain's client, the Sultan of Zanzibar. That drew London ever deeper into the affairs of East Africa.

But the extension of British rule to much of Africa followed from two great crises in the 1880s and 1890s, both connected with the security of the routes to India. In North Africa the stake was the great canal across the Suez isthmus that the Saint-Simonian engineer and promoter, Ferdinand de Lesseps, had completed in 1869. In 1876 the Khedivate, the regime of the successors of Mohammed Ali, collapsed in bankruptcy; it had attempted to modernize Egypt on European credit. The French and British governments took command of Egyptian finances and taxation to see their bondholders paid.

That intrusion was the latest of the series of defeats and exactions at the hands of unbelievers since Bonaparte. It generated a radical response; unlike the Indian Mutiny, that response was recognizably modern. In 1882 a movement in the partially Westernized Egyptian army overthrew its own government and defied the West to which that government appeared too subservient. The movement's ideological basis was a modernizing current of Islam; its program, Egypt for the Egyptians; its leader, the charismatic Colonel Ahmed Arabi Pasha.

That situation, now all too familiar, took Britain and France aback. A joint naval demonstration of the traditional sort merely provoked a massacre of for-

The strategic Suez Canal, in the 1890s.

eigners at Alexandria. The British responded with cannon fire. That was the point of no return: British prestige was committed, the prestige required to hold India. The pacific Liberal cabinet of William Ewart Gladstone (see p. 784) unhappily landed an army to restore a suitably cooperative Egyptian government. The French chamber and cabinet had no need of a route to India, and refused to follow.

The British convincingly crushed Arabi's army, and found themselves ruling Egypt. To Gladstone's dismay, the old techniques of informal empire no longer served. British interests appeared too great, Egyptian resistance too fanatical. If Britain withdrew, its discredited clients would again collapse, leaving Canal and debt at the mercy of anti-Western forces. Britain therefore stayed, despite the increasing hostility of the French, who illogically concluded that the British had slyly usurped the Egyptian empire that Bonaparte had failed to bequeath to France.

Worse, Egypt was not self-contained: the mighty river Nile upon which its agriculture depended rose in the Sudan, far to the south. That province was in theory Egypt's, held through isolated garrisons. But in 1881 an Islamic figure even more charismatic than Arabi had arisen there and had begun to weld the Dervish religious orders into an army and a state. The *Mahdi*, Mohammed Ahmad, swept the Egyptian garrisons out of the Sudan in 1883. In 1885 he destroyed at Khartoum

Nationalism against the West: Ahmed Arabi Pasha of Egypt (1839–1911).

The Scramble for Africa   1884/1914

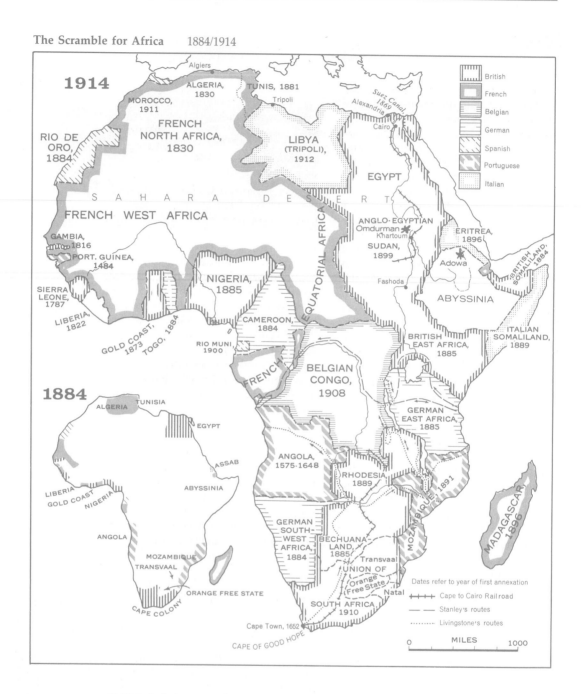

a British-led force under an eccentric soldier of fortune, General "Chinese" Gordon.

Gladstone, lamenting his "Egyptian bondage," left the *Mahdi* for later British governments to deal with. But British occupation of Egypt had unleashed French acquisitiveness in West Africa. Other powers also took a hand. The resulting "scramble" for protectorates and annexations divided the African continent, at least on paper, in the 20 years after 1882. In West Africa Britain left much to the French but kept Nigeria and a number of smaller river colonies. In East Africa the British were less generous to their rivals. Proximity to India impelled them to keep most of the coast, except for areas conceded, graciously or not, to Italians and Germans.

And a second great crisis far to the south drove Britain to extend its control still further. Britain's principal stake at the Cape of Good Hope was also in origin strategic. The Cape was an indispensable base, "the true centre of the Empire . . . clear of the Suez complications, almost equally distant from Australia, China, India, Gibraltar, the West Indies, and the Falklands," as a Colonial Office official put it in the 1870s. Unfortunately, the Cape had a land frontier. It also had non-British white inhabitants: the Dutch settlers that the Dutch East India Company had planted in 1652 to provide supplies for its shipping.

British relations with the Cape Dutch after annexation were amicable; the colony received representative self-government in 1872. Dealings with the Boer ("peasant") farmers of the inland frontier were less satisfactory; British humanitarians frowned on the Boer habit of enslaving the Africans. Between 1835 and 1844, hungry for land and determined to preserve a white supremacy they considered God had ordained, the Boers streamed north across the Vaal River and out of British control. The climax of that "Great Trek" came at the battle of Blood River in 1838. A Boer wagon train defeated the onslaught of the Zulu king Dingaan, heir of the great Shaka, who had created the mightiest army south of the Sahara. To the "*Trekboers*," reared in the stern Old Testament faith of the Dutch Reformed Church, victory proved that God had chosen them.

The twin Boer republics of the Orange Free State and Transvaal were thus in their very origins a reaction to British penetration, a reaction almost tribal in character and intensity. London hoped to pressure the Boer republics into a Cape federation that would eventually become a Dominion. Britain proclaimed the annexation of the Transvaal in 1877 and defended it against a new assault of the Zulu regiments in 1879. The Zulus lost, but in the process crushed a British force at Isandhlwana; the Boers bid for independence once the British had quelled the Zulu threat. At Majuba Hill in 1881, Transvaal Boer rifles picked off an isolated and ill-led British detachment. Gladstone conceded independence to the Transvaal while retaining only a vague right of veto over Boer relations with foreign powers. Unlike Egypt, the stakes were not high enough to warrant a major British commitment, and Boer nationalism was clearly too tough to take on lightly.

Gladstone's retreat postponed the struggle for mastery in South Africa. That development, like the climax of the British-French struggle for the Nile and the crises in East Asia around the turn of the century, is best left for discussion in its international context (see pp. 821–23). But even before the second round against the Boers, and despite doubts and hesitations in London, Britain had annexed most of a new empire in Africa. Egyptian revolt, the fanaticism of the *Mahdi*, and Boer proto-nationalism had marked the limits of informal influence. Africa's resistance drove Britain to defend by ever broader acquisitions what Britain already held. And the growing rivalry from the other European powers increasingly confirmed the British on the path they had chosen.

BRITAIN'S EUROPEAN RIVALS

The other European powers inevitably sought to imitate Britain. But each power did so in its own way. And they ultimately did so at Britain's pleasure, for neither separately nor in concert could they challenge British naval supremacy.

French imperialism, which created the second largest of the nineteenth-century European empires, was primarily military in inspiration. It began in 1830 with an attack on the pirate kingdom of Algiers. The moribund

Colonial troops: An Algerian officer in the French army of the 1880s.

Bourbon dynasty sought the prestige of conquest; Louis Philippe inherited some coastal outposts and a hinterland that resisted fiercely. The French army, in almost 20 years of bloody campaigns and hair-raising atrocities, prevailed by 1847 against the canny resistance leader Abd-el-Kader.

The Algerian outpost provided security for French Mediterranean shipping. Its conquest both demanded and gave a home to that quintessential French colonial force, the Foreign Legion. It offered a training ground for generations of colonial officers. And thanks to French and European immigration and agricultural settlement, Algeria almost began to pay for itself after the suppression of a further Moslem uprising in 1870.

But Algeria was no product of trade and industry, the power behind British expansion. And even if the French had aspired to an informal commercial empire in North Africa, Moslem intransigence would have thwarted them. The French empire did have economic functions. But its reason for existence lay above all in the belief of successive French governments before 1870 that France's claim to European primacy required colonial perquisites. And the loss of that primacy in 1870 made colonial self-assertion a welcome compensation for European humiliation.

Under Napoleon III, General Louis Faidherbe applied proven Algerian methods to make Senegal, France's most important West African outpost, a major source of native troops. In 1858–59 Napoleon made good longstanding French influence in Vietnam by seizing Saigon and Da Nang in reprisal for native killings of French missionaries. In the 1860s France annexed the southern areas of Vietnam. Napoleon III exploited the U.S. Civil War to impose with Foreign Legion bayonets an Austrian Archduke as Emperor of Mexico. Union victory and Mexican resistance brought French withdrawal and the Archduke's death by firing squad in 1867.

The Franco-Prussian war inevitably imposed a pause. But by the early 1880s France had again begun to expand. It forced a protectorate on Tunis, Algeria's difficult neighbor, in 1881. After the humiliation unintentionally inflicted on France in the Egyptian crisis, French consuls and officers on the West African rivers began feverishly staking claims that Paris until then had been unwilling to back. Collision with a series of unbending Moslem theocracies in the interior compelled the French to make good with Maxim guns their paper pretensions. The colonial army and France's formidable naval infantry happily bent to that task. By 1902 France had extended its control from Algeria to the Gulf of Guinea, and had annexed Madagascar on the Indian Ocean flank of the Cape of Good Hope.

The German and Italian empires had even less economic function than the French; as latecomers Germany and Italy could only aspire to territories so worthless that Britain and France had passed them by. Bismarck had utter contempt for the German colonial enthusiasts who had inevitably emerged after 1871. He nevertheless unleashed them in 1884–85 to claim Togo, Cameroons, South-West Africa, and German East Africa while he created artificial friction with London. At the 1884–85 Berlin colonial conference he also helped give the brutal King Leopold II of Belgium control of the Congo basin; British-French rivalry benefited other powers besides Berlin.

Bismarck's purposes in picking a quarrel with Britain were diplomatic and domestic, not colonial: rapprochement with France, a thumping nationalist vote in the 1884 elections, and re-insurance against dismissal by the mildly liberal and pro-British Crown Prince Frederick when William I ultimately died. Those passing needs saddled Germany with expensive and useless African territories and an assortment of Pacific islands. Bismarck's successors acquired a Chinese port. That unsatisfactory empire did not disillusion German opinion; it whetted its appetite for larger things.

Italy, as the least of the great powers, found even slimmer pickings than Germany. It acquired the Red Sea port of Assab in 1882 and asserted a protectorate over the Coptic Christian kingdom of Ethiopia in 1889. The Amhara rulers of Ethiopia appeared to acquiesce, then resisted further Italian encroachment. Menelik, the emperor, acquired large stores of European rifles and the assistance of French experts. On March 1, 1896, at Adowa he dealt the Italians the worst defeat inflicted upon a would-be European colonizer in the nineteenth century. In the face of an enemy that outnumbered them by five to one, the Italians had divided their forces and had struck out on divergent routes across unmapped mountains. They lost 6,000 dead and 4,000 wounded or captured; political chaos at home precluded any renewal of the war. Italy contented itself for a generation with the coastal enclaves of Eritrea and Somalia.

Finally, Russia rounded out an empire in central and east Asia in the course of the nineteenth century. That process was like French expansion in that it was military, and like that of the United States in that it pursued geopolitical "manifest destiny." The Crimean War checked Russia in Europe but sharpened its appetites elsewhere. In 1853–54 it annexed large areas around the Aral Sea. In the next 20 years it methodically crushed the central Asian nomad peoples and the surviving Tartar Khanates of Bukhara, Khiva, and Kokand. By 1884 Russia had reached the Afghan border. Further east, it pressed into Mongolia. And in 1858 and 1860, by the army's bayonets and the treaties of Aigun and Beijing (Peking), it seized from the Chinese the Amur and maritime provinces opposite Japan. At the southern tip of the maritime province it founded a naval base with a name that was a program: Vladivostok, "Ruler of the East." And from 1891 Russia began pushing a railroad

Tocqueville Foresees the World Domination of Russia and America 1835

There are at the present time two great nations in the world, which started from different points, but seem to tend towards the same end. I allude to the Russians and the Americans. . . . All other nations seem to have nearly reached their natural limits, and they have only to maintain their power; but these are still in the act of growth. . . . These alone are proceeding with ease and celerity along a path to which no limit can be perceived. The American struggles against the obstacles that nature opposes to him; the adversaries of the Russian are men. The former combats the wilderness and savage life; the latter, civilization with all its arms. The conquests of the American are therefore gained by the plowshare; those of the Russian by the sword. The Anglo-American relies upon personal interest to accomplish his ends and gives free scope to the unguided strength and common sense of the people; the Russian centers all the authority of society in a single arm. The principal instrument of the former is freedom; of the latter, servitude. Their starting-point is different and their courses are not the same; yet each of them seems marked by the will of Heaven to sway the destinies of half the globe.

From Alexis de Tocqueville, *Democracy in America* (New York: Vintage Books, 1953), Vol. I, p. 434.

across Siberia toward Vladivostok, to make that program reality.

A SECOND EUROPE: THE UNITED STATES

The Young Republic

By that point an entirely different sort of state had reached the New World's Pacific shores. The United States that emerged from the Revolutionary War of 1775–83 and the Constitutional Convention of 1787 was a unique experiment. It was a new state, not founded through the slow processes of dynastic accretion and military-bureaucratic consolidation that had made the states of Europe. Its sovereign people—"We the people of the United States"—did not claim to be a "nation," a political unit preordained by language, culture, and territory. America's language and culture were initially British and its territorial boundaries lost in the endless forests of the Appalachians and the swamps of southern Georgia. The foundation of the new state was principles: "We hold these truths to be self-evident, that all Men are created equal, that they are endowed by their Creator with certain unalienable rights, that among these are Life, Liberty, and the Pursuit of Happiness. . . . " The securing of those natural rights was the purpose of American government, the unity of the thirteen colonies was the means.

To their purpose the framers of the Constitution brought an understanding of human nature and of political practice laboriously acquired in town and county meetings, state assemblies, and the Revolutionary War. More experienced than the French revolutionaries who followed, the framers took a pessimistic view of humanity. James Madison of Virginia, one of the Constitution's principal architects, put it well: "If men were angels, no government would be necessary." Majority will unchecked by law meant tyranny over both individuals and states. Madison and others therefore built into the Constitution what a great American historian has described as a "harmonious system of mutual frustration": the separation of powers.

Legislature, executive, and judiciary checked and balanced one another, as did the new federal government and the thirteen states. Within Congress, the indirectly elected Senate moderated the potentially impetuous House of Representatives. Neither majority whim in Congress, nor the authority of that elected monarch, the president, nor any caprice of the Supreme Court's judges could prevail for long without cooperation of the other branches. That system, so seemingly cumbersome in theory, in practice usually forced the deliberate creation of the compromise and consensus without which demo-cratic polities fall into incoherence or despotism. The Constitution's paragraphs did not guarantee the success of the American experiment: that depended above all on the common sense, civic spirit, and political experience of the citizenry. But it did provide a framework that used those qualities to advantage.

The Constitution was above all a democratic document, although its framers were men of property and social distinction, and it made allowances for the South's "peculiar institution," slavery. In order to secure the assent of the southern states, the framers counted each slave, for purposes of apportioning representation, as three-fifth of a white. Despite that concession to inequality, the Constitution swiftly developed in the direction of yet greater democracy. To overcome opposition to its adoption, Madison and others put forward a further series of guarantees that the new federal government would not replicate the "tyranny" of George III. The first ten amendments or Bill of Rights, adopted in 1789–91, placed the rights of the individual against the state at the center of the new political system. Those rights gradually grew as the country expanded and the political weight of the socially stratified east coast states decreased. Most states that had restricted voting through religious tests or property qualifications enacted universal male suffrage by the 1820s.

The founders gradually passed from the scene, leaving a vacuum that political parties ultimately filled. The first alignment of importance was the "Federalists," whose advocacy of a strong central government helped push the Constitution through. Their leading light was Alexander Hamilton, first Secretary of the Treasury and prophet of the economic development of the United States. Their program implied the supremacy of industry and commerce over agriculture and of the cultivated elite over the masses. Thomas Jefferson and Madison of Virginia formed a "Democratic-Republican" party that opposed Hamilton with a vision of an egalitarian farmers' republic; great cities, Jefferson wrote, were "pestilential to the morals, the health, and the liberties of man."

That conflict of ideologies and interests persisted throughout the century and beyond. It soon became at least in part a sectional division. The egalitarian frontier triumphed in the 1828 election, the first fought by recognizable national parties. Andrew Jackson, "the People's Choice" against the Eastern elites, was ironically a Kentucky magnate. But his overwhelming popular vote victory at the head of the Democratic party was a mighty step toward the emergence of the system of two national parties, powerful engines of consensus, that still exists.

By 1828 the United States was well on its way to territorial consolidation. Jefferson, as president in 1803, had bought from Napoleon the Louisiana territory that commanded the mouth of the Mississippi and stretched west to the Rocky Mountains and north to the still unmarked Canadian border. In the aftermath of the war of 1812, Britain and the United States agreed to demilitarize the Great Lakes and establish the 49th parallel as their mutual border as far as the Rockies. In 1819 Spain sold Florida to the United States. By 1837 the original thirteen states had doubled in number. Jackson encouraged and speeded the "removal" by force of most of the remaining Indian tribes east of the Mississippi. Only Mexico to the south was now a potential rival.

Unassailable continentally, the United States even began to interest itself in Latin American affairs. Napoleon, by deposing the Bourbons in 1808, had cut the Spanish Empire in Latin America adrift. The ensuing revolts against Spain had produced by the early 1820s a collection of weak and internally divided states. After France's 1823 invasion of Spain to restore the Bourbons, French backing for Spanish efforts at reconquest appeared to threaten what Britain considered a promising market. Castlereagh's suc-

cessor as British Foreign Secretary, George Canning, suggested a joint British-United States declaration to ward off European intervention.

But President James Monroe preferred to act unilaterally, with a characteristically American statement of republican principles. He announced to Congress in December 1823 that the United States would regard attempts to establish or reestablish European control in the western hemisphere as signs of "an unfriendly disposition towards the United States." Canning could boast to Parliament that he had "called the New World into existence to redress the balance of the Old." But it was the Royal Navy, not the still minuscule seapower of the United States, that initially backed the Doctrine with force. Until the very end of the century the Royal Navy, in Britain's own interest, served as ultimate guarantor of the maritime security of the United States.

Expansion and Disunion

Economic and territorial expansion soon strained both the principles and

"Old Hickory": Andrew Jackson (1767–1845)

The Monroe Doctrine   1823

The political system of the allied [European] powers is essentially different . . . from that of America. . . . We owe it, therefore, to candor and to the amicable relations existing between the United States and those powers to declare that we should consider any attempt on their part to extend their system to any portion of this hemisphere as dangerous to our peace and safety. With the existing colonies or dependencies of any European power we have not interfered and shall not interfere. But with the [Latin American] governments who have declared their independence and maintained it, and whose independence we have, on great consideration and on just principles, acknowledged, we could not view any interposition for the purpose of oppressing them, or controlling in any other manner their destiny, by any European power in any other light than as the manifestation of an unfriendly disposition toward the United States.

From the message to Congress of President James Monroe, December 2, 1823.

The mechanization of the slave economy: Eli Whitney's cotton gin.

John C. Calhoun (1782–1850), the voice of the South.

the political fabric of the Republic. The trading Northeast, which acquired a merchant marine second only to Britain's, rapidly industrialized (see pp. 691–92). The Erie Canal and the railroad opened the Midwest to settlers, and gave those settlers new markets in the East for their grain.

The South, despite the qualms of figures such as Jefferson ("Indeed I tremble for my country, when I reflect that God is just"), further refined the slave economy established in the seventeenth century. Tobacco was less and less profitable, but after 1793 the cotton gin of the Yankee Eli Whitney made the short-fiber cotton that grew easily in the South into a fabulously profitable plantation crop. The slave economy spread rapidly westward, creating a "Cotton Kingdom" from Savannah to Mobile and New Orleans. By the 1820s the South was shipping 60 million pounds of raw cotton annually to the mills of Europe.

Old divisions between states blurred. Fissures between Puritan trading New England, the religiously and socially varied central Atlantic states, and the Anglican slave South had been less important than the fundamental divide between the settled and relatively hierarchical societies of the coastal plains and the egalitarian frontiersmen of the Appalachians and beyond. Now canal, railroad, and river steamer riveted North and South firmly to their respective hinterlands. Free

labor spread across the northern back-country, slave across the South.

Economic and territorial expansion brought to a head the fundamental conflict of principles: could a system founded on individual freedom ultimately tolerate slavery? By the 1830s stern New England voices had begun to attack the Cotton Kingdom at its most vulnerable point—its principles. Agitators such as William Lloyd Garrison and Wendell Phillips ceaselessly pounded at the irreconcilability of black slavery and white freedom. Garrison denounced the Constitution itself as "a covenant with death and an agreement with hell," for it permitted slavery. The Southern response was increasingly implausible and hysterical. John C. Calhoun, the South's greatest national political figure, told the Senate in 1837 that slavery was no evil, "but a good, sir, a positive good." The Abolitionists were and remained a tiny though noisy minority, but they inspired a persecution mania in the South that in the end drove it to revolt and ruin.

Economic issues also helped strain relations between the two sections. The South, as befitted a satellite economy of Britain, demanded free trade; the industrializing North with its Midwestern markets sought protective tariffs. In 1832 that conflict led to a great crisis. The "sovereign state" of South Carolina, under Calhoun's leadership, "nullified" a protective tariff that Congress had passed. President Jackson prepared to use force: "The laws of the United States must be executed." Since the issue was not slavery itself, the other Southern states were not prepared to back South Carolina. A compromise deferred until later the issue of "states' rights": the rebellious state withdrew "nullification" and Congress agreed to reduce tariffs. Nor did economics always pull the sections apart. Northern industry's dependence on Southern cotton led the South to bet heavily though in vain upon the existence of an implicit alliance between plantation chattel slavery and factory "wage slavery," between the "lords of the lash and the lords of the loom."

Territorial expansion, by constantly raising the stakes in the competition between two irreconcilable systems, ultimately brought the parting of the ways. Admitting new states created a series of ever greater crises. Missouri's admission as a slave state was only possible as part of an 1820 compromise that established latitude 36° 30', Missouri's southern border, as the future boundary between slave and free territories.

Then, in the 1820s and 1830s, settlers that included planters and their slaves flocked into the Mexican territories west of Louisiana, ironically at the invitation of the Mexican government. Attempts to reassert Mexican control led to settler revolt in 1835–36 and the proclamation of a "Republic of Texas." Eight years later the Democratic party under James K. Polk carried the presidential election on a platform of the annexation of Texas, which had asked to join the Union. Mexico's warnings that it would fight what it regarded as aggression, and clashes with Mexican patrols on the Rio Grande, brought war in 1846–48. The minuscule U.S. Army outclassed its adversary. It captured Mexico City and seized by force the entire Southwest from Texas westward to California.

The extension of U.S. power, and Polk's compromise with the British to extend the 49th parallel border with Canada westward to the Pacific across the Oregon territory, created a far greater crisis than had Missouri. Polk had promised the northern states an Oregon-Canada border ("Fifty-four forty or fight!") far to the north of the one he ultimately secured. Northern leaders retaliated by demanding that Congress exclude slavery from the territories wrested from Mexico. The South, which had contributed disproportionately to victory, replied with threats of secession from the Union.

The Compromise of 1850 failed to paper over the cracks. It admitted California as a free state but left the status of the lands between California and Texas to the choice of their eventual inhabitants. It also pledged the North to return fugitive slaves, thus forcing northern authorities to choose between conscience and federal law. And Harriet Beecher Stowe's popular novel, *Uncle Tom's Cabin* (1852), dramatized the nature and consequences of slavery for the Northern public. The conflict deepened.

Congress and the Southern-dominated Supreme Court tore up the Missouri Compromise in the Kansas-Nebraska act of 1854 and the Dred Scott decision of 1857. All territories, even those previously covered by the Missouri Compromise, could now choose to be free or slave. The consequence was a savage guerrilla struggle, punctuated with mob violence, in "bleeding Kansas," west of Missouri but north of the Missouri Compromise line.

Quasi-war over Kansas opened the door to the men of blood on both sides. There an Abolitionist extremist, John Brown, made a name for himself by a series of unsavory killings. In October 1859, impelled by visions of arming the slaves and provoking an immense revolt, he and a band of followers seized the federal arsenal at Harpers Ferry, Virginia. Colonel Robert E. Lee, U.S. Army, swiftly turned him out. Virginia as swiftly hanged him. Brown provided Abolition with a martyr and convinced the increasingly deluded South that it stood alone, for "states' rights" and slavery, against the rest of the Union.

The election of 1860 showed that political polarization was complete. Abraham Lincoln of Illinois ran for the new Republican party ("free soil, free men") that represented North and Northwest. He carried 17 of the 18 free states. The 15 slave states overwhelmingly opposed him. Lincoln sought to preserve the Union with conciliatory gestures. He abhorred slavery but was a practical politician, not a zealot. The

Slave States and Free States   1861

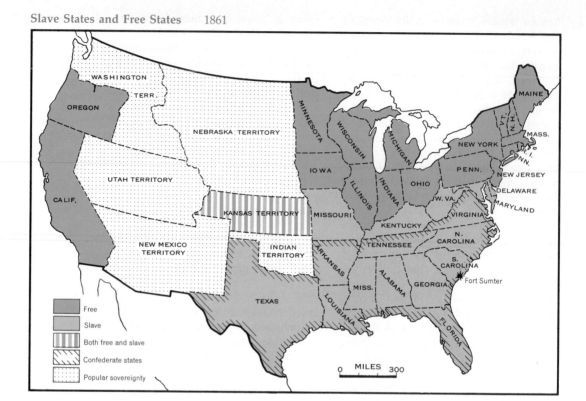

fire-eaters of the South, trusting in the economic power of "King Cotton" over both New England and Lancashire, and in their military spirit and talent as a planter aristocracy, determined on secession. Beginning on April 12, 1861, South Carolina bombarded and took Fort Sumter, the federal outpost in Charleston harbor. The "irrepressible conflict" had begun.

The Second American Revolution, 1861–65

The slave South's appeal to arms unleashed the world's first industrialized war, a war that ultimately became a second American revolution. The Crimean War had come too early and Bismarck's wars were too short to show what happened when industrialized powers collided. The U.S. Civil War was different. It was the first conflict between Western powers unlimited in aims since the Wars of Religion. To the South's limited war to assert the

"right" of states to preserve slavery, the North replied. Reestablishment of the Union required *unconditional surrender*—a war aim the French revolutionaries had hinted at but which even Napoleon had hesitated to pursue. Reestablishment of the Union ultimately demanded the total destruction of the South's military power, the elimination of slavery, and the remaking of Southern society.

Neither side possessed at the outset a military establishment serious by European standards. The 16,367 officers and men of the peacetime U.S. Army split. A quarter of the 1,066 regular officers went South, including Colonel Lee, who stood with Virginia when it seceded to join the Confederate States of America. The Confederacy used these defectors wisely, to train and lead the state militias that became its army. The Union inherited the regular army, and kept its officers with regular army units. The Northern militias, sketchily trained and led by political appointees and elected officers, paid in blood for that mistake. Not until 1863–64 did Union battlefield effectiveness begin to rival that of the "rebels."

The Confederacy faced a daunting but by no means impossible task. It initially produced 26,000 tons of mostly charcoal-smelted pig iron annually, to the Union's 160,000 tons made with coke. The Union had 22,000 miles of railroads to the Confederacy's 9,000. The Union included a population of 22 million; the Confederacy's whites were 6 million, with 3.5 million slaves. Weight of numbers and an almost infinitely expandable productive capacity were thus the Union's greatest assets. The Confederacy nevertheless coped in the short term. It improvised military-run war industries virtually overnight, in Birmingham, Selma, Atlanta, Richmond. And the new fire-power of the Minié rifle, deadly to a thousand yards, favored the tactical defensive.

Union morale was also anything but firm; the Confederacy's will to resist, at least in the early years, was unconditional. "Peace Democrats"—"Copperheads" to the supporters of the Union cause—sought with considerable success to undermine Lincoln. In the border states partisans of the Confederacy intrigued, plotted, and spied. The 1863 introduction of a draft in the North caused an insurrection in New York City; mobs burned government offices and killed blacks as scapegoats for the war. Putting these "draft riots" down required a Union army corps. To cope with Confederate sympathizers Lincoln took the drastic step of partially suspending the Bill of Rights and trying civilians in military courts. The Confederacy's purely negative war aim gave it a further advantage. A few striking victories might win the war. Northern opinion might desert Lincoln; Britain and France might recognize the Confederacy.

Lincoln had no military experience. Like so many of his troops and generals, he learned on the job and he learned well. He swiftly adopted the key elements of the "Anaconda plan" that the aged generalissimo of the Mexican war, Winfield Scott, had proposed. The Union navy would blockade the Confederacy's coasts and dominate the Mississippi. But Lincoln could not afford to wait for strangulation to do its work; Union opinion demanded action. He also soon concluded that strangulation alone could not produce unconditional surrender. Union armies had to penetrate the heart of the Confederacy and destroy it.

The Confederate armies in northern Virginia dominated the first phase of the war, which lasted until mid-1863. They threw back repeated but inept Union attempts to seize Richmond. The terrain was a hundred-mile stretch of wooded rolling hills between Chesapeake Bay and the Blue Ridge; numerous rivers flowing west to east favored the defenders. Lee nevertheless failed to exploit the inexperience of the Union armies to deliver the crushing counter-offensive blow needed to unseat Lincoln.

The Confederacy's two major attempts to invade the North ended in disaster. The first, in September 1862, led to the appalling bloody draw at Antietam Creek in Maryland. The Union won a strategic victory, for Lee had to retreat. That gave Lincoln the platform to launch a political offensive of momentous consequences. On September 23, 1862, he announced that after January 1863 all slaves in states still in rebellion would be free. And on New Year's Day he promulgated the Emancipation Proclamation. It made the war a crusade to end slavery. It captured for the Union the support of European liberal opinion. It threatened the cohesion of the Confederacy's home front. It gave the Union armies, by the end of the war, almost 180,000 black soldiers, an eighth of their strength.

Lee's second invasion of the North, in June–July 1863, ended at Gettysburg, the largest battle so far fought in North America. Lee's instinct for the Napoleonic tactical offensive betrayed

The strain of war: Abraham Lincoln, April 1865.

him. The artillery and rifle fire of the new industrial age shredded the ten brigades he launched at the Union center. His army, less over 20,000 dead, wounded, or missing, retreated through rain and mud to defend Virginia.

The Union had not merely checked Lee's last offensive. In the hitherto neglected western theater Lincoln had found a winning strategy and two generals equal to any who fought for the Confederacy. Ulysses S. Grant, a whisky-sodden failure in peace, had revealed himself in 1861–62 as a brilliant strategist and dogged tactician. On July 4, 1863, the day after Gettysburg, the Confederate citadel at Vicksburg in Mississippi fell after a long amphibious campaign to Grant and his subordinate William Tecumseh Sherman. The greatest river of the continent belonged to the Union from Ohio to New Orleans; the Confederacy was cut in two. After Grant and Sherman took Chattanooga at the end of 1863, the way was open for a Union drive through the Appalachians to cut the South in three and tear out its heart.

That task fell to Sherman, who practiced to the fullest his insight that "War

is hell." He marched on Atlanta, the hinge in the rail system that linked the arsenals of Alabama with the Richmond front. He took and burned Atlanta and its factories. Then he discarded his precarious rail links and marched to meet the Union navy at Savannah, cutting a 50-mile-wide swath of scorched earth across Georgia's richest plantations. Sherman's victories gave Lincoln the decisive edge against Democrats and Copperheads in the hotly contested 1864 election.

To the north, Grant had become commander-in-chief under Lincoln. He methodically ground Lee's forces down in a year of staggeringly bloody battles of attrition around Richmond. To deprive Lee of the often-used Shenandoah Valley route outflanking Washington, Grant sent Philip Sheridan with instructions to so waste the Valley that crows crossing it would need to carry rations. Lincoln had at last found the method appropriate to the Union's unlimited war aim. As Sheridan remarked to the Prussians while observing their 1870–71 campaign, the object was to leave enemy civilians with "nothing but their eyes to weep with over the war."

Industrial firepower: "The Dictator," a Union 13" mortar.

The ruins of Richmond, 1865.

The end came in March–April 1865. While Sherman savaged the Carolinas on his way north toward Lee's rear, the Confederate armies began to melt. Sherman's destruction of farms and livestock created an irresistible urge to desert. And the inexorable pressure of Grant's will and of the Union's immense manpower on the Confederate trenches at Petersburg near Richmond ultimately forced Lee out. Cornered in the open at Appomattox Court House, he surrendered to Grant on April 9, 1865. Five days later, a Confederate sympathizer assassinated Lincoln.

Reconstruction, the process of reintegrating the South into the Union, would have to go forward without the political genius of this greatest of presidents. The North faced a choice: it could simply concede amnesty, and return the South to the rule of the unrepentant planters in return for promises not to repeat the experiment of secession. Or it could attempt to reconstruct the South on a Northern pattern, ensuring that the newly freed slaves would receive the equality that blacks and many Northern whites had fought to achieve.

The first path was that of Lincoln's successor Andrew Johnson; it led to his impeachment at the hands of the Republican majority in Congress, which imposed the second alternative, "radical reconstruction." But martial law and federal aid for the ex-slaves were not enough to break the united resistance of planters and poor whites. The South's commitment to victory was as fierce after 1865 as before, and the North's staying power was limited.

Within twelve years, Ku Klux Klan terrorism and the more subtle opposition of the South's political class had won. To carry the disputed election of 1876 the Republicans in Congress agreed to end Reconstruction. Henceforth the white South, in return for being left alone, gave the Democratic party a bloc of safe congressional seats. Blacks in effect lost the guarantees of life, liberty, property, and the vote given them in the thirteenth through fifteenth amendments of 1865–70. Compulsory labor, sharecropping, and debt bondage to the landlord replaced the old slave order, and guaranteed a future of poverty. Sharecroppers and their masters do not innovate, nor do they give industry the markets needed to support growth. And in the course of the war Egyptian and Indian cotton had conquered the South's export markets; low cotton prices further slowed recovery from the devastation of war.

Despite its immense cost—roughly 359,000 Union and 258,000 Confederate dead—and a legacy of stagnation and resentment in the South, the Civil War had decided issues as vital as the Revolutionary War. The United States would remain united, rather than splitting into rival assortments of squabbling states; Napoleon III had to end his Mexican escapade. Slavery was dead; the United States would be a predominantly industrial society of free men and women. And Reconstruction was a battle better fought and lost than not fought at all.

Toward an Industrial Society

In the North and West, the years after the war were ones of unprecedented expansion and change. William H. Seward, secretary of state to Lincoln and Johnson, bought Alaska from Russia in 1867 for 7.2 million dollars. He also annexed the island of Midway, halfway across the Pacific. The completion of the first transcontinental railroad in 1869 welded California to the East. The Great Plains fell under the new steel plows or suffered division by barbed wire. By 1890 the frontier was passing.

The new age brought to the North and West the usual conflicts of industrialization. The towns and cities, in which over a third of the North's population already lived in 1860, asserted their power over the countryside. Railroads and banks dominated the farmers of the plains, setting freight rates and conceding credit on whatever terms they pleased. "Trusts," vertically integrated monopolies such as John D. Rockefeller's Standard Oil, and giant corporations, such as Andrew Carnegie's U.S. Steel, replaced old-style family firms. Wall Street buccaneers such as Jay Gould and Jim Fisk left behind them trails of looted companies.

Industry demanded and received from the most uproariously corrupt Congresses of U.S. history the highest protective tariffs in the world. But a reaction against monopolies eventually set in. The Interstate Commerce Act of 1887 sought to regulate the railroads in the interests of the farmers. The Sherman Antitrust Act of 1890 made a gesture toward controlling the trusts. And in national politics, farmers organized. From the National Grange of 1867 through the Farmers' Alliance of the

1880s to the People's party or Populists of 1891, they sought to defend the Jeffersonian vision of an agrarian republic. They stood against banks, cities, and the ever-growing masses of immigrants. The "prolific womb of governmental injustice," the Populists thundered, was breeding "two great classes—tramps and millionaires."

In the 1896 election the Populists coalesced with the Democratic party under the leadership of William Jennings Bryan, later famous as an opponent of the teaching of Darwinism. His florid oratory ("You shall not crucify mankind upon a cross of gold") failed to carry the Northeast and Midwest against the Republican and industrial candidate, William McKinley. Industry, which had already passed agriculture's share of the national product in the 1860s, had defeated agriculture for good.

In the cities the Populists so abhorred, new forms of organization were emerging. The Knights of Labor, formed in 1869, had over 700,000 members at its height. An 1886 episode of European-style anarchist bomb violence at the Haymarket in Chicago helped discredit the Knights, although they were not involved. The American Federation of Labor (AFL), an organization of skilled craft unions under the decidedly reformist Samuel Gompers, replaced them. The first major union actions inevitably brought defeat. The Pinkerton guards of Andrew Carnegie and his partner Henry C. Frick crushed their AFL opponents in the great 1892 Homestead steel strike in Pittsburg. Eugene Debs's American Railway Union likewise failed in its bitter confrontation with the Pullman Company in 1894. But the unions survived.

In politics, the industrial cities of the Northeast and Midwest were the scene of a vast social experiment—the creation of Americans out of speakers of languages other than English. This was relatively new, for until the 1870s the only non-English-speakers to arrive in large numbers had been Germans. The waves from eastern and southern Europe after 1870 soon learned; their children grew up as Americans, thanks to compulsory elementary schooling. Their political participation, with the hearty encouragement of the big city machines ("Vote early and often"), gave new meaning to the liberties proclaimed in the Constitution. A country as empty and short of labor as America, a country founded on principles rather than on notions of ethnic identity, lay open to anyone willing to subscribe to those principles—except for the Chinese and Japanese, excluded by racist public opinion in 1882 and 1907 respectively. Industry and immigrants together transformed the United States from farmers' republic into cosmopolitan industrial empire, another Europe in size, ethnic variety, and power.

RESISTANCE AND EMULATION, FAILURE AND SUCCESS

Others were less fortunate. The major non-European states that faced the Western challenge in the nineteenth century responded in a variety of ways. Some vegetated. Some collapsed. Some attempted to adapt Western technology while rejecting the ideas that had created that technology. And one, the empire of Japan, carried out a revolution from above that in 40 years, from 1854 to 1894, transformed it from victim into conqueror.

Latin America: Anarchy and Dictatorship

The states that emerged from the collapse of Spain's New World empire between 1808 and 1824 suffered from serious disabilities. Spain had created societies stratified by blood. First came the Spanish administrators, then the Creoles—native-born of Spanish blood—then the *mestizos*—those of mixed Indian and Spanish descent. At the bottom were the Indians and the black slaves or ex-slaves of the Caribbean and Brazil. These societies had no

tradition of self-rule; the jealous centralization of Spain, which distrusted the Creoles, had seen to that. And racial stratification meant weak states in which the masters had more in common with their counterparts in neighboring states than with their own peasants.

Repeated Creole revolts against Spain produced an unstable collection of 15 states. Only Brazil, which achieved independence under the heir to the Portuguese throne, escaped a major upheaval. The new states oscillated between anarchy and the rule of narrow landowner oligarchies or despotic *caudillos*. Simón Bolívar (1783–1830), liberator of half the continent, despaired: " . . . America is ungovernable." By 1826 he already foresaw the future: "Many tyrants will rise upon my tomb."

The inland state of Paraguay provided the most spectacular example of those tyrants. Three men ruled it mercilessly between 1811 and 1870: José Gaspar Rodríguez de Francia (1811–40), Carlos Antonio López (1840–62), and his son, Francisco Solano López (1862–70). Francia created a police state cut off from the outside world and an army that under his successors became the most powerful in Latin America. In 1864 López junior took that army to war against all three of Paraguay's neighbors: Brazil, Argentina, and Uruguay. By the end, in 1870, the population of Paraguay had fallen from over half a million to less than a quarter; almost all adult males were dead.

A few states, especially after mid-century, began to develop economically, as part of the British informal empire—Argentina, Brazil, Chile. Increased European immigration, especially to Argentina, speeded the pace of change. Elsewhere, savage struggles between peasants, rancher oligarchs, and the immensely powerful landowning Church produced repeated civil wars. Mexico changed chief executives 46 times in its first 30 years. It suffered a massive civil war and French intervention in mid-century, and the quasi-

Hero of the independence struggle against Spain: Simón Bolívar, el Libertador.

dictatorship of Porfirio Díaz from 1877 to 1911. Much of Latin America ended the century further behind the West in economic and social terms than it had been in 1800.

Egypt and the Ottoman Empire: Collapse and Survival

Closer to Europe, the Islamic world faced the full force of Western power. Algeria, Tunisia, and Morocco (in 1911) succumbed to French military colonialism. Persia and the weak states of the Persian Gulf fell under the protectorate of Britain's Indian Empire. Only Egypt and Turkey were strong enough to have a chance at survival.

Egypt failed. The cotton boom of the 1860s encouraged the successors of Mehemet Ali to launch ambitious public works such as the reconstruction of Cairo in the image of Napoleon III's Paris. By the 1870s the Khedive Ismail was spending annually twice Egypt's revenue and plugging his deficit with European loans. Bankruptcy and the fierce reaction of Egypt's partially Westernized elites to the Khedive's subservience to Britain and France produced the explosion that led an unhappy Gladstone to occupy Egypt. The country's vital strategic importance to Britain, its easily mastered terrain, and its still largely peasant society doomed it.

The Ottoman Empire was both more fortunate and less digestible than its sometime vassal Egypt. It faced stirrings of nationalism, reinforced by religion, among its Balkan peoples. Russia, despite defeat in the Crimea, remained a major threat. Bankruptcy and foreign financial controls, as in Egypt, followed upon incautious borrowing and frivolous expenditure in the 1870s. But the empire's international function and military tradition saved it from dismemberment in the nineteenth century. Britain propped it up to keep Russia from the Middle East. Austria supported it lest the demise of the Ottoman multinational empire free Balkan nationalities to turn against the multinational Habsburg empire. Germany supported it to stabilize Austria and as a field for German "informal empire." France supported it because France held much of the Ottoman debt. The powers would not tolerate one of their number monopolizing the empire, nor could they agree on how to divide it. Its poor but warlike peoples and its mountainous terrain made it an unpromising conquest.

Under the stubborn and wily Abd al-Hamid II ("the damned"), who ruled from 1876 to 1908–09, the empire survived war with Russia in 1877–78 (see p. 816). It acquired military equipment and training from Prussia-Germany. In 1908–09 a group of Westernized "Young Turk" officers on the pattern of Arabi made the Sultan a figurehead. In the following years they proved that the Ottoman warrior tradition could inspire a twentieth-century fighting force. That force ultimately upheld Turkish independence.

China: Resistance and Decline

The China that faced the Europeans in the middle decades of the nineteenth century was the most populous state on earth, with a tradition that stretched back three millennia. To the Manchu aristocrats of the Qing (Ch'ing) dynasty (1644–1911) and the Confucian scholar-gentry who ruled China, the "Middle Kingdom" was the center of the universe. The overseas "barbarians" who had first appeared around China's coasts in the sixteenth century seemed no different than the nomads of central Asia or the tributary kingdoms of Vietnam, Korea, and Tibet. Barbarians could only enter into relations with China by bringing tribute and prostrating themselves before the emperor. The dynasty kept them in their proper place in the eighteenth century by restricting them to the single trading port of Canton.

But China proved less and less capable of imposing Chinese norms on the seaborne barbarians or on the Russian land power to the north. Externally,

Sultan Abd al-Hamid II, known for his cunning and cruelty.

the barbarian technological lead lengthened decisively with the coming of steam and shell-firing cannon. Internally, the Qing dynasty appeared to be following the law of cyclical rise, crisis, and decay that had long shaped Chinese thought about history and politics. By 1800 the dynasty had passed its peak and was descending, amid secret society agitation, peasant rebellions, massive overpopulation, and immense natural catastrophes that took millions of lives. The sheer size of the empire, along with administrative inefficiency, corruption, and the inherent conflict between Manchu and Chinese, crippled efforts at reform.

The end of the East India Company's monopoly of the China trade in 1833 led to a rush by private British

China in the Nineteenth Century

merchants, and China's opening by force. British traders had developed a lucrative Chinese black market for the Indian-grown opium that paid for the West's imports of tea, silk, and the gleaming ceramics that had inspired envy and imitation in eighteenth-century Europe. To a desperate attempt of the Beijing (Peking) government to close down the opium trade for both fiscal and health reasons, the British replied with gunboats. The first and second Opium Wars of 1839–42 and 1856–60 flattened the dynasty's armed forces, opened numerous ports to European trade, delivered Hong Kong to Britain and vast northern territories to Russia, and gave foreigners immunity from Chinese law, with its custom of judicial torture. Traders, missionaries, and diplomats flocked in, rousing xenophobia. Killings of foreigners and frequent gunboat reprisals were the predictable result.

Internally, defeat in the First Opium War and the strains of dynastic decline unleashed an immense civil war. Hong Xiuquan (Hung Hsiu-ch'üan), the principal leader of the "Taiping Rebellion" that conquered south-central China in the 1850s, believed that he was the younger brother of Jesus and that his mission was to exterminate the Manchus. Hong's unstable blend of Western religious ideas and Chinese peasant millenarianism attracted a wide and fanatical following. But its foreign elements made it suspect to the Confucian provincial gentry. Eventually the dynasty rallied, thanks to armies the gentry raised and led. With help from foreign military experts such as "Chinese" Gordon, they crushed the Taipings by 1864. The European powers, in the end, preferred the Qing to chaos. Twenty million peasants perished in the war and its accompanying famines.

Qing survival now required drastic measures—not merely the adoption of Western techniques, but of the concepts on which they rested. The dynasty made a start in the late 1860s under the leadership of the Manchu

The Empress Dowager Ci Xi (T'zu Hsi) (r. 1861–1908), whose fierce resistance to change helped doom the Qing dynasty.

Prince Gong (Kung). But Gong lost a series of palace struggles to the pitiless Empress Dowager Ci Xi (Tz'u Hsi), who henceforth dominated court and central administration until her death in 1908. Her hostility to anything she did not control paralyzed the regime. And to a true Confucian, the West's material and military success was irrelevant; tradition and virtue were their own reward. China's "self-strengthening" program grudgingly acquired armament plants, railways, and a military academy, but it lacked conviction. Neither dynasty nor scholar-gentry created the leadership and institutions required to save China from further dismemberment at the hands of Europeans and Japanese.

Japan: The Meiji Restoration

Japan, until the arrival of Perry in 1853–54, was even more closed than China. The great lord Tokugawa Ieyasu (1542–1616) had unified it in a series of wars that lasted until 1600. He and his successors imposed peace, exterminated or forced underground the Christian communities the Jesuits had founded, and recognized only the Dutch—limited to one port and one ship a year—as trading partners. The Tokugawa discouraged and occasionally persecuted Japanese who pursued "Dutch learning," the new European knowledge.

The Japanese system was nevertheless very different from anything in China. Both Western scholars and their twentieth-century Japanese counterparts have frequently described it as "feudal," for its basis was some 250 domains, or *han*, whose lords were dependents or vassals of the Tokugawa. But a key element in European feudal institutions, the rights of the vassal against the lord, was largely lacking, and the system was infinitely more centralized than anything resembling it in Europe. Most of Japan's hereditary warrior caste, the samurai, did not even own land, but received stipends in rice from their *han*. Their ethos stressed above all service to their lord.

Japanese politics were thus far different from those of China. The Tokugawa ruled, at least in theory, as deputies (*Shōgun*) of the imperial house, which had reigned although rarely ruled from time immemorial. The emperor was both a figurehead for the Tokugawa and the most powerful symbol of Japanese unity. He might become a figurehead for others, legitimizing revolutionary transformation. And the division of Japan into domains offered regional bases for any movement to overthrow the Tokugawa.

Culturally, Japan had a tradition of borrowing. It acquired Confucianism and Buddhism from China and sixteenth-century guns from the Portuguese. The curiosity of Japanese scholars about the outside world had no parallel in China. And the practical warrior ethos of the samurai took precedence over Confucianism. On the bat-

tlefield virtue was irrelevant; the issue was victory or defeat. A leader in "Dutch learning," Sakuma Shōzan (1811–64), compiler of foreign language dictionaries and cannon-foundry master, put it caustically: China had lost the First Opium War "because foreign learning is rational and Chinese learning is not."

Structurally, Japan was small and ethnically homogeneous, with a fierce sense of distinctness. During the long Tokugawa peace, it had developed a flourishing agricultural economy and a large and growing merchant class. The Tokugawa, although still in control in 1854, were losing their grip upon an increasingly rich and diverse society. Like eighteenth-century Britain, Japan had the cultural and social potential for a vast leap in productivity.

Finally, Japan's economy, although dynamic, was—unlike China's—not conspicuously rich enough to attract Western greed from the beginning of the century. The opening of Japan was

A Japanese view: Commodore Matthew C. Perry, charged by President Millard Fillmore with opening Japan to Western trade, parades through the streets of Yokohama (1854).

1598		1868	1912
	Tokugawa Shogunate		Meiji Era

an afterthought; that was why Perry got there first. And the Japanese, in framing their response to Perry's peremptory demands, had the advantage of knowing what had happened to China. Collaboration, not resistance, was clearly wisest until Japan was stronger.

Perry's arrival created a revolutionary situation. The Tokugawa Shogunate grudgingly opened Japanese ports and conceded extraterritorial jurisdiction in "unequal treaties." Xenophobic "men of spirit" among the lower samurai replied by assassinating foreigners and the Tokugawa officials who collaborated with them. In 1863 Britain bombarded the city of Kagoshima in reprisal. The Shogunate's impotent collaboration with the West, like that of the Khedivate in Egypt, deprived it of the legitimacy needed to rule.

But Japan took a different path than Egypt or China. The Shogunate avoided open war with the West. And in the outer *han* of Satsuma, Chōshu, Tosa, and Hizen, middle and lower samurai with some notions of the outer world offered an alternative to supine acquiescence or self-destructive fanaticism. In 1868 they induced their lords to revolt in the name both of tradition and modernity; the Tokugawa Shogunate fell after a brief but bloody civil war.

The insurgents "restored" the emperor, who took the reign-title of Meiji. The new leaders were ruthless and clear-sighted—Ōkubo Toshimichi, Yamagata Aritomo, Kido Kōin, Ōkuma Shigenobu, and Itō Hirobumi. Backed by imperial authority and the newly invented tradition of the Shintō state religion, they swiftly swept away all perceived obstacles to a "rich country, strong army." Loyalty previously given to "feudal" superiors proved readily transferable to emperor and nation.

The Meiji oligarchs pensioned off the domain lords in 1871. In 1873 Yamagata began the creation of a Prussian-style conscript army, breaking the "feudal" samurai monopoly of arms. The oligarchs abolished their own caste, the samurai, to mobilize all energies in a race against time to ensure Japan's independence. In 1877 their new army pitilessly crushed a last great rising of dissident samurai under a former comrade, Saigō Takamori. The oligarchs created state enterprises with Western machinery, and sold them off to a merchant class that rose eagerly to the challenge of creating an industrial economy. The oligarchs imposed Western-style code law, and compulsory education to reinforce powerfully Japan's existing traditions of learning, hard work, and deference to authority. They secured French, Prussian, and British advisers for army and navy. They created a military-bureaucratic absolutism with a Bismarckian constitution (1889) as fig-leaf. And in foreign affairs, they succeeded in appearing meek until Japan was strong enough to face the West on equal terms. The Meiji oligarchs created a mighty modern state, a powerful engine of change and conquest. Its chief lack, it later emerged, was brakes.

Japan was an exception. It avoided Western domination in the nineteenth century and soon acquired the strength to create an empire of its own. The United States, thanks to mighty demographic and economic growth and Northern victory in the Civil War, likewise escaped the hegemony of Britain. Other states, from Latin America, to Egypt, Burma, and China, failed to rise to the challenge, and suffered colonial occupation or "informal" domination through gunboats and treaties. When

Britain's "followers" sought to rival it in the wider world, Africa too went under the knife, divided by diplomacy and Maxim gun in less than 20 years. But the world hegemony of Britain and of Europe was precarious, for it rested on narrow demographic foundations and on the long but increasingly fragile peace in Europe itself.

Suggestions for Further Reading

British and European Expansion

For much of the conceptual framework of this chapter, see the essays of J. Gallagher and R. Robinson in W. R. Louis, ed., *Imperialism* (1976), and D. Headrick, *Tools of Empire: Technology and European Imperialism in the Nineteenth Century* (1981). B. Porter, *The Lion's Share: A Short History of British Imperialism, 1850–1983* (1984), is useful on Britain. D. K. Fieldhouse, *The Colonial Empires* (1966), and *Colonialism, 1870–1945* (1981), offers a comparative perspective, as do S. K. Betts, *Europe Overseas* (1968), the sardonic V. Kiernan, *From Conquest to Collapse: European Empires from 1815 to 1960* (1982), and W.

Baumgart, *Imperialism: The Idea and Reality of British and French Colonial Expansion, 1880–1914* (1982). For Britain's "white" colonies, see D. G. Creighton, *Canada's First Century* (1970); E. McInnis, *Canada: A Political and Social History* (1947); and C. H. Grattan, *The Southwest Pacific to 1900* (1963). On India, see J. M. Brown, *Modern India: The Origins of an Asian Democracy* (1985), and S. Wolpert, *A New History of India* (1982). R. Robinson, J. Gallagher, and A. Denny, *Africa and the Victorians: The Climax of Imperialism* (1968), is delightfully provocative on the "scramble for Africa."

The United States

The literature on the United States is distressingly vast; J. M. Blum et al., *The National Experience: A History of the United States*, 7th ed. (1989), is an excellent introductory survey with detailed bibliographies. On the pre-Jacksonian period, see G. Dangerfield, *The Awakening of American Nationalism* (1965); J. C. Curtis, *Andrew Jackson and the Search for Vindication* (1976), covers the "Age of Jackson." For the road west, see R. A. Billington,

Westward Expansion (1967). On slavery, see especially E. D. Genovese, *Roll, Jordan, Roll: The World the Slaves Made* (1974). J. M. McPherson, *Battle Cry of Freedom: The Civil War Era* (1988), describes the greatest crisis in America's history; C. V. Woodward, *Origins of the New South, 1877–1913* (1951), deals with its long-term impact.

Latin America, the Islamic World, and East Asia

For general surveys of Latin America, see J. F. Rippy, *Latin America: A Modern History* (1958, 1968), and T. H. Skidmore and P. H. Smith, *Modern Latin America* (1984); J. Lynch, *The Latin American Revolutions, 1810–1826* (1973), describes the initial upheaval that brought independence. For the fates of Ottoman Turkey and Egypt, see respectively B. Lewis, *The Emergence of Mod-*

ern Turkey (1968), and J. C. B. Richmond, *Egypt, 1798–1952* (1977). On China and Japan see C. Schirokauer, *A Brief History of Chinese and Japanese Civilizations*; 2nd ed. (1989); J. K. Fairbank, *The Great Chinese Revolution, 1800–1985* (1986), *The Cambridge History of China*, Vols. 10 and 11 (1978, 1980); and W. G. Beasley, *The Modern History of Japan* (1981), and *The Meiji Restoration* (1972).

28
Europe in the Long Peace, 1871–1914

*T*he years between 1871 and 1914 were the longest period of uninterrupted peace in Europe since the "five good emperors" of the first and second centuries A.D. Only minor Balkan conflicts disturbed the peace. The workings of the balance of power and above all the self-restraint of the new Germany prevented war between great powers. Only after 1890 did the German bid for continental hegemony and world power status (see pp. 831–43) lead to a new age of world wars.

Internally, monarchy and its attendant aristocracy remained the preeminent form of government. Landed wealth still dominated state administrations, diplomatic services, and standing armies. Revolution was no longer practical politics, although faith in it persisted and even broadened. The demands of the working classes had little political weight until after 1900. The welfare state, with its bureaucracies, regulations, and taxes was still in its infancy. These conditions along with the immense strides of industry and commerce made these de-

Opposite: The golden age of the middle classes: a holiday in the park, late 1870s.

783

Queen Victoria on Her Prerogatives   1850

She requires: 1. That he [Lord Palmerston, the Foreign Secretary] will distinctly state what he proposes in a given case, in order that the Queen may know distinctly to *what* she has given her Royal sanction. 2. Having *once given* her sanction to a measure, that it be not arbitrarily altered or modified by the Minister: such an act she must consider as failing in sincerity towards the Crown, and justly to be visited by the exercise of her Constitutional right of dismissing that Minister. She expects to be kept informed of what passes between him and the Foreign Ministers before important decisions are taken. . . ; to receive the Foreign Dispatches in good time, and to have the drafts for her approval sent to her in sufficient time to make herself acquainted with their contents before they must be sent off.

From Queen Victoria to Lord John Russell (the Prime Minister), August 12, 1850, *The Letters of Queen Victoria,* ed. by A. C. Benson and Viscount Esher (London: John Murray, 1907), Vol. II, p. 315.

cades the golden age of the middle classes. Money, although it still sought to climb through marriage into families of noble birth, had become the foremost source of social status. The middle-class citizen of Europe, thanks to steam, electricity, and the absence of government restrictions on movement, could travel as never before or after. Letters of credit and British banknotes took the place of passports.

This golden age was short. Both liberal principles and the preservation of political stability after the coming of mass education and the second industrial revolution seemed to demand an ever-wider expansion of the franchise. Universal male suffrage in turn created the first workers' parties and encouraged women to demand the vote. In the realm of ideology and culture, a confident middle-class materialism compounded of Darwin, steel, and electricity provoked a response: outright hostility to the gospel of science and "progress." The rapidity of change itself created immense tensions, psychological as much as political and intellectual. Those tensions ultimately discharged in spontaneous rejoicing among the urban masses at the coming of war in August 1914.

EUROPEAN POLITICS AND SOCIETY

England: The Limits of Gradualism

By the 1860s Britain's spurt of dramatic economic growth was ending. From the 1870s its rivals began pressing ever more insistently at its heels. Yet as late as 1914 London remained the center of the world economy. Britain's money market was the largest, although upstart New York increasingly rivalled it. Britain dominated insurance and other services reserved for mature economies. Britain controlled the world's largest merchant marine. Britain's overseas investments rose from 1 billion to 2.5 billion pounds between 1870 and 1900; in 1914 they still dwarfed those of other powers, and underwrote economic growth on every continent. Britain's export of know-how and import of interest and insurance premiums increasingly rivalled its trade in goods. But financial dominance proved to be a poor substitute for the mastery of world manufacturing that was passing to others (see Figure 24-4, p. 688).

Politically, the Britain of Queen Victoria (r. 1837–1901) was a time of gradual adjustments to the demands of the new age. The irascible Palmerston had dominated a period of shifting factional alignments until his death in 1865. Parties remained incoherent collections of notables, without central machinery or discipline. The Queen, in this situation, was able to assert considerable powers as constitutional monarch. But under Palmerston's two great successors, Benjamin Disraeli and William Ewart Gladstone, Liberals and Tories (Conservatives) took on their modern shape, following a pattern also visible in the United States. The monarchy's influence receded as that of the mass electorate advanced.

The parties alternated in power, spurring one another in succession to

1714	1727	1760		1820	1830	1837		1901	1910		1936	1952
George I	George II	George III		George IV	William IV		Victoria		Edward VII	George V	George VI	Elizabeth II

Edward VIII (abdicated)

enlarge the franchise and appeal to the new electorate. Gladstone, "the People's William," took the initiative on the franchise in 1866. But it was Disraeli, son of a converted Jew, author of novels about the social question, and radical Tory, who preempted his rival with the Second Reform Bill of 1867 that almost doubled the electorate. Gladstone, during his governments of 1868–74 and 1880–85, then introduced the secret ballot in 1872 and a Third Reform Bill in 1884 that gave most adult males the vote.

The consequences of the coming of democracy were at least three. First, it created the modern machinery of mass parties. Disraeli pioneered a network of constituency organizations coordinated from the center in the 1874 election. Gladstone replied in 1880, damning Disraeli's foreign policy in Britain's first populist stump speeches by a major political leader. Such tactics, along with Gladstone's persistent inability to distinguish morality from foreign policy, had prompted Disraeli earlier to describe his rival as an "unprincipled maniac, and with one commanding characteristic—whether preaching, praying, speechifying or scribbling—never a gentlemen." The day of the gentleman in politics was indeed passing. The Liberal party machine, under "Radical Joe" Chamberlain, self-made businessman and reforming mayor of Birmingham, improved on Disraeli's 1874 example and converted Gladstone's "speechifying" into victory. Appeals to and organization of the new mass electorate replaced social standing as the key determinants of political success.

The second major consequence of democracy was to raise the problem of Ireland, Britain's earliest colony. Elizabeth I, James I, and Cromwell had imposed Protestant landlords on Ireland's Catholic peasants. An Irish nationalist revolt in the 1790s had failed. The famine of the 1840s had cut the population by a third, but the problem of peasant land tenure remained. A "Fenian Brotherhood" founded in 1858 in New York pressed the Irish cause with intermittent terrorism. And the Second Reform Bill and secret ballot between them brought over 50 Irish nationalist members to Parliament. There they obstructed proceedings with long speeches demanding rights for the peasantry, and autonomy within the British empire—"home rule"—for Ireland.

Gladstone's first administration (1868–74) made an inadequate start on the peasant question; his second (1880–85) settled it with the Land Act of 1881. But he was already too late. Exorbitant rents, arbitrary evictions, peasant boycotts, violence against landlords, and Irish nationalist assassinations of high British officials had created an atmosphere in which extremism on both sides prospered. Gladstone's conversion to Irish home rule and his attempts to implement it in 1886 and during his tragic last government in 1892–94 were in vain. Home rule meant placing Protestant landlords and the Presbyterian Scottish settlers of Ulster under the "Rome rule" of the Catholic majority.

To the delight of the Tories, who thereby gained uninterrupted power from 1895 to 1905, home rule split Gladstone's party. "Radical Joe" Chamberlain and his followers joined the Tories; Chamberlain became a spokesman for British supremacy in

The great antagonists: Disraeli and Gladstone (below).

David Lloyd George (1863–1945), the last of the great Liberal reformers and war prime minister, 1916–22.

South Africa. The Irish question, which had now become a religious-national conflict between Protestant Ulster and the Catholic south and west, festered. On the eve of World War I the Liberals made a final attempt to impose home rule. Ulster, armed to the teeth, defied London. The army officer corps, as closely connected to Ulster as its Prusso-German counterpart was to Prussia's Polish borderlands, resisted government policy in a fashion unprecedented since Cromwell. Then war in Europe postponed civil war in Ireland.

The ballot had brought the Irish question, which arguably had no peaceful solution, to a head. Ballot and Irish question together introduced the third major consequence of democracy, the rise of a worker's party. Until the 1890s the working-class movement had confined itself to trade unionism. Craft unions had organized the Trades Union Congress in 1868; unskilled workers won their first major victory in the great London dock strike of 1889. But Gladstone and Liberals to his left on social issues, such as Chamberlain, held the working man's vote—until the party split over home rule.

Chamberlain's defection to the Tories created the political space for a working-class party. Keir Hardie, Scottish leader of the miners, organized the Independent Labor Party (ILP) in 1893. In 1900 the ILP, the gradualist middle-class "Fabian Socialists" of Sidney and Beatrice Webb, and a variety of other groups coalesced to form what became the Labour Party. In the 1906 election it won 29 seats. Although the Liberals carried the election of 1906, they henceforth had to reckon with an increasingly formidable force to their left. That strengthened Liberal resolve in pressing expensive social reforms such as old age pensions (1908) and unemployment and health insurance (1911) under the leadership of the "Welsh magician," David Lloyd George.

When the unrepresentative Tory majority in the House of Lords balked at Lloyd George's "People's Budget," the Liberals rammed through a Parliament Act in 1911 that stripped the Lords of their veto over money bills. But the Liberals did not recapture Labour. Indeed, a wave of strikes after 1911 culminated in the ominous 1914 "Triple Alliance" of railwaymen, transport workers, and miners. Here also the coming of war rescued the Liberals from grave crisis—but that rescue proved only temporary.

France: The Third Republic Beleaguered

France entered the long peace with a difficult legacy. Since 1789 three constitutional monarchies (1789–92, 1815–30, 1830–48), two republics (1792–99, 1848–51), and two Bonaparte dictatorships (1799–1815, 1851–70) had attempted to rule it. All had collapsed within 20 years. Savage disputes divided Bourbon Legitimists, Orleanists, and Bonapartists, moderate "opportunists" and radical republicans, clericals and anticlericals. War, defeat, and the crushing of the Paris Commune in 1871 had created lasting bitterness. Yet by 1879 France had established a regime that weathered one world war and only succumbed after crushing defeat in a second.

The Third Republic would have gladdened the heart of Edmund Burke. It institutionalized the triumph of the provinces over radical Paris. Thanks to its middle-class leadership and its peasant voters, it proved remarkably conservative. And unlike its two predecessors it had no prefabricated constitution.

Its origin was Bismarck's demand for a French regime with a popular mandate to make peace. The universal male suffrage elections of February 1871 returned a chamber of monarchists because the republicans had discredited themselves by preaching war to the bitter end. But the monarchists failed to restore the monarchy. The Legitimist claimant, the childless Count of Chambord, refused to abandon the white flag with lilies of his royal forefathers. The country would

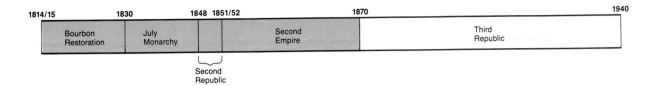

1814/15	1830	1848	1851/52	1870	1940

Bourbon Restoration | July Monarchy | | Second Empire | Third Republic

Second Republic

not give up the Revolutionary and Napoleonic tricolor. Nor while Chambord lived would the Legitimists support the more flexible Orleanist claimant, the Count of Paris.

The monarchy's moment soon passed. The monarchists had brought peace, but the peasantry feared that if left too long in office they might attempt to restore the old regime. Elections between 1871 and 1874 gradually tipped the balance in favor of the republicans. In 1873 the monarchist majority removed from power the grand old man who had made peace with Bismarck, Adolphe Thiers. In his place it installed Marshal MacMahon, who had become an Orleanist after an astounding demonstration of battlefield incompetence in 1870. MacMahon was to serve as provisional executive until Chambord died or otherwise resolved the monarchist deadlock.

But the republicans forestalled MacMahon. In 1875 they pushed through by one vote a motion establishing a procedure for choosing MacMahon's successor as president. That was the Third Republic's basic law; it made the provisional permanent. And when MacMahon dissolved the Chamber in May 1877 in order to seek a monarchist majority, the republicans won. When they captured the Senate in 1879, MacMahon resigned. France received, in Jules Grévy, its first republican president.

The republican president, however, was not to be the Third Republic's executive. A strong presidency might fall to another Louis Napoleon or MacMahon. Henceforth prime minister and cabinet, ever-changing according to the Chamber's whims, ruled France. The Third Republic so diffused power that paralysis sometimes resulted.

Yet it was capable of decisive action. Under the stern leadership of Jules Ferry, minister of education from 1879 to 1881 and prime minister in 1880–81 and 1883–85, the Republic created a national educational system independent of the implacably hostile Church. The mission of France's new school teachers was to nationalize and republicanize the rural masses, and to make France competitive with Prussia-Germany. In the villages, the "schoolmaster's party" now faced the "priest's party." Railways, another priority of Ferry and of his colleague Charles de Freycinet, likewise opened up the countryside to new ideas. The Republic finished the rail net that Napoleon III had begun, and at last consolidated France as a national market.

Its successes did not save the Republic from two major internal crises before the turn of the century. Despite the collapse of the royalists and the extinction of Bonapartist hopes with the death of Napoleon III's son in the Zulu War of 1879, the Right remained unreconciled. The agricultural downturn of the 1880s, the phylloxera vine blight that almost destroyed France's historic wine industry, and a slow-down in industrial growth sapped the regime's popularity. After 1885 the moderate "opportunist" republicans who had presided over the establishment of the Republic no longer had a majority. Three groupings of roughly equal size, the Right, the Opportunists, and the radical republicans, faced one another.

In this tense situation the chief figure among the Radicals, Georges Clemenceau, imposed his protégé, General Georges Boulanger, on the cabinet as minister of war. Boulanger, an impressive figure on horseback, cultivated popularity with the troops and

Statesmen of the Third Republic: Jules Grévy, president, 1879–87, and (below) Jules Ferry, prime minister, 1880–81, 1883–85.

The young Georges Clemenceau, "Tiger" of the Radicals and war prime minister, 1917–20.

made imprudent remarks about Germany, remarks Bismarck gleefully exploited. When the government fell in 1887, Boulanger intrigued with both Catholic Right and extreme Left. In his support the ferocious anti-Semite Edouard Drumont joined the demagogue Paul Déroulède, one of the first of those nationalist extremists, common in the twentieth century, whose politics failed to fit the classic nineteenth-century Left-Right distinction. Boulanger began posing as a potential Bonaparte—until a resolute Opportunist government frightened him into exile in 1889. There he committed suicide upon the grave of his mistress.

The Republic survived, despite continuing depression and a series of scandals that included revelations that de Lesseps's Panama Canal company, which had failed to repeat his triumph at Suez, had paid off numerous deputies. The Republic's second major crisis came from a different direction. In 1894 army intelligence recovered from a wastebasket at the German embassy a document suggesting that a member of the French general staff was selling war plans to Germany. The army immediately fixed upon a culprit, Captain Alfred Dreyfus, the only Jew on the staff. It court-martialled him without a shred of evidence, stripped him of his rank, and condemned him to imprisonment on Devil's Island off French Guyana. His family protested but failed to gain a hearing until evidence emerged that the leaks to Germany were continuing.

In 1898 the flamboyant novelist Émile Zola wrote an open letter to the president of the Republic entitled "J'accuse!" He accused the army of unjustly condemning an innocent man and of covering the real traitor. He challenged the authorities to sue him for libel. The "Affaire Dreyfus," or simply "the Affair," split France into warring camps. The clericals, who had in 1892 refused a pressing invitation from the reforming Pope Leo XIII to "rally" to the Republic, stood with officer corps, monarchists, anti-Semites, and the radical Right of the streets. For

them, Dreyfus was guilty; he must be guilty—for his innocence meant the guilt of army, aristocracy, and Church. The Left stood in general for Dreyfus, although nationalism impelled many Opportunists and Radicals to support the army.

The government, which had incautiously claimed in 1897 that "there is no Affaire Dreyfus," collapsed. The suicide of the officer who had forged the cover-up evidence and the flight of the real traitor, a Lieutenant Esterhazy, led to a succession of new trials and Dreyfus's eventual rehabilitation. A Déroulède coup attempt in 1899 failed. Anticlerical Radical governments dissolved religious orders that had attacked the Republic, took the Church off the state payroll, and purged the army. The Republic won its confrontation with the Right and carried to completion the process of secularization begun with the Civil Constitution of the Clergy of 1790.

Finally, the Republic even deflected or absorbed the rise of the workers' movement. The elections of 1893 brought almost 50 socialists into the Chamber. The economic upturn after 1896 eased France's domestic distress and encouraged socialist and trade-union struggles. France acquired, in the CGT or General Confederation of Labor and in a unified Socialist party after 1905, a workers' movement second only to that of Germany. Marxism, which the austere Jules Guesde had introduced into the French labor movement in the late 1870s, prospered. Yet the greatest of all French Socialists was only a Marxist by courtesy. Jean Jaurès, the man who unified the movement's quarreling sects, had concluded that capitalism did not necessarily lead to revolution. By temperament he preferred conciliation to violence. And in advocacy of violence the Marxists had a powerful rival—the anarchist myth of the revolutionary general strike, creation of the eccentric Georges Sorel, author of Reflexions on Violence (1908). Militants influenced by Sorel captured the CGT amid violent strikes in 1905–06.

Clemenceau and Aristide Briand, prime ministers in 1906–10, ruthlessly suppressed them and broke Sorel's myth. But the Republic demonstrated great powers of absorption as well as of repression. To the left of the now-respectable Radicals an exotic new hybrid, the "Radical-Socialists," sprang up. A genuine though non-Marxist Socialist joined a government for the first time in 1899. Others eventually followed.

The Republic, to the surprise of all, far outlasted it predecessors. It proved strong enough to face war squarely in 1914. As international tension mounted after 1911 the Chamber swallowed its qualms about leadership. It appointed as president Georges Poincaré, a dour, forceful, and logically uncompromising Alsatian. It increased compulsory military service from two years to three to compensate partially for Germany's population advantage. When war came, even the Socialists marched.

Germany: Bismarck and After

The new Reich was a hybrid—partly centralized and partly federal, part military dictatorship and part constitutional monarchy. The King of Prussia and German Emperor (Kaiser), as "All-Highest War-Lord," personally controlled the German army. The Emperor appointed and dismissed the Reich chancellor without reference to the Reich's legislature. Prussia, which made up over three-fifths of the Reich, dominated the upper house of that legislature, the representatives of the German princes. The lower house or *Reichstag*, elected under universal male suffrage, had the indispensable right of approving or disapproving the budget; that much the Prussian Liberals had won in the constitutional conflict of 1862–66. Nor could the Reich government levy direct taxes. The states retained that right, and made occasional contributions to Reich finances at their pleasure. Finally, the constitutions of the states, especially the inequitable "three-class" franchise law of Prussia,

---

Zola Accuses
January 1898

I accuse Lieutenant Colonel Du Paty de Clam [the investigating officer] of having been the diabolical author of the [original] judicial error—unknowingly, I may hope—and of thereafter defending his evil work, for the last three years, by the most bizarre and reprehensible machinations.

I accuse General Mercier [the former Minister of War] of having become the accomplice, at best through weakness of intellect, of one of the greatest iniquities of the century.

I accuse General Billot [the present Minister of War] of having had in his hands the indisputable proofs of the innocence of Dreyfus, and of having suppressed them. . . .

I accuse General de Boisdeffre and General Gonse [chief and deputy chief of staff of the army] of having become accomplices in that same crime. . . . .

I accuse the first court martial [of Dreyfus] of having violated the law by condemning the accused on secret evidence, and I accuse the second court martial of having covered up that illegality, on orders from above. . . .

In making these accusations, I am not unaware that I am placing myself in jeopardy under articles 30 and 31 of the press law of July 29, 1889, which punishes the crime of defamation of character. I do so voluntarily. . . .

I have only one passion, that of enlightenment, in the name of humanity, which has suffered much and has a right to happiness. . . . Therefore let them dare to take me to court, and may the investigation take place in the light of day!

I am waiting.

From Émile Zola, *Oeuvres Complètes* (Paris: Cercle du Livre Précieux, 1969), Vol. 14, pp. 930–31 (translation by M. Knox).

---

balanced the universal suffrage of the *Reichstag*.

This was a system of checks that only Bismarck could balance. Its complexity was in part a result of his desire to make himself indispensable, and in part a reflection of the strength of the various mutually antagonistic forces with which he had to deal. The "National" Liberals who had chosen to

The French army, determined to brand Dreyfus as a traitor, provides him with a "guard of dishonor" whose backs are turned (1899).

cooperate with Bismarck after 1866 initially controlled the *Reichstag*. The Conservatives, thanks to the weighting of votes by income in the Prussian elections, held Prussia. The states retained the power to paralyze Reich finances.

All three forces were losers in the long term. The National Liberals failed to make the leap from mid-nineteenth-century party of notables to mass party that British Liberals and Tories had made between 1868 and 1880. That failure doomed the German liberals to long-term electoral decline. The Conservatives, despite an increasingly populist style from the 1890s on, only survived thanks to the three-class franchise and the votes of the landless peasants of the great estates. Conservatism lost whatever Pietist ethical content it may have had, and became the party of Junker "agribusiness." And the states lost vitality as national integration proceeded. That left a vacuum into which other forces gradually moved.

First of those forces were the German Catholics, who made up over 30 percent of the Reich's population. They responded to Bismarck's Protestant "Greater Prussia" with a national Catholic political party, the Center. When Bismarck and the National Liberals attacked them in the early 1870s as "ene-

mies of the Reich" who took their orders from Rome, Catholics rallied to Church and Center party. This "*Kulturkampf*" or "cultural struggle" between the Prusso-German state and the Catholic Church consolidated German political Catholicism as a party that held as much as a quarter of the popular vote. That electorate, precisely because its bond was religion, came from all classes, although it concentrated regionally in the Catholic south and west.

The second German mass party was that of the workers. Various workers' parties had emerged in the course of the 1860s, and in 1875 they coalesced to form the Social Democratic Party of Germany (SPD). Like the Center, the SPD suffered a Bismarckian preemptive attack. In 1878–79, in the course of a major policy change that involved alliance with Vienna, heavy protective tariffs, and the deliberate splitting of his National Liberal allies, Bismarck induced the *Reichstag* to outlaw SPD propaganda and mass meetings. He and his successors attempted to wean the workers away from the SPD with factory legislation and with the world's first state sickness and accident insurance (1883–84) and old age and disability pensions (1889). Neither stick nor carrot checked the SPD's growth. The masses flooding into the new industrial cities voted, and voted Socialist.

By 1891, affiliated with highly disciplined trade unions and equipped with a Marxist program, the SPD was poised for expansion. By the Reich's last election in 1912, it had conquered 29 percent of the vote, the largest of any single party—and the largest vote for any workers' party in the world. This massive bureaucratic organization, with its women's and youth affiliates, its social clubs and workers' libraries, its newspapers and periodicals, was the mainstay of the international working-class movement, the "Second International" that emerged in 1889 after the collapse of Marx's "First International."

Despite its verbal commitment to revolution, its "proletarian internation-

Frederick III
1888

1871   William I   1918   1933
        Bismarck   William II   Weimar Republic
        1890
        Imperial Germany

alism," and its hostility to "militarism," the SPD was and remained a working-class copy of the organization, sobriety, and discipline of the Prussian army. But it was not monolithic. The "revisionists" of its center and right, under the leadership of Edouard Bernstein, proposed to "revise" Marx. Like Jaurès in France, Bernstein believed that revolution was neither inevitable nor necessary, for the standard of living of the workers was rising. Social reform could and should come through ballot box and trade union. The SPD left, whose leading theoretician was the formidable Rosa Luxemburg, replied with vituperation. Reform was a "bourgeois swindle" and the revolutionary general strike was the just and necessary weapon of the "proletariat." That split increasingly threatened to crack the party open.

Failure to strangle the SPD at birth was the greatest of Bismarck's domestic defeats, but not the only one. His turn to protection in 1878–79 missed its two main goals. It did not provide the Reich with an adequate source of revenue independent of the states. Nor did it give the government a stable *Reichstag* majority. The often stormy alliance between right National Liberals and Conservatives, industry and agriculture, "iron and rye" that Bismarck created around protective tariffs only gained an absolute majority once, in the 1887 elections. Without a Boulanger, without an emergency real or imagined with which to rouse the electorate with cries of "the Fatherland in danger," neither Bismarck nor his successors were able to dominate the universal suffrage *Reichstag* he had created.

Ultimately he was also unable to dominate the Kaiser. The dependable William I died in 1888 at age 91. His successor, the reputedly liberal Frederick III, died of throat cancer shortly after ascending the throne, and had no time to remove Bismarck. Instead, William I's brilliant and unstable grandson became Kaiser William II. His education, received from a dour Calvinist pastor and the Prussian Guards officers' mess, was poorly calculated to induce moderation. His mother, Queen Victoria's daughter, voiced forebodings: "My son will be the ruin of Germany."

William II did not merely lead the new German industrial military monarchy forward, as he put it, "toward glorious times." He personified its blend of manic self-confidence and inward self-doubt, of fear and aggression. He soon fell out with Bismarck. The old man, to render himself indispensable, even wrecked the *Reichstag* coalition of 1887; he also proposed to suppress the SPD with Maxim guns. In March 1890, after an exchange of insults, the Kaiser sent Bismarck into vengeful retirement.

Henceforth William II planned to rule personally. But he failed to fill Bismarck's heroic role, and he and his subjects increasingly lacked Bismarck's sense of limits. The Kaiser's frequent "oratorical derailments" created chaos in both foreign and domestic affairs. By 1897 he did acquire a team capable of translating his enthusiasms into coherent policy: the 78-year-old Prince Chlodwig von Hohenlohe-Schillingsfürst as figurehead chancellor, the slippery Bernhard von Bülow as foreign secretary, and the supremely devious Admiral Alfred von Tirpitz as chief of the navy that was to make the new Germany a world power (see pp. 829–30). But William's short attention span and inability to resist the influences of

William II, king of Prussia and emperor of Germany, 1888–1918, in a favorite uniform—that of the Death's Head Hussars.

the fire-eating young Guards officers of his entourage guaranteed further crises.

In 1908, after a series of scandals at court had sapped the monarchy's reputation, William gave an interview to the British *Daily Telegraph* in which he unwittingly offended British and German public opinion simultaneously. The ensuing outcry included criticism of the All-Highest in the *Reichstag*, and gave him a nervous breakdown. Henceforth his interventions were less frequent, although his fear of being thought weak played a fateful role in 1914.

The force that increasingly took the monarchy's place and filled the political vacuum that the failure of the National Liberals had left was German nationalism. The Liberals had themselves promoted the growing Bismarck cult to combat regional particularism. On the far right a variety of groups emerged with more extreme visions. The Farmers' League, a rabble-rousing spin-off of the Conservatives, began in the 1890s to mobilize the rural masses with anti-Semitism. Jews, money, machinery, cities, the SPD, modernity—all were allegedly ruining the world of authentic German values and destroying the *Volk* community.

This sort of racist "cultural pessimism" was not unique to Germany. French racist fanatics such as Count Arthur de Gobineau (*On the Inequality of Human Races*, 1859) and Drumont had thought up or propagated many of the notions that became current in Germany in the 1880s and 1890s. But France was industrializing less rapidly than Germany and was thus under less intense social strain. Above all, its political tradition since 1789 had stressed equality and rights. In Germany, once religious anti-Semitism met Darwin's ambiguous legacy in the 1880s, restraints collapsed. The Conservatives made anti-Semitism socially respectable, part of the ideological armory of the new nationalism.

Other groups, such as the Navy League to which Tirpitz played sorcer-

er's apprentice and the Pan-German League founded in 1890, increasingly put forward megalomaniacal foreign policy programs with domestic implications. Their more extreme members created a grass-roots right-wing politics of a new kind, independent of the parties and the government. This loose movement was increasingly divorced from the monarchy and from the nobility, whom the new nationalists saw as castebound and inadequate. Erich Ludendorff, non-noble general staff officer, anti-Semite, and personification of the new outlook, put it well after 1914. Asked for his views on the monarchy, Ludendorff replied "I prefer to call it Fatherland." All that such people lacked was a vehicle and an occasion for mobilizing the masses. The coming great war gave them that and much else.

Russia: Despotism and Revolution

"Russian government is an absolute monarchy tempered by assassination," wrote a French observer in the 1830s. Despite Catherine the Great's concessions to the nobility, the tsar, thanks to the Tartar autocratic tradition of the Muscovite state, remained a ruler more absolute than any eighteenth-century Western enlightened absolutist. Preserving autocracy as the nineteenth century drew on required ever-sterner measures.

Nicholas I succeeded the neurotic Alexander I in December 1825. Confusion over the succession prompted dissident noble officers under the influence of half-understood French liberalism to attempt a palace coup. After its failure, Nicholas had personally interrogated the surviving "Decembrist" leaders and had vowed to prevent a recurrence. His remedy was an ever more extensive and powerful secret police and laws against what the next century came to call "thought-crime." The tsarist criminal code of 1845 was unique in Europe. It devoted 54 pages to "crimes against the state" and decreed savage penalties for merely raising "doubts" about the authority of the tsar.

The autocracy nevertheless faced a fundamental contradiction. The preservation of its power rested on external success. Yet the bayonets of conscripted serfs were no longer enough; defeat in the Crimea in 1854–56 had proved that. The continuance of success, and thus autocracy, in the machine age required a society capable of economic growth. But growth in turn created demands for political participation that threatened autocracy.

The successor of Nicholas, Tsar Alexander II (r. 1855–81) chose development, but with what he hoped were safeguards. In 1861, following the example of Peter the Great, he imposed on Russia a revolution from above: the emancipation of the serfs. The end of bondage would permit universal military service, raise agricultural productivity, free labor for industrialization, and galvanize society into a prosperity that would restore Russia's threatened power position. Alexander's great Emancipation Edict of 1861 freed from the rule of their landlords the 22.5 million serfs that made up almost 38 percent of the Russian empire's population. What it did not do was free them from the land. To aid tax collection and to retain control of the peasantry, the autocracy kept the peasants bound to their village community, the *mir*. The landowners retained two thirds of the land and the former serfs received only a third, for which they had to pay through installments that extended over the following 49 years.

Land redemption debt, the stifling effects of the *mir* on enterprise among its members, and massive population growth ensured that emancipation merely turned a serf problem into a peasant problem. The rural population leapt upward from 50 million in the early 1860s to 82 million in 1897. Competition from newly created industries in the cities lessened peasant income from traditional village handicrafts. Peasants who stayed on rather than migrating to mines and cities waited expectantly for a final redivision of the land that would wipe the landlords out.

More immediately damaging to the autocracy than this growing potential for rural revolt was a loss of control over educated society. Russia had few cities and no middle class of any size in 1800. It developed them hesitantly, with the support of the autocratic state's efforts at industrialization. What it above all developed was an intelligentsia, a minority defined first by its education and then by its opposition to the autocracy. That minority produced some of the nineteenth century's greatest literature in any language, from the poetry of Pushkin to the novels of Turgenev, Tolstoy, and Dostoyevsky. But thanks to the autocracy that prevented it from acquiring political experience, it also developed, like the thinkers of Enlightenment France, a variety of dangerous utopias.

The generation that followed the Decembrists took their inspiration from Hegel rather than liberalism. They asked how Russia might contribute to the self-realization of the world spirit. In the 1840s and 1850s their dominant school, the "Slavophiles," argued that Russia's very differences from the West were Russia's strength. The Westernizing experiment of Peter the Great, they insisted, had been a disastrous mistake that had fortunately failed. Thanks to Orthodox Church and *mir*, Russia had not succumbed to rationalism, individualism, alienation. Russia's mission, they proclaimed, was therefore to give humanity back its soul. A variety of critics, often called "Westerners," pointed out that the *mir* was above all an invention of the autocracy's tax collectors, and suggested that talk of Russia's soul was utopian glorification of backwardness. But Slavophilism persisted, and furnished much of the substance of Muscovite "Great Russian" nationalism.

The generation that followed emancipation argued more about politics than about Russia's soul. By the 1860s non-nobles had reached the universi-

Alexander II, "tsar Liberator" of the serfs.

ties in numbers. The learned professions were beginning to proliferate, providing political radicalism with a social base. A Left emerged that derided the reforms of the 1860s as insufficient and dedicated itself to the autocracy's overthrow. In 1874 several thousand students went "to the people" to create a peasant revolutionary movement. Peasants reacted to these "populists" with suspicion and revealed a deep interest in private property that shocked students brought up on Slavophile visions of peasant communism.

Defeat in the countryside and mass arrests impelled some radicals toward terrorism. A tiny conspiratorial group, with the presumption characteristic of those who believe they possess the absolute truth, named itself "The People's Will" (*Narodnaya Volya*). It hunted the tsar himself and killed him in March 1881. The new tsar, Alexander III (r. 1881–94), crushed *Narodnaya Volya* and created the dreaded *Okhrana*, a secret police even more powerful than its predecessors. Repression froze what little political life Russia possessed. An anti-Semitic radical Right grew, with government support, to oppose the revolutionary intelligentsia. Slavophilism mutated into Russian nationalism and Pan-Slavism, the claim that the Russian state was the patron of Slavs everywhere. Right-wing opinion, as in Imperial Germany, began to place limits on the autocracy's flexibility in foreign affairs.

At home, after the defeat of *Narodnaya Volya*, the radicals turned increasingly to the "scientific" certainties of Marxism. But Marxism was a theory of revolution for advanced countries. That posed a dilemma in Russia, which still awaited both a "bourgeoisie" and a "bourgeois revolution." Vladimir Ilyitch Ulyanov, brother of a hanged member of *Narodnaya Volya* and son of an imperial bureaucrat, found the answer. Under the alias of V. I. Lenin, he embraced the voluntarism that was one part of Marx's legacy. It was the task of Russian Social Democracy, Lenin announced, to force the pace of history. It must take command of Russia's small but growing industrial working class and itself overthrow the autocracy.

The professional revolutionary: Vladimir Ilyitch Lenin (center) with associates (1895).

For that task, Lenin created a new kind of organization, the embryo of the twentieth-century one-party state. The history of Europe after 1848, Lenin saw, demonstrated that Marx had been wrong. The proletariat under capitalism was not spontaneously revolutionary. "The working class, exclusively by its own effort, is able to develop only trade-union consciousness," he wrote with contempt. Logically enough, Lenin recognized that the vehicle of socialist revolution was not the working class, but the "bourgeois intelligentsia: contemporary socialism was born in the heads of individual members of that class." Only the mobilization of that "class" could bring revolution. In 1902 he spelled out what was needed in a famous tract, *What Is to Be Done?* An organized minority of "professional revolutionaries" must serve as vanguard to the childlike masses. "Give us an organization of revolutionaries," wrote Lenin, "and we will overturn Russia!" That organization arose from Lenin's splitting of the Russian Social Democratic party at its conference in London in 1903. His faction henceforth claimed for themselves the title of "men of the majority," or *Bolsheviki,* and imposed on their irresolute opponents the demeaning title of *Mensheviki,* or "men of the minority." Lenin's narrow sect ("better fewer, but better") slowly grew.

Imperial Russia's first revolution owed nothing to the Bolsheviks. The autocracy sought reinforcement by courting "a victorious little war" against Japan in 1904 (see pp. 829–31). Defeat instead led to urban and rural revolt. Russia after 1890 had begun to industrialize at a startling rate under the impulse of French loans and of bureaucrats such as Sergei Witte, creator of the Trans-Siberian Railway. The opening up of the coal and iron of the Donetz basin and the oil of the Caucasus made Russia an industrial world power. In the cities of northern Russia, textile and mechanical industries grew feverishly. And an industrial work force torn from its villages and as yet

Lenin Invents the Dictatorship of the Vanguard Party — 1902

I assert:

(1) that no revolutionary movement can endure without a stable organization of leaders maintaining continuity;

(2) that the broader the popular mass drawn spontaneously into the struggle, which forms the basis of the movement and participates in it, the more urgent the need for such an organization, and the more solid this organization must be (for it is much easier for all sorts of demagogues to side-track the more backward sections of the masses);

(3) that such an organization must consist chiefly of people professionally engaged in revolutionary activity;

(4) that in an autocratic state, the more we *confine* the membership of such an organization to people who are professionally trained in the art of combating the political police, the more difficult it will be to unearth the organization.

From Vladimir Ilyitch Lenin, *What Is to Be Done? Burning Questions of Our Movement* (New York: International Publishers, 1969), p. 121.

largely unprotected by factory legislation proved far more radical than Lenin had suspected.

The shooting in front of the Winter Palace of an unarmed crowd petitioning the tsar on January 22, 1905, "Bloody Sunday," touched off a widespread anarchic revolt in the cities. But that spontaneous popular insurrection failed to find leaders. The Mensheviks lacked the will; they expected that in the fullness of time a "bourgeois revolution" would pave the way for their own socialist one. The Socialist Revolutionaries, heirs to the Populists, expected peasant uprisings and were unprepared to lead the workers. The Bolsheviks were too few, and naturally distrusted this spontaneous expression of the popular will. The last tsar, the fatuous Nicholas II (r. 1894–1917), was thus able to end the Revolution of 1905. He conceded his subjects a legislature or *Duma,* while loyal troops, bureau-

Bloody Sunday, January 22, 1905. Tsarist troops fire on a procession of workers, killing 70 and wounding 240.

crats, and police gradually suppressed the revolutionary workers' councils or Soviets that had given the revolution what little organization it possessed. The far Right, organized with official approval in the "League of the Russian People" or Black Hundreds, massacred Jews and opponents of the autocracy.

Constitutional experimentation soon ended. Two successive *Dumas* defied the government with demands for civil rights and reforms. Nicholas refused to surrender his autocratic power. Restriction of the franchise produced a Third *Duma* (1907–12) of "masters, priests, and lackeys" that proved more pliable. Under its last strong minister, Peter Stolypin, the autocracy attempted belatedly to finish the emancipation of the peasants from the *mir*, while suppressing all opposition. Stolypin died by assassination in 1911. More despotism bred further extremism and pushed Russia's few Liberals to believe naively that the far Left was preferable to the autocracy. As a new war approached in 1914, waves of massive strikes convulsed urban Russia.

Tsarism desperately needed victory, but victory might not suffice to save it.

Austria-Hungary: Dynastic Empire in an Age of National States

For Austria, 1866 was not merely a military defeat, but a portent. The breakthrough of the national state in central Europe threatened the break-up of the empire itself. Austria survived because Bismarck needed it. "If you ask me what we have promised Austria in return for her friendship, I should answer 'life,'" remarked Prussia's ambassador in Vienna to his Russian colleague in the fall of 1870. Austrian collapse would saddle Protestant Prussia with the Catholic Austrian Germans and with Austria's Balkan quarrels with Russia.

But German goodwill alone could not ensure Austria's long-term survival. That required an ideology, an "Austrian Idea," to counter the nationalism of the subject peoples. Preserving the economic integration of the Danube basin, the ties of agrarian Hungary to industrial Vienna and Bohemia, was not sufficiently inspiring. Good government from the most efficient bureaucracy of east central Europe was likewise no answer to the increasing clamor of the nationalities for rule—or misrule—by their own. And Austria's substitute for colonial expansion, its "civilizing mission" in the Balkans, encouraged the same sort of nationalist reaction that bedeviled the European powers in Asia and Africa.

Emperor Francis Joseph (r. 1848–1916) and his ministers faced a central paradox. Preserving Habsburg freedom of action, as always, required playing off the empire's provinces and nationalities against one another. But in the age of nationalism, that strategy could only encourage the nationalities to greater and greater mutual intolerance, and tear the monarchy apart. And if, by some miracle, the monarchy should successfully promote compromise between the nationalities, they would then be free to combine against the monarchy itself.

The dynasty therefore played for time. In 1866–67 Francis Joseph grudgingly struck a bargain with Hungary to prepare the way for a war of revenge against Prussia. That "*Ausgleich*" or compromise of 1867 gave the Hungarians what their moderates had sought in 1848: full control of affairs within the far-flung borders of a "greater Hungary" that included millions of Rumanians, Serbs, and Croats. The only institutions of importance that Hungary thereafter shared with the rest of the monarchy were the emperor and the ministries of foreign affairs and war. And Hungary received, in effect, a veto over Habsburg foreign and military policy.

When Austrian revenge on Prussia seemed possible in alliance with France in 1870, the Hungarians exercised that veto. Prussia had made the *Ausgleich* possible; a Habsburg reversal of the verdict of 1866 would automatically place Hungary's hard-won autonomy in question. The revolutionary alliance with Hungary against Vienna that Bismarck had toyed with in 1866 thereby became a tacit German-Magyar agreement to preserve the new status quo. Thus the provisional became permanent. The *Ausgleich* made Austria the "Dual Monarchy" of Austria-Hungary until 1918. In Hungary, the gentry ruthlessly Magyarized the subject nationalities and dominated the voteless and voiceless Hungarian peasantry. In the remainder of the empire, the German "ruling *Volk*" fought a losing battle against the rise of the Czechs.

After a series of unsatisfactory German liberal ministries, Francis Joseph turned in 1879 to an aristocrat of Irish extraction, Count Eduard Taafe. Taafe's formula was simple and for a time effective. In the *Reichsrat,* the legislature of the non-Hungarian parts of the empire, he created a government bloc of loyal Poles, clericals, and Czechs, the so-called "iron ring." With that support, and with the aim of keeping "all the nationalities of the empire in a balanced state of mild dissatisfaction," he kept the peace until his fall in 1893.

The German-Czech conflict over rich and rapidly industrializing Bohemia burst Taafe's framework. Since 1848 the Czechs had developed a high culture, complete with composers such as Bedřich Smetana and Antonín Dvořák, that put to shame German claims of cultural superiority. The Czechs had nationalized their masses with schooling in Czech and with a university at Prague. They were developing an industrial middle class. And their most advanced politicians, the "young Czechs" (shades of Mazzini) refused to subscribe to Taafe's proposed arrangement for sharing power with the Germans in Bohemia.

The Germans were equally obdurate. In Vienna, that cosmopolitan city of art and vice, a variety of anti-Slav and anti-Semitic demagogues arose. The fanatical Georg von Schönerer preached that "religion is irrelevant, *race* is the source of the swinishness" that he ascribed to the Jews. The mayor of Vienna, Karl Lueger, organized a "Christian Social" party that mixed populist clericalism with an anti-Semitism more decorous than that of Schönerer; its descendants still give Austrian politics their peculiar tone. Even Austrian social democracy divided into German and Czech national socialisms. Language and culture proved, there and elsewhere, more powerful than class.

In 1897 the dynasty tilted decisively toward the Czechs. It pushed through a decree requiring that state officials in Bohemia be bilingual in Czech and German. Since no German would deign to learn Czech, that excluded the Germans from state employment and from power. The Germans rioted. Schönerer thundered at the dynasty's betrayal of Germandom. He and other lesser fanatics looked to Prussia-Germany against a Habsburg state which they accused of submerging the Austrian Germans in Slavs and Jews.

In the short term the Germans won. The monarchy dismissed Count Casimir Badeni, responsible for the language decree, and rescinded the decree itself in 1899. Naturally the Czechs rioted in response. Slovenes and Italians fought in Trieste. Some Croats began to feel the pull of the notion of a "South Slav" (Yugoslav) state of Croats, Slovenes, and Serbs. The "South Slav" idea had little basis in history, culture, or religion, for Slovenes and Croats were Catholic and Western in orientation, Serbs Orthodox and Balkan. But it gradually spread; fear that independent Serbia might prove the "Piedmont of the South Slavs" provoked hysteria in Vienna.

In 1906–07 the dynasty at last fell back on universal suffrage, hoping to submerge the competing nationalisms in a flood of loyal clerical peasant votes. But universal schooling had made the peasants into Germans, Czechs, Croats, and Slovenes. After 1909 Francis Joseph and his ministers therefore ignored the *Reichsrat* and ruled by decree. Reformers floated a variety of federal or "trialist" plans to give Slavs equality with Germans and Magyars. But Germans and Magyars preferred to wreck the monarchy rather than suffer diminution of their "historic rights." In the face of ever-intensifying internal conflict, Austria-Hungary's "idea" remained Church, dynasty, bureaucracy, and army. By 1914 those institutions were strong but wasting assets.

Italy: Least of the Great Powers

The weight of Italy's historic greatness almost crushed the new Italian national state. Ideologues from the radical Mazzini rightwards insisted that the new Italy must be and act as a great power. The legacy of the Roman empire and of Italy's economic and cultural primacy in the Renaissance demanded no less.

Italian reality was ill-equipped to live up to such expectations. The South, where landlords' horses lived better than peasants, was two centuries or more behind the North. At unification in 1861, illiteracy ranged from 54 percent of the population over six years of age in the North to 89 percent in the South and the islands. Even the relatively prosperous North lacked an industrial base, for Italy had little iron and almost no coal.

The new state also had a narrow political base. In part this was deliberate. Cavour and his heirs feared the masses with their potential for anarchic radicalism or Bourbon-clerical revolt. Until 1882 the electoral law gave 2 percent or less of the population the vote; after that date 7 to 9.4 percent could vote. In part, narrowness was unavoidable. The illiterate, until they encountered conscription, had little idea that they even belonged to a national state. And after 1870, furious at his loss of Rome, Pope Pius IX had locked himself in the Vatican and ordered a Catholic boycott of Italian politics. That was no small loss for a state with a population that was nominally 99 percent Catholic.

Finally, the later stages of unification were demoralizing. War in 1866 brought Venetia into the state, but only because Prussia won at Königgrätz; Italy itself suffered humiliating defeats by land and sea. The taking of Rome from the Pope in 1870 was inglorious. The petty spectacle of parliamentary politics provoked the scorn of the aged Mazzini and of nationalists such as the poet Giosuè Carducci: "Oh for the days of sun, of liberty and glory in 1860. . . . Oh for the struggles of titans between Cavour and Garibaldi in 1861!" "What have we become?" asked Carducci despairingly.

What Italy had become was a moderately successful parliamentary regime under a series of centrist coalitions resembling those of France's Third Republic. Defeat in 1866 at least banished the specter of a revival of royal absolutism. Victor Emmanuel II and his army henceforth lacked the prestige for Bismarckian solutions. Under Cavour's heirs, the moderate liberal *Destra* or Right, Italy paid the immense debts of the wars of unification and balanced the budget. The money came mostly from the hard-pressed peasantry, but at least Italy did not follow Egypt and Turkey into debt bondage. The *Destra* reformed the army, although that institution still lacked the prestige needed to attract first-rate officer material. Finally, the *Destra* gave Italy some small voice in the councils of the great powers.

In 1876 a motley coalition of northern left-liberals and southern landowners, henceforth known as the *Sinistra* or Left, ousted the *Destra*. The *Sinistra* extended the franchise and made elementary education free and compulsory in law if not yet in fact. It also created a parliamentary tradition that outlasted the century, for the southern landlords, in return for patronage jobs and public works, gave the government of the day their votes. That bargain, rather like the tacit agreement that ended Reconstruction in the United States, helped stabilize parliament at the price of social and political stagnation in the South.

By the 1890s a variety of forces pressed against the system. The steamship brought in cheap grain and ruined southern agriculture, then bore away the resulting emigrants. Peasant unrest in Sicily unnerved the governments of the early 1890s. A socialist movement, Bakuninite in the 1870s and Marxist by the 1890s, gained ground. And unlike their counterparts elsewhere, the Italian socialists successfully organized parts of the countryside. By the first decade of the new century the unions of landless agricultural laborers of the rich Po Valley in north Italy were strong enough to stage bitter province-wide strikes.

Even Catholicism began to stir politically. Leo XIII (r. 1878–1903) weakened his predecessor's prohibitions of Catholic political participation in Italy, just as he had urged Catholics to "rally" to the Third Republic in France. Then his successor Pius X (r. 1903–14) revived some of Pius IX's denunciations of modernity. The entry of organized Catholicism into Italian politics

was thus slow. But by the 1913 election it was an accomplished fact.

The *Sinistra* had its last incarnation under the charismatic Sicilian and ex-Mazzinian, Francesco Crispi (prime minister, 1887–91, 1893–96). It fell resoundingly after catastrophe at Adowa ended Crispi's bid for a vast East African empire. Riots against the African war and hard times at home inaugurated a period of bayonets in the streets and right-wing governments. The king, Victor Emmanuel's son Umberto I, imposed a general as prime minister before his own assassination by an anarchist in 1900. Parliament fought back, and won decisively.

With the new century came economic takeoff and political stability under the greatest of Cavour's successors, Giovanni Giolitti (prime minister 1903–05, 1906–09, 1911–14). Giolitti despised rhetoric; that won him respect but no fanatical followers. He knew well that Italy's uneven economic and social development had produced bizarre political effects—including his own need to pay southern deputies for their support. If you cut a suit for a hunchback, he once remarked, you get a hunchbacked suit.

What he attempted was gradual reforms that would integrate the new mass forces, the Socialists and Catholics, into the Liberal parliamentary system without destroying it. He refused to persecute the Socialists. To the horror of Italy's industrialists, he did his best to keep the state neutral in labor disputes. His greatest monument was the enactment in 1912 of virtual universal male suffrage, which expanded the electorate from 3.3 million to 8.6 million. It was also his downfall.

The Catholics proved difficult and demanding allies. On the Left, extremists that included a certain Benito Mussolini (see pp. 914–919) captured the socialist party leadership and closed off any chance of cooperation with Giolitti. The prime minister's own supporters in parliament resented concessions he had made to the Catholics, and overthrew him in March 1914. "Red Week,"

Francesco Crispi, Mazzinian revolutionary and colonial enthusiast.

Facts, not rhetoric: Giovanni Giolitti (1842–1928), five times prime minister of Italy.

an immense wave of Anarchist and left-Socialist-led riots that swept north Italy in June 1914, soon made Giolitti's sober common sense and conciliation look outdated and naive.

Intellectuals of all stripes had long railed against his lack of charisma. The young literary firebrands of the Italian Nationalist Association lamented that Italy "had been too much made with diplomatic intrigues and foreign arms." They and others forcefully revived a myth widespread since the anticlimax of the *Risorgimento*. "Making Italians," the completion of national integration, required a great war. Giolitti's right-Liberal successor Antonio Salandra was soon to find that war, and with it destroy Liberal Italy.

BATTLES FOR WOMEN'S RIGHTS

The coming of mass politics for men inevitably raised the question of the rights of women. It opened an arena in which large numbers of women could for the first time press their case not merely for the vote but for equality between the sexes. That was a question that went far beyond politics.

Male domination of women has taken many forms. Its foremost mid-

Crusader for hospital reform: Florence Nightingale (1820–1910).

nineteenth-century incarnation was middle-class woman's role as pedestal-mounted "angel in the house." That notion was in part a consequence of the separation of life into work and home, male and female domains, that came with industrialization. But it also had pseudo-scientific underpinnings. Learned doctors discoursed on women's presumed lack of sexual passion and on the alleged "gigantic power and influence of the ovaries" over woman's whole being. For such pundits, women's position was biologically determined: "What was decided among the prehistoric Protozoa, cannot be annulled by Act of Parliament." What passed for science thus dispensed even liberals from giving women the same rights as men. Religion contributed as well to the myth of woman's domestic nature. In the 1820s the churches took to insisting that women, who were proving more resistant than men to the temptations of religious skepticism, were also "purer" than men. Preservation of that purity required their continued confinement to the home.

By the 1860s, especially in Britain, these notions were under attack. Women had penetrated previously male citadels such as hospitals and schools. Florence Nightingale made nursing a profession for women by her crusade against the British army's grotesque mismanagement of medical services in the Crimea. Soon a broad women's movement pressed for higher education and careers for single middle-class women. In the 1870s Girton and Newnham Colleges at Cambridge began giving women degrees. Pioneers opened up medicine and the law. Agitation led to reforms in the 1870s and 1880s of Britain's crude laws governing marriage, divorce, and the age of consent. Women's bodies and property ceased to belong to their husbands in a literal, legal sense.

The British "feminists"—the French word became current in the 1890s—also attacked the legal double standard in a more spectacular way. They crusaded successfully against the Contagious Diseases Acts (repealed 1886) that mandated venereal disease examinations and quarantine for prostitutes— but not soldiers—in garrison towns. The acts, they insisted, were government endorsement of the creation of "a *slave* class of women to minister to lust." The crusaders sought to do more than raise the status of women. They proposed to reform men and revolutionize the relationship between the sexes.

When the Liberals came to power in the 1906 election, the women's movement attempted to hold them to liberal principles. But the evasive Herbert Asquith (prime minister, 1908–16) and the even more slippery Lloyd George torpedoed women's suffrage legislation in 1910. The Women's Social and Political Union (WSPU), under the leadership of Emmeline Pankhurst and her daughter Christabel ("Votes for Women, and Chastity for Men"), thereupon declared war on government, Parliament, and men. "Suffragette" activists attempted to force police cordons in Parliament Square; the police and male bystanders replied with violence and sexual abuse. Christabel Pankhurst orchestrated a campaign of window-smashing, burning of country houses, attacks on art galleries, and bombs in Westminster Abbey. To trial and imprisonment, the WSPU replied with hunger strikes. The government countered with forced feeding. Opinion, including opinion among women, was overwhelmingly against WSPU defiance of the law. But WSPU tactics provoked the government to acts that weakened its position.

Finally, in June 1914, Asquith consented to receive a delegation of working women under the leadership of Sylvia Pankhurst, Christabel's sister and a labor activist. The specter of a potential mobilization of working-class women into a genuine mass movement apparently made Asquith quail. He lost all stomach for further warfare between the sexes, and undertook to support a women's suffrage bill. The war delayed it until 1918, but eased its passage. The

A policeman carries Mrs. Emmeline Pankhurst bodily off to jail during a 1911 suffrage demonstration.

contribution of women to the war effort made it impossible to deny them the vote.

Continental feminists faced societies far less tolerant than Britain (or than the United States, where suffrage agitation developed intertwined with evangelical religion and the temperance movement). And as with continental liberalism, continental feminism tended to be far less radical than its British counterpart. In France and Germany, middle-class feminists inclined toward the "equal but different" school. Woman's role as mother and her right to control reproduction was the focus of the work of widely influential figures such as Ellen Key (1849–1926) of Sweden or Nelly Roussel (1878–1922) of France. The most radical continental women tended to gravitate to the women's affiliates of the socialist parties, which took more interest in woman's presumed oppression by capitalism than her domination by man. Nevertheless, the socialist parties of the Second International were the first continental political parties to endorse women's suffrage. By the end of the great war that began in 1914 much of western Europe was ready to follow them.

RISE AND FALL OF THE CULT OF SCIENCE

The waning of traditional forms of religious belief helped open space for a variety of other faiths. Nationalism and socialism provided their adherents with many of the consolations that earlier generations had gained from religion. After mid-century a misunderstood science provided a third secular religion: the "cult of science."

The furious attacks of religious figures on Darwin and Lyell were misplaced; the rise of science did not challenge religion in any direct, logical sense. God is not subject to empirical proof or disproof. But the new science did provide a semblance of empirical underpinning for statements of faith—in science. The source of the cult was the Enlightenment vision of a machine-like universe in which everything was in principle knowable. The cult's nineteenth-century founder, Auguste Comte (1798–1857), attempted from the 1820s to the 1850s to systematize all of human knowledge. He postulated—like Hegel and Marx—a series of stages. For Comte, humanity's road led from theology to metaphysics and from metaphysics to science, which was the domain of what Comte called "positive" or empirically verifiable knowledge. The "Positivism" of Comte and successors enshrined science as the new diety. Comte was confident that even the messy affairs of humanity would eventually yield scientific general laws in the form of a discipline of "sociology."

That discipline has still to yield general laws. That did not stop Comte's most conspicuous successor, the indefatigable Herbert Spencer (1820–1903) from following in his footsteps. Spencer's *Synthetic Philosophy* (1862–96) attempted in ten volumes what Comte had attempted in six, the compression of all of human knowledge into a positivist framework. And Darwin was the centerpiece of Spencer's work, but a Darwin misapplied to social phenomena. Darwin himself was in part responsible for this misunderstanding. In *The Descent of Man* he incautiously speculated that "the wonderful progress of the United States, as well of that character of its people, are the results of natural selection; the more energetic, courageous, and restless men from all parts of Europe having emigrated during the last ten or twelve generations to that great country. . . . "

Alongside Spencer a wide variety of "social Darwinists" proliferated. Most argued (in the words of Walter Bagehot, high priest of the English constitution) that "the majority of the groups which win and conquer are better than that majority which fail and perish." That was a wonderfully convenient rationalization for "might makes right" among nations, social groups, and individuals. The oil king John D. Rockefeller trumpeted that business was "merely the survival of the fittest . . . the working out of a law of nature and a law of God."

In Germany the task of propagating and popularizing Darwinian biology fell to Ernst Haeckel (1834–1919). He followed in the footsteps of Feuerbach (whose materialism had influenced Marx) and of the best-selling crank Ludwig Büchner (1824–99). Büchner's *Force and Matter* (1852) confidently asserted that since matter and energy were eternal, it was "impossible that the world can have been created. How could anything have been created that cannot be annihilated?"

Haeckel, simultaneously Darwinist and social Darwinist, defied 25 centuries of Western thought by abolishing any distinction between humanity and nature; he called the cult he founded and led "Monism." In his international best-seller of 1899, *The Riddle of the Universe*, he mocked theological and metaphysical speculation. Questions not susceptible to empirical answers were not questions. And "Monism" meant that upon pain of degeneration humanity must live in harmony with "the laws of nature." Chief of those laws was natural selection. When Haeckel's notion of nature as legislator for man

The Thinker: Friedrich Nietzsche, the last great German philosopher.

met the ideas of racist cranks such as Gobineau, the results were intellectual high explosive. Marx had abolished all theoretical restraints on revolutionary dictatorship and on the elimination of the "class enemy." Haeckel, Gobineau, and Kaiser William II's friend, the racist-social Darwinist Houston Stuart Chamberlain (*The Foundations of the Nineteenth Century*, 1899) similarly abolished intellectual and moral restrictions on the liquidation of the "racial enemy."

The Revolt against Positivism

The domination of the positivist cult of science was shortlived, although its influence persists to our own day. In the realm of philosophy, a commanding figure soon emerged who denounced almost every aspect of the present, science and its idolaters included. Friedrich Nietzsche (1844–1900), son of a Protestant pastor, was the last great German philosopher of the nineteenth century. He was the antithesis of his system-building predecessors, whose work he ridiculed. From 1872 until his final collapse into syphilitic dementia in 1889 he bombarded a growing public with at least one work each year. One of the greatest masters of the German language, he leapt from one striking aphorism to the next. He frequently contradicted himself, and always contradicted others. He damned the smugness of the age.

Nietzsche's message was at bottom consistent. Contradiction was life. Philosophy was not systemic, but perpetual question and experiment. Morality—for Nietzsche in his eccentric way was the last great moralist—took precedence over knowledge. Scientific truth was valuable only insofar as it contributed to "life." And to Nietzsche the law of the modern world was not the survival of the fittest but that of ever-growing mediocrity. Darwin had it backwards. In reality "happy accidents are eliminated, the more highly evolved types lead nowhere, it is the average and below average types

---

Nietzsche Speaks

Truths are illusions that one has forgotten *are* illusions.

Nothing is true, everything is permitted.

Why morality, when life, nature, and history are "unmoral"?

The common man alone has the prospect of carrying on, of propagating himself—he is the man of the future, the only survivor; "Be like him! Become mediocre!" is now the only morality that still has a meaning or an audience. But it is hard to preach, this morality of mediocrity.

Objection, evasion, gleeful mistrust and irony are signs of health. Everything absolute belongs to pathology.

In individuals, insanity is rare, but in groups, parties, nations and epochs, it is the rule.

The thought of suicide is a powerful consolation; with it one can get through many a bad night.

Man must be trained for war and woman for the recreation of the warrior: anything else is silliness.

I have only rarely the courage of what I know.

Dear Professor, in the end I would have much preferred being a Basel professor to being God. But I did not dare carry my private egotism so far as to omit—for its sake—the creation of the world. . . . [Nietzsche's last letter, to the Basel historian Jacob Burckhardt, January 1889]

From *Friedrich Nietzsche, Werke in Drei Bänden*, ed. by Karl Schlechta (Munich: Karl Hanser Verlag, 1954–56), 3:314, 2:889, 2:645, 2:737, 2:637, 2:328, 3:1272, 3:1351 (translation by M. Knox).

---

which ineluctably ascend to power." Women's emancipation was "one of the worst developments of the general *uglification* of Europe." Nationalism was unbearably crass: the new Reich of 1871, bristling "hedgehog-fashion" with arms was "the most stupid, the most depraved, the most mendacious form of 'the German spirit' that ever was." Nietzsche likewise denounced anti-Semitism and the Germanic tribal cult of the composer Richard Wagner, whom he had originally admired.

Christianity, for Nietzsche, was worst of all. It stifled "life" and dragged down the exceptional individual with its "slave morality" of meekness and compassion. Nietzsche consoled himself by contemplating what he described as "the greatest event of recent times—that 'God is dead,' that the belief in the Christian God is no longer tenable." Nietzsche's morality was that of the isolated exception, the aristocratic *Übermensch* or "superman" living "beyond good and evil" and outside society and politics. "Life," the "will to power," was supreme over all else.

That proved a dangerous legacy. In the short term Nietzsche appealed to socialists, anarchists, and outsiders. His denunciations of German nationalism infuriated the pan-Germans. But Nietzsche's popularization, which ironically accelerated immediately after his descent into madness, ultimately made "the will to power" and the "superman" into myths of the new populist Right. "Everything is permitted" became a credo for political "supermen" riding the coming wave of war and revolution.

Other late nineteenth- and early twentieth-century philosophers, especially the Frenchman Henri Bergson (1859–1941), shared Nietzsche's abhorrence of rationalist system-building. But it was the world of medicine and scholarship that offered the most decisive rejection of positivism. In the mid-1890s a Vienna medical figure, Sigmund Freud (1856–1939) began publishing a series of works that offered the first serious attempt to understand the human mind. To the horror of a prudish age, Freud argued that sex was the root of human motivation. He pioneered the exploration of unconscious layers and processes in the mind, thus exploding the assumption of positivists and rationalists that "mind" meant the conscious mind. He tapped the unconscious with novel techniques: hypnosis, dream interpretation, and free association. What Marx did for economics as a historical force, Freud did for the unconscious.

Sigmund Freud, explorer of the unconscious mind.

Unfortunately for the further development of his new discipline of psychoanalysis, it soon emerged that Freud's elaborate theoretical structure was metaphor rather than a verifiable scientific theory. Freud warred with prominent disciples such as Carl Gustav Jung (1875–1961) and Alfred Adler (1870–1937) over key points of interpretation. Even more than Marxism, Freudianism and the larger psychoanalytic movement that it created has relished the hunt for error and deviation. That has placed in question its claim to be science; for good or ill science is about empirical proof. And Freud's attitude towards women, whom his odd theory of "penis-envy" consigned anew to biological inferiority, has not gone unchallenged. But Freud was in some ways a good prophet of the coming century, thanks to his experience of Austria-Hungary's vicious ethnic quarrels and to his membership in Vienna's most conspicuously persecuted minority, the Jews. Humanity, Freud asserted, was irremediably predatory.

A final challenge to positivism emerged in the social sciences. The man who actually founded the "sociology" that Comte had named was Max Weber (1864–1920), Prussian reserve lieutenant and professor. Weber, the "bourgeois Marx," was a realist: "All ideas aimed at abolishing the dominance of men over men are 'Utopian.'" He began by asking a question that Marx had neglected: how did "capitalism" originate? Weber hit upon religion as the key variable that distinguished societies that had industrialized from those that lagged. And within Western society he found a close historical association between the "Protestant ethic," especially that of Calvinism, and the joyless drive to accumulate ever-greater masses of capital. This "Weber thesis" has proved a fruitful source of argument from his day to the present, although critics have pointed out that the earliest European capitalism—in the Italian city-states—was Catholic.

Weber's other major contribution was his attempt, in a massive and often obscure unfinished work entitled *Econ-*

omy and Society, to make sense of the relationships between economics and social and political forms. But unlike many later sociologists, Weber rejected the Comtean notion that the social sciences, like the natural sciences, must formulate general laws. In the human sciences, Weber pointed out, verification through controlled experiment was unfeasible. The researcher's own value system inevitably intruded on the results. Truth was only possible within narrow limits. Weber's work on method demolished the positivist approach to society and history. Humanity would have to make do with lawlike hypotheses such as the "Protestant ethic."

Finally, Weber was in his way a prophet, although a self-limiting and modest one. Like Marx but without Marx's dogmatism, he saw goal-oriented movement in history: the "disenchantment of the world," the decay of traditional religious and social certainties in the face of ever-increasing rationalization and bureaucratization. Weber feared that in the new century that process would end with humanity bound in a static "iron cage of serfdom" under immense self-perpetuating state and capitalist institutions. His prophecy ignored both the growing freedoms of the West's democratic societies—of which Weber the Prussian lieutenant had little understanding—and the dynamism of technological change. But Weber's "iron cage" metaphor proved far less off-center than the prophecies of Marx.

ART IN AN AGE OF SCIENCE

In the realm of culture, the last half of the nineteenth century was a period of crisis. Romanticism had broken all restraints on form or content. Everything was permitted. A bewildering proliferation of styles and radical disagreement about the purposes of "art" was the ultimate result. That proliferation destroyed the dominant idea of Western art since Plato and Aristotle, the notion that art should imitate reality or nature.

Architecture and design were the principal exceptions to this growing stylistic confusion. The fragmentation of architecture had begun well before that of literature and the visual arts. In the late eighteenth century, a profusion of "revivals" had succeeded the dying Baroque. As the nineteenth century drew on, Greek temples mutated into churches, museums, and banks; Gothic cathedrals provided models for hideous town halls in grimy industrial cities; Romanesque arches adorned the massive temples of science at the universities. Furniture became ever heavier, ever more overstuffed and hideously carved. But by the end of the century a reaction had set in.

In design, the opening of Japan in 1854 was as important to the nineteenth century as the influence of Chinese art had been to the eighteenth. The geometric shapes and absence of ornament of Japanese interiors were a revelation to European designers and architects. Simultaneously, the machine stimulated new thought. Some, such as England's William Morris (1834–96), revolted against mass production. Morris's politics were a romantic socialism, his taste an attempt to relive a lost golden age of craftsmanship now submerged in shoddy machine-made furniture. His "Arts and Crafts Movement" created a spare geometric style that was the beginning of modern home furnishing. German designers in the *Werkbund* or Craft League that flourished from 1907 to 1914 pioneered a style that in some ways resembled Morris's—but they did not share his irrational hostility to the machine.

Architecture developed in a like manner. Steel and glass were its materials. The Crystal Palace of the 1851 Great Exhibition, the immense canopy of St. Pancras station in London (1863–65), and the Eiffel Tower (1889) pioneered their use. But it was America, thanks to sheer technological exuberance and to the high property costs in its new city centers, that invented the steel-framed skyscraper in the 1880s. The Americans Louis Sullivan (1856–1924) and his pupil Frank Lloyd Wright (1869–1959) gave the new architecture its slogan: "form follows function." Sullivan did not disdain ornament, although he aspired to buildings that would be "comely in the nude." After 1890, his buildings took on a geometric grid-like pattern. German architects associated with the *Werkbund*, especially Walter Gropius (1883–1969) and Bruno Taut (1880–1938), had also begun before 1914 to design functional steel and glass buildings. The "international style" of the twentieth century, the first unified style in Western architecture since the Baroque, had arrived.

The fate of literature and the visual arts was entirely different. Old conventions of form and substance collapsed, but fragmentation instead of unity was the consequence. The novel, the nineteenth century's foremost art form, passed from the psychological "realism" of Gustave Flaubert (1821–80) to the pseudo-positivist "naturalism" of Émile Zola (1840–1902). Flaubert, in his great *Madame Bovary* (1856), dissected the consciousness of a small-town doctor's wife whose dreamy reading of romantic novels leads her to adultery and destruction. Both subject and technique scandalized contemporaries. The far less talented but infinitely more prolific Zola churned out a sequence of 20 novels between 1871 and 1893 that traced "the social and natural history of a family" during the Second Empire. Zola kept careful track of his "facts," and propounded laws of human nature. But his sometimes lurid style suggested the opposite of scientific detachment. His Naturalism was above all social criticism; his intervention in the Dreyfus case and brief exile to escape prison was the high point of his career.

The work of the great Russians, Count Leo Tolstoy (1828–1910) and Feodor Mikhailovitch Dostoyevsky (1821–81) showed a similar tension between psychological observation and social and political commitment. Tolstoy eventually repudiated his greatest works, *War and Peace* (1869) and *Anna Karenina* (1871), and turned his back on Russian society in favor of a mystical New Testament asceticism and pacifist "non-resistance to evil." Dostoyevsky migrated from advanced revolutionary beliefs to a mystic Slavophilism. In *The Possessed* (1871–72) he drew on his youthful experiences and his deep psychological insight to suggest the demonic nature of revolutionary messianism—just as much of the Russian *intelligentsia* embraced that messianism.

One conspicuous exception to this pattern of ideological commitment was the great American expatriate, Henry James (1843–1916). His many novels, novellas, and short stories combined Flaubert-like psychological observation with penetrating commentary on the contrast between European and American manners and morals. James's European-style novels earned him an international reputation; his most conspicuous American contemporaries, Herman Melville (1819–91) and Mark Twain (1835–1910), remained curiosities to Europeans. Melville's great symbolic epic of whaling and the struggle between evil and good, *Moby Dick* (1851), derived from the Protestant biblical tradition, not the European novel. Twain achieved the impossible. In *The Adventures of Huckleberry Finn* (1884) he rendered backwoods dialect—or rather a carefully contrived illusion of dialect—into art, in a comic yet often grim tale of life on the Mississippi against the ominous background of the slave South. Twain was deliberately and aggressively provincial; he frequently spoofed European social and linguistic snobbishness.

While Flaubert, James, and the Russians between them seemingly exhausted most of the novel's possibilities, the Norwegian Henrik Ibsen (1828–1906), the Swede Johan August Strindberg (1849–1912), and the Russian Anton Pavlovitch Chekhov (1860–1904) did the same for drama. Ibsen mercilessly attacked social pretension and the oppression of women. He depicted the quest of the modern individual for self-understanding. The truth, he suggested, could destroy as well as free. But humanity was not irredeemable; love was still conceivable. Not so for Strindberg, who created increasingly dreamlike plays in which unlovely characters, "bound together by guilt and crime," inexorably destroyed one another. Chekhov, who depicted symbolically the dissolution of Russian aristocratic society, pioneered a drama that turned its back on conventional notions of plot. He gave artistic form to the anarchy of life. Chekhov's characters speak in seemingly disconnected remarks, dramatic development occurs within the characters themselves, and action is inconclusive.

It was in poetry, music, and painting that the breakthrough to the artistic fragmentation of the twentieth century was most dramatic. In poetry, late Romantic lyricism dissolved into Symbolism. Intended for a few initiates rather than for a mass audience, Symbolism was in part a reaction to the dreary Naturalist notion that art should serve social and political betterment. Symbolism's predecessor was the dissipated "accursed poet," Charles Baudelaire (1821–67), and its banner "art for art's sake." The Symbolists, above all the schoolboy prodigy Arthur Rimbaud (1854–91), Stéphane Mallarmé (1842–98) and Paul Verlaine (1844–96), wrote a poetry of deliberate obscurity and musical effects. Their style influenced the two greatest German poets of the new century, Rainer Maria Rilke (1875–1926) and Stefan George (1868–1933). It furnished the basis for much twentieth-century poetry.

In music, Richard Wagner's "total work of art," his four evening long *Ring of the Nibelungen* opera cycle (1853–74), was the end of romantic music as well as one starting point of the new German *Reich's* political mythology. Gustav Mahler (1860–1911) and others continued Wagner's tradition of orchestral excess and startling effects, but with less conviction. In France, Claude Debussy (1862–1918) and Maurice Ravel (1875–1937) pioneered a new style that deliberately paralleled Symbolist poetry. The irregular rhythms and harsh dissonances of Igor Fëdorovitch Stravinsky's *Rite of Spring* caused a riot at its Paris première in 1913. Arnold Schönberg (1874–1951) and his pupils attempted to create a new "atonal" music that defied traditional notions of melody.

In painting, an entire epoch in Western art ended with the school known as the Impressionists. Claude Monet (1840–1926) and Auguste Renoir (1841–1919) were its originators and greatest masters. They discarded the age-old attempt to render reality on canvas literally. Photography, invented in the 1820s, had by the 1860s rendered "realism" seemingly superfluous. Instead, the Impressionists sought to use the play of light, represented with dabs of color, to show scenes as they appeared to the mind's eye. Their paintings shocked contemporaries accustomed to increasingly sterile imitations of ancient or Renaissance models. But the Impressionists were not revolutionaries; they were the brilliant end of a long tradition.

After them came Paul Cézanne (1839–1906), proclaiming both in words and on canvas that "all of nature is formed by the cylinder, the sphere, and the cone." Vincent Van Gogh (1853–90) reproduced a tortured life in violent colors and swirling shapes. Georges Seurat (1859–91) composed

From realism to impressionism and beyond: *The Shepherdess* by Jules Dupré (1880).

A pioneering landscape, *Montagne Sainte-Victoire* (*ca.* 1885–90) by Paul Cézanne.

The "Yellow Press": A Novelist's View

In *New Grub Street* (1891), the English novelist George Gissing presented through the mouth of his fictional editor, Whelpdale, a view of the mass media's conception of its audience that is still surprisingly up-to-date.

No article in the paper is to measure more than two inches in length, and every inch must be broken into at least two paragraphs. . . . Let me explain my principle. I would have the paper address itself to the quarter-educated; . . . the young men and women who can just read, but are incapable of sustained attention. People of this kind want something to occupy them in trains, and on buses and trams. . . . What they want is the lightest and frothiest of chit-chatty information—bits of stories, bits of description, bits of scandal, bits of jokes, bits of statistics, bits of foolery. Am I not right? Everything must be very short, two inches at the utmost; their attention can't sustain itself beyond two inches.

From George Gissing, *New Grub Street* (London: Eveleigh Nash & Grayson, 1927), p. 419.

chine-driven rotary press permitted the first truly cheap newspapers, the first modern "mass media" based on advertising. Great press barons arose, profiteers of ignorance with a secret contempt for their public. Alfred Harmsworth (later Lord Northcliffe) of the London *Daily Mail* first achieved a daily circulation of over a million, with a paper that combined gossip and crude xenophobia in equal proportions. Publishers churned out vapid "best-sellers" by the hundreds of thousands. The mass press was not responsible for its readers' lack of sophistication, but it worked hard to perpetuate it. That narrowed the market for genuine art, and gave it a snobbish exclusiveness that further deepened the gap between high and low culture characteristic of the new century.

Like the aristocrats who after 1789 lamented a lost golden age, the middle classes of Europe were soon to mourn the long peace. The years from 1871 to 1914 were the peak of Europe's power and wealth relative to the other continents. The cultural brilliance of Europe's capitals, above all Paris and Vienna, made the last decades of peace a *"belle époque,"* a delectable era. But powerful forces were working against equilibrium and tolerance. Those forces, above all the impetus of nationalism and the growing economic power of the new Germany, slowly undermined the stability of the European state system. That shift, invisible to peoples engrossed in their everyday lives, in the end proved a matter of life and death for millions of Europeans.

stiff, flat figures out of thousands of tiny colored dots. And after 1900 Pablo Picasso (1881–1973), Wassily Kandinsky (1866–1944), the "Cubists," and Italy's fiercely irreverent "Futurists" began to cut painting's links with visual reality. The art of the twentieth century was to be an art of increasing abstraction and of ever-proliferating schools and slogans.

It was also increasingly an art for the few rather than the many. Until the nineteenth century Western art had always spoken to a unified audience, a cultivated and largely aristocratic elite. Mass literacy and mass market ended that. Wood-pulp paper and the ma-

Suggestions for Further Reading

General

E. J. Hobsbawm, *The Age of Capital, 1848–1875* (1975), and *The Age of Empire, 1875–1914* (1987), are outstanding works of synthesis. Readable surveys include N. Rich, *The Age of Nationalism and Reform, 1850–1890* (1977), C. J. H. Hayes, *A Generation of Materialism, 1871–1900* (1941), and O. J. Hale, *The Great Illusion, 1900–1914* (1971).

Domestic Affairs

On Britain, see above all A. Wood, *Nineteenth Century Britain* (1960), G. Dangerfield, *The Strange Death of Liberal England, 1910–1914* (1935), and F. Bédarida, *A Social History of England, 1851–1975* (1979). The most accessible discussions of France are A. Cobban, *A History of Modern France*, Vol. 2 (1957), and R. D. Anderson *France, 1870–1914: Politics and Society* (1977); E. Weber, *Peasants into Frenchmen: The Modernization of Rural France* (1976), is full of wonderful material. For Germany, H. U. Wehler, *The German Empire, 1871–1918* (1985), is short and provocative, but the relevant portions of G. Craig, *Germany, 1866–1945* (1978), are a better guide to what actually happened. For Russia see R. Pipes, *Russia under the Old Regime* (1974); H. Seton-Watson, *The Russian Empire, 1807–1917* (1967);

A. Ulam, *Lenin and the Bolsheviks* (1966); and the intelligent popular account of E. Crankshaw, *The Shadow of the Winter Palace: Russia's Drift to Revolution, 1825–1917* (1976). On Austria-Hungary, C. A. Macartney, *The Habsburg Empire* (1969), is lucid and balanced; A. J. P. Taylor, *The Habsburg Monarchy, 1809–1918* (1948), is one-sided and entertaining. On Italy, the best treatment is C. Seton-Watson, *Italy from Liberalism to Fascism, 1870–1925* (1967), but see also the pertinent portions of D. Mack Smith, *Italy, a Modern History* (1959–), and M. Clark, *Modern Italy, 1870–1982* (1984). J. A. Thayer, *Italy and the Great War: Politics and Culture, 1890–1914* (1964), describes the fatal fascination that a last great war to achieve national integration exercised over Italy's elites.

Society and Culture

On the rise of feminism, see especially R. Bridenthal et al, *Becoming Visible: Women in European History* (1987), and S. K. Kent, *Women and Suffrage in Britain, 1860–1914* (1987). The best introductions to Nietzsche are J. P. Stern, *Nietzsche* (1978); W. Kaufmann, *Nietzsche: Philosopher, Psychologist, Antichrist* (1956); and R. Heyman, *Nietzsche: A Critical Life* (1980). On Freud and his legacy, see especially R. Wollheim, *Sigmund Freud* (1971), and the critical treatment of H. J. Eysenck, *The Decline and Fall of the Freudian Empire* (1984). On Freud's environment, see above all

C. Schorske, *Fin-de-Siècle Vienna: Politics and Culture* (1980). W. J. Mommsen, *The Age of Bureaucracy* (1974), offers an excellent short introduction to Max Weber and his ideas. E. Wilson, *Axel's Castle: A Study in the Imaginative Literature of 1870–1930* (1931–), is still the best introduction to literature from the Symbolists onward. R. Raynal, *The Nineteenth Century: New Sources of Emotion from Goya to Gauguin* (1951), with fine illustrations, and F. Mathey, *The World of the Impressionists* (1961), remain excellent introductions to the new painting.

29

From Balance to Breakdown, 1871–1914

In international politics, neither fear of revolution nor "concert of Europe" secured the long peace. Princes and standing armies had crushed the myth of revolution in 1848–49, and the concert of Europe had died in the Crimea. Europe, Bismarck scoffed, was a mere "geographic expression": "I only hear a statesman use the word 'Europe' when he wants something for himself." The long peace from 1871 to 1914 was rather the classic age of the balance of power, a mechanism as ostensibly self-operating as the free market. Excesses by one power led to the automatic combination of others against it, and its enforced retreat.

But the balance was above all a balance in Europe alone, and by the 1890s the European system ceased to be self-contained. The rise of two great powers outside Europe, the United States and Japan, created for the first time a world balance. At the same time it undermined the European equilibrium. Developments within Europe worked in the same direction. The new Germany's explosive economic growth surpassed Britain's between 1900 and 1913. And Prussia-Germany, already the greatest land power, challenged Britain after 1897 for world mastery at sea. New technologies of war and transport privileged the great continental powers and increasingly threatened Britain's ability to bring its seapower to bear. The tilt of the balance in Germany's favor and Germany's imprudent attempt to exploit that shift eventually drove Britain to ally with Germany's neighbors, France and Russia. Germany answered with war.

THE FORCES BEHIND DIPLOMACY

The economic development and gradual democratization of Europe also meant the mechanization and democratization of war and foreign policy. Generals, admirals, and diplomats resisted but could not reverse those forces. The war of 1866 was the last "cabinet war." Thereafter victory required and nationalism inspired the participation of the masses. The expansion of literacy and extension of the franchise meant that the masses began to intrude on foreign policy as well.

Toward Mass Armies and Industrial War

Until 1871 only Prussia possessed a genuine mass army based on the concept of universal military service. The French, despite or because of the revolutionary effects of the *levée en masse* of 1793, preferred long-service professional forces after 1815. Long-service troops were more effective than conscripts on the battlefield, and infinitely more trustworthy in suppressing domestic disturbances. The other European powers had in general imitated *la grande nation*.

Then the Prussian mass army, created in 1814 and doubled in size in William I's military reforms in the 1860s, crushed the French. That compelled others to follow Prussia if they hoped to remain or become great powers. Austria-Hungary, thanks to its lesson in 1866, introduced universal service in 1868; France, Italy, Russia, and Japan

Opposite: Sarajevo, June 28, 1914: Archduke Francis Ferdinand and his wife walking to the automobile in which they were to die.

811

followed in the 1870s. Only Britain and the United States, which faced no major land threats, basked in the luxury of volunteer services. Britain's medium-sized army was an imperial police force; the U.S. Army, a dwarf service tailored to fighting Indians.

Military power thus rested more than ever on demographic strength. That weakened the position of France even more than had defeat in 1870, for France's population growth slowed after 1800, while Germany's rapid increase continued (see p. 679). By 1911 France needed 83 percent of its available manpower to produce the same sized army that Germany achieved by conscripting only 53 percent. Only Russia and the remote and self-absorbed United States surpassed Germany in total population. And Russia's economic weakness and political decrepitude rendered numbers its only great asset.

A revolution in destructiveness paralleled the revolution in numbers. Alfred Nobel's nitrated powder gave higher pressures than the old unsatisfactory mixture of charcoal, saltpeter, and sulfur that had propelled musket and cannon balls since the fourteenth century. The result was unheard-of muzzle velocities, lightweight small-caliber bullets, and trajectories virtually flat for 300 to 400 yards. With the new

powder, unlike classic gunpowder, combustion was virtually complete. Nitrated powder neither gummed weapons with soot, nor gave away the rifleman's position, nor fogged the battlefield with smoke. Combined with the bolt-action rifle and Maxim's machine gun, smokeless powder created the modern battlefield, astoundingly empty because all visible movement draws fire.

Artillery changed more slowly than small-arms, but as dramatically. Nitrated powders flattened trajectories and multiplied range. Nitrated explosives made possible shells of unprecedented destructive power. The recoil-absorbing gun carriage, first employed effectively on the legendary 75mm French field gun of 1897, speeded fire dramatically by making it unnecessary to resight the gun after each shot. The *soixante-quinze* or "French 75" had a peak rate of fire of 20 rounds per minute.

Leveling devices, telescopic sights, surveying techniques, and the field telephone, which allowed forward observers to "walk" shells from distant hidden guns onto a target, made possible unprecedented accuracy and timeliness of fire. By the end of the century European armies had heavy guns with an effective range of 6 miles—compared to half a mile for the cannon of the Napoleonic wars. And by 1914 the first precariously droning aircraft could conduct reconnaissance or direct artillery fire. Cannon and small-arms between them reversed the advantage the offensive had enjoyed in the days of the great Napoleon. Attackers could now prevail only with crushing superiority of fire and numbers. Success might extend only so far as the next belt of enemy positions.

By 1900 the railroad had also worked a revolution. It had vastly increased the potential strategic mobility of land powers. In the Napoleonic wars, Wellington's sea communications proved better than the road links of his French adversaries. The railroad changed that; land powers could now rapidly meet

The French 75mm field gun.

amphibious threats with overwhelming force. And the new mass armies could mobilize with unprecedented rapidity. Mobilization and concentration for battle became a single continuous operation. Speed, as the Prussians had demonstrated in 1866 and 1870, was all-important. The power that mobilized first and fastest, the general staffs of Europe concluded, would win.

What the staffs ignored was that industrialization and the new firepower it had created made swift decision increasingly unlikely. Prussia's victory in 1870 had been a fluke, a consequence of France's disorganized mobilization and its ineptitude in the first battles. War between industrial powers, as the U.S. Civil War had demonstrated, tended inexorably toward immense struggles of attrition. The outcome of such protracted wars turned not on rifle strength in the first battles, but on industrial might and financial stamina. And in total industrial potential, by 1913, one power had surpassed all others except the United States: the Germany of William II. That was a momentous shift in the balance of power (see Figure 29-1).

Technology also revolutionized war at sea and threatened Britain's position. Napoleon III had embarrassed his British allies and rivals in 1859 by introducing the world's first armored warship, the frigate *Gloire.* Armor and shell-firing cannon made the wooden ships that had won at Trafalgar obsolete. The 1862 success of the Confederate ironclad *Merrimac* in smashing Union wooden ships drove the point home. The Union answer, the *Monitor,* with its all-iron construction and revolving turret, was the ancestor of all subsequent armored warships. In the 1870s and 1880s the European navies, with Britain in the lead, dropped auxiliary sails and adopted steel cannon and armor.

Numbers counted alongside quality. The Eastern crisis of 1885–87 (see p. 818) prompted scrutiny of Britain's neglected navy. The result was the Naval Defense Act of 1889, which mandated the construction of ten capital ships over three years. Britain adopted a permanent yardstick of naval strength: the Two-Power Standard. British strength had to equal that of the two next-ranked naval powers. Neither

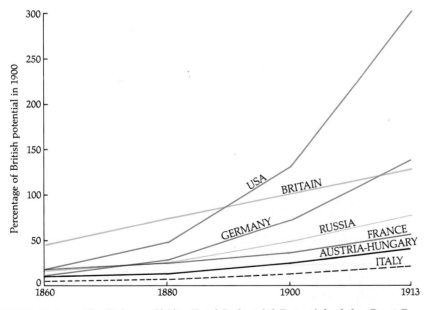

FIGURE 29-1   The Balance Shifts: Total Industrial Potential of the Great Powers

The first duel between armored warships: the *Monitor* against the *Merrimac* (renamed *Virginia*) at Hampton Roads, March 1862.

the protests of Gladstone at a further "monstrous scheme of the admirals" nor his resignation in 1894 checked the Royal Navy's expansion. Britain laid down an average of seven battleships a year throughout the following decade. And by 1900 those battleships each mounted four 12-inch guns, displaced 14,000 tons, and were capable of 18 knots. Then the British, to outpace all rivals, introduced in 1904–05 the first all-big-gun ship, H.M.S. *Dreadnought*.

With its ten 12-inch guns and 21-knot speed, it could stand off at long range and batter any earlier battleship into flaming scrap.

But Britain's rivals followed: by 1912 every great power had Dreadnoughts. And other weapons challenged the supremacy of the battleship and thus of Britain. An Englishman, Arthur Whitehead, invented a self-moving steam torpedo in the 1860s; the Russians first used it effectively in the Russo-Turkish

The ten 12-inch guns of the H.M.S. *Dreadnought* (launched 1906), outclassed all previous warships.

war of 1877–78. Torpedo boats posed an increasing threat to battleships close to shore. Mines, an unglamorous but highly effective weapon proven in the U.S. Civil War and thereafter also a Russian specialty, were even more menacing. Finally, the French, always on the lookout for technological shortcuts that might embarrass their British rivals, drew on U.S. Civil War precedents. By 1899 France had developed the first practical torpedo-firing submarine, the *Gustave Zédé*. Torpedoes, mines, submarines, and eventually aircraft evened the contest between Britain and its rivals, between the greatest sea power and the land powers.

Technology also inevitably raised the cost of warfare and of preparation for war. Britain's defense expenditure more than doubled between 1890 and 1914. Germany's almost quadrupled. But since their economies were also expanding, the burden of military expenditure as a percentage of gross national product did not increase as sharply as did the absolute amounts spent. What many contemporaries perceived as an uncontrolled upward-spiralling "arms race"—to use a metaphor that became current in the decade before 1914—was in reality a slow climb. Nevertheless, the weaker or slower-growing powers, Italy, Austria-Hungary, Russia, and France, found it harder to become or remain great powers than did the economic giants. In a long war, those that had difficulty keeping up before 1914 might well go to the wall.

Public Opinion and Foreign Policy

Educated opinion naturally first began to affect foreign policy in Britain and the United States. Opinion made the Crimean War and unmade the cabinet that bungled it. Opinion was decisive in making and—under Lincoln's inspired leadership—in deciding the U.S. Civil War. Gladstone mobilized opinion against Disraeli's foreign policy in the 1880 election; his command of Parliament began to crumble when the public discovered how his muddling had sent Gordon to his death at Khartoum.

As public opinion broadened, it began to affect policy in a variety of ways. First, its frequent ambiguity increasingly provoked—or excused—the indecision of policymakers. As Gladstone's Conservative successor Lord Salisbury lamented in 1895, "when the great oracle speaks, we are never quite certain what the great oracle said." Democratic opinion often appeared to want no foreign policy at all.

Second, reversals of opinion made continuity of policy increasingly difficult. Democracy, as Tocqueville pointed out in the 1830s, "can only with great difficulty regulate the details of an important undertaking, persevere in a fixed design, and work out its execution in spite of serious obstacles. It cannot combine its measures with secrecy or await their consequences with patience." The British foreign office made the fickleness of Parliament a virtue, a ready excuse when other powers inconveniently pressed for British commitments. The French Chamber destroyed its government for attempting to cooperate with Britain in Egypt in 1882, then paradoxically held a grudge against the British for going ahead alone. In 1885 the Chamber suddenly overthrew Ferry after a minor defeat in Tonkin; colonial entanglements momentarily appeared a betrayal of France's "lost provinces" of Alsace-Lorraine. Italian governments fell for "losing" Tunisia to France in 1881 and for losing at Adowa in 1896. Lack of continuity and of patience was no argument against democracy, but it did place increasing constraints upon makers of foreign policy.

Third, Liberal opinion in Britain and Socialist opinion on the continent tended to confuse morality with policy, to the dismay of self-proclaimed realists such as Disraeli and Bismarck. State interests often appeared to require actions, such as the threat of war, or clients, such as the Turks, that were distasteful to an electorate under the influence of Gladstonian moralizing. Extreme moralists rejected the rules of the international game altogether. Richard Cobden and John Bright, middle-class crusaders against Britain's Corn Law tariffs, denounced the Crimean War and lost their seats in Parliament. They shared a faith that free trade would act "on the moral world as the principle of gravitation in the universe—drawing men together, thrusting aside the antagonism of race, and creed, and language, and uniting us in the bonds of eternal peace." Free trade triumphed, but eternal peace did not appear. Cobden and Bright blamed that "foul idol," the balance of power, and the aristocracy, a historical fossil for which the diplomatic service allegedly served as a gigantic welfare system.

Socialist utopianism saw a different villain. Capitalism, the root of all evil, must also be the cause of war, not its cure (as Cobden and Bright had claimed). "For this system, not a man or a penny," ran the slogan of Germany's Social Democrats. Rosa Luxemburg and Lenin clashed over whether the party's leadership or the spontaneity of the masses were the key to revolutionary struggle, but they fervently agreed that imperialism and war were fruits of capitalism. They and others in the revolutionary wing of the Second International proclaimed that capitalist-imperialist war would and must lead to socialist revolution. Less dogmatic continental thinkers merely deplored expenditure on armaments. Countess Bertha von Suttner, an Austrian writer, gained wide success with her pacifist novel, *Lay Down Your Arms* (1889), and helped inspire the guilt-ridden Alfred Nobel to establish the prizes that bear his name. In 1905 she was the first woman to receive a Nobel peace prize.

Even states played to pacifist opinion. Nicholas II of Russia, fearing that his ramshackle finances would not support re-equipping his army with the French 75 or its equivalent, proposed a ten-year "holiday" on armaments in

Bertha von Suttner (1843–1914), recipient of the 1905 Nobel Peace Prize.

1898. But the 1899 disarmament conference at The Hague in Holland failed. That meeting, and a second in 1907, merely produced a World Court charged with deciding minor disputes involving "neither honour nor vital interests," a series of agreements on treatment of neutrals, prisoners, wounded, and non-combatants, and the stipulation that small-arms bullets must have full metal jackets rather than the more lethal expanding lead tip. Most rulers and military figures were secretly grateful to William II for sabotaging the conferences. The Kaiser scoffed rudely in private, and proclaimed his reliance "on God and on my sharp sword." Sir John ("Jacky") Fisher, the reforming admiral responsible for the *Dreadnought*, was equally forthright: "The essence of war is violence. Moderation in war is imbecility." What counted was winning, and winning required the swift application of overwhelming force without regard for niceties.

William II and Fisher need not have worried. In the age of nationalism, the more democracy, the more nationalism. That was the fourth major consequence of the growth of the power of public opinion. Pacifist sentiment remained confined to powerless minorities. The principal prewar leader of the SPD, August Bebel, admitted in 1892 that even his own party was "a sort of preparatory school for militarism." In Britain and France, "jingoism" (see p. 818) and Boulangism testified that even the public opinion of universal male suffrage was not necessarily pacific.

And even authoritarian regimes had to consider the views of their publics and officer corps. Nationalist opinion had driven Napoleon III, against his better judgment, to war and his doom in 1870. Nationalist opinion, originally unleashed with government support, helped drive Imperial Germany after 1905 to make good its bid for the mastery of Europe. By the 1870s, Slavophilism had mutated into Russian nationalism and had taken the cloak of "pan-Slavism." Russia was the patron and protector of its Slav "little brothers" everywhere—a sacred duty that extended the Russian state's potential claims far into central Europe and the Balkans. Journalists such as Nikolai Katkov of the *Moscow Gazette* preached that duty and those claims in a manner the tsars, given Russia's tradition of assassination, found increasingly difficult to ignore. Even in Japan, the oligarchs and their successors were responsive to opinion, especially military opinion. Assassination sometimes struck down those who appeared insufficiently resolute in defending Japan's security and rights.

BISMARCK THE CONSERVATIVE, 1871–90

German victory in 1870–71 dismayed Disraeli: "The balance of power has been entirely destroyed. . . ." The prophecy was 30 years too soon. Bismarck had harnessed German nationalism to Prussian state purposes. He was not about to loose that nationalism after 1871. The new Germany, he explicitly declared, was a "satiated" power. Bismarck henceforth sought to preserve the quasi-hegemonic position in Europe that he and Moltke had won.

That meant keeping the peace. In a future great war the powers whose mutual antagonisms had neutralized them in 1866 and 1870 might yet combine against Germany. France, unreconciled to the loss of Alsace-Lorraine, was the chief threat. If France found allies, Germany would face a dangerous coalition. And if Russia's Balkan friction with Austria-Hungary led to open conflict in eastern Europe, Germany might have to support Vienna, while St. Petersburg would bid for French support. The annexation of Alsace-Lorraine meant that an Austro-Russian conflict might well become a general European war in which Germany would have to fight on two fronts.

Bismarck the conservative.

Bismarck therefore sought, as Lord Salisbury uncharitably remarked, to use "his neighbors to pull out each other's teeth." He encouraged the powers' mutual tension to keep them dependent on Berlin. He diverted conflict to Europe's periphery, away from Alsace-Lorraine. Bismarck's policy, as much as the new Germany's strength, made Berlin the center of European diplomacy for a generation.

To freeze the status quo, Bismarck attempted above all to restore the unity between Vienna, St. Petersburg, and Berlin that had guaranteed stability before the Crimean War. His two "Three Emperors' Leagues" of 1872–73 and 1881 were above all devices to prevent Austria-Hungary and Russia from clashing in the Balkans. Bismarck was less successful than Metternich; neither league held for long.

In early 1875 Bismarck also attempted to bully a fast-reviving France with press warnings ("Is War in Sight?") and private threats of war. That provoked a crack in the first Three Emperors' League: Russia, for the first time since its resistance to Prussia's thrusts against Denmark in 1848–50, joined Britain. The tsar and Disraeli jointly warned Berlin that they would not allow Germany to crush France. Bismarck retreated. Unlike Moltke, he was not an apostle of the Prussian doctrine of "preventive" war, which went far beyond the preemption of *impending* enemy attack, and sanctioned wars to strike down *potential* future enemies before they became too strong. The balance of power, the mechanism that 30 years later was to bring Britain, Russia, and France together once more, had shown Bismarck his limits—limits he had himself established in 1871.

The Great Eastern Crisis and the Congress of Berlin, 1875–78

The "war-in-sight crisis" was transitory, despite its ominous undertone for Germany. It was the Balkans that wrecked both Three Emperors' Leagues. And the great Balkan crises of 1875–78 and 1885–87 were entirely different than their predecessor, the Crimean War. Not the great powers but the subject nationalities now threatened the Ottoman Empire. Balkan nationalism had come of age.

The Christian Slavs of Bosnia triggered the first and greatest crisis by rising in revolt against the Ottomans in July 1875. The revolt spread to the province of Bulgaria and the Turks replied with massacres. Tsar Alexander II, under pressure from pan-Slav opinion, prepared to rescue Russia's Balkan "little brothers"—and secure Constantinople. Unlike the clash in 1854, France abstained. Britain was paralyzed: Gladstone, in opposition, used the "Bulgarian horrors" to undermine Disraeli and Britain's traditional policy of supporting Turkey to keep Russia from the Dardanelles. Austria-Hungary likewise stood aside. Vienna feared that the triumph of Balkan nationalism over Turkey would make Austria-Hungary itself the next "Sick Man" of Europe. But in the absence of British support, Vienna made the best bargain it could. The Russians offered

Austria-Hungary territorial compensation in the western Balkans, and promised not to create a "large compact Slav state" that would threaten Vienna.

To everyone's surprise, the Turks held when Russia went to war in April 1877. At the entrenched camp of Plevna that blocked the main pass leading to Constantinople, their British magazine rifles stalled the ill-equipped Russians until December. Osman Pasha, the Turkish commander, gave the Ottoman Empire another 40 years of life. The Russians reached the outskirts of Constantinople exhausted. Britain's fickle opinion swung decisively: the Turks were no longer butchers of Christian Slavs but plucky defenders of Plevna. That freed Disraeli to send the British fleet to face Russia at the Straits, and gave the world a new word for populist bellicosity, "jingoism":

> We don't want to fight,
> But by Jingo, if we do,
> We've got the ships,
> We've got the men,
> We've got the money too.

Russia was now in no condition to fight Britain, but the tsar's peace treaty of San Stefano with Turkey (March 1878) nevertheless overreached. It created a great Bulgaria covering the entire eastern Balkans. That "large compact Slav state" and Russia's failure to offer the promised compensation induced Vienna to join Disraeli. Then Bismarck stepped in as "honest broker," and convened an international "Congress of Berlin" in June–July 1878. Its location symbolized the new Germany's decisive voice.

Disraeli returned from Berlin triumphant, with Turkish Cyprus as a sort of payment for saving Constantinople. Russia grudgingly divided the great Bulgaria of San Stefano into three: Bulgaria, an "Eastern Roumelia" technically under Turkish suzerainty, and a "Macedonia" that returned to Turkey. Austria-Hungary received its compensation—the Serb-inhabited provinces of Bosnia and Herzegovina to administer as a sort of trust. Serbia officially became independent of Turkey, although in 1881 Austria-Hungary made it a client state for a generation. The Congress of Berlin patched up a map of the Balkans that endured with minor modifications until 1912. Russia turned to expansion in Central Asia.

Bismarck's Alliances

In the aftermath, Bismarck accepted the logic of his policy of giving Austria-Hungary life. He took the very step for which he had reproached the Prussian governments of the 1850s: he tied the trim Prussian frigate to the "moth-eaten Austrian galleon." In September 1879 he signed at Vienna a defensive military alliance against Russia that endured until 1918.

This first peacetime alliance between great powers since the eighteenth century served several purposes. Bismarck hoped to reassure Vienna about its security and thus in theory make it more conciliatory to Russia. Since the alliance was defensive, Bismarck could always imply that he would leave Austria-Hungary to its fate if it actively provoked Russia. Domestically, the Dual Alliance gave German nationalism a surrogate for the "greater Germany" that Bismarck's creation of a greater Prussia had blocked. The existence of the alliance was immediately publicized, although its terms were secret until Bismarck published them in 1888.

Bismarck's solution held great dangers. Assurance of German backing if its survival was at stake increased rather than decreased Vienna's aggressiveness. And Bismarck's coupling of alliance politics with nationalist public opinion made it less and less possible for him to threaten Vienna with abandonment. Bismarck's successors considered themselves bound to Vienna by German nationalist "*Nibelung* loyalty"— a doom-laden Wagnerian motif that presided over the destruction of both empires in 1914–18. Finally, the alliance irrevocably tied Alsace-Lorraine

The Treaty of San Stefano   1878

The Congress of Berlin   1878

and the "Eastern Question" together, if doubt still existed about their connection. Germany, bound to Austria-Hungary by alliance and divided from France by an insoluble quarrel, was the link between east and west. Germany and Austria-Hungary would face France and Russia no matter how the war started.

To put off that day, Bismarck followed the Dual Alliance in 1881 with his second Three Emperors' League. Russia agreed not to join France in a Franco-German war and the three powers agreed to tolerate no Balkan changes except by mutual consent. The League rested on even weaker foundations than its predecessor. Tsar Alexander III, in power thanks to his father's assassination, was a narrow autocrat of nationalist bent. Monarchical solidarity meant little to him and still less to Vienna, which Bismarck had to pressure into signing.

To compensate Vienna for this enforced cohabitation with Russia, Bismarck made yet another treaty. In 1882 he roped the Italians into a Berlin-Vienna-Rome triangle, the Triple Alliance. Rome, humiliated over French seizure of Tunisia in 1881, was delighted at recognition of Italy's importance, however insincere. Vienna received an unconvincing Italian promise not to seek Trento and Trieste if Russia attacked Austria-Hungary. Bismarck paid the bill by guaranteeing Italy against French attack, a contingency he thought unlikely to arise.

In 1883 Bismarck added Rumania to his increasingly bizarre structure. That for the first time directly contravened his assurances to Russia that he was merely underwriting Austria-Hungary's existence, not its Balkan interests. The Rumanian treaties blocked Russia's land route to Constantinople. The Balkans, as Bismarck had told the *Reichstag* in 1876, contained no German interests worth the "bones of a Pomeranian musketeer." Yet Bismarck had now committed Germany to their defense against Russia.

Eastern Crisis and Reinsurance Treaty, 1885–87

Bismarck's diplomacy increasingly resembled an elaborate conjuring trick. The second of the great Balkan crises of these years, which opened in 1885, tested his ingenuity to the fullest. The issue, fortunately, was less explosive

than in 1877–78. Russia's fundamental goal was now mere security against British naval attack in the Black Sea and free passage through the Dardanelles for its growing grain exports from the Ukraine.

Nevertheless, Russia found occasion to quarrel with Britain in 1885–87, first by encroaching on Afghanistan, India's vital buffer, then by pressing Bulgaria, the gateway to the Straits. The first crisis blew over after the powers unanimously warned Gladstone against attempting to imitate Palmerston and Disraeli by threatening Russia in the Black Sea. The second crisis lasted longer. Russia sought to dominate Bulgaria with threats and military advisers. When it found it could not, it attempted to block the efforts of the Eastern Rumelians to join Bulgaria—ironically reaffirming the partition of the "great Bulgaria" of San Stefano that the powers had originally forced on Russia in 1878. In late 1887, Russia appeared poised for intervention in Bulgaria; then it accepted a face-saving solution. East Asia beckoned.

The crisis drove Britain, under Gladstone's Conservative successor, Lord Salisbury, towards the Triple Alliance. In two "Mediterranean Agreements" of 1887, Salisbury joined Italy and Austria-Hungary in guaranteeing—against Russia and France—the territorial status quo in the Mediterranean and Black Sea. That blocked Russia at Constantinople, with Bismarck's blessing. Bismarck added the final touch to this eccentric combination by negotiating a secret agreement with the Russians to replace the collapsed Three Emperors' League. The three-year "Reinsurance Treaty" of June 1887 pledged support for an eventual Russian drive on Constantinople. The parties also promised benevolent neutrality should war come, except if Germany attacked France or Russia attacked Austria-Hungary.

That assurance contradicted the spirit if not the letter of the Dual Alliance linking Berlin and Vienna. And by promising Russia the Straits, the Reinsurance Treaty contradicted the second Mediterranean Agreement between Bismarck's allies. Bismarck had created a system of mutually contradictory commitments that froze the Austro-Russian quarrel while keeping Germany's "line to St. Petersburg" open. If treaties could not keep the Balkans quiet, he would have to choose. His choice could only be Austria-Hungary, and a German clash with Russia.

The Collapse of Bismarck's System

Running a system of such complexity taxed even Bismarck. It also had unforeseen effects. France, weary of isolation, reluctantly drew closer to Russia. Tsarist Russia, annoyed at Bismarck's renewed backing of Austria-Hungary and at his closing of the Berlin loan market during the Bulgarian crisis, swallowed its qualms about the French Republic's money. The Russians secured their first sizable French loan in October 1888. In January 1889 they ordered a large quantity of French rifles after promising not to use them against France.

In Berlin, Bismarck was no longer sufficiently in control to counter this threat. The new Kaiser, William II, was under the influence of Moltke's successor, the warlike Count von Waldersee, who consistently counseled "preventive" war against Russia before it became too strong. In fall 1889 William II assured Vienna, without Bismarck's approval, that German mobilization would immediately follow that of Austria-Hungary, whatever the source of the quarrel. He also visited Sultan Abd al-Hamid II at Constantinople, a gesture implicitly hostile to Russia. Germany was abandoning its Russian connection.

Then Bismarck and the young emperor quarreled over domestic policy in March 1890. When the Russians anxiously proposed renewal of the Reinsurance Treaty, the man who had made it was gone. Bismarck's successor was a conscientious but limited general, Count Leo von Caprivi. He found

Alliances and Alignments before 1914

Austro-German (Dual) Alliance, 1879

Triple Alliance, 1882

Turkish-German Alliance, 1914

Reinsurance Treaty, 1887-90

Franco-Russian Alliance, 1894

Triple Entente, 1904/07

Anglo-Japanese Alliance, 1902

Franco-Italian Agreement, 1902

Russian-Serb Friendship

Bismarck's foreign policy too complex and self-contradictory. He feared that St. Petersburg might leak word of Germany's promise to support Russia at the Straits. That would irreparably damage German ties with Russia's adversary Britain. Nor would German opinion or the Vienna government take kindly to Germany's sins against the "*Nibelung* loyalty" supposedly enshrined in the Reinsurance Treaty.

Germany therefore declined the Russian offer and drew closer to Britain with an 1890 colonial agreement that traded nebulous German claims to Zanzibar for the British-controlled North Sea island of Helgoland. The end of the Reinsurance Treaty and Germany's wooing of Britain accelerated Russia's move toward France. In July 1891 a surly Tsar Alexander III stood at attention for the playing of the *Marseillaise,* hymn of revolution, during a visit of the French fleet. Bismarck had deliberately isolated France; William II and Caprivi had left Russia isolated. In August of 1891 France and Russia agreed to coordinate their foreign poli-

Tsar Alexander III, the French Republic's grudging alliance partner.

cies. Both sought the independence from Berlin that Bismarck had denied them.

By 1892 French and Russian negotiators had hammered out a military pact that pledged France to attack Germany if Germany attacked Russia, and Russia to attack Germany if Germany attacked France. If Austria-Hungary alone mobilized, France also pledged to mobilize. That provision broke with France's previous reticence in Balkan quarrels, but Paris agreed because it desperately wanted security against Germany and considered an isolated Austro-Hungarian move improbable. The alliance was to last almost as long as the Triple Alliance of its adversaries.

The ratification of this Franco-Russian Alliance in December–January 1893–94 did not, as often suggested, make a general war inevitable. The annexation of Alsace-Lorraine and Bismarck's Dual Alliance had already done that. The effect of the Franco-Russian alliance was rather to end the German political hegemony in Europe that Bismarck had established. The young Kaiser might as late as 1892 confide to associates his vision of erecting "a sort of Napoleonic supremacy" in Europe "in the peaceful sense." But after the Franco-Russian alliance, a German "Napoleonic supremacy" could come only through war.

THE BREAKTHROUGH TO WORLD POLITICS, 1890–1905

Europe nevertheless continued to enjoy unprecedented peace. The Franco-Russian alliance made both parties feel relatively secure in Europe. A new Near Eastern crisis in 1895 over Turkish massacres of Armenians failed to embroil Russia with Austria-Hungary. Indeed, in 1897 the two powers agreed to put the Balkans "on ice." For a generation Europe turned to Africa and east Asia. And for the first time non-European great powers, Japan and the United States, made their presence felt. That made the Eu-

ropean balance a world balance. Such a system, commentators discerned, suddenly made dwarves of powers such as France that were merely European in scale.

Theories of World Politics

Theorists such as Sir Charles Dilke and Sir John Seeley had begun to notice that even the British Empire lacked the vast territorial and demographic base of continent-spanning powers such as the United States and Russia. Britain could only compete, argued Seeley in the 1880s, if it welded the often wayward white colonies and Britain into a world-spanning trans-national federation, a "Greater Britain." That remedy appeared less and less plausible, for the white colonies were developing away from Britain, not toward it. Particularly after 1900, informed British opinion inclined toward anxiety about preserving the Empire from disintegration.

In Germany, the professorial elite provided a conceptual framework suitable for a "rising" power. From the summit of the German historical profession, the liberal Johann Gustav Droysen and the far less liberal Heinrich von Treitschke declared that unity under Prussia was the culmination of all previous German history. Droysen's fourteen-volume *History of Prussian Policy* (1853–86) and Treitschke's five-volume *History of Germany in the Nineteenth Century* (1879–94) portrayed the past, in good Hegelian fashion, as the upward struggle of a Prussian state embodying the world spirit. They also looked forward to higher things: Germany's mission in the world paralleled Prussia's pre-1871 mission in Germany. An entire generation absorbed their outlook.

Max Weber, in a famous 1895 speech, suggested that German unity had been a waste of time unless it served as prelude to a "German world power policy." The founder of the odd quasi-discipline of geopolitics, Friedrich Ratzel, suggested in his *Political*

Geography (1897) that state boundaries were fluid and ephemeral. Organization and numbers were the key elements in an eternal struggle for "space." A variety of theorists proclaimed that Britain's decline was Germany's opportunity to break through into the charmed circle of true world powers, alongside Russia and the United States. The Kaiser himself remarked hopefully in 1899 that "old empires are fading away and new ones are about to be formed."

In Russia, figures such as Katkov temporarily set aside pan-Slav fantasies for a Russian nationalist "manifest destiny" in East Asia. Russia in Asia, Katkov argued, was "as much at home as in Moscow." The Russians were not "foreign intruders from afar, as England is in India." As the Trans-Siberian Railroad crept eastward, the tsar and his subordinates began to look to control of northeast Asia as the foundation of Russia's world power status.

In the United States, pundits urged a search for new frontiers beyond the seas to replace the land frontier that was passing. "Manifest destiny," a phrase that a Southern journalist had coined in 1850, appeared to extend beyond the Pacific shores to "universal empire." But America's most influential prophet of empire was more modest. When Captain Alfred Thayer Mahan of the U.S. Naval War College published *The Influence of Seapower Upon History, 1660–1783* in 1889, it enjoyed instant success. Mahan derived two laws from the age of British naval supremacy. One he merely implied: seapower, from Roman empire to British empire, made for supremacy. The second he stated baldly: seapower meant a battle fleet, not commerce raiders. The France of Louis XIV and successors had sinned against both precepts with its "false policy of continental extension" and its preference for privateering over fleet actions. Both notions made Mahan's book the bible of the U.S. Navy and of its great-power counterparts. The Kaiser "devoured" it, and decreed that every German ship re-

ceive a translation. Mahan offered a recipe for success in the new age of world politics: build battle fleets and seize overseas bases and colonies to protect and foster an ever-expanding commerce. Mahan, ironically, achieved prominence just as railroad, torpedo, mine, and submarine were evening the contest between land and sea power, and non-European nationalism was making colonies an increasingly doubtful investment.

The Struggle for Mastery in Africa

The new age of world politics after 1890 involved two principal theaters of action. Britain and France confronted one another in the culmination of the "scramble for Africa" begun with the British occupation of Egypt in 1882. In East Asia, China's failure to keep pace with Japan or with the European powers led to a decade of bitter conflict.

In Africa, France's refusal to accept British control of Egypt led it into dangerous paths. In 1897 Paris sent a small expedition under Captain Jean-Baptiste

Kitchener, victor over the Dervishes—and the French.

Marchand of the French naval infantry to stake a diplomatic claim on the upper Nile, the key to Egypt's water supply. But London, after Salisbury and the Conservatives returned to power in 1895, had decided to avenge the Mahdi's 1885 defeat of Gordon at Khartoum. Egypt's security demanded command of the Sudan.

A British army under Sir Herbert Kitchener ascended the Nile by steamer to face the Dervishes of the Mahdi. That made the issue between Britain and France one of power alone. At Omdurman, in September 1898, Kitchener crushed the Dervishes. Three weeks later, Kitchener found Marchand and his small force at Fashoda on the upper Nile. To make good its claim, France would now have to go to war. Salisbury refused to negotiate: "We claim the Sudan by right of conquest . . . ." The Dreyfus affair crippled Paris politically, and France remained mindful that Britain still held that control of the Mediterranean won in 1798 at the battle of the Nile. Marchand received orders to withdraw.

Fashoda was not the end of London's African woes. The great conflict between Britain and the Boers, which Gladstone had postponed by retreating in 1881, finally erupted. The discovery of gold on the Rand in 1886 made the Boer Transvaal republic the greatest power in southern Africa. British entrepreneurs rushed in to exploit the mines—but every ounce of gold they extracted strengthened the Boers. After

1894 the Transvaal secured an independent link to the outside world by a railroad to Delagoa Bay in Portuguese East Africa. German political and economic influence flowed in, to the alarm of the British.

Most alarmed was Cecil Rhodes, the great robber baron of the Kimberley diamond mines and Rand gold fields. In a departure from custom, London had allowed Rhodes to become prime minister of the Cape Colony and had thus put British policy in the service of Rhodes's investments. Rhodes of course saw it differently: his failed efforts to outflank the Transvaal and lessen its economic preponderance by finding gold in "Rhodesia," to the north, were service to the empire.

In 1895 Rhodes at last decided to destroy the Transvaal before its growing strength imperiled Britain's control of the Cape and Rhodes's own interests. With the connivance of the ex-Liberal Joseph Chamberlain, now Salisbury's secretary for colonies, Rhodes prepared a raiding force. Under the leadership of a Dr. Jameson, the raiders were to attack the Transvaal in support of a planned uprising of British settlers and miners inside the Transvaal itself. But the "Uitlanders," as the Boers called them, failed to rise. Boer mounted infantry efficiently rounded up Jameson and his raiders in January 1896.

The Jameson Raid fiasco sent Rhodes into eclipse, but Chamberlain persisted. The mercurial Kaiser had sent the president of the Transvaal, the bearded patriarch Oom Paul Kruger, a telegram of congratulations that seemed to presage German meddling in southern Africa. Chamberlain began preparing British opinion for war. Chamberlain's new deputy at the Cape, Sir Alfred Milner, sought and prepared for war itself. The Cape Dutch, he feared, would in the long run desert Britain for the Transvaal. Economic and political trends were running strongly in favor of the Boers. Britain must fight before it was too late. Salisbury was unhappy: "I see before

Architects of empire, and of the Boer War: Joseph Chamberlain (above) and Cecil Rhodes (relaxing in the bush during the Matabele war, 1896).

us the necessity for considerable military effort, and all for people whom we despise and for territory which will bring no power and profit for England." Chamberlain and Milner had their way. In October 1899 Milner succeeded in provoking the Boers into a declaration of war.

Contrary to Milner's expectation, the war was no walkover. Britain commanded the seas; despite European disapproval and violent pro-Boer agitation in Germany, Britain's European rivals were powerless. Not so the Boers. Unlike Dervishes or Zulus they did not obligingly charge into British Maxim guns. The Boers instead allowed the British to attack, and sent them reeling with Mauser rifles and Krupp field guns. Boer knowledge of the country and mounted mobility gave them operational as well as tactical superiority in the early engagements. Not until June 1900 did a huge and clumsy British army conquer the Boer capital, Pretoria. Britain, to defeat a few backwoods farmers, had found it necessary to commit a grand total of 450,000 men.

Milner was now master of Pretoria and the Rand, but not of southern Africa. The Boers persisted in a bitter guerrilla struggle. Boer commandos of 50 or 100 mounted raiders smashed British outposts and railroad lines. The British replied with African and Boer defector scouts, irregular cavalry given to savage reprisals, and "concentration camps": barbed-wire open-air prisons for the Boer civilian population and their black dependents, to cut off supplies to the commandos. Roughly 20,000 Boers and 12,000 blacks died behind the wire from typhoid, measles, dysentery, and British mismanagement. The Liberal opposition damned the government for defending civilization with the "methods of barbarism." Soon all except the most determined "jingoes" were heartily tired of the brutality and sacrifices that empire entailed.

In the end, attrition and Britain's increasing use of Boer turncoats and

Three generations of defiant Boers, with their Mauser rifles.

native auxiliaries induced the commandos to give up in May 1902, and acknowledge British sovereignty. The greatest colonial war of the century was over. But the fierceness of Boer resistance compelled London to conciliate its new subjects. In 1910, Britain conceded Dominion status to a Boer-dominated Union of South Africa. The Boers had won in all but name.

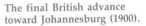

The final British advance toward Johannesburg (1900).

Asia in 1880

Britsh colonies
Protected states (in India)
• Treaty ports (in China)

MILES
0   1000

The Struggle for Mastery in East Asia, 1894–98

African struggles were still largely part of the inherited framework of European and colonial rivalries. East Asia was different. There a new power, Japan, burst upon the scene by attacking China in September 1894. In the 1870s the Meiji oligarchs had restrained Japan's extremists, who had urged a war with China's dependent kingdom, Korea. Japan had been as yet too weak for conquest; it had settled for "opening" Korea, Perry-fashion, to Japanese trade in 1876. It had smoothed over a crisis with China over Korea in the mid-1880s. Now it was ready, and friction over Korea provided the occasion.

Japan's new army threw the Chinese out of Korea and invaded Manchuria. Japan's new navy battered the poorly trained Chinese fleet off the mouth of the Yalu River; the Empress Dowager had spent much of China's naval budget to build the Summer Palace in Beijing (Peking). Japan seized the vital base of Port Arthur on the Liaodong Peninsula. By the Treaty of Shimonoseki of April 1895, Japan imposed on China the cession to Japan of Port Arthur and recognition of Korea's independence—from China, not from Japan.

Then disaster struck. Russia and its French ally took the occasion to pose as China's protectors. Their adversary in Europe, Germany, joined them in

Asia in 1914

hopes of currying favor with the Russia it had estranged in 1890. The three powers "advised" Japan against keeping Port Arthur and the Liaodong Peninsula. The resentful Japanese disgorged; their one major prize was Taiwan, which they henceforth ruled as a colony.

Japan's victory over China opened a new scramble for concessions and ports that seemed to presage the final collapse of the ramshackle Chinese empire. Russia made its own bid for control of northern China and Korea. Count Witte, architect of the Trans-Siberian Railway, plied the Chinese with loans. Russian emissaries negotiated the right to build a railway spur directly across Manchuria to Vladivostok. In December 1897 Russia seized

and "leased" the prize the Japanese had sought, the ice-free naval base of Port Arthur, and secured the right to connect it to the new railroad. In 1897–98 Germany and Britain acquired ports on the Shandong Peninsula, opposite Port Arthur. Italy demanded a port, but China had learned enough about Europe to know that it could safely refuse. The powers divided China into spheres of influence: Manchuria to Russia, southwest China to France, the Yangtze Valley to Britain, and the Shandong area to Germany.

The United States as a World Power

While the powers stripped China to the bone, a power potentially greater than any of them began to acquire a foreign policy. That was a novelty, and not always a welcome one, for the United States. Thanks to its ocean boundaries and the indirect protection of the British fleet, the United States had largely ignored the European balance throughout the century. But a new assertiveness emerged in the 1890s, as industrial America reached maturity. In 1895 President Grover Cleveland's secretary of state intervened in a boundary dispute between Britain and Venezuela with the uncivil but accurate claim that "the United States is practically sovereign on this continent, and its fiat is law . . . ."

In 1898 the second of two Cuban revolts against Spain tempted the United States to make good that assertion of hegemony. The battleship *Maine*, anchored in Havana harbor, exploded and sank in February 1898—the new nitrated powders tended to instability in hot climates. The jingoist press of William Randolph Hearst claimed a Spanish plot: "Remember the *Maine!*" That agitation and the coming election pressed the invertebrate President William McKinley to act.

The shining new U.S. Navy, built up on Mahanian lines since the early 1890s, swept the decrepit fleets of Spain from the seas. A hastily improvised U.S. expeditionary force landed on Cuba and eventually prevailed, despite inadequate training and logistical chaos. Theodore Roosevelt, soon to succeed McKinley, made a name leading the dashing "Rough Riders." The navy reached out across the Pacific toward China, following Mahan's precepts. Commodore George Dewey crushed the Spanish fleet in the Philippines at the battle of Manila Bay. He then challenged a German squadron that was loitering nearby in hopes of snapping up a coaling station. The Germans wisely declined.

The Filipinos proved more difficult than Spain or the Germans. Already in revolt against Spain, they failed to see the charm of United States domination, enlightened though it might be. It required up to 70,000 troops, three years, and all the U.S. Army's Indian-fighting expertise to defeat the insurgency of Emilio Aguinaldo. Anti-imperialists at home fervently denounced the war. Ultimately the United States mastered its empire in the Philippines and in nominally independent Cuba by political solutions. In return for the loyalty of the planter oligarchy Spain had created, the United States promised order. That guaranteed stability, but offered no long-term release from the fierce conflicts inherent in such sharply stratified societies.

The United States thus acquired an overseas empire, rounded out with the annexation of Guam, Puerto Rico, and Hawaii. It also intervened diplomatically—with a pronouncement mixing moralism and American interests in the style of the Monroe Doctrine—in faraway China. In 1899 McKinley's secretary of state, John Hay, asserted the "Open Door" to trade, and China's territorial integrity, against the projects of the powers for exclusive spheres. The powers humored the newcomer and agreed. Paper promises were cheap, and easy to disavow later.

Closer to home, the United States also made good the claim to an exclusive sphere in Latin America first asserted in the Monroe Doctrine. Britain tacitly conceded United States hegemony in the Caribbean in the Hay-Pauncefote treaty of 1901. Under Roosevelt and his successors William Howard Taft (1909–13) and Woodrow Wilson (1913–21), the United States engineered the secession of "Panama" from Colombia, and between 1904 and 1914 carried through the Panama Canal project that had defeated de Lesseps. U.S. Marines brought imperial order to Central America and the Caribbean while diplomats sought, in Wilson's words, to teach the inhabitants "to elect good men." A navy of Dreadnoughts, with bases stretching from Manila Bay to Norfolk, assured the security of the new empire and of America's growing trade. And America's immense and still-growing share of the world's industrial production buoyed up its power claims.

The Western powers line up for their slices of China (from a German cartoon, 1900).

The Struggle for Mastery in East Asia and the European Balance, 1899–1905

Meanwhile, the unprecedented scale of Western intrusion into China after 1897 triggered the greatest spontaneous anti-Western rising since the Indian Mutiny of 1857–58. The "Righteous and Harmonious Fists" or "Boxers" originated as an antidynastic secret society. It claimed Daoist magic powers that made its adherents impervious to Western bullets. In 1898–99 it spread across northern China as a mass movement to "expel the foreign bandits and kill the Christian converts." The Dowager Empress and her conservative advisers tacitly encouraged the Boxers, who obligingly ceased opposition to the Qing dynasty.

International intervention to protect the missionaries triggered a Boxer-led rising that bottled up the Westerners in Beijing in the embassy quarter. Boxers assassinated the German minister. The Qing declared war on the powers. Boxers sought to exterminate all Westerners they could catch. As an Italian nationalist cynically remarked a year or two later, only an invasion from Mars could unite humanity. China briefly fulfilled the same function: Europe, Japan, and the United States momentarily forgot their quarrels. William II dispatched Field-Marshal Waldersee to lead the conquest of northern China. The Kaiser sent the troops off with an impromptu speech that exhorted them to take no prisoners, and to rival the fearsome reputation of Attila and his Huns. That phrase Germany's enemies long remembered.

Even before Waldersee's arrival, Daoist magic had succumbed to Maxim guns. The victorious powers exacted a stiff settlement, but preserved the Qing by endorsing the fiction that the Boxers had been an anti-Manchu rebellion. The dynasty staggered on; the death of the Empress Dowager in 1908 and a

revolution of provincial armies and westernized intellectuals in 1911 ultimately destroyed it.

In the short term, Russia remained in possession of Manchuria and for a while of Beijing itself. That disquieted Britain. London now felt little need of allies in Europe, for in the mid-1890s Salisbury had at last felt strong enough to weaken Britain's commitment to defend the Turkish Straits. Revived British naval power and the possession of Egypt had made "splendid isolation" practical. But to resist Russia in China, Britain needed a land ally. Between 1899 and 1901 Chamberlain therefore sought agreement with Germany. The Germans proved slippery, for good reason. British goodwill and Germany's small stake in China were no recompense for risking Russia's enmity. Germany shared European borders with Russia and with Russia's French ally; Britain did not.

In January 1902 Britain found a different partner, that other "island empire," Japan. The parties pledged to fight only if their ally faced *two* great powers in East Asia. That meant Britain and Japan would fight side by side only if France intervened alongside its Russian ally. Britain's role was to hold the ring while Japan, if necessary, stood up to Russia. And the Russians soon made war inevitable. In March 1903 the first train across the Trans-Siberian Railway reached Port Arthur. The tsar dismissed Witte, and appointed a dangerous fanatic for Asian expansion, A. M. Bezobrazov, to office. A member of Bezobrazov's circle, Vice-Admiral E. I.

Alekseev, became viceroy of Russia's Asian possessions. Alekseev pressed forward: Bezobrazov had established Korea as Russia's ultimate objective. But Korea, as a Prussian general staff adviser had taught his Japanese pupils, was of supreme geopolitical importance. It was "a dagger pointed at the heart of Japan." Yamagata Aritomo, founder of Japan's modern army and most Prussian of the surviving oligarchs, pressed for war.

St. Petersburg rejected Japan's offer that Russia recognize Japanese preponderance in Korea in return for a more qualified Japanese acknowlegment of Russia's position in Manchuria. In reply, Japanese torpedo boats attacked and crippled the Russian fleet at Port Arthur on February 8, 1904. Japan thus secured command of the sea. In May 1904 a Japanese army invaded Manchuria from Korea while Japanese forces laid seige to Port Arthur. Russian machine-gun fire piled thousands of dead Japanese attackers on the new barbed wire obstacles. The Japanese persisted, and took Port Arthur in January 1905. By March they had worn the Russians down in immense battles of attrition in Manchuria. The Trans-

A Japanese view of the sinking of the Russian flagship *Petropavlovsk* at Port Arthur, 1904.

Siberian Railway was as yet single-tracked, and Russian supplies and reinforcements were precarious. The Russians retreated northwards from Mukden.

And at the end of May 1905 the Russian Baltic fleet, dispatched half way around the world to rescue Port Arthur, met the Japanese off the island of Tsushima, south of Korea. Admiral Togo Heihachiro "crossed the T" of the advancing Russian fleet, sweeping the leading Russian ships with the long-range broadsides of his entire force. The annihilation of that last Russian fleet and the revolution that broke out in European Russia in January 1905 (see pages 795–96) forced Russia to cease fighting. "Teddy" Roosevelt, trying out America's new status as Pacific great power, stepped in to mediate and to preserve a balance that would keep China alive. The Treaty of Portsmouth (New Hampshire) of September 1905 recognized Japan's "paramount interests" in Korea, forced Russia to return Manchuria to China, and presented Japan with Port Arthur, its railway, and the southern half of the island of Sakhalin. Within five years Japan had annexed Korea. A non-European power had for the first time defeated a European great power.

The Russo-Japanese war decisively altered the European scene. The approach of war caused the French deep anxiety: would Russia's conflict with a British ally drag France into hostilities with Britain? Theophile Delcassé, France's canny foreign minister, turned in the course of 1902–03 toward Britain. The British, for similar reasons, turned toward France. Queen Victoria's successor, the high-living Edward VII, wooed French opinion with a state visit in 1903 and with less official gastronomic and amorous cross-Channel excursions. By April 1904 the parties had arrived at a settlement of the colonial disputes that had divided them since the occupation of Egypt in 1882. France traded its existing interests in Egypt for a British promise to support its eventual annexation of Algeria's western neighbor, the decrepit Sultanate of Morocco. This Anglo-French *"Entente Cordiale"* was thus East Asian in origin and colonial in nature. But it soon became an alliance in all but name, facing the greatest European power, Germany.

That fateful development was a consequence of a second major repercussion of the Russo-Japanese war: the disruption of the European naval and military balance thanks to Russia's defeat. Until Russia recovered, Germany was supreme on the continent. Its naval buildup soon outpaced the Franco-Russian alliance and threatened to outpace Britain. Its land forces, freed temporarily from the two-front threat, held France hostage. And its consequent efforts to reduce France to vassalage impelled Britain, for the first time since Waterloo, to contemplate committing British forces to a great land war in western Europe.

GERMANY ON THE LOOSE, 1905–14

The German Challenge at Sea

The restless Kaiser spent much of the 1890s seeking a means to achieve the "Napoleonic supremacy" to which he aspired. The Franco-Russian alliance barred the way on the continent. Germany's future, the Kaiser concluded, lay "on the waters." Personal rivalry with his English naval cousins, identification with the world-spanning goals of German middle-class nationalism, and a dilettantish interest in naval technology made him from early 1890s the chief advocate of enlarging Germany's coastal defense navy into something larger and more impressive. The Kaiser read Mahan in 1894 and became a convert to the gospel of the battle fleet. But not until 1897 did he find the team capable of translating his wishes into budgets and battleships: Bernhard von Bülow at the foreign office and Admiral Alfred von Tirpitz at the Reich naval office.

Bülow provided the foreign-policy cover for the fleet effort. Germany was to preserve a "free hand" and avoid entanglement with either of the two great antagonists, England and Russia, while creating a fleet that would alter the world balance of power. It was the task of Tirpitz, who possessed an impressive bifurcated beard and the wiliest political mind of William II's Germany, to provide that fleet. The admiral's opponents did not call him "the Father of the Lie" for nothing.

To convince the *Reichstag* of the need for a battleship navy, he mounted Germany's first modern advertising campaign. Charts showing Germany's comparative naval strength appeared in dentists' waiting rooms all over Germany. School children chipped in pennies for the fleet. Professors and industrialists spoke and wrote fervently of Germany's "sea interests" and world mission. In 1898 the *Reichstag* passed a first naval law providing 19 battleships, and in 1900 accepted a second that doubled the fleet to 38 battleships and stepped up the building tempo to three ships each year.

To justify to the *Reichstag* both the enormous expense and a program of advance appropriations stretching over decades, Tirpitz claimed that Germany's increasing foreign trade and colonial empire required a fleet for its security. Only a fleet capable of placing "the greatest naval power" at serious risk would provide that security. Tirpitz's so-called "risk theory" thus appeared on the surface to be defensive, a strategy of deterrence. But no power threatened Germany's commerce or its largely useless colonial empire. Nor was deterrence Tirpitz's aim. In his internal memoranda for the Kaiser and others, he preached decisive battle "between Helgoland and the Thames." For the "greatest naval power," the opponent Tirpitz had chosen, was Britain.

Victory over Britain, Tirpitz calculated, depended on four conditions. Rivalry with France and Russia would continue to bind the British navy in

Admiral von Tirpitz, who built the fleet against Britain.

China and the Mediterranean, leaving Britain weak in the North Sea. The effete British would neither pay for nor be able to man—with expensive volunteers—the additional ships needed to keep pace. Technology, Tirpitz assumed, would remain static; German battleships built in 1900 would be roughly equivalent to later British and German ships. Finally, in the event of war the British fleet would charge into the mine- and submarine-infested German waters and mount the traditional close inshore blockade of enemy ports. That would give the Germans their opportunity to fight on advantageous terms.

The Kaiser was enthusiastic. The fleet would assure him his place in Prusso-German history. Just as his grandfather William I—thanks to Bismarck—had used the Prussian army to give the new Germany a semi-hegemonic position in Europe, so he would use the navy to break through into the circle of true world powers. And just as William I and Bismarck had mastered Prussian Liberalism by victory abroad, so he and his "second Bismarck," Bülow, would master Social Democracy. And his fleet, thanks to provisions in the naval laws that automatically replaced over-age ships, would ultimately be independent of the hated *Reichstag*. William II would become a naval "People's Kaiser" ruling a "German world empire."

The British were not amused. Britain by 1900 had progressed farther than Germany along the road to becoming an industrial society; over half of Britain's food was imported, and those imports inevitably came by sea. Naval supremacy was for Britain not a luxury but a matter of survival. The British navy scrapped its Chinese river gunboats and its Caribbean squadron to free manpower for the North Sea. After 1903 it created new naval bases facing Germany at Rosyth in Scotland and at Scapa Flow in the Orkneys. Admiral "Jacky" Fisher, reforming Admiralty chief after 1904, supervised Britain's technological leap to the all-big-gun

ship, the *Dreadnought*—and urged destruction of the German fleet in harbor, before it was strong enough to challenge Britain. The British foreign office sought closer ties with France and eventually with Russia. By 1905, the principal assumptions of Tirpitz's plan were thus proving false. Germany had summoned up a naval competition that its British opponent dared not lose and had isolated itself diplomatically except for alliance to an increasingly ramshackle and dependent Austria-Hungary.

The First Morocco Crisis, 1905–06

Germany might have sought to loosen by good behavior the "encirclement"—as the Germans now began to call it—that Germany had itself summoned up. Britain, France, and Russia were an odd assortment: two parliamentary regimes, one brutal autocracy. Britain and Russia might still clash anywhere from China to Persia, if Germany lay low. But Bülow and the chief brain at the German foreign office, the secretive Friedrich von Holstein, chose to break "encirclement" with threats. Russia's defeat at the hands of Japan removed France's continental backing. Bülow and Holstein sought to exploit that weakness by picking a quarrel with France and reducing it to vassalage by proving that it could not rely on Britain.

They chose French encroachment on derelict Morocco as a pretext. The "First Morocco Crisis" was in reality not colonial, but a crisis of the European balance. In March 1905, with Russia in chaos, Bülow and Holstein diverted the Kaiser's habitual Mediterranean cruise to Tangier. The "All-Highest" landed reluctantly, and asserted Germany's non-existent "great and growing interests in Morocco." Tension mounted as summer, the season for war, drew near. In June the French cabinet cracked, and dismissed Delcassé as foreign minister.

Germany appeared to have won; William II made Bülow a prince. And in July William II succeeded during a yachting encounter off the Finnish island of Björkö in persuading his cousin "Nicky"—Tsar Nicholas II—to sign an alliance with Germany. Nicholas agreed in the hope that German backing would help him get better peace terms from Japan. Germany had apparently broken the Franco-Russian alliance, and achieved supremacy on the Continent.

But Russia in defeat and revolution needed French money more than ever before. France's price was naturally Russian repudiation of Björkö, which the Russians in any event found less necessary after making peace with Japan in September 1905. The Germans also made a fatal error. Instead of pressing for a bilateral Moroccan bargain with France that would recognize their victory, they sought an international conference.

At Algeciras, opposite Gibraltar, the representatives of the powers met in January 1906. Germany found itself isolated except for Austria-Hungary. Even its Triple Alliance partner Italy stood with France. In 1900 Italy had secretly secured French acquiescence to Italian designs on Libya in return for Italian support in Morocco. In 1902 Rome had even sinned against the Triple Alliance with a secret promise of neutrality in the event Germany "provoked" France to a declaration of war.

The Algeciras conference therefore handed Germany a major diplomatic defeat. And Britain had already taken secret steps to bolster the French. When the Liberals took office in December 1905, talks were already underway between the British and French army staffs about committing a British army on the left wing of the French, if Germany attacked. The crisis Germany had launched had mightily reinforced the "ring" forming around Germany. Bülow and Holstein had converted an Anglo-French colonial entente into a quasi-alliance against Germany to preserve the European balance of power. And on August 31, 1907, Russia and Britain, the two most persistent antag-

The German Challenge: The View from London

On January 1, 1907, Sir Eyre Crowe, the best brain in the British foreign office, dissected Imperial Germany's motives and policies in a long and prescient memorandum for his superiors. His analysis was potentially applicable to the armament programs and foreign policies of later expansionist powers.

Either Germany is definitely aiming at a general political hegemony and maritime ascendancy, threatening the independence of her neighbors and ultimately the existence of England; Or Germany, free from any such clear-cut ambition, . . . is seeking to promote her foreign commerce, spread the benefits of German culture, extend the scope of her national energies, and create fresh German interests all over the world wherever and whenever a peaceful opportunity offers, leaving it to an uncertain future to decide whether the occurrence of great changes in the world may not some day assign to Germany a larger share of direct political action over regions not now a part of her dominions . . . .

In either case Germany would clearly be wise to build as powerful a navy as she can afford. The above alternatives seem to exhaust the possibilities of explaining the given facts. The choice offered is a narrow one, nor easy to make with any close approach to certainty. It will, however, be seen, on reflection, that there is no actual necessity for a British Government to determine definitely which of the two theories of German policy it will accept. For it is clear that the second scheme (of semi-independent evolution, not entirely unaided by statecraft) may at any stage merge into the first, or conscious-design scheme. Moreover, if ever the evolution scheme should come to be realized, the position thereby accruing to Germany would obviously constitute as formidable a menace to the rest of the world as would be presented by any deliberate conquest of a similar position by "malice aforethought."

From *British Documents on the Origins of the War, 1898–1914*, (London: His Majesty's Stationary Office, 1928), Vol. III, p. 417.

onists of the nineteenth century, signed a colonial entente settling their long-standing disputes in Tibet, Afghanistan, and Persia. The "Triple Entente" of Britain, France, and Russia now faced the Triple Alliance of Germany, Austria-Hungary, and Italy.

Naval Race and Bosnian Crisis, 1907–09

The Germans learned little from the first Morocco crisis. The noisy diplomacy of Bülow and Holstein had contradicted Tirpitz's need for quiet in which to build a fleet against Britain. Now Tirpitz's fleet cut across Germany's far greater need to lie low. By 1908 Tirpitz faced the possibility that he might fail. The Liberals in Britain, despite their detestation of "great armaments" and their desire to increase social spending, would not give up Britain's lead over the German fleet. Tirpitz, amid clamorous anti-British propaganda from the German Navy League, therefore pushed a third naval law through the *Reichstag*. The German building tempo rose to four Dreadnoughts per year.

Britain replied with a proposal for a one-year "naval holiday." Berlin rejected it. Except for the pacifist Cobdenite wing of the Liberals, British opinion was now unanimous. Britain must keep its lead whatever the cost. "We want eight [Dreadnoughts] and we won't wait!" clamored the popular press. In 1909–10 Britain laid down ten battleships and battle cruisers. When the time came to pay the bill, the Liberals raised the income tax, instituted inheritance taxes, and overrode the protests of the House of Lords. In Germany, Bülow's attempt to raise taxes to cover the vast increases in fleet costs led to the defection of the Junker Conservatives and the collapse of the government's *Reichstag* majority. The Reich's antiquated fiscal structure proved unequal to the strain, while the knowledge that naval superiority was a matter of life and death strengthened British resolve.

As Anglo-German tension mounted, Germany's ally Austria-Hungary made its own contribution to the growing European crisis. For a decade it had held to its 1897 agreement with Russia to keep the Balkans quiet. But in 1903 a group of fanatical Serb officers slaughtered Vienna's clients, King Alexander and Queen Draga Obrenovitch of Serbia. Austria-Hungary's relations with Serbia deteriorated. French capital fortified Serbia against an Austro-Hungarian tariff war. By 1908 the Austro-Hungarian foreign minister, Count Aehrenthal, had concluded that Vienna's prestige was at stake.

As a blow against Serbia he sought Russia's acquiescence to the annexation of Bosnia and Herzegovina, the largely Serb-inhabited provinces bordering Serbia that the Congress of Berlin had allowed Austria-Hungary to occupy in 1878. Aehrenthal's Russian counterpart, Count Isvolsky, agreed, on condition that Austria-Hungary help secure a long-standing Russian goal, the opening of the Turkish Straits to Russian warships.

Aehrenthal was too clever. He announced the annexation of the provinces in October 1908, before the Russians had time to secure the agreement of other powers to the opening of the Straits. The other powers, in any event, did not agree. Aehrenthal pocketed Bosnia and Herzegovina, while Isvolsky grumbled and threatened, and the Serbs agitated against Austria. Eventually William II appeared, as he himself put it, "in shining armor" alongside Austria-Hungary. Berlin cabled St. Petersburg to accept the annexation, or else: "We would have to consider an evasive, conditional, or ambiguous reply as a refusal." The Russians accepted; they had not yet recovered from war with Japan. What from Berlin appeared a triumphant reassertion of German and Austro-Hungarian prestige seemed to the other powers dramatic evidence of German aggressiveness. Bülow, leaving office after a personal clash with William II, claimed to have given this sound advice: "Do not repeat the Bosnian Crisis."

The Second Morocco Crisis, 1911

Bülow's successors, Chancellor Theobald von Bethmann Hollweg and foreign secretary Alfred von Kiderlen-Wächter, did not act on it. Instead, Kiderlen again attempted to use Morocco as a pretext to bully France, in the hope of breaking the Entente and riding nationalist enthusiasm to victory in the 1912 German elections. In May 1911 the French occupied Fez, the capital of Morocco, after the usual disorders threatening European businessmen. Kiderlen met with the pan-Germans and enlisted them as propagandists for his policy. He then dispatched a gunboat, the *Panther*, to the Moroccan Atlantic port of Agadir on the pretext of protecting German lives, which were not threatened. The German nationalist press was ecstatic: "Finally, a Deed!"

Kiderlen, a jovial Swabian given to canary-yellow vests, conducted a policy so secretive that the austere and bureaucratic Bethmann Hollweg had to ply him with drink to find out what he had told the French. Kiderlen had threatened war while offering to settle for the entire French Congo in compensation for France's seizure of Morocco and as symbol of France's dependence on Germany. But the French and Russian armies were stronger than in 1905. Britain, through the mouth of Lloyd George, whom the Germans had thought was a pacifist Liberal, stiffened the French with Jingo oratory.

Although Bethmann Hollweg shared what his private secretary described as "the authentic and fitting German idealist conviction that the *Volk* needs a war," the Kaiser was less enthusiastic. Kiderlen had to settle for several strips of French Congo swamp. France retained its independence. The pan-Germans vented their fury on the Reich government for this "new Olmütz." And the crisis brought Britain to make further secret commitments to France. London reaffirmed its plans to send a British Expeditionary Force (B.E.F.) in the event of German attack. Sir Edward Grey, the foreign secretary, authorized increasingly binding military discussions with the French while keeping the Cobdenites in the cabinet in the dark. And Sir Winston Churchill, civilian chief of the navy after 1911 and a distant descendant of the great Duke of Marlborough, called the Mediterranean fleet home to face the Germans in the North Sea. The French took over Britain's Mediterranean duties in return for a secret British undertaking to protect the coasts of northern France against the German fleet. That was Britain's most far-reaching commitment against Germany to date.

Germany Prepares, 1912–13

The German response to defeat in the Second Morocco Crisis was retrenchment—of a sort. Tirpitz lost the unchallenged right to funding which his navy had enjoyed. In 1913 and 1914 the German building tempo fell to two ships a year. Berlin at last recognized that it must secure its continental base before defeating Britain. The Kaiser and Bethmann Hollweg now gave the army priority. Radicals on the general staff such as Erich Ludendorff broke down aristocratic inhibitions against expanding the army with non-noble officers. In 1912 and 1913 two army bills added 165,000 first-line troops. The *Reichstag* at last passed an inheritance tax over Conservative objections. Tirpitz's only consolation was the Kaiser's rejection of yet another British "naval holiday" proposal.

The army increase was necessary, if Germany were to implement its chosen strategy in war. Waldersee's successor as Chief of the Great General Staff, Count Alfred von Schlieffen (1891–1905), faced the same nightmare of a two-front war as his predecessors. But his answer was different. Instead of attacking in Russia and defending in fortified Alsace-Lorraine, as both Moltke and Waldersee had proposed, Schlieffen planned to strike France first. France, he reasoned, was vulnerable to a swift decisive blow, whereas the Russians could always retreat into their limitless spaces as they had in 1812.

Schlieffen's Plan

Schlieffen had studied military history, classifying battles as a bug-hunter does insects. Decisive battles, he concluded, were all envelopments. The most perfect was Hannibal's crushing double envelopment of the Romans in 216 B.C. at Cannae in southern Italy. But mountains, French fortifications,

"War the sooner the better": Helmuth von Moltke the younger, Prussia-Germany's chief of join staff, 1906–14.

and the absence of space for Germany's million-man army did not permit a double envelopment on the Franco-German border. Instead, Schlieffen planned a holding action there to distract the French. Meanwhile an immense right wing, three-quarters of the entire German army, would swing down through neutral Belgium upon the unfortified and undefended French rear.

Timing was everything. If Germany did not mobilize in time, or failed to knock France out immediately, the "Russian Steamroller" would crush Germany's skeleton force in East Prussia, and drive on Berlin. And Schlieffen, in his admiration of Hannibal, had forgotten one vital fact: Rome had ultimately defeated Hannibal. It had destroyed Carthage through attrition and through command of the sea.

Schlieffen's plan dictated that any German war, even one stemming from a Balkan quarrel, would begin with an attack on France that staked Germany's future on a single card. And the violation of Belgium, whose neutrality the powers had guaranteed in 1839, virtually ensured that Britain would join

Germany's enemies. To Schlieffen that seemed unimportant. Britain had no mass army, and the war would be over—*must* be over—before it had time to raise one. Those were dangerous misapprehensions.

Schlieffen retired in 1905, leaving his plan to Helmuth von Moltke the younger, high-strung and indecisive nephew of the great Moltke. The new chief of staff had doubts about Schlieffen's "infallible recipe for victory" but kept them to himself. He added additional troops to both wings of the German deployment; later charges that he "watered down" Schlieffen's plan were unjust.

And at the end of 1912 the German leadership apparently decided to act. A British warning that Britain would stand by France in the event of war enraged the Kaiser. On December 8, 1912, he presided over a conference of his military advisers at Potsdam. Moltke, according to the diary of the Kaiser's chief naval aide, counseled a Prussian-style preventive war "the sooner the better" to crush Germany's

adversaries while Germany could still do so. New Russian railways in Poland and rearmament of the Russian army with modern weapons would make the Schlieffen plan impractical by 1917. Tirpitz advised restraint—for the moment. His navy was not ready. Only in June 1914 would the vital canal across Jutland between the Baltic and the North Sea be widened for Dreadnoughts, and the submarine pens on Helgoland be ready. The conference, without consulting Bethmann Hollweg, decided to mobilize the press to prepare the German public for war. With government encouragement, stories increasingly hostile to Russia began appearing.

And at the general staff, Moltke and his assistant Ludendorff made two fateful changes in 1913. First, they discarded Germany's one remaining alternate plan, which had provided for an offensive deployment against Russia and defense against France. Second, Ludendorff added to the Schlieffen plan the requirement that German troops must move immediately upon

The Dissolution of the Ottoman Empire   to 1914

The Balkan Wars: Turkish infantry moves up.

mobilization into neutral Luxembourg and Belgium to seize the key rail junction of Liège. If the war for which Moltke was pressing came, Germany would violate Belgium upon mobilization and attack France regardless of the war's origin.

The Balkan Wars, 1912–13

While the Germans prepared, the great powers lost control of the Balkans. France's absorption of Morocco produced a chain reaction. Giovanni Giolitti of Italy, fearing that the French now no longer needed to honor their promise to support Italy's acquisition of Libya, acted. No Italian government could survive if it failed to assert Italy's great-power status. In September 1911 Italy declared war on Turkey, Libya's nominal overlord, and sent its fleet to Tripoli. A hastily improvised landing failed to subdue the warlike Arabs or their Turkish advisers. Italy therefore seized Turkish islands in the Aegean

and attacked the Dardanelles. Not until October 1912 did the Turks cede a still unpacified Libya to Italy.

The Italian example emboldened the Balkan states. Serbia and Bulgaria, with Russia as godfather, signed an alliance in March 1912. Greece and Montenegro joined. The Russians thought of the new alliance as defensive; the Balkan states had other ideas. In September the Balkan League attacked Turkey and swiftly partitioned Turkey's territory in Europe. Then the victors fell out over the division of the spoils. Bulgaria attacked Serbia in the hope of seizing the province of Macedonia, of which it claimed the powers had defrauded it in 1878. Serbia, Greece, Montenegro, Rumania, and Turkey smashed the Bulgarians.

The Serbs gained most from the wars, although Austria-Hungary fiercely barred them from the Adriatic in Albania. The powers, under the leadership of Sir Edward Grey of Britain, cooperated in holding Serbia back and in creating an independent Albania. The victory of Balkan nationalism had ended the multinational Turkish empire in Europe. That made the new "Sick Man" of Europe, Austria-Hungary, increasingly desperate to reassert its shrinking prestige against Serbia, the "Piedmont of the South Slavs." The Balkan Wars were clearly not the last Balkan crisis.

"EVEN IF WE END IN RUIN"— JULY 1914

On June 28, 1914, at Sarajevo in Bosnia, a Bosnian-Serb terrorist assassinated Archduke Francis Ferdinand, heir to the throne of Austria-Hungary. The terrorists, following a pattern common later in the century, were connected with a secret society—the "Black Hand"—under the sponsorship of Serbia's military intelligence department. Vienna did not know that, but it reacted with predictable fury. The chief of staff, the bloody-minded Conrad von Hötzendorff, looked for a war to restore Habsburg prestige and crush Serbia for good. Austria-Hungary's foreign minister, the frivolous Count Leopold von Berchtold, concurred. Only the Hungarians, appalled by the thought of annexing yet more Slavs, opposed action.

Berlin broke the deadlock. When Berchtold's envoy called upon the Kaiser on July 5, William II counseled immediate war against Serbia, regardless of Russia's reaction. He repeatedly assured a confidant, Krupp von Bohlen, that "this time I will not chicken out [*Diesmal falle ich nicht um*]." Bethmann Hollweg told his closest confidant on July 8 that Germany would probably win a general war. If Russia pulled back, Germany would nevertheless split the Entente, and achieve a decisive diplomatic and strategic victory. In Vienna, Berchtold used Berlin's so-called "blank check"—in reality a virtual order to act—to break Hungarian opposition. Since 1866–67 Greater Hungary had owed its independence

Sarajevo, June 28, 1914: The arrest of the assassin, Gavrilo Princip.

The Kaiser Spurs Vienna On   July 5, 1914

The Kaiser's message, as reported by Austria-Hungary's ambassador, Count Ladislaus Szögyény, was no simple "blank check" or assurance of support. It was an incitement to war.

After lunch, when I once again underscored with the greatest emphasis the seriousness of the situation, His Majesty [Kaiser William II] authorized me to report to our most gracious Majesty [Emperor Francis Joseph] that in this case as in others we could count on Germany's full support. . . . He (Kaiser William) was of the opinion that this action must not be delayed. Russia's attitude will in any event be hostile, but he had been prepared for that for years, and should it come to a war between Austria-Hungary and Russia, we could be assured that Germany would stand by our side with its usual faithfulness to its alliances. . . . He understands full well that His royal and imperial Apostolic Majesty [Emperor Francis Joseph] would be reluctant, given his well-known love of peace, to march into Serbia. But if we had really become convinced of the necessity of military action against Serbia, he (Kaiser William) would regret it if we allowed the present highly favorable moment to pass unused.

From Immanuel Geiss, ed., *Julikrise und Kriegsausbruch 1914* (Hannover: Verlag für Literatur und Zeitgeschehen GmbH, 1963), pp. 83–84 (translation by M. Knox).

Conrad von Hötzendorff, Austria-Hungary's chief of staff, contemplates war on three fronts (1914).

to Berlin; it could not refuse Berlin's order.

But partly out of Viennese languor and partly out of calculation, Berchtold delayed issuing the ultimatum to Serbia until July 23. That gave Austria-Hungary's action an appearance of cold premeditation that weakened Vienna's moral position. And the 48-hour ultimatum itself appeared a deliberate provocation. One German ambassador could not believe that Vienna had drafted the document; its brutal tone was "Prussian to the very bones." Berchtold made the deliberately humiliating demand that Austro-Hungarian police enter Serbia to join the hunt for the terrorists and their accomplices. Vienna also announced that it would treat refusal of any single condition as a total rejection. The Serbs made a conciliatory answer. But perhaps thanks to Russian reassurances, they refused to accept Austro-Hungarian intervention inside Serbia itself.

That was enough for Vienna, and for Berlin, where official circles, in the words of a participant, "worried only that the Serbs might swallow the note." Bethmann Hollweg sabotaged efforts by Grey to arrange a conference of the kind that had prevented the Balkan Wars from growing into great power conflict. On July 28, with strong German encouragement, Austria-

Hungary declared war on Serbia. Austro-Hungarian mobilization was too slow to permit an invasion for several weeks, but Vienna and Berlin were determined to present the powers with a violent *fait accompli*. Austria-Hungary therefore shelled Belgrade, the Serb capital.

Russia now had to respond or suffer a humiliation far worse than the Bosnian crisis. Nicholas II and his Foreign minister, Sergei Dimitrievich Sazonov, reluctantly attempted to deter Vienna. On July 28 they fatalistically ordered mobilization of the four Russian military districts opposite Austria-Hungary. Then the generals reported that Russia's cumbersome mobilization system permitted only a general mobilization. On July 31 Russia published the order for general mobilization. That proved the point of no return, although the Russian purpose was deterrence, not war.

In Berlin, the news was welcome indeed. The Kaiser had begun to waver, while Moltke pressed Bethmann Hollweg with increasing vehemence to mobilize before Russia. Bethmann Hollweg himself feared the domestic consequences of mobilizing first; it was his task to keep the German Social Democrats loyal to the coming war effort. Russia's mobilization appeared heaven-sent. "The mood is brilliant," wrote the Kaiser's naval aide in his diary on August 1, "The government has succeeded very well in making us appear as the attacked." Germany dispatched an ultimatum to Russia summoning it to demobilize. Russia refused.

On August 1 Germany declared war on Russia and mobilized. France responded to its alliance obligations to Russia by mobilizing. A German ultimatum to Paris demanding French neutrality followed. The ultimatum was for show only; German strategy dictated war on two fronts. If France dared to upset the Schlieffen plan by abandoning its Russian ally and remaining neutral, the German ambassador in Paris was to ask provocatively for the surrender of French border fortifications. That would force France to fight. In the event, France did not accept the ultimatum. On August 2 Germany invaded Luxembourg and summoned Belgium to give free passage to German troops. Belgium refused. On August 3 Germany declared war on France. On the morning of August 4 German troops entered Belgium—and pushed the indecisive British cabinet into war. The violation of Belgium allowed the Liberals to feel moral about a war to defend British security and the balance of power; the Cobdenite pacifist Liberals resigned. At midnight on August 4 London's ultimatum to Berlin expired. As the Kaiser addressed the *Reichstag* amid stormy applause, the war minister, Erich von Falkenhayn, was overcome by emotion: "Even if we end in ruin, it was beautiful." That was a fitting epitaph for Imperial Germany and for the long peace.

"War Guilt"

Later, after 1918, it became fashionable to dispute Germany's preeminent responsibility for the war of 1914–18. German scholars rallied around their foreign office, and accused Russia or Britain. Anglo-Saxon "revisionists" did their best to charge Vienna, St. Petersburg, Paris, and even London with "war guilt." Guilt is a notion best left to psychoanalysts and theologians—but causation and responsibility are of interest to the historian.

Nor, for all the oceans of ink spilled over the origins of this conflict, is apportioning responsibility difficult. The long-term causes of the war were two: Austria-Hungary's decline and Germany's rise. Balkan nationalism threatened an Austria-Hungary embroiled in perennial struggle with Russia. German nationalism, after 1890, proved not at all "satiated." Bismarck, with the dual alliance of 1879, had inextricably tied together these two principal sources of European conflict. After

---

Bethmann Hollweg's Calculations   July 1914

Kurt Riezler, Bethmann Hollweg's private secretary and author of a work on politics with the symptomatic title of *The Necessity of the Impossible* (1913), recorded in his diary his July 1914 conversations with the Chancellor. They leave little doubt about the extent of Bethmann Hollweg's, and Germany's, responsibility for the outcome.

July 7, 1914. . . . In the evening a long talk about the situation . . . [Bethmann sees] Russia's military power swiftly growing; once [the] strategic buildup in Poland [is] complete, [our] situation untenable. Austria ever weaker and less dynamic. . . . I was appalled; I did not see things that darkly. . . . [Bethmann:] The future belongs to Russia, which grows and grows. . . .

July 8, 1914. . . . The Chancellor thinks the old Kaiser [Francis Joseph of Austria] may not decide to go ahead. If war comes from the East, so that we have to go to war for Austria-Hungary rather than Austria-Hungary for us, we have the prospect of winning. If war does not come, if the Tsar doesn't want it or France, appalled, counsels peace, then we nevertheless still [doch noch] have the prospect of maneuvering the Entente apart through this action.

July 14, 1914. . . . For him [Bethmann Hollweg] action is a leap in the dark, and a heavy duty. Kiderlen always said we would have to fight. Berchtold is considering the timing [of the ultimatum], whether before or after the visit of Poincaré [the French president] to St. Petersburg. Better before, for then the chance is greater that France, panicked by the sudden appearance of the specter of war, will warn Russia to keep the peace.

From Kurt Riezler, *Tagebücher, Aufsätze, Dokumente* [Göttingen: Vandenhoeck & Rupprecht, 1972], pp. 182–84 (translation by M. Knox).

1905 they interacted explosively. Balkan nationalism sapped Austria-Hungary just as the German threat drove the Entente powers to coalesce against Germany.

In the final crisis, responsibility was unevenly divided. Britain merely intervened once the Germans invaded Belgium. Contrary to later German accusations, Grey scarcely hid the likelihood that Britain would act if Germany sought to crush France—but fear of Britain did not deter Berlin. France merely accepted a war that Germany forced on it. The Serb government did not seek war, although it nurtured the terrorists. St. Petersburg encouraged Serb expansion in 1912 and after, and possibly nerved Belgrade to refuse Austria-Hungary's most humiliating demands. Russia also mobilized first, although its intention was not war, but getting Vienna's attention.

Austria-Hungary's responsibilities were more serious. It sought war with Serbia, made sure that its ultimatum meant war, and shelled Belgrade. But it was Berlin that took the key decisions: without German pressure, Austria-Hungary would never have acted. Since late 1912 Germany's leaders had inclined toward a general war, given a suitable occasion. Moltke actively sought war "the sooner the better." His purpose was to strike down Germany's *potential* enemies before they

became too strong—a goal little different from outright aggression. Bethmann Hollweg, obsessed with the specter of the ever-growing—though hollow—Russian colossus, and inclined to optimism about German military prospects if general war came soon, was more than willing to risk it. All trusted in a "fresh and joyous war" (in the phrase of the Kaiser's obstreperous son, Crown Prince William), short and victorious in the style of 1870.

Germany's minimum goal was a small Balkan war to bolster a flagging Austria-Hungary and split the Triple Entente. Its maximum goal was the domination of Europe. And the Schlieffen plan—after 1913 Germany's *only* war plan—ensured that war against Russia would begin with an attack on France through Belgium. That guaranteed British intervention. Germany made a Balkan war, then turned it into a world war.

Suggestions for Further Reading

Europe in the Age of Bismarck

The relevant chapters of L. C. B. Seaman, *From Vienna to Versailles* (1955), offer a good brief guide to international politics after 1871. A. J. P. Taylor's indispensable *The Struggle for Mastery in Europe* (1954), gives a detailed and brilliantly sardonic account, but see also P. Kennedy, *The Rise and Fall of the Great Powers* (1987), for the underlying trends. W. L. Langer, *European Alliances and Alignments, 1871–1890* (1950), is still useful on the diplomacy of Bismarck's conservative phase. M. Hurst, ed., *Key Treaties for the Great Powers*, vol. 2, *(1871–1914)* (1972), gives English texts of agreements such as the Triple Alliance. Among the many accounts of the policies of the different powers, see especially G. Bourne, *The Foreign Policy of Victorian England* (1970); B. Porter, *The Lion's Share* (1984); and D. Geyer, *Russian Imperialism* (1987). On military affairs, see the relevant chapter in H. Strachan, *European Armies and the Conduct of War* (1983); G. Ritter, *The Schlieffen Plan* (1958); and P. Kennedy, ed., *The War Plans of the Great Powers, 1880–1914* (1979).

World Politics

For the rise of "world politics," see especially the chapter on international affairs in G. Barraclough, *An Introduction to Contemporary History* (1964). W. L. Langer, *The Diplomacy of Imperialism* (1950), covers the 1890–1902 period in informative detail. H. W. Morgan, *America's Road to Empire* (1965), provides a convenient summary of America's entry into world politics; see also C. S. Campbell, *The Transformation of American Foreign Relations, 1865–1900* (1976), and H. K. Beale, *Theodore Roosevelt and the Rise of America to World Power* (1956). R. Van Alstyne, *The Rising American Empire* (1960), offers a jaundiced view of U.S. motives. T. Pakenham, *The Boer War* (1978), and I. Nish, *The Anglo-Japanese Alliance* (1966), are excellent.

The Road to World War I

The best single work on the origins of the First World War remains L. Albertini, *The Origins of the War of 1914* (1952). P. Kennedy, *The Origins of the Anglo-German Antagonism, 1860–1914* (1980), is a model of analysis. V. Berghahn, *Germany and the Approach of War in 1914* (1973), and Z. Steiner, *Britain and the Origins of the First World War* (1977), offer parallel accounts that emphasize German responsibility. On France, Russia, Austria-Hungary, and Italy see J. Keiger, *France and the Origins of the First World War* (1983); D. Lieven, *Russia and the Origins of the First World War* (1983); F. R. Bridge, *From Sadowa to Sarajevo: The Foreign Policy of Austria-Hungary, 1866–1914* (1972); and R. Bosworth, *Italy and the Approach of the First World War* (1983). V. Dedijer, *The Road to Sarajevo* (1967), throws some light on Serb machinations. For the final crisis, I. Geiss, ed., *July 1914* (1967), is indispensable. F. Fischer, *Germany's Aims in the First World War* (1967), and *War of Illusions* (1975), makes a strong case for a premeditated German war of aggression.

30
War and Revolution, 1914–1929

*T*he war that began in August 1914 irrevocably changed Europe and the world. Contrary to almost unanimous expectation, neither Jena-Auerstädt nor Sedan repeated themselves. Instead, as in the U.S. Civil War, industrialized states mobilized their full reserves of human and machine power, and battered one another into collapse. In the process, Europe forfeited a world economic leadership that the growth of the United States already threatened. The nationalism of the colonial peoples received powerful reinforcement. The four great empires of Europe and the Middle East perished. One of them, Russia, suffered a revolution of utopian claims and unparalleled ferocity, the first Marxist revolution. The European balance of power broke down: victory over Russia potentially gave Germany the mastery of Europe. Only the intervention of a power from outside Europe, the United States, brought Germany's final defeat. And swift U.S. withdrawal after 1919 left the exhausted victors, Britain and France, face-to-face with a vengeful Germany that did not acknowledge defeat. Those conditions made the war of 1914–18 merely the *First* World War.

THE WAR OF MOVEMENT, 1914

The dead Schlieffen's stupendous gamble failed. The initial coup at Liège went well. The great German right wing, a million men in four armies, began to swing. The French, fervent for the offensive, obligingly attacked the German fortifications in Lorraine and thus plunged deeper into the German trap. There, France lost 300,000 dead, wounded, and missing, a loss never made good.

But Schlieffen and his successor, Moltke the younger, had allowed neither for enemy reaction nor for "friction," that force of chance and circumstance that makes even the simplest plans in war excruciatingly difficult to execute. The Belgians wrecked their railroads. Belgian civilians, despite German massacres in reprisal, fired on German columns. German transport beyond the railheads was increasingly inadequate. The immense march distances exhausted the reservists, who were of necessity not in peak condition. By September, wrote an officer of the German army with the farthest to travel, "the men stagger forward, their

Machine warfare: a British
tank moves up, 1917.

faces coated with dust, their uniforms in rags, looking like living scarecrows. They march with their eyes closed, singing in chorus so as not to fall asleep. . . . It is only the delirium of victory that sustains our men."

Delirium was not enough. As the Germans neared the Franco-Belgian border, they encountered both the French and the 120,000 professionals of the British Expeditionary Force (B.E.F.). The Kaiser exhorted his commanders to "exterminate the treacherous English" and walk over their "contemptible little army." The B.E.F. replied with rifle fire so rapid and accurate that the Germans thought they faced a new form of machine gun. German numbers eventually flanked British and French, and forced withdrawal southwards. But the price of German victory was high. It increased further as the French commander in chief, the imperturbable "Papa" Joseph Joffre, gave up the Lorraine offensive and switched forces by rail to face the German right wing. Schlieffen had simply assumed the French would be too paralyzed to outflank the German right wing; the French decided otherwise.

The Germans, footsore in the August heat, found by the end of the month that they lacked the troops to envelop Paris as Schlieffen had originally hoped. The Russian threat in East Prussia had forced diversion of two corps to the eastern front; even had they stayed, they would have been too few to cover the front and flanks of a drive around Paris from the west. And as the outermost German army swung inside Paris, it exposed its flank and rear to French forces in the city. Joseph Galliéni, conqueror of Tonkin and Madagascar, threw his troops onto the German weak point and mobilized the taxis of Paris to bring up reserves. Alexander von Kluck, the German army commander, frantically turned his five corps back to the northwest to counter Galliéni; that opened a fatal gap between Kluck's army and its neighbor to the east. On September 8–9, thanks to the persistence of Joffre ("the honor of England is at stake"), the battered B.E.F. staggered forward into that gap and threatened to roll up von Kluck. On September 9 the outflanked and exhausted German armies withdrew northward toward the river Aisne. Moltke, who had urged war for so long, suffered a nervous breakdown. France's defensive victory on the Marne meant that Europe faced a long war.

Moltke's replacement as Germany's chief of staff, the moody Erich von Falkenhayn, might yet have flanked the British and French north and west of Paris and have seized much of France's Channel coast. But he refused to withdraw further than the Aisne, and thus lacked the mass of troops needed for a concentrated drive. Instead, he dissipated German reserves in a series of piecemeal attacks north of Paris. The B.E.F. and the French held with difficulty, but they held.

This "race to the sea" ended in October–November 1914 with a huge slaughter in Flanders. At Langemarck, near Ypres, Falkenhayn committed scarcely trained volunteers, fresh from school or university, against the remains of the B.E.F. It was a "massacre of the innocents." Little remained of the volunteers, of whom Germany had much need later, or of the B.E.F., the main repository of experienced leaders for Britain's coming mass armies. In mid-November Falkenhayn admitted to Bethmann Hollweg that the Imperial German Army was "a broken instrument," incapable of forcing a decision. By year's end Germany had lost almost a million dead and wounded, and France at least 900,000. Trenches and barbed wire stretched from the Channel to Switzerland. Until early 1918 the lines scarcely moved, despite unparalleled carnage.

In eastern Europe the Germans had better fortune. The "Russian Steamroller" rolled into East Prussia and broke down. When the outnumbered German defenders gave way, Moltke dragged a senior general, Paul von Hindenburg, out of retirement and

The First World War   1914–18

gave him Ludendorff as chief of staff. Ludendorff, with the help of intercepted Russian radio communications, concentrated all German forces against one of the two Russian armies and crushed it at Tannenberg by August 29. Russia lost 92,000 men and 400 guns. Then Ludendorff turned on the other Russian army and drove it back in disorder. That made Hindenburg and Ludendorff much-needed symbols of German invincibility, compensation for defeat on the Marne.

Germany's ally fared less well. Austria-Hungary's first invasion of Serbia

was a fiasco and the main Russian attack in Galicia drove Conrad von Hötzendorff's armies back to the Carpathian mountains in confusion. But by the end of the year German troops had retrieved the situation. In the vast spaces of eastern Europe, movement was still possible, although here too siege warfare around key fortresses and rail junctions dominated.

To the south, one member of the Triple Alliance did not go to war in August 1914: Italy. Its grounds were eminently reasonable, for the alliance did not require it to share a war of aggres-

Victors on the eastern front: Hindenburg (left) and Ludendorff.

sion about which Berlin and Vienna had failed to consult it in advance. But Italian neutrality did not prevent the spread of the war beyond Europe. A German Mediterranean detachment, the battle cruiser *Goeben* and the cruiser *Breslau*, evaded an inept British pursuit and sought refuge at Constantinople in August 1914. The Turkish government thereupon gambled on the victory of Germany, its longtime patron, over Russia, its perpetual enemy. When *Goeben* and *Breslau* bombarded Odessa in October, Russia declared war and attacked Turkey in the distant Caucasus. The entry of Turkey extended the war to the entire Middle East, from the Caucasus to Suez to the Persian Gulf.

Farther afield, British seapower was supreme. Britain swept the seas of German surface raiders by the end of 1914. And the Grand Fleet did not charge into the mines and submarine ambushes off the German fleet base of Wilhelmshaven, as Tirpitz had expected. Instead, it established blockade lines at the Channel and from Scotland to Norway, a "distant blockade" outside the effective reach of the fleet that Tirpitz had built. Britain, thanks to its geographic position, could cut Germany off from the outer world without

fighting the fleet action on German terms for which Tirpitz had planned.

Thanks to seapower, the Dominions were free to join Britain and the German colonies were easy prey. Even the Boer leaders cooperated with London, and themselves suppressed a short-lived backwoods anti-British revolt. French and British seized Togo, Cameroons, and South-West Africa. Only in and around German East Africa (now Tanzania) did the Germans hold out for long. There, until 1918, Paul von Lettow-Vorbeck and his native *askaris* repeatedly made fools of their British, Indian, British-African, and Boer pursuers. The "war of the white tribes" of Europe and the sight of Lettow-Vorbeck's *askaris* defeating whites proved a major stimulus to African nationalism.

And in Asia the war was Japan's opportunity to reverse the verdict of 1895, when the powers had forced it to relinquish its gains in China. Tokyo enthusiastically offered Britain its support in August 1914. It gobbled up the German outpost in Shandong, and the German island possessions in the Pacific that did not fall to Australia. In January–May 1915 it imposed on derelict China the famous "twenty-one demands" that consolidated Japanese control of the Shandong Peninsula and claimed southern Manchuria, Inner Mongolia, and an industrial region in central China. British persuasion secured the "postponement" of the most extreme claims, such as a right to impose advisers on China's central government. But protests could not remove Japan's continuing threat to China, and to Europe's domination of Asia and the Pacific.

THE INDUSTRIAL AND GEOGRAPHIC BALANCE

The sources of the stalemate that begun in 1914 are clearer in retrospect than they were to contemporaries. Railways allowed the mobilization and movement to battle of immense armies. The size of those armies allowed the occupation of ever-wider defensive frontages. Finding an enemy flank upon which to launch a decisive attack, as the "race to the sea" demonstrated, was now almost impossible. And on the battlefield itself, the storm of steel and lead, the ever-thicker coils of barbed wire, and the absence of transport for troops, ammunition, and food, immobilized the mass armies. Cars, trucks, and motorcycles were neither bulletproof nor available initially in adequate numbers. Reserves, thanks to railroad, telephone, and radio, could always reach a threatened point faster than attackers could break through on foot. Air reconnaissance and air photography allowed defenders to detect offensive preparations, and made surprise difficult. Strategic mobility checkmated tactical decision, firepower crushed movement, communications and air reconnaissance removed surprise.

Two other factors made the war of 1914–18 an unprecedented struggle of attrition. First, although the staffs of Europe had largely ignored it, the U.S. Civil War had demonstrated that industrial powers fought long wars even when one contender was far stronger industrially than the other. In the absence of striking military ineptitude of the sort the French had displayed in 1870, only attrition could decide the outcome. And the coalition nature of the 1914–18 war likewise prolonged the struggle. As in the world wars of the eighteenth century but unlike 1859, 1866, and 1870–71, the belligerents of 1914–18 had great-power allies. When the weak faltered, their allies usually sustained them. And although Russia indeed collapsed in 1917, the United States simultaneously intervened to shore up a flagging France and Britain with money, food, munitions, and troops.

The keys to victory in this world struggle were industrial might, geographic position, and access to raw materials. The three Allied powers, Britain, France, and Russia, had in 1913 a total industrial potential a third greater than that of the Central Powers, Germany and Austria-Hungary. But the Central Powers were superior to France and Russia alone and after 1914 probably also to Britain and France combined. The Schlieffen Plan had accomplished one major if unsought objective: it deprived France of a fifth of its wheat, half of its coal, and two-thirds of its iron production. Only U.S. intervention in 1917 gave the Allies the better than two-to-one margin in total industrial power that brought victory.

In geographic position, the Central Powers enjoyed one decided advantage and one serious but not insuperable drawback. The advantage was the obverse of Germany's two-front predicament; German possession of "interior lines" allowed swift transfer of forces from west to east to meet successive threats. Given the stalemate at the tactical level, that was no small advantage. The Allies, conversely, were unable to link their major source of manpower, Russia, with the weapons and ammunition produced in the West.

But "encirclement" also had a major disadvantage for the Central Powers: it cut them off from the world market. Shortages of vital materials such as nitrates, rubber, and copper developed immediately. The Germans at first coped. Holland and Scandinavia served as transshipment points for German imports and exports. A German Jewish research chemist, Fritz Haber, broke the nitrate bottleneck with his nitrogen fixation process, perfected in 1913: the inexhaustible nitrogen of the atmosphere gave Germany the explosives it needed to continue the war.

In the long run, Germany suffered. Command of the sea allowed Britain and France to draw on munitions made in the United States and on loans with which to pay for those munitions. The United States, at least at first, would have gladly done business with the Germans as well. But German shipping remained locked in the Baltic and North Sea. And Britain slowly overcame U.S. resistance to "rationing" neutrals near Germany to their pre-war levels of imports. The loss of overseas food and fertilizer imports, the forced slaughter of livestock to save fodder, and farm labor shortages crippled German agriculture. First potatoes and then turnips became the staple of the German diet. The blockade failed to paralyze German industrial production, but it did slowly sap civilian morale through hunger.

On balance, the Germans had the advantage until 1918. German possession of northern France deprived the Allies of key assets and forced them to take the offensive. Under prevailing tactical conditions and given the dogged ineptitude of most Allied generals, that meant immense slaughter for no gain. Geography isolated Russia and political and industrial weakness made it increasingly vulnerable. Finally, the quality of German leadership at the tactical and operational levels compensated for the Central Powers' two-to-three disadvantage in total potential against the Triple Entente. Germany, by 1917, had virtually won the war it had started. It went under only because it started another war with another continent, the United States.

POLITICS, SOCIETY, AND THE "HOME FRONT"

All powers, except perhaps Italy or Rumania, entered the war with the certainty—in some cases spurious—that they were victims of unprovoked aggression. That conviction—and the sense of sudden release from the cares, frustrations, and social tensions of Europe's rapidly changing yet narrowly class-bound societies—brought widespread rejoicing. Everywhere, especially in the cities, reservists marched to the stations through crowds waving flags and pelting them with flowers. As the trains rolled, the troops chalked "To Paris!" or "To Berlin!" on the boxcars. They expected to be home before the autumn leaves fell.

Those who lived through the August days never forgot the spontaneous outpouring of a national enthusiasm that momentarily abolished social distinctions. Bethmann Hollweg's assistant, Riezler, noted with wonder on August 14: "War, war, the *Volk* has risen! . . . All deeply joyful, to live, for once, caught up in a great cause." And a recent immigrant to Munich from Austria-Hungary, a certain Adolf Hitler, later wrote in his memoirs that "overpowered by stormy enthusiasm, I fell down on my knees and thanked Heaven from an overflowing heart for granting me the good fortune of being permitted to live at this time." Then as later, he expressed a widespread emotion.

That emotion everywhere guaranteed national cohesion across class and party lines. The socialist Second International collapsed amid the mutual recriminations of its members. In Germany, the government declared a political truce, the *Burgfrieden* ("peace inside the fortress"). Even revolutionary Social Democrats, at the request of the SPD leadership, voted for the first war appropriations. Good Marxists could not refuse a seemingly defensive war against tsarist Russia, the European state Marx had hated above all others. But Germany's unity was short-lived.

For the Reich, despite its public protestations, fought to create an immense central European empire as the basis for German world mastery. In September, as the German armies began their retreat from the Marne, Bethmann Hollweg drafted a confidential memorandum setting forth Germany's aims: annexations in France and Belgium that would reduce them to vassalage, the absorption of Luxembourg, and the creation of a central European customs union that would guarantee Germany's economic as well as military supremacy on the continent. German war aims in eastern Europe did not take concrete shape until 1915, but they were even more voracious. And the leaders of the Reich looked beyond Europe to vast African annexations and to a victory that would give Britain's world position to Germany. The war, as Riezler noted in his diary in mid-1916, was in part a "struggle with England for world mastery."

Public discussion of Germany's aims, despite the attempts of Bethmann Hollweg to still it, increasingly broke into the open. By 1915 politicians, business figures, and pan-Germans were vying with one another to claim ever-larger areas of Europe and ever-tighter control over the small states, Germany's vassals-to-be. Racist pan-Germans urged the removal of inconvenient Poles from the annexed lands. Much of the Left soon concluded that the war was a war of conquest. The Right coupled demands for total victory and immense annexations with total refusal to reform the unequal Prussian franchise. Germany's lack of cohesion at home was its weak point. But only military defeat could transmute weakness into collapse.

In France, all political forces joined a *Union Sacrée* against the German invader. In Britain, German aggression against Belgium utterly discredited the Cobdenite pacifist Liberals. Volunteers swamped the British army. In Austria-Hungary, quarreling nationalities loyally answered the call to the Habsburg colors. Even the Russian autocracy gained a brief reprieve: the pre-war strike wave subsided and the peasant reservists marched. Only Italy, which chose intervention in 1915 without disguising it as national defense, faced from the beginning an internal struggle against those who failed to see the necessity of war.

Parliamentary regimes showed greater staying power than their autocratic counterparts. Warfare in the age of the masses required popular support and only political participation reliably guaranteed that support. That was one secret of France's survival, despite the death or wounding of 60 percent of all Frenchmen who reported for duty between 1914 and 1918. Britain, with amazing unanimity, abolished cherished traditions of *laissez-faire*. When

volunteers began to fall short in 1916, the British cabinet took the radical step of conscription. Conversely, once the war turned sour in 1915–16, internal social and national tensions placed Austria-Hungary, Russia, Italy, and even Germany at risk.

Parliamentary regimes also proved surprisingly successful at directing their war efforts. At first the soldiers dominated in Britain, France, and Italy, thanks to their allegedly esoteric professional wisdom. But much of that wisdom proved wrong. When the generals failed to force a decision, the civilians took a hand. In December 1916 the feeble—or too humane—Asquith gave way to a Liberal-Conservative-Labour coalition under Lloyd George, a man known to have "fire in his belly." Lloyd George reasserted, not always successfully, London's control over Britain's intractable commander on the western front, Sir Douglas Haig. The French Chamber made Joffre a figurehead in December 1916. The national emergency of 1917 made the cynical and iron-willed Clemenceau, "the Tiger" of the Radicals, prime minister and virtual dictator by consent of the Chamber and the nation. Vittorio Emanuele Orlando, a less compelling figure, assumed some of the

Britain recruits a mass army, 1915: the appeal, and the result (below).

same powers in Italy's dark winter of 1917–18.

The autocracies took two paths. In Russia and Austria-Hungary, the monarchies held jealously to power, while inefficiency and defeat sapped their store of prestige and public trust. The essential question on the eastern front until 1917 was which of the two great empires would win the race to military collapse and political disintegration. Germany traveled another road. The Kaiser's blood-curdling asides and blustering orders of the day imperfectly concealed his indecision and proneness to nervous collapse. By 1916 he had become a figurehead. In his place Germany received a military rather than a parliamentary dictatorship.

Socially, the war marked the real beginning of the "century of the common man." Until 1914 aristocrats and landowners had dominated the bureaucracies, diplomatic services, and officer corps of Europe. The war did not end that domination everywhere, but it made a mighty start. The military aristocracies paid in blood for their privileges. Pomeranian Junkers, Ulster landowners, Russian nobles, Hungarian gentry, and the impoverished aristocracy of France led their peasant soldiers from in front, and suffered accordingly. Noble families that lacked daughters died out, their sons fallen on the Marne, in Galicia, or in the great 1915–16 battles of attrition in the West. By 1916 the professional officers of 1914 were mostly dead. Those who survived graduated gratefully to staff jobs and higher commands.

The middle classes took their place as company and battalion officers. The lower middle classes, which in peacetime had rarely aspired to ranks higher than sergeant, suddenly became lieutenants. These "temporary gentlemen" suffered the sneers of the officers' mess at their accents and demeanor. The Germans created a special indeterminate rank of "officer substitute" to avoid giving deserving sergeants commissions. But the new men proved themselves in battle. The Great War,

along with death and bereavement, brought social promotion to an entire class. That sudden increase in social mobility, along with the classless society of shared danger at the front, was the origin of powerful myths. Finally, the war integrated the peasantry into the nations of the middle and upper classes far more than universal schooling or even peacetime military service had done. Enforced travel, mixing with men from different regions and backgrounds, and above all the experience of fighting together for the national cause made Pomeranian, Swabian, or Bavarian peasants into Germans and made Bretons, Normans, or Gascons into Frenchmen.

At home, industrial mass warfare dictated a new sort of labor force. With men at the front, women and unskilled adolescents joined the work force in numbers not seen since the early industrial revolution in Britain. Almost a quarter of the workers in France's war industries were women, as were 60 percent of the workers in Britain's munitions plants. British craft unions fought jealously against this "dilution" of the work force, but lost. War work expanded women's horizons and gave them a new sense of confidence and competence.

Industrial mass warfare also dictated an unprecedented intensity and extent of state action. The autocracies already had strong traditions of "state capitalism." The democracies mobilized their economies with similar and often more drastic methods: a bewildering variety of war-production and raw-materials allocation boards and bureaucracies, and close coordination between the state, the labor unions, and the military. The wartime industrial state incarnated Weber's "iron cage" of bureaucracy and furnished the model for the welfare state of the later twentieth century.

Finally, mass warfare dictated the mobilization of mass opinion. German propaganda damned the barbaric British "hunger blockade" and stressed the German world cultural mission that overrode the rights of "parasitic" small nations such as Belgium. British, French, and (after 1917) U.S. propaganda dwelt on "Hun" barbarism: poison gas and Zeppelin or submarine warfare against noncombatants and neutrals. Opinion was as powerful as high explosive, and both sides sought to exploit it to the full.

ATTRITION, 1915–16

In 1915 the belligerents made a series of confused attempts to break the unexpected deadlock. The Germans were most successful. In the West Falkenhayn stood on the defensive. He remained so until 1916, except for a brief experiment of Fritz Haber's with chlorine gas near Ypres in April 1915. The German command failed to mass reserves to exploit the unexpected gap the gas opened in the Franco-British lines. Introduction of this new and apparently barbaric weapon profited the Germans nothing and mightily helped the Allies in the battle for neutral opinion.

For most of the year, Britain and France attacked. Their strategic goal was to drive Germany out of France and win the war; that dictated the offensive. But their generals had no better method for restoring movement to the battlefield than ever heavier weights of high explosive shell to blast the German wire flat and silence the machine guns. At Neuve Chappelle, and Loos, and in the repeated French "pushes" in Artois and Champagne, the Allies suffered repeated bloody reverses and gained virtually no ground. The Germans became ever cannier at sheltering their troops in dugouts and in positioning reserves and artillery in depth. In 1915 the French lost 1,500,000 dead and wounded, Britain 300,000, and the German defenders perhaps 875,000.

In eastern Europe, Generals August von Mackensen and Hans von Seeckt broke through the Russian front in Galicia. By September 1915 they had sent

the tsar's armies reeling back 300 miles with a loss of 1.7 million dead, wounded, and captured. Yet Falkenhayn did not believe that the eastern front offered a chance of decisive victory. He declined to press on, although the immense defeat of 1915 had opened wide the political fractures within Russia that the German declaration of war had temporarily closed in 1914. The Germans, totally discarding what little remained of European traditions of monarchical and elite solidarity, attempted to widen those fractures by covert action. SPD leaders with ties to their Russian counterparts funneled large sums into Russia to foment disorder. And in the Middle East, German agents based in Turkey sought with some success to raise Islam against the Allies.

Far to the southeast, new fronts opened. Britain, thanks to the impulsive genius for war of the young Winston Churchill at the Admiralty, attempted to seize Constantinople and open a year-round warm-water supply route to Russia. The muddled British high command proved unequal to the task of coordinating a simultaneous land and sea assault. The British navy, using expendable pre-Dreadnought battleships, failed to force the shore batteries and mines defending the Dardanelles in February–March 1915. The

Gas! British troops blinded by mustard gas (1918).

Between the Turks and the sea: Gallipoli, 1915.

Turks ran out of ammunition just as the admiral in charge pulled back. Then it was the turn of the army. British and Australian landings on the Gallipoli Peninsula in April soon bogged down; the Turks proved unexpectedly dogged and skillful. The only British success was the brilliantly planned and coordinated evacuation of the failed beachheads by January 1916; France and Britain retained a toe-hold at Salonika in Greece.

The Gallipoli landings, before British bungling became apparent, impelled the least of the great powers to take a hand. In October 1914 Salandra, Italy's prime minister, had incautiously announced that henceforth "holy national egoism"—*sacro egoismo*—would guide Italy's course. In winter–spring 1914–15 he proved as good as his word. Salandra and his foreign minister, Sidney Sonnino, secretly auctioned Italy to the two groups of powers. The Allied bid was inevitably higher: Trento, Trieste, and Dalmatia (where Italian-speakers were a tiny minority) from Austria-Hungary, a piece of Turkey, and unspecified colonial gains. On May 24, 1915, Salandra, Sonnino, and King Victor Emmanuel III took Italy to

war against the will of parliament. Italy's armies crossed the Austro-Hungarian border and ran headlong into long-prepared defenses on the Isonzo River. There the Italians stalled, despite repeated bloody offensives.

And in fall and winter 1915 the Germans confirmed the verdict of Gallipoli. Bulgaria joined the central powers after an auction similar to that in Rome. German, Austro-Hungarian, and Bulgarian armies attacked Serbia from three sides. By enticing Bulgaria into the war and by smashing Serbia, Germany had secured its communications through the Balkans to Turkey. Russia would receive no Allied aid through the Straits. Only the icy sea route to Murmansk and Archangel and the single track of the Trans-Siberian Railway linked Russia to the West.

Yet by December 1915 Falkenhayn was understandably not satisfied. Germany's immense losses had brought it no closer to its goal: a strategic decision over one of its three adversaries. In his 1915 "Christmas Memorandum," Falkenhayn concluded that Britain was the keystone of the enemy alliance. To strike it required the intensification of submarine warfare against merchant shipping, which the Germans had introduced in February 1915, and of terror attacks on British civilian targets with Zeppelin airships.

Falkenhayn identified French morale as Germany's second, and most promising, objective. Its collapse would "strike England's best sword from her hand." The method he chose was attrition, and he sought an objective "for the retention of which the French leadership will commit their last man. If they do this, France's strength will be bled white, since once committed to such a course there is no alternative for them, whether we reach the objective itself or not." Limited German infantry attacks would pin the French defenders under a giant mincing machine: the German artillery. Falkenhayn baptized his brainchild Operation GERICHT—"execution place."

1916: Verdun and the Somme

On February 21, 1916, the army of the German Crown Prince attacked the objective Falkenhayn had selected, the fortified city of Verdun at the hinge of the French line. German guns that eventually numbered over 2,200 tore the French to pieces with the heaviest artillery fire so far seen. As the French cracked, Joffre appointed Henri Pétain, a master of the defensive, to command Verdun. "Courage! We'll get them!" was his watchword. In the course of the next eight months, over three quarters of the French army passed down the muddy truck route to Verdun and emerged shattered.

Yet France held. By May 1916, despite German innovations such as flamethrowers, phosgene gas shells, and masses of fighter aircraft, Falkenhayn was caught fast in the snare he had rigged for the French. The Germans had themselves invested so much prestige, morale, and blood at Verdun that they had to take the city. The French fought them to a standstill by July, then counterattacked in October, November, and December to regain the lost ground. Verdun cost the French 377,000 dead, wounded, and missing and the Germans at least 337,000. Neither army, but especially that of France, was ever the same again.

The agony of France had repercussions. As in 1914, Russia sought to help its ally. Russia's most noteworthy commander, Alexei Brusilov, launched a major offensive in the Ukraine in June. Shortage of ammunition dictated a short bombardment, and Brusilov spread his preparations over a broad front to preserve surprise. Austria-Hungary's eastern armies collapsed; the Russians took 200,000 prisoners. Conrad von Hötzendorff had to break off a promising "punitive expedition" against his favored victim, Italy. Falkenhayn loosened his grip at Verdun and sent divisions eastward to prop up Austria-Hungary.

Then, on July 1, 1916, Sir Douglas Haig attacked on either side of the Somme River. On a day of "intense blue summer beauty," after a seven-day bombardment of unprecedented weight, the infantrymen of Britain's volunteer "New Armies" climbed from their trenches. Loaded with a minimum of 66 pounds of gear per man, aligned in rigid formations, they walked toward the German wire, which in most areas the British artillery had failed to cut. As the British bombardment lifted, German machine-gunners scrambled unhurt from their deep concrete-lined dugouts and massacred the British infantry. German artillery observers had never before seen such tempting targets. The French, further south, advanced in small groups,

Pétain of Verdun.

Verdun 1916:
The Return from the Front

I have never seen anything more heart-rending than the passage of the two regiments of the brigade that flowed past me on that road [from Verdun] the whole day long. . . .

First came skeletons of companies, sometimes with a surviving officer in front, propping himself up with a cane; all walked or rather moved with short steps, bent knees forward, folded into themselves, staggering as if gripped by drink. Then came groups that were perhaps squads, or even platoons; there was no telling. They advanced, head down, staring blankly, crushed under their rucksacks, holding by the slings rifles red with mud. The color of their faces scarcely differed from that of their overcoats. Mud had covered everything and dried, then more mud had covered them once more. . . . Cars thundered past in close-packed columns, scattering this pitiable flotsam, survivors of the great slaughter. But [the troops] said nothing, made no sound. They had lost even the strength to complain. . . .

Some reservists, from the roadside, looked on somberly. . . . I heard one saying: "It's not an army; it's corpses!". . . . Two of the reservists cried silently, like women.

From Georges Gaudy, *Les trous d'obus de Verdun (février-août 1916)* (Paris: Plon, 1922), pp. 233–34 (translation by M. Knox).

taking cover wherever possible. They did rather better.

Haig's army lost 57,470 dead and wounded—nearly half the men engaged—on the first day. But Haig, "brilliant to the top of his army boots" (as Lloyd George later put it) remained convinced that German losses were so severe that the enemy was bound to crack. Using the same unimaginative tactics, he persevered until the battlefield became a sea of icy mud in November. The maximum British penetration was less than 6 miles. British losses were 419,000, those of the French, over 200,000. The German defenders lost over half a million.

As Brusilov's push petered out and the British pressed on the Somme, a sudden emergency provoked Falkenhayn's downfall. Rumania, like Italy, had been associated with the Triple Alliance; it had likewise chosen neutrality in 1914. Now, in August 1916, Brusilov's success inspired the Rumanians to join the Allies. Their timing was remarkably poor. The Kaiser dismissed Falkenhayn as chief of staff but gave

him Rumania as consolation prize. Falkenhayn, Mackensen, and Seeckt rolled up the inept Rumanians within four months.

At German supreme army headquarters, a new team took control—Hindenburg and Ludendorff. Hindenburg, the "wooden Titan," was content to be a symbol of national resistance. Ludendorff, the dominant partner, brought a new ethos to the supreme command, the ethos of the pan-German "right opposition." He despised the Kaiser as a weakling. His devious aide, Colonel Max Bauer, cultivated pan-Germans and right radicals. Domestically, Ludendorff and Bauer soon erected a virtual dictatorship over the war economy and increasingly over the civilian political leaders. The Kaiser feared his nominal subordinates; Hindenburg and Ludendorff alone commanded the confidence of the masses. Once he had appointed them, the Kaiser could only remove them at the risk of his throne.

The new team had two principal recipes for victory. First, total war demanded total mobilization. Under the "Hindenburg Program," Germany planned to double its production of shells and treble that of artillery and machine guns. The army, with the assistance of the SPD unions and of the industrialists, applied compulsory service to the work force. Substitute—*ersatz*—materials would make up for shortages. Germany, by a supreme effort of will, would submerge its opponents in fire and steel. The new team's second major innovation was to stake Germany's future on one card, in the manner of Schlieffen. The card they chose was the submarine.

THE WAR IN THE BALANCE, 1917

Germany Challenges America

The U-boat question had been long in ripening. Tirpitz soon realized that the distant blockade had neutralized his

British troops fix bayonets before going "over the top" on the Somme, 1916.

battle fleet. He therefore pressed for the use of submarines, which he had scandalously neglected before 1914, against British merchant shipping. But submarines were only effective if used from ambush. Attempts to board and search merchant ships before sinking them, as international law required, might expose the surfaced submarine to deadly fire from camouflaged guns on the merchant ship. The Germans therefore adopted in February 1915 a policy of "sink on sight" around the British isles. On May 7, 1915, Germany's U-20 sank the British liner *Lusitania* off the southern tip of Ireland and killed 1,198 people, of whom 128 were U.S. civilians. The Germans struck a medal to commemorate their feat of arms.

President Woodrow Wilson, a dour ex-academic of messianic bent, had no intention of leading the United States into war. Unlike his rival, "Teddy" Roosevelt of the Rough Riders, Wilson took pride in being "too proud to fight." He was soon to run for reelection in 1916 on the slogan "He kept us out of the war." But the *Lusitania* outrage prompted even Wilson to bombard Berlin with stern summonses to obey international law.

U.S. opinion had long been suspicious of Imperial Germany. Germany's treatment of Belgium and first use of poison gas had appalled it. The *Lusitania* sinking swung it heavily against the Central Powers. Bethmann Hollweg persuaded the Kaiser and the navy to retreat and postpone confrontation. Then Falkenhayn, in his "Christmas Memorandum," urged the renewal of unrestricted U-boat warfare. In February 1916, the Germans synchronized "intensified" submarine warfare around Britain with their attack at Verdun. The inevitable sinking involving U.S. citizens followed in March, and Wilson's typewriter clattered threateningly once more. The Germans again retreated. Bethmann Hollweg, at least, was now aware that further sinkings might goad Wilson into "a sort of crusade against Germany."

The German navy tried to make do with surface action. On May 31, 1916, Admiral Reinhard Scheer took the German High Seas Fleet out. But the British had intercepted Scheer's radio messages, and Admiral John Jellicoe's Grand Fleet was waiting off Jutland. Tirpitz's Dreadnoughts and their British rivals faced one another for less than 30 minutes, until the outnumbered Scheer frantically turned away into clouds and smoke and ran for Wilhelmshaven. The Germans lost fewer ships, and claimed victory. But the British were the strategic victors, for they still controlled the exits from the North Sea. And the Germans concluded from their narrow escape that surface action offered no means of breaking the blockade.

Thus when Hindenburg and Ludendorff arrived on the scene in August 1916, they found the navy once more pressing for a decision to unleash the submarines. Tirpitz had resigned over the issue in March and had raised a fanatical public outcry for U-boat war. To buy time and to preempt a mediation attempt by Wilson, Bethmann Hollweg launched a Central Powers "peace offer" in mid-December 1916. The offer failed to mention the restoration of Belgium, and was thus unacceptable to the Allies. Its inevitable re-

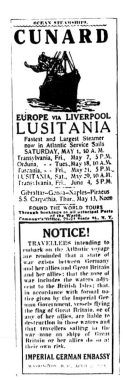

U-boat warfare: Germany warns neutral travelers that it will sink the *Lusitania* if it can. U-boats at sea in the Mediterranean (below).

jection, Bethmann Hollweg apparently hoped, might turn Wilson's wrath on Paris and London, and give Germany a convincing pretext for launching unrestricted submarine warfare.

At the Castle of Pless in Silesia, on January 9, 1917, the Germans took the decision that doomed them. The navy sang its usual tune: U-boats would bring Britain "to its knees" in a few months. Hindenburg and Ludendorff argued fiercely for action, regardless of consequences. They made the same error with the United States that Moltke had made with Britain in 1914. Because their prospective enemy had no mass army, they assumed that it was safe to defy it. Germany's U-boats received orders to sink all shipping around Britain after midnight on January 31, 1917. Wilson broke relations with Germany but still hoped to keep the United States neutral in order to mediate a "peace without victory."

But by 1917 the powers had invested too much blood and money to settle for peace short of victory or defeat. Nor, thanks to the Germans, did U.S. neutrality remain tenable. The Reich foreign secretary, Arthur Zimmermann, soon proved that the stresses of total war had caused Berlin to take leave of its senses. Using the telegraph channel that Wilson had thoughtfully provided the Germans for possible peace negotiations, he cabled the German ambassador in Mexico City. The ciphered message offered the Mexicans a war alliance and the recovery of Texas and the Southwest. The British intercepted it, deciphered it, and delivered it to Wilson along with proofs of its authenticity. It arrived at the end of February, along with news that a U-boat had sunk the British liner *Laconia* with the death of three Americans, two of them women.

Wilson gave the Zimmermann telegram to the press on March 1. Zimmermann compounded his amazing blunder by admitting that the telegram was genuine. Even voices of the isolationist Midwest such as the Chicago *Tribune* and the Cleveland *Plain Dealer* accepted war. A Germany that incited Mexico to attack the United States was intolerable. On April 2, Wilson, to repeated applause, addressed Congress: "The world must be made safe for democracy." The United States declared war on Imperial Germany. The New World was coming, somewhat belatedly, to restore the balance of the old.

The Russian Revolutions: February and October

While Wilson debated his course, events in eastern Europe disclosed the full magnitude of Germany's blunder in provoking the United States. Russia ceased to count as a belligerent, and Germany faced only a weakening

---

The Zimmermann Telegram   January 19, 1917

[To German Ambassador, Mexico City]
Top Secret—Decipher Personally

We intend on 1 February to begin unrestricted U-boat warfare. We shall nevertheless attempt to keep America neutral. Should that not succeed, we propose to Mexico an alliance on the following basis. Joint conduct of the war. Joint peace settlement. Lavish financial support and agreement on our part that Mexico should reconquer its lost territories in Texas, New Mexico, and Arizona. We leave settlement of the details to your Excellency.

Your Excellency should disclose the above offer in the greatest secrecy to the President [of Mexico, Don Venustiano Carranza] as soon as outbreak of war with the United States seems certain, and add the suggestion that he should on his own initiative invite Japan to join the alliance, and [that he should] simultaneously mediate between Japan and ourselves.

Please call to the President's attention the fact that merciless use of our U-boats now offers the prospect of forcing England to make peace within a few months.

Acknowledge receipt.

Zimmermann

From Herbert Michaelis, Ernst Schraepler, eds., *Ursachen und Folgen vom deutschen Zusammenbruch 1918 und 1945* (Berlin: Dokumenten-Verlag Dr. Herbert Wendler, 1958), Vol. 1, pp. 151–52 (translation by M. Knox).

France and Britain. In 1916 munitions strikes paralyzed industry in Moscow and Petrograd (the new, non-German name given to St. Petersburg in 1914). Russia's railroads broke down. Refugees and wounded swamped tsarism's decrepit administrative machinery. Food ran short in the cities; conscription and government purchases of food at artificially low fixed prices alienated the peasantry. The ultimate failure of the Brusilov offensive and the antics of the tsarina's favorite, the faith-healing charlatan Grigorii Rasputin, lost the autocracy what little public support it still possessed. Strikes and food riots by workers and housewives in Petrograd challenged the autocracy in early March 1917 (February by the "old style" Julian calendar that symbolized Russia's apartness from Europe). The peasant soldiers deserted the autocracy on March 12; it fell without a struggle.

A provisional government of liberals, Mensheviks, and Socialist Revolutionaries born from the last *Duma* attempted to fill the vacuum the "February Revolution" had left. But in Petrograd the Soviets, or councils of workers, soldiers, and sailors, now controlled the streets. On March 14, 1917, the central Petrograd Soviet addressed to the war-weary world a proclamation that blamed "monarchs, landholders, and bankers" for the war, and demanded an immediate end to the "horrible slaughter." Similar appeals in 1915 and 1916 from the wrangling representatives of the parties of the Second International had lacked resonance. The call of the Petrograd Soviet was different: it came from a body with power. And its claim to world ideological leadership conflicted with the call for "war to end war" that Wilson was soon to issue from Washington.

Soon after the Petrograd Soviet's peace message, the Germans made a further contribution to the disruption of Russia. They shipped Lenin and a few chosen Bolsheviks home to Russia from their place of exile in neutral Switzerland in a sealed boxcar ("like a plague bacillus," as Winston Churchill later observed). Lenin arrived at Petrograd's Finland Station on April 16, 1917, and dictated to his small and hitherto confused party a few simple policies: support of the Soviets, implacable hostility to the provisional government, and an immediate end to the war.

In June 1917, Lenin launched a slogan of vast appeal to the peasantry that made up 80 percent of Russia's population and to the overwhelming majority of Russia's 7 million troops: "Bread, Peace, Land." His aim was as simple as his slogan. He proposed to seize power and hurl backward Russia directly into socialism. Revolutionary breakthrough in Russia would then trigger the revolution in western Europe without which a socialist Russia, isolated, would inevitably perish.

The provisional government was divided and inexperienced, thanks to the stifling effect the autocracy had had on Russian political life. The new government shared power uneasily with the Petrograd Soviet while seeking to continue the war against Germany. The government's most conspicuous personality, the Socialist Revolutionary Alexander Kerensky, identified himself with a final bungled offensive in July 1917. Bolshevik appeals spread through the army and undermined what little discipline remained. Peasants, weary of war and obsessed with the notion that revolution meant the long-awaited final redivision of the *mir* land (see p. 793), "voted with their feet." Many went home; those that stayed demanded an end to the fighting.

A spontaneous Petrograd quasi-insurrection against the provisional government in July showed that the Bolsheviks were gaining ground. In their unyielding utopian radicalism they proved better attuned to the mood in the cities than their more responsible or faint-hearted opponents. Kerensky arrested some Bolsheviks but lacked the ruthlessness or perhaps the power to suppress them outright. Then, in August, General Lavr Kornilov, Keren-

"The Russian Ruling House": a contemporary cartoon of Rasputin manipulating Tsar Nicholas II and Tsarina Alexandra.

The new master: Lenin in Moscow, 1917.

sky's commander in chief, marched on Petrograd to restore order. Workers and mutinous troops from the capital persuaded Kornilov's forces to defect.

Kornilov's failed coup from the Right further weakened Kerensky and his allies. Mensheviks and Socialist Revolutionaries, by their association with the Provisional Government and the continuing war, forfeited much of the popular support they had enjoyed in Petrograd in the spring. The Bolsheviks painted the disintegrating provisional government and its parties as Kornilov's accomplices; Bolshevik numbers swelled.

On November 6–7 (October 24–25 by the Russian calendar), Lenin and his dashing ex-Menshevik associate, Leon Trotsky, launched their own coup from the Left. The Military Revolutionary Committee of the Petrograd Soviet, of which Trotsky had gained control, seized key points with picked troops. On the evening of November 7 (October 25), the provisional government's last stronghold, the tsar's Winter Palace, fell. Kerensky fled. The Bolsheviks had acted in the name of the Soviets against the provisional government. The Bolsheviks soon infiltrated or cowed the Soviets while taking for themselves the mantle of legitimacy

The Logic of the Red Terror   1918

M. Y. Latsis, the terrifying Latvian who was Dzerzhinsky's chief subordinate at the CHEKA, spelled out in a 1918 newspaper article the logic under which his organization acted.

We are not carrying out war against individuals. We are exterminating the bourgeoisie as a class. We aren't looking for evidence or witnesses to reveal deeds or words against the Soviet power. The first question which we ask is—to what class does he belong, what are his origins, upbringing, education, or profession? These questions define the fate of the accused. This is the essence of Red Terror.

Quoted in Harrison Salisbury, *Black Night, White Snow: Russia's Revolutions, 1905–1917* (Garden City: Doubleday, 1978), p. 565.

that the Soviets provided. And in January 1918 Bolshevik bayonets dispersed Russia's first and last democratically elected parliament, the Constituent Assembly.

The Bolsheviks had won less than 25 percent of the seats in the Constituent Assembly. But they had guns and organization, and they briefly commanded a popular majority in Petrograd and Moscow. Above all, they moved swiftly to institutionalize terror. In December 1917 Lenin's security officer, the fanatical Pole Feliks Dzerzhinsky, became chief of a new organization, the "All-Russian Extraordinary Commission for the Struggle Against Counterrevolution and Sabotage," known by its acronym of CHEKA. Its task was to exterminate the enemies of the revolution; their place, in Lenin's words, was "against the wall."

In January 1918 the Socialist Revolutionaries, whose peasant loyalists had given them more votes than any other party, fought back against the dissolution of the Constituent Assembly. They rose against Bolshevik dictatorship— and Lenin and Dzerzhinsky massacred them. In July 1918 the Bolsheviks likewise shot the ex-Tsar Nicholas II and his entire family. By that point Lenin and his CHEKA had discarded the concept of individual responsibility for actions, the basis of Western and even tsarist law. The CHEKA defined its enemies by class, and killed them not as individuals but as members of a category. The bourgeoisie was "objectively"—by its very existence—guilty of counterrevolution. That was a logic not seen in action in the West since the September massacres of 1792 and the Jacobin Terror of 1793–94. It was the logic of genocide.

Terror worked well internally. Externally, Lenin faced an immediate crisis. The German masses did not overthrow their rulers in response to the "Decree on Peace" that Lenin and Trotsky published immediately after the October Revolution. Instead, Russia's peasant armies continued to melt, while the

Germans advanced toward Petrograd. Lenin therefore sought a breathing-space for the Revolution, to give time for the western European and world revolution he unrealistically expected; he had predicted in September 1917, before taking power, that "to secure an armistice means *to conquer the world.*"

He secured that armistice from the Germans in December, and began negotiation at Brest-Litovsk in Poland for a Russo-German peace. But the Bolshevik negotiators soon found that "self-determination," as the Germans interpreted it, meant stripping away the conquests of all tsars since the seventeenth century. The border peoples, from Finland through the Ukraine to the Caucasus, were to become independent under German "protection." When the Bolsheviks balked, the Germans resumed their effortless advance on Petrograd. Lenin then dragooned his wavering comrades into signing; the Revolution had to swallow the German terms if it hoped to survive. On March 3, 1918, the Bolsheviks signed. The treaty of Brest-Litovsk deprived Russia of a quarter of its European territory, a third of its population, over half of its coal and iron, and a third of its industry. But it left the Bolsheviks in power.

The Crisis of the Allies

The collapse of Russia came close to wrecking the Allies. The October Revolution, which took Russia definitively out of the war, followed an unmitigated series of catastrophes. Germany's submarines almost throttled Britain's Atlantic supply line between March and August 1917. Sinkings peaked in April at 881,000 tons. British food stocks, despite rationing, fell to a mere two months' worth. But the German navy soon found that it was unable to sink ships faster than the United States could construct them. Lloyd George stormed into the Admiralty and compelled it to institute convoys, which it had originally despised as a "defensive" and therefore inferior form of war. Mine barriers partially closed the exits from the North Sea even to U-boats. The U.S. Navy, with its eight Dreadnoughts and its indispensable escort craft, reinforced the British.

As the U-boats battered Britain, France faltered. Joffre's replacement, Robert Nivelle, was convinced that he had found the secret of victory: surprise. The discovery was not original. And Ludendorff dislocated Nivelle's offensive of April 1917. In Operation ALBERICH, named after the malevolent dwarf in Wagner's *Ring of the Nibelungen,* Ludendorff withdrew to a new line 12 to 25 miles behind the original front. And the Germans had a further surprise for the French: flexible defensive tactics far superior to the thin and brittle trench lines of 1914–16. The German "defense in depth"—deep belts of strongpoints interlocked by fire, coordinated artillery barrages, and swift and terrifying counterattacks—broke Nivelle's offensive and inflicted 200,000 casualties. The French army had believed in Nivelle; now its morale cracked. From the end of April until June 1917, units mutinied. Some waved red flags; the example of the Petrograd Soviet, with its call for immediate and unconditional peace, was contagious.

Fortunately, German intelligence was characteristically poor. Had Ludendorff known of the mutinies, he could and doubtless would have driven France from the war. Instead, Pétain, who had saved France at Verdun, now had time to save it once more. He suppressed the mutinies with a judicious combination of firing squad and conciliation. He listened to the troops and gave them what they wanted: leaves, better food, and no more offensives. The French army would do its part in defense, but others would have to break Germany.

The mutinies gave Haig what he thought was his opportunity. In the third battle of Ypres, from July to December 1917, Haig threw his troops again and again at the German lines as

Before and after:
Passchendaele, 1917.

heavy artillery and rain churned the soil of Flanders into "a porridge of mud." As in 1916, Haig suffered from the delusion that the Germans were about to crack. The maximum British and Canadian penetration was about 5 miles around the village of Passchendaele; the cost, perhaps 400,000 dead and wounded. By the end of the year British morale was scarcely higher than that of the French.

Finally, far to the south, the Germans showed that they were developing a tactical answer to the riddle of the trenches. On October 24, 1917, after a brief surprise bombardment, an Austro-German army crashed through the Italian defenses on the Isonzo around the village of Caporetto. The Germans moved in small, stealthy groups equipped with light machine guns. Instead of advancing on a broad front and slowing to tidy their flanks, they pushed rapidly through weak points and on into the Italian rear, sowing alarm and despondency. Positions too difficult to take they simply bypassed.

The Italian army crumbled and withdrew almost to Venice. Then, to the surprise of Germans and Austrians, it held on the Piave River even before British and French troops arrived to prop up Italy. Caporetto and the resulting loss of most of Italy east of Venice at last made the unpopular war a war of national defense.

On the home front, 1917 was equally disastrous for the Allies. Commodity shortages and the indiscriminate printing of money to finance the immense war expenditures drove prices steadily upward. Inflation and scarcity gener-

ated popular discontent (although troops on leave found civilian complaints about rationing increasingly tiresome—the civilians were safe from shell fire.) The extreme left of the European socialist parties took up with enthusiasm the slogans of the Petrograd Soviet and of the Bolsheviks. Shortly before Caporetto, a socialist-led revolt convulsed one of Italy's principal industrial centers, Turin. Civilian disturbances and demonstrations accompanied the French mutinies. Agitators at the Paris railway stations incited the troops to desert. Even Britain experienced unrest.

Nevertheless, the outlook was not totally bleak either on the western front, in the Middle East, or in central Europe. In November 1917, at Cambrai, Haig for the first time committed en masse that bizarre British invention, the tank. The British high command had failed to find a tactical answer to the trench deadlock, but a few innovators, among them Winston Churchill, had found a technological one. The combination of the internal combustion engine, caterpillar track, armor, and machine guns or cannon might yet restore mobility to the battlefield. Unfortunately, Haig had squandered surprise by using a few isolated tanks on the Somme in 1916. At Cambrai, the 400 tanks that Haig committed overwhelmed the terrified Germans. But the characteristic British failure to coordinate infantry, artillery, and reserves left the tanks exposed to a German counterattack that regained most of the ground lost.

In the Middle East, Turkey was beginning to crack, despite its victory at

Gallipoli and an appalling series of British blunders in Mesopotamia in 1914–16. Sir Edmund Allenby, perhaps the most imaginative British commander of the war, took Jerusalem in November 1917 after a push northwards from Egypt into Ottoman Palestine. Simultaneously, Britain issued the Balfour Declaration, which appeared to promise "the establishment in Palestine of a national home for the Jewish people." London sought to mobilize Zionist—Jewish nationalist—support in Europe and to create a buffer between the Suez Canal and the postwar sphere allotted to the French in Syria. With the aid of Arab irregulars led by the eccentric T. E. Lawrence (later "Lawrence of Arabia"), Allenby pressed on for Damascus and Constantinople.

Finally, Austria-Hungary too was beginning to crumble. Allied statesmen had already reluctantly dabbled in the subversion of Austria-Hungary as early as 1916. The "old Kaiser," Francis Joseph, who had reigned since 1848 and had become the symbol of the Dual Monarchy, died that November; his death deprived Austria-Hungary of its essential symbol of unity. In 1917 the Petrograd Soviet and the Bolsheviks, among their many slogans, launched that of "self-determination." Wilson took it up, lest the Bolsheviks monopolize it. In his statement of American war aims of January 1918, the famous "Fourteen Points," he demanded "autonomous development" for the peoples of Austria-Hungary and the recreation of the Polish state destroyed in 1795. Self-determination was a powerful political weapon in the hands of the Allies. But it was a weapon of desperation that might well destroy all prospect of postwar order in central and eastern Europe.

As the year 1917 closed, the Allied leaders contemplated their position with alarm. Russia had dissolved. Britain, France, and Italy had each in turn come close to collapse. Germany was victorious in eastern Europe and in Italy. It seemed poised to attack in the

West. The home front was wavering. The "Yanks," Allied propaganda insisted, were coming. Would they come in time?

GERMANY'S LAST THROW, 1918

"Michael"

Ludendorff might have played for time and trusted to Germany's defensive expertise to blunt Allied offensives in 1918. But time appeared to be working against Germany. Since the "turnip winter" of 1916 the British blockade had bitten ever-deeper into German civilian morale and health. Austria-Hungary, Bulgaria, and Turkey were on the verge of collapse. Time would allow the Americans to mobilize a mass army and would fortify the Allies with U.S. food and munitions. Ludendorff also rejected a political solution that the war-weary Allies might have had to accept in the dark winter of 1917–18: German withdrawal from Belgium and northern France in return for a peace that conceded to Germany its immense gains in eastern Europe—and thus the mastery of the Continent.

With defense and negotiation ruled out, the remaining solution was attack. Russia's collapse freed enough German forces to ensure a temporary rough equality in France by March 1918—although Ludendorff's megalomania nevertheless kept a million Germans in eastern Europe to bring in the grain of the Ukraine and seize the oil of the Caucasus. Ludendorff proposed to use the reinforcements and the methods proven in Russia and at Caporetto to "hack a hole" in the western front. The rest, Ludendorff insisted, would "take care of itself." The great German offensive, in the words of a member of his staff, "would not be a battering ram, pounding head-on against a wall, but rather like a flood of water, flowing around obstacles, isolating them, and following the path of least resistance

T. E. Lawrence, greatest of English eccentrics, in Bedouin dress.

March 21, 1918: Germany Attacks

Ernst Jünger, winner of Germany's highest decoration, the *Pour le Mérite*, and of its foremost literary award, the Goethe Prize, led a *Stosstrupp* in the 1918 offensives. His vision of war, set forth in post-war memoirs such as *Storm of Steel*, was very different from the laments over war's futility and waste frequently found in British and French war writing. Here he describes Ludendorff's stunning opening bombardment and the initial German assault.

The minute hand moved closer and closer; we counted off the last minutes. Finally it stood at 0505. The hurricane broke loose.

A fiery curtain rose high in the air, supported by sudden, unceasing upwellings. A raging thunder, into which even the heaviest shell-bursts merged, shook the earth. The gigantic eruption of annihilation from the innumerable [German] cannon [firing overhead from] behind us was so frightful, that the greatest of the battles we had passed through before this seemed like children's games. . . . The enemy artillery remained dumb; it was flattened as if by a single blow from a giant's club. . . .

It had become day. Behind us the immense din still grew. Before us rose an unpierceable wall of smoke, dust and gas. Men ran through the trench and yelled joyfully in one another's ears. Infantry and artillery, combat engineers and field telephone linemen, Prussians and Bavarians, officers and men, all were overmastered and gripped with enthusiasm by this elemental outpouring of our power, and were burning for the assault at 0940. . . .

Even the laws of nature seemed to have lost their validity. The air shimmered as on a hot summer day and its varying density [with the shockwaves] made solid objects seem to dance back and forth. The din had become so absolute that we ceased to hear. . . .

The great moment had come. The barrage rolled across our first line. We attacked. . . . The overpowering desire to kill gave my feet wings. Rage squeezed bitter tears from my eyes. The immense desire to destroy and annihilate that hovered over the battlefield thickened our minds and dipped them as if in a red haze. We called to each other stumbling and stammering disjointed phrases, and an outside observer might perhaps have believed that we were overcome by an excess of joy.

From Ernst Jünger, *In Stahlgewittern* (Berlin: E. S. Mittler, 1941 [1st. ed., 1920]), pp. 253–57 (translation by M. Knox).

deep into the enemy's territory." Throughout the winter the German staffs pulled divisions out of the line, formed assault battalions (*Stosstruppen*), trained them in the new "infiltration" tactics, and rested them for a last supreme effort. Ludendorff knew the risks. When a politician asked him what would happen if he failed, he was frank: "Then Germany is finished."

The German leadership's irreducible objective of dominating Europe, the German style of all-or-nothing gambles, and the immense expectations that victory over Russia had aroused in the German public all dictated action. No political check on Ludendorff existed. In January 1917 Bethmann Hollweg had given up his small remaining authority by acquiescing in unrestricted submarine warfare. In July 1917 Hindenburg and Ludendorff forced Bethmann Hollweg's resignation by threatening their own. The intimidated Kaiser appointed an unknown bureaucrat as Chancellor. Tirpitz organized the political underpinnings of the Hindenburg-Ludendorff dictatorship. On Sedan Day, September 2, 1917, a "Fatherland Party" (*Vaterlandspartei*) emerged, proclaiming pitiless war until final victory over both Allies and SPD, and massive annexations in east and west to secure that victory for all time. Germany's mission, Tirpitz announced, was to lead Europe against the "all-devouring tyranny of Anglo-Americanism." The *Vaterlandspartei* soon had more members than the SPD. It was the first—but not the last—fanatical mass party of German nationalism. Its spirit momentarily galvanized the home front in the expectation of final victory.

On March 21, 1918, the first of Ludendorff's offensives, baptized MICHAEL, struck the British line between St. Quentin and La Fère. The British defenders massed in their forward trenches and German high explosive and gas shells massacred them. Haig had failed to learn from the German defense in depth that had cost the Allies so dear in 1917. Then the new German infantry tactics—attack in depth—tore a hole in the British 30 miles deep. It was the greatest gain on the western front by either side since 1914. The French prepared to withdraw to defend Paris.

But the British ultimately held. Ludendorff broke his own rule of always bypassing resistance, and shattered his reserves against the stubborn British defense of Arras. In April a second German offensive in Flanders took back the gains Britain had achieved at heartbreaking cost in the 1917 Passchendaele offensive. A third attack, in May–June 1918, drove the French back to the Marne and came within 40 miles of Paris. Each time, Ludendorff achieved operational freedom but failed to translate it into a strategic victory that would force the Allies to make peace before the Americans came.

The Yanks arrive: General John J. ("Black Jack") Pershing (right) meets Haig.

The Yanks Arrive

And on the Marne, U.S. Army and Marine Corps units joined the French in counterattacks at Belleau Wood and Château-Thierry. The Americans lacked experience. But they were willing to die in a manner not seen since 1914–16, the manner of Langemarck and the Somme. That spirit, and American numbers and weight of artillery terrified the Germans even as they shot the Americans down in droves.

Ludendorff's fourth and fifth offensives failed miserably, at great cost. The American counterattacks helped divert German reserves from the fourth, in early June, and the French dislocated the fifth with a tactical withdrawal of the sort that had crushed Nivelle in 1917. Ludendorff had bled the German army to death. In March his forces in the West had numbered 3,800,000. By July they had suffered 2,000,000 casualties; the cream of the German army was dead or wounded. German troops shipped in from Russia as replacements began to vote with their feet and jump from the slow-moving troop trains before they reached the western front. Yet in the face of hunger, desertion, demoralization, and defeat, Ludendorff still refused to allow negotiations with the Allies.

In July, August, and September, the Allies began to counterattack in a series of carefully limited operations. An inter-Allied high command under the hard-driving Marshal Ferdinand Foch of France at last began to coordinate Allied actions effectively. Allied infantry, often with tank support, would break into the German lines until German reserves arrived and resistance stiffened. Then the Allies would shift the battle to another sector.

These attacks slowly nibbled away the German gains of the spring and further demoralized the Germans. On August 8, the "black day of the German army," German units surrendered whole for the first time to British tanks and infantry. In September, Haig, at last using intelligent tactics, broke through the strongest German defenses in the West, the "Hindenburg Line." By now the U.S. Army in France was 1,500,000 strong and under its own commander, John "Black Jack" Pershing. It pinched out the St. Mihiel salient east of Verdun and prepared for a massive drive into Lorraine to roll up the German front and meet the British in central Belgium.

At the end of September, Ludendorff's fears about Germany's allies at last proved correct. The Franco-British army at Salonika broke the Bulgarians and drove north through the Balkans, threatening Austria-Hungary and Germany's southern border. Ludendorff panicked and demanded the appointment of a German civilian government to take the blame for defeat. He insisted that Germany seek an armistice from Wilson before total collapse ensued. The Fourteen Points, Ludendorff slyly assumed, would allow Germany to keep at least some of its gains. Pershing foresaw that the Germans would deny they had lost, unless the Allies dictated peace at Potsdam. Wilson, less prescient, entered negotiations in October.

Then events took command. Italy attacked on October 24 and reached Trieste by November 3. Austria-Hungary collapsed into a chaotic mass of seething nationalities, each attempting to carve out its own state. The German naval command, knowing the war was lost and hoping to create a suitably Wagnerian legend for the future, attempted to send the High Seas Fleet on a death ride down the English Channel. The sailors understandably mutinied and seized Kiel naval base. Revolution spread to Munich and Berlin. The SPD leaders in Berlin proclaimed a German Republic on November 9; the Kaiser abdicated and fled ignominiously to Holland. And the Allies, under pressure from Wilson and from their own war-weary public opinion, conceded the Germans an armistice while Germany still occupied most of Belgium and some French territory.

On the "eleventh hour of the eleventh day of the eleventh month" of 1918, silence at last descended on the western front. As the armistice terms commanded, the Germans withdrew to the Rhine, demobilized, and sailed their fleet to Scapa Flow. The war had cost at least 20 million lives. Germany suffered 2 million military dead, Russia 1.7 million, France 1.3 million, Austria-Hungary 1.1 million, Britain and its empire 750,000 and 250,000 respectively, Italy about 500,000, Turkey somewhat less, and the United States 114,000. Civilian casualties included 100,000 killed by U-boats and air raids, 30,000 Belgians killed by German forced labor, reprisals, or artillery fire, and at least 1.5 million Armenians whom the Turks had massacred in 1915. A further 20 million died in the great influenza pandemic that struck the world in 1918.

TREATIES WITHOUT PEACE

The first general European peace conference since Vienna in 1814–15 met at Paris in January 1919. It faced a more difficult task than had Metternich and Castlereagh. They had merely attempted to return the world "to peaceful habits" and reestablish a balance of power that France had upset. The peacemakers at Paris in 1919 faced similar requirements, and far more.

Scores of outraged nationalities, mercifully silent at Vienna, now clamored for self-determination and "rights"—including the right to oppress minorities or neighboring nationalities. Public opinion, mobilized to hate for four long years and politically potent thanks to universal suffrage, made moderation difficult. Bolshevism, a revolutionary threat without parallel in 1814–15, appeared to menace central Europe. War and self-determination had disrupted complex industrial economies; the permanence of peace might depend in part on the economic solutions the peacemakers found. And Wilson, who insisted on attending the conference in person, rejected a French proposal for drafting a clear agenda and order of business. The "Big Four," Wilson, Lloyd George, Clemenceau, and Orlando, leapt from issue to issue. Out of confusion, they created chaos.

Germany's fate was the chief issue facing the conference, and its chief failure. In the abstract, two courses were available that might prevent Germany from again attempting the experiment of 1914. The Allies and the United States could conciliate the new German republic by offering a lenient peace. Or they could fasten on Germany a genuinely Carthaginian peace that would undo Bismarck's work and divide Germany into two or three: Prussia, Catholic south Germany, and an independent Rhineland. Clemenceau, who had seen two German invasions of France in his lifetime, naturally preferred the second alternative. But neither Lloyd George nor Wilson were neighbors of Germany. Britain had already interned the German fleet; it could calmly disparage Clemenceau's fears and reject the open-ended military commitment needed to enforce his drastic solution. And Germany was an economic unit essential to European and British prosperity, and the only remaining counterweight to Bolshevik Russia in eastern Europe.

The Big Four therefore compromised. Bismarck's Reich remained in existence, and Britain and the United States calmed France with the offer of an Anglo-American security guarantee, a military alliance against German resurgence. But having decided to preserve Germany, the Allies failed to adopt the corollary of that decision, a peace as lenient as that offered to Bourbon France in 1814–15. Allied public opinion, even in Britain, shouted "Hang the Kaiser!" The disorderly procedure of the Paris conference meant that demands on Germany accumulated piecemeal and found their way into the treaty without any weighing of their cumulative effect. And their own disunity prevented the Big Four, despite initial good intentions, from inviting the Germans to help draft the treaty, as the French had in 1814.

Not that the treaty that the German delegation grudgingly signed in the Hall of Mirrors at Versailles on the fifth anniversary of Sarajevo (June 28, 1919)

The "Big Four" at Paris, 1919: Orlando makes a point to Lloyd George, while Clemenceau (center) and Wilson (far right) look on.

was severe, compared to Brest-Litovsk. Germany lost a mere 13.5 percent of its 1914 territory, mostly areas inhabited by Poles, Danes, and French. The Allies piled on (1) financial "reparations"; (2) disarmament to a force of 100,000 men without heavy equipment, aircraft, or general staff; (3) the end of Tirpitz's navy; (4) temporary Allied occupation and permanent demilitarization of the Rhineland; (5) the loss of the Silesian coal fields; (6) the temporary cession to France of the Saar; (7) the loss of Germany's useless colonies; and (8) a prohibition on union with German-speaking rump Austria. The essentials of Bismarck's Reich nevertheless remained intact.

Yet compared to German expectations, the "Diktat" or dictated peace the Germans received at Versailles was a nightmare. For four years German propaganda had told the German people that a savage ring of aggressors had attacked Germany out of Cossack bloodlust, French thirst for revenge, and British "trade envy." Germany's leaders had assured their public that victorious occupation of Belgium, northern France, and vast stretches of Russia guaranteed Germany a victorious peace. And the Germans had also, quite without justification, expected a

Wilsonian "peace without annexations or indemnities" as their reward for proclaiming a republic. They had evidently not read Wilson's Point 13, which specified the creation of a Poland with access to the sea, inevitably across German territory.

The abrupt transition in 1918 from the expectation of victory to the reality of defeat, of territorial loss and national humiliation, lessened German opinion's already tenuous grip on reality. Germany, its political leaders at its head, denied the obvious. Germany, they claimed, had not provoked the war—although numerous German documents soon emerged indicating precisely the opposite, and few could deny that Germany had attacked Belgium without provocation. The Germans damned as a "war guilt lie" the Allied attempt, in Article 231 of the Versailles Treaty, to establish the financial responsibility of Germany and its allies for "loss and damage" resulting from the war imposed on the Allied Powers "by the aggression of Germany and its allies." The Germans, from the beginning, furiously denied the Treaty's moral validity.

Nor had Germany suffered military defeat, according to most German leaders, including the new SPD president of the republic, Fritz Ebert. Through the mouth of Hindenburg, the Right added the crucial corollary. If the Allies had not defeated Germany, the culprits could only be the "November Criminals" of the SPD, whose Revolution had allegedly stabbed the heroic troops "in the back." The twin legends of Allied victory through trickery and German defeat through a "stab-in-the-back" ensured that Germany would have the will to reverse the verdict of 1914–18.

And the Versailles Treaty's relative lenience ensured that it would have the means. For east-central Europe was now a power vacuum. The collapse of Austria-Hungary brought into being five miniature Austria-Hungaries: rump Austria, a diminished Hungary, Czechoslovakia, Poland, and a Serb-dominated kingdom of Serbs, Croats, and Slovenes that later took the name of Yugoslavia. Rumania, which now absorbed both Transylvania and the Rumanian-inhabited ex-Russian territory of Bessarabia, formed a sixth weak state between Germany and Russia. Italy, by seizing Trento and Trieste, became the seventh "successor state" of the defunct Habsburg empire.

With Russia temporarily in eclipse and German economic and demographic power virtually intact, only the

The Peace Settlements in Europe   1919–20

Territories lost by:
Germany
Bulgaria
Austria-Hungary
Russia
Plebiscite areas
Demilitarized Rhineland zone of Allied occupation

United States could balance Germany once it began to revive. The war, despite Germany's defeat, had paradoxically made Germany potentially stronger *in relative terms* than in 1914. The states of eastern Europe, the Germans correctly judged, were *Saisonstaaten*, "states for a season" destined to wilt in the hot sun of renewed German greatness.

And Wilson soon hastened that sunrise by destroying the prospect of continued U.S. participation in the European power balance. In the course of 1917–18 the notion of a "League of Nations," brainchild of British pacifists such as Lord Robert Cecil, captivated the President. He saw in the League an alternative to the alleged evils of the balance of power and of secret treaties that Cobdenite mythology blamed for the war.

In the Paris negotiations Wilson therefore devoted an increasing portion of his energy writing the League's "Covenant" into the Versailles Treaty, thus confusing further the process of settlement with Germany. The League, Wilson increasingly hoped, would remedy admitted imperfections in the German clauses of the Treaty, bind the potentially isolationist United States to Europe, and ensure the perpetual peace that Wilson had promised would emerge from this war to "make the world safe for democracy."

In pursuing the mirage of the League, Wilson destroyed the prospect that the United States would underwrite European stability by a permanent commitment of its power, the power that had defeated Germany. The Republicans took control of the Senate in the fall 1918 elections. They balked at the open-ended global commitments that League "collective security" entailed. Their leader, Henry Cabot Lodge, was no isolationist; he favored a continued commitment of American power to prevent Germany from renewing its "war of world conquest." But Wilson rejected Lodge's offer to ratify the Treaty with reservations. Wilson—professorially dogmatic about

National Minorities in Central Europe   1919

presidential prerogatives, always rigid of character, and now increasingly ill— defied an essential feature of the Constitution: the requirement that the President lead rather than command the Congress.

Wilson's reward, after he had suffered nervous collapse and an incapacitating stroke while taking his case to the people, was Senate rejection of the Treaty in March 1920. The British economist John Maynard Keynes influenced the Senate with his vitriolic pamphlet against Wilson and the Treaty, *The Economic Consequences of the Peace.* Wilson himself ensured rejection by ordering his loyalists to vote against the amended version the Republicans proposed. And the wreck of Wilson's policy and presidency destroyed any prospect of an Anglo-American security guarantee for France. The Republican presidential candidate, Warren G. Harding, summed up the rising national yearning for a return to the womb with a word of his own invention. America needed "normalcy." Harding carried the 1920 election. The United States retreated into resentful isolation, except for its petulant demands for repayment of Allied war debts.

The Pacific proved the one area in which the United States continued to play a great-power role. Wilson had sought unsuccessfully at Paris to move the Japanese from Shandong and compel them to rescind the "twenty-one demands" they had forced on China in 1915. U.S. opinion also looked unkindly on the Anglo-Japanese alliance, and U.S. admirals saw in it a two-ocean threat that demanded a fleet larger than the navy second to none projected in 1916, after the first submarine outrages. The United States, with the help of Canada, forced Britain to choose between its alliance with Japan and its friendship with the United States. Britain, in no condition to engage in a naval "race" with the United States, acquiesced. Britain had abandoned the "two-power standard" to face the German challenge; now it abandoned its alliance with Japan and accepted formal parity with the greatest naval power, the United States.

At the Washington Conference on arms limitation and Pacific affairs in 1921–22, the powers laid down a new naval and East Asian order. The Washington Naval Treaty of February 1922 apparently froze the world hierarchy of naval power. It decreed a ten-year "holiday" in battleship construction and limited total tonnage of capital ships to 500,000 each for Britain and the United States, 300,000 for Japan, and 175,000 each for France and Italy. The powers relieved China of most Japanese encroachments and reaffirmed the "Open Door." The Anglo-Japanese Alliance dissolved into a meaningless Four-Power Treaty in which Britain, France, Japan, and the United States pledged to preserve the Pacific status quo. Japan acquiesced to the Washington settlement in return for British and American pledges not to build fortified bases north of Singapore and east of Hawaii. Tokyo retained both naval supremacy in northeast Asia and Hong Kong and the Philippines as hostages. The Washington treaties seemed to promise an era of peace. Their real results were a perilous complacency in the democracies and the cutting loose of Japan from the restraining influence of its alliance with Britain.

WARS AFTER THE WAR, 1919–23

Meanwhile, U.S. withdrawal left Europe on its own. Peaceful habits did not return. Social and national struggles convulsed Europe until 1923. The League of Nations generated immense masses of paper and gave small nations a forum for interminable talk. But it proved impotent whenever it faced a great power. Even Italy defied it in 1923 over an incident with Greece.

In Germany and Hungary, short-lived Left-extremist uprisings or regimes perished when faced with ruthless counteraction from the Right. The SPD government of the German republic, unable to impose order with the debris of the Imperial German Army, authorized the recruitment of right-wing freebooters, the *Freikorps.* Such units appealed to Germans of the Ernst Jünger type, who had enjoyed the Great War and were reluctant to give it up, and to nationalist students too

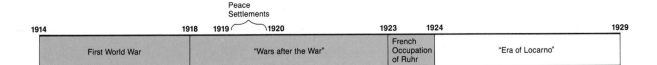

1914		1918	1919	Peace Settlements	1920		1923	1924		1929

First World War	"Wars after the War"	French Occupation of Ruhr	"Era of Locarno"

young to fight in 1914–18. In January 1919, after an abortive Communist ("Spartacist") coup in Berlin, the *Freikorps* shot Rosa Luxemburg and other leaders of the far Left "while attempting to escape." That was a euphemism much imitated later. A *Putsch* or military coup by *Freikorps* elements and a subsequent Communist uprising in the Ruhr almost destroyed the German republic in 1920.

In Italy, the Liberals failed to master the mass political forces that Giolitti had unleashed by conceding virtual universal male suffrage in 1912–13. The Italian socialists succumbed to the delusion that Italy was Russia. Their verbal threats of revolution and occasional violence against landowners and veterans soon provoked a virtual civil war, which they naturally lost (see pp. 914–17).

Further east, Bolshevik Russia fought for survival. The 1918 Armistice had forced Germany to disgorge the gains of Brest-Litovsk, but the Bolsheviks continued to proclaim the goal of World Revolution, without which they expected a Communist Russia to succumb to "capitalist encirclement." Lenin and associates split the European socialist parties by founding their own Third ("Communist") International in March 1919. They also appealed to the colonial peoples, furthering the disruption of the European empires that the war had begun.

Trotsky raised Bolshevik armies and fought with increasing success against "White Russian" forces under former tsarist generals who sought to restore the old regime. The Allies landed troops in 1918 at Vladivostok and Murmansk to secure the supplies they had sent to the tsar and to support the Whites. Except for the ever-acquisitive Japanese, who remained at Vladivos-

tok until 1922, the Allies soon found their position untenable and withdrew. By 1920 the Red Army had defeated the Whites, but the Poles made the error of attempting to seize the Ukraine. In July 1920 the Red Army drove into Poland with hopes of continuing westward. Then the Poles under Marshal Josef Pilsudski held at Warsaw. Russia's borders stabilized. Finland, Estonia, Latvia, and Lithuania kept their newly acquired independence; Rumania kept Bessarabia. In other respects Bolshevik Russia preserved the inheritance of the tsars.

In the vacuum between Germany and Russia, the successor states quarreled. The diplomats at Paris did their best to draw new borders for Germany's former allies by the treaties of St. Germain (September 1919) for Austria, of Neuilly (November 1919) for Bulgaria, and of Trianon (June 1920) for Hungary. These frontiers, although

Postwar wars: street fighting in Berlin, 1919.

much criticized as a source of conflict, in most cases merely ratified or systematized what the nationalities of eastern Europe had done in pulling Austria-Hungary down. The great powers thereafter showed little ability to moderate the squabbles of the small. Poland and Czechoslovakia disputed the border town of Teschen. Lithuania quarreled over its borders with Poland and Germany. Hungary claimed territory from all three of its neighbors—Rumania, Czechoslovakia, and Yugoslavia. The neighbors sought security through alliances with one another, a combination the Hungarians disparaged as the "Little Entente." France, seeking an eastern ally to replace Russia, itself contracted alliances with Poland and Czechoslovakia, and consultative pacts with Rumania and Yugoslavia.

Germany and Bolshevik Russia, the pariahs of the international scene, sought solace together. In 1922, at Rapallo, they publicly and demonstratively canceled their mutual debt and reparations claims. Secretly, Red Army and German *Reichswehr* contracted a profitable bargain. Germany furnished the Bolsheviks with modern military technology and in return received an opportunity for secret experiment in Russia with weapons such as gas and aircraft, forbidden under the Versailles Treaty.

Far to the south, the Turks reacted to the collapse of their empire by creating a national state, under the leadership of the victor of Gallipoli, Mustafa Kemal Pasha. A foolhardy Greek advance into Turkey in pursuit of the "Great Idea" (*Megali Idea*) of a Greek empire from the Adriatic to the Black Sea led to disaster in 1922. The Turks then massacred or expelled the 1.35 million Greeks of Asia Minor whose ancestors had lived there for three millennia. The Greeks in turn drove almost half a million Turks from Greek Thrace. This "exchange of populations," as League bureaucrats euphemistically described it, still appeared conspicuously barbaric in the 1920s.

Unfortunately it did not appear so for long.

After a confrontation with British troops at Chanak near Constantinople that brought down Lloyd George's government in October 1922, the Turks permitted the Allies to leave them alone. The 1923 Treaty of Lausanne recognized the independent Turkish state. Kemal, who later took the name Atatürk ("father of the Turks"), abolished the Ottoman Sultanate and ruled ruthlessly until his death in 1938. The "Eastern Question" was closed. Its worthy successors were the merciless struggles throughout the Middle East between the Ottoman's Empire's former subjects.

Meanwhile, France and Germany fought a deadly although as yet largely bloodless struggle. The issue was simple: would Germany accept the apparent demotion to second-rate power visited upon it in 1918? Germany refused to acknowledge as final the loss of Posen, West Pussia, and Upper Silesia to Poland. Above all, it refused to pay promptly and fully the reparations that the Allies had fixed in 1921 at a theoretical total of $32 billion dollars.

The French faced immense expenses to repair the devastation that the war and the methodical German wrecking during the 1917 and 1918 retreats had wrought. France also hoped that heavy reparations would make it harder for Germany to rearm. It therefore attempted to hold Germany to its obligations, especially since the $32 billion reparations total set in 1921, by a feat of bureaucratic sleight-of-hand, in actuality amounted to only $12.5 billion, a figure well within German capacity to pay.

When the Germans defaulted massively in late 1922, France and its ally Belgium acted. Poincaré sent French troops into the Ruhr Valley to seize Germany's mines and factories. Mining coal with bayonets was expensive, but the French made a modest profit. The German government of Wilhelm Cuno decreed passive resistance. Cuno began printing marks feverishly, fuelling an inflation already underway thanks to Germany's immense internal war debt. Cuno wrecked Germany's currency to prove that Germany could not pay. What he proved was that Germany would not pay.

In August–September 1923 Cuno and passive resistance collapsed as the mark rose from 4 million to 160 million to the dollar. Gustav Stresemann, a crafty ex-National Liberal with an extreme annexationist past, took power as Chancellor. He mastered internal disorder, which included a radical nationalist uprising in Bavaria under the leadership of a fanatical ex-corporal and winner of the Iron Cross, Adolf Hitler.

Stresemann sought a compromise with France that would give Germany a breathing space. Britain and the United States, concerned at the economic repercussions of chaos in Germany, helped. They threatened economic reprisals if Poincaré did not withdraw from the Ruhr. By spring 1924 Stresemann had stabilized the currency by introducing a new mark. Poincaré gave way to a left-wing coalition in the May 1924 French elections; his successor, Aristide Briand, was a weaker and more conciliatory man. An emissary of the United States, Charles G. Dawes, patched together a temporary reparations settlement, the Dawes Plan. It lowered payments to a level Germany consented to pay and underwrote Germany's solvency with a U.S. loan, the first of many. Henceforth U.S. credit to Germany indirectly furnished the sums Germany paid as reparations. The last French troops left the Ruhr in August 1925. France had lost a great trial of strength.

THE ILLUSIONS OF LOCARNO, 1925–29

Worse, from the French viewpoint, followed. Austen Chamberlain, Britain's foreign secretary, had thought to prevent a repetition of the Ruhr occupation by giving France security against

France occupies the Ruhr, 1923.

Germany in an Anglo-French pact that would replace the failed 1919 Treaty of Guarantee. Stresemann got wind of the project, and slyly preempted it with an offer of a general western security pact that Germany would also sign.

Instead of a revival of the Anglo-French Entente Cordiale, the French received the multilateral Treaty of Locarno (October 16, 1925). France, Germany, and Belgium pledged to respect their mutual borders, as drawn in the Versailles Treaty, and to preserve the demilitarization of the Rhineland. Britain and Italy acted as outside guarantors against "unprovoked attack," a singularly vague and elastic phrase. And France could now only respond militarily to "flagrant violations" of the demilitarization of the Rhineland. That phrase significantly weakened a key provision of Versailles.

Despite Stresemann's professions of conversion to being a "good European," Locarno was an immense German victory. It prevented a repetition of the Ruhr experiment: if France sought to use force to uphold the Ver-

Having restored Germany's international respectability, Stresemann addresses the League of Nations in 1929.

sailles Treaty, Britain might be treaty-bound to fight France! Locarno thus precluded Anglo-French staff talks on the pre-1914 model, much to the relief of the British army and government. And Locarno covered only the West. Germany retained freedom to redraw, by force if necessary, its eastern borders.

A brief Indian summer of illusion, the "era of Locarno," followed the treaty. France and Britain repeatedly ignored massive German violations of the Versailles Treaty's disarmament provisions. They gave up their right of on-site inspection of German violations. Germany entered the League of Nations. In 1929, in a second reparations settlement (the "Young Plan") negotiated under U.S. auspices, Germany agreed to make modest payments until 1988. France in turn undertook to evacuate its Rhineland occupation zone by summer 1930, five years ahead of the Versailles Treaty schedule.

Western public opinion demanded from its political leaders forgetfulness and illusion, and received them. The

Great War, Western opinion concluded, had been an exercise in criminal futility that must never be repeated. Alliances and armaments—not German aggression—had caused the war. Therefore alliances and armaments (except semi-clandestine German armaments) were evil. Enlightened international public opinion, working through the League of Nations, would prevent war.

Illusion reached its height with the famous pact "outlawing war" that Aristide Briand and Frank B. Kellogg, the U.S. secretary of state, drafted in 1928. Briand hoped the pact would bind the United States, however tenuously, to Europe. But the Kellogg-Briand Pact, which 62 nations happily signed, contained no enforcement provisions whatsoever. It also included an escape clause wide enough to accommodate entire tank armies: signatories could still fight in self-defense. The pact had all the force of a pious declaration against sin.

Fifteen years of war and revolution had broken for good the "peaceful habits" acquired in the nineteenth century. For four years millions of men had killed one another in mud holes while Europe had transmuted its vast accumulated wealth into steel and high explosives. Those who returned from the front took the language and habit of violence into politics. In the East, a pitiless utopian sect had taken control of a great power of immense economic and military potential. In central Europe, the greatest European power of all had emerged from the war unreconciled to defeat. The victors had checked at heartbreaking cost the German bid for European and world mastery, but had left a Germany capable of repeating that bid. Soon—with the onset of the Great Depression in 1929—the world economy collapsed. That enfeebled the democracies and unleashed voracious "have-not" powers in Asia and Europe. The Great War receded into memory, but others took its place.

Suggestions for Further Reading

General

No adequate one-volume history of the war exists. M. Ferro, *The Great War, 1914–1918* (1973), A. J. P. Taylor, *The First World War* (1972), and G. Hardach, *The First World War, 1914–1918* (1977), offer intelligent surveys. Z. Zeman, *The Gentlemen Negotiators* (1971), covers war diplomacy with style. P. Kennedy, "The First World War and the International Power System," *International Security*, 9 (1984), analyzes the relative strength of the powers. On life in the trenches, see especially the chapter on the Somme in J. Keegan, *The Face of Battle* (1976).

War and Revolution

For Germany's war, see above all F. Fischer, *War of Illusions* (1975), and *Germany's Aims in the First World War* (1967); H. W. Gatzke, *Germany's Drive to the West* (1950); T. Lupfer, *The Dynamics of Doctrine: the Changes in German Tactical Doctrine During the First World War* (1981); and J. Kocka, *Facing Total War: German Society, 1914–1918* (1984). On Britain, see especially E. L. Woodward, *Great Britain and the War of 1914–1918* (1967); also useful are P. Guinn, *British Strategy and Politics, 1914 to 1918* (1965), and A. Marwick, *The Deluge: British Society and the First World War* (1965). For France, see especially P. Bernard and H. Dubief, *The Decline of the Third Republic, 1914–1938* (1985), and A. Horne, *The Price of Glory: Verdun, 1916* (1962). S. Fitzpatrick, *The Russian Revolution, 1917–1932* (1982), offers a useful overview; A. Ulam, *Lenin and the Bolsheviks* (1965), and L. Schapiro, *The Russian Revolutions of 1917* (1984), are more detailed; L. Trotsky, *History of the Russian Revolution* (1936), is an unparalleled history-memoir by a key participant. On U.S. intervention, see especially B. Tuchman, *The Zimmermann Telegram* (1958); E. May, *The World War and American Isolation, 1914–1917* (1959), and D. Smith, *The Great Departure: The United States and World War I* (1965).

Settlement and Aftermath

On the power consequences of the war, see Kennedy, "The First World War" cited above; G. Weinberg, "The Defeat of Germany in 1918 and the European Balance of Power," *Central European History* 2 (1969); and H. Holborn, *The Political Collapse of Europe* (1954). P. Birdsall, *Versailles Twenty Years After* (1941), remains the best treatment of the peace conference, but see also K. Schwabe, *Woodrow Wilson, Revolutionary Germany, and Peacemaking, 1918–1919: Missionary Diplomacy and the Realities of Power* (1985). On the aftermath, S. Marks, *The Illusion of Peace: International Relations in Europe, 1918–1933* (1976), is unsurpassed. C. A. Macartney and A. W. Palmer, *Independent Eastern Europe* (1962), is excellent. S. Marks, "The Myths of Reparations," *Central European History* 11 (1978), demystifies a widely misunderstood issue.

31

The Interwar World,
1919–1939

*T*he virtual withdrawal of the United States and Russia from world politics fostered a moment of illusion. The victorious powers of western Europe, Britain and France, appeared to dominate Europe and the wider world as they had in the early nineteenth century. But France's failure to cow even a disarmed Germany and Britain's economic and imperial troubles soon revealed the hollowness of appearances. Germany enjoyed a brief prosperity after 1924, thanks to U.S. credit. But political stability eluded it. Few of the new states of central and eastern Europe enjoyed either stability or prosperity. The United States enjoyed an unprecedented prosperity—in isolation.

Then came the Great Depression. It extinguished the few surviving parliamentary regimes between Germany and Russia. It virtually destroyed world lending and trade. It mortally wounded the great democracies, confirmed the United States in its isolationism, and freed unsatiated or defeated powers to attack the West both in Europe and Asia. Fascist Italy under Benito Mussolini, a racist Germany under Adolf Hitler, and a militarized Japan destroyed the Versailles-Washington Treaty order while Lenin's implacable successor, Joseph Stalin,

The guardians of the peace: negotiators at a 1930 reparations conference caught napping by the mischievous photographer Erich Salomon.

sought to profit from the resulting chaos. Britain, France, and the United States met these global challenges demoralized and disunited. France went under; Britain nearly perished; the United States paid dearly for its irresponsibility after 1919.

THE TWENTIES: A GOLDEN AGE?

Britain: Stability and Stagnation

War and aftermath broke the Liberals. In 1916 Asquith gave way to Lloyd George. In May 1918, Asquith attacked Lloyd George in the House of Commons and split the Liberal party. In the "khaki election" of December 1918 Lloyd George led his wartime Liberal-Conservative coalition to crushing victory over both Asquith and Labour. That condemned the divided Liberal party to permanent opposition and decline.

But the Conservatives soon found Lloyd George's leadership galling. His brinkmanship in the Chanak crisis with Turkey in October 1922 gave the stolid foot soldiers of the Conservative party their opportunity. The comfortable, avuncular, pipe-smoking Stanley Baldwin rose up and denounced Lloyd

George as "a great dynamic force"—"a very terrible thing." By 1923 Baldwin, whose enemies disparaged him as "a man of the utmost insignificance," was prime minister.

He remained so until 1929, except for a brief Labour minority government in 1924. Baldwin was the tweedy personification of a largely defunct rural England. A master of conciliation, of fudging issues, he defused social conflict with the soothing syrup of his "fireside chats" on that new medium, the radio. He found foreign policy boring. The Locarno treaty seemed to make foreign policy superfluous; he did his best to have none.

The mass army that had broken the Hindenburg Line shrank to a numerically insignificant imperial police force. The new Royal Air Force remained a hollow shell. The navy languished. In 1928 Britain adopted as permanent a 1919 budgetary invention of Lloyd George—the "ten year rule." All defense expenditure and planning was to rest on the assumption that Britain would not fight a great power for at least ten years. That assumption proved a rationalization for unilateral disarmament.

At home, Baldwin's government weathered in 1926 the general strike feared since the miners, dockers, and railwaymen had formed a "triple alliance" in 1914. The Polish and German mining industries had recovered from war and disruption, and had forced coal prices down. Britain's miners struck to protest the resulting pay cuts. Transport and other workers joined the miners in sympathy. But the Cabinet did not need the armored cars that Churchill, by then a defector to the Baldwin cabinet from the dying Liberals, gleefully displayed in Hyde Park. Baldwin supervised a conciliatory settlement for the transport workers; the miners, left to their own devices, eventually surrendered.

The General Strike of 1926 left a legacy of bitterness, especially among the miners. But in other industries it brought to the fore conciliatory union leaders. Baldwin's tranquilizing manner preserved Britain's traditions of

The General Strike, 1926: London police protect delivery workers from possible reprisals by strikers.

gradualism and relative social peace, despite the rise of Labour and the strain of a structural unemployment in declining areas and industries that idled over 10 percent of Britain's labor force in every year except 1927. But Baldwin was certainly no "dynamic force." Neither he nor his Labour successor of 1929–31, Ramsay MacDonald, were the men to counter the decay of Britain's heavy industry or arrest Britain's military decline.

France: Instability and Resilience

France, at least superficially, contrasted sharply with Britain's orderly alternation between Conservatives and Labour. France enjoyed the dubious benefits of 17 governments between 1920 and 1929. Once the war emergency was past, the Chamber reasserted its dislike of leaders; it did away with Clemenceau in 1920. The Ruhr crisis with Germany over reparations brought Poincaré to the fore in 1922–24. Then *"Poincaruhr"* departed when the May 1924 victory of the moderate left *Cartel des Gauches* displaced the nationalist chamber elected in the enthusiasm of 1919. The Cartel, in turn, displayed political incoherence; Radical-Socialists and Socialists squabbled. The Communists, who had captured from the Socialists most members of the largest union, the General Confederation of Labor (CGT), gleefully attacked the Cartel from the left. Moscow demanded then and later that all Communist parties concentrate their fire not on the Right but on their Socialist rivals. A "cascade" of short-lived Cartel ministries proved incapable of governing in 1925–26, as the franc declined catastrophically thanks to the repercussions of the Ruhr crisis. Poincaré returned in July 1926; his authority saved the franc. Remarkably, he remained—and retired voluntarily in 1929.

The appearance of chaos, except under Poincaré, was deceptive. The Third Republic succeeded in rebuilding the war-devastated areas by the end of the 1920s. The return of the coal and iron of Lorraine fuelled a sharp rise in steel production. André Citroën pioneered—in Europe—the mass production of automobiles, an innovation the British were slow to follow. Hydroelectric power and bauxite deposits in southern France made it a major producer of that new light metal, aluminum. While unemployment laid waste to Britain's mining and shipbuilding areas, France suffered a labor shortage. Prosperity and the immense wartime losses created openings; 1.5 million immigrants from eastern Europe and the colonies filled them.

But France's position was precarious; it rested above all on German disarmament. For as in 1914, France's industrial economy was about half the size of Germany's, and three Germans of military age still faced every two Frenchmen. After the Ruhr and Locarno, which barred France from invading western Germany, the French sought security in defense, and implicitly abandoned their eastern alliances. In 1929, the government initiated a gigantic engineering project to seal France's eastern borders and protect its vital industries from a repetition of 1914. The Maginot Line, named for the minister of war of the moment, André Maginot, was an immensely strong crust of obstacles and fortresses linked with tunnels and underground rail-

Underground in the Maginot Line.

1871		1918	1933	1945
German Empire ("Second Reich")		Weimar Republic	Hitler ("Third Reich")	

ways. It had one weakness: it did not cover the Belgian border. Belgium was a French ally and had its own fortifications facing Germany. If Belgium ceased to be an ally, both the Maginot Line and France might fall.

Germany: *Republic without Republicans*

Germany's new democracy showed neither British stability nor French resilience. The SPD, Center, and German Democratic (left Liberal) parties received 70 percent of the vote in the January 1919 elections, thanks to Germany's need to appear democratic for the Paris peace conference. That coalition repaired to the provincial town of Weimar, safe from the Spartacists in Berlin, and drafted the most democratic constitution conceivable. It provided votes for both sexes at age 20 and an extreme form of proportional representation that measured, like a delicate seismograph, every quirk and blip of public opinion. Any party that could collect 60,000 votes in all of Germany

Seeckt, planner of German victories over the Russians and Rumanians in 1915–16, made Germany's post-war 100,000-man force an elite "army of leaders," cadres for a future mass army.

could have a *Reichstag* seat. That was an invitation to political fragmentation; by 1928 Germany had at least 45 parties.

The Weimar constitution contained a further decisive weakness, which in the end proved fatal. Max Weber, who helped draft the constitution, saw in a strong American-style presidency a guarantee of leadership that would ward off what he took to be democracy's tendency toward incoherence. Thanks to Weber and to Germany's monarchical tradition, the Republic received *both* a Chancellor responsible to the legislature *and* a popularly elected Reich President. And the Reich President had something his American counterpart did not have, although Lincoln at war had in practice claimed it: emergency powers to make law by decree.

The Weimar constitution failed to work because its drafters superimposed it upon a state and an electorate that were anything but democratic. The officer corps, core of the old Reich, saved itself in 1918–19 by cooperation with the SPD. Thereafter, under General von Seeckt, it supported the Republic grudgingly so long as the Republic tolerated the army's semi-independent status as a "state within the state." As for the electorate, it voted its convictions in the 1920 election, which placed the founding parties of the Republic in a permanent minority. Democracy had failed as a means of ensuring a lenient peace. Middle-class Germans had no natural love of democracy for its own sake, and therefore deserted the German Democratic party for the Right. Even the SPD and Center parties were scarcely democratic by vocation. The SPD had to retain its Marxist rhetoric to prevent further defections to the increasingly vocal Communists to its left; the Center had a built-in authoritarian bent.

That the Republic survived as long as it did, and that it provided the backing for Stresemann's moderate foreign policy from 1923 to 1929, was almost miraculous. This was a political system unable to reach agreement on the colors of the national flag; a cabinet fell over the issue in 1926. Coalitions, to command a *Reichstag* majority, had to extend so far left or right that they were prone to breakdown at any moment.

Nevertheless, three factors preserved the Republic. No alternative commanded support. The monarchy was politically dead; Communist risings failed in 1919, 1920, and 1923; *Putsches* from the Right collapsed in 1920 and 1923 because Seeckt was neutral or hostile. Second, the Republic acquired an unexpected respectability in 1925. Tirpitz, in his last contribution to German politics, persuaded Field Marshal von Hindenburg to run for Reich President. Hindenburg's triumphant election compelled the traditionalist Right to moderate its hatred for the Republic. Finally, Germany after 1924 began to recover its pre-1914 prosperity, thanks primarily to U.S. short-term loans. But if a political alternative arose, if Hindenburg disappeared, if the army turned against the Republic, or if prosperity ended, Weimar might end as well.

The Successor States: Democracies and Dictatorships

German democracy, however precarious, was an earthly paradise compared to conditions further east. The states of eastern Europe greeted 1919 clothed in Wilsonian democratic garb. Within a decade, the absence of native parliamentary traditions and the pressures of nationalism and peasant-landlord conflict had made most of them dictatorships.

As Austria-Hungary collapsed, its nationalities had erected national states. Inevitably, given central and eastern Europe's mixed pattern of settlement, the new borders included large national minorities. Rumania

The dreariness of Weimar depicted by Georg Grosz, an artist of the Left who bitterly attacked the Republic.

forcibly incorporated the 1.5 million Hungarians of Transylvania, and returned with interest the treatment the Hungarians had meted out to the minorities of pre-1914 greater Hungary. The Poles sometimes dealt arrogantly with their German minority, despite the danger of provoking the German state. Orthodox Serbs lorded it over Catholic Croats and Slovenes, former subjects of Austria-Hungary. Virtually everyone mistreated the Jews. League of Nations safeguards for ethnic minorities proved mere scraps of paper.

Social oppression was almost as pervasive as national oppression. Except in industrial Czechoslovakia and rump Austria (which consisted of Vienna and an assortment of Alps), the chief class was the peasantry. It ranged in size from 80 percent of the population in Bulgaria to 55 percent in Hungary. Controlling it was the chief preoccupation of eastern Europe's landholding ruling classes. In the Baltic states of Estonia, Latvia, and Lithuania the landlords were predominantly Russians, Germans, or Poles; the new nationalist governments happily took their land. Elsewhere, peasant land

"Strong men" of eastern Europe: Horthy of Hungary (above) and Pilsudski of Poland (below).

hunger and landlord resistance contributed mightily to political instability.

By 1930, Hungary, Poland, Lithuania, Yugoslavia, Bulgaria, and Rumania were all essentially dictatorships. Hungary went first. From March to November 1919 it suffered the Bolshevik dictatorship of Béla Kun, Rumanian invasion, and finally a bloody reconquest by the Right under the leadership of Austria-Hungary's greatest naval leader, Admiral Nicholas Horthy. The result was a gentry-controlled sham parliament that cloaked a narrow oligarchy with Horthy at its head. A nationalist dictatorship of the peasant Right emerged in Lithuania in 1926. Poland's parliamentary interlude yielded to a 1926 coup by that ex-socialist "man on horseback," Marshal Joseph Pilsudski. In Yugoslavia, the assassination in parliament of the chief Croat leader in 1928 rendered the country ungovernable. King Alexander imposed a royal dictatorship that rested upon Serb bayonets; some Croats replied with terrorism. And in Bulgaria, a military coup in 1923 displaced the ruthless peasant leader, Alexander Stambolisky, who had ruled since 1919. Stambolisky and some 10,000 of his followers perished in ensuing uprisings and massacres. In 1925 a Communist bomb dropped the roof of Sofia cathedral on the representatives of the Right. Enough survived to massacre the Left and impose a royal and military dictatorship with parliamentary trimmings. In 1930 the dissolute King Carol of Rumania returned from exile and adopted a similar solution.

Two exceptions to this pattern existed. Austria, despite the economic ruin of separation from Hungary and Bohemia and a built-in cleavage between "Red Vienna" and the *Freikorps*-like hearties of its Alpine valleys, managed to last out the decade as a parliamentary regime. Czechoslovakia, although a veritable patchwork of nationalities, was an island of relative freedom and prosperity under the enlightened leadership of its Czech founders, Thomas Masaryck and Eduard Beneš. But no eastern European state was equipped to face the coming storm.

The United States: The "Roaring Twenties"

Unprecedented domestic prosperity appeared to reward the international irresponsibility of the United States. The economy grew steadily after the brief worldwide slump of 1920–1921. By 1929 the real per capita income of the average American had improved by more than a third compared to 1921. The automobile came into its own as the engine of growth and symbol of the "American way of life." By 1926, Henry Ford had sold 16 million Model T's, the first true mass-production automobile. By 1929, the United States had one car for every five people; European automobile production was a mere 13 percent of the U.S. level. The U.S. electrical industry followed suit: radios, refrigerators, and vacuum cleaners deluged a public that displayed an apparently insatiable appetite for consumer goods.

Politically, the 1920s were a placidly Republican decade. President Harding died suddenly in 1923 during the revelation of financial scandals that involved his associates. His Vice President, Calvin ("Silent Cal") Coolidge, then presided in masterful inactivity until 1928. A man of few words but pithy ones, he made no secret of his conviction that "the business of America is business."

The 1920s were also a decade of stern intolerance. As Wilson lay paralyzed, his attorney general, A. Mitchell Palmer, mercilessly hunted foreign-born "Reds." In laws of 1921 and 1924, under the guise of immigration quotas, Congress extended to southern and eastern Europeans the policy of exclusion adopted earlier against Chinese and Japanese. The Ku Klux Klan revived, and lynched blacks and Jews. And after 1917, temperance crusaders

1913		1921	1923		1929	1933		1945
Wilson (D)		Harding (R)	Coolidge (R)		Hoover (R)	FDR (D) and the "New Deal"		

dragooned the state legislatures into ratifying an Eighteenth Amendment that prohibited "the manufacture, sale, and transportation of alcoholic beverages."

Prohibition—not repealed until 1933—was the revenge of rural and Protestant America upon the great cities and their immigrants. But Prohibition also took revenge upon its proponents. The Eighteenth Amendment and the Volstead Act of 1919 that enforced it created an immense illegal beer and liquor industry under the control of the very immigrants whom the temperance movement had sought to discipline. Prohibition made the great "families" of organized crime, and made them a permanent feature of American life.

License accompanied intolerance. War, Prohibition, and prosperity broke down inherited standards. Prohibition, an unenforceable law, led to contempt for all laws; it also increased the attraction of alcohol. Relief from the strain of war, the emancipation of women not merely politically but sexually, and the freedom that affluence and automobiles conferred created a hectic and exhilarating "Jazz Age." But all things end. The 1920s ended in an economic catastrophe that appeared to place capitalism itself in question.

Prohibition in action: Federal agents destroy barrels of liquor (1920s).

THE GREAT DEPRESSION

The collapse of the New York stock market in October 1929 helped trigger a depression that lasted until the next great war, for which it was partially responsible. The Great Depression's ultimate causes, a subject of much dispute, were essentially three.

First, the war distorted the fabric of world trade, and political rigidities thereafter prevented readjustment. Britain and Germany hurled the products of their industries at one another for four years. When they resumed peacetime production the result was worldwide overcapacity, thanks to a vast economic expansion in the United States and Japan that had filled the wartime gap in the world market. The same process operated in agriculture: the United States, Canada, Argentina, Australia, and New Zealand had multiplied their agricultural production after 1914. After 1919, governments dared not permit the market to curtail the resulting surpluses. Industrialists and bankers made their money talk; workers and farmers voted. Instead of allowing production to fall, most states chose price subsidies and tariffs—a choice that simply prolonged overproduction. Despite the best efforts of the bureaucrats, agricultural prices turned irrevocably downward. Cotton peaked in 1923, and grain in 1924–25; by 1927 the slide in prices was general.

Second, the war burned up the capital needed to propel Europe's growth. France lost over half its 1914 foreign investments—a quarter had been in Russia. Britain took on a debt of $1 billion in paying for U.S. supplies. Britain's allies owed it $1.7 billion. The resumption of economic growth depended on renewed U.S. lending.

And the policies of the United States—the third major cause of the Great Depression—were irresponsible and self-contradictory. In the war, America replaced Britain as the world's greatest creditor; U.S. foreign investments rose from $2 billion in 1913 to $15 billion in 1930. But the isolationist United States of the 1920s refused to play the part that its wealth thrust upon it, the part of leader and ultimate guarantor of the stability of the world market. It rejected any thought of cancellation of the crushing burden of war debts, incurred in a common cause, under which its allies labored. Coolidge well expressed the implacable American view of those debts in a famous remark in his Vermont twang: "They hired the money, didn't they? Let them pay it!"

Worse, the United States barricaded itself behind the Fordney-McCumber tariff in 1922. High tariffs were traditional, but now they deprived Europe of a market desperately needed to earn profits from which to pay war debts. The president of the Chase National Bank put it well: "The debts of the outside world to us are ropes about their necks, by means of which we pull them towards us. Our trade restrictions are pitchforks pressed against their bodies, by which we hold them off."

Not that the United States did not have a foreign economic policy of sorts. Well-meaning emissaries such as Dawes and Young attempted to rationalize reparations and stabilize Europe economically. But in the absence of tariff reduction and debt cancellation they merely produced a financial merry-go-round. U.S. short-term loans fuelled the German economic expansion that underwrote reparations to France, which in turn paid war debts to Britain. Both Britain and France then paid war debts to the United States. But what if Europe's economy turned downward or U.S. lending ceased?

Both began to happen in 1927–28. Germany's agricultural prices crumbled and its industrial growth stopped. In the United States the Federal Reserve System, an innovation of Wilson's first administration designed to stabilize the banking system, made existing economic instability worse. Since 1921 it had happily pumped in credit, creating hectic growth. In mid-1927, sensing a possible downturn, the "Fed" pumped harder than before.

Easy credit helped stimulate an already foolhardy stock market to the greatest speculative boom in history. The Dow Jones index doubled in value, from 191 to 381, between early 1928 and September 1929. The Wall Street boom put pressure on Europe by diverting money from foreign lending. It squeezed U.S. banks and industry by sucking funds out of bank savings, industrial investment, and consumer spending.

In spring and summer 1929, U.S. economic activity turned downward. Production outran demand as speculative mania drained cash from the pockets of businesses and consumers. The market continued vertiginously upward. Then the bubble burst. Wall Street slipped on October 3, 1929. By the end of the month, after "Black Thursday" (October 24) and "Black Tuesday" (October 29) the Dow index was falling free. Investors who had bought stocks on credit trampled each other to sell, or leapt from high places into Wall Street. Business activity, commodity prices, foreign trade, and the vital lending to Europe all collapsed.

Congress reacted predictably. In March–June 1930 it passed the notorious Smoot-Hawley Tariff, the highest in U.S. history. Coolidge's successor, the unlucky and unloved Herbert Hoover, signed that tariff into law despite a monster petition from a thousand U.S. economists beseeching him to veto it. The tariff and the cut-off of American short-term credit upon which Europe depended were the principal forces that transmuted the Wall Street crash into the Great Depression.

All nations sought to keep their industries and farmers afloat by excluding imports. In spring and summer of 1931, the year of wrath, the banking system of central Europe collapsed. A subversive German scheme for economic union with Austria—a disguised annexation—provoked French financial retaliation. An already frail Austrian bank, the Credit Anstalt, failed. The resulting sudden flight of U.S. short-term loans from Germany almost

destroyed a banking system that agricultural depression and industrial malaise had already enfeebled. The German economy, the motor of central Europe, stalled; 17,000 industrial enterprises shut down.

Britain, after a last despairing gesture toward Austria—a credit offer of a mere $7 million for a week—itself came under pressure. In September 1931 London suspended payments in gold, which it had discontinued during the war and painfully reestablished in 1925 only thanks to U.S. help. The pound sterling became just another paper currency, rather than the unchanging world standard it had been throughout the nineteenth century. That was the end of Britain's already shattered claim to leadership. Hoover belatedly and half-heartedly laid claim to Britain's role by proposing a one year morato-

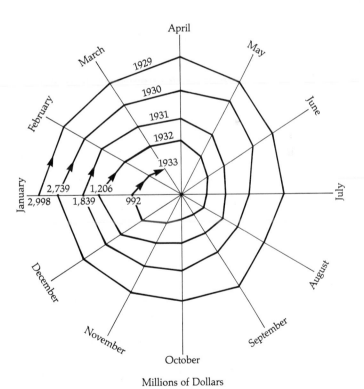

FIGURE 31-1   Down the Drain: The Contracting Spiral of World Trade, 1929–33

From Charles P. Kindleberger, *The World in Depression, 1929–1939* (Berkeley: University of California Press, 1973), p. 172.

rium on reparations and war debt payments in June 1931. Cancellation would have been more appropriate but U.S. opinion would not permit it. Regardless of U.S. wishes, war debt and reparations payments effectively ceased, although negotiations lingered until 1932–33.

Governments sought to promote recovery by drastic expenditure cuts to balance their budgets. That further depressed their economies by lessening demand. All, especially Germany, feared inflation so much that they fought deflation with more deflation. Tariff and currency devaluation wars continued, further deepening and widening the Depression. Britain, formerly the world bastion of free trade, adopted tariffs in 1932. The United States left the gold standard and devalued the dollar in 1933. In Germany and the United States, the worst-hit powers, roughly one worker in four was unemployed by the time the Depression reached bottom in 1932. The Great Depression cut world industrial production by almost a third and world trade by two thirds. The world market almost ceased to exist (see Figure 31-1). Then the precarious peace of 1919 collapsed.

THE WEST AND THE WIDER WORLD, 1919–39

The war discredited empire as well as destroying empires. The victors received German colonies, chunks of the Ottoman empire, or Pacific islands not as outright possessions, but as "mandates" from the League of Nations. In theory the purpose of colonialism was now to prepare the subject peoples for independence. That colonialism now needed fig-leaves was a sign of its impending demise.

And especially in Asia and the Middle East, war and Bolshevism encouraged the ultimate agent of that demise— nationalism. Japan's economic expansion encouraged it to press its claim to hegemony in East Asia. China's reac-

tion and the Great Depression soon impelled Japan to make good that claim by force. That challenge undermined the essential foundation of colonialism everywhere, the prestige won in the nineteenth century through the West's effortless domination of the wider world.

Culmination and Twilight of the Colonial Empires

In 1919, Britain appeared more supreme outside Europe than at any time since the 1870s. Along with its South African and Australian dominions, Britain had taken the lion's share of the colonial booty. It had at last secured the east coast of Africa from the Cape to Cairo. It had triumphantly completed the partition of the Ottoman empire that the Balkan nationalities had begun in 1878. Its major rivals were out of the running. Germany was defeated, Russia was in chaos, and the United States had no desire for further colonial acquisitions; in 1933–34 it pledged to give the Philippines independence by 1945 and renounced unilaterally its treaty right to intervene in Cuba. Britain's only remaining competitors were its allies, France and Japan.

But Britain's position was hollow. By May 1920 the chief of the general staff, Sir Henry Wilson, noted despairingly that "in no single theater are we strong enough—not in Ireland, nor England, not on the Rhine, not in Constantinople, nor Batoum, nor Egypt, nor Palestine, nor Mesopotamia, nor Persia, nor India." Nationalist revolts, Britain's shattered economic position, and the domestic priorities of its mass electorate made it impossible to hold either the immense gains of 1914–18, or Britain's first colony, Ireland.

At Easter 1916 a band of Irish nationalists had risen in Dublin with German promises of support. British troops put the rebels down and tactlessly executed the movement's leaders. That "blood sacrifice" destroyed the position of moderate Irish proponents of home rule, and made the radical nationalist

The Easter Rising, 1916: ruins in central Dublin after British artillery bombardment.

Sinn Fein a mass movement. In 1919 an offshoot of Sinn Fein, the "Irish Republican Army," launched a campaign of assassination and urban guerrilla war. The British responded. The feared "Black and Tans," former western front desperadoes, reinforced the Royal Irish Constabulary. Anonymous gangs caused suspected I.R.A. members and sympathizers to disappear. Even partition in 1921–22 between an Irish Free State in the south and Protestant Ulster in the north did not end "the troubles." I.R.A. diehards refused to accept partition, continued to assassinate British officials, and forced on the Free State itself a civil war more savage than the one the British had waged. A semblance of peace did not return until 1923, and in Ulster sporadic violence has continued to the present.

In Egypt, pivot of the empire, nationalist riots and assassinations in March 1919 likewise showed the limits of British power. Britain gave Egypt nominal independence in 1922 while retaining control of foreign policy, defense, and the all-important Suez Canal. In Iraq the British conceded sham-independence, inexpensively enforced by punitive raids with the fighter-bombers of the infant Royal Air Force.

Palestine was more difficult. The Balfour declaration of 1917 and the war itself speeded Jewish emigration from Europe to Palestine. The ideal of a Jew-

ish state was a creation of Theodor Herzl, who in 1897 had founded a Zionist Organization to promote it. Jewish immigation and aspirations to state-

The Balfour Declaration

Foreign Office
November 2nd, 1917

Dear Lord Rothschild,

I have much pleasure in conveying to you, on behalf of His Majesty's Government, the following declaration of sympathy with Jewish Zionist aspirations which has been submitted to, and approved by, the Cabinet.

"His Majesty's Government view with favour the establishment in Palestine of a National Home for the Jewish people, and will use their best endeavors to facilitate the achievement of this object, it being clearly understood that nothing shall be done which may prejudice the civil and religious rights of existing non-Jewish communities in Palestine, or the rights and political status enjoyed by Jews in any other country."

I should be grateful if you would bring this declaration to the knowledge of the Zionist Federation.

Yours sincerely,
(Signed) Arthur James Balfour

Quoted in L. Stein, *Zionism* (London: Ernest Benn, 1925), p. 377.

hood inevitably cut across the claims of Palestine's Arab inhabitants, many of whom, paradoxically, had moved to Palestine to benefit from the economic upsurge the Jews brought. In 1929 Arab-Jewish conflict erupted in the "Wailing Wall" riots in Jerusalem. After 1933, thanks to Adolf Hitler, Jewish immigration to Palestine doubled the Jewish population in three years. After 1936–37, a guerrilla struggle between Arabs and Jews tied down two British divisions sorely needed elsewhere. A British ban on Jewish immigration in 1939 failed to placate the Arabs and aroused the fierce hostility of the Zionists.

Worse still for Britain, India repeatedly erupted. Among the many ambiguous British promises of the dark year of 1917—when a mere 15,000 troops upheld British rule on the subcontinent—was a pledge of "responsible government" as reward for India's notable contribution to the war effort. Postwar British conduct appeared to betray that pledge. In April 1919, after a series of attacks on British civilians at Amritsar in the Punjab, General Reginald Dyer ordered his troops to disperse a crowd with rifle fire. In this "Amritsar Massacre" at least 379 died and over 1,200 suffered wounds. The massacre, and the ensuing celebration of Dyer in British Conservative circles as the man who had prevented a second Indian Mutiny, opened an unbridgeable gulf between Britain and educated Indian opinion.

Amritsar impelled Mohandas K. Gandhi, a Hindu lawyer who had made his name as a leader of the Indian community in South Africa, to launch the Congress party on a campaign of nonviolent civil disobedience. That collapsed in 1922, but British concession of self-government was slow; Gandhi revived his movement in 1930. The imprisonment of 60,000 demonstrators and Gandhi's rejection of British compromise offers again led to the movement's collapse; Gandhi had outrun Indian opinion. Then Britain gave in. The Government of India Act of 1935

The young Gandhi (1910).

conceded a constitution and a firm promise of independence, despite fierce opposition in London from Conservative diehards such as Winston Churchill. The Congress party swept the 1937 elections. But by that point, despite Gandhi's charismatic appeal, Indian nationalism had divided along the Hindu-Moslem line. A Westernized Moslem lawyer-politician, Mohammed Ali Jinnah, created a Moslem League that by 1940 was demanding partition of the subcontinent into Hindu and Moslem states.

Not even the white Dominions showed the unquestioning loyalty for which British imperialists hoped. Their share in Britain's 1914–18 sacrifices and victory gave the Dominions claims on Britain. With Canada and South Africa in the lead, the Dominions sought full sovereignty at the Imperial Conference of 1926. By the Statute of Westminster of 1931 they received it. The British Empire took the ambiguous title of "British Commonwealth of Nations." And in 1932, Eamon De Valera, sole survivor of the leaders of Easter 1916, became prime minister of the Irish Free State. In 1937 he took the Free State out of the Commonwealth in everything but name, and set a powerful example.

France preferred the Foreign Legion bayonet to the subtleties of negotiation. It was little more successful than Britain. Its 1919 acquisitions, Syria and Lebanon, proved combative and unrewarding. The French thought themselves compelled to batter Damascus with artillery as late as 1925. The Berbers of Morocco destroyed a Spanish army in 1921, and attacked the French. It took Pétain, tanks, and four years of fighting to reestablish colonial order. Algeria and Tunisia were intermittently restless.

In Indochina, under a placid surface, nationalist and Communist clandestine organizations spread, with encouragement from China. The Depression brought starvation to the Vietnamese peasantry and offered occasion for the first serious insurrections since French conquest in the nine-

Revolution 1911		1916		1921		1929	First Communist Republic Set Up 1931			1945		Communist Victory 1949
	Rule of General Yuan		Chaos		Guomindang Campaigns to Unify China		Guomindang Nominally in Control				Civil War	

teenth century. At Yen Bay, north of Hanoi, nationalists rose in 1930; Communists organized strikes and risings. Ho Chi Minh ("the bringer of enlightenment"), agent of the Communist International for Southeast Asia, founded a Communist party of Indochina. French reprisals were brutal even by French standards. Ho escaped to China and Moscow, and dryly observed that had the nonviolent Gandhi been born in a French colony he "would long since have entered heaven." France's control appeared unshaken. But soon white power everywhere in East Asia was at risk.

The Struggle for Mastery in East Asia Renewed

The Depression unleashed a struggle for supremacy in Asia that pitted Japanese imperial claims against both Chinese nationalism and the remnants of European domination. That struggle was long in the making. The decrepit Qing dynasty had expired in 1911–12 in the face of military revolt in southern and central China. The leading proponent of a Western-style Chinese nationalism, Sun Yat-sen, blessed that outcome—which destroyed what little prospect remained for a Japanese-style revolution from above that harnessed dynastic loyalty to the task of transformation. Sun instead helped found a political party, the Guomindang, and strove to give China constitutional government.

But power in the new China—as in most other societies whose traditional order collapsed under the impact of the West—now came from the barrel of a gun. The end of the dynasty and the crumbling of Confucianism in the face of Western ideas left no other form of

legitimacy. Yuan Shikai, most successful leader of the Western-armed provincial armies, had the most guns. He attempted to make himself emperor. Regional warlords resisted; Yuan fell ill and died in 1916. Thereafter warlord armies fought obscure struggles the length and breadth of China; those around Beijing (Peking) contended for the honor of manipulating a sham parliament. Chinese nationalism, outraged at the persistence of European and Japanese encroachments, sought in vain for a political vehicle.

Two contenders soon arose. Sun discarded parliamentarism for Leninism without Marxism. The Soviet Union, seeking a sphere of influence in China, delightedly offered advisers and arms. With the help of Michael Borodin, the Communist International's man in China, Sun drafted a new statute for the Guomindang that made it a centralized "vanguard party"—but one without a coherent ideology. Sun's military assistant, Chiang Kai-shek, created a party army in southern China with Soviet rifles and advisers, and inherited the Guomindang upon Sun's death in 1925. But the Soviet Union had a second string to its bow: the Chinese Communist Party (CCP) that groups of Beijing and Shanghai intellectuals had founded with Soviet advice in 1920–21. Those groups included the sturdy and pugnacious son of a rich peasant, Mao Zedong (Mao Tse-tung).

In 1927, as Chiang extended Guomindang control to central China, the collaboration that Moscow had imposed between Communists and Guomindang broke down. Chiang crushed the Communists in Shanghai and elsewhere with much slaughter; soon the CCP had forfeited its original base, the embryonic working classes of

Sun Yat-sen, theorist of Chinese nationalism (1923).

Rivals for the mastery of China: Chiang Kai-shek and Mao Zedong (below).

the industrializing coastal cities. Mao escaped to the hills on the Jiangxi-Hunan border, created a Party army of peasants and bandits, and ultimately purged his remaining rivals in the Party leadership. Lenin had adapted Marxism to a largely peasant country but had kept Marx's notion of the industrial proletariat as chosen people. Mao discarded even that; his Marxism for Chinese conditions made it an ideology of peasant revolt *against* the cities.

After temporarily suppressing the Communists, Chiang Kai-shek defeated the northern warlords and seized Beijing in 1928. That nominally unified China. But Chiang's rule was precarious; the Guomindang absorbed a variety of quarrelsome warlord elements as it expanded. The Communists in the hills remained a threat, despite five Guomindang "bandit-extermination campaigns." In 1934–35 Mao's forces escaped from south-central China and in an epic "Long March" of 6,000 miles sought refuge at Yenan in the remote northwest.

By that point, Chiang had another adversary to occupy him. Japan had yielded up most of its claims on China in the Washington treaties of 1922. The Western-style political parties that had arisen under Japan's Bismarckian constitution of 1889 were at the height of their influence in the early and middle 1920s, despite occasional assassinations of politicians by ultra-nationalist sects. But Japan's era of liberalism within and peace without was brief, thanks to both external and internal pressures. At Paris the powers had humiliated Japan by refusing its request to incorporate into the Versailles Treaty a declaration on racial equality. The corollary of that refusal was the banning of Japanese immigration to the United States and to Australia. Simultaneously, U.S. tariffs constricted Japanese exports and U.S. pressure dictated in 1921–22 the end of the alliance with Britain that had tied Japan, how-

ever tenuously, to the international status quo.

Inside Japan itself, by the late 1920s, explosive economic growth, population increase, and radical ideologies pressed against that status quo. Economic growth between 1900 and 1929, at 4.2 percent a year, was faster than that of any other power. Population grew from 43.8 million in 1900 to 71.1 million in 1940. American tariffs and immigration restrictions pushed Japan toward dependence on mainland raw materials and emigration outlets, especially in coal- and iron-rich Manchuria.

Ultra-nationalist sects, a feature of the Japanese scene since the "men of spirit" of the 1850s, proliferated. Ideologues such as Kita Ikki (1883–1939) proposed vague syntheses of Marxism and nationalism, and looked forward to a world-dominating Japan with vast colonial possessions and a population of 250 million. In the military such ideas prospered, especially among middle-level and junior officers with rural backgrounds. Ishiwara Kanji, most formidable of the middle-level officers, foresaw world conquest by stages. Japan would seize Manchuria, then fight Russia, Britain, and the United States in turn. Each victory would bring Japan the resources needed for the next step: "war can maintain war." Ishiwara was no isolated dreamer; he had the ear of the army's chiefs. And the army, like its German counterpart during the Hindenburg-Ludendorff dictatorship, soon became the decisive force in the state, responsible only to a figurehead emperor.

Chiang's conquest of northern China and the Depression almost coincided. Together they triggered this explosive mixture. Chinese nationalist boycotts of Japanese goods, Chinese aspirations to regain full control of Manchuria, and the Depression-borne collapse of Japan's already stagnant peasant economy impelled the Japanese army officer corps to strike, to secure Japan's vital Manchurian hinterland before it was too late. In September 1931, Ishiwara and a group of like-minded officers acting with the connivance of the staff in Tokyo planted explosives on Japan's railway in Manchuria and blamed the Chinese. The army swiftly cleared Manchuria of Chinese forces and created the puppet state of Manchukuo. The navy collided with the Chinese at Shanghai and extricated itself by ruthlessly bombarding the Chinese quarters of the city—in front of Western newsreel cameras. The cabinet in Tokyo, divided and terrified of assassination, acquiesced. When the League of Nations mildly reproved Japan in February 1933, the Japanese delegation stalked out, never to return.

The West failed to do anything effective, despite outrage over Shanghai. Britain now faced the same unpleasant situation that Russian occupation of northern China had created in 1900. London could not realistically fight a great war to preserve distant China; no vital British interest was at stake. In 1901–02 London had therefore taken on Japan as junior partner. But now Japan itself was the threat, and its relative strength was immeasurably greater

Mao Proposes a Peasant Revolution   1927

Mao's "Report on an Investigation of the Agrarian Movement in Hunan" of March 1927 was his earliest attempt to persuade his Party that it must either lead China's peasantry, or succumb to it.

The force of the peasantry is like that of the raging winds and driving rain. It is rapidly increasing in violence. No force can stand in its way. The peasantry will tear apart all nets which bind it, and hasten along the road to liberation. They will bury beneath them all forces of imperialism, militarism, corrupt officialdom, village bosses and evil gentry. Every revolutionary party, every revolutionary comrade will be subjected to their scrutiny and be accepted or rejected by them. Shall we stand in the vanguard and lead them or stand behind them and oppose them? Every Chinese is free to pick his answer. However, destiny will force us to pick an answer soon . . . .

From Benjamin I. Schwartz, *Chinese Communism and the Rise of Mao* (Cambridge: Harvard University Press, 1964), pp. 74–75.

than in 1902. This time Britain's only potential allies were the Soviet Union and the United States. But the Soviets were as great a threat to British interests in China as was Japan. And while Washington sternly refused to recog-

Japanese troops in Shanghai, 1933.

nize Japan's acquisition of Manchuria, it refused with equal sternness to back its moralistic talk with economic reprisals, much less with force. Braving U.S. disapproval, Britain soothed the Japanese and attempted to limit the damage.

Japan made that difficult. Its navy embarked on a new and massive program; in 1934 Japan withdrew from the Washington naval treaty. The elaborate structure of interwar naval disarmament came crashing down. Japanese politicians increasingly deferred to the military. Some who deferred with insufficient speed suffered the fate of prime minister Inukai Tsuyoshi in 1932, assassination. In 1936 junior officers, with the collaboration of Kita Ikki, attempted a coup in Tokyo and slaughtered several ministers. The high command reasserted itself with loyal troops and executions.

That ended the day of junior officers and freelance ideologues. Senior generals such as Tōjō Hideki increasingly directed Japanese policy in rivalry with the admirals. And in July 1937 an accidental brush with Guomindang forces near Beijing swiftly escalated into an open-ended China war. A militarized Japan, fighting under the unintentionally ironic slogan of "Asia for the Asians," sought to make China a Japanese colony. The first of the wars that ultimately converged to make the Second World War had begun.

THE THIRTIES: THE DEMOCRACIES FALTER

The Japanese threat caught the democracies as the Depression and their own demoralization touched bottom. Japan's success soon emboldened others. Fascist Italy, the Germany of Adolf Hitler, and ultimately even the Soviet Union broke the peace (see pp. 917–36). They met little opposition until very late.

Britain: Highmindedness and Decline

The Depression destroyed Ramsay MacDonald's second Labour government, which had taken office in 1929. Labour, trembling at the displeasure of the financial markets and lacking imagination, met the Depression by imposing balanced budgets. That required cuts in unemployment payments and provoked a cabinet and labor-union revolt in the catastrophic month of August 1931. MacDonald stayed on at the head of a "National Coalition" with Liberal and Conservative backing; Labour went into opposition.

As in Lloyd George's coalition, the Conservatives were the dominant partner. Baldwin flattered and mollified parliament and public; Neville Chamberlain provided the efficiency and drive. He was Austen Chamberlain's unlovable and iron-willed younger brother, in Lloyd George's unkind words "a good mayor of Birmingham in an off-year." In 1935 an enfeebled MacDonald retired, and Baldwin led

---

Churchill Warns MacDonald and Baldwin   1932

On November 23, 1932, in the House of Commons, Churchill commented scathingly on MacDonald's continued pursuit of Western disarmament in the face of the growing German threat:

Do not delude yourselves. Do not let His Majesty's Government believe—I am sure they do not believe—that all Germany is asking for is equal status. . . . That is not what Germany is seeking. All these bands of sturdy Teutonic youths, marching through the streets and roads of Germany, with the light of desire in their eyes to suffer for their Fatherland, are not looking for status. They are looking for weapons, and, when they have the weapons, believe me they will then ask for the return of lost territories and lost colonies, and when that demand is made it cannot fail to shake and possibly shatter to their foundations every one of the countries I have mentioned [France, Belgium, Poland, Rumania, Czechoslovakia, Yugoslavia], and some other countries I have not mentioned. . . .

From Martin Gilbert, *Winston S. Churchill*, Vol. V, *1922–1939. The Prophet of Truth* (Boston: Houghton Mifflin, 1977), p. 451.

the Conservatives to victory over Labour by shamming action to block Italy's conquest of Ethiopia (see p. 918). Then Baldwin bequeathed his iron-clad House of Commons majority to Chamberlain in 1937.

By that point Britain's world position was precarious. Japan's thrust into Manchuria had prompted the scrapping of the "ten year rule" and the creation of a committee to look into defense needs—but nothing more concrete. MacDonald, a quasi-pacifist during the First World War, deferred to the World Disarmament Conference that met in 1932–34, just as the revolt of the discontented powers took shape. Not until March 1934, after the Conference's inevitable collapse, did the British cabinet begin to debate rearmament. And only Winston Churchill, ceaselessly harassing the cabinet from outside, looked on the German threat with any urgency. Conservative opinion considered him "unsound" since his association with the Dardanelles fiasco (which others had mismanaged); his fierce opposition to the government over India had not enhanced his reputation. Baldwin's indolence and Chamberlain's niggling defense of financial orthodoxy triumphed. Large-scale British rearmament did not begin until

1936–37. It proved too little and too late.

France: Cynicism and Decline

Highminded professions of faith in the League and in disarmament accompanied the decline of Britain. The French were more cynical; the only disarmament that interested them was that of Germany, and that collapsed in 1932–1933. Yet France failed to react. The Depression struck France later than Britain or Germany, thanks to France's lesser degree of industrialization. But it hit hard and kept hitting. Industrial production stagnated at between 80 and 90 percent of its 1928 level from 1931 to mid-1939 (see Figure 31-2). Economic stagnation inevitably worsened drastically the central vice of French politics, ideological polarization. The always disorganized Third Republic tottered.

The Communists polled a million votes in 1928 and gained another half million by 1936. A further sharpening of Moscow's anti-Socialist line in 1928 produced open war between Communists and Socialists. That stopped the Socialists from collaborating for long with the Radical-Socialists to their right, for fear of losing yet more voters

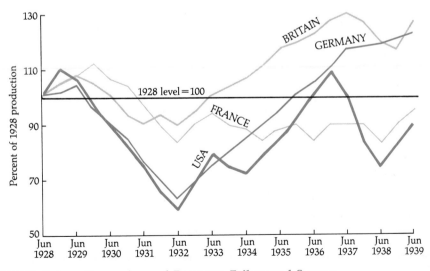

FIGURE 31-2   Depression and Recovery: Failure and Success
(Industrial Production as a Percentage of 1928 Production)

and union members to the Communists. Nor were the deputies of the center numerous enough to command the Chamber. And alongside the old Right of the Dreyfus era and the "two hundred families" that supposedly controlled French industry, a new populist Right emerged. The "Leagues," bands of trench-coated anti-Semitic thugs with lead pipes and revolvers, professed ideologies ranging from monarchism to extreme nationalist authoritarianism.

In January 1934, after two years of weak governments of the Left that rivalled the "cascade" of 1925–26, one of the Republic's characteristic scandals erupted. A shady financier of eastern European extraction, Alexander Stavisky, committed suicide or was murdered after the exposure of frauds apparently committed with the backing of prominent politicians. The Republic seemed even less reputable than usual. On February 6, 1934, the Leagues attacked parliament while Communists rioted in the industrial suburbs of Paris. Police firepower saved the Republic amid tension not seen in Paris since Boulanger and Dreyfus. The *"six février"* served notice that the Republic lived on borrowed time.

A change of line in Moscow gave the Left a second wind. In 1935 the Communist International, faced with the rise of Hitler's Germany, reversed its previous attempt to stamp out its Socialist rivals. In France the result was a "Popular Front" coalition of Radical-Socialists, Socialists, and Communists. Léon Blum, a vacillating Socialist intellectual, led the government that emerged from the Popular Front's election triumph of April–May 1936. Blum suppressed the Leagues. To the accompaniment of sit-in strikes and industrial turmoil he decreed paid vacations, the 40-hour week, and other concessions that French workers considered long overdue. Those restrictions on industry slowed rearmament and caused French investors to move their capital into harder currencies than the franc. That in turn brought Blum down in June

1937. The Left could win elections but could not govern.

Nor did Blum, torn between abhorrence of war and the pressing need for rearmament to face Germany, find a coherent foreign policy. Not that the Right would have necessarily performed better; much of it mouthed the slogan "better Hitler than Blum." Blum's foremost successor, Edouard Daladier, was a Radical of Napoleonic appearance but less than Napoleonic strength. His minister of finance, Paul Reynaud, saved the franc in the manner of Poincaré. But that success proved irrelevant. Under Daladier and Reynaud, France first abandoned its eastern allies, then itself collapsed.

The United States: Political Success and Economic Failure of the New Deal

Hoover appeared helpless as the economic fabric of the United States disintegrated. Stock prices continued to slide, wiping out much of the savings of a generation; U.S. Steel plunged from $262 a share in 1929 to $22 in 1932. U.S. industrial production dropped by 1932 to half of its 1929 level. Only unemployment rose: from 5 million in December 1930 to 13 million in December 1932. The unemployed and their families sought refuge in shantytowns, named with bitter irony "Hoovervilles."

Hoover lost the 1932 election. His threadbare protestations that prosperity was "just around the corner" were unconvincing. His spending on public works, although far greater than that of any previous administration, proved insufficient to spark the economy. His Democratic opponent, the New York grandee Franklin Delano Roosevelt, accepted the nomination with a pledge of a "new deal for the American people." But before Roosevelt could take office the overstrained banking system followed the rest of the economy, as panicked depositors stormed the tellers' windows. On inauguration day, March 4, 1933, Roosevelt shut the re-

The impact of the Depression: a "Hooverville" in Seattle, 1933.

maining banks before they collapsed. Capitalism itself seemed in ruins.

Roosevelt brought a short-term remedy that had eluded Hoover: force of conviction. "So first of all let me assert my firm belief that the only thing we have to fear is fear itself—nameless, unreasoning, unjustified terror . . . ," rang his presidential address. In a mere five days he pushed through Congress a Hoover plan to shore up the banks. In the first of a series of radio "fireside chats" that gave the nation back some of its lost self-confidence, he announced that the banks would reopen. By June 1933 he had averted the threat of total economic collapse. Industrial production briefly equalled the level of 1929.

Roosevelt and his "brain trust" of young intellectuals directed at Congress a torrent of legislation that established public works programs far vaster than those of Hoover, and recruited the unemployed into a quasi-military Civilian Conservation Corps; the first New Deal administration created 6 million jobs. To raise agricultural prices, government paid farmers not to plant crops. Government extended to farmers and householders some protection from the mortgage foreclosures that meant economic ruin, and gave unemployment benefits to workers. Government ultimately guaranteed the right to organize unions and created the compulsory pension plan known as Social Security. And thanks to the free-trade convictions of Roosevelt's otherwise ineffectual Secretary of State, Cordell Hull, U.S. trade barriers dropped after 1934. That was too late to save the fragmented world market—but better later than not at all.

The New Deal's European-style welfare-state measures seemed revolutionary—and aroused the bitter enmity of business interests. Soon the Republican establishment was denouncing Roosevelt as a "dictator" and traitor to his class. Labor, blacks, and most middle-class Americans took a different view. Roosevelt won his second term in 1936 by an unprecedented margin of 11 million votes; his Republican opponent carried only Maine and Vermont.

But stability and prosperity failed to return. Production briefly surpassed 1928 levels in 1936–37, then dropped again catastrophically (see Figure 31-2 on p. 893). By December 1937, the largest steel industry in the world was operating at 26 percent of capacity. Roosevelt had vastly increased the role of government in the economy—but until 1938 he held to the Hoover orthodoxy of balanced budgets. Unfortunately, unbalanced budgets were precisely what the economy required to stimulate demand. Not until his 1938 recovery plan did Roosevelt halfheartedly opt for deficits. And it was not New Deal economic policies but necessity that generated recovery after 1939. Armament production for global war dragged the United States out of the Depression as the revolt of the discontented powers in Europe and Asia dragged it back again into world affairs.

THE AGE OF UNCERTAINTY

The 20-year truce was not merely a time of demoralization for the democracies or of triumph for savage dictatorships—a theme taken up in the following chapter. It was also an era of disorienting intellectual, social, and cultural change. Science continued its rapid expansion of human knowledge of the cosmos and of the building blocks of matter itself. Technology transformed everyday life. The state took on vast new duties. The war had accelerated the rise of workers' parties and the political, economic, and sexual emancipation of women. It had speeded the breakdown, among much else, of previous notions of what constituted art. A new writing, art, and architecture, reflecting disenchantment with the certainties of the pre-1914 era and rejection of the war, flourished. The mass culture born before the war reached maturity, especially in the United States, to the horror of many

traditionalist intellectuals. And the war acted as catalyst for new and terrifying ideologies.

Science: The End of Certainty

By 1900, and still more by 1919, phenomena had emerged that were puzzling or inexplicable to physicists. Neither electromagnetism nor light conformed precisely to the traditional Newtonian framework. Worse, the theorists soon had to cope with X-rays (1895), radioactivity (1896), and Ernest Rutherford's 1911 discovery that atoms were not solid, as assumed since the first atomic theories had emerged in ancient Greece. Atoms apparently contained electrons, nuclei, and much empty space. Radioactive decay emerged in 1913; uranium and thorium, it appeared, turned into lead. Atomic nuclei might contain further particles.

Matter, considered fixed and untransmutable since the birth of modern chemistry in the eighteenth century, was thus again in flux. In 1919 Rutherford bombarded nitrogen with helium nuclei, and produced oxygen. Researchers discovered neutrons and positrons in 1932 and 1933. The "cyclotron" or racetrack-like particle accelerator first proposed in 1932 allowed, among much else, the laboratory creation of the "transuranic" heavy elements. The first were neptunium and plutonium in 1940.

The theorists soon attempted to explain some of what the researchers were finding. Max Planck of Berlin suggested in 1900 that energy from warm bodies did not radiate at uniform levels across the spectrum, but jumped in steps or *quanta*; the amount of energy released varied with its wavelength. Albert Einstein, at that point an obscure patent examiner in Switzerland, suggested in 1905 that light too was "quantized." Niels Bohr of Denmark applied the quantum concept in 1913 to Rutherford's new atom, and explained both atomic structure and the differing spectra that various elements emitted. In 1927 Werner Heisenberg of Leipzig,

Giant of the new physics: Albert Einstein in Berlin, 1920.

in the course of researches on quantum theory, suggested that the very act of measuring the position, velocity, or mass of a particle interacted with the particle, introducing uncertainty into the measurement. Prediction of the action of subatomic particles fell back on mere statistics—a most un-Newtonian and disquieting state of affairs.

By that point Einstein had established the theory of relativity, the foundation, along with quantum theory, of modern physics. In 1905, in a paper that outlined his "Special Theory of Relativity," Einstein asserted that time and space were not absolute entities, as Newtonian physics required, but rather varied relative to the observer's velocity and location. The only absolute in Einstein's new universe was the speed of light—186,300 miles per second—which was the absolute limit of velocity. Mass increased with velocity, and mass, times a constant squared, was equivalent to energy: $E = mc^2$. That fateful notion as yet lacked empirical confirmation.

By 1916 Einstein had incorporated gravitation into his theory, which now became the "General Theory of Relativity." And in 1919 an eclipse permitted the first confirmation of the General Theory. Starlight passing through the sun's gravitational field bent by the amount Einstein's theory predicted. Newton's tidy universe gave way to a four-dimensional and curved "space-time continuum." Attempts to unify the General Theory of Relativity with quantum theory, and to explain everything from gravitation to the birth and death of the cosmos and the ever-expanding world of subatomic particles, proliferated.

It soon emerged that Einstein's insights had dramatic practical application. In January 1939, building on work by Niels Bohr, Enrico Fermi, and others, Otto Hahn and Fritz Strassmann of Berlin announced that they had split the nuclei of uranium atoms by bombarding them with neutrons. The process transmuted the uranium into barium and a small amount of the uranium's original mass into an as-

tounding amount of energy, as Einstein's formula suggested. The race to create a self-sustaining atomic chain reaction—and weapons of unprecedented destructive power—began.

Biology and medicine experienced the same accelerated pace of advance that was visible in physics. Even before the First World War, the first crude antibiotics—organic poisons that killed disease organisms but not their human hosts—appeared. Salvarsan, an arsenic compound that revolutionized the treatment of syphilis, became available as early as 1909. The sulfonamides, effective against pneumonia and gangrene, followed in 1935–38. Penicillin emerged in the laboratory in 1929; its first medical use in 1940 proved it startlingly effective against a wide range of diseases and infections.

Advances in immunization had in 1914–18 at least spared western Europe the typhoid epidemics that had accompanied previous great wars. In the interwar period inoculations for diphtheria, yellow fever, typhus, and bubonic plague became available. The discovery of hormones such as insulin (1922) and cortisone (1936) permitted the development of therapies for such previously untreatable conditions as diabetes. The identification and isolation of vitamins helped eradicate deficiency diseases such as pellagra. Thanks to improvements in blood typing, transfusions became normal procedure after 1940. And insecticides, especially DDT (1939) showed promise of eliminating insect carriers of disease. For the Germans, who first developed them, the new insecticides also showed promise of another sort. In 1936 the great German chemical trust, I. G. Farben, began a crash program to develop, from a family of insecticides that killed by disrupting nerve impulses, a weapon for use against humans: the first nerve gas.

Technology: Steel, Oil, and Electricity

The war and the interwar period accelerated dramatic changes in materials and energy sources that were already underway. Steel remained king, thanks to a bewildering variety of new stainless or extremely hard alloys with metals such as chromium, vanadium, tungsten, nickel, and molybdenum. Concrete, reinforced with steel rods, came into its own as a structural material that permitted the most astounding architectural shapes. Aluminum, refined with electric power, became the material of choice for everything from aircraft to cooking pots. Plastics developed rapidly; by 1939 they provided everything from transparent canopies and windows for aircraft to flexible insulation for electrical cables. Synthetic rubber, another German innovation, became vitally important both to Germany and to the United States after 1939. Artificial fibers such as rayon and its numerous derivatives made possible garments even less expensive than cotton. But artificial yarns made from wood or cellulose fibers were only the first step. In the 1930s the first truly synthetic fiber, derived from oil, became available—nylon. Its great strength made it ideal for everything from stockings to parachutes.

In the realm of energy sources, oil and electricity now triumphed, along with their associated technologies. The First World War had made demands for transport that only the internal combustion engine could meet, and had immensely accelerated motorization. Trucks, tanks, and tractors supplemented and in many cases superseded the horse. Oil-fired high-compression steam turbines or diesel engines replaced clumsy coal, which required stokers and prevented refueling at sea. By the mid-1920s aircraft had ceased to be underpowered kite-like objects of wood, cloth, and wire. By the early 1930s the first multiengined all-metal airliners were carrying passengers rich and daring enough to try them. Even humanity's oldest form of combustion-propelled projectile revived. In 1926 the visionary Robert Goddard developed the first practical liquid-fuelled rocket. His work attracted little attention in his native United States, but

observers in Russia and Germany found it intriguing.

Electricity revolutionized communications and created new mass media: motion pictures, sound recordings, radio, and television. Motion picture technology originated in the 1890s in the United States and France; by 1914 "movie houses" were common. Record players and radios, thanks to Lee DeForest's triode amplifier tube (1906–07), were widespread by 1928, the year of the first "talkie." Television—images electronically scanned, transmitted by radio, and displayed on a cathode ray tube—emerged in U.S. and British laboratories in the mid-1920s, although it did not begin to reach the public for another two decades.

Electronics had more deadly uses: the detection of submarines by sound ranging (sonar) and above all of aircraft and surface ships by radio ranging (radar). After 1935 Britain and Germany raced one another for mastery over those vital auxiliaries to air and sea warfare. As the unquiet truce ended, science was developing a potential it had not yet possessed in 1914: the potential to decide the outcome of war between great powers.

The State in Crisis

The First World War ended for good the state that governed best by governing least. The state henceforth took responsibility for guaranteeing the survival and welfare of the individual. Prewar measures such as old age pensions and industrial-accident insurance expanded. Unemployment benefits became law. In Germany, workers briefly gained a state-sanctioned voice in management decisions. The United States of Coolidge and Hoover resisted such allegedly socialist measures; then Roosevelt adopted many of them.

The war had also introduced management of currency and foreign exchange, and vast bureaucracies to plan investment and allocate raw materials. Peace had dismantled that planning

The RCA Victor trademark, symbol of the new recorded sound.

"HIS MASTER'S VOICE"
REG. U.S. PAT. OFF.

machinery, but the example of the Hindenburg Program lived on in the Soviet Union (see pp. 911–12). The Depression, a crisis in some ways more severe than the war, gave the state back its wartime role—in "peace." The state grudgingly took responsibility for the fate of the economy.

Most democracies adopted a degree of economic planning. But as Roosevelt's confused experimentation suggests, they lacked a theory. In 1936, John Maynard Keynes at last provided a theory for an era in which laissez-faire appeared to lead ever deeper into the abyss. In his *General Theory of Employment, Interest, and Money*, Keynes argued that government deficit financing—the creation of money by decree—was the obvious antidote to deflation and unemployment. Government spending put people to work; their spending, through the "multiplier effect," put others to work. Ideas require time to penetrate, and Keynes's arrived too late. The old orthodoxy dominated as late as 1937, when a tax increase and a tightening of the money supply produced a renewed economic nosedive in the United States. To recover, Roosevelt adopted by trial and error a mild version of deficit financing. Within a decade, Keynes's theories had become conventional wisdom, the charter for continuous state management of market economies.

Workers: Expectations Disappointed

At the outbreak of war in 1914, Britain's Liberal foreign secretary, Sir Edward Grey, dolefully foretold its political and social consequences: "There will be Labour governments everywhere after this." Britain, France, and Weimar Germany indeed received governments that workers' parties led or dominated. But those governments, and the labor unions that furnished their largest single bloc of support, operated under severe limitations.

First, the workers were themselves divided. Regional and craft lines fractured the unions of Britain and the United States; racial and ethnic lines also divided U.S. workers. On the Continent, Communists sought to destroy Socialists in both the unions and the political arena. In Germany, as described in Chapter 32, the Communist offensive after 1928 helped kill the Weimar Republic; both Socialist and Communist parties perished in a common ruin.

Second, the Depression dramatically lowered morale. Especially in Europe, it weakened the main weapon of industrial workers, the strike. Few strike when one worker in four has no job. Finally, industrial workers, contrary to the predictions of Marx, found themselves in the minority in advanced capitalist societies. Except in egalitarian Scandinavia, political parties claiming to represent workers consistently failed to achieve more than a third of the vote. Insuperable social and ideological barriers prevented further growth—a profoundly demoralizing situation.

If the workers accepted democratic rules, socialism was clearly impossible, for the "bourgeoisie" would hardly vote its own demise. But if the workers chose the path of revolution, the other two-thirds of society, with the help of the state apparatus, would inevitably prevail. These constraints and the moderate instincts of western Europe's social democrats confined unions and workers' parties in the interwar period to a "war of position"—a trench struggle for gradual reform of the economic system rather than for its overthrow. Given their minority status, those workers' parties that did achieve power rarely governed long. In the Depression many even failed to prevent their political adversaries from balancing government budgets by reducing unemployment benefits and state employee salaries.

Women: New Predicaments for Old

Women in Britain, Germany, Scandinavia, and the United States likewise discovered that the vote and the workings of the political system changed their status only slowly. Giving the vote prevented a repetition of the prewar confrontations in Britain. It channeled women's political activities to the existing parties. It helped women's groups to lobby for full equality before the law and for legislation protecting mothers and children. But the onset of the Depression and the coming of a new war soon diverted politically active women from "women's issues" to more general ones.

Many countries, among them France, Italy, Belgium, and Switzerland, did not concede even the vote, thanks to the weight of male opinion and of the Church. And women's economic position between the wars was even more precarious than that of men. Demobilization of the mass armies and conversion to peacetime production led to mass dismissals of women from industry. Structural changes—the continuing decline of peasant agriculture and of "mom and pop" retailing—likewise narrowed women's employment possibilities.

But women were unwilling to give up their new-found economic independence. Many had to earn a living in any case: their husbands were dead. The interwar growth of business bureaucracies and of that temple of consumption, the department store, offered a substitute for industrial employment. Women penetrated the professions at a greater rate than before, especially in the United States, Britain, and Scandinavia. They maintained their positions in fields such as nursing, primary-school teaching, and librarianship. They nevertheless normally received less money than men—for the same work.

In one vital area the interwar period was the scene of truly dramatic change—control of reproduction. During and immediately after the war, pioneers such as the American Margaret Sanger (1883–1966) and the Englishwoman Marie Stopes (1880–1958) made contraceptive information available to a mass audience for the first time. A Dutch invention, the diaphragm, joined the condom, an eighteenth century device popularized—like cigarettes—in the First World War.

Women thus for the first time acquired efficient means to determine when and by whom they had children. Improved childbirth techniques and nutrition ensured that fewer of the children born subsequently died. Fewer children in turn meant that the average woman now spent four years or less—instead of fifteen or more—pregnant or nursing. That was a historic achievement that allowed some women, for the first time, to aspire to have both a career and a family.

Most men still objected. And the new science of the mind offered small improvement over nineteenth-century medical notions of female inferiority. In Freud's view, woman's unconscious yearning for a penis allegedly led her to seek a penis-substitute: babies. Above all, the course of interwar politics menaced emancipated women; Fascists and Nazis sought to crush all challenges to male supremacy. The mission of the allegedly "inferior sex of the master race" was to breed large broods of heroes. But even those regimes failed to reverse the decline of the birth rate that industrialization had brought and contraception accelerated.

The High Culture of Disenchantment

The war broke down inhibitions in literature and art as well as in life. William II had insisted that "an art that transgresses the laws and barriers recognized by me ceased to be an art." Now he was gone; censorship, both formal and informal, diminished in intensity throughout northern Europe. Avant-garde literary and artistic trends that had originated before 1914 now became dominant, at least in high culture.

The prevailing mood was one of disenchantment. The war was the formative experience of an entire generation. Its apparent futility marked their writing, especially in highminded Britain, where the sordid brutality of war had come as a greater shock than elsewhere. British "war poets" such as

Margaret Sanger, pioneer of birth control for the masses, about to appear in court (1917).

Wilfred Owen, Robert Graves, and Siegfried Sassoon wrote eloquent verse that damned the war and the western front. The peculiar conditions of the war, the stark contrast between apparently futile slaughter at the front and almost complete safety beyond artillery range, engendered a fierce hatred of all symbols of authority. Sassoon, a highly decorated officer, railed with particular bitterness at generals, staffs, politicians, and civilians. French war writing, especially *Under Fire* (1917) by Henri Barbusse, who later became a Communist, reflected France's immense losses. Even German war literature occasionally sounded a despondent note, as in Erich Maria Remarque's *All Quiet on the Western Front* (1929).

But Germany was different from the West. There, heroic nihilists of the Ernst Jünger stamp dominated. Works such as *Battle as an Inner Experience* (1922), *Fire and Blood* (1925), and *Artillery Barrage Around Germany* (1928) convinced the German young that they had missed something. Jünger spoke or claimed to speak for his generation: "War, the father of all things, is also our father; it has hammered, hewn, and tempered us into what we are. And so long as the spinning wheel of life turns within us, this war will be the axis about which it whirls."

In England, the aesthetes of the "Bloomsbury Group" devoted themselves to the destruction of what little remained of Victorian morality in their own private lives. Freud appeared to suggest that conventional morality was an elaborate hypocritical cloak over unconfessable desires. He appeared to legitimate not merely confessing but advertising and even gratifying those desires. And his doctrines were an inexhaustible source of small talk. Freud's works now became a popular success.

Bloomsbury also attacked the symbols of Victorianism. Lytton Strachey's *Eminent Victorians* (1918), with its inaccurate but compelling demolitions of Florence Nightingale, "Chinese" Gordon, and other national totems, was an instantaneous success. Keynes, a Bloomsburyite by adoption, expiated his guilt—in Bloomsbury's eyes—for having worked for the government during the war by savaging his former chief, Lloyd George, in *The Economic Consequences of the Peace* (1919).

In poetry, two transplanted Americans and an Irishman—T. S. Eliot (1888–1965), Ezra Pound (1885–1972), and William Butler Yeats (1865–1939)—gave English poetry a modern shape that ultimately derived from the French Symbolists: loose in structure and playing on layer upon layer of symbolism and allusion to mythology and literature. Eliot's greatest work, a manifesto for the new English poetry, was *The Waste Land* (1922). Its bleak vision of London and modern life as Dante's *Inferno* fitted precisely the post-war mood among intellectuals:

> Unreal City,
> Under the brown fog of a winter dawn,
> A crowd flowed over London Bridge, so many,
> I had not thought death had undone so many.

Pound, more difficult and allusive even than Elliot, eventually succumbed to an obsessive anti-Semitism and took Fascist Italy as his adopted country. Yeats, like the others, wove symbols and bizarre occult or cosmological references into his poems. But he also wrote some of the most lucid and musical English verses of the twentieth century, such as the famous lines of "The Second Coming" (1921) that prophesied the interwar triumph of political barbarism:

> Things fall apart; the centre cannot hold;
> Mere anarchy is loosed upon the world,
> The blood-dimmed tide is loosed, and everywhere
> The ceremony of innocence is drowned;
> The best lack all conviction, while the worst
> Are full of passionate intensity.

In the novel, a new technique, the "stream of consciousness," prevailed briefly. Marcel Proust pioneered it in his monumental *Remembrance of Things Past* (1913–27), in which he abandoned narrative in favor of an apparent reconstruction of the thoughts and memories of the novel's protagonist. Virginia Woolf, the one great literary talent of Bloomsbury, experimented with it. But its greatest master was the Irish expatriate, James Joyce. His *Ulysses* (1921) was a minute reconstruction of a day in the life of a Dublin salesman, Leopold Bloom, organized around themes from Homer's *Odyssey*. Its occasional passages about sex prevented it from appearing in England or the United States, much less in Ireland. Banning, and its spread through copies smuggled from Paris, only enhanced its reputation. It was the most influential English novel of the century. In its sequel, *Finnegan's Wake* (1939), Joyce pushed his language beyond comprehensibility and left his audience behind.

On the Continent, Thomas Mann confirmed his position, acquired before the war, as Germany's greatest living man of letters. His monumental symbolic novel, *The Magic Mountain* (1924), was an ambiguous saga of good and evil that conveyed despair in the power of reason in human affairs. Despair in reason was a step forward for Mann. During the war, he had actively urged the rejection of reason, democratic politics, and the West in a long tract entitled *Reflections of an Unpolitical Man* (1918).

German writers of the "Expressionist" school experimented with a drama of unbridled emotion, Freudian symbolism, and Left politics. Expressionist

sons messily murdered their fathers and the other figures of authority that the lost war had discredited. The greatest talents of the school were Bertolt Brecht (1898–1956), and the novelist and short story writer Franz Kafka (1883–1926). Brecht soon exchanged Expressionism for Leninism. Kafka constructed a symbolic world in which fear, guilt, and the merciless arbitrariness of incomprehensible forces torture the isolated individual. Kafka's novella, "The Metamorphosis" (1915), sums up Kafka's view of humanity's fate in the modern world. His hero, Gregor Samsa, wakes up one morning and discovers that he has inexplicably become a giant cockroach.

In the visual arts and architecture, new schools proliferated. The Great War slaked Italian Futurism's thirst for violence and change; it emerged enfeebled. "Dada," a Parisian fashion of the teens and twenties, poked fun at art itself and celebrated the absurd and unpredictable. Its progeny, "Surrealism," sought to represent inner reality in paintings strewn with half-melted pocket watches and Freudian symbols. The center of excitement in the visual arts moved briefly from Paris to Berlin and Munich, thanks to Expressionist masters such as Paul Klee (1879–1940). And in architecture, Walter Gropius, Mies van der Rohe, Bruno Taut, and others secured the first large-scale commissions for the new functional architecture, the "international style." The architects at least were optimists; they sought to remake humanity by remaking its environment. The last was too ambitious a project—but they did revolutionize architecture and design.

Mass Culture and Its Critics

One source, beside the shock of the great war, of the despondency that afflicted many intellectuals in the 1920s was the appalling discovery that this was indeed the "age of the masses." A variety of German thinkers stigmatized democracy as the "rule of the inferior." Ortega y Gasset, a Spanish philosopher and literary critic, won immediate fame

The Bauhaus school of architecture and design, Dessau, Germany (1926).

with his denunciation of *The Revolt of the Masses* (1929). Ortega complained that unwashed legions, half-educated through universal primary schooling and given power through the vote, were besieging the citadel of Western civilization. The liberal elites born in the nineteenth century had ceased to lead; chaos had resulted.

The reason for that failure of leadership was obscure to Ortega. But it was plain enough. Liberals deplored as an affront to their own cultural standards or to human dignity the methods seemingly needed to exert leadership. Others were less squeamish. Georges Sorel, the pre-1914 French seer of revolution, had developed the concept of "political myths" that mobilized the masses. The French psychologist Gustave Le Bon (1841–1931) had argued that "the crowd" was "feminine" and had claimed that it demanded the domination of a charismatic male. And in the Anglo-Saxon countries, vast engines of publicity sold everything from soap to vacuum cleaners to wartime hatred of "the Hun." The foremost characteristic of the operators of that machinery was their contempt for the public they manipulated.

The "age of the masses" was thus to be an age of emotion, not reason. Advertising used the same techniques to sell a charismatic leader or a Lucky Strike. New media such as film, radio, and illustrated magazines proved especially effective at conveying and appealing to emotion. Politics in Fascist Italy and in Germany after 1933 took on quasi-religious overtones as vast regimented throngs hailed their leaders.

What most critics of interwar mass culture failed to remember was that historically speaking, the alternative to semiliteracy had been no literacy at all. Until the nineteenth century only narrow elites had fully enjoyed the written word. Its extension to the majority of the population inevitably involved a lowering of standards, by the standards of the elite. But that was not the end of the world; one answer to semiliteracy was better mass education. Nor was the thrust of the mass market toward the lowest common denominator an all-encompassing and uniform thrust.

The continuing rise in living standards, except during the Depression, did not invariably foster mediocrity and uniformity. It also permitted excellence and diversity. Bauhaus architecture and design was a genuine popular success. In film, German directors before 1933 created popular successes that were also works of art. Even Hollywood, which established an absolute dominance over the world film industry in the 1930s, occasionally made movies that were not totally frivolous. And in politics, as Roosevelt's radio talks demonstrated, genuine democrats could mobilize a mass public as effectively as the new barbarians.

The Revolt against Reason

War and Depression unleashed those barbarians. In Germany above all, defeat and revolution made anti-Semitic conspiracy theories seem plausible to a wide audience. The wartime propaganda of Tirpitz's *Vaterlandspartei* against the West, the Left, and the Jews found its logical continuation in scores of radical nationalist prophets and sects.

An eccentric Munich schoolmaster, Oswald Spengler (1880–1936), provided a pseudo-historical legitimation for the new barbarism of the racists and of the visionaries of "soldierly nationalism" such as Jünger. In the summer of 1918, Spengler published the first volume of a turgid 900-page work entitled *The Collapse of the West.* For Spengler, history was a vast cyclical process in which civilizations, the products of creative minorities of Nietzschean supermen, rose, decayed, and collapsed. The West was nearing the end of its cycle. Amid chaos and the brutal self-assertion of new creative minorities a new civilization might soon be born.

As history, Spengler's grandiose vision was oddly compelling although sometimes laughably distorted. As prophecy it proved almost self-fulfilling. The book's coincidence with Germany's defeat ensured its success. To many Germans, war and an unwanted revolution indeed seemed like the collapse of civilization. And in ensuing years, in works such as *Prussianism and Socialism* (1920) and "The Political Duties of German Youth" (1924), Spengler spelled out in detail the ruthless commitment he thought the new age demanded.

German philosophy added its authority to the chorus of unreason. Nietzsche had denounced Judeo-Christian values as a "slave morality" and had subordinated all morality to "life." His most prominent successor, Martin Heidegger (1889–1976), altogether denied that moral values had a rational basis. In Heidegger's *Being and Time* (1927), the individual was utterly alone, imprisoned in time. The only certainties were *Angst* (usually translated, too strongly, as "dread") and death. Only by living in full awareness of *Angst* and death could a select few define themselves and live "authentically"—a claim that ironically smacked of moral judgment.

Spengler on the Political Duties of German Youth   1924

Whether one is right or wrong—that doesn't amount to much in history. Whether or not he is superior to his adversary in a practical way, that is what decides whether he will be successful. . . . To be honorable and nothing else—that's not enough for our future. . . . To train oneself as material for great leaders, in proud self-denial, prepared for personal sacrifice, that is also a German virtue. And, given the case that, in the hard times ahead, strong men will appear, leaders to whom we must entrust our fate, then they must have something upon which they can rely. They need a generation such as Bismarck did not find, which appreciates their kind of action and does not reject it for romantic reasons, a dedicated band of followers who have, by way of long and serious self-training, come to the point of understanding the necessary and do not—as would doubtless be true today—reject it as un-German.

From Gordon A. Craig, *Germany 1866–1945* (Oxford: Oxford University Press, 1978), p. 491.

This quest for "authenticity"—in a world where values apparently have no foundation or validity outside the individual—had curious consequences. It often led to self-affirmation through radical politics: the more radical, the more self-affirming. Heidegger himself made his choice in 1933. Academic freedom, he announced in his inaugural speech as rector of Freiburg University, was "inauthentic." Like Spengler, he enthusiastically urged German youth to serve German radical nationalism and a leader. Unlike Spengler, Heidegger had a specific leader in mind—Adolf Hitler.

Others chose different leaders. Bertolt Brecht and the literary critic György Lukács (1885–1971) picked Stalin, to whom Lukács made embarrassing obeisance. Lukács's commitment to an irrational political faith did not make him self-conscious; he later wrote an entire volume lovingly demolishing German "irrationalism" from the romantics to Heidegger and Hitler. Brecht, in one of his Depression plays, used his unmatched command of German to celebrate the omniscience and ruthlessness of the Leninist "vanguard of the masses" in verses that the German Communist Party found excessively enthusiastic and frank.

Even in strongholds of middle-class values such as Britain and the United States, the war, the Depression, and the crises of the 1930s prompted intellectuals to irrational enthusiasms. Freud, although he claimed to be a rationalist, undermined reason through his faith in the overwhelming power of the savage forces he saw in the unconscious mind. Those who nevertheless retained a faith in "progress" and reason tended to lean leftward. Lincoln Steffens, a crusading American journalist, returned in 1919 from Russia with a jubilant announcement: "I been over into the future, and it works!" He was the first of many. Widespread loss of faith in the future of Western society engendered an irrational desire to believe in progress *somewhere*. Visiting Western liberals noisily embraced the Soviet Union and resolutely ignored all evidence that contradicted the facade behind which their jolly Soviet hosts hid a reality of mass executions and starvation. In the mid-1930s American Communism successfully wooed some disenchanted liberals; it claimed to be "twentieth century Americanism."

War and Depression together created a disorienting and demoralizing world. Empires fell. Political and social landmarks crumbled. Religious, moral, political, and even scientific certainties undermined in the nineteenth century now collapsed. An exaggerated faith in the power of reason gave way to the fanatical celebration and cynical manipulation of emotion. The "best," the defenders of Western civilization and of democracy, lacked the conviction to squarely face the "passionate intensity" of their enemies, the nationalist-racist and Marxist-Leninist dictatorships. The 1920s were no golden age, even in western Europe. The 1930s opened with war in East Asia. They closed with the greatest war in history.

Suggestions for Further Reading

Interwar Politics

A good introduction to interwar Europe is R. J. Sontag, *A Broken World, 1919–1939* (1971). S. Marks, *The Illusion of Peace: International Relations in Europe, 1918–1933* (1976), is excellent on relations between states; for eastern Europe see C. A. Macartney and A. W. Palmer, *Independent Eastern Europe* (1962). On Britain, A. J. P. Taylor, *English History, 1914–1945* (1965), is highly readable; see also M. Muggeridge, *The Thirties* (1940), and G. Orwell, *Down and Out in Paris and London* (1933), and *The Road to Wigan Pier* (1937). On France, see especially P. Bernard and H. Dubief, *The Decline of the Third Republic, 1914–1938* (1985), and

A. Adamthwaite, *France and the Coming of the Second World War* (1977). On the United States, W. E. Leuchtenburg, *The Perils of Prosperity, 1914–1932* (1958), is still rewarding, but see also E. W. Hawley, *The Great War and the Search for a Modern Order* (1979); for the 1930s, R. S. McElwaine, *The Great Depression: America, 1929–1941* (1984), is excellent. For Germany's brief democratic experiment, see especially A. J. Nicholls, *Weimar and the Rise of Hitler* (1968); E. Eyck, *A History of the Weimar Republic* (1967); and the relevant portion of G. Craig, *Germany, 1866–1945* (1978).

The Great Depression

For the causes and course of the Great Depression, J. K. Galbraith, *The Great Crash, 1929* (1955), and C. Kindleberger, *The World in Depression, 1929–1939* (1973), are useful; D. Landes, *The Unbound Prometheus* (1972), places the event in long-term perspective. For events in the colonial empires, see especially E. Monroe, *Britain's Moment in the Middle East, 1914–1956* (1963); A. Williams, *Britain and France in the Middle East and North Africa, 1914–1967* (1968); B. N. Pandey, *The*

Break-Up of British India (1969); and J. M. Brown, *Modern India: the Origins of an Asian Democracy* (1985). On China, see J. K. Fairbank, *The Great Chinese Revolution, 1800–1985* (1986); *The Cambridge History of China*, Vol. 12, Part I (1983); and J. E. Sheridan, *China in Disintegration* (1975). For Japan, see especially W. G. Beasley, *Japanese Imperialism, 1894–1945* (1987), and J. B. Crowley, *Japan's Quest for Autonomy* (1966).

Culture Between Two Wars

On the intellectual impact of the war, the broad survey of R. Wohl, *The Generation of 1914* (1979), and the relevant portions of H. S. Hughes, *Consciousness and Society: The Reorientation of European Social Thought, 1890–1930* (1958), are excellent. For the sharp contrast between Britain and Germany, compare the writers discussed in P. Fussell, *The Great War and Modern Memory* (1975), with the widely shared views expressed in E. Jünger, *The Storm of Steel* (1920). H. S. Hughes, *Oswald Spengler: A Critical Estimate* (1952), is perhaps too

kind to Spengler. For Germany's decisive contributions to interwar high culture, see especially P. Gay, *Weimar Culture* (1968); J. Willett, *Art and Politics in the Weimar Period: The New Sobriety, 1917–1933* (1979); and B. M. Lane, *Architecture and Politics in Germany, 1918–1945* (1968). For the many interwar intellectuals who despaired of their own societies and sought solace in Moscow, see P. Hollander, *Political Pilgrims: The Travels of Western Intellectuals to the Soviet Union, China, and Cuba, 1928–1978* (1981).

32
The Totalitarian States

By 1933 the demoralized democracies faced not only a militant Japan, but three great dictatorships: the Soviet Union of Joseph Stalin, the Fascist Italy of Benito Mussolini, and the National Socialist Germany of Adolf Hitler. Dictatorship was not new. Lenin, an expert, defined it as "a power that is not limited by any laws, not bound by any rules, and based directly on force." Despots from the god-emperors of the ancient world to the tsars of Russia had ruled without laws or rules that limited the sovereign. But custom, the merciful inefficiency of their bureaucracies, and the inadequacies of the technologies at their command had limited their power.

Robespierre and the Committee of Public Safety had briefly wielded, in the name of the General Will, power more total than that of any preceding European state. Now, in the twentieth century, war and revolution made possible the perfection of the dictatorship of the General Will sketched out in 1793–94. It soon acquired a name. Giovanni Amendola, an Italian liberal later murdered by the thugs of the Italian dictatorship, coined in 1923–24 the adjective *"totalitario"* to describe Fascist election methods. Mussolini happily

Opposite: Totalitarian mass politics: Hitler (on platform, center) greets his following at a 1936 party rally.

plagiarized it in 1925; he relished its brutal sound.

"Totalitarianism" thus became a generic term for the dictatorship of the age of mass politics, a dictatorship that set itself a limitless goal: *total power over the individual*. That goal distinguished it from earlier despotisms, and from "authoritarian" regimes such as the dictatorships of interwar eastern Europe or Latin America, which sought above all to conserve their power. The totalitarian states sought instead to create a "new man." And their external goals were almost equally limitless, for the example of freedom anywhere was a mortal threat for all such regimes.

Yet distinctions did exist between the three regimes, despite their frequent imitation of one another and their ultimate collaboration in producing the Second World War. Russia, the only Marxist-Leninist state of the three, was also the most economically and socially backward. Russia's middle class was small and the Orthodox Church relatively weak, even before the Bolsheviks decided to exterminate the one and virtually abolish the other. And Bolshevik power came from victory in a merciless civil war; from the beginning it was "based directly on force." Lenin and his successor Stalin thus faced none of the constitutional or social obstacles to total power present in the more developed societies of the West.

Mussolini and Hitler, by contrast, came to power in apparent legality in societies that in theory still had parliamentary regimes. They faced mighty entrenched interests and institutions—armies, industrialists, and churches—whose assistance was necessary for the consolidation and expansion of the regime. In Russia the regime was free from birth to begin the total transformation of Russian society accomplished by the late 1930s. All that it lacked was an implacable will, and that Stalin supplied. In Italy and Germany the despots had to purchase their freedom. The method they chose was war.

RUSSIA: FROM REVOLUTION TO GENOCIDE

From Tsarist to Communist Autocracy

Within five years of the collapse of tsarism in 1917, Russia was once again an autocracy. After October 1917, Lenin systematically crushed all opposition—the short-lived Constitutional Assembly, the other left-wing parties, and the counterrevolutionary "Whites." The workers' Soviets withered away; the secret police (CHEKA) swelled to 30,000 and the Red Army to 5.3 million. Soon all that remained of the workers' Soviets was the name, which the Party appropriated for its new state: the Union of Soviet Socialist Republics.

In 1921, with the civil war against the Whites virtually won, the Bolsheviks faced still graver crises. War, revolution, and civil war had cost Russia over 10 percent of its 1913 population of 159 million. At least 2 million had died in the First World War, a million had emigrated, up to 10 million had died in the civil war and accompanying famines, and as many as 5 million had perished in drought and famine in 1921–22. Between 1917 and 1920, food shortages, the brutalities of Bolshevik mismanagement, and civil-war chaos had cut Russia's "proletariat" in half, from 3 million to 1.5 million. The industrial work force, recently recruited from the peasantry, simply returned to the villages. The peasantry itself fiercely resented the ruthless Bolshevik confiscation of crops to feed the cities. Externally, defeat in Poland in 1920 and the failure of world revolution to materialize meant isolation and peril.

In February 1921 strikes against the self-proclaimed "workers' state" swept Petrograd. In March, sailors at Kronstadt, the nearby naval base that had once furnished fanatical recruits to Bolshevism, rose against Bolshevism on behalf of the half-starved remnant of Russia's workers. Millions of peasants in central Russia were already in armed revolt against the exactions of "war communism," the forced requisition of food. The regime appeared close to collapse.

Lenin and the Party acted. Mass arrests clamped Petrograd down. Trotsky besieged Kronstadt and annihilated the sailors at the cost of 10,000 Red Army casualties. Lenin outlawed internal "factionalism" and reproved those comrades who still took seriously the Party's claim to represent the *existing* Russian proletariat. In the Party's eyes, the workers and Kronstadt sailors who demanded free elections to the Soviets had ceased to be proletarians.

To placate the peasantry, the only great social group the Party was not yet strong enough to crush by force alone, Lenin and his associates retreated from "war communism." The "new economic policy" or NEP of 1921–28 restored a degree of free enterprise to the countryside and even to industry. It was a recognition of reality—external isolation and internal weakness—that ended for the moment Lenin's attempt to force the pace of history and leap directly from tsarism to Communism.

The NEP was an economic success. Agricultural production passed 1913 levels in 1924. Enterprising peasants prospered. By 1926–27 even the cities had begun to revive. But the NEP proved a brief respite. In May 1922, Lenin suffered the first of a series of incapacitating strokes. In January 1924 he died. By that point the struggle for the succession had already begun; Trotsky was the leading candidate. But his Menshevik past, Red Army ties, and lack of modesty alienated a fiercely clannish Party that feared "Bonapartism"—the rule of a successful general. Trotsky's rival was that self-effacing bureaucrat from Georgia in the Caucasus, Joseph Stalin, a former seminary pupil and revolutionary bank robber. Lenin had placed Stalin in charge of the central Party machine, and thus of recruitment. Stalin soon allied himself with Trotsky's rivals on the Party

Trotsky, victorious Commissar for War, reviews his troops (1920).

"Left," Grigorii Zinoviev and Lev Kamenev.

Stalin craftily cloaked his ambition in mock humility, and easily deflected Lenin's dying demand that the Party demote the uncouth Georgian, who was "too rude," a fault "insupportable in a general secretary." Stalin's deluded allies of the "Left" found him less threatening than Trotsky, and the new Party rank and file with whom Stalin was rapidly swamping the "Old Bolsheviks" owed their careers to him alone.

Stalin was careful always to speak in the name of the Party while consolidating his own power. Since Lenin had forbidden "factionalism," opponents of Stalin were automatically opponents of the Party. They thereby forfeited both legitimacy and self-confidence; Stalin used the Party's cult of unity against them to force humiliating recantations and "self-criticisms." The CHEKA, renamed GPU, then OGPU, and finally NKVD, became Stalin's ally and chosen instrument; it soon overshadowed the Party. And Stalin had Lenin embalmed, and placed on exhibit as a holy relic of the new state religion: "Leninism." Petrograd became Leningrad; all across the Soviet Union statues of the prophet arose. The cult of Lenin legitimated Bolshevik power and created the role that Stalin himself was soon to fill.

In 1925 Zinoviev and Kamenev led the pack against Trotsky, and expelled him from his Party and army offices. In 1926 Stalin turned on his allies and demoted them with the help of the Party "Right" formed around the theorist Nikolai Bukharin. Trotsky had urged continued conflict: "permanent revolution" abroad and, at home, increased pressure on the peasants to squeeze from them capital for a crash industrialization program to achieve the Communist utopia. Zinoviev, though personally fiercely hostile to Trotsky, had in essence agreed. Stalin and Bukharin triumphed within the Party by asserting a seemingly moderate course: "socialism in one country" and continuance of the NEP.

Once Trotsky, Zinoviev, and Kamenev were disposed of, Stalin took over their domestic policy. The naive Bukharin suddenly discovered that Stalin was "an unprincipled intriguer who . . . changes his theories depending on whom he wants to get rid of at any particular moment." Terrified, Bukharin belatedly sought alliance with Kamenev and Zinoviev: Stalin was "a new Ghenghis Khan; he will strangle us all." In 1927–28, Stalin began warning that the Soviet Union faced war at the hands of the encircling capitalist powers. A five-year plan of crash industrialization was therefore imperative. But the NEP was already failing to provide enough grain for the towns, as the peasantry resisted Party attempts to keep agricultural prices artificially low. Stalin could therefore argue that the NEP, if it continued, would make it impossible to extract from the peasants the surplus needed to finance industrialization and feed a larger factory work force. Party and OGPU pressure on the most prosperous peasants—the so-called *kulaks* ("fists")—increased.

By early 1929, Stalin had forced Trotsky into exile (and had him murdered in 1940, after expunging his name from the history of the Bolshevik Revolution). Stalin then demoted Bukharin and the "Right" by exposing their attempts to ally with the discredited "Left," and ended the NEP. Lenin's party had erected a new autocracy over Russia. Stalin, whom his press increasingly hailed as the "Great Leader," was now close to erecting an autocracy over the Party. In the absence of laws and rules, Bolshevik dictatorship over the proletariat was swiftly becoming the dictatorship of an individual. And that individual, because he commanded the instrument of terror and embodied the purported will of the proletariat and

Stalin Demands Crash Industrialization

Stalin shrewdly blended Marxism-Leninism and Russian nationalism in his rationale for crash industrialization. He advanced his thesis most forcefully in a speech of early 1931.

To reduce the tempo [of industrialization] would mean to fall behind. And those who fall behind get beaten. But we do not want to be beaten. No, we refuse to be beaten! One feature of the history of old Russia was the continual beating she suffered because of her backwardness. She was beaten by the Mongol Khans. She was beaten by the Turkish beys. She was beaten by the Swedish feudal lords. She was beaten by the Polish and Lithuanian gentry. She was beaten by the British and French capitalists. She was beaten by the Japanese barons. All beat her—because of her backwardness, military backwardness, cultural backwardness, industrial backwardness, and agricultural backwardness. They beat her because to do so was profitable and could be done with impunity. . . . It is the jungle law of capitalism. You are backward, you are weak—therefore you are wrong; hence, you can be beaten and enslaved. You are mighty—therefore you are right. . . . We are fifty or a hundred years behind the advanced countries. We must make good this distance in ten years. Either we do it, or we shall be crushed.

From Basil Dmytryshyn, *USSR: A Concise History* (New York: Charles Scribner's Sons, 1978), p. 158.

the supposed laws of history, could do anything he pleased.

The Great Famine, 1929–34

On December 27, 1929, as the first Five Year Plan went into effect, Stalin informed Russia of its fate: "either we go backward to capitalism or forward to socialism. What does this mean? It means that after a policy that consisted in limiting the exploitative tendencies of the *kulaks*, we have switched to a policy of liquidating the *kulaks* as a class."

Crash industrialization and the consolidation of Soviet power, for Stalin, required the transformation of the landowning peasantry into a rural proletariat—serfs of the Soviet state—working the land with state-owned machinery. The goal of "complete collectivization" that Stalin announced in December 1929 would end forever the mortal internal threat that Lenin had discerned: "Capitalism begins in the village market-place." It would also provide external might, to defend and advance the Revolution. With collectivization, Stalin made good his claim to be Lenin's true heir—despite the doubts Lenin had expressed about Stalin's manners. Stalin proposed to force the pace of history and complete the revolution that Lenin had launched in 1917.

Nor was Stalin's choice of the word *liquidate* an accident. The Party activists, army, and OGPU troops who forced the peasants into state-controlled collective farms received orders to designate fixed quotas of *kulaks* and "*kulak* henchmen." Between 5 and 20 percent of the rural population, depending on the area, suffered deportation to Siberia and Central Asia. Most of those deported died, either on the march or under the care of the OGPU's newly established "Main Administration of Corrective Labor Camps," best known by its sinister acronym, GULAG. The remaining peasants resisted. They slaughtered and ate their livestock rather than deliver it to

The "Mutability of the Past"

In his novel *1984*, published in 1949, the British essayist and novelist George Orwell (1903–50) depicted a nightmare totalitarian future that drew on Stalin's attempts to *control the past*.

The mutability of the past is the central tenet of Ingsoc [Orwell's fictional state ideology]. Past events, it is argued, have no objective existence, but survive only in written records and in human memories. The past is whatever the records and the memories agree upon. And since the Party is in full control of all records, and in equally full control of the minds of its members, it follows that the past is whatever the Party chooses to make it. It also follows that though the past is alterable, it never has been altered in any specific instance. For when it has been recreated in whatever shape is needed at the moment, then this new version *is* the past, and no different past can ever have existed. . . . At all times the Party is in possession of the absolute truth, and clearly the absolute can never have been different from what it is now. . . .

From George Orwell, *1984* (New York: Signet, 1961), p. 176.

the collective farms. They refused to plant more than a bare minimum of crops. Villages and entire regions defied the regime. Red Army sweeps and mass executions gradually subdued them.

Stalin's war on the Soviet Union's 120 million peasants culminated in a devastating famine in the Ukraine and elsewhere in 1931–32. Stalin barred relief shipments, to bring home to the peasantry the cost of defying him; Soviet food *exports* during the famine exceeded those during the prosperous years of the NEP. With macabre relish Stalin publicly commanded merriment: "Life has become more joyous, comrades; life has become gayer." Privately he remarked much later, to Winston Churchill, that 10 million had suffered death or deportation. Soviet demographers later admitted a population loss of 7.5 million; the true figure may have been as high as 15 million. Not accidentally, figures for livestock deaths—149.4 million head between 1929 and

1917		1924	1928		1953
	Lenin	Stalin against Trotsky		Stalin	

1934—are more readily available than those for people.

Stalin's war on the peasantry so devastated Soviet agriculture that in per capita terms it produced scarcely more in 1953 than it had in 1913. The catastrophic losses to agriculture probably exceeded the gains of the rapidly expanding industrial sector. Conciliation of the peasantry and continuation of the NEP, as Bukharin had urged, would in all likelihood have led to a higher over-all rate of economic growth than Stalin actually achieved.

But the terror-famine achieved its political purpose. The Party broke the one great social force in Russia. By 1932 the state had seized 88 percent of Russia's farmland; by 1937 collectivization was almost total. And Stalin did extract the labor and some of the needed capital for the Five Year Plan. According to some estimates, "de-kulakized" slave laborers furnished over 5 percent of the Soviet labor force by 1933. Peasants fled the land for the industrial cities and mines of the Don Basin and the Urals. Food extracted from the peasantry at gunpoint helped the regime to more than triple Russia's industrial work force. Terror and propaganda whipped the exhausted workers onward, amid immense waste and confusion. Vast hydroelectric dams and steel mills arose, based on technology bought from the West with exported grain and with gold that camp inmates dug from the arctic tundra. The first Five Year Plan increased Soviet capital-goods production two and a half times. At the "Party Congress of Victors" in January 1934 Stalin savored a success he had bought through the crippling and stunting of his society: "The line of the Party has triumphed."

Joseph Stalin at his desk: "To choose one's victims, to prepare one's plans minutely, to slake an implacable vengeance, and then to go to bed . . . there is nothing sweeter in the world."

The Great Terror, 1934–39

As the crisis of collectivization passed, Stalin nevertheless found himself under attack. In 1932 opponents circulated a long document full of devastating criticism of his wasteful and erratic economic leadership, and of the Party's alienation of the working class it claimed to incarnate. Stalin responded with orders to scrutinize the Party membership and purge those suspected of opposition. But he failed to persuade his colleagues on the Party's ruling committee, the Politburo, to redefine dissent within the Party as "counterrevolutionary activity," which carried the penalty of death.

That impasse ended on December 1, 1934. A dissident Party member, with the apparent complicity of the NKVD, assassinated Sergei Kirov, boss of Leningrad and rising young star of the Party. Much later, after Stalin's death, Soviet leaders hinted broadly that Stalin was behind the murder. It gave him a pretext to clamp down once more. Having enserfed the peasantry, he now set as his goal the destruction of the doubters and of all *potential* sources of future opposition. Hitler had set the example that June with a massacre of associates who had become politically inconvenient (see p. 923).

In the aftermath of Kirov's assassination, the NKVD under Stalin's personal direction received the power to shoot summarily anyone it pleased. It soon discovered a mythical "terrorist center" in Leningrad. In early 1935 it dredged up Zinoviev and Kamenev for the first of a series of show trials, an art form already perfected in trials of Socialist Revolutionaries, Mensheviks, and foreign engineers falsely accused of sabotage. Calls went out to the Party to unmask "Trotskyites" and "Zinovievites." Soviet law, a flexible instrument, soon provided swift death not only for alleged spies and "parasites," but also for those who had knowledge of their activities and failed to denounce them—including children of 12 years or older. The families and children of those arrested became hostages, liable to punishment—a further extension of the genocidal notion of "class justice" that Dzerzhinsky and Latsis of the CHEKA had pioneered. *Pravda* began to carry stories that praised children who had reported their parents to the NKVD.

In August 1936, amid mounting anxiety, Stalin announced a new Soviet constitution that contained lavish guarantees of individual freedoms. But woe to those who failed to exercise those freedoms "in accordance with the interests of the workers and for the purpose of strengthening the socialist system." The same month, Zinoviev and Kamenev obligingly admitted to having planned Stalin's assassination; the court had them shot. Terror became all-pervasive.

But Stalin was not content. He accused the NKVD leadership of footdragging and moved the appointment of a new man, the "bloodthirsty dwarf," Nikolai Yezhov. In January 1937 Yezhov mounted yet another Moscow show trial, of the fancifully named "terrorist counterrevolutionary Trotskyite-Zinovievite bloc." Mass arrests and lesser trials occupied the rest of the year. The NKVD and its informers feverishly invented conspiracies, beat prisoners into confessions that implicated ever more suspects, and shot in the prison cellars those who were no longer of use.

Stalin also turned on the Red Army, which he apparently feared might threaten his power in the event of an ever more probable European war. The generals proved tougher than the Party; they refused to confess to being in league with Germany and Japan.

Stalin had his own high command shot in secret in June and July 1937, and announced the executions after the event.

The last great trial, in March 1938, was that of the so-called "bloc of anti-Soviet rightists and Trotskyites." It included a wide range of victims, from Bukharin to Genrikh Yagoda, the ex-head of the NKVD whom Stalin had replaced in 1936 for insufficient zeal. Old Bolsheviks confessed to sabotaging butter production with ground glass and to conspiring with Trotsky, Germany, Japan, Britain, and Poland. Western observers, including Roosevelt's ambassador and the correspondent of the *New York Times*, swallowed these absurd tales whole. Bukharin was puzzling, however. He confessed to almost everything, then implicitly retracted. Above all, he refused to admit to having plotted Lenin's murder, as Stalin's vindictive prosecutor, Andrei Vishinsky, alleged. The court had Bukharin shot with the rest, but he had marred the illusion of guilt that Stalin sought to create.

The great terror, like the terror-famine that preceded it, accomplished its objective. It remade the Party. Seventy percent of the Central Committee of 1934 perished; Stalin wiped out the leading Old Bolsheviks, and any alternative within the Party to his own domination. Terror remade the armed forces. Half of the officer corps, 35,000 men, fell victim: 3 of 5 marshals of the Soviet Union, 13 of 15 army commanders, 57 of 80 corps commanders, 70 of 190 division commanders, all 11 vice commissars for war, and all 8 admirals. And only 10 percent of those destroyed in the great terror were members of the Party and army. The rest were victims of chance associations, of neighbors' denunciations, of family relationships to suspects, of the envy of subordinates at work, of membership in national minorities. The victims of Stalin's genocide died not because of anything they had done, but because of what they were. They perished *by categories*, from *kulaks* and "*kulak* henchmen," to Ukrainians, to Old Bolsheviks, to suspects of "Trotskyism," to relatives of suspects, to individuals whose only "crime" was that they belonged to a generation that remembered Russia before 1917.

The replacements of those "purged" were younger, with fewer such memories than their predecessors. They were unlikely to question Stalin's leadership. Above all they were bound to Stalin: they owed their rapid promotions to the vacancies that he and his NKVD had created. In many cases they had helped, by opportune words to the NKVD about their superiors—for Stalin was not the sole author of the terror. He had millions of helpers, bound irrevocably to their master by fear, gratitude, and complicity. Stalin had created a new ruling class in his own image.

The cost was high. The secret 1937 census, according to some accounts, showed that the Soviet Union had 21.5 million people less than the second Five Year Plan had forecast. Stalin, furious, had the demographers denounced as a "serpent's nest of traitors" and shot or sent to GULAG for having allegedly "exerted themselves to diminish the numbers of the population of the Soviet Union." Stalin reserved that privilege to himself. By 1939, the GULAG concentration camps held an estimated 10.4 million people—10 percent of the Soviet labor force. The death rate in the camps was as high as 10 percent each year. By 1940, Stalin's genocide had through famine, terror, and slave labor killed between 12.7 and 22.1 million people—on top of the immense losses between 1914 and 1922. He had also signed a pact with Hitler.

ITALY: FROM DICTATORSHIP TO EXPANSION

To achieve total power in a developed Western society was a challenge more difficult than that facing Stalin. But the First World War created conditions that made it thinkable. The war into which Antonio Salandra, Sidney Sonnino, and King Victor Emmanuel III had flung Italy in 1915 caught the country as it made the delicate transition to mass politics after Giolitti had greatly enlarged the suffrage in 1912.

The Crisis of Liberal Italy

War and the example of the Russian revolution mobilized the masses; the 1919 election destroyed the hegemony of the Liberals. Two great mass parties, the Catholic People's Party (*Popolari*) and the Socialists, henceforth commanded between them a majority in parliament. But unlike Weimar Germany, the mass parties refused to coalesce and rule. Socialists embraced the half-understood example of Lenin. The *Popolari*, under Vatican influence, had in part entered politics to counter the Socialist threat. Parliamentary deadlock and a series of weak Liberal cabinets resulted. And for the Right, the Liberal regime had lost its small stock of prestige when the Allies at Paris had "mutilated" Italy's victory by refusing to concede Sonnino's colonial and Balkan claims.

Outside parliament, the Socialists confusedly took the offensive in the "two red years" of 1919–20. Their agricultural unions and political machines organized the landless laborers and soon ruled Italy's richest farming region, the Po Valley. Landowners who refused to hire labor at the rates and in the numbers that the Socialists decreed suffered boycotts, arson, mutilation of livestock, and worse. Factory and transport workers struck repeatedly. But incessant Socialist talk of revolution, violence against landowners, and public abuse of veterans as warmongers and capitalist dupes inevitably backfired.

In October 1914 Benito Mussolini, whom Lenin had seen as the future leader of Italian Socialism, had quarreled with the party over its refusal to support war. Mussolini, the brutal and charismatic son of a village blacksmith, had agitated for war, then served in the infantry until wounded. In March 1919, he founded a movement to carry the war into politics: the *Fasci di Combattimento* ("combat leagues"). Its initial recruits were a curious mixture of former shock troops, wartime junior officers, nationalist students, and ex-socialists who had opted for war in 1914–15. "Fascist" ideology was and remained amorphous, but its principal components were two: fierce hostility to the Left and a resentful expansionist nationalism.

The Socialist offensive in the Po Valley flatlands and agitation by the Slovenes of newly annexed Trieste made the summer of 1920 "the hour of Fascism." Fascist gangs in black shirts or wartime field-gray attacked Socialists and Slavs with clubs, knives, pistols, and hand grenades. Landowners and the occasional industrialist happily contributed funds. Army commands secretly provided trucks and weapons. The numerous landowning peasants, whom the Socialists had alienated with talk of collectivization of the land, joined the Fascist *squadre*. Some Liberals in Rome deplored Fascist violence, but lacked the resolve to restore order. Other Liberals, among them Giovanni Giolitti, saw the Fascists as a healthy patriotic reaction against the excesses of the Socialists and the encroachments of the *Popolari* on the Liberal state.

By the summer of 1921 Fascism had smashed the Socialists in the Po Valley and Tuscany, and had set itself the task of conquering Italy. In Rome, Fascist deputies took the battle into parliament thanks to an electoral alliance that Giolitti offered. In the countryside, "punitive expeditions" of truck-borne blackshirts grew ever larger and more ferociously effective. But mutual hostility between Socialists and *Popolari* still prevented them from joining hands against the Fascist threat.

By October 1922 Liberal Italy was in dissolution. Right Liberals such as Salandra sought to co-opt Mussolini, to tame him by admission to government.

In a two-track maneuver that combined an insurrectionary "March on Rome" with negotiations with Salandra and others, Mussolini demanded the prime ministership. The last Liberal cabinet feebly attempted to persuade the King to command the army to restore order. Victor Emmanuel III consulted his generals, who answered that the army would do its duty, but that it would be better not to put it to the test. King, army, and Right Liberals chose Mussolini over a civil war that they feared would strengthen the Left. They made Mussolini prime minister of Italy on October 31, 1922.

The Fascist State

As Mussolini admitted privately in 1924, the "March on Rome" was no revolution: "The revolution comes later." He initially had no majority in parliament and therefore took fellow-traveling Liberals and *Popolari* into his cabinet. He depended on Italy's industrialists and on foreign bankers to keep the economy from faltering. And to the end his authority ultimately derived from the king who had appointed him. The Fascist regime remained a "dyar-

Mussolini, surrounded by the commanders of the "March on Rome," strikes a pose before assuming power.

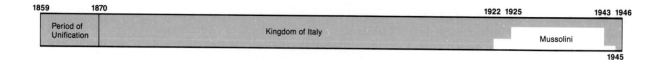

chy," a system in which dictator and king shared power. The regime was thus the least "totalitarian" of the three great dictatorships: Mussolini's "NEP" lasted until 1935–36.

But Mussolini nevertheless aspired to total power and moved to achieve it by stages. From the beginning he chipped away both at opponents and at conservative "flankers" who sought to use him merely to tame the Left. Fascist violence continued in the provinces; a new electoral law guaranteed a Fascist majority in the 1924 elections.

That victory led Mussolini to overreach. His most conspicuous opponent, Giacomo Matteotti, rightly claimed to parliament in June 1924 that the Fascist election majority was the product of force and fraud. A few days later, Mussolini's "CHEKA," as he only half-jokingly called his bodyguard of thugs, took Matteotti for a fatal ride in the country. Bystanders noted down the license plate of Matteotti's abductors; the police, not yet fully under Fascist control, traced the vehicle to Mussolini's entourage. The perfect political crime had failed.

Mussolini himself preserved what a later age was to call "plausible deniability." Pressure for his resignation nevertheless mounted among Liberals in the cabinet and in parliament. Mussolini privately railed at the Italian people's "absurd fuss" over the death of one man. Then and later he secretly envied the Bolsheviks, who faced no such constraints.

Socialists, *Popolari*, and Left Liberals, briefly united, seceded from parliament in protest. That was suicidal; it split the opposition between those who seceded and those who stayed. Mussolini bought off with concessions some of the Liberals remaining in parliament. He faced down waverers in the cabinet by threatening to fight rather than yield power. As in 1922, he offered the Italian establishment a simple choice: him or civil war.

On January 3, 1925, with the King's acquiescence, Mussolini announced that he would remain in power indefinitely. The police closed the opposition press. A succession of botched attempts to assassinate Mussolini soon gave welcome pretexts to rule by decree and outlaw all opposition parties. Within the Fascist party, Mussolini abolished the few shreds of internal democracy that survived from 1919–21: "The Revolution has one Leader." By 1928 he had grafted the party into the state and had given the party's highest organ, the Grand Council of Fascism, power to regulate the succession to the throne. He created a Fascist youth movement to imbue the coming generations with a brutish nationalism and a pagan "sense of virility, of power, of conquest."

Mussolini also secured a prize that had eluded his Liberal predecessors: a settlement of Italy's festering quarrel with the Church. The Lateran Pact of February 1929 created a Vatican City mini-state and gave the Vatican a large sum in Italian state bonds as indemnity for the territory seized in 1870; a Concordat between Church and state made Catholicism the state religion. In return, Pope Pius XI hailed Mussolini as "the man whom Providence has placed in Our path." That blessing and the enthusiastic support of the rural clergy for the regime made Mussolini's position unassailable. A plebiscite and one-party election in March 1929 gave Mussolini an overwhelming and mostly genuine majority, and returned a black-shirted parliament. The dictatorship rested on monarchy, military, and police, but also on the acclamation of the masses and the blessings of the Church.

Mussolini Breaks Through:
Ethiopia and After

Yet control of government and the growing cult of the *Duce* was not enough. In 1925 Mussolini had expressed many of his ultimate goals in a speech to the party. Fascism's "fierce totalitarian will" would "'fascistize' the nation, so that tomorrow Italian and Fascist, more or less like Italian and Catholic, will be the same thing." He also discerned a method for achieving that goal. Like the Girondin orator Isnard, who in 1792 had foreseen a war "indispensable for completing the revolution," Mussolini saw a connection between war and revolution. In 1914–15 he had demanded a "revolutionary war." That war had destroyed Liberal Italy and placed him in power. Only more war could make that power total.

And from the extremists of Italy's Nationalist party and from his navy, Mussolini acquired a vision of Italy's goals in that war. "A nation," he informed a group of high officers in 1926–27, "that has no free access to the sea cannot be considered a free nation; a nation that has no free access to the oceans cannot be considered a great power. Italy must become a great power." Britain and France, and Italy's ties to the world market, stood in the way of Mediterranean domination and of what Mussolini later described as Italy's "march to the ocean." By 1923–24, if not before, Mussolini had already foreseen that a vengeful nationalist Germany would be Italy's most promising ally in that march.

Waiting for Germany was tedious. Between 1922 and 1931 Mussolini crushed with massacres and concentration camps the Arabs of Libya, whom the Liberal state had been unable to subdue. He dabbled with plans for attacking Turkey, and sponsored Croat and Macedonian terrorist forays against neighboring Yugoslavia. But British disapproval, Italy's economic and financial weakness, and the Depression forced Mussolini to sham a deep love of peace—but the Depres-

Mussolini: War, Revolution, and Empire   1925

At times I look with favor in the idea of [creating] generations in the laboratory, of creating, in other words, the class of the warriors, who are always ready to die, the class of the inventors, who pursue the secrets of the mysteries [of nature]; the class of judges; the class of the great captains of industry; of the great governors. It is through this sort of methodical selection that one creates the great elites that in turn establish empires. . . . War and revolution are two terms that are almost always linked. Either war produces revolution or it is revolution that leads to war. Even the strategy of the two movements is alike: as in war, in revolution you do not always attack. Sometimes you must make more or less strategic retreats. Sometimes you must rest for long periods on positions you have conquered. But the goal is there: empire.

Speech to the Fascist party congress, June 22, 1925, from *Opera Omnia di Benito Mussolini* (Florence: La Fenice, 1956), Vol. 21, pp. 362–63 (translation by M. Knox).

sion also ended the foreign loans that bound Fascist Italy to the status quo.

In early 1933, as Hitler came to power, Mussolini briefly thought he had blackmailed the French into abandoning their support of their Yugoslav ally, a Mussolini target since the 1920s. Then the king and generals vetoed a

Mussolini harangues a Roman crowd, 1931.

Balkan war that would risk French retaliation and "a lesson that would last us for a century." It was nevertheless France, terrified at the rise of Hitler, that finally gave Mussolini the opening he sought. In July 1931 its prime minister, the unscrupulous and gullible Pierre Laval, had suggested to an Italian emissary that Italy might assuage its thirst for expansion in Ethiopia. France would acquiesce, in return for Italy's help in maintaining the status quo in Europe against Germany.

Mussolini at first rejected this offer as a French trick to bog Italy down in Africa just as Germany was opening up possibilities in Europe. Then, in early 1934, he reversed himself. He had quarreled with his would-be ally, Hitler, over Austria. If war in Europe was impossible, war in Africa might yet serve his purpose. The king, the military, and the Italian establishment were lukewarm rather than actively hostile, as they had been over Yugoslavia. They were willing to "avenge Adowa" if Mussolini insisted and no great power objected.

In January 1935, Mussolini and Laval signed the Rome Agreements, which conceded Italy a "free hand" in East Africa in return for the abandonment of Italian colonial claims on France and for Italian backing for France in Europe. The last part of the

bargain Mussolini regarded skeptically; to Berlin he confided through intermediaries that "he would exploit the French, if they offered him anything, without becoming dependent upon them."

Large Italian forces, the first of almost half a million troops and laborers, began shipping out for East Africa. Britain feebly objected. War in Africa would make cooperation with Italy against the German threat impossible, and in an election year Baldwin could not abandon the League of Nations, of which Ethiopia was a member. When Mussolini wrecked British efforts at compromise, London reluctantly sent additional battleships to the Mediterranean to deter him. The League, impotent in the Manchurian crisis, rallied behind Britain—and the overwhelming power of the British fleet. But Baldwin's foreign secretary secretly assured Mussolini that Britain did not intend war. That pledge, and intercepted British radio messages suggesting the fleet was short of ammunition, allowed Mussolini to overrule his hesitant military and overawe the King. On October 3, 1935, Italy attacked Ethiopia.

Britain reacted with economic sanctions against Italy organized through the League of Nations. Sanctions proved easy although expensive to evade, and thanks to a British failure of nerve they did not cover the imported oil that fuelled Italy's armed forces. Their main consequence was to cut Italian dependence on British coal—in favor of the coal of the Ruhr. London also pressed on the French and on Mussolini yet another compromise that gave the Duce only parts of Ethiopia. When this "Hoare-Laval Plan" leaked to the press in December 1935, British and French opinion damned it as a sellout of Ethiopia and forced its abandonment. Mussolini was much relieved; his war could proceed.

On the battlefield, the armies of emperor Haile Selassie almost routed the Italians in December–January 1936; then Italy's lavish use of tanks, artillery, aircraft, and mustard gas crushed them. At the beginning of May 1936,

Italian troops depart for Ethiopia, 1935.

Italian forces entered the Ethiopian capital, Addis Ababa. Mussolini hailed before a delirious crowd the "reapparition of empire, after fifteen centuries, on the fateful hills of Rome." War and the brutal Italian occupation of 1936–41 cost the lives of a million Ethiopians.

War also made Mussolini "founder of the Empire." Ex-Liberal or Nationalist flankers, generals, and king now counted for less. Mussolini listened less and advisers dared offer less and less advice. Sanctions inflamed Italian opinion against the West and made it easier for Mussolini to overawe the industrialists and militarize the Italian economy under the banner of "autarky," the illusory pursuit of self-sufficiency in raw materials. And Italy's quarrel with the League and subsequent intervention in the Spanish Civil War in July–August 1936 gave him the opportunity to move closer to Berlin. In October 1936, he and Hitler inaugurated the "Rome-Berlin Axis." In 1938 he imitated Hitler's anti-Semitic legislation.

In 1940, after long struggle with the generals, king, and moderate opinion, Mussolini led Italy into the Second World War. Only war, he told the crowd on June 10, 1940, would "resolve . . . the problem of our maritime frontiers" and "break the military and territorial chains that suffocate us in our sea, for a people of forty-five million souls is not truly free unless it has free access to the ocean." Victory would give him the prestige needed to smash the monarchy and to break the grip of the Church on Italian society. Defeat instead hurled the regime and Italy itself into the abyss.

GERMANY: FROM WAR TO WAR

Adolf Hitler

The man who opened the road for Mussolini and invited Stalin into central Europe began as modestly as his fellow dictators. Son of an Austro-Hungarian customs official, Adolf Hit-

ler imbibed pan-Germanism and anti-Semitism from his surroundings. He failed admission to the Vienna Art Academy in 1907–08—no loss for art, but unfortunate in view of his subsequent career. He drifted to Munich in 1913 rather than serve in the armies of the Habsburg dynasty he despised for its compromises with Slavs and Jews. War in 1914 he regarded as a deliverance (see p. 850). Always a loner, he found in the German army a home and in battle a vocation. From October 1914 to October 1918 he served at the front in the most dangerous job the infantry offered: battalion messenger. He earned two Iron Crosses, decorations rarely given to lance-corporals.

Word of revolution and defeat reached him as he lay in hospital, temporarily blind from British gas; the news roused him to fury. As the army demobilized, he remained in service at Munich for lack of anything better. The army's propaganda branch took him in. There he made a discovery that changed Europe and the world: "I could 'speak.'" And in September 1919 his superiors sent him to listen in at a meeting of a radical rightist sect of Munich railway workers, the German Workers' Party (DAP).

There Hitler immediately attracted attention and an invitation to join. News of his talent for the spoken word spread rapidly in Munich's right radical circles. By July 1921 he had taken the DAP away from its founders, had changed its name to National Socialist German Workers' Party (NSDAP), and had made himself its sole dictatorial leader. By late 1923 his party had 55,000 members and a paramilitary mass army, the brown-shirted SA (*Sturmabteilungen*, "storm troop sections") under the leadership of Ernst Röhm, a fiercely politicized ex-army officer.

The "*Führer*," as Hitler now became, spoke powerfully to a nation that had become convinced, however perversely, that it had suffered foreign aggression and unmerited demotion to second-class power. Hitler's ideological delusions and those of his ever larger audiences coincided, thanks to Germany's defeat. His starting point was the extremist form of social Darwinism that had long been popular in Germany. Following pseudo-biological prophets such as Ernst Haeckel (see pp. 802–803), Hitler assumed that nature's laws—the "survival of the fittest" or the "free play of forces"—offered the sole "healthy" rule for human conduct. Humanity was one with nature, not apart from it or above it; biology was supreme in all spheres of human activity.

That insight, Hitler insisted, was science. Like his rivals the Marxist-Leninists, Hitler and his followers combined materialist pseudo-positivism with bizarre ideological claims. For Communists, economics was the secret essence of human history, the history of class struggle. For Hitler, biology held the key: race—not class—was "the driving force of world history." History was the history of race struggle. And like the Marxist-Leninists, who saw "the capitalist" as demon, Hitler too saw a historic villain.

For Hitler, the Jewish people were a "race-tuberculosis of nations" who had supposedly lived "parasitically" throughout history from the labors of peoples that had given them shelter—especially the "Aryan" or "Nordic"

peoples of Europe to whom Hitler ascribed biological superiority. Throughout history, the Jews had allegedly sought the "eternal Jewish goal—world domination." They were responsible for Germany's internal weakness and thus for its defeat through the purported stab-in-the-back of 1918. The alleged Jewish threat, Hitler informed his beer-hall audiences, now placed the world before a stark alternative: "either victory of the Aryan side or its annihilation and victory of the Jews." Only Germany could ensure "Aryan" victory; Germany's "historic mission" was to found "an Aryan world order." Hitler's goal was racist world revolution.

More immediately, recovery from the lost war required a new state: "We need a dictator who is a genius, if we want to rise again." But in the age of mass politics, even dictatorship required pseudo-democratic phrases and mass enthusiasm or mass terror to make it workable. Hitler therefore proclaimed that nationalist dictatorship was "Germanic democracy." His mass following, and many in Munich's social elite, appeared to agree.

The Ruhr crisis of 1923 shook Weimar's authority and led Hitler to bid for power before inaction could sap the enthusiasm of his increasingly fanatical following. On the night of November 8–9, 1923, Hitler and the SA seized key points in Munich and sought to launch a "March on Berlin" modelled on Mussolini's October 1922 exploit. But unlike Mussolini, Hitler failed to secure the support of army and police; they soon crushed this "Beer Hall *Putsch*." Hitler's oratory at his subsequent high treason trial nevertheless turned defeat into victory. His allies, who included Ludendorff, sheepishly evaded their responsibilities. Hitler affirmed his own and appealed to a higher court: Weimar judges might condemn the rebels, but history would triumphantly acquit them. He emerged from the trial as uncontested leader of German radical nationalism.

His short term in prison was a welcome rest, a chance to "confirm his

Hitler and associates in prison after the "Beer Hall *Putsch.*"

ideas by the study of natural history." There he began a memoir and political tract entitled "A Four and One-Half Year Struggle against Lies, Stupidity, and Cowardice." A merciful editor later shortened the title to the catchier *Mein Kampf*—"My Struggle." Its 600 turgid pages included much wisdom about propaganda technique, expressed with a cynical frankness that distinguished Hitler from the theorists of commercial advertising. It also suggested that Hitler saw himself as that rare phenomenon, a combination of prophet and political leader.

Last but not least, *Mein Kampf* offered a foreign policy program. In late 1922, Hitler had already formulated in private how he proposed to go about fulfilling Germany's world mission: "We should attempt the carving up of Russia with English help." In *Mein Kampf* Hitler laid out this program in detail, beginning with a critique of William II's too ambitious foreign policy, which had alienated Britain, France, and Russia all at once. Germany should instead proceed to world domination by stages, smashing one adversary at a time: first the internal enemies, then France, and finally Russia, where Germany would seize the *Lebensraum* or "living space" it required, the vast blockade-proof empire Ludendorff had briefly grasped in 1918. Britain and Italy, both hostile to France during the Ruhr crisis, appeared available as allies; Hitler had inevitably conceived an admiration for Mussolini, who furnished a welcome prototype for nationalist dictatorship. In an unpublished "second book" of 1928 Hitler also discovered Germany's final adversary in the quest for world domination: the United States.

For the moment, such vistas were beside the point. Prosperity and the success of Stresemann's foreign policy lessened the appeal of radical nationalism. The NSDAP, which Hitler had reorganized as a tightly centralized "Führer-party" after his release from prison, received a mere 12 *Reichstag* seats in the 1928 election. But two

---

Hitler, Master of Propaganda   1925

Hitler set forth four mutually reinforcing principles for effective propaganda: it addressed "the most limited intelligence" in its audience, it appealed to emotion rather than intellect, it was relentlessly repetitive, and it displayed and fostered a fanatical one-sidedness.

All propaganda must be popular and its intellectual level must be adjusted to the most limited intelligence among those it is addressed to. . . . The more modest its intellectual ballast, the more exclusively it takes into consideration the emotions of the masses, the more effective it will be. . . . The art of propaganda lies in understanding the emotional ideas of the great masses and finding . . . the way to the attention and thence to the heart of the broad masses. . . .

The receptivity of the great masses is very limited, their intelligence is small, but their power of forgetting is enormous. In consequence . . . all effective propaganda must be limited to a very few points and must harp on these in slogans until the very last member of the public understands what you want him to understand. . . .

What . . . would we say about a poster that was supposed to advertise a new soap and that described other soaps as "good"? We would only shake our heads. Exactly the same applies to political advertising. The function of propaganda is . . . not to make an objective study of the truth . . . ; its task is to serve our own right, always and unflinchingly. . . . It does not have multiple shadings; it has a positive and a negative: love or hate, right or wrong, truth or lie, never half this way and half that way. . . .

From Adolf Hitler, *Mein Kampf*, trans. by Ralph Manheim (Boston: Houghton Mifflin, 1943), pp. 180–83.

---

things suggested that it was ready for further growth: its relentless emphasis on organization and propaganda, and its increasing success with the hard-hit peasantry of north Germany as the agricultural depression deepened after 1927.

The Nazi Revolution

Hitler's breakthrough into national politics came in 1929–30, even before the Depression hit Germany in full force. The press and film magnate Alfred

Hugenberg, an extreme pan-German, had taken over the party of the traditional Junker Right, the German National People's Party (DNVP). Hugenberg, unlike the DNVP's preceding leaders, was fanatically committed to bringing Weimar down. The Young Plan reparations settlement of 1929 offered him an occasion for a massive propaganda campaign against the Republic that had consented to the alleged "enslavement of the German people" through reparations.

Hugenberg enlisted the help of Hitler and the NSDAP—and firmly established Hitler on the national political scene. Then the last Weimar coalition government collapsed; the SPD, like Labour in Britain in 1931, rejected balancing the budget by cutting unemployment benefits. It successor, the government of the authoritarian Center Party leader, Heinrich Brüning, lacked a firm *Reichstag* majority. Brüning therefore committed an act of folly. He called an election for September 1930.

The French had evacuated their last Rhineland occupation zone that June; Germans were now free to vote their views without fear of consequences. Brüning's deflationary measures against the deepening Depression made him unloved. Hugenberg's campaign against the Young Plan had allowed Hitler to create an agitation and propaganda machine that utterly outclassed that of the other parties. The 1930 vote was therefore an electoral earthquake: 107 Nazi *Reichstag* seats, and 6.4 million Nazi votes of 34.9 million votes cast.

The NSDAP was now Germany's second largest party, after the SPD. It tailored its appeals to every conceivable interest group, but its program was above all a name: Adolf Hitler. Hitler offered to fill the role that Bismarck had created and that William II had failed to fill, the role of national *Führer*. He symbolized a radical alternative to Weimar's economic misery, dreary indecisiveness, class and religious division, and national humiliation. The NSDAP, ranted one of Hitler's lieutenants, was

"the opposite of everything that now exists." Increasing numbers of Germans found that deliberately vague appeal compelling.

The principal question in German politics after September 1930 was when, and under what conditions, Hitler would achieve power. In the next two years, as the Depression shrank Brüning's authority, the Junker kitchen cabinet around Reich President Hindenburg became increasingly desperate. They applauded the NSDAP's nationalist fanaticism and sought to use it to buttress their own power, while resisting Hitler's increasingly pressing demands for the chancellorship. But like the similar efforts of Salandra and Giolitti in 1921–25, repeated conservative attempts to domesticate Hitler failed.

In spring 1932, Brüning sponsored Hindenburg's reelection for a second seven-year term, and Hitler unchivalrously ran against the "Old Gentleman." Hindenburg won, but only thanks to the votes of the SPD, which preferred even a Prussian field marshal to Hitler. After the election, Hindenburg dismissed Brüning, who had outlived his usefulness and had provoked Hitler by attempting to abolish the SA. The army, which played an increasing political role, resisted curbs on what it naively perceived as the SA's young "idealists."

A *Reichstag* election in July 1932 gave the NSDAP an unprecedented 230 seats, amid SA violence that left hundreds dead. With the help of the 89 Communists, who opposed democracy as bitterly as the NSDAP, Hitler now had a *Reichstag* majority not merely against any cabinet or chancellor, but against the Weimar Republic itself. NSDAP obstruction and Hitler's demand for the chancellorship produced political paralysis. Hindenburg as yet refused to hand over Germany "like a laboratory rabbit" to the bold experimenters of the NSDAP. But Brüning's two successors as chancellor failed to master the Depression, the *Reichstag*, the continuing violence, and back-biting in the conservative camp. On January 30, 1933, Hindenburg gave in and made Adolf Hitler chancellor of the German Reich in a coalition cabinet with Hugenberg and numerous other conservatives.

Hitler soon disabused his conservative allies of the illusion that they had "hired him" as their front man. He established a direct alliance with the military high command on February 3 with promises to "exterminate Marxism root and branch," reawaken the German people's "will to arms," and create a new armed forces (*Wehrmacht*) once more based on universal military service. He extracted from Hindenburg permission to hold a new election and emergency presidential powers that restricted press and other freedoms. The SA and its elite offshoot, the SS (*Schutzstaffel* or "security echelon"), terrorized political opponents and German Jews with the approval of the Prussian police, which was now under the management of Hitler's close associate Hermann Göring.

On February 27, 1933, the *Reichstag* building in Berlin mysteriously burned; Hitler and his propaganda chief, the malevolent Joseph Goebbels, seized on this as evidence of a "Communist plot" that justified the suppression by presidential decree of all remaining constitutional freedoms. After the election on March 5, 1933, gave the conservative-NSDAP coalition a majority, Hitler bullied the new *Reichstag* into voting an "Enabling Act" that gave the chancellor himself the power to make law by decree. That made him independent of both *Reichstag* and of Hindenburg. By July 1933, Hitler had abolished all parties other than the NSDAP, including the DNVP of his conservative allies. He had purged the civil service of political opponents and Jews—a measure that initiated an intensifying effort to define who was a Jew and to isolate those so defined from the rest of the population.

Hindenburg and the army acquiesced. They approved heartily of Hitler's crushing of Communists and SPD, and swallowed whatever modest qualms they may have had at the anti-Jewish measures, which roused a storm of protest abroad. Hitler also received the blessings of the Vatican, which abandoned the Catholic Center party as it had the Italian Catholic *Popolari* and signed in July 1933 a Concordat with Hitler similar to its 1929 arrangement with Mussolini. In November 1933 a plebiscite and *Reichstag* election gave Hitler a brown-shirted parliament and an 87.8 percent majority. Hitler had achieved in nine months what Mussolini, with far less mass support in 1922 than Hitler had in 1933, had needed seven years to accomplish.

But while Hindenburg lived, Hitler still faced an authority higher than his own. In preparation for the "Old Gentleman's" demise, Hitler consolidated his alliance with the army, that "state within the state" equally indispensable to his domestic power and to his plans for war. When the SA under its chief Ernst Röhm challenged the army for leadership of the rearmament effort, Hitler opted decisively for the army. On June 30, 1934, with trucks and weapons the army provided, Hitler's SS forces rounded up and shot over 200 of the SA leadership, Röhm included. That "night of the long knives" sealed with blood Hitler's alliance with the military leadership. On August 2, after the ailing Hindenburg finally died, the *Wehrmacht* took an oath to Hitler personally. As "*Führer* and Reich Chancellor," a position that united his own prerogatives with those of the Reich President, Hitler now enjoyed powers that far surpassed Mussolini's.

In the ensuing years Hitler consolidated and extended that power. The NSDAP did its best to mobilize the population, including the industrial workers, who received membership in a Nazi "German Labor Front" in place of the smashed SPD trade unions. German youth, by 1936, was subject to compulsory membership in the "Hitler Youth" and "League of German Maidens." And the SS proved a far more formidable rival to the army than had Röhm's SA. Its fanatically loyal and

On Hitler's order, the party organized a boycott of Jewish shops and offices in April 1933. The placard reads: "Germans! Defend yourselves! Don't buy from Jews!"

Heinrich Himmler (left) and
Ernst Röhm a few months
before Himmler had Röhm
shot at Hitler's order.

state bureaucracy and with Hitler's approval gradually usurped its powers. The SS, with Hitler's explicit backing, encroached on both army and judiciary. "Political free enterprise," as one scholar has well described it, was the ruling principle of Hitler's Reich. From his villa in the Bavarian Alps, far above the struggle, Hitler encouraged the rivalries of his subordinates. Internecine struggle strengthened his own power and served as a form of "natural selection" in molding the new National Socialist governing elite. The regime's dynamism was in part a consequence of this system, which contrasted with the more rigid top-down style of Stalin and even Mussolini. Hitler defined the goal of competition—to fulfill the *Führer*'s will—and left it to his subordinates to guess that will and strive frenetically to implement it. That was his most original contribution to the technique of total power.

"Everything for the Wehrmacht!"

Nazi Germany's road to that power led through massive rearmament and conquest. On February 3, 1933, five days after taking office, Hitler addressed a private meeting of his generals and admirals. As well as promising them the elimination of the Left and rearmament, he announced that the power of the new *Wehrmacht* would serve for "the conquest of new *Lebensraum* [living space] in the East and its ruthless Germanization." The generals did not take that statement seriously until much later, but they were delighted that he proposed to give them arms once more.

fastidiously precise leader, Heinrich Himmler, had by 1934 seized control of the Reich police forces, established a network of concentration camps outside the control of the normal judiciary, and set up a small but growing private army that included an SS bodyguard regiment for the *Führer*. By 1936, Himmler was officially "Reich leader of the SS and chief of the German Police," a unique party-state hybrid. And the regime struck once more at Germany's half-million Jews. In September 1935, at the annual Nuremberg party rally, Hitler proclaimed a "Reich citizenship law" that made the German Jews less than full citizens and forbade the intermarriage of "Germans" and "Jews." The definition and increasing segregation of the "racial enemy" proved a mighty step toward extermination.

By 1936–37, within the shell of the Weimar constitution, Hitler had created a system that German jurists described as a "*Führer*-state." Party organizations proliferated alongside the

In the following year the army, Germany's dominant service, accelerated the clandestine rearmament plan upon which it had already embarked under Weimar. When the Disarmament Conference of the League of Nations threatened to get in the way of that plan, Hitler left both Conference and League in October 1933, with the unanimous support of his generals, ex-conservatives, and diplomats. His establishment "flankers" enabled him to rearm and to launch the war that culminated in their own ruin.

Externally, rearmament inevitably led Germany into a "danger zone" in which it ran the risk of preventive war. Hitler warned his generals in February 1933 that they would soon find out "if France has statesman; if so, it will not give us time but will attack us (presumably with [its] eastern hangers-on)." France had no statesmen, and Hitler neutralized Poland with a surprise non-aggression pact in January 1934. Each time Western outrage at Germany's anti-Jewish measures or its rearmament reached dangerous heights, Hitler soothed foreign opinion with a "peace speech" that played on the credulity and yearning for peace of the democracies.

That tactic served even to cover Germany's March 1935 declaration that it had unilaterally torn up the disarmament provisions of Versailles. Germany, Hitler triumphantly announced, had an air force—the *Luftwaffe*—and would soon have a vast mass army based on universal service. London and Paris made feeble protests; then Britain legalized Germany's violations of the Versailles treaty by conceding to Hitler a fleet a third the size of Britain's in the Anglo-German Naval Agreement of June 1935.

Internally, Hitler broke the opposition to breakneck rearmament that emerged in 1935–36, as the economy achieved virtual full employment. Germany's steel barons, whose excess capacity had almost ruined them in the Depression, balked at investing in new plants. Big business leaders warned that the armament boom was overheating the economy; labor and raw material shortages would soon lead to massive inflation and financial ruin. Hitler treated the doubters with contempt. He was secretly confident that the *Wehrmacht*'s future loot would keep the economy going. He also had the support of the army leaders, who wanted armaments and did not share the industrialists' qualms. Hitler gave Her-

mann Göring, now chief of the *Luftwaffe* and second man in the Nazi state, full powers over the economy in mid-1936, and simple orders: "Within four years the German *Wehrmacht* must be ready to fight; within four years the German economy must be ready for war."

The rearmament effort itself proceeded rapidly, gobbling up an ever-greater portion of Germany's gross national product (see Figure 32-1). By 1939, despite the belated beginnings of rearmament in the democracies, Germany was out-spending all its Western rivals combined by a factor of almost two to one. Hitler's effort produced results: the most powerful air force and army in the world. All that remained was to use them. As Hitler remarked retrospectively in November 1939, "I did not create the *Wehrmacht* in order not to strike."

Germany's first and last "Minister for Public Enlightenment and Propaganda," Joseph Goebbels.

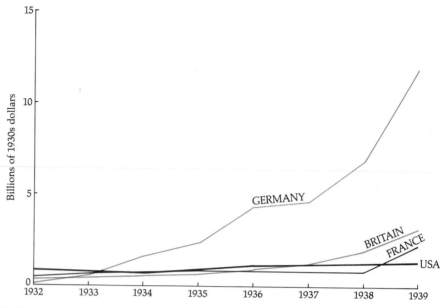

FIGURE 32-1   Hitler Rearms, the Democracies Falter:
Military Expenditure, 1932–39

THE ROAD TO WAR

The massive extent of German rearmament soon made it the decisive driving force in world politics. But what did the *Wehrmacht* mean? The powers sought to divine Hitler's intentions but shrank from the obvious answer, that German rearmament served the purpose announced in *Mein Kampf*, the conquest of *Lebensraum*. Recognizing Hitler's warlike intentions required abandonment of the cherished myth that World War I had been so terrible that another great war was inconceivable. Recognizing Hitler's warlike intentions dictated war to stop Hitler before he was too strong. The Western powers shrank from that conclusion. Their reward was war once Hitler was too strong to stop.

Diplomatic Revolution in Europe, 1936

By 1936, Germany's growing might and the Ethiopian quarrel between Italy and the West offered Hitler a unique opportunity. In February 1936

he sounded the Italian attitude toward Locarno; Mussolini made clear that he would not object to a German breach of that treaty, of which Italy was a guarantor. On March 7, 1936, Hitler's forces occupied the Rhineland demilitarized zone without warning. Germany had broken not only the "dictated peace" of Versailles, but Locarno, a treaty Germany had freely signed.

Hitler's action was by far the greatest risk he had yet taken. The German army was in the initial phases of massive expansion and was correspondingly disorganized. The French could have brought overwhelming force to bear. Victory would not have been bloodless; Hitler had given orders to fight, and to hold the line of the Rhine. But Germany was not yet ready to put up lengthy resistance.

It did not have to. Britain, tied up facing Italy, pressed Paris not to take rash action. As *The Times* of London indulgently put it, Hitler's coup was no more than the occupation of "territory indisputably under German sovereignty." The French military made clear to its politicians that it too preferred inaction. The politicians in turn happily seized on Britain's pusillanimity as excuse for their own. Hitler, who launched the crisis despite wavering among his generals, saw the outcome as confirmation of his own superior judgement. He now had the measure both of the West and of his own timid high command.

The remilitarization of the Rhineland was a strategic and diplomatic revolution. Now Hitler could fortify Germany's western border and prevent France from defending its eastern allies

Europe before the Second World War   1930–39

by attacking Germany. The smaller powers rushed to seek favor with the new master. Belgium, convinced of the futility of its French alliance, retreated into neutrality in November 1936. That potentially uncovered France's northeastern border, which the Maginot line did not protect. Austria, which Mussolini had tacitly abandoned to Hitler in January 1936, contracted in July 1936 a treaty that gave Hitler a voice in its foreign and domestic affairs. The Balkan states expanded their already close economic ties with Germany. Stalin, apparently after reading *Mein Kampf*, had in 1934 become a belated convert to the League of Nations and "collective security"—but he now made intensified efforts to tempt Hitler into a mutually profitable arrangement. Hitler saw no need as yet to answer. He had the initiative.

Spain and China, 1936–39

Hitler was not the sole source of conflict, but he found the quarrels of others tactically useful. Mussolini's Ethiopian adventure had distracted attention from German rearmament and offered an opportunity to pocket the Rhineland. New conflicts in Spain and China offered similar advantages.

In July 1936, a group of traditionalist generals rose against the republic that had taken the place of Spain's enfeebled monarchy in 1931. Popular resistance blocked the coup in most of Spain. Generals Francisco Franco and Emilio Mola then appealed to Fascist Italy and Nazi Germany for assistance. They received it. Mussolini had visions of dominating the western Mediterranean and saw conflict in Spain, as in Ethiopia, as a means of increasing Fascist power at home through what he described as the "permanent revolution" of warfare. He sent aircraft and a ground force that ultimately amounted to four divisions.

Hitler simply wanted a conflict in Spain that would prevent the West from following too closely his doings in central Europe; he sent arms and *Luft-waffe* units. Even Stalin, who apparently saw the Spanish Civil War as a vehicle for keeping the "capitalist" powers at one another's throats, intervened on the side of the Republic with arms, advisers, and Communist-organized "International Brigades." Only Britain and France abstained. London viewed both sides with distaste and feared that the Spanish Civil War might lead to general war. Léon Blum's France offered hesitant unofficial assistance to the Republic but shrank from greater risks.

In the ensuing three years, over half a million Spaniards died in massacres of prisoners and civilians, in battles around Madrid in 1936–37, in bloody winter fighting in 1937–38, and in the final campaigns in southeastern Spain that ended with the collapse of the Republic in March–April 1939. The war became a symbol. For Germany and Italy, the battle against the Republic was a struggle against "Bolshevism"— a convenient propaganda theme to cloak the Italian and German threat to the status quo. For the Left of western Europe and the United States, the war was a struggle against "fascism"—a generic concept that the Communist International had popularized to distinguish "capitalist" from Soviet dictatorship. Few recognized that this was above all a *Spanish* civil war, last of a long series of struggles between military-clerical Right and liberal or socialist Left that had convulsed Spain since Napoleon's invasion in 1808. It ended with the victory of the clerical-military dictatorship of Francisco Franco, who cannily outlasted his Nazi and Fascist patrons and died in power, and in bed, in 1976.

Full-scale war in East Asia soon overshadowed in bloodshed and extent the events in Spain. In July 1937, a shooting incident between Japanese and Guomindang troops at the Marco Polo Bridge near Beijing (Peking) led both sides to reinforce. Chiang Kai-shek had grudgingly agreed in 1936 to a temporary alliance with the Chinese Communists against the Japanese; he now felt compelled to fight. The Japanese army welcomed the chance to reduce all China to colonial subjection. The Tokyo government, under a prime minister who had made his name as an expansionist ideologue, Prince Konoe Fumimaro, backed the army.

A Japanese landing force took Shanghai with much slaughter. In a series of swift campaigns, the Japanese forced Chiang southward. In December 1937 they seized Chiang's capital at Nanjing and massacred between 100,000 and 300,000 Chinese amid scenes of mass rape and displays of swordsmanship against unarmed prisoners. Almost simultaneously, Japanese aircraft sank the U.S. gunboat *Panay* on the Yangtze River. That was an unambiguous warning to the West. China was Japan's preserve: "Asia for the Asians."

The West showed small resolve. Baldwin's successor, Neville Chamberlain, hoped to avoid provoking Japan until he had conciliated Hitler and Mussolini. American opinion, after abandoning Europe in the 1920s, had justified itself by creating the myth that bankers and armaments barons—rather than Ludendorff and Zimmermann—had forced the United States into war in 1917. Between 1935 and 1937 an isolationist Congress passed three "Neutrality Acts" to prevent U.S. sales of arms and ammunition to belligerents, and thus supposedly avoid another war.

When Roosevelt vaguely urged nations to "quarantine" the aggressors in an October 1937 speech, a fierce isolationist chorus attacked him. His modest rearmament plan of January 1938 provoked a furor in Congress, but eventually passed. Roosevelt did join the British in January 1938 in secret naval talks directed against Japan. He contemplated imposing economic sanctions on Tokyo, and eventually entering hostilities undeclared and, by stages, bypassing the isolationists in Congress—both notions that came into their own in 1941. But Roosevelt was a master of ambiguity, of avoiding commitment until it was inescapable. Chamberlain found no reason to reverse his judgment of late 1937 that it was "always best and safest to count on *nothing* from the Americans except words."

Japan's China war therefore proceeded without Western interference. By 1939 the Guomindang had retreated to Chongqing (Chungking) in Sichuan province in the far southwest. Japan had won the war but could not end it. The "New Order in Asia" that Konoe proclaimed in November 1938 remained an order upheld only by Japanese bayonets. Japan neither subdued China nor secured the resources that its own economy lacked.

Alliances against the West

By late 1937, Hitler had reached a number of conclusions and decisions. He recognized that Britain was willing to acquiesce in the peaceful achievement of German aspirations in Austria, Czechoslovakia, and the Polish Corridor. But it was unlikely to fall in with the far wider program put forward in *Mein Kampf* and to become junior partner in a German quest for *Lebensraum* and world domination. Hitler therefore recognized the need for alliances against Britain, to deter it or distract it militarily.

In the fall of 1936, thanks to Mussolini's parallel search for allies against the West and to Italo-German cooperation in Spain, Hitler and Mussolini contracted a "Rome-Berlin Axis." Mussolini's triumphal visit to Germany in September 1937 confirmed that alignment. Footdragging by Mussolini's conservative flankers and fear of becoming a satellite of the Reich kept him from seeking a formal military alliance until early 1939. But he pledged his good faith to Hitler by ostentatiously adopting German-style laws against Italy's 50,000 Jews in the summer–fall of 1938, over opposition that included powerful elements within the Fascist party. Japan signed on with Hitler in November 1936, in an agreement ostensibly directed against the Communist International. That "Anti-Comintern Pact" in reality involved a secret military commitment against the Soviet Union and an unspoken hostility to Britain. Italy joined the Anti-Comintern Pact in November 1937 when it followed the German and Japanese example, and left the dying League of Nations.

None of these "Hitler coalition" pacts as yet offered firm guarantees that Germany would have allies. But they scared London, which intensified—in the hope of binding Hitler to the status quo—its efforts to "appease" what it regarded as his legitimate claims in central Europe. Hitler inevitably viewed such efforts as signs of British irresolution and as an incitement to further German coups. On November 5, 1937, he informed his high command and his conservative foreign minister that Germany might have the opportunity to seize Austria and/or Czechoslovakia in the near future. War with Britain and France must in any event come before 1943–45. Germany was ready to move from rearmament to war.

His listeners, except Göring of the *Luftwaffe* and Admiral Erich Raeder of the navy, found Hitler's resolve to launch a war of aggression imprudent. They grumbled that Germany's strategic situation was as yet unfavorable. Hitler took note, and in January–February of 1938 he exploited questions about the moral character of his minister of war and army commander-in-chief to dismiss both them and his conservative foreign minister. He himself became minister of war and chose new military subordinates pathetically eager to please their *Führer*. Joachim von Ribbentrop, the former champagne salesman and NSDAP foreign policy pundit who had negotiated the Anglo-German Naval Treaty and Anti-Comintern Pact, became the new foreign minister. Hitler had cleared the way for further expansion by consolidating his control over the German army and foreign office, the last preserves of the conservatives who had brought him to power.

Bloodless Victories: Vienna, Munich, Prague, 1938–39

External opportunity immediately arose. In February 1938 the prime minister of Austria, Kurt von Schuschnigg, visited Hitler to attempt to placate him. Hitler bullied Schuschnigg unmercifully and extorted his agreement to take two Austrian NSDAP leaders into his cabinet as ministers of war and of the interior. Once back in Vienna, Schuschnigg thought better of his promise to thus hand over Austria to Hitler. But British and French support was not forthcoming, and Italy had given up its claim to be Austria's protector in 1936. On March 11–12, 1938 the *Wehrmacht* rolled bloodlessly across the Austrian border.

The Austrians received the *Wehrmacht* and its *Führer* with flowers and delirious applause. Hitler responded by proclaiming the immediate *Anschluss* ("merging") of Austria into Germany. Savage SS persecution of Vienna's Jews began immediately; the Austrian army received new uniforms and Prussian drill instructors. And Austria's northern border allowed the new "Greater Germany" to surround Czechoslovakia on three sides.

Unlike Austria, Czechoslovakia had a military alliance with France, 35 well-equipped divisions, and fortifications that in some areas rivalled the Maginot line. But like Austria, it lacked Western support. The France of Daladier shamefacedly sought a way of avoiding fulfillment of its alliance obligations. A prominent Englishman privately advised a German contact not to shoot Czechoslovakia, but to strangle it.

Strangulation, or what his diplomats jokingly described as an ethnic "chemical solution," was indeed Hitler's first thought. The German minority of 3.25 million in Czechoslovakia's northern border area—the Sudetenland—was his chosen instrument. In April he instructed the political leadership of the Sudeten Germans to press on Prague a series of ever-escalating demands that would lead ultimately to the dissolution of the Czech state. "Autonomy" for the Sudetenland would render Czechoslovakia indefensible by depriving it of its border fortifications and industries.

When the Czechs mobilized their army in May 1938 in response to bogus rumors of an impending German attack, Hitler changed his policy and resolved on force instead of subversion: "It is my unalterable intention to smash Czechoslovakia by military action in the near future." He set a target date of October 1, 1938, and intensified work on Germany's fortified *Westwall*, to keep the French at bay while he crushed Czechoslovakia.

By early September, as Goebbels's propaganda about fictitious Czech atrocities against the Sudeten Germans reached a crescendo, a covert German mobilization had readied the *Wehrmacht* for use. Sudeten Germans rioted on orders from Berlin, and Hitler demanded their "self-determination" at the close of the last Nuremberg party rally on September 12. Mussolini, on a speaking tour of northern Italy, derided the Czechs and pledged his support to Hitler. The Czechs, despite intense pressure from London and Paris, readied themselves to fight for their existence.

This crisis impelled Neville Chamberlain to act, to carry to its logical conclusion the policy of active, preemptive "appeasement" he had followed since becoming prime minister in 1937. He flew to Germany twice and urged the

Hitler receives the applause of the Vienna crowd, March 14, 1938.

dictator to accept the Sudetenland by slices rather than all at once. Hitler naturally responded to Chamberlain's attempts at conciliation with further demands: the entire Sudetenland by October 1. But Chamberlain failed to bend his cabinet colleagues to accept that humiliating ultimatum. Hitler, in a speech at the Berlin Sports Palace on September 26, then raved at the Czechs and offered them a stark choice: "Peace or war!" Chamberlain's reply was a mournful radio address to the British people in which he confessed his dismay over this "quarrel in a far away country between people of whom we know nothing." Chamberlain's cabinet colleagues displayed greater resolve; they ordered the Royal Navy mobilized and the blockade prepared. The French unhappily followed. Hitler's insistence on unilateral violent solutions appeared to have at last summoned up a coalition capable of blocking Germany before it achieved European hegemony.

Then Hitler had second thoughts. German crowds greeted the approach of war with a sullen silence far different from the delirious enthusiasm of August 1914. Germany could crush the Czechs. But Czech fortifications would exact a stiff price and the army was still far from ready for general war; it was not scheduled to reach its projected full strength until 1940–41. Finally, Germany in 1938 lacked the oil and raw materials that a long war against Britain and France would demand.

When Chamberlain proposed a further compromise through Mussolini, Hitler therefore resentfully acquiesced to a four-power conference at Munich on September 29–30, 1938. There Chamberlain and Daladier pressed on him a phased occupation of the Sudetenland by October 10. Roosevelt, from the background, urged London and Paris to avoid war. To save the West's face, the dictatorships agreed to an unenforceable four-power guarantee of the mutilated and militarily defenseless remainder of Czechoslovakia.

The Munich agreement was an immense moral, political, and strategic defeat for the West, a defeat that made

The Munich Conference, September 29–30, 1938. Chamberlain, Daladier, Hitler, Mussolini, and Ciano decide Czechoslovakia's fate.

possible Hitler's destruction of the European and world order in 1940–41. The West abandoned its one industrialized eastern European ally, and Germany's annexations in the Sudetenland included a rich booty: over 70 percent of Czechoslovakia's major industries.

Chamberlain nevertheless returned from Munich bearing what he claimed was "peace with honor," "peace for our time." Churchill and a small band of dissident Conservatives thought otherwise. So did Hitler, who immediately and publicly rejected British attempts to hold him to the Munich agreement: "We will suffer the tutelage of governesses no longer!" He was privately furious that his "entry into Prague had been spoiled." In a secret speech to his press representatives on November 10, he regretted that his peace speeches had misled the German people: "Force of circumstances was the reason I spoke for years only of peace." Now the task was to turn the *Volk* around: it must stand like "formed-up troops" behind his leadership. Doubters in the "intellectual strata" unfortunately still possessed necessary skills: "otherwise one could exterminate them, or whatever." As Hitler spoke, party activists devastated synagogues and Jewish shops all over Germany at his command, in the regime's last public attempt to mobilize the German people against the Jews.

By early 1939, Hitler had begun to see the realization of his program within his grasp. He inaugurated a new naval building plan: by the mid-1940s Germany would have an 800-ship fleet far superior to Britain's and capable of taking on the United States. He accelerated an immense construction plan to remake Germany's city centers within ten years. Huge domes and halls, designed so that their ruins would be impressive thousands of years hence, were to fit Berlin for its new status as capital of the world. To his officer corps, he insisted that Munich was not an end but a beginning; Germany was bound for world domi-

nation. It must move forward as it had since 1933, "without letup, exploiting every opportunity, however small, to move immediately toward a new success." And he publicly warned that "international Jewry" was the source of foreign accusations that he sought war. He promised retribution.

Convinced of the feebleness of Western resistance, Hitler saw no reason to resist the temptation to absorb the remainder of Czechoslovakia. On March 14–15, 1939, he bullied its hapless government into placing itself under German "protection." Hitler and the *Wehrmacht* entered Prague. Germany's overheated war economy received a fresh infusion of booty. But Hitler had at last gone too far. His con-

---

Churchill on Munich   October 5, 1938

To the accompaniment of heckling from Chamberlain loyalists, Churchill sought unsuccessfully to convince the House of Commons that "peace for our time" was defeat without war.

CHURCHILL: . . . I will . . . begin by saying the most unpopular and most unwelcome thing. I will begin by saying what everybody would like to ignore or forget but which must nevertheless be stated, namely, that we have sustained a total and unmitigated defeat, and that France has suffered even more than we have.

VISCOUNTESS ASTOR: Nonsense.

CHURCHILL: When the Noble Lady cries "nonsense," she could not have heard the Chancellor of the Exchequer [Sir John Simon, speaking for the Chamberlain government] admit in his illuminating and comprehensive speech just now that Herr Hitler had gained in this particular leap forward in substance all he set out to gain. The utmost my right hon[orable] Friend the Prime Minister [Chamberlain] has been able to secure by all his immense exertions . . . the utmost he has been able to gain—[*Hon Members*: "Is peace."]. . . . The utmost he has been able to gain . . . has been that the German dictator, instead of snatching his victuals from the table, has been content to have them served to him course by course. . . .

From Martin Gilbert, *Winston S. Churchill*, Vol. V, *1922–1939*: *The Prophet of Truth* (Boston: Houghton Mifflin, 1977), p. 997.

"Peace for our time"? Chamberlain returns from Munich, 1938.

The morning after *Kristallnacht* ("plate glass night"), the Nazi party attack on synagogues, Jewish businesses, and Jews which Goebbels organized on November 9–10, 1938.

quest of territories inhabited almost entirely by Czechs made a mockery of his claims that he sought only self-determination for Germans. His breach of the Munich agreement and of his September 1938 promise that the Sudetenland was his "last territorial demand in Europe" showed that he was utterly untrustworthy. The Prague coup crystallized opinion in Britain, which had turned increasingly against Germany after Munich and the November 1938 attack on Germany's Jews.

The Totalitarians United, and the Coming of Hitler's War

A storm of public protest enveloped Chamberlain, who had initially sought to avoid a response to the Prague coup. His response, when it came on March 31, 1939, was ill-considered. Britain and subsequently France guaranteed Poland, which appeared to be Hitler's likely next victim, against threats to its independence. They soon extended similar guarantees to Rumania and to Greece, which Mussolini appeared to

menace by his annexation of helpless Albania on April 7. Chamberlain, with Paris in tow, belatedly attempted to create a structure of diplomatic deterrence that would halt Hitler.

But Hitler played by war-fighting rules. Paper guarantees of states that the Western powers could not help in war did not impress him. The Western pledge to Poland simply convinced him that the Poles, who had resisted secret German territorial demands, should definitely be his next target. On April 3 Hitler set September 1, 1939, as the planning date for the attack on Poland.

The Western guarantee to Poland also made Stalin the man of the hour: the "capitalist" powers were now pledged to fight among themselves. All Stalin had to do was to await bids for his support. He had made clear his policy as early as 1925: "We will have to intervene, but we will intervene last [of all the powers], in order to throw a decisive weight onto the scales." But Soviet participation in war might not be necessary; the Soviet Union and Nazi Germany might exercise joint domination of the Eurasian land mass. Stalin's daughter, who later defected to the West, testified to her father's conviction that "together with the Germans, we would have been invincible!"

In May 1939, Stalin removed his foreign minister, Maxim Litvinov, lest his Jewish antecedents complicate negotiations with Berlin. Stalin's creature Vyacheslav Molotov took Litvinov's place and renewed Moscow's long-standing secret proposals for a German-Soviet political agreement. The British and French also explored cooperation with Russia, but sent their negotiators to Leningrad by slow boat. Chamberlain lacked enthusiasm for a Bolshevik alliance, and London, thanks to Stalin's removal of half the Soviet officer corps, doubted the military usefulness of that alliance.

Hitler also moved to secure Italy, which would serve to distract Britain and France in the Mediterranean while he attacked Poland. Thanks to Mussolini's impatience, the Axis powers concluded a war alliance, the so-called "Pact of Steel," on May 22, 1939. It was to operate automatically if either power "became . . . involved in warlike actions," regardless of who had provoked the conflict. Mussolini privately attempted to limit his commitment by pointing out that Italy needed another three years to strengthen its armaments; Hitler was silent.

The day after the signing of the Pact of Steel, Hitler addressed his generals. The German-Polish border dispute over West Prussia and the German-inhabited city of Danzig was merely the occasion for war; the issue was "the enlargement of *Lebensraum* in the East." That was necessary soon; Germany had a choice between continuing rise, or decline. And this action would be different from Czechoslovakia: "There will be fighting." If the West objected, he would fight it as well.

By mid-August, as the Goebbels propaganda machine barraged the Poles, the *Wehrmacht* had again covertly mobilized. Talks in Moscow progressed well: Hitler and Stalin spoke the same language. On August 20 Hitler wrote urging Stalin to receive Ribbentrop to put the finishing touches on a Russo-German "non-aggression" pact. Stalin agreed. The British and French negotiators in essence offered Stalin war with Germany and no gains. Hitler offered him no war and a division of eastern Europe into Nazi and Soviet spheres. Stalin thereby achieved objectives sought since the beginnings of the Soviet state. The foundation of the Non-Aggression Pact, Stalin later informed the British ambassador with amazing openness, was the common Russo-German aim of destroying the "old balance" of power that had existed in Europe.

On the night of August 23–24, in the Kremlin, Ribbentrop and Molotov signed the Nazi-Soviet Non-Aggression Pact in Stalin's presence. Its contents belied its name: it promised benevolent neutrality in the event that either power became involved in war, even a war of aggression. And its se-

---

Hitler "Foresees" the Holocaust   1939

In his *Reichstag* anniversary speech of January 30, 1939, Hitler made clear publicly that he reserved a special fate for Europe's Jews.

I have in my life very often been a prophet, and was generally laughed at. In the period of my struggle for power it was the Jewish people who first of all received my prophecies exclusively with laughter, [when I said] that I would one day take over the leadership of the state and thus of the entire German people, and that I would among many other things also bring to solution the Jewish problem. I believe that the laughter of German Jewry that then resounded has since died in their throats.

I will today once more be a prophet: if international finance Jewry inside and outside Europe succeeds in plunging the nations into a new world war, the outcome will not be the Bolshevization of the earth and thus the victory of Jewry, but the extermination [*Vernichtung*] of the Jewish race in Europe.

From *Hitler: Reden und Proklamationen 1932–1945*, ed. by Max Domarus, (Munich, 1965), Vol. 2:1, p. 1058 (translation by M. Knox).

---

cret protocol drew a line through eastern Europe and Poland that divided the two parties' respective booty in "the event of a territorial-political remodeling of the territories belonging to the Polish state." At the close of the negotiations, Ribbentrop ventured a joke: Berlin humorists were saying Stalin was about to join the Anti-Comintern Pact. Stalin too offered a witticism: "The Germans wanted peace. . . ." And Stalin toasted both Hitler and Heinrich Himmler, that "guarantor of order in Germany."

Even before Ribbentrop had closed with the Russians, Hitler again harangued his generals: "We must act." Now was the point of Germany's greatest relative strength. His own leadership was irreplaceable: "I can at any time be removed by an idiot or criminal." In a few years British and French armaments would begin to catch up, while Germany's war economy would run down for lack of raw materials. Hitler's sole fear, according to one ac-

Stalin and Ribbentrop enjoy a joke at the signing of the Nazi-Soviet Pact, August 23–24, 1939.

count of his remarks, was "that Chamberlain or some other swine [*Saukerl*] might arrive at the last moment" with peace proposals. He ordered the attack on Poland for August 26.

Britain's signing on August 25 of a military alliance confirming the guarantee to Poland and Mussolini's concurrent confession that Italy was too weak to fight led the *Führer* to waver briefly. Then, surrounded by SS advisers, Hitler confirmed his choice for war. Germany's long-term situation was "very difficult, perhaps hopeless." But as he had written in *Mein Kampf*, Germany would "either be a world power, or would cease to be." At 4:45 A.M., German summer time on September 1, 1939, the *Wehrmacht* attacked Poland from north, west, and south.

In the next two days a disconsolate Chamberlain and the fearful French sought to promote, with Italian help, yet another conference. But the House of Commons balked. The Labour opposition and dissident Conservatives combined to "speak for England" and demand that Chamberlain honor Britain's pledge to Poland. The March guarantee had perhaps been a tactical diplomatic error, but it had one great virtue at the end. Hitler, in challenging it, forced Chamberlain to declare war or suffer the certain collapse of his government. The British ultimatum to Germany expired at 11:00 A.M. on September 3. The last European war had begun.

The causes of the war of 1939 have generated less dispute than those of World War I, of which it was a continuation. Britain, France, and the United States made a second war possible by failing either to dismember or conciliate Germany in 1919. Subsequently, their supine inaction and preemptive concessions permitted Hitler to rearm and strike. The Prusso-German conservatives helped Hitler to power and collaborated enthusiastically with him in creating the *Wehrmacht* that destroyed the European and world balance. Stalin sought alliance with Hitler for the overthrow of the European balance and the extension of Soviet power. Stalin gave Hitler the chance to strike when he did. But in the end, it was Hitler's drive toward total power and his vision of racist world revolution that made this greatest of wars: "The decision to strike was always in me."

Suggestions for Further Reading

Totalitarianism

H. Arendt, *Totalitarianism* (1951), remains the classic description of the phenomenon, but is often eccentric. W. Laqueur, *The Fate of the Revolution*, rev. ed. (1987), conveniently summarizes current debate about the concept and about the Soviet regime. G. Orwell, *1984* (1949), and *Animal Farm* (1946), offers biting analysis in fictional form of totalitarianism in general and of Stalin in particular.

Stalin

On the Soviet Union, M. Heller and A. Nekritch, *Utopia in Power* (1982), is a lively introduction; B. Dmytryshyn, *USSR: A Concise History* (1978), provides a brief narrative and key documents. H. Carrère d'Encausse, *Lenin: Revolution and Power* (1981), and *Stalin: Order Through Terror* (1981), offer clearsighted analysis. On Stalin see especially A. Ulam, *Stalin* (1973). On Stalin's consequences see R. Conquest, *The Harvest of Sorrow* (1986); *The Great Terror* (1968); *Kolyma: the Arctic Death Camps* (1978); and A. I. Solzhenitsyn, *The*

GULAG Archipelago (1973). The numbers Stalin killed remain a subject of hot debate; the most convincing estimates are S. Rosefielde, "An Assessment of the Sources and Uses of GULAG Forced Labour, 1929–56," "Excess Mortality in the Soviet Union," and "Incriminating Evidence: Excess Deaths and Forced Labour Under Stalin," *Soviet Studies*, 1:1981, 3:1983, 2:1987. On Stalin's foreign policy, see above all A. Ulam, *Expansion and Coexistence* (1968).

Mussolini

The Italian dictatorship is insufficiently studied. C. Seton-Watson, *Italy from Liberalism to Fascism* (1967), offers an excellent introduction to the circumstances that made it possible. A. Lyttelton, *The Seizure of Power* (1973), describes ably its first decade. M. Knox, *Musso-*

lini Unleashed, 1939–1941 (1982), and "Conquest, Foreign and Domestic, in Fascist Italy and Nazi Germany," *Journal of Modern History*, 56:1 (1984), explore where it was going.

Hitler and War

The best introduction to Nazi Germany remains K. D. Bracher, *The German Dictatorship* (1970). K. Hildebrand, *The Third Reich* (1984), and P. Ayçoberry, *The Nazi Question* (1981), are excellent on the interpretive issues. On Hitler himself, see first of all his own words: A. Hitler, *Mein Kampf* (Ralph Manheim translation, 1943), and *Hitler's Second Book* (1961). J. Fest, *Hitler* (1975), is by far the best biography. On the inner workings of the regime, M. Broszat, *The Hitler State* (1981), is outstanding. W. Deist, *The Wehrmacht and German Rearmament* (1981), is the best introduction to Hitler's war preparations. K. Hildebrand, *The Foreign Policy of the Third Reich* (1973), and G. Weinberg, *The Foreign Policy of Hitler's Germany* (1970, 1980), are excellent on foreign policy. W. Murray, *The Change in the European Balance of Power, 1938–39* (1984), provides outstanding analysis of the strategic consequences of Munich and dissects

the West's failure to stop Hitler before he became too strong. On Hitler's responsibility for and movement toward genocide, see especially G. Fleming, *Hitler and the Final Solution* (1982), and R. Hilberg's classic, *The Destruction of the European Jews* (1961; revised and expanded, 1985).

Finally, A. J. P. Taylor's *The Origins of the Second World War* (1961), raised a storm by arguing that Hitler had no long-term vision and that war in 1939 was simply a result of opportunism and miscalculation. That view has found few supporters; Hitler's words, both public and private, demonstrate otherwise. C. Thorne, *The Approach of War, 1938–39* (1967), remains the best short narrative; G. Martel, ed., *The Origins of the Second World War Reconsidered* (1986), offers mostly hostile retrospective comment on Taylor.

33
From Second World War to Cold War, 1939–1949

The war that began on September 1, 1939, grew within two and a half years into a global conflict. Hitler destroyed Poland, invaded Scandinavia, and crushed France. That victory permitted Mussolini to overrule his flankers and begin a Mediterranean and Balkan war. It also encouraged Japan to move southward on a collision course with Britain and the United States. And it gave Hitler the strategic and economic base needed to begin "his" war for *Lebensraum* in the East and racist world revolution.

On June 22, 1941, Germany attacked the Soviet Union. That at last brought into existence an "anti-Hitler coalition" powerful enough to bring the Reich down. On December 7, 1941, Imperial Japan completed that coalition by forcing into war a still reluctant United States. Hitler and Japan made the "last European war" of 1939–41 a global struggle; henceforth others beside Europeans would decide Europe's fate.

Only Hitler united his enemies. As the Reich began to fail in its desperate battle against three world powers, those enemies diverged. Stalin sought to expand his power far beyond the eastern European sphere that Hitler had conceded him in 1939. Britain and America hesitantly sought the Soviet despot's cooperation in a postwar system of world order, a successor to the defunct League of Nations. Given that fundamental divergence, "cold war" predictably succeeded war once Hitler was dead. By 1947–48, what remained of eastern Europe after Hitler's end had suffered yet another revolution from above—Soviet style. But this time, unlike 1919, the United States did not withdraw from Europe. It reluctantly committed forces to hold in "peacetime" against Stalin the positions stormed in war against Hitler. Global war gave way to global confrontation between the new superpowers, under the shadow of weapons of unimaginable power, atomic and then thermonuclear bombs.

THE NEW WARFARE

The internal combustion engine gave the Second World War an entirely different character from its predecessor. When combined with armor, radios, and airpower, it gave back the battlefield mobility that industrial firepower had taken away in 1914–18. The second German war was a war of movement; its pace at times rivalled or exceeded the campaigns of Napoleon. Only in fortified areas and when evenly matched forces met head-on did the fighting congeal for months at a time into something that resembled Verdun.

The tank came into its own. British theorists had suggested in the 1920s

Opposite: The face of a new world war: German mechanized infantry destroys a Russian village, 1941.

939

that large armored formations might restore movement to the battlefield. But cavalry conservatism, Chamberlain's budget stringency, and his government's resolve before 1939 to never again fight on the Continent killed innovation in Britain. In Germany the tank caught on during the rapid expansion after 1933; in 1935 Germany set up its first *Panzerdivisionen* or armored divisions. By September 1939 it had six of them.

Contrary to myth, Germany's armored forces did not arise in response to a Hitler demand for tools with which to implement a "*Blitzkrieg*" or "lighting war" strategy that would substitute short decisive campaigns for the grinding attrition of World War I. Until 1938, Hitler gave the army its head. He was fortunate and Europe and the world unfortunate that his professionals successfully combined motors, armor, radios, and the German deep penetration tactics of 1917–18 into an instrument capable of smashing the European balance of power.

At sea, oil-fired turbines and diesel engines gave the great fleets far greater range than their coal-fired predecessors. A new capital ship, the aircraft carrier, rivalled and soon replaced the Dreadnought as the backbone of seapower. The fast fleet carriers of the Imperial Japanese and U.S. navies could by 1941 reach out several hundred miles beyond the horizon to rain armor-piercing bombs on the enemy. Refuelling at sea gave the fleets combat ranges of many thousands of miles. And the amphibious techniques that the U.S. Marine Corps pioneered— partly to ward off raids on its budget between the wars—allowed Americans and British to fight their way back after the opening Allied disasters.

In the air, the scene was likewise entirely changed. Airpower was no longer an infant. It proved capable of a multiplicity of missions, from "strategic" bombing of the enemy's homeland, to transport of troops and supplies, dropping of parachute or glider infantry, close support of ground troops, deep photoreconnaissance, attack on opposing fleets, antisubmarine patrol, and air defense. Air superiority was the key to rapid forward move-

Fleet carrier: the USS *Lexington* in 1939.

ment whether by land or sea, and was indispensable for amphibious landings. Only the Germans, in the last phases of the war, proved tough and expert enough to fight successfully for long without air cover.

The greatest novelty of all was the role of science and technology. Fritz Haber's nitrate process had made Germany's survival possible until 1918. But in World War I science had in other respects been a mere auxiliary. By 1939 that was no longer true. Decisive or potentially decisive weapons such as radar, liquid-fuel ballistic missiles, jet aircraft, computers to decipher enemy signals, and the atomic bomb required a high level of scientific skill, technological expertise, and economic power.

The bomb's practical realization was only possible thanks to an unprecedented commitment of scientific talent and resources, a commitment only the United States was equipped to make. The spur for this first example of "command science"—a vast government-directed research project aiming at a goal—was the fear that the Germans would reach that goal first. Fortunately, German physicists advanced slowly and hesitantly, and Hitler gave priority to projects that promised us-

able weapons soon. The American "Manhattan Project" spent a staggering $2 billion and drained away the hydroelectric power of the Tennessee Valley and Pacific Northwest. But by July 1945 it had produced uranium and plutonium bombs usable against Japan. Science made possible and war demanded weapons of mass destruction that were for the first time potentially capable of annihilating humanity.

THE INDUSTRIAL AND GEOGRAPHIC BALANCE

Even more than its predecessor, the war was a struggle between opposing war economies. Germany began at a slight disadvantage in total industrial potential compared to that of Britain and France. But its unassailable geographic position, control of Rumania's oil, and economic aid from Stalin more than compensated. A major proportion of Germany's rubber requirements flowed in through Vladivostok. The oil of Baku fuelled the Reich's U-boats, aircraft, and tanks. Turkey's chrome and Finland's nickel hardened the armor of the *Panzer* divisions. In 1940 Sweden provided almost half of Hitler's iron ore

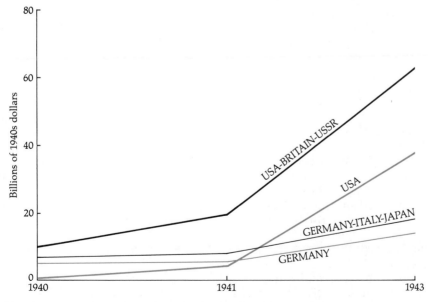

FIGURE 33-1   The Axis Defeated: War Production, 1940–43

through the Baltic and the coastal waters of Norway. This time, the British blockade was ineffective.

The collapse of France brought much booty, and France's industries, which henceforth worked for the Reich rather than against it. But Italy's consequent entry into the war extended Germany's military and economic liabilities without compensation; Britain now had an enemy it could defeat in Africa and the Mediterranean. And by the fall–winter of 1940, the economic power of the United States had begun to swing against Germany.

That threat helped decide Hitler for war against the Soviet Union, which he expected would swiftly crumble. But the Soviets held, although barely; Germany thereafter faced a coalition of world powers with at least three times Germany's industrial potential. The addition of Japan to the Axis powers in December 1941 was small gain; Britain, the United States, and the Soviet Union still had over two and a half times the potential of the "Hitler-coalition" of Germany, Italy, and Japan (see Figure 33-1). The Soviet refusal to collapse and Hitler's rejection of Stalin's secret bids for an armistice left one alternative: the eventual destruction of the Reich under a rain of fire and steel from the east, the west, and the skies.

FROM EUROPEAN TO GLOBAL WAR, 1939–41

Poland: Defeat and Vivisection

Poland fought bravely, but not long. The *Luftwaffe* savagely bombed railroads, roads, refugees, and cities. German armored units stormed forward in north and center, and sliced the Polish forces into pockets. The slower masses of German infantry divisions crushed everything in their path. By September 15 the most serious fighting was over. Stalin attacked the Poles in the rear on September 17 and claimed the Polish territories due him under the secret protocol to the Nazi-Soviet pact. Rib-

bentrop returned to Moscow and ironed out with his hosts, "as if in conversation with old party comrades," the new Russo-German border. The Germans also agreed to take in several hundred thousand ethnic Germans from the Baltic States of Estonia, Latvia, and Lithuania, upon which Stalin now forced a Soviet protectorate.

In Poland, Soviets and Nazis indeed showed a remarkable similarity of method. As Stalin remarked much later to a Yugoslav Communist, "This war is not as in the past; whoever occupies a territory also imposes on it his own social system. . . . It cannot be otherwise." Beginning in September 1939, Stalin deported to the GULAG over a million Polish prisoners of war and civilians. To decapitate any future Polish national resistance, Stalin's secret police (the NKVD) shot roughly 11,000 Polish officers in April 1940; the bodies of many of them turned up in 1943 in a mass grave in the Katyn forest in western Russia. The Baltic States suffered similar deportations and massacres when the Soviet Union swallowed them totally in June–July 1940. And Stalin, who so loved foreign Communists that he had liquidated many of them in the Great Terror, also handed over to the SS hundreds of German and Austrian Communists who had sought refuge in the Soviet Union. Stalin was not joking when he publicly hailed "Russo-German friendship, cemented by blood."

Himmler and his sinister subordinate Reinhard Heydrich lacked Stalin's long experience in truly large-scale killing; they found in Poland a convenient proving ground. With the advancing *Wehrmacht* forces came *Einsatzkommandos* ("task forces") of SS and Police, with the mission of killing both Jews and Poles with an education, especially priests. Thousands perished in experimental massacres; German army protests led to a brief halt. Then the army sheepishly handed over control of occupied Poland to the party and SS.

Hitler himself, on October 18, spelled out what he expected of the

Poles: "cheap slaves." Himmler concentrated the Jews of Poland in artificially created ghettos as a "first prerequisite" for an as yet unspecified "final goal." He also shipped in Baltic Germans and carpetbaggers from the "Old Reich" to fill areas cleared of Poles and Jews. And war freed Hitler even inside Germany. In October 1939 he ordered, in secret, the killing of mental patients and the handicapped in order to rid the "race" of "worthless life." The totalitarian reshaping of Europe had begun.

Grossdeutschland Triumphant

The West made no attempt to help the Poles, despite repeated pre-war French pledges to attack Germany from the west. The French instead peered fearfully from their casemates and ventured a few inept patrol actions. By the end of September 1939 the Germans were happily redeploying their forces from Poland to the French and Belgian borders.

Hitler immediately demanded of his generals an attack in the west. Time was against Germany. The British were belatedly creating a new mass army; Allied war production was rising; America "was still not dangerous to us because of her neutrality laws," but that might change. Germany must "choose between victory or defeat. I choose victory." The generals grumbled that they needed more time. Some hesitantly plotted against the regime.

Unfortunately for the West, weather forced repeated postponements on Hitler. That unsought breathing space gave the German army time to add additional vehicles, draw lessons from the fighting in Poland, and train relentlessly. Hitler and a brilliant junior general, Erich von Manstein, also had time to replace the army staff's hastily improvised copy of the Schlieffen Plan with an unexpected armored thrust through the hills around Luxembourg.

Distractions in Scandinavia, where the Soviets were active, also dogged Germany throughout the winter. Stalin misjudged the Finns: they did not tamely acquiesce to Soviet demands for military bases and territory as had the defenseless Baltic states. On November 30 Stalin therefore attacked Finland and proclaimed a puppet Finnish Communist government in a captured border town. The League of Nations, in its last memorable act, expelled the Soviet Union. But the Finns and the great powers, not world opinion, determined the outcome. Russian numbers finally wore the Finns down in February–March 1940, but not before Stalin's ineptly led troops had suffered several hundred thousand casualties. Fearing that Soviet occupation of Finland would lead to continued fighting and Allied intervention in Scandinavia, Stalin imposed on the Finns only the small amputations he had demanded at the outset.

War in Scandinavia indeed attracted Allied and German hopes and fears. Paris sought to expand the war on the periphery, away from the plains of northern France. Winston Churchill, whom Chamberlain had found himself compelled to take into the cabinet as chief of the Royal Navy, urged attacks on Germany's vulnerable iron ore supply line to neutral Sweden. The Germans prepared to parry; they in turn coveted for their submarines and commerce raiders a window on the Atlantic in Norway.

The Germans struck first. On April 9, using the *Luftwaffe* to compensate for their naval inferiority, they seized key points in Norway with brilliant amphibious and airborne coups. German ground troops also swiftly bagged Denmark. Britain and France belatedly landed forces in central and northern Norway but German speed, skill, and air superiority drove them out by early June.

Defeat in Scandinavia at last destroyed the doleful Chamberlain as a war leader. On May 10, 1940, Winston Churchill came to power at the head of an all-party coalition. Labour, which had damned Churchill in earlier years for his uncompromising hostility to striking miners, Gandhi, and Hitler,

Victor and vanquished, June 1940: British troops await shipping on the Dunkirk beaches; Hitler tours Paris.

now staunchly refused to serve under Churchill's appeasement-minded conservative rival, Lord Halifax. Churchill, it now appeared, had at least been right about Hitler.

But Churchill arrived almost too late. The day of his appointment, May 10, 1940, was the day of the long-awaited German offensive against France and the Low Countries. The Germans had prepared well. The *Luftwaffe*, despite heavy losses, swept the skies of French aircraft and savagely bombed Rotterdam to cow the Dutch. German infantry swiftly crushed the small and inexperienced armies of Holland and Belgium. Seven *Panzerdivisionen* and three motorized infantry divisions struck through Luxembourg and the Ardennes hills, and reached the Channel on May 20, cutting off 40 of the best-equipped Allied divisions in the Low Countries. Of that huge force, 1.2 million fell prisoner; only 226,000 British and 112,000 French escaped from the beaches of Dunkirk.

On June 17, after the Germans had seized Paris, a new French government under the aged Marshal Pétain sued for armistice. By June 24 France was out of the war; only small "Free French" forces under the command of a charismatic junior general, Charles de Gaulle, fought on overseas with British help. Hitler occupied the north and west of France, and conceded to Pétain only an enclave in the south with a capital at Vichy. Greater Germany—*Grossdeutschland*—now controlled Europe from the North Cape of Norway to the Spanish border. Hitler had apparently succeeded where William II and Ludendorff had failed. In the intoxication of victory and looted champagne, the German generals and Hitler's remaining conservative opponents forgot their earlier doubts. War, as he had hoped, had made Hitler *Führer* indeed.

Britain, America, and the German Strategic Impasse

Victory in France did not end the war. Hitler expected Britain to "see reason" and join the Reich as a junior partner. But Churchill refused to give in: "Nations that went down fighting rose again but those which surrendered tamely were finished." He carried the cabinet against Chamberlain and Halifax, who in the name of "realism" sought negotiations from weakness. Churchill was confident that rising British fighter production would keep the Germans from achieving air superiority and invading Britain.

He also bid ruthlessly for the American support needed to fight on; better Roosevelt as senior partner than Hitler. On May 20 Churchill secretly warned the U.S. president that failure to support Britain might lead to a new British government, committed to negotiations. Such a government might swing the British fleet to the Axis side and mortally threaten the United States in the North Atlantic. And to show Roosevelt and the world that Britain would fight so long as he led it, Churchill on July 3 crippled with coordinated naval attacks the fleet of Britain's ex-ally, France. That blow removed the possibility that the new Pétain regime in

France might swing the Mediterranean and Atlantic naval balance in favor of the Axis.

The fall of France at last galvanized American opinion; Roosevelt belatedly responded both to Churchill's polite blackmail and to his demonstration of resolve. Congress conceded America's first peace-time military draft in August 1940; America's dwarf army of 280,000 thus had the means to once more become a serious force—in a few years. For the present, Roosevelt defied the spirit of a congressional ban on weapons sales. In September 1940 he traded 50 obsolete U.S. destroyers for base rights in Newfoundland, Bermuda, and the Caribbean, and for a pledge that Britain would never turn its fleet over to the Germans. In November 1940 Roosevelt rode triumphantly over his Republican opponent, Wendell Willkie, to an unprecedented third presidential term.

Hitler drew the moral from these events as early as July 31: "England's hope is Russia and America. If hope in Russia falls away, America too falls away, for after elimination of Russia an immense increase in Japan's power in East Asia follows." If Germany destroyed the Soviet Union, Japan would be free of threat on its northern flank and would keep the Americans busy in the Pacific. Hitler thus sought an immediate attack on the Soviet Union. War in the East was not only "his" war, sought since 1922, to secure for Germany a vast blockade-proof eastern empire, a "German India." It was also the answer to the increasing support of the United States for Britain. A German "world *Blitzkrieg*" would make Germany unassailable by conquering the Soviet Union before Roosevelt could bring to bear the immense economic and military potential of the United States.

But Hitler's planners soon told him that weather would not permit an eastern campaign that fall. He therefore fell back on stopgaps. Germany launched a sea and air war against Britain's Atlantic supply lines, but that struggle of at-

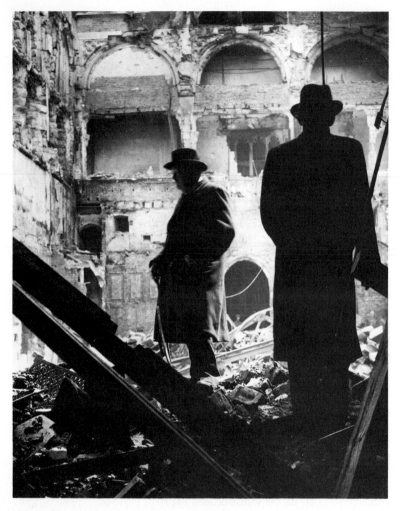

Churchill inspects the ruins of the House of Commons after a German attack.

trition offered no prospect of immediate results and threatened to speed Roosevelt's drift toward war. A second possibility was operation SEA LION, an invasion of Britain for which the Germans began preparation in July. But in vast battles over southern England that reached their climax on September 15, the Spitfires and Hurricanes of the Royal Air Force (RAF) denied the *Luftwaffe* air superiority. The Germans, in a fury at RAF nuisance raids on Berlin, switched to the night bombing of the winter 1940–41 "Blitz." They razed large areas of London and killed civilians by the thousands but failed to break British morale.

The German navy and Ribbentrop offered other options. The Navy pressed for a Mediterranean campaign that would seize Britain's outpost at Gibraltar with the help of Franco's Spain and would galvanize the Italians to take Suez. Ribbentrop attempted to create a world coalition from Madrid to Tokyo against the Anglo-Saxon powers. On September 27, 1940, Ribbentrop succeeded in enlisting the Japanese and Mussolini in a "Tripartite Pact" that pledged all three powers to come to one another's aid in the event of war with America. But Franco and Mussolini between them wrecked the navy's plan and the European part of Ribbentrop's planned coalition. Franco set his price for intervention higher in supplies and territory than Hitler was willing to pay. That scotched the Gibraltar operation. Mussolini, at the end of October 1940, threw the Mediterranean theater into chaos. He attacked Greece without Hitler's approval; the Greeks hurled the ill-trained Italians back into Albania in confusion. British torpedo bombers subsequently sank three Italian battleships at anchor and British armored forces from Egypt crushed the large but ill-led Italian army in Libya between December 1940 and February 1941.

Italy's disasters compelled Hitler to intervene in the Mediterranean—not to achieve final victory over Britain, but merely to rescue his ally. U-boats, a *Luftwaffe* air corps, and armored units under the brilliant but erratic Erwin Rommel arrived in time to prevent the collapse of Italy's position in northern Africa, and of Mussolini's regime. In spring 1941 Hitler extricated the Italians from Greece by striking south through Rumania and Bulgaria into Greece, and by dismantling with much slaughter a potentially hostile Yugoslavia.

These new victories did not offer Germany a long-term strategic alternative. No defeat in the Mediterranean or Middle East could force Britain to make peace, so long as it held the North Atlantic and the support of the United

States. And Roosevelt, despite a continuing isolationist opposition that trumpeted that "the British, the Jew[s], and the Roosevelt administration" sought to force America into war, was at last achieving results. In February–March 1941, Anglo-American staff talks secretly established the strategic principle that was to govern the future U.S. war effort—*"Germany first."* If and when the United States entered the war, it would concentrate its power against the West's most dangerous enemy. In March 1941 Congress passed a "Lend-Lease Act" that offered to a financially exhausted Britain, and thereafter to other U.S. allies, an almost unlimited supply of arms on long-term credit. Credits later turned into outright gifts, and ultimately amounted to $43 billion.

Racist War of Annihilation: BARBAROSSA

Even before Lend-Lease offered unambiguous evidence that the United States was moving toward Britain, Hitler had decided on his response: "his" war, the war in the East. Ribbentrop had invited the Soviets to Berlin to explore the possibility of Soviet participation in the Tripartite Pact. The uncouth Molotov's visit, on November 12 and 13, 1940, was decisive. To Ribbentrop's fantasies about a Soviet outlet to the warm seas through Iran and British India, Molotov replied with a long shopping list in Europe. Stalin wanted Soviet bases at the Turkish Straits, the addition of Bulgaria to the Soviet "security zone," the removal of tacit German protection over Finland, and joint Soviet-Danish—but not Soviet-German—control over the exits from the Baltic. Molotov also stressed the Soviet Union's "interest" in Rumania, Hungary, Yugoslavia, Greece, and even the portion of Poland currently assigned to Germany under the Nazi-Soviet Pact. The tactlessness and breadth of Molotov's demands suggested that Stalin expected the Anglo-

Spitfire!

Saxon powers to defeat Germany and was claiming his booty in advance.

Hitler was relieved. Stalin had "let the cat out of the bag." The Russo-German "marriage of convenience" was over. On December 18, Hitler issued a directive for the greatest land war in history, Operation BARBAROSSA: "The German *Wehrmacht* must

St. Paul's Cathedral, London, under *Luftwaffe* bombardment, January 23, 1941.

be prepared to *overthrow Soviet Russia in a swift campaign,* even before the end of the war with England." BARBAROSSA would annihilate all Soviet forces in European Russia and seize a line from Archangel to Astrakhan. Hitler and his planners assumed that stroke would crush the Soviet regime and would ultimately give Germany world mastery.

The generals bent to planning and deployment with a will. They shared Hitler's racist contempt for the Red Army and found the destruction of the Soviet Union an "intriguing" operational problem. But for Hitler it was more than that. "The coming campaign," he told his subordinates on March 3, "is more than a mere armed conflict; it also entails a struggle between two ideologies." And since, by Hitler's racist logic, Bolshevism was an outgrowth of Judaism, the ideological struggle required "racial" measures: "The Jewish-Bolshevik intelligentsia . . . must be removed."

What that meant in practice soon became clear. Hitler's military assistants issued orders empowering Himmler of the SS to accomplish "special tasks" in the coming area of operations. *Einsatzgruppen* ("task groups") of the SS and Police, with army cooperation, would take "executive measures with respect to the civilian population" of Russia. The army itself, under the "Commissar Order" of May–June 1941, became for the first time a direct extension of Hitler's racial goals. That order required the shooting upon capture of all Red Army political officers and Communist party members. The *Wehrmacht* estimated that it would take 3.5 million prisoners of war but allocated rations for only 790,000; the rest would presumably starve. And the experts of Göring's economic planning staff established the principle that the territories to be conquered would have to feed the *Wehrmacht*—leaving no food for the cities of European Russia. "X millions of people will die out," noted the bureaucrats dispassionately. BARBAROSSA was to be a racial and ideological war of extermination, a war that

trampled underfoot all limits on interstate violence established in Europe since the Thirty Years' War. Colonial war had come home to Europe.

On June 22, 1941, the *Wehrmacht* struck the Soviet Union on a front that stretched from the Baltic to the Black Sea. Germany had deployed 3 million troops, 625,000 horses, 600,000 motor vehicles, 3,380 tanks, and 7,184 artillery pieces. Stalin received numerous warnings, but spurned them as "capitalist provocations" designed to involve him in an unwanted and unnecessary war with Hitler. The German deception plan held. Until the last, thanks to numerous rumors that the Germans had planted to make their deployment appear a gigantic attempt to extort more raw materials from the Soviet Union, Stalin expected a German ultimatum.

He instead received an attack. "What shall we do?" he reportedly asked the Politburo before suffering a nervous collapse. Not until July 3 did he belatedly take to the radio and in a broken voice exhort his Soviet "brothers and sisters" to resist to the last. Stalin evidently had difficulty believing that those whom he had terrorized would fight for him. They fought above all for biological survival and Great Russian nationalism. Immense German massacres of prisoners of war and Jews stiffened Soviet resistance. And the Soviet regime now appealed not to "proletarian internationalism" but to something far stronger. It invoked the Russian traditions that Stalin had himself fostered through the historical rehabilitation, in the 1930s, of past rulers whose methods resembled his own: Ivan the Terrible and Peter the Great.

The Germans nevertheless advanced swiftly, thanks to strategic surprise and to their overwhelming advantages in doctrine, experience, and *Luftwaffe* airpower. By the first days of August they had taken Smolensk, halfway to Moscow, and had killed or taken prisoner well over a million Soviets. Hitler looked to the future; he believed he had won. He ordered German armament efforts shifted to air and sea warfare against the Anglo-Americans. Subordinates drafted a directive for German thrusts in "the period after BARBAROSSA" through the Caucasus to the Middle East oilfields. Germany, Hitler privately declared, would raze Moscow and Leningrad to the ground, exterminate much of the population of European Russia, and replace it with German settlers. The term "Greater German World Empire," which Goebbels had banned from his press in 1940 as premature, no longer seemed inappropriate.

July–December 1941: The Culmination of the War

Others saw different vistas. Churchill and Roosevelt immediately offered aid to a surprised Stalin. The despot accepted it in the spirit in which it was offered; as he once remarked, "In war I would deal with the Devil and his mother." But the Western powers nevertheless assumed that the Germans would destroy Russia. Roosevelt and Churchill met on shipboard near Newfoundland in mid-August 1941, and produced an "Atlantic Charter," a declaration of war aims in the style of Woodrow Wilson.

The Charter implied that the United States would eventually enter the war. It proclaimed that Britain or America sought "no aggrandizement, territorial or other" and desired "no territorial changes that [did] not accord with the freely expressed wishes of the people concerned." It announced that both powers would seek free markets, freedom of the seas, and "freedom from fear and want" for all humanity. The Western powers made no reference to the third member of the new "Grand Alliance," or to that power's entirely different principles and methods. Roosevelt and Churchill evidently expected that they alone would dictate the outcome of the new world war. The United States prepared to do its part by planning an army that would surpass

the *Wehrmacht:* 215 divisions of which 61 would be armored.

The Newfoundland meeting was the outward and political expression of a halting change in Roosevelt's policy. In the conviction that the aid "short of war" promised with Lend-Lease was not enough to defeat Hitler, he began to take steps toward war itself. Without the formal approval of Congress, Roosevelt embarked between July and September on an undeclared naval conflict in the North Atlantic. U.S. forces relieved the British troops occupying Iceland, an outpost Hitler coveted, and Roosevelt agreed to convoy British shipping from Canada to Iceland. In September, after the inevitable naval incident, he gave the U.S. Navy orders to "shoot on sight" at U-boats.

Immediately before sailing to meet Churchill, Roosevelt also moved against Japan. Hitler's May–June 1940 victory in Europe had encouraged Tokyo to turn southward toward the vital oil of the Dutch East Indies. That thrust, and gestures such as the Berlin-Rome-Tokyo Tripartite Pact alliance of September 1940, had freed Roosevelt to react. Then a Soviet-Japanese nonaggression pact of April 1941 and Hitler's attack on the Soviet Union in June ended Tokyo's latent fear of a Soviet threat on its northern flank in Manchuria. In July 1941, Japan occupied bases in the southern part of French Indochina and prepared for further moves toward the oil of the Dutch East Indies. Roosevelt in reply ordered all Japanese assets in the United States frozen, and restricted the U.S. oil exports upon which Japan depended. The Dutch took similar measures. Japan in the space of a week lost 90 percent of its oil supplies. Roosevelt himself seems to have intended only to throttle back those supplies as a warning; zealous subordinates were responsible for the total cutoff.

Tokyo responded with an offer to moderate its activities in China and Indochina. Roosevelt and his advisers judged Japan insincere and its offer impossible of fulfillment given the Jap-

Before the rains came: the German drive on Moscow, October 1941.

Pearl Harbor, December 7, 1941.

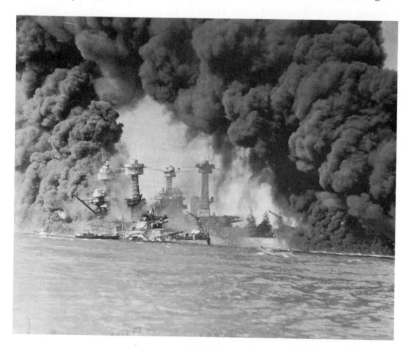

anese army's long record of dominating governments in Tokyo. The Japanese army privately concurred; it refused to give up its Chinese colony. Tokyo decided in September to go to war with the United States while its navy still had oil stocks and before U.S. naval rearmament was complete, unless a breakthrough occurred in negoti-

ations. None did. In mid-October the military rulers of Japan dropped their facade; Prince Konoye's civilian cabinet gave way to the government of General Tōjō Hideki. On November 26, as Roosevelt again insisted on Japanese withdrawal from China, Japan's fast carrier forces secretly sailed.

In Russia, the Germans belatedly closed on Moscow. Hitler had in July and August diverted armored forces south to the Ukraine, where they took another 650,000 prisoners in a great encirclement at Kiev. The Ukraine operation, troop exhaustion, and logistical difficulties delayed the final drive on Moscow until early October. But once lauched, operation TYPHOON made dramatic progress. The Germans demolished yet another Soviet army group and seized a further 600,000 prisoners in the great battles of Vyazma and Bryansk.

In the Soviet capital, the NKVD disappeared from the street-corners. Bonfires in the ministry courtyards consumed mountains of files. Bureaucrats fled for Kuibyshev on the Volga River, designated as alternate capital. The announcement that Stalin remained in the Kremlin and a few exemplary shootings stabilized the situation briefly—but the Soviet regime appeared close to collapse. Then the fall rains bogged the *Panzerdivisionen* and their supply echelons in Russian mud. The ensuing freeze briefly speeded the advance again, although Soviet resistance stiffened. German reconnaissance units reached the outskirts of Moscow; they could see the flashes of the anti-aircraft guns on the Kremlin roof. But the Germans were desperate. By early December, only a quarter of their original tank force could move and 23 of every 100 German soliders who had invaded the Soviet Union were dead, missing, or wounded. On December 5 Hitler consented to halt. The next morning fresh Soviet troops counterattacked and threw the Germans into confusion. Hitler had failed to destroy the Soviet Union.

The following day, December 7, 1941, came news that the Japanese naval air arm had struck the U.S. base at Pearl Harbor and had crippled the battleship force of the Pacific fleet. The military logic of the Japanese attack was as impeccable as its execution was flawless—except that it missed the fleet carriers, which were at sea. The U.S. Navy was the main obstacle to a Japanese southward advance to the oil of the Dutch East Indies. A preemptive strike to eliminate it had therefore appeared necessary. But the Japanese in their desperation had given small thought to Pearl Harbor's political and strategic consequences. It freed Roosevelt of the delicate task of persuading Congress to declare war in defense of British and Dutch colonies, and produced instantaneous unanimity in the United States. Isolationists, many of whom regarded themselves as defenders of American ethnic purity against contamination from the outside world, took up with a fierce racism the cause of crushing Japan. Nor had Tokyo, thanks to its own racist disdain for outsiders and its consequent underestimation of American resolve, given much thought to methods of ending the war it had begun, a war that it entered at an economic disadvantage of at least six to one.

Hitler closed the circle on December 11, 1941; he declared war on the United States. He apparently hoped that a simultaneous two-ocean war would prevent America from concentrating its power decisively in either theater. His decision, like that of the Japanese, handed Roosevelt an immense political-strategic victory. The president now had no need to persuade Congress to declare the war on Germany that he needed to implement America's long-decided strategy of "Germany first." Hitler's declaration of war compelled an American effort in Europe and guaranteed that it would be wholehearted. Hitler and Tokyo between them ensured the defeat of the Axis and the end of Europe's independence.

THE "FINAL SOLUTION"

The realization that Germany might lose spurred Hitler to greater military efforts. It also led him to make sure of one thing: the accomplishment of the "historic mission" he had defined for Germany, the elimination of the alleged threat of "Jewish world domination." The "executive measures" of the SS against the civilian population of Russia that Hitler ordered in March–April 1941 took effect during the head-

---

Hitler Gloats Openly over the Extermination of the Jews   1942

Few Germans later admitted to having known about it, but Hitler publicly boasted in scarcely veiled language about the "Final Solution" on four occasions in 1942 (January 30, February 24, September 30, and November 8):

I told the *Reichstag* session [January 30, 1939; see p. 935] two things:
First, that once they had forced the war upon us, neither armed force nor passage of time would bring us down, and second, that if Jewry were to unleash an international world war for the purpose of exterminating the Aryan peoples of Europe, then it would not be the Aryan peoples that would be exterminated, but Jewry. . . . The Jews in Germany once upon a time laughed at my prophesying. I do not know if they still laugh, or whether their laughter has already ceased. I can however now assure you that they will never laugh again [*es wird ihnen das Lachen überall vergehen*]. And *that* prophecy of mine will also be confirmed.

You will still remember the Reichstag session in which I declared:
If Jewry thinks it can produce an international world war to exterminate the European races, then the consequence will not be the extermination of the European races, but rather the extermination [*Ausrottung*] of Jewry in Europe. People have always laughed at my prophecies. Of those who laughed, innumerable ones no longer laugh, and those who still laugh will perhaps in a little while also no longer laugh.

Hitler speeches at Berlin and Munich, September 30 and November 8, 1942, in *Hitler: Reden und Proklamationen 1932–1945*, ed. by Max Domarus, (Munich, 1965), Vol. II:2, pp. 1920, 1937 (translation by M. Knox).

long *Wehrmacht* advance from June to December. SS and Police *Einsatzgruppen* rounded up and shot as many of European Russia's 4.7 million Jews as they could catch.

The *Wehrmacht* protested far less now than it had over the 1939 killings in Poland. Hitler's victories had immeasurably reinforced his authority and that of his ideology, and the army too had its *Freikorps* tradition, the shooting of Bolsheviks "while attempting to escape." Until the war turned in December 1941, high German commanders such as Manstein or Walther von Reichenau had no qualms about ordering subordinates to shoot Soviet prisoners and Jews: "The [German] soldier must be fully convinced of the necessity of harsh, but just expiation by the Jewish-Bolshevik subhumans."

But the Jews of Russia were only part of the target. At the height of his victories in July 1941, Hitler remarked of the Jews of Europe that "if any [European] state . . . permits a Jewish family to remain, that [family] will become the bacteria-breeding-ground for a new infection." On July 31, 1941, Himmler's subordinate Heydrich received orders to organize, "with the

participation of all necessary German central bureaucracies, all preparations for a general solution of the Jewish Question in Europe."

Hitler himself was apparently careful not to sign a document authorizing what soon became known in the SS and the German ministries as the "Final Solution of the Jewish Question." But both his public remarks and private actions leave little doubt that he was the driving force behind it. He repeatedly demanded reports of the progress of the killings, and in November 1941 promised the Grand Mufti of Jerusalem, leader of the Palestinian Arabs, that when Germany conquered the Middle East he would "annihilate" the Jews there as well.

In September–October 1941 the SS began deporting the Jews of Germany and Austria to Poland and occupied Russia. The SS shot many in mass executions. But that method soon proved cumbersome given the immense numbers of Jews anticipated. In the fall, winter, and spring of 1941–42, Himmler and his subordinates therefore set up camps in occupied Poland designed as factories of death, with gas chambers and crematoria: Auschwitz-Birkenau, Treblinka, Lublin, Sobibor, Belzec, Chelmno. In January 1942, at a conference in the flossy Berlin suburb of Wannsee, Heydrich asked the major Reich ministries to assist him in deporting the Jews—men, women, and children—to the death camps: "Europe will be combed through from west to east."

The "Final Solution" did not end until November 1944, when Himmler, on his own initiative, suspended it as the Reich neared collapse. Its consequence was the murder of over 6 million Jews including a quarter of a million from Germany, well over a million from Russia, 3 million from Poland, 200,000 from western Europe, and at least 750,000 from eastern Europe.

But the Jews were only the victims with the highest priority. The Gypsies of Europe also suffered deportation to the death camps on "racial" grounds;

The "Final Solution": Jewish deportees arrive at Auschwitz.

hundreds of thousands perished. German experts tested killing factory techniques on German mental patients and handicapped as well as on Jews. Between 1941 and 1945 the SS and *Wehrmacht* between them killed the staggering total of 3.3 million Red Army prisoners from shooting or maltreatment. The Poles suffered over 2 million dead during German conquest and occupation. And Hitler's intention in the event of military victory was to remove most of the population of eastern Europe and European Russia. Hitler's genocide was not simply a Holocaust of the Jewish people. It was part of a pseudo-biological attempt to remodel humanity—a racist world revolution.

It also went unchallenged, except on distant battlefields and in a doomed 1943 uprising in the Warsaw ghetto. French police and Dutch SS helped round up Jews for deportation. Slovaks, Greeks, and Hungarians cooperated with greater or lesser enthusiasm. Rumanians and Croats organized their own massacres of Jews; Latvians, Lithuanians, and Ukrainians provided the SS with valuable auxiliaries. The major exceptions were Denmark, Norway, Bulgaria, and even Fascist Italy; those governments and peoples faced the Germans with bureaucratic roadblocks and passive resistance, and saved many of their Jews.

The churches and the Allies did little. Protestants were generally silent except in Scandinavia. Pope Pius XII, despite excellent information about the death camps, offered only generic condemnations of the killing of civilians. Even the October 1943 deportation to Auschwitz of the Jews of Rome—"from under his windows," as the German ambassador put it—did not move Pius XII to public protest, although the Church did help to hide Jews. Stalin was himself a longstanding and virulent anti-Semite. Many high British and American bureaucrats harbored a poorly concealed distaste for Jewish refugees.

The Allies initially disbelieved the reports of the killing; deliberate, mech-

The "Final Solution"

The first train arrived . . . 45 freight cars with 6,700 people, of which 1,450 were already dead on arrival. . . . A large loudspeaker blares instructions: undress completely, take off artificial limbs, glasses, etc. Hand in all valuables. Shoes to be tied together (for the clothing collection). . . . Women and girls to the barber, who cuts off their hair in two or three strokes and stuffs it into potato sacks.

Then the line starts moving. . . . At the corner a strapping SS-man announces in a pastoral voice: Nothing will happen to you! Just breathe deeply inside the chambers, that stretches the lungs; this inhalation is necessary against the illnesses and epidemics. When asked what would happen to them, he replies: Well, of course the men will have to work, build houses and roads, but the women won't have to work. If they want to they can help in the household or the kitchen. For a few of these unfortunates a small glimmer of hope which suffices to have them take the few steps to the chambers without resistance—the majority knows what is ahead, the stench tells their fate. . . .

The wooden doors are opened. . . . Inside the chambers, the dead are closely pressed together, like pillars of stone. . . . Even in death one recognizes the families. They still hold hands, so they have to be torn apart to get the chambers ready for the next occupants. The corpses are thrown out—wet with sweat and urine, covered with excrement, menstrual blood. Children's bodies fly through the air. . . . Two dozen workers use hooks to pry open mouths and look for gold. . . . Others search genitals and anuses for gold, diamonds, and valuables. Wirth [an SS-guard] motions to me: Just lift this can of gold teeth, this is only from today and the day before! . . . .

From an eyewitness account of mass gassings, in *Vierteljahrshefte für Zeitgeschichte*, (1953), Vol. I, pp. 190–91.

anized mass murder seemed too monstrous even for Hitler. Britain did issue a declaration describing the deportations in December 1942, and Churchill pressed for air attacks on the rail lines leading to Auschwitz. But the great distances to the target, the military demands of the bomber offensive and of the Normandy invasion, and the bureaucratic sabotage of his subordinates prevented action.

Churchill did not resort in this case to the public threat with which he had greeted rumors in early 1942 that Hitler contemplated using poison gas against Britain's Soviet ally. Then Churchill had promised reprisals: a deluge of mustard gas from the air upon Germany. That all too credible threat had deterred Hitler, although the Reich had secretly stockpiled large quantities of nerve gas, a weapon far more powerful than anything in the Allied chemical arsenal. Unlike the Soviet Union, the Jews of Europe were not a state, a British or United States ally. They thus had last call on Allied resources. The victims of Hitler's genocide, like those of Stalin's, perished without even token assistance from that elusive force, world public opinion.

THE HOME FRONT: BUREAUCRACY, PROPAGANDA, TERROR, DEATH

On the home fronts, the war in part followed precedents laid down in World War I and in the Great Depression that had succeeded it. All major belligerents mobilized immense masses of men for war and industry. Women again joined the work force in vast numbers, except in Germany, where the regime's ideology dictated that they remain at home. The Reich filled the gap with up to 12 million Soviet prisoners of war, slave laborers, and foreign workers.

The totalitarian states had conducted themselves even in "peace" as if they were at war. Their economies, even when "capitalist" in formal terms, were largely state-directed even before 1939. War itself provided justification in Germany for ever greater state and Nazi party intervention in the economy and in daily life, and the occasion for ever more intense barrages of lies from Goebbels's "Ministry of Public Enlightenment and Propaganda."

As the ring around Germany grew tighter, terror itself became a key ingredient in the war effort; Hitler was fanatically determined to prevent a repetition of Germany's 1918 political

collapse. Civilians who expressed doubts about "final victory" disappeared into Himmler's camps; military personnel guilty of "undermining the will to fight" perished by the thousands on *Wehrmacht* portable gallows. Conversely, Stalin in 1941 and 1942 gave survival priority even over domestic terror. NKVD pressure on the population and the army briefly relaxed. But once the Soviet Union gained the upper hand after 1943, arrests gradually increased once more.

The democracies, as in 1914–18, improvised after 1939 vast bureaucracies to guide public opinion and to ration food, raw materials, and labor. Press, radio, and film became an arm of the war effort. Censorship, often voluntary, normally prevented the publication of news deemed harmful to morale. Photographs of American battle dead rarely appeared. And as in the previous war, public discussion of war aims aroused excessive expectations. At home, especially in Britain, the vehicle of those expectations was planning for a post-war "welfare state" that would banish the misery of the Great Depression. In international politics, the new "United Nations" fulfilled a similiar propaganda function. A new and better League would replace that supposed evil, the balance of power, and secure peace through universal goodwill without excessive effort by the democracies. British and American war propaganda also encouraged a curious unrealism about the allegedly lovable nature and supposed agreement with the principles of the Atlantic Charter of jovial, pipe-smoking "Uncle Joe" Stalin.

Traditional democratic freedoms also suffered partial eclipse, especially for groups that appeared connected with the enemy. Churchill's government rounded up 30,000 German and Italian "enemy aliens" during the great invasion emergency of 1940 and imprisoned them not for offenses committed, but for *suspected* disloyalty. The United States faced an external threat far less immediate than Germans across the Channel. Pearl Harbor nevertheless triggered a hysterical racist clamor against the Japanese-American minority on the West Coast. Roosevelt ordered 112,000 of them deported to the interior; many lost farms and businesses. Deportees of military age put those responsible for this shabby treatment to shame by volunteering to fight. Many served as linguists in the Pacific. Their unit in Europe, the 442nd Regimental Combat Team, terrified the Germans and earned more decorations for valor than any American force of its size and time in combat.

Except for fortunate North America and distant Australia and New Zealand, all major belligerents suffered either occupation or devastation from the air. Many suffered both. That was the most striking difference between the two world wars. In the first, those behind the front had been virtually immune from violent death. In the second, scorched earth and famine, guerrilla warfare and assassinations, reprisals and massacres, and the rain of high explosive, magnesium, white phosphorus, and jellied gasoline from the skies bound "front" and "rear" in shared danger. This was a "total war" far more total than its predecessor.

THE SECOND WORLD WAR, 1941–45

The global war of December 1941 turned swiftly against the Axis. By summer–fall 1942 Germany and Japan were stalled everywhere, from the Don steppe to the South Pacific. Then Allied counterattacks drove the Axis back while air bombardment and submarine blockade wrecked the economies that sustained the Axis forces. As the Allies advanced, the divergences between them became increasingly visible.

The Last Successes of the Axis

While the Germans sought to rebuild the forces shattered in the 1941–42 winter fighting, Japan seized a perimeter from India's western border to Wake Island, west of Hawaii. Hong Kong, the Philippines, Singapore, and the Dutch East Indies rapidly fell to expertly executed air and amphibious operations. Douglas MacArthur, photogenic commander of U.S. forces in the Philippines, retired in March to Australia at Roosevelt's order. His troops fought on until overwhelmed in May. The inglorious surrender on February 15 of over 80,000 British and Empire troops at Singapore—to a smaller Japanese force—was the deathblow to "white" imperial prestige in Asia. By summer 1942 Japan appeared poised to attack India from Burma, while Gandhi inspired a new wave of demonstrations and riots against British rule.

But after a thrust south at New Guinea that led to a first indecisive action between carrier fleets, Japan struck at Midway Island, west of Hawaii. The decipherment of Japanese orders allowed Chester Nimitz, the U.S. theater commander, to lay an ambush. On June 3–6, 1942, the fleets traded air attacks near Midway—and the outnumbered U.S. Navy almost miraculously destroyed four Japanese fleet carriers and their highly trained pilots. The Battle of Midway tore the heart from the Japanese naval air force, and made Japan's far-flung perimeter untenable.

By June 1942, Hitler was himself ready for a last major offensive thrust, toward the oil of the Caucasus region. The *Panzerdivisionen* once again ripped immense gaps in the Soviet front. But as in 1941 Hitler failed to seek one objective and stick to it. As the Soviets crumbled, he ordered simultaneous drives on the Caucasus and on the key Soviet communications point on the Volga, Stalingrad. Both thrusts bogged down. At Stalingrad, the Germans soon found themselves in desperate street fighting in the rubble, where German armor and skill was little use. Bitter Soviet resistance turned Stalin's city into the Verdun of World War II.

Counterattack! Soviet infantry in the ruins of Stalingrad, 1943.

Hitler had lost the strategic initiative in December 1941. He had now lost even the operational initiative; Germany lacked the troops and equipment for wide-ranging offensives. Even in Africa, where Rommel had improvised a modest *Blitzkreig* at the end of a long and precarious supply line, the Germans halted in July 1942 at El Alamein, 75 miles short of Alexandria.

The Allies Strike Back

Allied counterblows soon came. In the Pacific, a Japanese threat to the long and precarious U.S. supply line to Australia provoked a Marine Corps landing at Guadalcanal, at the southern tip of the Solomon Islands. In a savage land, sea, and air battle of attrition that lasted from August 1942 to February 1943 the Marines and the U.S. Army forced the Japanese out. U.S. submarines began a ruthless campaign against Japanese merchant shipping that eventually cut Japan's seaborne empire into isolated fragments.

Rivalry between MacArthur and the Navy dictated a two-pronged thrust back across the Pacific. MacArthur laboriously ascended the Solomons and New Guinea toward the Philippines, to which he had theatrically vowed to return. The Navy, with Marine and U.S. Army landing forces backed by battleship gunfire and carrier aircraft, seized from late 1943 on a succession of blood-stained central Pacific islands: Tarawa, Kwajalein, Eniwetok, Saipan, Guam, Ulithi, Palau. In fall 1944 MacArthur and the Navy joined to invade the Philippines. From Saipan, Tinian, and Guam, the shining new B-29s, the largest and farthest-ranging bombers in existence, could henceforth batter the Japanese homeland.

British and Americans soon drove the Germans from northern Africa. In October–November 1942 the British desert commander, Bernard Montgomery, at last attacked Rommel at El Alamein. Montgomery deliberately fought a 1918-style methodical battle. Weight of fire, not skill, bore down his more nimble opponent. Rommel escaped to face an unexpected attack on his rear after an American-British task force landed in French northern Africa on

November 9, 1942. The slow-footed Allies failed to take Tunis before the Germans, but thereafter methodically laid siege to Rommel and his Italian allies by land, sea, and air. In May 1943 the Axis bridgehead around Tunis collapsed; Hitler and Mussolini lost almost a quarter of a million irreplaceable veterans. The Allies leapt to Sicily in July. As Mussolini's regime crumbled and Italy fled the war, they seized positions south of Rome in September–October 1943.

On the eastern front, the Soviets launched the greatest counteroffensive of all. On November 19, 1942, the Red Army struck from north and southeast of Stalingrad, and encircled 300,000 Germans and German allies in and near the city. Hitler, as was his habit,

ordered implacable resistance on the spot—no withdrawal or breakout, and no surrender. By the end, in February 1943, only 93,000 Germans remained alive to surrender, as food and ammunition ran out. In July 1943 Hitler ventured a last local offensive at Kursk, south of Moscow. Surprise was absent and Soviet antitank guns smashed the Germans in the greatest armored battle in history. Germany had lost even the tactical initiative in the East.

In the Atlantic, the U-boats that had savaged British and U.S. shipping in 1941–42 soon found themselves beleaguered. British microwave radar, British decipherment of the German navy's communications, and the addition of U.S. escorts and airpower to those of Britain won the "Battle of the Atlantic"

The Road to Tokyo Bay   1942–45

by May 1943. In that month the Germans sank 50 merchant ships at too steep a price: 41 U-boats and crews. The defeat of the U-boats made possible the American build-up in Britain for the coming assault on Hitler's "Fortress Europe."

That beleaguered fortress, as Churchill pointed out in a speech, lacked a roof. Stalin's increasing clamor for an Allied "second front" in Europe impelled Britain to pour vast resources into heavy bomber forces; only in the air could Britain strike directly at Germany. Since German fighters made daylight bombing suicidal, RAF Bomber Command concentrated on night raids. And at night, it emerged by the summer of 1941, British bombers lacked the precision navigation aids needed to hit any target smaller than a German city. The bomber offensive, for lack of alternatives, therefore sought to dislocate the German economy indirectly through what the chief of RAF Bomber Command described with relish as "de-housing" the Germans.

The Reich now paid dearly for having broken down, among the many conventions of "civilized" European warfare that it had violated, inhibitions against bombing cities: Warsaw, Rotterdam, London, Coventry, Belgrad. From March 1942 RAF massed bomber raids devastated the cities of western and central Germany: Lübeck, Rostock, Cologne, Essen, Bremen, Düsseldorf. In July–August 1943, the RAF burned most of Hamburg, killing 50,000 civilians and "de-housing" 800,000 others. The *Luftwaffe*, overcommitted on all fronts, took on the bombers in a bitter struggle of attrition. But fresh Allied aircraft and crews joined the battle faster than the Germans could destroy them.

Hitler and Goebbels took the fall of Stalingrad and the coming of the bombers as the occasion to demand total mobilization for "total war" from the German people. SS terror, loyalty to a still revered *Führer*, and fear of retribution for Germany's war of extermination in the East henceforth kept the German people in the war to the bitter end. War production, thanks to fanatical German efforts and to the mobilization of millions of foreign workers, slave laborers, and prisoners of war, rose until 1944. New "reprisal" weapons, such as the V-1 "buzz-bomb" and V-2 ballistic missile, poured from slave-built underground factories. Jet-propelled fighters, by late 1944, briefly challenged Allied control of the skies. But the Reich failed to overcome the combined forces of the coalition it had created.

That coalition, by fall 1943, had begun to define its war aims. By December 1941, when Churchill's foreign secretary, Sir Anthony Eden, visited Moscow, Stalin had recovered fully from his panic of the previous summer. The Soviet Union was going to survive. Eden discovered, as had Hitler and Ribbentrop before him, that Stalin had ambitions. The Soviet dictator insisted upon retaining the Baltic states that Hitler had delivered to him. That was a violation of the Atlantic Charter promises of self-determination that the Soviet Union had accepted with reservations in September 1941. But Stalin jovially sought to reassure Eden: he was different from Hitler, whose "fatal defect" was that "he does not know where to stop. . . . I can assure you that I will always know where to stop."

Subsequently, Stalin capitalized on the Soviet Union's immense casualties and on its status until June 1944 as the sole member of the coalition that faced large German land forces. Stalin incessantly demanded from Roosevelt and Churchill the establishment of a "second front" in Europe—the front that had existed in 1939–40 and had collapsed thanks in part to Stalin's support for Hitler. Stalin also played masterfully on Anglo-American fears of a Russo-German separate peace that would leave the Western Allies facing Hitler alone. He repeatedly approached Hitler clandestinely with offers of an armistice that would restore the borders of 1939 and the Russo-German quasi-alliance against the Western powers.

Roosevelt and Churchill failed to parry Stalin's diplomacy effectively. They almost apologetically asked Stalin to declare war on Japan, with whom the Soviet Union had contracted a non-aggression pact in April 1941. Stalin fobbed them off with a variety of excuses. Roosevelt, too anxious to please, promised a "second front" in Europe in 1942, a logistical and military impossibility. Partly to placate Stalin, Roosevelt also proclaimed at his January 1943 conference with Churchill at Casablanca that the Allies would accept nothing less than "unconditional surrender" from Germany, Italy, and Japan. A further purpose of that policy, which Roosevelt explicitly derived from the U.S. Civil War tradition, was to prevent a repetition of 1918–19. This time the Western Allies proposed to smash Germany for good and stamp out any "stab-in-the-back" legend or desire for yet another rematch. Stalin responded with an inexpensive gesture: in May 1943 he dissolved the Communist International, which had become superfluous now that he had placed his own men firmly at the head of the International's "fraternal parties."

As with Chamberlain's 1939 guarantee to Poland, Roosevelt's assurances that the "capitalists" would fight Hitler to the bitter end only encouraged Stalin to continue his secret courtship of Hitler. What the Anglo-Americans apparently did not know was that Hitler adamantly refused all compromise; Germany's Lebensraum was at stake. Hitler remained willing to strike a deal with the Anglo-Americans—but they demanded Germany's total defeat. Stalin offered Hitler a chance for survival— but Hitler refused to bargain in the East. That deadlock ensured that the war would continue until Germany won, or ceased to exist.

By November–December 1943, when the ill-assorted Allies met for the first "Big Three" conference at Teheran, Stalin held the advantage. British and Americans were stalled in bloody fighting against a handful of German divisions at Cassino, south of Rome; the Red Army was driving back some 2.5 million Germans. Lend-Lease aid, which gave the Red Army the 700,000 U.S. and British trucks that made it capable of the far-ranging offensive thrusts of 1944–45, was no substitute for a large Western ground effort. And the United States drastically weakened its diplomatic position by scaling down its projected army from the 215 divisions planned in 1941 to a mere 89 by early 1944. Roosevelt sought to avoid war-weariness and his own defeat in the 1944 election. But the American decision meant that the Western Allies now *needed* the Soviet Union to defeat Germany, and perhaps even Japan.

Churchill therefore offered preemptive concessions. To give Stalin once again the western border he had secured from Ribbentrop in 1939, the Allies proposed that Poland "move westward" into Germany, whose ultimate dismemberment they agreed on in principle. Stalin, for his part, formally undertook to enter the Pacific war after the defeat of Germany. That was a prize the Anglo-Americans need not have paid for, since the Soviet Union was certain in any event to take booty in Manchuria and Korea after Germany's defeat.

The Reconquest of Europe, 1944–45

Throughout 1943 the Reich had been strong enough to throw into the sea any green American and British troops that might land on the mined and fortified shores of "Fortress Europe." By spring 1944, that had changed. The U.S. Army had acquired in northern Africa and Italy some experience of the Germans and of amphibious landings, the most difficult operation in war. The long-range P-51 Mustang fighters of the U.S. Army Air Corps had secured daylight air superiority over France and

D-Day: Normandy, June 6, 1944.

the western parts of the Reich. Precision heavy bomber attacks on Germany's vital synthetic oil and gasoline plants followed. British decipherment of German signals (code-named ULTRA) gave the Allies forewarning of German operations. Allied deception plans fooled the German command into thinking that the main attack would come near Calais—and might come as far north as Norway.

On June 6, 1944, British and American forces under the supreme command of an American, Dwight D. Eisenhower, landed on the Normandy beaches. Three airborne divisions descended on the German rear. Overwhelming air superiority, Allied logistical mastery, and messy ground fighting resembling that of 1918 expanded the Allied beachhead. Then, in late July, the U.S. First Army broke through at St. Lô and launched the Third Army of George S. Patton around the German western flank. Patton, unlike his cautious superior Eisenhower, understood mobile warfare as well as his German adversaries. By

August he had overrun Paris and was reaching for the German border. Charles de Gaulle, now head of a sizable Free French army, returned to claim the presidency of a new French republic. Even Montgomery, commanding the British and Canadians, showed unexpected speed in pursuit of a thoroughly beaten enemy. For a brief moment Hitler's subordinates despaired of halting the Allies short of the Rhine. In the East, the *Wehrmacht*'s Army Group Center folded up in the face of a massive Soviet summer offensive that advanced over 400 miles, from Smolensk to the outskirts of Warsaw, and cost the Germans half a million troops.

But Hitler himself held on, despite the shock of an assassination attempt on July 20 by a conspiracy of anti-Nazi staff officers. Himmler received the welcome task of purging army and bureaucracy. The Prussian conservatives who had invited Hitler into power and then thought better of it now perished in the concentration camps they had made possible. Goebbels and the NSDAP spurred the German population to fanatical resistance.

Eisenhower reined Patton in and gave Montgomery most of the shrinking stream of supplies reaching the Allied armies from their beachheads and improvised ports. In mid-September Montgomery launched three U.S. and British airborne divisions in a straight line across Holland toward the Ruhr and sent his armored divisions forward to link up. The attack's purpose was transparent and Montgomery's armor was slow. An SS *Panzer* division resting near the Arnhem drop zone crushed the British paratroops and derailed the Allied thrust. Bitter positional fighting amid the minefields and camouflaged bunkers of Hitler's *Westwall* ran on into winter.

Hitler still hoped that a last stunning blow at the Western Allies would break the unnatural coalition and leave him to face Stalin. In the Ardennes, scene of his May 1940 victory, Hitler flung in mid-December 1944 a last offensive at the Americans, whom he considered soft. His luck was no better than Ludendorff's in 1918, despite a penetration of 50 miles and an SS massacre of U.S. prisoners. The U.S. 101st Airborne division, outnumbered and ringed by German armor, defiantly held the key road junction at Bastogne. Patton spun the Third Army by 90 degrees in mid-winter and within a week struck northward at the German flank. The skies cleared; Allied fighter-bombers hunted the roads clear of German tanks and trucks. This "Battle of the Bulge" consumed most of Ger-

many's reserves of armor, ammunition, and gasoline.

In the East, Stalin had by that point gone far toward the objectives staked out in 1939–40. By late July the great Soviet drive that crushed Army Group Center had seized the Polish city of Lublin. There Stalin established a Communist puppet regime (the "Lublin Committee") like that he had attempted to force on Finland in the 1939 Winter War. On August 1, 1944, as the Red Army approached Warsaw for the second time in a quarter-century, the Polish resistance movement allied

The Road to Berlin   1942–45

Allied airpower in the Bulge: a supply drop to the 101st Airborne Division at Bastogne, December 1944.

with the Polish government-in-exile in London answered Stalin's bid for political control of Poland. It rose against the Germans inside the city in a desperate effort to liberate the capital before the Red Army and NKVD arrived.

Stalin halted his army across the Vistula River and gave Himmler's pitiless counterinsurgency forces time to crush the Poles in a two-month struggle. The SS eliminated on Stalin's behalf much of the remaining national leadership of Poland. The Soviet dictator met Churchill's protests with denunciations of the Polish resistance as "criminals." He denied to British and American aircraft the use of his airfields to drop supplies to the Poles. Despite pleas from Churchill, Roosevelt refused to use the considerable leverage over Stalin that the great Allied victories in France now gave. And while it marked time in Poland, the Red Army drove Rumania and Finland from the war, overran Bulgaria, and slowly conquered Hungary. Soviet troops seized Belgrade, but the Yugoslav Communist guerrilla army of Josip Broz Tito largely cleared the rest of Yugoslavia of Ger-

mans by its own efforts—a fact of much political importance later.

As Stalin carved out a Soviet empire, Churchill made a last attempt to secure a modest measure of independence for eastern Europe. He faced Stalin in the Kremlin in October 1944 and reached an agreement—to which Roosevelt never subscribed—dividing Europe into spheres of influence. By this informal "percentage deal" Stalin conceded Britain a 90 percent preponderance in Greece, where Communist partisans were soon to attack the British and the Greek government that had returned from exile in London. Stalin received a similar preponderance in Rumania and slightly less in Bulgaria. Yugoslavia was to be split "50-50." On Poland, Churchill failed to shake Stalin from his support of the Lublin Poles.

When the "Big Three" met, for the second and last time, in February 1945 at Yalta in the Crimea, Stalin's position was even stronger than it had been the preceding fall. Roosevelt was mortally ill, and even in good health lacked Stalin's relentlessness and mastery of detail. Churchill was now totally dependent on the United States; Britain was financially and militarily exhausted.

Above all, the Red Army now held practically all of Poland. It was advancing into East Prussia amid rape and slaughter of civilians, while the Anglo-Americans were still grinding their way painfully through Hitler's *Westwall* fortifications. Roosevelt's advisers still assumed that they needed Stalin's assistance against Japan, and that they must pay for that assistance with concessions both in Europe and Asia. Finally, Roosevelt himself, although no zealot for world government, assumed that only a new and better League, the United Nations, could prevent a new American retreat into isolationism. The success of the United Nations clearly required Soviet postwar cooperation.

Yalta was thus the masterpiece of Soviet war diplomacy. Stalin had already brushed aside Western objections and had recognized his Lublin Committee as Poland's government. He conceded at Yalta that a few London Poles could enter that government as individuals—and as hostages to the Red Army and NKVD. And he secured a firm commitment to the division of Germany into occupation zones, one for each major ally. He also presumably noted with interest Roosevelt's unguarded remark that United States troops would probably remain in Europe less than two years after the war.

In Asia, Roosevelt capitulated to Stalin's demands for Russia's pre-1904 perquisites and more: railroad rights in Manchuria, the vital warm-water base of Port Arthur, and the annexation of southern Sakhalin and the Kurile islands north of Japan. Roosevelt even accepted the delicate task of securing the acquiescence of Chiang Kai-shek to this renewal of tsarist colonialism. In return, Stalin magnanimously promised to enter the war against Japan three months after Germany's defeat. He pledged Soviet cooperation in founding the United Nations, which eventually came into being at a conference at San Francisco between April and June 1945. Finally, Stalin agreed at

Yalta to a vaguely worded "Declaration on Liberated Europe" that promised free elections in all countries the Allies occupied. Within a month of that promise, Stalin's tanks forced on Rumania a Communist-led government; NKVD roundups in and deportations from Poland intensified. The Western Allies made ineffectual protests.

In early March 1945 Americans and British at last forced the Rhine at several points; it was the Soviet turn to mark time while the Red Army cleared up the Baltic coast. British in the north and Americans to the south swiftly encircled 325,000 German troops in the Ruhr. Patton drove across central Germany toward Czechoslovakia. The U.S. Ninth Army reached the Elbe River, 60 miles from Berlin, two weeks before the Soviets surrounded the city. Two battle-tried U.S. airborne divisions stood ready to descend upon the rubble of Hitler's capital.

But Eisenhower and his superiors in Washington, in the disarray of Roosevelt's last illness and death on April 12, failed to grasp the opportunity to seize Berlin. George Marshall, the U.S. chief

The "Big Three" at Yalta, February 1945.

The Soviet flag rises over the *Reichstag*, April 1945.

tisans who captured the *Duce* shot him "in the name of the Italian people." On May 7 and 9, the *Wehrmacht* capitulated unconditionally to Anglo-Americans and Soviets. Germany, as Hitler had half-promised, had ceased to exist.

Japan in Ashes

As the members of the "anti-Hitler coalition" faced one another across the rubble of central Europe, the United States readied itself for the final assault on Japan. Hundreds of B-29s were now in action. On the night of March 9–10, they turned central Tokyo into a sea of fire and killed between 80,000 and 120,000 civilians. By July 1945 the United States had burned out half of the surface area of urban Japan.

In February–March and April–June, two huge and bloody amphibious landings seized first Iwo Jima and then Okinawa, within fighter range of the Japanese home islands. Japanese pilots, following a tactic tested in the Philippines the previous fall, sought to crash explosive-laden *kamikaze* ("divine wind") aircraft into U.S. carriers, transports, and escorts. They sank 21 U.S. ships and damaged more than 60 others. On land, the Japanese were equally merciless toward themselves and toward the prisoners they rarely took. The Marines replied in kind; only 212 of the 22,000 Japanese on Iwo Jima surrendered successfully. The coming landings on the Japanese home islands, in the view of Truman's advisers, might cost as many as a million U.S. casualties, and many millions of Japanese. The war, U.S. planners assumed, could last until mid-1946.

The Japanese cabinet saw defeat impending. But the army, the decisive force now as earlier, refused to accept defeat. It still held Southeast Asia and much of China, as well as Manchuria, Korea, and Japan. Japanese peace feelers through Moscow, deciphered by U.S. intelligence, suggested the diplomats now sought peace, but feverish Japanese military preparation for a last-ditch defense of the home islands told

of staff, opposed the sacrifice of American lives for "purely political purposes"—an oddly innocent remark, given that war itself is politics "by other means." Marshall and Eisenhower abandoned to the Red Army the symbol of victory over Germany and vital German territory. The United States ignored Churchill's desperate urging that it counter Stalin's all too obvious appetites by meeting the Soviets as far east as possible.

The Red Army took Berlin against fanatical SS and *Wehrmacht* resistance, while Hitler committed suicide on April 30 in his bunker under the Reich chancellory. Mussolini preceded him on April 28; the Italian Communist para different tale. And the apparent Allied insistence on "unconditional surrender," which implied the removal of the Emperor, gave the military diehards an apparently unanswerable argument.

It fell to Harry S. Truman, Roosevelt's vice-president and successor, to face this difficult situation. Truman, a man of resolve ("the buck stops here") whose contemporaries underestimated him, entered the presidency with no experience of foreign affairs. He gradually turned against Stalin, but too slowly to affect the outcome in Europe. On July 1, 1945, the U.S. Army, despite further pleas from Churchill, swiftly withdrew from the wide areas it had conquered to the east of the foreordained Western occupation zones.

On July 17, at Potsdam in the center of conquered Prussia-Germany, Truman met Stalin and Churchill at the last wartime conference. Stalin confirmed his promise to enter the war in Asia. He secured half of a scheduled $20 billion in German reparations for the Soviet Union, but pledged in return to deliver food from agricultural eastern Germany to the industrial Western zones. He also demanded a voice in the Ruhr occupation; the Western Allies refused. And he voiced a series of disquieting desires: fleet bases in Greece, a United Nations mandate over the Italian colony of Libya, an interest in French Syria and Lebanon, and a role in the international administration of Tangier. When Churchill congratulated Stalin on his military successes, the Soviet ruler revealed a mild disgruntlement. At least one predecessor in the Kremlin had done better: in 1814 "Tsar Alexander got to Paris." That was an aspiration far beyond anything disclosed to Hitler in the Berlin talks of November 1940.

In the course of the conference, a British election replaced Churchill with the leader of Labour, Clement Attlee. That redoubled the burden on Truman. But Truman had discovered that the United States possessed an asset that Roosevelt had concealed from him—

the still highly secret atomic bomb. Hitler had died before it was ready, but it might speed Japan's collapse. Stalin, informed of it officially for the first time at Potsdam, feigned indifference and expressed the wish that it be used on the Japanese. His own bomb project had begun secretly in 1942, after Soviet intelligence had alerted him to the British, American, and German nuclear efforts.

Truman shared the impatience of most citizens of the democracies. The war must end soon, so that "our boys" could return and happily demobilize. Neither Truman nor his planners explored the possibility of inducing Japan to surrender by siege, without an invasion; that course would require too much time. Nor, despite prompting from some State Department experts, was Truman willing to abandon publicly the demand for "unconditional surrender." That formula had long outlived its supposed usefulness in conciliating Stalin, but it had acquired a life of its own: the public overwhelmingly supported it as a fitting revenge for Pearl Harbor.

Truman and Churchill did attempt to warn Tokyo with a declaration from

Stalin, radiating self-confidence, with Churchill and Truman at Potsdam, July 1945.

The ruins of Hiroshima, August 1945.

Potsdam that promised "prompt and utter destruction" unless Japan surrendered and hinted at Allied flexibility on Japan's postwar form of government. The Japanese ignored it. Truman therefore ordered the first two bombs dropped on Japanese industrial cities. He could not "disinvent" the weapon upon which the United States had spent $2 billion. U.S. opinion, from extreme Left to far Right, was in 1945 virtually unanimous in approving its use to end the war. Most thankful of all were the infantry awaiting orders to storm the mined and barbed-wired beaches of the Japanese home islands.

On August 6 and 9, B-29s from Tinian dropped two atomic weapons on Hiroshima and Nagasaki, in southwestern Japan. Roughly 120,000 Japanese perished outright and many died later from long-term radiation injuries. The Hiroshima bomb failed to persuade, but the shock of the Nagasaki bomb and the simultaneous Soviet declaration of war and *Blitzkrieg* in Manchuria produced crisis in Tokyo. The prime minister, Suzuki Kantarō, urged acceptance of the Potsdam declaration before worse followed. The war minister, General Anami Korechika, de-

manded continued resistance; most of the high command concurred. To break the deadlock, Suzuki made an unprecedented appeal to Emperor Hirohito, who by ancient but disused custom could in exceptional circumstances decide vital issues.

The Emperor, speaking softly, reproached his military for a wartime performance that had fallen far short of its promises. He insisted that Japan had no choice; it must "bear the unbearable." On August 15, after the suppression of a die-hard military revolt, Japan's god-emperor broadcast to a people who had never before heard his voice and informed them that Japan would end the war. On September 2, 1945, Japan surrendered unconditionally to MacArthur and Nimitz on the deck of the battleship *Missouri*, at anchor in Tokyo Bay.

After six years and a day, the Second World War was over. It had cost the Soviet Union approximately 17 million military and civilian dead. Germany had lost 6.2 million; Poland, 6 million including its Jews; China, perhaps 4 million not counting victims of famine and disease; Japan, 2 million; Yugoslavia 1.7 million; France somewhat over and Italy somewhat under half a million. Britain lost 325,000; the United States escaped with combat losses of only 292,000. Over 50 million people had perished in the most destructive conflict in history. Germany and Japan lay in ruins; tens of millions of destitute refugees, prisoners of war, slave laborers, and concentration camp survivors thronged central Europe. Economic chaos and political vacuum followed the defeat of the Axis in both Europe and Asia.

THE COLD WAR

As in 1918, victory did not bring peace. In bringing order out of chaos the United States and Soviet Union collided. Their ensuing "Cold War" has in most respects continued to the present. Its origins, chronological boundaries, and nature have provoked bitter ideological debate, at least in the West. But its origins were no mystery. Conflict between great powers of differing aims and interests was neither new nor startling. What was surprising about the Cold War was its long-deferred outbreak. It took two years of ever more brutal Soviet measures in eastern Europe, of Soviet demands and encroachments in divided Germany, and of Soviet pressure on its neighbors on Europe's flanks to provoke the United States to a coherent response.

Before the Cold War: 1945–46

As in 1939–41, Stalin imposed his system on his new territories. As in his destruction of his domestic rivals in the 1920s, he proceeded by stages, keeping his goals deliberately ambiguous. These "salami tactics," as Stalin's man in Hungary, Matyás Rákosi, aptly described them, also owed a debt to Mussolini and Hitler, who had pioneered the technique of "legal" revolution through the power of the state apparatus. Stalin's relative caution, as Rákosi explained to a secret party meeting in May 1945, was a product above all of the need to divide Britain and the United States. If not provoked, Stalin apparently thought, the United States might follow Roosevelt's prediction at Yalta and withdraw its troops from western Europe. That would concede continental hegemony to the Soviet Union.

The Sovietization of eastern Europe therefore proceeded cautiously, in three phases. First came Red Army and NKVD control in 1944–45, then in 1945–47 a slow slicing away of the noncommunist parties. Finally, after the United States showed that it was prepared to stay in Europe and resist, came the creation of one-party communist dictatorships in 1947–49.

In Rumania and Bulgaria, Stalin's proconsuls rapidly imposed Communist-dominated coalition governments. Churchill had in essence conceded both countries to Stalin in the "percent-

age deal" and Stalin rightly assumed that action there would not unduly provoke the United States. Stalin was almost equally cavalier in Poland. That unhappy country was his vital land bridge to the Soviet occupation zone in Germany. Inconvenient individuals such as the political leaders of the Polish resistance who surfaced in March 1945 disappeared into NKVD custody. But Stalin was nevertheless careful to

Territorial Adjustments After the Second World War   1945

The boundaries shown on this map date from the beginning of World War II.

Axis nations after World War II

Lands which changed hands after World War II

maintain a façade; until 1947 the leader of the London Poles, Stanislaw Mikolajczyk, remained as "second deputy prime minister" in the government of Stalin's Lublin Committee puppets.

Hungary and Czechoslovakia enjoyed relatively free elections in 1945–46. Especially in Czechoslovakia, Stalin did not at first need force. The Czech government-in-exile of President Beneš chose collaboration from the beginning; unlike the Poles, the Czechs had no prior experience of Russian occupation. The Czech Communist Party of Kliment Gottwald achieved a plurality of 38 percent in the 1946 election.

In his zone of Germany, which he rightly regarded, even in ruins, as Europe's greatest power, Stalin applied similar methods. The day after the Red Army hoisted its flag on the remains of the *Reichstag*, a small group of German Communist émigrés under the leadership of the ice-cold and ruthless Walter Ulbricht landed in Berlin from Moscow. The Western Allies at first largely shut down German political activity in their zones and gave priority to the large-scale hunt for war criminals that culminated in trials of the surviving

Nazi leaders at Nuremberg in 1945–46. The Soviets shot a few prominent Nazis but gave priority in their zone to the creation of a regime around Ulbricht.

In early 1946, Ulbricht's resurrected German Communist Party cajoled and coerced the much larger SPD organizations in the Soviet zone into a merger that produced a "Socialist Unity Party," the SED. That tactic, which Stalin attempted to apply unsuccessfully through other Communist parties in western as well as eastern Europe, ultimately aimed at a Communist united Germany—a goal Stalin and his associates disclosed to Yugoslav and Bulgarian Communist leaders in early 1946.

Stalin's gradual destruction of non-Communist forces both in the Soviet zone of Germany and elsewhere in east-central Europe was not the only Soviet policy that aroused alarm in the West. Stalin insisted on receiving reparations from the Western zones of Germany without in turn delivering the food from East Germany that he had pledged at Potsdam. He continued to demand a Soviet share in the occupation of the Ruhr while blocking with unacceptable conditions the fitful inter-allied negotiations over a German peace treaty. That provoked the United States, in September 1946, to announce that its occupation force would remain in Germany indefinitely.

On the Soviet Union's borders, Stalin continued to seek gains far beyond those the Red Army had already secured. He pressed the Norwegians for bases on their island outpost of Spitzbergen, and repeatedly demanded bases at the Dardanelles and parts of the Caucasus from Turkey. In Greece, the Communist guerrilla movement that had suffered defeat in December 1944 after attacking the British in Athens renewed the struggle in May 1946. Tito of newly Communist Yugoslavia provided weapons and supplies. Stalin remained in the background but at first made no objection. Communist victory in Greece would isolate Turkey and assure the Soviet Union the foothold in the eastern Mediterranean that Stalin

Göring (left), Ribbentrop (third from left), and associates on trial at Nuremberg, 1945.

had demanded in vain from Britain and the United States.

In three areas Stalin made tactical retreats. In Austria, he refrained from Sovietizing his occupation zone, probably for fear of provoking an *Anschluss* of the Western zones with the Western zones of Germany. In Finland, he contented himself with imposing a military alliance that left Finland's parliamentary institutions intact. That compromise, which rested on Finland's proven willingness to resist Soviet invasion, Finland's political caution, and Sweden's continuing neutrality, has endured. Finally, in March 1946 Stalin suddenly and belatedly agreed to honor his Teheran promise to evacuate the northern parts of Iran that he had occupied in 1941.

That swift—and unique—postwar withdrawal was symptomatic of Stalin's policy. Churchill, out of office but still forceful, had just spoken eloquently under Truman's sponsorship of an "Iron Curtain" that had descended across Europe. U.S. protests over Soviet creation of satellite "republics" in Iran and Churchill's call for a new Anglo-American alliance to block further Soviet expansion apparently made a temporary retreat seem advisable to Stalin. It was his last.

"Containment" against Expansion, 1947–48

Within the ever-disorganized policy machinery in Washington, those who distrusted Soviet intentions gradually gained the upper hand after 1945. Truman, who had remarked in June 1941 that he hoped that Nazis and Soviets would kill each other off, was temperamentally so inclined. But in the absence of Soviet acts of direct hostility to the United States, domestic opinion prevented the translation of sentiment into policy. U.S. wartime propaganda stressing Stalin's amiability and world peace through the United Nations had succeeded too well. That "Uncle Joe" was as merciless though more cautious than Hitler and that no disunited

Churchill: "The Iron Curtain"   March 1946

In a speech given at Fulton, Missouri, with Truman in the audience, Churchill sought to educate the American public:

From Stettin in the Baltic to Trieste in the Adriatic, an iron curtain has descended across the Continent. Behind that line lie all the capitals of the ancient states of Central and Eastern Europe. Warsaw, Berlin, Prague, Vienna, Budapest, Belgrade, Bucharest and Sofia, all these famous cities and the populations around them lie in what I must call the Soviet sphere, and all are subject in one form or another, not only to Soviet influence but to a very high and, in many cases, increasing measure of control from Moscow. . . .

The Russian-dominated Polish government has been encouraged to make enormous and wrongful inroads upon Germany, and mass expulsions of millions of Germans on a scale grievous and undreamed-of are now taking place. The Communist parties, which were very small in all these Eastern States of Europe, have been raised to pre-eminence and power far beyond their numbers and are seeking everywhere to obtain totalitarian control. Police governments are prevailing in nearly every case. . . . These are sombre facts for anyone to have to recite on the morrow of a victory gained by so much splendid comradeship in arms and in the cause of freedom and democracy; but we should be most unwise not to face them squarely while time remains. . . . I do not believe that Soviet Russia desires war. What they desire is the fruits of war and the indefinite expansion of their power and doctrines.

From Lewis Broad, *Winston Churchill 1874–1951* (London: Hutchinson & Co., 1951), pp. 574–75.

"United Nations" could repeal the balance of power came as a rude shock.

While the education of the American public proceeded with help from both Churchill and Stalin, the military power of the United States shrank dramatically. The 12.1 million men under arms in August 1945 clamored for release. By June 1946 those vast and battle-hardened forces had dwindled to 3 million, and by June 1947 stood at a mere 1.4 million, most of them without combat experience. Possession of the bomb served on balance as an excuse for complacency. And Stalin's demobilization was far less rapid than that of the United States. By 1948–49 the Soviet armed forces were the largest in the world, with roughly 4 million men. An estimated 30 or more Soviet divisions under unified command in eastern Europe faced a scratch assortment of 2 U.S. and 9 British, French, and Belgian divisions in western Europe. The West lacked a high command, and Soviet tank forces held a crushing edge in numbers and quality.

In the United States, the Republicans achieved majorities in both houses in November 1946 and paralyzed Truman. But to the surprise of the doomsayers, the U.S. economy, which now briefly accounted for half of world industrial production, did not relapse into depression. In the course of the war the United States had finally taken up the role of economic leadership spurned in 1919. At the Bretton Woods Conference of July 1944, the Western powers agreed under U.S. sponsorship to a new international economic order, complete with a World Bank and International Monetary Fund. The Bretton Woods system offered a framework for the expansion of U.S. exports that had not existed between the wars. But a prerequisite for that expansion was the recovery of Europe. By the bitter winter of 1946–47 that recovery was worryingly overdue.

Stalin's appetites and Europe's distress, which might strengthen the large Communist parties in France and Italy as well as checking the expansion of world trade, ultimately impelled Truman to act. Britain furnished the occasion. As in 1919, nationalist revolts from Egypt to India beleaguered its Labour government, which sought at home to implement the long-promised welfare state on the back of a faltering economy. In February 1947 Britain confessed that it could no longer bear the weight of shoring up Turkey and of supporting the Greek government against the Communist partisans. The collapse of the British position in the eastern Mediterranean left a power vacuum. If Truman did not fill it, Stalin clearly would.

On March 12, 1947, after assuring himself of Republican support in Congress, Truman announced the "doctrine" that bears his name. The United States would help Greece, Turkey, and all "free peoples" against "armed minorities or . . . outside pressures." The Republicans, under the leadership of Senator Arthur Vandenberg, enlisted with enthusiasm. But Vandenberg and U.S. public opinion exacted a price. As Vandenberg explained to Truman, Congress would only spend money if Truman "scared hell out of the American people." Truman therefore transformed an essentially pragmatic decision to support two strategic countries into something entirely different: a worldwide ideological struggle between light and darkness. And Truman's choice of words unwittingly placed an intolerable burden on many of America's allies-to-be. To qualify for U.S. aid, they now had to seem virtuous and "free," rather than merely strategically important.

In the short term, Truman succeeded brilliantly. Truman Doctrine aid to Greece and Turkey passed Congress. In June 1947 Truman's new secretary of state, the ex-chief of staff George Marshall, announced a second major initiative. The United States offered to both western and eastern Europe, including the Soviet Union, a massive infusion of economic aid to set the postwar recovery in motion at last. While Congress would never have approved aid to the Soviets, the Marshall Plan's authors left to Stalin the burden of refusal.

A senior state department official, George Kennan, simultaneously supplied a much-needed statement of the Truman Doctrine's underlying rationale. Writing as "Mr. X" in the July 1947 issue of *Foreign Affairs*, Kennan urged a "policy of firm containment, designed to confront the Russians with unalterable counterforce at every point where they show signs of encroaching upon a peaceful and stable world." Containment, Kennan argued, would ultimately foster "either the break-up or the gradual mellowing of Soviet power." He later explained with embarrassment that by "counterforce" he had not necessarily meant the use of force, and that not *"every* point" at which the Soviet Union might seek expansion was equally vital to the United States. But his article, and other semiofficial and official pronouncements from Washington, in theory made U.S. commitments virtually unlimited.

To uphold those commitments, the United States reorganized its armed forces in July 1947, creating a nuclear-armed air force independent of army and navy and a Department of Defense. And America acquired new institutions that until now, alone of the great powers, it had disdained. Permanent peacetime secret services, the Central Intelligence Agency (CIA) for foreign intelligence and "covert action" (1947) and the National Security Agency (NSA) for codebreaking (1952), arose from the debris of the wartime intelligence effort.

Europe Divided

Stalin did not disappoint the framers of the Marshall Plan. Molotov attended the initial conference of the Plan in Paris but soon uttered his characteristic stone-faced *"nyet."* Stalin commanded his satellites to decline Marshall aid, and ordered the Communist parties of western Europe to oppose the Plan with strikes and riots. The Cominform, a replacement for the defunct Communist International, emerged to enforce ideological discipline.

In the fall and winter of 1947–48 Stalin swiftly completed his "revolution by conquest" in the Soviet Union's new central and eastern European empire. In Hungary, Rákosi arrested key opposition leaders in May 1947. Mikolajczyk fled Poland in fear of his life in October. In December King Michael of Rumania abdicated. In Czechoslovakia, Kliment Gottwald and his Communist party seized control in February 1948 from within the popularly elected government. Jan Masaryck, the protégé of Beneš at the foreign ministry, fell, jumped, or was pushed from a window to his death. Beneš, as in 1938, declined to fight; Gottwald shunted him

aside. The new regimes took the remarkable name of "people's democracies"—Stalin too was a master of packaging dictatorship for the age of mass politics.

The United States, Britain, and France now went ahead rapidly with the reestablishment of economic and political life in their sectors of Germany. When they attempted to include the Western part of Berlin in the creation of a new currency that foreshadowed a West German state, Stalin reacted wrathfully. In June 1948 he violated the wartime interallied agreements providing for free access to Berlin, and blockaded the Western sectors with Soviet tanks.

Truman and his advisers contemplated sending their own few tanks down the *Autobahn*. But in the face of the Soviet Union's crushing ground superiority (roughly 20 Soviet against 2 U.S. divisions in Germany), they opted in characteristic American fashion for an engineering remedy to a political or military problem. To keep alive the same West Berliners that they had bombed three years before, the Allies organized an endless chain of transport

The Berlin airlift, June 1948–May 1949.

aircraft that delivered millions of tons of food, coal, and gasoline. In November 1948, Truman won reelection against all odds. In May 1949 Stalin abandoned the Berlin blockade.

Its effects remained. Stalin's blockade provoked the creation in April 1949 of the North Atlantic Treaty Organization (NATO), the military alliance between the United States and the western European democracies that Wilson had failed to create in 1919. The blockade also impelled the United States and its Allies to hasten the creation of a "Federal Republic of Germany" in the Western zones. The Federal Republic adopted a constitution in May 1949 and held its first election that August. Ulbricht's "German Democratic Republic" arose in response. The two superpowers now confronted one another with unbending hostility from northern Norway to the Turkish Caucasus.

As well as provoking—in the form of NATO—the "unalterable counterforce" Kennan had prescribed, Stalin also failed to Sovietize one key nation in east-central Europe. In early 1948 he attempted to reduce Tito of Yugoslavia to the same subservience as Ulbricht, Gottwald, and Rákosi. When Tito balked, Stalin expelled Yugoslavia from the international Communist movement for "nationalist tendencies." Then he sought to orchestrate a pro-Soviet coup from within the Yugoslav party: "I shall shake my little finger and there will be no Tito." But Tito remained. That first break in the international Communist movement scuttled the Greek insurgency. Stalin had already told the Yugoslavs that it should be "rolled up" as unprofitable now that the United States had made clear its determination in Greece. After the break with Moscow, Tito abandoned the Greek guerrillas; he needed Western economic support to survive.

Increased tension with the United States and the quarrel with Yugoslavia gave Stalin the occasion to tighten further his control at home. An alleged external threat and genuine internal terror went together, as in the 1930s, to force the population to accept the privation that Stalin's military-economic priorities and crash reconstruction of the wartime devastated areas demanded. In war and aftermath, Stalin deported to Siberia and central Asia millions from nationalities—Crimean Tartars, Volga Germans, and the Baltic and Caucasus peoples—that he accused of collaboration with the German invaders. He vengefully transferred to his own concentration camps all returned Soviet prisoners of war ("In Hitler's camps there are no Russian prisoners of war, only Russian traitors, and we shall do away with them when the war is over.") He demoted prominent military leaders once he no longer needed them, and arrested many whose sole crime was having seen with their own eyes the wealth of the world west of the Soviet borders. The GULAG had suffered a labor shortage after 1941; by 1950 it once more held an estimated 8 to 10 million prisoners.

After war's end, Stalin's lieutenant Andrei Zhdanov began a purge of Soviet writers and scientists that continued even after Zhdanov died a sudden and perhaps unnatural death in 1948. Zhdanov's rival Georgi Malenkov and Yezhov's sinister successor at the NKVD, Lavrenty Beria, subsequently had Zhdanov's former associates in the Leningrad party apparatus liquidated. The gradually intensifying purge, which Stalin extended to the new eastern European satellites, soon took on an overtly anti-Semitic character. "Rootless cosmopolitanism" and "Zionism" were the chief charges under which prominent satellite leaders, many of them of Jewish descent, went to gallows or execution cellars after show trials in 1951–52. Stalin thus applied to the satellites the remedy imposed at home after Kirov's murder in 1934: the removal of all who were not his creatures and the creation of a new ruling class of grateful accomplices.

As Tocqueville had foreseen in the 1830s, America and Russia had each come to "sway the destinies of half the globe." Their confrontation in 1947–49 resulted from and ended a century of ever more destructive European national struggles. Hitler, the most extreme of all nationalist prophets, had invited the superpowers onto the scene. Then he had created a chaos and destruction so vast that at the end only superpowers could master it.

That they proceeded to do and their solutions were mutually exclusive. Here too Tocqueville had seen clearly: "The principal instrument of [America] is freedom; of [Russia], servitude." The democracies of western Europe, despite occasional grumbling, conceded hegemony to Washington. They repeated, against Stalin, the choice Churchill had made in 1940: better to serve as junior partner to another democracy, the United States, than to suffer the domination of a continent-wide slave state. In east-central Europe, Stalin's new multinational empire replaced the Habsburg order that had collapsed in 1918. Supranational American-Soviet confrontation dwarfed and repressed the largely spent forces of European nationalism and froze the borders of 1945. But outside Europe both geography and the alignment of forces were far different. There Stalin failed to discern "when to stop," and nationalism, Europe's most successful export, opened new worlds of violent conflict.

Suggestions for Further Reading

The Second World War

As with World War I, no comprehensive, up-to-date, and readable one-volume history of World War II exists. G. Wright, *The Ordeal of Total War, 1939–1945* (1968), is still a useful survey. J. Lukacs, *The Last European War, September 1939/December 1941* (1976), offers a brilliant synthesis of everything from grand strategy to the intellectual impact of the first two years of war. K. Hildebrand, *The Foreign Policy of the Third Reich* (1973), and A. Hillgruber, *Germany and the Two World Wars* (1981), lay out German strategy and objectives, but see also H. R. Trevor-Roper, ed., *Hitler's Secret Conversations, 1941–1944* (1953), and N. Rich, *Hitler's War Aims* (1973–74). A. Seaton, *The Russo-German War 1941–45* (1971), remains the best one-volume work on BARBAROSSA. G. Fleming, *Hitler and the Final Solution* (1982), and R. Hilberg, *The Destruction of the European Jews* (1961; revised and expanded, 1985), cover the "Final Solution" and Hitler's responsibility for it in chilling detail. M. van Creveld, *Fighting Power* (1982), suggests why the Germans were so difficult to defeat. Among the many excellent books about aspects of the European war, see especially W. Murray, *Luftwaffe* (1984), and M. Hastings, *Overlord: D-Day and the Battle for Normandy* (1984).

Of Hitler's principal enemies only Churchill left memoirs: his wonderfully readable *The Second World War*, 6 vols. (1948–1953), remains the best existing history of the war as seen from London. On Roosevelt and American policy, see R. Sherwood, *Roosevelt and Hopkins* (1950); R. A. Divine, *The Reluctant Belligerent: American Entry into World War II* (1965); and G. Smith, *American Diplomacy in the Second World War, 1941–1945* (revised, 1985). On the Pacific war, see especially A. Iriye, *The Origins of the Second World War in Asia and the Pacific* (1987), and *Power and Culture: The Japanese-American War, 1941–1945* (1981); H. P. Willmott, *Empires in the Balance: Japanese and Allied Pacific Strategies to April 1942* (1982); R. H. Spector, *Eagle Against the Sun: The American War Against Japan* (1985); C. Thorne, *Allies of a Kind: The United States, Britain, and the War Against Japan, 1941–1945* (1978); and R. Butow, *Japan's Decision to Surrender* (1954).

The Cold War

On wartime diplomacy and the origins of the Cold War, H. Feis, *Churchill, Roosevelt, Stalin* (1957), still provides useful narrative; D. S. Gaddis, *The United States and the Origins of the Cold War, 1941–1947* (1972), and V. Mastny, *Russia's Road to the Cold War* (1979), use a wider selection of sources. H. Seton-Watson, *The East European Revolution* (1951, 1956), is still the best overview of the Communist seizure of power in eastern Europe; A. Ulam, *The Rivals: America and Russia Since World War II* (1971), provides a succinct and witty narrative; P. Seabury, *The Rise and Decline of the Cold War* (1967), introduces some of the interpretive issues.

34
The Age of Containment, 1949–1975

The Prague coup and Berlin Blockade marked the beginning of the "classic" Cold War, the fiercest phase of the superpower confrontation that remains the axis of international politics. In Europe, the "war" remained cold. In Asia, by Stalin's choice, cold war became a shooting war in Korea in June 1950. Then military stalemate and Stalin's death in March 1953 ended the most acute period of United States-Soviet hostility.

But truces in Korea and elsewhere in Asia did not end conflict. Anti-Soviet revolts in the satellites and recurrent Soviet threats over Germany marked the post-Stalin "thaw." Superpower tension culminated in 1962 with the attempt of Stalin's successor, Nikita Sergeyevich Khrushchev, to shift the strategic balance by placing nuclear missiles in Cuba. Khrushchev's shamefaced withdrawal and U.S. distraction in Southeast Asia after 1962 inaugurated a period of gradual "détente" or "relaxation of tension," despite wars in the Middle East. The Soviet Union looked on in masterful inactivity as the United States, convulsed at home, ultimately abandoned "containment" in Vietnam in 1972–75.

Unheard-of prosperity in the United States, western Europe, and a resurgent Japan accompanied superpower conflict. American-style material culture—appliances and automobiles, Hollywood films, television serials, and rock and roll—enveloped the world. A new generation arose in the West that remembered neither Depression nor war, and fiercely attacked its elders. A transnational women's movement that originated in France and the United States at last pushed the boundaries of women's rights beyond the vote. For the democracies the age of containment was an age of unprecedented material advance and broadening of wealth. But as in previous ages, the price of change and economic growth was unease and dissatisfaction.

CONFRONTATION IN EUROPE AND ASIA, 1949–53

Stalin's Temptation in Asia

Japan left the Western Allies a difficult legacy. Its slogan of "Asia for the Asians" had been an instrument of Jap-

Opposite: America in Vietnam. U.S. helicopters lift off after delivering South Vietnamese infantry to the battlefield, March 1965.

974

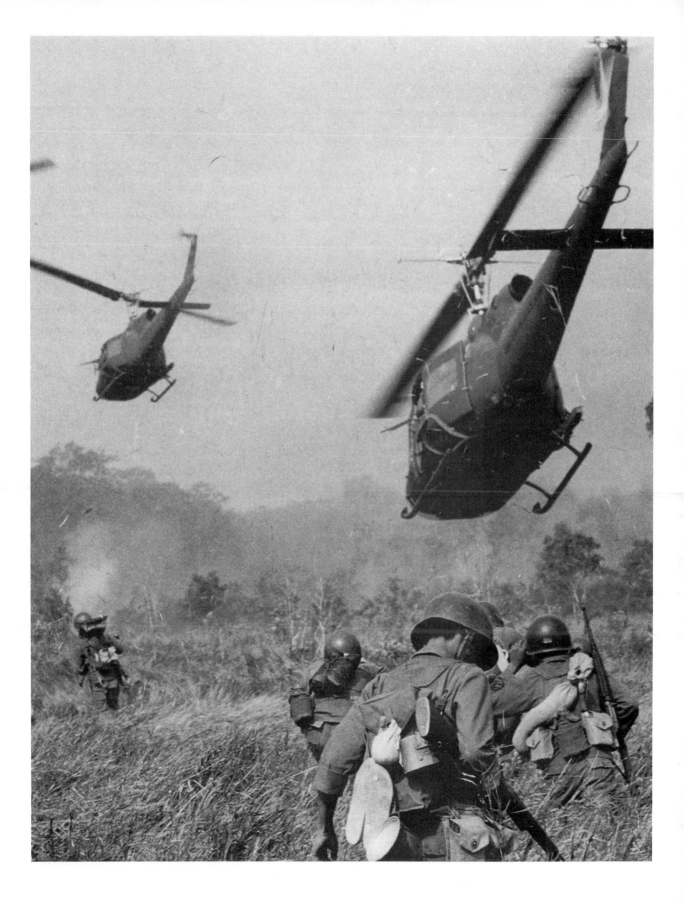

anese colonialism. But that slogan and the inglorious defeat of the British at Singapore in February 1942 had nevertheless mightily encouraged Asian nationalism. Thanks to the "Germany first" strategy, Southeast Asia had enjoyed the lowest priority of all the Allied theaters of war. In August 1945, when Imperial Japan collapsed, the British had only half reconquered Burma. The Guomindang was still hiding in a remote enclave in southeastern China. Indochina and the Dutch East Indies remained under Japanese control. Japan handed that control over not to the former colonial masters, but to armed native movements.

The Dutch ultimately gave up in 1949, under U.S. pressure, and granted Indonesia its independence. In Vietnam, Ho Chi Minh's Communist Party of Indochina assassinated non-Communist nationalist rivals and in September 1945 declared Vietnam's independence from France. The return of French troops led to fierce guerrilla conflict after November 1946.

To the north, the Soviets took Manchuria in their twelve-day war of August 1945 and remained until 1946. They took only half of the former Japanese colony of Korea; the United States, after hard experience in Europe, insisted on dividing that strategically

vital peninsula at the 38th parallel into Soviet and U.S. zones. By 1947–48, two Korean states, one Communist and one with American "advisers," were locked in bitter hostility and intermittent guerrilla warfare. Japan itself fell to the United States alone. Douglas MacArthur, installed in Tokyo as a sort of American Shōgun, contemptuously dismissed Soviet bids to share in the occupation. In the Pacific, unlike Europe, Moscow's contribution to victory had been minimal.

In China, the Guomindang of Chiang Kai-shek and the Chinese Communist Party (CCP) of Mao Zedong (Mao Tse-tung) ended the war as nominal allies. That marriage of convenience inevitably turned to renewed civil war in July 1946. China could not have *two* dictatorships. Truman and his subordinates wavered between attempting to reestablish a Guomindang-CCP coalition, backing the Guomindang, and abstaining. Washington tried all three in succession. Stalin initially sought to maintain a balance between CCP and Guomindang favorable to the Soviet Union, as in the 1920s. But once CCP victory seemed certain he opted for Mao.

In January 1949, Mao's "People's Liberation Army" entered Beijing (Peking). That October Mao proclaimed the People's Republic of China (PRC). Chiang and the remnants of the Guomindang took refuge on Taiwan.

Something resembling a new dynasty, after almost 40 years of war, turmoil, and famine, had replaced the Qing. Mao traveled to Moscow and, after difficult negotiation, signed in February 1950 a "treaty of friendship" with Stalin that promised the return to China of the Manchurian railway and Port Arthur, and allied China and the Soviet Union against Japan.

The "loss" of China and the contemporaneous explosion of a first Soviet atomic bomb in August 1949 created turmoil in the United States. Truman now paid for having "scared hell out of the American people," for having funded resistance to Soviet expansion

The Cold War comes home: McCarthy at work, October 1951.

in Europe by a pledge of aid to opponents of "armed minorities" everywhere. The Republican Right, in the unsavory person of Senator Joseph McCarthy of Wisconsin, out-trumped the president by claiming that he was not anti-Communist enough. McCarthy and his many supporters were convinced of American omnipotence. For them neither Chinese Communists nor Soviets were serious enemies. Only treason at home by U.S. officials could have delivered China to Mao and the "secret" of the atomic bomb to Moscow. They saw above all an internal menace—"Caaamunism" (as McCarthy and his supporters pronounced it) at the State Department and in the academic world of "pointy-headed intellectuals." The public's sudden realization that it faced a Soviet nuclear threat added to the hysteria. The pattern of ideological witch-hunts and populist-isolationist demagogy visible in the 1920s and 1930s reasserted itself. McCarthy's wild charges discredited him in 1954; in the long term he gave resistance to Communism a bad name.

In response to the new situation of 1949–50, Truman decided in the affirmative the contentious issue of whether to build a thermonuclear, or hydrogen, bomb. Stalin, unknown to the Americans, had initiated his own H-bomb research in 1948. The new weapon was orders of magnitude more destructive than the Hiroshima bomb, which had been equivalent to a mere 20,000 tons of high explosive. Truman also called for a review of U.S. defense preparations and strategy; his advisers embodied their conclusions in National Security Council paper NSC-68. It urged a major U.S. conventional as well as nuclear build-up to maintain a balance of power that the Soviet Union's bomb, its ever-growing military, and its alliance with China now threatened.

The recommendations of NSC-68 were politically impractical. The Republicans in Congress persisted in demanding budget cuts while simultaneously damning the administration

for being "soft on Caaamunism." Then Stalin, by an ill-timed display of appetite in Asia that repeated the error of the Berlin Blockade, allowed Truman to counter the Soviet build-up. At the end of 1949 (as Stalin's successor Nikita Khrushchev disclosed in his memoirs) Stalin received Kim Il-Sung, former Soviet Red Army major and chief of the Soviet-sponsored "Democratic People's Republic of Korea." Stalin authorized Kim to attack South Korea. Mao concurred. Stalin supplied weapons, including the T-34 tank that had opened the road to Berlin. On June 25, 1950, Kim's tanks crossed the 38th parallel and rolled the South Korean army up.

Wars in Asia and the Rearmament of Europe

Truman scarcely hesitated. On June 30, 1950, he ordered American ground troops from Japan into combat. Both U.S. control of Japan and the credibility of the U.S. commitment to Europe appeared to be at stake. Like Roosevelt in

Korea   1950–53

One of Kim Il-Sung's T-34s meets the U.S. Marine Corps (1950).

the Atlantic in 1941, Truman acted without a congressional declaration of war and without congressional opposition. A Soviet walk-out allowed the United Nations Security Council, for the first and last time in its history, to vote with the necessary unanimity to fight in defense of a member. The United States provided supplies and a force that eventually grew to 350,000. South Korea provided up to 400,000, and under the U.N. flag 44,000 troops from 14 nations also served.

The North Koreans, well-trained by their Soviet advisers, stormed south and almost swallowed the peninsula in one gulp. But by early August, with some embarrassment and much air and naval support, an Army, Marine, and South Korean force ground them to a halt around the vital port of Pusan, in the far southeastern corner of Korea. Then MacArthur landed Marines and Army at Inchon, halfway up Korea, cut the North Koreans to shreds, and reached the old border on the 38th parallel. Truman and the United Nations imprudently authorized him to conquer North Korea unless Chinese or Soviet intervention appeared immi-

nent. Containment briefly became "rollback." To MacArthur, who knew neither doubt nor humility, permission to cross the parallel was a blank check. As winter deepened he drove headlong for the Yalu River that divides Korea and China, stringing his forces out on North Korea's icy mountain roads.

Beijing conveyed through a variety of channels the message that it would fight to avoid becoming MacArthur's neighbor. MacArthur disregarded a sudden appearance of Chinese "volunteers" in mid-October. A massive Chinese counteroffensive in mid-November took him completely by surprise, and flung U.N. forces back below the 38th parallel. Only the Marines who walked out from Chosin reservoir near the Yalu—through snow and seven Chinese divisions—emerged with credit from the disaster.

MacArthur, to redeem his reputation, demanded the bombing and blockade of China. Truman relieved him of command in April 1951 for insubordination; in a letter to a Republican congressman, MacArthur had criticized his commander-in-chief by insisting that "in war there is no substitute for victory." Truman and his advisers saw no profit in a wider war against China that would pin down an ever-increasing proportion of U.S. forces and might lead to a direct U.S.-Soviet clash. That would be "the wrong war, at the wrong place, at the wrong time, and with the wrong enemy." The ultimate stakes were western Europe and Japan, the largest non-Communist concentrations of economic power and talent in the world beside the United States. And as in Europe, Washington sought to fill a dangerous economic and political vacuum by encouraging the resurgence of former enemies. In 1952 the United States returned sovereignty to a newly democratized Japan, linked to the United States with military bases and a security treaty.

After MacArthur's defeat, Truman thus fought a "limited war" in Korea. U.S. reinforcements and firepower pushed the Chinese back above the parallel. By July 1951, U.S. and allied forces had inflicted immense casualties and had stabilized the front. Acrimonious truce talks began, while trench raids and nibbling operations continued on Korea's bare and jagged hills. Chinese and North Koreans sought to wear down the resolve of an impatient and pacifically inclined democracy by simultaneously talking and fighting. Stalin willed that the war continue. In January 1951, immediately after MacArthur's catastrophe, he told a secret conclave of satellite Communist leaders that the United States was so feeble militarily that the opportunity for a Soviet stroke against Western Europe would come in the next three to four years. Tying U.S. forces down in Asia served that strategy. In western Europe the Communist parties and their sympathizers mounted a "peace" campaign that played on fears of nuclear annihilation and sought to divide Europe from the United States.

But Stalin was not immortal. He had apparently begun in 1952 to prepare a last purge; the Kremlin doctors, most of them of Jewish extraction, stood falsely accused of plotting to murder the Soviet leadership. Their coming trial, like that of Zinoviev and Kamenev in 1936, promised to unleash a flood of denunciations, arrests, and liquidations. Stalin's associates trembled for their heads. "The Boss" was apparently about to inaugurate yet another round of social mobility, Soviet style.

But on March 5, 1953, Stalin died of a stroke. His heirs inaugurated a "collective leadership" that sought hesitantly to retreat from Stalin's terror within and confrontation without. In the United States, impatience with the Korean stalemate ("die for a tie") carried the Republican candidate, Dwight D. Eisenhower, to victory in the 1952 presidential election. He promised to apply his military experience to ending the war. Stalin's death gave the Communist side flexibility; Eisenhower's expressed willingness to use nuclear weapons in Korea helped concentrate minds in Beijing. On July 27, 1953, the two sides finally signed an armistice that established the de facto boundary that still separates North and South Korea. After three years and the deaths of a million Chinese, perhaps 2 million Koreans, and 52,246 Americans, the war was over. Only a little over a third of the 10,000 Americans whom the Communists had captured returned alive.

Containment in northeastern Asia had succeeded, but at a price. Part of that price was that after mid-1950 Washington perceived all Communist actions, even unrelated ones, as part of a grand design. Truman deployed the U.S. Navy to shield Taiwan from Mao's forces on the mainland, although Washington had earlier shunned Chiang Kai-shek. The United States looked on approvingly as Britain tamed a Communist insurgency among the overseas Chinese of Malaya. Mao's victory in China impelled Truman in May 1950 to order aid to France in Indochina, a cause of which Washington had earlier disapproved. The North Korean attack impelled Washington to flood Indochina with weapons and funds that amounted to $1 billion a year by 1954.

The French lost. Ho Chi Minh skillfully identified Vietnamese Communism with national resistance to colonial rule. The Vietnamese Communist regular army that Mao's forces trained and equipped in southern China after 1949 showed unparalleled fighting power. U.S. prodding drove Paris to foster non-Communist Indochinese nationalist forces by making promises of eventual independence. More Vietnamese indeed fought on the French side than on Ho Chi Minh's, but few fought as hard. In late 1953 the French staked everything on luring Ho's forces to attack an isolated French outpost in a valley on the Laos border, at Dien Bien Phu. There the excellent artillery that the United States had given Chiang, who had lost it to Mao, who had given it to Ho, trapped the French instead. Dien Bien Phu fell in May 1954. France agreed to withdraw, sub-

Ho Chi Minh ("the Bringer of Enlightenment"), architect of Vietnamese Communism (1954).

ject to a satisfactory truce. The United States, Soviet Union, China, France, and Britain met at Geneva in the first major East-West conference since 1946 and agreed to a cease-fire and the division of Vietnam at the 17th parallel. Laos and Cambodia were to be independent and neutral. The First Indochina War was over.

Contrary to later myth, the Geneva conference did not reach a general agreement that required free elections and reunification of all Vietnam by 1956. The United States rejected elections without United Nations supervision to ensure a fair vote. Nor did Ho's newly minted "Democratic Republic of Vietnam" (DRV), north of the 17th parallel, subscribe to the conference's unsigned face-saving declaration that called for elections. Ho and associates were the least satisfied of the parties at Geneva; they felt that Beijing and Moscow had sold them out by failing to deliver all of Indochina. An unquiet peace nevertheless descended on Asia.

The attack of Stalin's North Korean clients on South Korea thus had worldwide repercussions. It at last roused the United States to attempt to right the military imbalance that its precipitate demobilization in 1945–46 had caused. A rearmed United States and West Germany were the Soviet Union's ultimate rewards for its Korean escapade. The 1950 emergency allowed Truman to persuade Congress to commit to Europe additional U.S. divisions and much military aid. The Germans received back their sovereignty in a peace treaty with the Western powers in 1954 and began rearming in 1955.

Thanks to Stalin's blunder, the United States implemented many of the recommendations of NSC-68. America acquired its first large-scale peacetime draft, a standing military establishment twice the size of that of 1949, and a network of bases that ringed the Soviet Union. By the late 1950s, NATO at last had the forces, both American and German, needed to stop a Soviet armored thrust short of the Rhine. The Soviet Union answered with more armored divisions, intermediate-range nuclear missiles, and an alliance against NATO, founded in 1955, the Warsaw Pact.

THE PERILS OF NIKITA SERGEYEVICH KHRUSHCHEV, 1953–64

In Moscow, Stalin's death apparently prevented a last great purge, a new stage in the totalitarian remodeling of Soviet society. Instead, the Soviet Union fell back into a drab bureaucratic "failed totalitarianism." The messianic claim to remake humanity remained. The will to do so by terror and war henceforth diminished.

"Thaw" at Home and Abroad

Indeed, Stalin's heirs and beneficiaries vied with one another to lead the "thaw" that ensued after March 1953. Lavrenty Beria, master of the security apparatus, moved first. His ministry announced that the confessions of the Kremlin doctors had been fraudulent and extorted by force. That appeared to open the road to the wholesale rehabilitation of millions of other victims of Stalin—and of Beria. Beria's colleagues reacted poorly to their rival's shameless bid for popularity. They coalesced, called on Red Army support, and had Beria shot, possibly in the Kremlin basement. The new "collective leadership," under Georgi Malenkov for the state apparatus and Nikita S. Khrushchev for the Party, then announced implausibly that Beria had been an agent of British intelligence since 1919. Some of Stalin's habits survived him.

Beria's liquidation was nevertheless the last. When the canny Khrushchev displaced Malenkov in 1955, he did no more than demote him. When Malenkov, Molotov, and Stalin's most bloodstained surviving associate, Lazar Kaganovich, combined against Khrushchev in 1957, he merely dismissed them from their Party and government posts. Thanks to Khrushchev, the new Soviet ruling class that Stalin had created at last acquired a degree of job security. Amnesties gradually deflated the GULAG after a series of prisoner revolts.

And Khrushchev, whose deliberately uncouth peasant exterior concealed both shrewdness and a moral courage he had been careful to repress while Stalin lived, soon took on the legacy of his former "Boss." As the Twentieth Party Congress of February 1956 approached, mention of the former "great leader" and "guide of progressive humanity" dropped from the Soviet press. At the Congress, Khrushchev in a secret speech damned Stalin so severely as to place in question the very bases of the Soviet system.

Khrushchev was careful to claim that Stalin's "cult of personality" and his "extreme methods and mass repressions," were an exception, a historical accident that owed nothing to Lenin, much less Marx. But Marx had justified dictatorship and terror. Lenin had authorized terror against the "class enemy" and had erected the dictatorship of a Party that he insisted must be monolithic. Stalin had merely followed that logic to its conclusion and had attempted to make the Party itself monolithic through terror.

Despite its slant, Khrushchev's secret speech contained a wealth of information about the purges, from the technique of extorting false confessions to the startling numbers of victims in the higher ranks of the Party. It soon leaked to the outside world and devastated Communist parties and sympathizers everywhere. Some departed sadly disillusioned with Communism. Others attacked Khrushchev for betraying the faith. In the Soviet Union, as Khrushchev had apparently intended, the speech made a return to Stalin's methods difficult. Dissidents who eventually raised their heads now risked labor camp or punitive psychiatric hospital but rarely immediate death. The "thaw" replaced mass terror with subtle and calculated repression by the

reorganized secret police and intelligence service, the Committee for State Security (KGB).

Externally, "de-Stalinization" made Soviet policy less rigid. Khrushchev announced that "war was not fatalistically inevitable" between the "socialist camp" and the Western "capitalist" powers. In a belated attempt to woo rather than terrorize German and European opinion, he agreed to withdraw Soviet forces from Austria in 1955. He visited Tito in 1955 and apologized for Stalin's intemperance against Yugoslavia; the Soviet Union thus recognized that the "Soviet path" was not the sole road to Communism. That was the beginning of a development later described as "polycentrism": the splitting of the formerly monolithic world Communist movement.

But de-Stalinization had limits abroad as well as at home. In the Soviet

Khrushchev on Stalin   February 24–25, 1956

Khrushchev sought above all to differentiate between Lenin and Stalin, to present Stalin's terror and "cult of personality" as an accident rather than as a logical consequence of Lenin's party autocracy.

Lenin used severe methods only in the most necessary cases, when the exploiting classes were still in existence and were vigorously opposing the revolution, when the struggle for survival was decidedly assuming the sharpest forms, even including a civil war.

Stalin, on the other hand, used extreme methods and mass repressions at a time when the revolution was already victorious, when the Soviet state was strengthened, when the exploiting classes were already liquidated. . . . It is clear that here Stalin showed in a whole series of cases his intolerance, his brutality and his abuse of power. Instead of proving his political correctness and mobilizing the masses, he often chose the path of repression and physical annihilation, not only against actual enemies, but also against individuals who had not committed any crimes against the party and the Soviet Government.

From Basil Dmytryshyn, *USSR: A Concise History* (New York: Charles Scribner's Sons, 1978), p. 501.

Soviet tanks dominate the streets of Berlin after crushing the East German workers' revolt (June 1953).

The Hungarian uprising, 1956: insurgents burn Russian books and magazines.

Union, the "great patriotic war" of 1941–45 and Stalin's rehabilitation of the Tsarist past had partially merged Great Russian nationalism with Communism. In the satellites, Communism was a Red Army import and nationalism was from the beginning its mortal enemy. The "people's democracies" consequently suffered repeated waves of unrest. In East Berlin, Stalin's death and Ulbricht's imposition of wage cuts

in June 1953 triggered a new Kronstadt 1921—a desperate workers' revolt that spread to much of the DDR. The "People's Police" and Soviet armor crushed the workers.

Khrushchev's secret speech led to further ferment. In Poland, workers at Poznán demonstrated against wage cuts in June 1956. Street fighting between workers and troops then triggered a struggle within the Polish Communist Party between Stalinists and "moderates." Street agitation against the regime mounted. But instead of sending tanks, Khrushchev grudgingly accepted assurances from the chief of the "moderates," Wladyslaw Gomulka, that Poland would remain within the Soviet empire. Gomulka then persuaded the population to subside in the name of national survival.

In Hungary, similar events led to tragedy. Rákosi, Stalin's man in Budapest, clung to power until Khrushchev ordered him to resign in July 1956. But his successor was another lesser Stalinist. When Hungary's equivalent to Gomulka, Imre Nagy, at last came to power in late October 1956, the Communist regime was disintegrating in the face of spontaneous revolt. Demonstrators toppled the immense statue of Stalin in Budapest. Communist leaders hid or ran for the Soviet border. A small contingent of Soviet tanks withdrew from Budapest in the face of popular fury. Nagy attempted to persuade Moscow to hold back, while simultaneously seeking to moderate popular demands for a multiparty political system and an exit from the Warsaw Pact.

Nagy failed. Like the Habsburgs whose role he now filled, Khrushchev could not permit the "rollback" of his power by one nationality, lest others follow. Simultaneous disarray in the West over the Suez crisis (see pp. 1013–14) made the decision to act easier. On November 4, 1956, Moscow committed its armored divisions against Budapest and crushed the revolt. In the fighting and aftermath, the Soviets and their collaborators killed thousands of Hungarians; 190,000 refugees fled west. Khrushchev had maintained Stalin's empire by the methods by which Stalin had established it.

The Sino-Soviet Split

To the east, where the Soviet Union faced a new phenomenon, a second Communist great power, such methods were of doubtful use. Stalin had preserved an uneasy ascendancy over Mao even after 1949. Khrushchev and his colleagues could not. Mao was his own Lenin and Stalin; he regarded Stalin's puny successors with poorly concealed contempt. The Chinese also felt slighted by having to carry the military burden of Stalin's Korean misjudgment and vexed at the poor quality and small quantity of Soviet economic aid. They nevertheless bore with Khrushchev, despite de-Stalinization, which Mao read as implicit criticism of his own thriving "cult of personality."

The parting of the ways, the greatest single defeat to Soviet policy since 1941, soon came. In October 1957, in a final bid to keep Beijing a loyal vassal, Khrushchev signed a secret treaty providing China with assistance in developing the atomic bomb. The following year, Mao staked a claim to world ideological leadership of the Communist movement. He launched an economic "Great Leap Forward" complete with collectivization and crash industrialization. The "attainment of Communism in China is no longer a remote future event," the CCP Central Committee trumpeted. That statement was a direct challenge to Moscow, which had not dared promise the rapid attainment of Communism—the blissful end of history amid untold abundance—to its long-suffering subjects. And Mao also challenged the United States by seeking confrontation in the Taiwan straits in the fall of 1958.

In June 1959, Soviet aid to China's nuclear program abruptly ended: Khrushchev had thought better of giving the bomb to his over-mighty and apparently reckless vassal. Soviet mili-tary and industrial experts left China. By 1960 the Sino-Soviet split was half public. By the summer of 1963 the two "fraternal parties" were trading mortal insults and mass displays of ritual hatred. Moscow damned Beijing for fanatical rigidity ("dogmatism"). Beijing denounced Moscow for betraying the Marxist-Leninist gospel ("modern revisionism").

From Berlin to Cuba

On the Soviet Union's western front, Khrushchev simultaneously took the offensive. His objective was probably to settle the question of Germany—to end the West's non-recognition of Ulbricht's shaky puppet regime with a German peace treaty and thereby consolidate Soviet control of East Germany and east-central Europe. But Khrushchev's methods lacked subtlety. He had already, in the Suez crisis of 1956, gleefully brandished the Soviet Union's small but growing arsenal of nuclear missiles. In October 1957 the Soviet Union's triumphant launching of the first artificial satellite, Sputnik, gave further proof that Soviet military technology could under some circumstances surpass that of the United States. The following month Khrushchev delivered to the West an ultimatum demanding a German peace treaty within six months.

That ultimatum became a rolling one, always extended. The exuberant Khrushchev accompanied it with a drumfire of nuclear threats that punctuated four years of steadily increasing superpower tension. Khrushchev's declared commitment to "peaceful co-existence" did not inhibit him from occasionally predicting in ominous tones the ultimate triumph of Communism: "We will bury you." In September 1959 Khrushchev nevertheless became the first Soviet ruler to visit the United States, for an inconclusive summit with Eisenhower accompanied by acrimonious exchanges with U.S. reporters. After a Soviet anti-aircraft missile knocked down a U-2 high-altitude

The "New Frontier":
Kennedy takes office (1961).

Khrushchev makes a point
(1962).

gan courting Moscow. Khrushchev happily responded during a visit to the United Nations at which he distinguished himself with uncouth shoe-pounding interruptions of a United Nations speech by the British prime minister.

Along with the Cuban problem, Kennedy inherited from Eisenhower a solution: an amateurish CIA-organized invasion of Cuba by anti-Communist Cuban exiles seeking to trigger an uprising against Castro. The landing at the Bay of Pigs on Cuba's south coast began on April 17, 1961. Castro's Soviet tanks swiftly crushed it. Kennedy denied the naval air support that alone could have given the 1,300 lightly armed attackers a chance of survival.

In the aftermath of that delectable humiliation of the "Yanquis," Castro consolidated his dictatorship. He took over for his own purposes the pre-existing Cuban Communist Party, secured increased military, police, and economic aid from the Soviet Union, and hastened the export of the most educated and articulate 15 percent of Cuba's population to southern Florida. The Soviet Union acquired a Caribbean satellite, complete with vanguard party, secret police, and GULAG; the United States received in the course of the decade up to a million enterprising new citizens.

Kennedy, sheepish over failure, met Khrushchev at a summit at Vienna in June 1961. There Khrushchev bullied the president unmercifully and apparently emerged with the notion that Kennedy lacked resolve. On August 13, 1961, Khrushchev solved his German difficulties unilaterally. East German forces with Soviet armor behind them sealed East Berlin off from the Western sectors with a massive wall of prefabricated concrete and electrified barbed wire. That closed the last avenue of escape from Ulbricht's "German Democratic Republic," which had lost 3 million citizens to the West in the preceding decade.

Kennedy and other western leaders had no answer to that unexpected So-

reconnaissance aircraft of the CIA over Sverdlovsk in central Russia, Khrushchev aborted the return summit in May 1960 by staging a propaganda circus, complete with personal slurs on Eisenhower.

The 1960 U.S. presidential election brought in a new Democratic administration under the debonair young Boston-Irish grandee, John Fitzgerald Kennedy. That offered Khrushchev new opportunities. Kennedy inherited from Eisenhower a Caribbean problem: Cuba. There a fanatically anti-American revolutionary adventurer, Fidel Castro, had come to power when the military regime of the incompetent Fulgencio Batista collapsed in January 1959. Castro later claimed not entirely implausibly to have been a life-long Marxist-Leninist. He immediately be-viet stroke, although Kennedy called up U.S. reserve forces as a warning to Khrushchev not to press his luck. Worse followed. Khrushchev ordered nuclear tests that violated both assurances he had given to Kennedy and a moratorium on atmospheric testing to which the nuclear powers had subscribed in 1958. In October 1961 the Soviet Union triumphantly detonated a bomb twice as large as any U.S. competitor, a weapon equivalent in power to 58 million tons of high explosive.

In mid-1962, with Ulbricht's regime at last on the way to consolidation behind barbed wire, the irrepressible Khrushchev launched a spectacular Caribbean gamble. In July he persuaded the Cubans to accept a Soviet garrison of 22,000 troops and technicians, to be armed with at least 48 medium-ranged and 24 intermediate-ranged ballistic missiles capable of striking most of the United States. The 72 missiles would more than double Soviet capacity to deliver thermonuclear weapons to United States targets. A successful *fait accompli* would also open the road for deployment of additional missiles that might give the Soviet Union parity or superiority. And success would shift the psychological superpower balance in favor of the Soviet Union. Khrushchev had evidently failed to learn one lesson of Korea—that the United States, if aroused, might act unpredictably.

By early September 1962, the missile sites were under construction and clearly visible. Khrushchev and his subordinates lied repeatedly to Kennedy: the Soviet Union was merely installing anti-aircraft rockets, not offensive missiles. But on October 14, 1962, photographs from a high-flying U-2 showed patterns already familiar from pictures of intermediate-range missile sites in the Soviet Union. Khrushchev's gamble that he could install the weapons before the United States noticed had failed.

Kennedy and his advisers consulted feverishly. The more militant urged immediate air strikes and an airborne

Berlin divided by concrete and barbed wire: the Berlin Wall.

and amphibious invasion of Cuba. Others pleaded for a predictably futile appeal to the United Nations. Robert McNamara, "boy wonder" of the Ford Motor Company turned Secretary of Defense, claimed with characteristically mechanical logic that the new missiles made little difference to the balance: "a missile is a missile," whether in Cuba or elsewhere. McNamara's analysis showed a peculiar blindness to the devastating effects that Khrushchev's coup, if successful, would have had on U.S. ability to deter further Soviet actions.

Kennedy finally chose a naval blockade; it would give Khrushchev time to climb down without excessive humiliation. But Kennedy also prepared air strikes and invasion, should they be necessary to prevent the 42 missiles already in Cuba from becoming operational. His television announcement on October 22 of a U.S. Navy "quarantine" of Cuba initiated a week of crisis that many in the West feared was the prelude to a "nuclear holocaust." Khrushchev was not that ambitious. When the blockade took effect on October 24, the Soviet ships carrying additional missiles stopped.

MISSILE ERECTOR

CABLE

MISSILE SHELTER TENT

TRACKED PRIME MOVERS

FUEL TANK TRAILERS

The Soviet ballistic missile site at San Cristóbal, Cuba (October 1962).

Khrushchev belatedly admitted having the missiles, but retreated behind the threadbare claim that he had placed them in Cuba to prevent a United States invasion—a threat the Bay of Pigs fiasco had dissipated, and which only revived thanks to the missiles. He offered to withdraw them in return for a U.S. agreement not to invade Cuba. But work on the sites in Cuba continued feverishly; the first missiles were apparently approaching operational readiness.

On October 27 Kennedy therefore sent his brother Bobby, the administration's enforcer, to tell the Soviet ambassador that "the point of escalation was at hand." If Moscow did not agree to withdraw the missiles, the United States would itself remove them. That threat, backed with a strategic nuclear superiority of at least 4 to 1 and by overwhelming air, sea, and ground power in the Caribbean, belatedly persuaded Khrushchev to climb down. The Soviet Union withdrew its missiles. It left behind advisers and a mechanized brigade based near Ha-

vana as a praetorian guard for Castro. The United States in turn agreed not to invade Cuba.

Like Stalin's death, the Cuban missile crisis marked the end of a phase in the Cold War. It was the closest that Soviet and U.S. forces had come to fighting since the Berlin blockade—but on that occasion the United States had possessed a nuclear monopoly. In the aftermath of the far more dangerous Cuban crisis, both powers sought to bring their mutual antagonism within bounds. A 1963 treaty banning nuclear tests in the atmosphere and in space was the first result of that effort.

In other respects, the rivals drew divergent lessons from the confrontation. The United States, temporarily reassured about the superpower balance, overcommitted itself in Asia. It also sought to limit nuclear weapons, and by 1969 had by deliberate inaction discarded the superiority that had helped checkmate Khrushchev in Cuba. Nuclear "parity," McNamara and others theorized, would make the Soviets more amenable to arms control and eventual reductions. Thermonuclear weapons, U.S. academics suggested, were so destructive that they had ceased to be usable as weapons. Their only purpose was to deter the use of nuclear weapons by others.

The Soviets took an entirely different view. "You will never be able to do this to us again," a Soviet diplomat grimly informed an American counterpart in the aftermath of the crisis. Khrushchev's colleagues forcibly retired him in October 1964, in part because he threatened the prerogatives of the Party elite, but also for mishandling the missile crisis. The stone-faced new leadership of Leonid Brezhnev and Alexei Kosygin tightened KGB controls at home and increased the Soviet defense budget from an already heavy 10 percent of gross national product in 1965 to 20 percent or more by 1980.

The Soviet Union's accelerating missile programs aimed at nuclear superiority (see Figure 34-1). Unlike Western pundits, the Soviets considered that superiority both militarily meaningful and politically useful. The United States and its allies relied on the U.S. strategic nuclear "umbrella" to hold back superior Soviet ground forces. If the Soviet Union could threaten the United States itself with destruction, the U.S. threat to use nuclear weapons in defense of its overseas allies lost credibility. Superiority would also give the Soviet Union a global reach, and greater latitude in supporting "wars of national liberation" that indirectly sapped the West's position. Finally, the growth of Soviet power would presumably cow the Europeans and Japanese, and separate them politically from the United States.

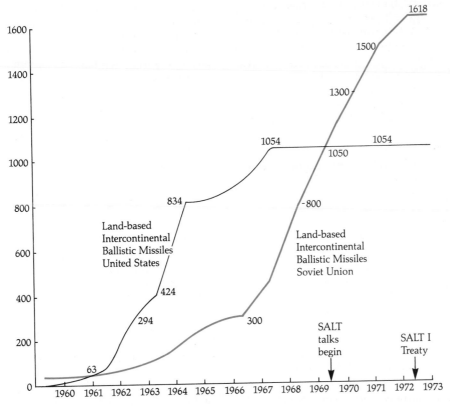

FIGURE 34-1   After Cuba: Missile Power, 1962–72
Adapted from *Le Monde*, November 22, 1972, p. 2.

PEACE AND WAR IN THE SHADOW OF THE COLD WAR

While the superpowers contended, Japan and the once-great powers of Europe enjoyed unprecedented economic growth. Not so the Middle East, where the West ceased after 1945 to fill the vacuum that Ottoman decay had created. The foundation of a Jewish state and the conflicting ambitions of the Arabs led to two generations of bitter wars.

The Mid-Sized Powers in Eclipse

The revival of world trade was the first prerequisite for the recovery of Europe and Japan. In the previous long peace, from 1871 to 1914, world trade had grown by an annual average of 3.4 percent; then the German bid for world mastery had dropped growth to an average of 1 percent per year from 1913 to 1938. But after 1948, over $20 billion in Marshall Plan and other U.S. aid along with the inevitable Korean War boom galvanized the world economy. The Bretton Woods system installed in 1944–47 brought a stability and predictability unknown in the 1920s and 1930s.

The result was stunning growth. From 1950 to 1960, the volume of world trade grew by 6.4 percent each year. Europe and Japan rebuilt under the military protection and economic leadership of the United States. The West German "economic miracle" was the most dramatic in Europe, at 7.7 percent growth per year. France followed, then Italy, which started as a far poorer country. Last, thanks largely to a continuing failure to put its best brains into its economy, came Britain at 2.6 percent.

But despite the aspirations of Europe's technocratic visionaries, no "United States of Europe" emerged. The European Economic Community (EEC) or European Common Market, founded at Rome in 1957, slowly developed a transnational political superstructure and a European Parliament. But its powers remained small indeed. The nation-state remained the principal focus of loyalty. And France crippled the EEC for a decade by checkmating a halfhearted British attempt to enter it in 1963.

Britain after 1945 displayed its usual orderly alternation between Labour and Conservative parties. Labour under Attlee nationalized major industries, thus protecting them from much-needed rationalization and modernization. Government health care and social insurance extended "cradle to grave" security to the entire population. When the aging Churchill returned to power in 1951, he left the welfare state intact but sold off some nationalized industries. His foreign secretary and successor, Anthony Eden, suffered collapse in the Suez crisis of 1956 (see p. 1014), but the reassuring leadership of Harold Macmillan kept the Conservatives in office until 1963–64. Labour then returned under the bland Harold Wilson, Labour's answer to Stanley Baldwin. Both Labour and Conservatives pursued roughly similar policies: the welfare state at home, a "special relationship" with the United States abroad, and retention of as much empire as Britain could hold without debilitating effort.

France, as always, was more lively. The Fourth Republic was roughly similar in political habits and alignments to the Third Republic that died in 1940. The Republic's founders pushed de Gaulle, the savior of his country, into premature retirement in early 1946. He repaid the compliment by damning the political system as "the convolutions of this absurd ballet." His successors halfheartedly waged the Indochina war into which de Gaulle's pro-consuls had blundered in 1945–46. The Fourth Republic's one hour of glory was the 1954–55 premiership of Pierre Mendès-France, who set a deadline for French withdrawal and made it stick.

But the Mendès-France government soon collapsed over the Algerian insurrection against France (see pp. 1015–18)

Fall of France
1940

Provisional Government
under de Gaulle

1958

| Vichy Government and German Occupation | | Fourth Republic | Fifth Republic |

1945 1946

that erupted less than six months after the Indochina settlement. That second great colonial war wrecked the Fourth Republic. The French Right supported NATO, but claimed that Algeria was part of France, despite its Moslem majority. Left-wing opinion and a strong Communist Party opposed NATO but —after some hesitation—favored Algerian independence. Parliamentary deadlock ensued. The army in Algeria was already restless; those who had served in Indochina grimly reproached the politicians for France's long record of defeat. A sense of betrayal impelled the army to swing its support behind de Gaulle's tumultuous return in a quasi-coup in May 1958.

De Gaulle demanded and received from parliament the right to draft a new constitution. His Fifth Republic endured better than its predecessor; de Gaulle as president took stronger powers than any French executive since Napoleon III. De Gaulle used those powers wisely. He led France out of the Algerian war in 1962 without splitting the highly politicized army or provoking the civil war between Right and Left that had seemed imminent in 1958. He gave France unprecedented economic growth. The France of landowning peasants consolidated in the Revolution of 1789 at last became a land of urban workers.

West Germany was Western Europe's most dramatic success. Bonn— the Federal Republic's provisional capital, chosen in the expectation of an eventual move to Berlin—was not Weimar. The constitution of 1949 barred from parliament any party that received less than 5 percent of the vote. That ended the political fragmentation that had helped destroy Weimar. The new presidency, unlike the presidency of Weimar that had made Hitler chan-

cellor, was a purely ceremonial position. And Hitler had through war, terror, and defeat destroyed—along with much else—the conservative elites that had so despised Weimar democracy that they had brought the Nazis to power.

The new Republic's first chancellor was an aged but vigorous former mayor of Cologne and pre-1933 opponent of Hitler, Konrad Adenauer. His party, the Christian Democratic Union/ Christian Social Union (CDU/CSU), was a successor to the Catholic Center party that also appealed to Protestants. It became the mass party of the German urban and rural middle classes and ruled uninterruptedly from 1949 to 1966 in coalition with a small liberal grouping, the Free Democrats (FDP).

The Social Democratic Party (SPD), the only major party survivor from Weimar, opposed the CDU/CSU. After publicly discarding Marxism in 1959, the SPD at last broke the class barrier that had stunted its growth before 1933. Like the CDU/CSU, it appealed to an ever larger and more prosperous middle and working class; it offered "good government" and the welfare state. Under Willy Brandt, a dynamic mayor of Berlin who had passed the Hitler years in political exile, the SPD achieved by 1966 a share of power in coalition with Adenauer's successors in the CDU/CSU. In 1969, in alliance with the FDP, Brandt and the SPD took power in place of the CDU/CSU. West Germany had achieved an orderly alternation between large coherent parties. Antidemocratic fringe groups persisted on the far Right and far Left, but their clamor was infinitely greater than their influence.

Italy also surprised everyone. It achieved stability and unprecedented prosperity. Political parties reemerged

De Gaulle in Algiers (1958).

Two generations of post-war German leaders: Konrad Adenauer (chancellor, 1949–63) and Willy Brandt (1969–74).

after the collapse of Fascism. The Catholic *Popolari*, renamed Christian Democrats, were the largest; they faced small middle-class parties and a Socialist-Communist alliance. Thanks to its collaboration with Mussolini, the monarchy failed to win a majority in a 1946 referendum; Italy became a republic. By 1947–48, as the lines of the Cold War became clear, Italy's politics had set. The shrewd Alcide De Gasperi of the Christian Democrats dominated government. The Communist-Socialist alliance lost heavily in the decisive election of April 1948, which the Christian Democrats fought with massive U.S. and Vatican support and a remarkable platform: "For or Against Christ."

De Gasperi gave way in 1953 to a series of revolving door governments. But more than in France, the "absurd ballet" in parliament cloaked underlying continuity. The Communist Party, western Europe's largest, formed a permanent "disloyal opposition" capable of overthrowing the system if admitted to government. By parliamentary arithmetic, therefore, only a coalition centered on the Christian Democrats could govern. With modifications such as the addition of the Socialists to the coalition in 1963 after they broke with the Communists, that formula gave Italy a government that showed remarkable stability behind a facade of incoherence. And by the late 1980s Italy's gross national product had according to some estimates passed that of the first industrial nation, Britain, and possibly that of France as well. That was an astounding achievement for a society that in 1913 had possessed less than a quarter of Britain's industrial power.

Finally, Japan amazed its American occupiers. MacArthur's democratic revolution from above, the greatest internal upheaval since the Meiji Restoration of 1868, was a success. Drawing on the precedents of the parliamentary 1920s, Japanese politicians created a powerful machine of electoral consensus, the Liberal Democratic party. Its ruling oligarchy achieved and maintained a parliamentary majority based on the votes of Japan's peasantry and urban middle classes. That permanently excluded from power a fragmented opposition that included Communists, Socialists, and a Buddhist political cult. This "half democracy," as Japanese critics described it, provided political stability and fostered spectacular economic growth.

The United States provided other ingredients as well: the technology that U.S. corporations offered their Japanese subsidiaries and markets and raw materials to replace Japan's lost empire in China and Southeast Asia. Direct U.S. aid to Japan after 1954 totalled some $2 billion, but the expenditure by 1970 of over $10 billion in military orders for the wars in Korea and Vietnam was more significant. The goods the U.S. military ordered were predominantly civilian; their production fostered the techniques that Japan used to storm the world's export markets after the mid-1960s. In Japan the United States, even more than in Europe, provided the catalyst for the "economic miracle" of the 1950s and 1960s. But it was the relentless hard work of the Japanese themselves, their highly skilled and educated labor force, that by the 1970s had made Japan the third largest economy in the world after the United States and the Soviet Union.

The New Eastern Question, 1947–73

Hitler failed to kill all the Jews of Europe. Instead, paradoxically and unintentionally, he made possible the first Jewish state since the Roman reconquest of Jerusalem in A.D. 70. His genocide inspired a disgust for Europe in many Jews who survived and provoked a flood of emigration to Palestine. His genocide taught the lesson that only a Jewish state, weapons in hand, could ensure Jewish survival. His genocide discredited anti-Semitism in western Europe and the United States, and inspired guilt in those who had failed to aid the Jews of Europe in time. That unspoken guilt dissipated with time, but it was a powerful source of international support for the creation of a Jewish state.

In the aftermath of Hitler's war, Britain attempted to uphold its 1939 ban on further Jewish immigration to Palestine (see p. 888). British interests in the Arab world—the world of oil—appeared to demand that Britain block the Zionist aspiration to a Jewish state. But by 1945 the 600,000 Jews of Palestine were a third of the population. Many of them had fought for Britain against Hitler. They now resisted Britain as they had resisted the Arabs in the guerrilla conflict after 1936. By 1946 Zionist guerrilla groups, the Irgun, and the "Stern Gang," were at war with both Arabs and British. Chaim Weizmann, the Zionist leader who had secured Balfour's promise in 1917, indefatigably lobbied the powers.

By 1946, Britain's position was untenable. As in Ireland after 1919, the British army could not control a spreading guerrilla war without using methods that no democracy could easily defend. Truman backed the creation of a Jewish state. Even Stalin, who despite his anti-Semitism initially saw the Jews of Palestine as possible allies against Britain, did not oppose it. In 1947 the Labour government therefore thankfully handed over the poisoned gift of Palestine to the United Nations. The U.N. proposed partition along ethnic-religious lines. The Jewish organizations accepted. The Palestinian Arabs and their supporters in the Arab states refused. An Arab "Liberation Army" attacked Jewish communities. In May 1948, as in Greece and India (see pp. 970 and 1012), the exhausted British withdrew.

That left Palestine to anyone that could dominate it. David Ben-Gurion, charismatic veteran of the Jewish settler communities, proclaimed a Jewish state—the state of Israel—on May 14, 1948. The armies of Egypt, Jordan, Syria, Lebanon, and Iraq invaded Palestine with the announced intention of driving the Jews into the sea. Israel, outnumbered and outgunned, fought that "Arab League" to a standstill and drew precarious borders by force. Many Palestinian Arabs heeded calls from their leaders to leave the Jewish areas, in expectation of a swift return with the Arab armies. In some cases Jewish forces drove Arab civilians out. Arab defeat left some 600,000 embittered refugees, and Arab states more committed than ever to expelling the Jews from Palestine.

The core of the new "Eastern Question"—the struggle between the successor states of the Ottoman Empire—was the irreconcilable conflict between the Palestinian Arabs, the Arab states, and Israel. But the antagonism also drew nourishment from a broader and longer-term conflict. The Arabs regarded Israel as yet another intrusion from the West, a successor to the Crusader kingdoms of the twelfth and thirteenth centuries and to the European imperialism of the nineteenth. Israel was a galling symbol of the Islamic world's humiliating weakness, first laid bare by Napoleon's 1798–99 campaign in Egypt. Only Israel's destruction, many Arabs henceforth felt, could restore their own self-respect.

Arab hostility was counterproductive. Relentless external threat welded Israel's disparate inhabitants together and consolidated its parliamentary system under the hegemony of Ben-Gurion's Labor party. Thanks to native ingenuity and money from Jewish organizations abroad, a modern economy took shape. In 1951 the gross national product of Egypt, most prosperous of the Arab states, was three to four times that of Israel; by 1966–67 that ratio had declined to 1.6 to 1.

War gave birth to Israel, a Jewish state, the only democracy in the Middle East. Only war could preserve it, for the Arab League powers refused to recognize the "Zionist entity" as a state and made no secret of their continuing desire to destroy it utterly. Egypt took the lead. Abdel Gamal Nasser, a visionary who dreamed of uniting the Arabs from the Atlantic to the Persian Gulf, emerged as dictator of Egypt after an army coup in 1952. From 1955 on he secured lavish supplies of arms from the Soviet Union.

Twice, in 1956 and 1967, Nasser provoked Israel with Palestinian raids from Gaza and closure of the straits of Tiran that commanded access to Israel's Red Sea port of Eilat. Twice Israel struck first and routed the Egyptians. Indefensible borders and immense numerical odds left Israel no alternative to preemptive war. Nasser's proclaimed desire for a "war of annihilation" suggested that the price of failure would be a new "Final Solution."

In 1956, thanks to the sheepish withdrawal of its British and French allies, Israel had to leave the conquered Sinai to a United Nations "peacekeeping" force that subsequently failed to keep the peace. In 1967, Israel therefore refused to withdraw after victory—and not only from the Sinai and Gaza. Syria and Jordan had joined Egypt in that "Six Days' War" and had lost the west bank of the Jordan River and the strategic Golan heights from which Syrian artillery had routinely shelled the farming settlements of northern Israel. The conquests of 1967 brought strategic security, but also a poisoned gift: a million new Arab inhabitants in the "occupied territories" of the West Bank and Gaza.

The Palestinian "resistance" drew a lesson from the 1967 war: it could not look to the Arab states for victory. In 1968 the "Palestine Liberation Organization" (PLO) and its offshoots therefore launched a campaign of terror against soft targets such as Israeli airliners. Israel replied with air attacks on Palestinian refugee camps and open season on PLO leaders. Israeli reprisals against Jordan moved Jordan's King Hussein to act against the armed Palestinians that constituted a state within his state. In "Black September" 1970 Hussein's highly professional army

crushed them. Lebanon, a state too weak to defend itself, became the last stronghold of the PLO.

An embarrassed Soviet Union soon replenished Nasser's arms and manned his radars, anti-aircraft missiles, and fighters. In 1969–70 Nasser and the Soviets waged a "war of attrition" against Israel's forward defenses along the Suez Canal. Negotiations sponsored by the United Nations and United States proved predictably futile. Nasser died of a heart attack in September 1970 after Egypt had suffered 30,000 casualties, and Washington and Moscow—again embarrassed—had together imposed a cease-fire along the Canal. Nasser's successor, Colonel Anwar Sadat, prepared for yet another round against Israel. The increasing economic power of the Arab oil states had begun to isolate Israel from the timid and oil-dependent western Europeans. But this time, instead of a "war of annihilation," Sadat planned a limited attack to take back the east bank of the Canal and bloody the Israelis.

The Soviet Union supplied advanced antiaircraft and antitank missiles by the shipload. But Sadat was careful to distance himself from his patrons, who for their part perhaps feared that too close association with a new Arab war might damage the newly developing "détente" with the United States. In July 1972 Sadat asked for the withdrawal of most of his Soviet "advisers." In 1973, with Egypt's army mobilized and deployed and with Syrian armor drawn up opposite the Golan, Sadat attacked. The date he chose was Yom Kippur, the Jewish Day of Atonement, October 6, 1973.

As Sadat had hoped, Israel's political isolation deterred it from a repetition of the preemptive strikes of 1956 and 1967; the more favorable borders seized in 1967 also induced overconfidence. In 1973 the Israelis thus found themselves compelled to mobilize under Arab attack and to hope for the best. Sadat's carefully planned crossing of the Canal crumbled Israel's thinly held static defenses. Sadat's Soviet an-titank missiles broke the first hasty Is-raeli armored counterattacks. Then the Egyptians ventured too far from the Canal and found themselves fighting a battle of movement which the Israelis dominated with their usual skill and drive. Outnumbered Israeli forces in the Golan routed some 1,000 Syrian and Iraqi tanks and advanced to within artillery range of Damascus. In the south, Israel soon crossed the Canal into Egypt and encircled one of Sadat's two armies. The road to Cairo lay open. Then the superpowers imposed a cease-fire, although not before an unprecedented Soviet threat to commit paratroops in Egypt had provoked a worldwide U.S. nuclear alert.

Militarily the Yom Kippur War was yet another crushing defeat for the Arab cause. But unlike 1967, it was not a total humiliation. Sadat's initial suc-cess along the Canal allowed him to claim a moral victory. That made Egypt's position—although not that of the Palestinians or the other Arab states—more flexible, while Israel's near disaster compelled rethinking in Jerusalem. The ultimate result of 1973 was the first break in the wall of Arab hostility surrounding Israel and the transition from war to grudging peace between Israel and Egypt (see p. 1050).

In international terms the Yom Kip-pur War was nevertheless ominous. It encouraged the oil-producing states of OPEC (Organization of Petroleum Ex-porting Countries) to more than double the real (inflation-adjusted) price of oil from October 1973 to 1975 while plac-ing a total embargo upon the United States as retribution for its support of Israel. The Europeans cowered. They cut off trade with Israel and, except for Portugal, refused to allow the United States to use NATO bases to support the massive airlift of ammunition that helped the beleaguered Jewish state to survive. Only Holland failed to comply swiftly enough with Arab demands; it suffered both Arab oil embargo and ostracism by its EEC partners. That dis-play of NATO and European disunity inevitably encouraged adversaries of the West to whom events in Southeast Asia had already given heart.

THE AGONY OF CONTAINMENT: AMERICA IN VIETNAM

The United States emerged from its vic-tory in the Cuban missile crisis with a sense that nothing was impossible. Then Kennedy's brilliant rhetoric, the intellectual self-confidence of the aca-

---

Kennedy: "Ask not . . ." 1961

Kennedy's inaugural address contained some of the most stirring phrases ever spoken by an American president. It also unwisely proclaimed a willingness to "pay any price."

Let the word go forth from this time and place, to friend and foe alike, that the torch has been passed to a new generation of Americans, born in this century, tempered by war, disciplined by a hard and bitter peace, proud of our ancient heritage, and unwilling to witness or permit the slow undoing of those human rights to which this nation has always been committed, and to which we are committed today at home and around the world.

Let every nation know, whether it wishes us well or ill, that we shall pay any price, bear any burden, meet any hardship, sup-port any friend, oppose any foe to assure the survival and the success of liberty. . . .

In the long history of the world, only a few generations have been granted the role of defending freedom in its hour of maxi-mum danger. I do not shrink from this responsibility; I welcome it. I do not believe that any of us would exchange places with any other people or any other generation. The energy, the faith, the devotion which we bring to this endeavor will light our country and all who serve it, and the glow from that fire can truly light the world.

And so, my fellow Americans, ask not what your country can do for you; ask what you can do for your country.

From Theodore C. Sorensen, *Kennedy* (New York: Harper & Row, 1965), pp. 245–48.

demic elite that he had drawn into government, and the pressures of domestic politics combined to commit the United States to a second war of containment in Vietnam.

The Illusion of Omnipotence, 1962–68

Containment by war had proved an effective though costly answer to Stalin's adventure in Korea. Against indirect methods, against insurgency, it was less promising. Those familiar techniques were the choice of Ho Chi Minh and his associates. In 1954 they established themselves in Hanoi and consolidated their "Democratic Republic of Vietnam" (DRV) north of the 17th parallel. In 1955–56 they killed as many as 50,000 peasants who resisted collec-

tivization. Above all, they maintained their network of party cadres south of the 17th parallel, in South Vietnam.

There Ngo Dinh Diem, a Catholic anti-Communist from the pre-colonial Mandarin ruling class, established at Saigon a "Republic of Vietnam." Diem's regime rested on the traditional landowning elite and on the Vietnamese army that France had raised to fight the Communists. Eisenhower, after much hesitation, committed the United States to support Diem. If South Vietnam fell to Hanoi and to its apparent backers in Beijing, Eisenhower theorized, other Southeast Asian "dominoes" such as Laos, Cambodia, Thailand, Malaya, and Indonesia would also fall.

The United States had first tolerated France's Indochina war, then after 1950

War in Southeast Asia   1954–88

had funded it. After 1954 the United States gradually became France's successor. It failed to foresee the sacrifices that course might entail. Nor did it fully recognize that Vietnam was unlike Korea in two essential ways. Vietnam was not a peninsula, surrounded on three sides by a sea the U.S. Navy owned. And Vietnam was peripheral to the fundamental American goal of maintaining its allies in Europe and Japan.

In January 1959, in deep secret, Ho Chi Minh and his associates on the North Vietnamese central committee decided to resume "armed struggle" in South Vietnam with the aim of annexing it to the DRV. A party army, called "Viet Cong" (Vietnamese Communists) by its enemies, took shape in the South and assassinated over 3,000 Diem administrators or civilians connected with the government between 1961 and 1963. Hanoi announced in December 1960 the creation of a political cover for that army, the "National Liberation Front" (NLF), a "popular front" that included many non-Communists but secretly took its orders from Hanoi. It was important, both to secure wide support in South Vietnam and to delude Western public opinion, that NLF and Viet Cong activities appear to be a Southern revolt against what Hanoi described as the "U.S.-Diem dictatorship."

Diem's regime crumbled in 1962–63. His Catholicism, his autocratic manner, and his sinister brother and police minister Ngo Dinh Nhu alienated the influential Buddhist clergy. Monks burned themselves to death in protests well-publicized on U.S. television. Diem's association with the Americans offended South Vietnam's urban, educated elite. His closeness to the landowners alienated the peasants. The NLF offered the urban elite a romantic nationalism and disingenuous assurances that the Front's victory would mean autonomy for the South. To the peasants the NLF offered land, but made no mention of the fate of the collectivized peasants of the DRV. Viet Cong units

Lyndon Baines Johnson takes the oath of office after Kennedy's assassination, November 22, 1963.

and political cadres established control over ever-wider areas.

Kennedy, an aficionado of spy novels and irregular warfare, raised the 900 advisers he inherited from Eisenhower to over 15,000, including helicopter and fighter-bomber units. That was not enough. When the Buddhist crisis provoked unrest among Diem's generals, Washington tacitly encouraged them. Kennedy made known in Saigon that if Diem did not dismiss Nhu "we must face the possibility that Diem himself cannot be preserved." That was a green light to the Vietnamese military plotters, who overthrew Diem on November 1, 1963. Contrary to Kennedy's intentions, but all too predictably, the coup forces shot Diem and Nhu.

The United States, in the illusion that it could control events in a society of which it was sadly ignorant, thus took total responsibility for the fate of South Vietnam. Kennedy himself died three weeks after Diem, on November 22, 1963, assassinated in Dallas in circumstances that remain unclear. His vice president and successor, Lyndon Baines Johnson of Texas, proved wily and resourceful in his domestic policy. He accomplished what Kennedy had begun, the belated abolition of the "Jim

Crow" segregation laws of the southern United States and the launching of a federal "war on poverty." But Johnson's irresolute attempts to cope with the disaster that he inherited in Vietnam wrecked his presidency.

The impending 1964 presidential election and the legacy of Chinese-American war in Korea made disengagement unthinkable. "Who lost Vietnam?" was a charge that Johnson dreaded as much as Eisenhower and Kennedy before him. Beijing, where Mao and associates were proclaiming a worldwide peasant revolutionary war against the urban capitalism of the West, appeared to loom behind Hanoi. And China appeared all the more menacing after its explosion of its first atomic bomb in October 1964. Withdrawal from Vietnam, the Washington policy elite and press assumed, would weaken the credibility of U.S. guarantees to other allies and unleash a wave of Communist expansion that would engulf "dominoes" from the rice fields of Thailand to the oil fields of Indonesia.

Johnson therefore sought to dissuade Hanoi from pursuing its ambitions in the South. He chose his instruments from the arsenal of the academic armchair strategists that Kennedy had brought from Harvard to Washington— carefully calibrated South Vietnamese commando operations against the DRV and U.S. air strikes at DRV supply routes to South Vietnam. Those operations began in secret in the spring of 1964. Hanoi, undeterred, began sending units of its regular army south.

In August 1964, DRV torpedo boats attacked a U.S. destroyer off North Vietnam shortly after a South Vietnamese raid in the same area. At Johnson's urging, Congress thereupon authorized "the use of armed force" to "prevent further aggression" anywhere in Southeast Asia. Congress later regretted that "Tonkin Gulf Resolution," which gave a broader measure of congressional approval than either Roosevelt or Truman had sought in the Atlantic in 1941 or in Korea in 1950. But

unlike a declaration of war—which Johnson could probably have had in 1964 but did not want—it neither committed the nation as a whole nor defined the enemy.

In the 1964 election Johnson handily defeated the Republican candidate, Barry Goldwater, whom he depicted as an irresponsible warmonger. Then Johnson discovered that massive DRV infiltration down the "Ho Chi Minh Trail" in Laos and the incompetence of the Saigon generals faced the United States with defeat. In March 1965 Johnson therefore began a major air campaign, hopefully named ROLLING THUNDER, to warn off the DRV. That effort delivered by the end of 1967 some 864,000 tons of bombs, far more than the 503,000 tons dropped in the war against Japan. But it delivered them intermittently on targets of secondary importance. Johnson and his advisers had learned from Korea that they must not under any circumstances strike the DRV hard enough to provoke Chinese intervention. The DRV had learned a different lesson: U.S. opinion would not tolerate a long war.

Johnson's use of the military to "send a message" by increments, interspersed with 16 bombing pauses and 70 peace initiatives, hardly impressed Hanoi with American resolve. It also sacrificed aircraft and crews in ever larger numbers. Failure to bring U.S. air power to bear massively and all at once, as Roosevelt and Truman had done against Japan in 1945, allowed Hanoi to acquire from its Soviet and Chinese friends the world's best air defense network. Nor did the bombing have any noticeable effect on the level of fighting in the South.

Ground intervention soon followed Johnson's air war. The North Vietnamese regulars arriving through Laos threatened the demoralized South Vietnamese army with swift destruction. In March 1965 Johnson landed Marines to guard the key airfield at Da Nang on the central coast. In May he committed U.S. Army paratroopers around Saigon. By the end of 1965, almost 200,000 U.S. combat and support troops were again fighting a land war on the Asian mainland alongside troops from South Korea, Australia, and New Zealand.

But the vast army that ultimately reached 543,000 men and women in April 1969 was mostly support troops; of the half million, perhaps 75,000 American infantrymen and 50,000 artillerymen and helicopter crewmen actually fought. The infantry, by comparison with earlier American wars, had everything—excellent weapons, superb communications, crushing air and artillery support, prompt medical evacuation, and rotation back to the United States if they survived their 365 allotted days in Vietnam. What they lacked was a strategy, a means of translating hard-bought battlefield victories into political success. Especially after 1967, they also lacked a sense that the public back in "the World"—the far distant United States—was behind them. Frustration and endless casualties inflicted by unseen enemies sometimes provoked explosions. The most notable was the 1968 massacre of up to 400 Vietnamese civilians by an ill-led battalion of the Americal Division at the hamlet of My Lai 4. Commanders attempted to cover up the atrocity, but once the news leaked the U.S. Army tried those responsible for war crimes.

In Washington, the leadership vacuum persisted. Johnson feared the sacrifice of his domestic "war on poverty"; he therefore attempted to fight cheaply, without the economic mobilization that Truman had demanded and received for Korea. Johnson's repeatedly proclaimed war aim was to force Hanoi to negotiate. That was even less inspiring than "dying for a tie." Nor did the military bureaucracies offer Johnson intelligent choices. The U.S. Navy and Air Force competed to drop ever more bombs on strategically irrelevant targets in and around the North. The Army pursued a war of attrition against the Viet Cong and North Vietnamese in the South. That war maximized *American* attrition.

U.S. intervention nevertheless bought time. Saigon's battlefield performance and political stability slowly improved. In January–February 1968 the victor of Dien Bien Phu, General Vo Nguyen Giap, launched Viet Cong and North Vietnamese forces at the cities of the South. Timed for Tết, the Vietnamese lunar new year, Giap's "General Uprising" was a stinging operational and tactical reverse for Hanoi. U.S. troops held and counterattacked. Saigon's troops, their backs to the wall, stood and fought. Contrary to Giap's expectation, the population of the cities did not join his troops. The Viet Cong and North Vietnamese suffered devastating losses. In many areas of the South, the Tết Offensive led to the collapse of the Viet Cong. Henceforth North Vietnam alone carried the weight of the war and South Vietnam's forces gained a measure of self-confidence. At Hue on the central coast, retreating North Vietnamese took re-

The War of Attrition: Dak To, Central Highlands, 1967

The battle for Hill 875 was over, and some survivors were being brought in by Chinook to the landing strip at Dak To. The 173rd Airborne had taken over 400 casualties, nearly 200 killed, all on the previous afternoon and in the fighting that had gone on all through the night. It was very cold and wet up there, and some girls from the Red Cross had been sent up from Pleiku to comfort the survivors. As the troops filed out of the helicopters, the girls waved and smiled at them from behind serving tables. "Hi, soldier! What's your name?" "Where you from, soldier?" "I'll bet some hot coffee would hit the spot about now." And the men from the 173rd just kept walking without answering, staring straight ahead, their eyes rimmed with red from fatigue, their faces pinched and aged with all that had happened during the night. One of them dropped out of line and said something to a . . . girl who wore a Peanuts sweatshirt under her fatigue shirt and she started to cry. The rest just walked past the girls and the large, olive-drab coffee urns. They had no idea of where they were.

From Michael Herr, *Dispatches* (New York: Avon Books, 1978), p. 169.

Têt, 1968: Marines advance warily through the ruins of Hue.

Johnson had failed to define a war aim. Now he concurred with his critics. Under a rough and profane exterior, the president concealed a fatal desire to be loved. Increasing fire from the press and the growth of raucous demonstrations against the war effort ("Hey, hey, LBJ, how many kids did ya kill today?") deeply wounded him. Subordinates such as Secretary of Defense McNamara had concluded that the war was "unwinnable" because the enemy's commitment to victory was total while their own was not. The Têt fighting and the strong showing of an "anti-war" candidate in the New Hampshire presidential primary broke what little nerve Johnson still retained. Polls nevertheless suggested that many Americans supported "staying the course" if the president would only lead.

On March 31, 1968, Johnson appeared on television and announced three things: that the United States would cease bombing the North except for the area immediately north of the 17th parallel, that the United States would seek to negotiate an end to the conflict, and that he himself would not run for reelection that fall. Assassination brought Johnson to power; he departed by political suicide. His public confession that he thought the war unwinnable changed the terms of debate. Americans henceforth battled over how to leave Vietnam, not over how to win or whether to fight.

Defeat, 1968–75

Johnson's hapless vice president, Hubert Humphrey, lost the 1968 presidential election. Jim Crow took its final revenge on Johnson's domestic policy, for a racist third-party revolt of George Wallace on the Right deprived the Democrats of their usually solid Southern vote. On the Left, violent student demonstrations against Humphrey outside the Democratic Convention in Chicago and the abstention of many "dovish" voters in protest against Johnson's Vietnam policy had a similar

venge for defeat by massacring 2,800 civilians.

Yet out of tactical defeat Hanoi gained strategic victory. The confusion and bloodshed of Têt shocked the American press and television representatives in Saigon. They had sought to cover the war from the comfort and safety of their hotel bars. They interpreted fighting in the cities as a massive U.S. defeat. Walter Cronkite, father-figure of CBS News, intoned funereally that the United States must find an exit.

effect. To the horror of the "doves," the Republican victor was a former associate of Senator McCarthy, Richard M. Nixon.

Nixon had claimed during the campaign to have a "secret peace plan." It remained secret. He did announce in March 1969 the "Vietnamization" of the war and the gradual withdrawal of American troops. He formalized the new policy in July 1969 as the "Nixon Doctrine"—the United States would continue to provide air support and supplies, but would henceforth allow its allies to do their own ground fighting. U.S. troop levels declined from 543,000 in April 1969 to 24,200 in December 1972. To buy time, Nixon in May–June 1970 launched a last offensive thrust, a brief invasion of Cambodia, where up to 300,000 North Vietnamese had set up housekeeping at the southern end of the Ho Chi Minh trail.

Nixon and his devious National Security Adviser, Henry Kissinger of Harvard, may have deluded themselves as well as others that "Vietnamization" would achieve a Korea-style stalemate. More probably they aimed from the beginning at a gradual retreat from Vietnam in the style of the withdrawal from Algeria of de Gaulle, whom Kissinger admired. The principal obstacle was Hanoi: it spurned negotiation. Its delegates to the Paris talks that began in May 1968 demanded instantaneous and total withdrawal by the United States and the dismantling of its ally, the Saigon regime. Hanoi also refused to offer assurances that it would release U.S. prisoners, mostly Navy and Air Force crews, held in its concentration camps. The death of Ho Chi Minh in September 1969 made no difference. The Leninist party he had created lived on.

But by now the international situation that had attended the U.S. plunge into Vietnam had entirely changed. A Communist *Putsch* in Indonesia had failed in 1965; the Indonesian military and Islamic activists had in response massacred perhaps 500,000 Indonesian Communists and sympathizers. *That*

vital "domino" and its oil was not going to fall. As for China, it had ironically ceased to need "containment." Mao had reduced it to chaos with his "Great Proletarian Cultural Revolution" of 1966–69, a cataclysm similar in causes and consequences to Stalin's Great Terror (see p. 912). And the Sino-Soviet split had ripened into a full-scale military confrontation between the two Communist giants along their 5,000 miles of border.

In the spring and summer of 1969 Soviet and Chinese troops fought bitterly on the Ussuri River, north of Vladivostok. A Soviet journalist with close ties to the KGB wrote ominously in the British press that "Marxist theoreticians" were discussing the possibility of full-scale Sino-Soviet war. Soviet spokesmen secretly approached the United States, suggesting that a Soviet strike against China's infant nuclear weapons program would be in the interests of both superpowers. But Nixon sternly warned Moscow off. Kissinger opened a line to Beijing, which he visited in July 1971 for talks with the shrewd Zhou Enlai (Chou En-lai), the second man in China. Kissinger sought

The opening to China: Nixon and Mao (1972).

to exploit Beijing's fears of Moscow to put pressure on Hanoi and to secure from Moscow both arms control agreements and settlement of the still contentious Berlin issue.

In February 1972, Nixon visited Beijing in person and ended the Chinese-American enmity that had endured since war in 1950. Ideology took a back seat to power relationships. The enemy of my enemy—as the Middle Eastern saying has it—is my friend. The U.S. "opening to China" so worried Brezhnev that he agreed to a Nixon visit and gave ground both in Germany and on strategic arms limitation.

Immediately before the Moscow summit of May 1972, Nixon blocked the vital North Vietnamese port of Haiphong with air-dropped mines in reprisal for a failed North Vietnamese offensive aimed at Saigon. The mines and the fact that Brezhnev, like Mao, received Nixon, apparently provoked thought in Hanoi. Nixon's probable victory in the fall 1972 presidential election over the dovish Democrat, George McGovern, made it seem wise to negotiate now. Hanoi therefore dropped its demand for the dismantling of the Saigon regime and agreed to return the U.S. prisoners that had survived its camps.

Then the president of South Vietnam, General Nguyen Van Thieu, raised obstacles. He foresaw abandonment by the United States. Nixon and Kissinger attempted to calm him with secret assurances that the United States would again intervene if Hanoi broke the coming truce. Hanoi sensed American weakness and likewise stalled, even after Nixon's landslide reelection in November. In December 1972 Nixon therefore ordered attacks on vital targets in and around Hanoi with the full firepower of the B-52 heavy bombers of the U.S. Air Force. Nixon's domestic opponents accused him of genocide for this so-called "Christmas bombing" and compared it to Auschwitz and Hiroshima. In actuality Nixon's bombing killed perhaps 1,100 DRV civilians and military, and at last brought Hanoi to

release the United States from the war on terms that did not appear utterly and immediately humiliating.

On January 27, 1973, the DRV representatives signed a peace agreement in Paris that provided for the return of U.S. prisoners, the withdrawal of the U.S. advisers that remained in South Vietnam, and a precarious truce. Publicly, Nixon and Kissinger claimed they had achieved "peace with honor," a phrase rich in historical irony. Privately they apparently hoped for a "decent interval" between U.S. withdrawal and South Vietnamese collapse.

The interval was indecently short. Nixon, like Johnson, aspired to be loved. Incessant personal attacks from his domestic opponents and endless leakages to the press from within his administration warped his sometimes eccentric judgment. During the 1972 election campaign he ordered the "plumbers," a secret White House unit formed to combat leaks, to plant electronic listening devices in the national Democratic party headquarters in Washington's Watergate Hotel. In June 1972, an alert security guard caught the inept "plumbers" breaking and entering. In the spring–summer of 1973 Nixon's frantic attempts to cover up his own role in this "Watergate Affair" collapsed. Televised hearings before Congress left his administration in shambles. On August 9, 1974, he left the presidency by a unique route—resignation to escape impeachment, criminal prosecution, and probable imprisonment.

Internally, the outcome of Watergate was a triumph for the rule of law. Externally, it allowed Congress to seize control of foreign policy, a role the Constitution had not allotted it, and which Congress could not successfully fill. In November 1973 Congress passed over Nixon's veto a "War Powers Resolution" that required congressional approval both before and during the commitment of U.S. forces to combat. Congress drastically cut aid to South Vietnam and to anti-Communist forces in Laos and Cambodia. Fierce congressional opposition paralyzed Nixon's vice president and successor, Gerald R. Ford.

In January 1975 the Politburo in Hanoi took the measure of Congress and of Ford: "Having withdrawn from Vietnam, the United States could hardly return." Hanoi, newly re-equipped with Soviet heavy weapons, prepared a North Korean-style offensive across South Vietnam's northern and western borders. In April 1975, that *Blitzkrieg* crushed the exhausted and demoralized South Vietnamese army with over 700 Soviet tanks. The United States assisted impotently, then organized one last operation: the evacuation from Saigon of all remaining Americans and a few of the many South Vietnamese who had worked for the United States.

On April 30, 1975, Saigon fell to DRV armor. The North annexed the South and renamed Saigon "Ho Chi Minh City." The Second Indochina War was over. It had cost the lives of perhaps 725,000 North Vietnamese, 525,000 South Vietnamese, and 58,000 Americans. Its end brought not peace but immense massacres, millions of refugees, and a Third Indochina War between the Communist victors (see pp. 1044–46).

A "GENERATION OF PEACE"?

As they disengaged from Vietnam, Kissinger and Nixon proclaimed that a new international order was being born. The opening to China would not only extricate the United States from Southeast Asia. It would also open the road to a lasting "détente," or relaxation of tensions, between Moscow and Washington.

Talk of détente was not new. The atmospheric test ban treaty of 1963 was its first monument. Johnson had pursued negotiations and in 1968 had signed with Moscow a nuclear nonproliferation treaty that China and France had rejected in favor of exploding their own hydrogen bombs. Strategic arms

The eve of Saigon's fall: Refugees storm the U.S. embassy to secure places on the last helicopter flights out, April 29, 1975.

talks and a 1968 summit with Brezhnev proved abortive. But in Europe, the West Germans abandoned Adenauer's rigid policy of nonrecognition of Ulbricht's DDR. Willy Brandt of the SPD, upon his entrance into Bonn's governing coalition in 1966, inaugurated a new "eastern policy." Brandt's *Ostpolitik* sought rapprochement both with the DDR and with the nations of eastern Europe upon which Germany had trampled in 1938–45. Extreme versions of *Ostpolitik* looked forward to an end to NATO and the Warsaw Pact, and the reunification of Germany.

As a French intellectual once remarked, Germany's neighbors loved Germany so much that they were delighted to have two of them. *Ostpolitik* was nevertheless a modest success. It suffered a brief setback in August 1968, when the Soviet Union and its Warsaw Pact allies invaded Czechoslovakia to crush the "Prague Spring," a liberalization movement in the Czech Communist party. But embarrassment at Soviet brutality did not long deter Brandt, Johnson, or Nixon from seeking further negotiations.

Brandt became Chancellor of West Germany in 1969, and concluded nonaggression treaties with the Soviet Union, Poland, Czechoslovakia, and the DDR in 1970–73. Kissinger's opening to China helped impel the Soviet Union in 1971 to sign a treaty with the United States, Britain, and France that formally guaranteed Western access to Berlin. In theory that precluded a renewal of Stalin's blockade or of Khrushchev's threats to West Berlin.

Kissinger judged that Brezhnev badly needed reinsurance against Beijing and an infusion of Western technology and money to bolster Soviet economic growth, which had peaked in the 1950s and declined thereafter. Kissinger assumed, in essence, that the West could bribe the Soviets. Economic ties and arms control would in good Cobdenite fashion (see p. 816) enmesh Moscow in a structure of "interdependence." As Kennan had hoped in 1947, the Soviet Union would at last "mellow" and became a status quo power. The need for containment would end, and the world, in Nixon's self-inflating phrase, would enjoy a "generation of peace."

The Soviet view was quite different. Despite Moscow's sensitivity about Kissinger's dalliance with Beijing, the Soviets did not consider China a near-term threat. The vast bulk of Soviet divisions continued to menace western Europe. Brezhnev sought détente as a tool for achieving Soviet objectives, not as an occasion to abandon them. Western money, technology, and grain would shore up his flagging centrally planned economy and upgrade Soviet weapons technology. Détente need not constrain the Soviet Union outside Europe, as the Soviet Union immediately demonstrated by backing Sadat's October 1973 war. Nor did détente mean the end of ideological struggle.

The two greatest monuments of détente, the strategic arms limitation treaty of May 1972 (SALT I) and the Helsinki security treaty of 1975, were thus profoundly ambiguous. SALT I and its accompanying "ABM Treaty" limiting antimissile defenses wrote into international law the quantitative advantage that the Soviet buildup had gained since 1962. The Soviets retained 1,618 land-based and 950 submarine-launched intercontinental ballistic missiles to the 1,054 and 710 of the United States. SALT I limited numbers of mis-

siles only, and placed no restrictions on the "multiple independently targeted" warheads (MIRVs) that soon equipped those missiles. The treaty appeared to make the superpower arms competition more predictable than before, but did little to end it. SALT I's duration was only five years.

The Helsinki treaty of 1975, the final cap on the eastern treaties of 1970–73, was equally problematic. The West, in a Europe-wide conference at Helsinki that included neutral powers, at last conceded legitimacy to Stalin's conquests of 1944–45. In return Moscow offered cultural exchanges, and promises, immediately violated, of respect for human rights and of free movement of people and ideas across the borders of the Soviet empire.

MASS CULTURE AND "COUNTERCULTURE"

Socially and politically, the 1950s were placid times in the West. Pundits prematurely hailed the "end of ideology," the demise of messianic political faiths in the wake of Khrushchev's 1956 revelations. Then worldwide communications, anti-American discontents, a student generation of unprecedented size and affluence, and the twin catalysts of the Vietnam War and the independence struggles in the "Third World" (see pp. 1011–19) created a wave of disturbances unprecedented since 1848.

The Americanization of the World

The growth of the world market in undreamed-of prosperity also meant the rapid worldwide spread of the mass culture of the leading state. Two things speeded that process: the dying British empire's legacy of English as the universal language of commerce, and a new revolution in transportation and communications that paralleled the coming of steam and the telegraph in the nineteenth century. In 1950, almost all intercontinental travel was by ship. By 1960 four-engined jet aircraft had cut the trip from Paris to New York to eight hours; no spot on the globe was more than 24 hours away. By the 1970s satellite television relays provided instantaneous transmission of pictures and sound from anywhere on Earth.

American film and television conveyed sparkling images of affluence and made few intellectual demands on their audience. Suitably dubbed into local languages, they acquired a wide following wherever governments allowed their citizens to view them. They also aroused appetites for wealth and growth that most societies found difficult to satisfy. Even the relatively rich Europeans did not duplicate the credit-card prosperity of the American middle classes until the 1970s.

Along with Hollywood movies and television serials came the gray legions of corporate America, from General Electric to ITT to Coca Cola. They established or widened beachheads for American commerce in Europe, Japan, and the "Third World." That massive expansion of America's cultural and economic visibility aroused a variety of reactions. European business at first gratefully embraced the Marshall Plan and private American investment in Europe. Welcome turned to distrust by the 1960s. U.S. capital export was so massive that Europeans feared losing control of their economies to America's allegedly sinister "multinational corporations." Then the burden of Vietnam undermined U.S. economic performance. Europeans created multinationals of their own and acquired assets in the United States.

Culturally, reaction was likewise mixed. The defeated nations of Germany, Italy, and Japan embraced some elements of American democracy or industrial organization. But especially in Britain, France, and the Islamic world, native traditions resisted fiercely. Britons such as the philosopher and unilateral disarmament crusader Bertrand Russell looked down their noses at what they took to be American provincialism and irresponsibility. Conservative critics, from tra-

ditionalist Catholics to stern Gaullists to Shi'ite Moslems, decried "Coca-colonization" and the moral laxity that American wealth allegedly brought. The academic Left, from Mexico City and Tokyo to the cafés of the Left Bank in Paris, turned withering Marxist scorn on America, the leading capitalist state.

Student Revolt and Middle Class Terrorism

After 1945 the United States attempted to create the first society in history in which a majority of citizens had some higher education. In the 1960s much of western Europe began to follow. Rapid university expansion created a shortage of faculty that consigned students to boredom in immense factory-like classrooms. Affluence apparently removed any pressing need to work. Leisure and the outrageous bohemian example of "beat generation" rebels of the 1950s such as the novelist Jack Kerouac fostered the rise in the early 1960s of a youth "counterculture." Its adherents were passionately contemptuous of inherited standards of behavior and dedicated to the joys that contraceptive pills, mind-distorting drugs,

Demonstrators confront military police outside the Pentagon (October 1967).

and the electric guitar had recently made available.

The rebellion of the youthful rich began appropriately enough in the richest country, the United States. In 1964, the University of California at Berkeley exploded in violent confrontation between a rigid central administration and a radical "Free Speech Movement" determined to shock and provoke. Vietnam loomed on the horizon as early as 1963, but it was Johnson's plunge into full-scale war in 1965 that gave the rebels their cause and mass base. College students received draft deferments, but those who graduated or flunked out faced call-up unless they discovered a convenient medical condition.

In these circumstances a "New Left" arose that mocked predictions of an "end of ideology." From 1964–65 on it savaged the American political and academic establishment from the Left with a zeal that recalled the 1950s attacks of Senator McCarthy from the Right. It proclaimed a "second American revolution" against "imperialism" in Vietnam and middle-class society at home. Student insurrections paralyzed Columbia, Harvard, and other campuses in 1967–68. Nixon's 1970 thrust into Cambodia inspired an immense wave of protest.

By then the most determined student radicals had formed a terrorist group that called itself the "Weathermen." The name came from a line of the folk-rock cult figure Bob Dylan: " . . . you don't need a weatherman to know which way the wind blows." The Weathermen sought to "bring the war home," to imitate the "armed struggle" of the Viet Cong and of urban guerrillas such as the Tupamaros in Uruguay (see p. 1031). The most striking Weatherman achievement was the accidental demolition in 1970 of a Greenwich Village townhouse and bomb factory belonging to the parent of a member. And the broader "Movement" deflated swiftly after 1970, thanks to the virtual end of the draft and to the inherent contradiction between Leninist commitment and countercultural hedonism. "Make love not war" also meant making love not revolution. Not "armed struggle" but drugs, sex, rock-and-roll, and imported Buddhist or Hindu mysticism were the most widespread forms of protest against middle-class America.

The American example helped inspire disturbances in Europe far more serious than mere campus revolts. The European rebels were heirs to a tradition of romantic student radicalism stretching back into the nineteenth century. They also drew on the discipline and doctrine of their countries' Communist parties, although they condemned those parties as stodgy. Even more than their American counterparts they found inspiration in the "noble savages" of "Third World" revolutionary movements (see p. 1011).

The Paris "days" of May 1968 turned back the clock to the Paris Commune of 1871; urban insurrection once more appeared practical politics. A student uprising with support from the industrial workers briefly controlled the Left Bank of Paris. Hundreds of thousands marched demanding de Gaulle's overthrow. The general flew in disgust ("reforms yes; bed-messing no") to visit his army and secure the support of the officer corps. He then returned to Paris and rallied the "forces of order" with a television speech that brought millions into the streets singing the "Marseillaise"—a revolutionary anthem transmuted into a call to arms against revolution. The student movement deflated. The Left lost votes in the ensuing election. De Gaulle resigned in 1969 when a referendum went against him, but he resigned in favor of a hand-picked successor. The modern state had again shown its ability to tame upheavals from below.

In Germany, student revolt was in deadly earnest—as it had been under Weimar, where the Nazis had captured the student movement long before they seized the state. Some German "New Left" radicals, Freudian-Marxist in ideology and Stalinist in practice, turned to "armed struggle" in the late 1960s. Their most prominent group, the "Red Army Faction" or "Baader-Meinhof gang," attacked U.S. bases in West Germany and assassinated industrialists, judges, and politicians with ruthless precision. But computerized tracking of suspects eventually demolished the guerrillas. In 1976–77 Andreas Baader, Ulrike Meinhof, and other "Red Army Faction" leaders committed suicide in prison to embarrass "the system." Bombings, assassinations, and revolution by suicide failed to inspire the placid West German "masses" to revolt. After 1979, the German student Left largely abandoned "armed struggle" for ecological and antinuclear protest (see p. 1049).

Italy's student radicals mounted the most determined challenge to the democratic state. Students and industrial workers combined in 1969 to make a deadly serious "hot autumn" of riots, strikes, and factory or university occupations. Throughout the 1970s terrorist groups of ex-students from both leftist and Catholic backgrounds sought to provoke the Italian parliamentary regime into revealing its allegedly "Fascist" nature. Some had received training in KGB-sponsored schools in Czechoslovakia, others with the PLO in Lebanon. Their instrument was the "knee-capping" or assassination of judges, factory managers, journalists, and politicians. In 1978 the terrorist "Red Brigades" kidnapped and killed a former prime minister, the Christian Democrat Aldo Moro. That stroke united Italian opinion against the terrorists and galvanized police and prosecutors. The "Red Brigades" and their offshoots ended in prison. Throughout the West youthful rebellion gave way to middle-class careers.

The Feminist Revolution

Among the movements that flourished in the 1960s alongside student and "countercultural" protest was a renewed and militant feminism. The vote, the Depression, and two world

The power of the state: French police beat Paris students (May 1968).

wars had damped feminist agitation from the 1920s to the 1950s. But in the heady atmosphere of the 1960s, the continuing growth of women's share in the work force—often in poorly paying part-time or temporary jobs—helped ignite protest. The contradiction between women's claims to rights and the facts of male power in the family, at work, and in politics inspired radical theorists, especially in the United States and France. Precursors such as Simone de Beauvoir, France's leading woman intellectual and author of The Second Sex (1949), soon appeared insufficiently militant. Beauvoir's elegant and learned analysis of "the slavery of half of humanity" appeared to lack a political program.

Numerous theorists and groups sought to supply one. In the United States, where women entered the labor force earlier and in greater numbers than in Europe, a broad front of women's organizations had arisen by the mid-1960s. It sought to open hitherto male professions to women and to secure "reproductive freedom": the removal of restrictions upon contraception and abortion. This "first wave" of

The new feminism: women march in New York City (1960s).

feminists ranged in its politics from mild liberalism to New Left radicalism. But in practice it took its cue from the Lockean natural rights tradition, as Harriet and John Stuart Mill (see p. 722) had applied it in the nineteenth century—women should enjoy by right the same autonomy as men. To at last assert that autonomy, women now had to learn to compete successfully with men in all fields of human activity. The most radical "first wave" theorists concluded that women's autonomy demanded the destruction of the "patriarchal" family and the liberation of women from childbirth and child rearing.

As the euphoria of the late 1960s subsided, a "second wave" of American feminist theorists began to celebrate—rather than seeking to eliminate—women's differences from men. The new "woman-centered" school had counterparts in western Europe and was related to the "equal but different" tradition of the nineteenth century (see p. 722). It asserted the superiority of women's nature, which was allegedly more intuitive, warm, compassionate, "nurturing," peace-loving, and practical than that of the purportedly cold, calculating, competitive, violent, power-mad male. It dismissed masterful women leaders from Margaret Thatcher of Britain to Indira Gandhi of India (see pp. 1026 and 1050) as victims who had in effect become men. It proclaimed that women were a "sex class" whose shared nature and experience overrode all ideological, social, national, and racial divisions. "Universal sisterhood" would inaugurate a new and purely female culture that would ultimately save humanity. Ironically, that vision caught on just as ideological, social, ethnic, and racial divisions fractured the women's movement—and as a counteroffensive by fiercely antifeminist "pro-family" women sought to roll it back.

But despite internecine struggles and external opposition, the feminist revolt had decisive consequences. In the United States and western Europe, it spurred reforms that gave women a greater measure of formal equality than ever before. It inspired the creation of institutions such as day-care centers that helped to free women to join the work force in ever greater numbers. Above all, it provided middle-class women with encouragement to pursue careers equivalent to those of men, encouragement that their mothers had lacked. Demographically, the consequence was later marriages and fewer children. Emotionally, the attempt to "have it all," to pursue a career and raise a family, sometimes provoked intolerable strain. Men inevitably proved slow to adjust to the equality in practical matters that the new "two-career family" demanded. But change was nevertheless perceptible. The feminist revolution brought closer to reality than ever before the nineteenth-century ideal of equality between the sexes.

Protest within the West was merely one sign of the passing of the "age of containment." The Middle East explosion of 1973 revealed the full extent of Western disunity. The ensuing swift escalation of oil prices struck a stinging blow to the world economy. U.S. foreign policy succumbed temporarily to paralysis as Congress sought to demolish the "imperial presidency" that it blamed for Vietnam. Geographic and strategic circumstances had favored containment in Korea, at a price. The agony of containment in Vietnam hastened the end of America's strategic dominance over the Soviet Union and of its economic edge over Japan. By the mid-1970s the pundits saw a new age of another kind emerging. Détente, they proclaimed, had ended the Cold War. In place of superpower conflict they discerned a growing international class struggle between rich and poor states.

Suggestions for Further Reading

The Superpower Conflict

Few intelligent syntheses cover the post-1945 period. Recent events arouse too much retrospective passion and carry too heavy a weight of current hopes and fears. Sources are simultaneously too wide and too shallow. Much remains buried in the archives, especially the Soviet archives. A. Ulam, *The Rivals: America and Russia Since World War II* (1971), is nevertheless excellent on the central U.S.-Soviet conflict. P. Seabury, *The Rise and Decline of the Cold War* (1967), is acute on that conflict's nature and dimensions. R. Aron, *The Imperial Republic: The United States and the World, 1945–1973* (1974), is both brilliant and detached; F. Schurmann, *The Logic of World Power* (1974), is less detached but full of unusual insights. On the Soviet Union, see first the inside views of M. Djilas, *Conversations with Stalin* (1962), and (with caution) N. Khrushchev, *Khrushchev Remembers* (1974). A. Ulam, *Expansion and Coexistence* (1968–) and *Dangerous Relations: the Soviet Union in World Politics, 1970–1982* (1983), are characteristically well-argued and delightfully written. D. Holloway, *The Soviet Union and the Arms Race* (1983), is indispensable. F. Fejtö, *A History of the People's Democracies* (1971), intelligently covers eastern Europe from Stalin to Brezhnev. For the Cuban missile crisis, see especially G. Allison, *Essence of Decision* (1971).

The Mid-Sized Powers

W. Laqueur, *Europe Since Hitler* (1970), offers a masterful synthesis both of events and of European political and intellectual trends; on the latter, see also J. F. Revel, *The Totalitarian Temptation* (1977). M. Schaller, *The American Occupation of Japan* (1985), traces the process that put Japan back on the road to supremacy in East Asia; E. O. Reischauer, *The Japanese Today* (1988), offers a sympathetic picture of postwar Japan. H. C. Hinton, *Three and a Half Powers: The New Balance in Asia* (1975), places Japan in its international context.

The Middle East

The Middle East arouses even more passion than the Cold War; no reliable narrative history of the area since 1945 exists. L. C. Brown, *International Politics and the Middle East* (1984), is a fine introduction to how it got the way it is. P. Mansfield, *The Middle East: A Political and Economic Survey* (1980), is a useful handbook. Y. Harkabi, *Arab Strategies and Israel's Response* (1977), offers one Israeli view; for Arab difficulties both with Israel and with the modern world, see especially F. Ajami, *The Arab Predicament: Arab Political Thought and Practice Since 1967* (1981). W. Laqueur, *Confrontation: The Middle East War and World Politics* (1974), remains the best book on the Yom Kippur War.

From Korea to Vietnam

Few dispassionate accounts of America's wars of containment exist, but see D. Rees, *Korea: The Limited War* (1964), and G. Lewy, *America in Vietnam* (1978). R. E. M. Irving, *The First Indochina War: French and American Policy, 1945–54* (1975), surveys the antecedents; W. J. Rust, *Kennedy in Vietnam* (1985), contains new material on the early years and the coup against Diem. G. Race, *War Comes to Long An* (1972), is indispensable on the Viet Cong. M. Herr, *Dispatches* (1978), conveys the atmosphere of Vietnam with unparalleled skill. P. Braestrup, *Big Story* (1977), describes with candor and irony the role of the U.S. press. H. Summers, *On Strategy* (1982), is a not always successful attempt to figure out what went wrong. For détente and the opening to China, see A. Ulam, *Dangerous Relations: The Soviet Union in World Politics, 1970–1982* (1983), and (with caution) H. Kissinger, *White House Years* (1979) and *Years of Decision* (1982).

Students and Feminists

The transnational student revolt still awaits its historian. D. Caute, *The Year of the Barricades: A Journey Through 1968* (1988), and R. Johnson, *The French Communist Party Versus the Students* (1972), are nevertheless useful. On the women's movement, see especially J. Mitchell and A. Oakley, *What is Feminism?* (1986); C. Duchen, *Feminism in France* (1986); and H. Eisenstein, *Contemporary Feminist Thought* (1983).

35
The "Third World"

*U*nder the shadow of superpower conflict, "new nations" arose in unprecedented numbers in the years after 1945. The collapse of the European empires under the pressure of that most successful of European exports, nationalism, ultimately produced over 120 states. Most adhered neither to the Soviet empire nor to the group of developed nations of western Europe, North America, and the Pacific that were allied to the United States.

The new states were for the most part poor compared to the developed West. That was their most noteworthy common characteristic. Theorists inevitably sought to lump them together. Alfred Sauvy, a French economic historian, coined in 1952 the name that stuck: the "Third World." Sauvy took his terminology from 1789, from the Abbé Sieyès. The "Third World" was allegedly "ignored, exploited, despised, like the Third Estate." That analogy suggested a conclusion: it was the duty of the "Third World" to follow the revolutionary example of France's Third Estate, and to launch a global revolution against the capitalist "First World."

In the ensuing 30 years, theorists of "Third World" revolution elaborated political myths on that theme. Marxist-Leninist voices from the Soviet bloc, soon known as the "Second World," cheered them on. The economic development of the West, prophets of revolution intoned, was responsible for "Third World" poverty. The "Third World," they insisted, should rise and smite the West, or compel it to give "reparations" that would raise the "Third World" to a developed world standard of living.

Neither revolution nor massive transfers of assets occurred. The "Third World" was neither united nor particularly militant, except verbally at the United Nations. "Third World" states fought one another more readily than they did developed countries. Internal bloodshed between tribal, religious,

The "Third World"
assembled—the Bandung
Conference of "non-aligned"
African and Asian states,
1955.

and social groups took precedence over struggle against the "imperialist" West or "North." And after 1979, the Soviet Union's massacres of Afghans (see p. 1044) showed many in the "Third World" that the West was far from being the most ruthless "imperialist" force in the contemporary world.

By the late 1980s, the "Group of 77," chief lobbying organization of "Third World" nations, had begun to accept Western contentions that states bear responsibility for their own fates and that the chief sources of economic development—or its absence—were internal. Simultaneously, dissatisfaction began to grow with the term itself, for "Third World" lumped together states radically different in history, culture, politics, economic structure, and wealth. The bankruptcy of the concept— the collapse of the notion of a unified "Third World" or southern hemisphere with interests implacably opposed to those of the West or "North"—has slowly opened the way for dispassion-

ate analysis of the sources of economic development and of the sharp historical and cultural differences between "Third World" states. The process of "decolonization" that gave birth to most "Third World" states is one place to begin that analysis.

DECOLONIZATION: IDEOLOGICAL "WINDS OF CHANGE"

The force of ideas was the most powerful of the "winds of change" that swept over the colonial empires in the two decades that followed Britain's defeat at Singapore in 1942. Nationalism, the secular religion of the nation-state, had arisen spontaneously in the "Third World" whenever native elites sought to resist Western power by acquiring Western ideas. From China to Ghana, nationalism offered an ideology to replace the old beliefs and communities that Western power had shattered in the nineteenth century. The creation of nation-states, independent and sovereign externally and focus of *all* loyalties internally, would wipe out the humiliation that Western domination had brought, provide a sense of belonging, and help nationalist intellectuals to power and wealth. That social function, indeed, was a mighty reason for nationalism's dramatic success. As in Europe, the cult of the nation-state rewarded well those who served it. At best they became the new rulers, borne to power on a wave of popular enthusiasm. At worst they could make a living as bureaucrats and schoolteachers, building the state or molding the new generations to its faith.

Some areas took to the new dispensation more readily than others. The states of East Asia were cultural units of long standing. That facilitated their conversion into nation-states on a pattern resembling Europe. In the Islamic world, loyalties were simultaneously too wide and too narrow to fit the new pattern easily. "Arab unity," "Islamic solidarity," or "Islamic revolution" coexisted uneasily with centuries-old tribal, religious, and linguistic-ethnic rivalries. In Latin America, the oldest group of "new nations" other than Holland and the United States, the persistence of stratification by blood—Creole, Indian, black—meant that the elites were often closer to their counterparts in neighboring states than to their own peasants. And in black Africa, state borders bore little relationship to the ethnographic map.

As an ideology of revolt against the West, nationalism inevitably had competitors, of which Marxism-Leninism was the most popular. In formal terms it was an ideology of class war, but outside Europe it often merged in practice with nationalism. As Sun Yat-sen had recognized (see p. 889), nationalism and Leninist organizational techniques were a powerful combination. In the "Third World" as in the Soviet Union, Marxism-Leninism provided the legitimation for all-dominating "cults of personality" and for unlimited power for

Party elites. The resulting regimes were the most brutally regimented and fiercely nationalist regimes in history: China, North Vietnam, North Korea, Cuba, Ethiopia. And those strange progeny of the European traditions of nationalism and Marxism were nationalist with a difference. They paradoxically belonged to the "socialist camp," to a multinational empire based on the denial of the importance of nationalism. Only China, Yugoslavia, and Albania ultimately developed Marxist-Leninist nationalisms *against* Moscow.

A variety of "pan-movements" likewise competed with nationalism. The Islamic world gave birth to two mutually contradictory ones—Arab nationalism and pan-Islamism. Arab nationalism, whose chief manifestation was the Arab League of States with its periodic meetings and communiques, proved weak indeed. Pan-Arab sentiment, even if wielded by charismatic figures such as Gamal Abdel Nasser, failed to unify the Arab world politically. Its religious counterpart, pan-Islamism, suffered from even greater weaknesses. Of the more than 800 million adherents of Islam only a quarter are Arabs; the remainder, from Senegal through Iran, Pakistan, and India to Indonesia and the Philippines, include such a wide variety of linguistic and ethnic groups that common action even in the United Nations has rarely proved possible. Islam itself, like Christianity, also has built-in divisions, above all hostility between the minority Shi'ites—10 percent of all Moslems—and the majority Sunni (see p. 220). South of Islam, "pan-Africanism" gave birth in 1963 to an inappropriately named "Organization of African Unity"; the organization has persisted but unity has been absent.

A final contender was—for lack of a better term—"Third Worldism"—the ideology that proclaimed the division of humanity into a rich and oppressive capitalist "North" and an innocent victimized agrarian "South." In 1955, at Bandung in Indonesia, 29 African and Asian states met and inaugurated a series of "Third World" conclaves that promoted the notion of "non-alignment" in the Cold War and made increasingly insistent demands that the West atone for its "imperialist" past.

"Third Worldism," as it developed in the 1960s and 1970s, was a heady mixture. First of its ingredients was the notion that the reduction of the "Third World" to poverty had been the precondition of Western development and wealth. Second came a romantic faith in revolution and its supposed modernizing effects; that faith rested in part on a misreading of the history of the Soviet Union. The third component of "Third Worldism" was psychological, the invention of Frantz Fanon, a French–West Indian intellectual who joined the Algerian rebels and wrote an impassioned work, *The Wretched of the Earth* (1961), that sold millions of copies to the professors and students of Western universities. Fanon celebrated violence, not merely as a means to a political end, but as a good in itself. He proclaimed bloodshed "a cleansing force," a psychotherapy for the oppressed. The final component of "Third Worldism" was the claim that the "Third World" itself was a cohesive unit, that its internal solidarity against "imperialism" overrode divisions of language, tribe, religion, or culture. Those were powerful myths, but they proved less powerful than the cult of the nation-state.

DECOLONIZATION: VIOLENT BIRTH OF THE "THIRD WORLD"

The collapse of the colonial empires was foreordained once the colonized peoples revolted. The empires that remained after World War II had extraordinarily narrow demographic bases. Britain, with roughly 41 million inhabitants in 1939, dominated an empire of over 500 million. The empires of France, Holland, Belgium, and Portugal were less disproportionate in size to the European powers that held

Fanon on Violence

Fanon theorized that violence liberated minds as well as bodies. He predicted prematurely that the masses, initiated politically through violence, would not tolerate post-colonial regimes under "demagogues," "opportunists," or "magicians."

At the level of individuals, violence is a cleansing force. It frees the native from his inferiority complex and from his despair and inaction; it makes him fearless and restores his self-respect. Even if the armed struggle has been symbolic and the nation is demolished through a rapid movement of decolonization, the people have the time to see that the liberation has been the business of each and all and that the leader has no special merit. . . . When the people have taken violent part in the national liberation they will allow no one to set themselves up as "liberators." They show themselves to be jealous of the results of their action and take good care not to place their future, their destiny or the fate of their country in the hands of a living god. Yesterday they were completely irresponsible; today they mean to understand everything and make all decisions. Illuminated by violence, the consciousness of the people rebels against any pacification. From now on the demagogues, the opportunists and the magicians have a difficult task. The action which has thrown them into a hand-to-hand struggle confers on the masses a voracious taste for the concrete. The attempt at mystification becomes in the long run practically impossible.

From Elie Kedourie, ed., *Nationalism in Asia and Africa* (New York: Meridian Books, 1970), p. 536.

them. But even there colonial rule rested on the continuing willingness of the colonized to submit and collaborate.

Overwhelming European power, the power of the Maxim gun, had produced submission and collaboration in the past. But now the correlation of forces had changed. The rise of the Soviet Union and of Mao's China, and their widening reach, gave colonial nationalists powerful allies. The dependable Soviet AK-47 assault rifle, copied from a German weapon of 1943–44, became the Maxim gun of *decolonization*. Economic growth and Western schooling produced native intellectuals who sought ways both peaceful and violent to induce the colonizers to go.

The partition of British India, 1947: Moslem refugees on a road near New Delhi strewn with Moslem dead.

These intellectuals created nationalist mass movements far better adapted to reconquering independence than the precolonial order had been retaining it. In Europe, the vast bloodletting of the two world wars and the economic unprofitability of many colonies persuaded most European democracies to let their empires go once native nationalists mounted a serious challenge.

British decolonization began first and lasted longest, thanks to the size and bizarre variety of Britain's possessions. In relative terms British decolonization was the least traumatic, thanks to London's empiricist willingness to concede, graciously or not, what it no longer had the power to withhold. Ireland went first in 1921–37 (see pp. 886–87). Its leader, the ex-rebel Eamon De Valera, was the first of many nationalist leaders whose road to power passed through British jails.

In the aftermath of World War II, Britain found itself even more beleaguered than in 1919–21. Mohandas Gandhi—fortunately for India—had failed to drag down British rule in 1942 with the Japanese at the gates. But after 1945 the Labour government of Clement Attlee had no alternative but to quit India; it lacked the troops and money to hold down by force a subcontinent of over 400 million inhabitants. Two mass movements fought Britain and each other: Gandhi's Congress Party and Mohammed Ali Jinnah's Moslem League. Congress claimed all India, by right of Hindu nationalism; the Moslem League claimed a Moslem-inhabited "Pakistan" around Karachi and in Bengal, east and west of the Hindu majority. By March 1947, in the words of a subordinate of Britain's last viceroy, the Indian empire was "a ship on fire in mid-ocean with ammunition in the hold." In August 1947 Britain simply left; the excellent British-trained armies of the two successor states, India and Pakistan, fought over the province of Kashmir. Hindu and Moslem populations on the wrong side of the partition lines fled for their lives. Independence brought 15 million refugees and 500,000 to 750,000 dead in religious-ethnic massacres.

Possession of India had impelled Britain to acquire Ceylon, Burma, Malaya, and the north coast of Borneo; the end of empire in India led London to concede independence to Burma and Ceylon (later Sri Lanka) in early 1948. Britain stayed on until 1957 in Malaya and Singapore, thanks to the Communist insurgency based on Malaya's overseas Chinese minority. Britain conceded independence to its possessions in Borneo in 1963, and retained only Hong Kong, which it pledged in 1984 to transfer to China in 1997.

In the Middle East, whose oil was essential to Britain and western Europe, London attempted to hang on until the mid-1950s. It gave up its thankless task in Palestine in 1948 and in 1945 left Egypt. It held only the irreducible minimum: the crucial base of

Cyprus, the oil states of the Persian Gulf, and a zone around the Suez Canal that connected the oil with Europe. But soon the sad tale of 1882 repeated itself—with a different outcome. Like the Khedive before him, Britain's Egyptian client King Farouk succumbed to a nationalist officers' revolt. After Farouk's departure for the French Riviera in 1952, a charismatic figure on the model of Arabi Pasha took command, Colonel Gamal Abdel Nasser.

Nasser set himself the task of unifying "the Arabs" from Morocco to Iraq. He sought as first steps to evict Britain from the Canal and to lead the Arab destruction of Israel. In June 1956, weary of terrorist attacks on British sentries, Britain evacuated the Canal Zone. Nasser thereupon confiscated the canal from its European owners while simultaneously challenging Israel with guerrilla raids from the Gaza strip and provoking the United States

South and East Asia since the Second World War

The antagonists of 1956: Anthony Eden (above) and Gamal Abdel Nasser (below).

by arms purchases from the Soviet Union. Anthony Eden, Churchill's wartime foreign secretary and successor, took up the challenge: Nasser was another Hitler. Had he not written a booklet, *Philosophy of the Revolution* (1953)? Was the Suez Canal in 1956 not the Rhineland in 1936? (But in 1936 Eden himself had merely thought Hitler's action "deplorable.") The French, mired in war against the Algerian insurrection and convinced that Nasser the pan-Arab was behind it, were happy to cooperate.

British and French airborne and amphibious forces, in secret cooperation with Israel's land thrust in the Sinai, landed at the Mediterranean end of the canal on November 5–6, 1956. But Eden, thanks to his own pigheadedness and to the ambiguity of Eisenhower's Secretary of State, John Foster Dulles, failed to understand that Washington sought to conciliate "Arab nationalism" and would not tolerate a Franco-British reconquest of Egypt. A U.S. attack on the stability of the British pound caused Eden to panic and withdraw. The French, fuming at British pusillanimity, resentfully followed.

The Suez fiasco allowed Nasser to claim victory, although his army had suffered its usual rout and Cairo was defenseless. Suez, a British military victory, ended Britain's prestige in the Middle East as defeat at Singapore had done in Asia. Coups against British-backed regimes in Iraq, unrest in Jordan, and an incipient civil war between Moslems and Maronite Christians in Lebanon followed in 1958. Iraq bloodily left the British orbit; British paratroops and U.S. Marines briefly landed in Jordan and Lebanon to maintain "stability." In Cyprus, a campaign by Greek guerrillas after 1954 led to Britain's departure in 1959–60. The successor to that struggle was a low intensity war within Cyprus between the Greek majority and the Turkish minority that ended only in 1974, with a Greek coup that provoked a Turkish invasion and the forcible partition of the island.

If the 1940s was for Britain the decade of decolonization in southern Asia and the 1950s that of the Middle East, the 1960s was the decade of Africa and the Caribbean. Harold Macmillan, Eden's successor, spoke grandly in January 1960 of the "wind of change" sweeping the continent. In the next five years, in a remarkable "scramble for Africa" in reverse, Britain and France gave their tropical empires away. In 1956–57 Britain had already conceded independence to the Sudan and to Ghana and the Gold Coast in West Africa. Independence for Nigeria, black Africa's richest and most populous "new nation," came in 1960. The principal retarding force was London's concern about the white settler population in Rhodesia, whose interests it attempted to serve by an abortive Central African Federation. The nationalists of Zambia and Malawi refused to accept the continuance of white privileges and brought the federation down by breaking away in 1964. In 1965 the whites of Rhodesia unilaterally declared their independence of Britain, defied Harold Wilson's Labour government and the United Nations, and fought to preserve their control over the black majority. That proved impossible; negotiations ultimately transformed Rhodesia into black-ruled Zimbabwe in 1978–79.

South of Rhodesia, the Union of South Africa under Boer leadership had achieved virtual independence after World War I, but its politics remained balanced precariously between English-speakers, pro-British Boers, and unreconstructed backwoods *Trekboers*. In 1948 the latter came to power, and imposed in law a rigid system of racial oppression called *Apartheid* ("apartness") that had largely existed in fact. The Boers met black demonstrations such as that at Sharpeville in 1960 with firepower. In 1961 South Africa withdrew from the British Commonwealth rather than listen to further criticism of its peculiar institutions.

Britain took the decisive final steps in its abandonment of empire in the late 1960s and early 1970s. The crucial base at Aden at the entrance to the Red Sea went in 1967, after a bloody guerrilla war by Arab tribal "Marxists." Soviet ships at anchor replaced those of the Royal Navy. Aden mutated into a "People's Democratic Republic of Yemen," complete with AK-47 massacres at Politburo meetings. And in 1971 Britain in essence handed over its oil-bearing clients in the Gulf, from Kuwait in the north to the United Arab Emirates in the south, to the mercy of the Shah of Iran (see pp. 1051–52).

All that remained of the British empire were a few small Caribbean, Atlantic, and Pacific islands along with outposts whose populations feared independence would lead to annexation by covetous neighbors: Hong Kong, Gibraltar, the Falkland Islands off Argentina, and Belize in Central America (which received independence in 1981). The Commonwealth, to which many of Britain's ex-colonies continued to belong, became a debating society.

France did not give up as easily as Britain. Its second colonial empire, acquired after defeat by Germany in 1870–71, was a symbol of national vitality. French schoolteachers had zealously propagated the political myth of France's "civilizing mission" in Africa and Indochina. French politicians, Right, Center, and Left, refused to give their empire up. De Gaulle inaugurated the failed reconquest of Indochina after 1945. Socialists such as prime minister Guy Mollet, who dispatched the task force to Suez, sought at least to hold Algeria. The French army, miserably defeated in 1940, committed its soul to victory in Indochina. It had failed at Dien Bien Phu (see p. 979). The survivors of Indochina returned in 1954 convinced that the Fourth Republic's politicians had stabbed the army in the back: *"On nous a fait le coup"* ["they shafted us"].

In November 1954, Algerian insurgents who took the name of the National Liberation Front (FLN) attacked

The Collapse of the British Empire

1947 India
1948 Ceylon [later Sri Lanka], Burma, Palestine
1956 Sudan
1957 Ghana, Gold Coast, Malaya
1960 Cyprus, Nigeria, British Somaliland [joined ex-Italian Somalia]
1961 Sierra Leone, Cameroons, Tanganyika, Kuwait
1962 Jamaica, Trinidad and Tobago, Uganda
1963 Kenya, Zanzibar [joined Tanganyika to form Tanzania, 1964], Singapore, North Borneo, Sarawak [joined Malaya to form Malaysia; Singapore broke away in 1965].
1964 Malawi, Malta, Zambia
1965 Gambia
1966 Guyana, Botswana, Lesotho, Barbados
1967 Aden, Leeward Islands, Windward Islands
1968 Mauritius, Nauru, Swaziland
1970 Fiji
1971 United Arab Emirates, Bahrein, Qatar

French settlers and police stations. That inaugurated a war that was both colonial and civil, a war that destroyed the Fourth Republic and created an Algerian nation. For Algeria was not simply a colony. Alongside 140,000 Jews and a swiftly growing Moslem population of 9 million lived slightly over a million European settlers, the *"pieds-noirs"*: privileged immigrants from France, Spain, Italy, Malta. Administratively, Algeria was part of France.

France reacted to the Algerian revolt by reinforcing its army there, bombing Moslem villages, and cutting its commitments elsewhere. It conceded independence to Tunisia and Morocco in 1956. The FLN, with some arms from outside but more self-help, soon found a winning strategy. At Philippeville in August 1955, FLN guerrillas and Arab crowds killed some 70 *pieds-noirs*; the French obligingly killed over 1,200 Moslems in reprisals. FLN assassination teams sought out and eliminated all Moslems who maintained contacts

The Sharpeville massacre, 1960: blacks flee the guns of the South African police.

with the French. FLN enforcers cut off the noses of Moslems who smoked tobacco, a French monopoly. The FLN divided the European and Moslem communities with a river of blood; that was the prerequisite for its own domination of the Algerian "camp."

By 1955–56, the two communities were at war. *Pieds-noirs* launched vengeful "rat-hunts" against any and all Moslems, even those entirely unconnected to the insurgents. FLN time-bombs shredded young Europeans in the cafés of the once pleasant city of Algiers. To end the bloodshed, the Fourth Republic abdicated to the army. In January 1957 it called in the *paras*, the army's pride, and made them secret policemen. In the ensuing "Battle of Algiers" the paratroops cordoned the Arab quarters into blocks, swept up suspects at random, tortured them with electric shock and water, and gradually ran the FLN bomb networks to earth. Many thousands of Algerian suspects simply "disappeared."

Torture won the "Battle of Algiers" but helped lose the war. In France, intellectuals of the Left but also of the Center and Right denounced the army. Officers resigned in disgust. FLN spokesmen abroad and states sympathetic to the FLN—including the United States—denounced French methods. And the civilian ministers who had ordered the army to win by any and all methods were already seeking negotiations with the FLN. The army had vowed that *this* time it was going to win; if winning required removal of the politicians before they "betrayed" the army, so be it. In May 1958, amid a proliferation of *pied-noir* and military plots, the armed forces commander in Algeria, General Raoul Salan, demanded the recall to power of Charles de Gaulle.

De Gaulle came once more to save France. But to the chagrin of the army and of the *pieds-noirs*, he soon gave signs of a hidden agenda. In 1958–59 the army crushed what remained of the FLN in the countryside and sought to win Moslem loyalty with promises of "integration." More Moslems, indeed, fought for France than against it. But the FLN maintained its political structures and its claim to represent the Moslem majority. And it began to dawn on French opinion that winning through "integration" would mean a large and ever-growing Moslem presence in the French parliament; the Moslem birth-rate was ten times that of the *pieds-noirs*. De Gaulle, with perfect timing, said the magic word in a speech of September 1959: "self-determination."

Pieds-noirs and army reacted with fury. In 1961 the high command in Algiers, the *paras*, and the Foreign Legion rose against de Gaulle as they had risen against the Fourth Republic. De Gaulle held fast, appealed by radio to the half million draftees in Algeria, and convinced the generals that they were isolated. The Algiers *Putsch* collapsed. In 1962, despite a *pied-noir* terrorist campaign against the army itself and a rising in the European quarter of Algiers, de Gaulle achieved a negotiated settlement. In effect he conceded independence unconditionally, and left the *pieds-noirs* to choose "the suitcase or the coffin." Most chose the suitcase.

The Algerian war was traumatic for France, and still more for the Algerians who suffered by far the largest portion of the war's million or so casualties. It was a graphic illustration of the lengths to which communities driven by nationalism will go to defend or assert control of territory. It also decolonized France. In the course of the war, de Gaulle conceded independence to almost all of France's colonies in sub-

Africa and Southwest Asia in 1988

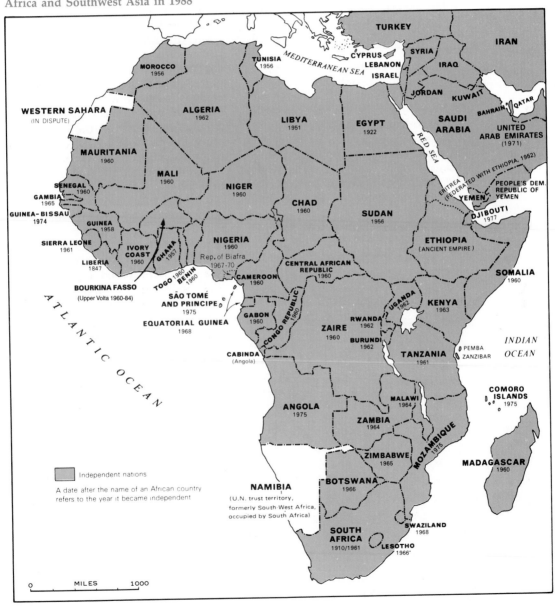

Saharan Africa: Guinea in 1958, and Cameroun, Chad, the Central African Republic, Congo-Brazzaville, Dahomey, Gabon, Ivory Coast, Mali, Niger, Senegal, and Togo in 1960.

The lesser empires of Holland and Belgium passed more quietly than did that of France. The Dutch found a "Republic of Indonesia" barring their return to the East Indies in 1945. Its leader was Achmet Sukarno, a charismatic nationalist who had collaborated with the Japanese to gain Indonesian independence. Four years of intermittent negotiations and "police actions" by the Dutch armed forces ultimately led under U.S. pressure to an agreement in November 1949 that granted independence, except for the Dutch territory of West Irian (the Dutch half of New Guinea), which Sukarno seized from the Dutch in 1962–63.

The Belgians gave the most spectacular example of irresponsible decolonization. Their Congo empire, which the Berlin Conference of 1884–85 had graciously assigned to King Leopold, had long been a by-word for relentless brutality. Its rubber plantations,

worked by native forced labor, were the subject of international protest even before World War I. And the Belgian state, which took the colony over from Leopold's private Congo Company, did far less than other colonizers to create a Western-educated elite. When the approaching independence of the neighboring French Congo (Congo-Brazzaville) inspired nationalist riots, the Belgians panicked, packed, and left in mid-1960. The Belgian-officered Congolese army mutinied. A multi-cornered civil war and massacres of both tribal enemies and whites followed. Belgian mining companies hired mercenaries to hold the copper-rich province of Katanga. It required four years and 20,000 United Nations troops to restore even a semblance of order. The victor was ultimately the head of the Congolese army, Joseph Mobuto, who established a corrupt but durable dictatorship in 1966, and changed the country's name to Zaire.

Portugal's colonies were the first European seaborne empire; they were also the last. The Portuguese military-clerical dictatorship of Antonio Salazar (1932–68) lost Indian enclaves such as Goa to an unprovoked Indian attack in 1961. In Africa—in Angola, Mozambique, and the west African mini-colony of Guinea-Bissau—Portugal elected to fight. The resulting commitment of 150,000 troops from the early 1960s until 1974 bled Portugal's already backward economy. In the end, Salazar gave way to a less effective successor. The Portuguese army, politicized by its long struggle in Africa, overthrew the government in Lisbon in 1974 and dismantled Portugal's empire.

A bloody scramble followed. Indonesia invaded the Portuguese island of East Timor, and in subjugating it killed up to a third of its almost 700,000 people. In Angola, Portugal's withdrawal led to the flight of most remaining whites, economic collapse, civil war between rival groups, and the intervention of the Soviet Union, Cuba, and South Africa (see p. 1040). In Mozam-

Chaos in the Congo, 1963: government paratroopers chase a mutinous policeman.

bique the Marxist-Leninist *Frelimo* ("Front for the Liberation of Mozambique") of Samora Machel took power. In Guinea-Bissau, the Lisbon-educated Amilcar Cabral, the most skillful of Portugal's adversaries, built a movement that grasped independence in 1973–74 without a civil war. But by then Cabral himself had already perished by assassination, a victim of rivalries within his own movement. As he had foreseen, the real test of his movement—as of the rulers of all "new nations"—came after independence.

RICH AND POOR

The new nations, for the most part, were and remain desperately poor in relative terms. In the 1960s, at independence, the poorest had annual per capita levels of gross national product (GNP)—the best indicator of a society's aggregate wealth or poverty—of 100 or less 1965 dollars. That compared unfavorably with Britain's level in 1700, before industrialization, of roughly 300 1965 dollars. Only Japan, with a per capita national product in the 1870s of a mere $74 (1965) was significantly lower than the West at the beginning of its industrialization.

Was widespread "Third World" poverty a consequence of Western wealth, as "Third Worldist" theoreticians have maintained? Little evidence supports that view. The West had been rich, inquisitive, and technologically sophisticated *before* its expansion. The capital and markets that fuelled Britain's development, and still more that of Britain's European competitors, were overwhelmingly internal. The West found the "Third World," with the exceptions of India, China, and Japan, already poor and weak. And India and China failed to match the growth rates of the West after 1800 not because of Western colonial occupation—which was not complete in India until the 1850s and was confined to coastal enclaves in China—but because

they failed to develop machine power on their own.

Europe's world supremacy was a byproduct not a cause of its industrial revolution, a byproduct of Europe's increasing mastery over nature and of the vast disparity in *power* that mastery created. Europeans rarely disdained plunder, but plunder extracted from the conquered played a minor role in Europe's growth; from 1492 to the late seventeenth century, Spain seized more plunder than any other state, but its economy became ever more poor and backward compared with those of the Netherlands and Britain.

If Western wealth was not a major cause of "Third World" poverty, might not colonial occupation itself have set the "Third World" back? A variety of "Third Worldist" theorists have argued that colonialism, by creating dependent economies based on commodities such as gold, silver, copper, tobacco, sugar, rubber, grain, and livestock, distorted the economic growth of the "Third World." The critics have maintained that without European interference, "Third World" growth would have been both better balanced and more rapid than it has been. They have also argued that colonialist "cultural imperialism" or "deculturation" of the "Third World" has discredited traditional cultures without offering adequate replacement. The consequent cultural and psychological disorientation, they have suggested, is itself a cause of slow growth.

Neither hypothesis is verifiable, since Europe *did* intervene and the native states did collapse under its impact. But the evidence from what actually happened speaks against it. Eighty years or less—the typical period of colonial domination in Africa—is a short time indeed for domination to have produced the fundamental changes that the critics allege. One of the very poorest states, Ethiopia (1985 per capita GNP of $110), only suffered occupation for six years, from 1936 to 1941. The Italians massacred Ethiopians with a will, but had no time for serious eco-

nomic exploitation or "deculturation."
And most "Third Worldist" critics,
while drawing inspiration from Marx,
appear to have forgotten that Marx
hailed British rule in India as the triumphant "annihilation of old Asiatic society, and the laying of the material
foundations of Western society in
Asia." Marx, wrong-headedly or not,
saw colonialism as the *precondition* for
sustained economic growth in much of
the non-Western world.

But, the critics have replied, has the
West not throttled "Third World"
growth after independence through
continuing "neocolonialism," through
a relationship of "informal empire"
with dependent "Third World" economies? Again, the evidence suggests the
contrary. In the nineteenth century, it
was precisely the most dependent

economies, those most closely tied to
Britain's "informal empire" of trade
and overseas investment—the United
States, Argentina, Canada, Australia,
New Zealand—that developed fastest.
In the late twentieth century the
fastest-developing "Third World"
economies have been those most ori-
ented toward the world economy dominated by the "First World" industrial
democracies.

States such as Indonesia and Malaysia (with oil) or Brazil (without it) have
forged ahead between 1965 and 1985 at
annual per capita growth rates of over
4 percent. South Korea, Taiwan, and
the Chinese-populated mini-states of
Hong Kong and Singapore, at between
6 and 8 percent a year, have made the
most spectacular gains of all. Even in
Africa, some states that have started
poor have made remarkable advances:
Cameroons and Congo-Brazzaville had
per capita growth rates over the 1965–
85 period of over 3 percent. Conversely, Argentina, which in 1900 appeared poised to be another Australia
or New Zealand, has stagnated since
the 1914–18 collapse of Britain's "informal empire." By 1985 Argentina's per
capita GNP had dipped below that of
South Korea, which had been desperately poor at the turn of the century.

The fortunes of states naturally vary
with those of the world economy.
Booms, such as the one that bore world
trade upwards from the 1950s until the
"oil shock" of 1973, benefit almost all
states. Downturns such as the savage
declines that followed 1973 and the
renewed disruption of oil supplies in
1979 (see p. 1060) disproportionately affect the very poorest, which depend on
imported oil but have few exports with
which to pay for that oil. The peculiar
cure the rich offered after 1973 was, if
anything, worse than the disease—
"petrodollar recycling." The OPEC
states took payments for oil in dollars.
They deposited their immense profits
in U.S. or European banks. The banks,
oblivious to risk, then happily lent
those "petrodollars" at high interest
rates to "Third World" countries. The

Losers . . .

At least 16 countries achieved a negative per capita growth rate
from the 1960s to the 1980s; in other words, they got steadily
poorer.

	Popu-lation (millions)	Annual per capita GNP (1985 $)	1965–85 growth in annual per capita GNP	Life expect-ancy at birth	Literacy (percent) (1982–84)
Uganda	14.7		−2.6	49	52
Chad	5.0		−2.3	45	17
Ghana	12.7	380	−2.2	53	30
Zaire	30.6	170	−2.1	51	46
Niger	6.4	250	−2.1	44	10
Nicaragua	3.3	770	−2.1	59	66
Madagascar	10.2	240	−1.9	52	53
Zambia	6.7	390	−1.6	52	54
Liberia	2.2	470	−1.4	50	24
Somalia	5.4	280	−.7	46	60
Jamaica	2.2	940	−.7	73	76
Senegal	6.6	370	−.6	47	10
C. African Rep.	2.6	260	−.2	49	20
Bolivia	6.4	470	−.2	53	63
El Salvador	4.8	820	−.2	64	65
Chile	12.1	1430	−.2	70	94

Source: World Bank, *World Development Report 1987* (New York: Oxford
University Press, 1987), pp. 202–203.

"Third World" countries in turn spent the money as much for prestige projects as for oil. Their resulting debts rose daily by compound interest and amounted to $1.25 trillion by 1988. "Petrodollar recycling" ominously resembled the reparation—war debt—U.S. loan merry-go-round of the 1920s. It also suggested that Western bankers and their regulators were deeply ignorant of the history of international debt—a history of repudiation.

As an alternative to loans, "Third World" critics and Western development economists have suggested large-scale gifts from the rich. Unfortunately, little empirical evidence suggests that massive infusions of capital would help. The West did not develop as a result of capital pumped in from outside. The post-1945 economic growth of nations as disparate as Germany and Japan suggests that capital is unimportant compared to human capital. In the "Third World" itself, Ethiopia received $2.26 billion in Western aid between 1979 and 1985, and got steadily poorer. The Sudan received $5.35 billion from 1979 to 1985—80 percent of its 1985 GNP—with similar results. Aid goes almost inevitably not to the peoples of the "Third World" or to their entrepreneurs, but to their ruling bureaucracies, the very organizations whose policies arguably prolong poverty. Even large amounts of aid have failed to make many poor countries capable of exporting to pay for their imports. Much aid has instead funded magnificent and useless new capitals, superhighways for the cars of single-party elites, and bankrupt steel mills rising like "cathedrals in the desert."

Perhaps growth or its absence is chiefly a function of the *internal* conditions within "Third World" states and economies, rather than of their subordinate position in the world market or of their shortages of capital. Perhaps political, social, and economic traditions, the extent of literacy, and the policies of "Third World" governments themselves are predominantly responsible for growth or its absence. Explor-

Winners . . .

Some economies, despite a position of "dependence" on the larger economies of the "First World," have made gains that range from considerable to spectacular.

	Population (millions)	Annual per capita GNP (1985 $)	1965–85 growth in annual per capita GNP	Life expectancy at birth	Literacy (percent) (1982–84)
Botswana	1.1	840	8.3	57	35
Singapore	2.6	7420	7.6	73	84
South Korea	41.1	2150	6.6	69	90+
Lesotho	1.5	470	6.5	54	60
Hong Kong	5.4	6230	6.1	76	75
Hungary	10.6	1950	5.8	71	98.9
Jordan	3.5	1560	5.8	65	71
Oman	1.2	6730	5.7	54	20
North Yemen	8.0	550	5.3	45	15
Indonesia	162.2	530	4.8	55	62
China	1040.3	310	4.8	69	65
Malaysia	15.6	2000	4.4	68	65
Brazil	135.6	1640	4.3	65	76
Yugoslavia	23.1	2070	4.1	72	90.5
Syria	10.5	1570	4.0	64	47
Tunisia	7.1	1190	4.0	63	62
Thailand	51.7	800	4.0	64	82

Source: World Bank, *World Development Report 1987* (New York: Oxford University Press, 1987), pp. 202–203.

ing the validity of that hypothesis requires dividing the "Third World" into its cultural, political, and economic components.

NEW STATES AND OLD: THE "THIRD WORLD" DIVIDED

The "Third World" contains at least five major groups of states: the Chinese cultural area, the Islamic Middle East, South Asia, Latin America, and Africa south of the Sahara. Politically, "Third World" states range from Right authoritarian military regimes, such as those of South Korea or Chile, through attempted democracies, such as the Philippines after 1986, to hermit "socialist" states such as Burma, to the Marxist-Leninist dictatorships of the "second Soviet empire" (see pp. 1040–41). Economically, "Third World" states range from market economies with some government direction (South Korea, Singapore, Ivory Coast) through "African socialist" experiments (Tanzania, Ghana), to "de-Stalinizing" socialist economies (China and possibly Vietnam), to Stalinist centralized economies (North Korea, Cuba). These characteristics intersect in manifold ways, and help account for the wide diversity of outcomes.

Confucian East Asia

Culturally, China has influenced its neighbors—Vietnam to the south and Korea and Japan to the northeast—from the beginning of recorded history. The Confucian pattern that China exemplified placed a high value on literacy, hierarchy, the subordination of the individual to the group. Those qualities made densely populated rice-growing economies work. At least in nineteenth-century China, that pattern may initially have retarded growth by its very success and durability. Japan, which rose to the Western challenge most readily, was always less Confucian than China, thanks to its hereditary warrior ruling caste. China and its neighbors, highly developed cultures with an ethos of literacy, duty, and relentless hard work, were nevertheless best equipped for economic growth of all the non-Western world.

But politics imposed differing outcomes. In Japan, small size helped in the consolidation of a modern state; a fortunate combination of centralization (the Tokugawa Shogunate and the traditions of the Imperial house) and decentralization (the "feudal" domains) gave innovators both their political vehicle for change and their opportunity to seize power. In China, the empire's unwieldiness, the rigidity of its Manchu rulers, and its initial choice of armed resistance rather than accommodation to the "barbarians" all conspired

to produce collapse, according to the recurring historical pattern discerned by the Chinese themselves. The immense Taiping rebellion of the 1850s and 1860s prefigured the far greater upheaval of the twentieth century: four decades of devastating civil war, Japanese invasion, and war in Korea with the United States (1911–53).

Mao Zedong (Mao Tse-tung) and his Party mobilized the peasantry by appealing to land hunger and roused the urban intellectuals by offering a vehicle for nationalism. That was a winning combination. But Mao, intoxicated with revolutionary messianism, soon sought to pioneer in economic development as he had in the adaptation of Marxism-Leninism to a peasant society. In two disastrous experiments, the "Great Leap Forward" (1958–59) and the "Great Proletarian Cultural Revolution" (1966–69), he almost destroyed both the Chinese economy and his own party. "Politics in command!" was Mao's guiding principle; the death by famine of up to 27 million in the "three lean years" of 1959–61 was the result. The forcing of China's peasantry into "communes" and a crash industrialization based on amateur back-yard blast furnaces reduced the economy to a shambles. After that débâcle, Mao's comrades sought to remove him from power while retaining him as a living symbol of the Revolution and of the Party's legitimacy.

But Mao did not resign himself to being thus embalmed and placed on display like the dead Lenin. With the help of Jiang Qing (Chiang Ch'ing), the former Shanghai film actress who had become his second wife, and of the Red Army political leader Lin Biao (Lin Piao), Mao took power back in 1966 through a coup in Beijing (Peking). He then launched an all-out struggle in the provinces against his own Party and government bureaucracy. The stake as Mao conceived it was the continuation of the Revolution: "There were two possibilities. There could be a continued development of the Revolution towards communism. The other possi-

The cult of Mao: National Day celebrations, 1966.

bility was that youth could negate the Revolution and do bad things: make peace with imperialism [the West] . . . and take a stand beside the small percentage of counter-revolutionaries still in the country."

The "Great Proletarian Cultural Revolution" enthused Western student radicals; to China it brought chaos. Groups of youthful fanatics, the "Red Guards," attacked foreigners, high Party figures, government bureaucrats, and one another. The economy again threatened to disintegrate. Another 10 to 20 million may have perished from Red Guard purges, internecine fighting, and malnutrition. The army ultimately restored order while Mao's associates such as the durable Communist mandarin, Zhou Enlai (Chou En-lai), sapped the power of the radicals. Mao himself lost his grip with increasing age and died in 1976. But his work, as one successor summed it up in the mid-1980s, had been catastrophic: "We have wasted twenty years." Only in the late 1970s did China begin to "de-Maoize" and show its economic potential (see pp. 1046–47).

North Korea and Vietnam, although they began under foreign rule rather than under informal domination, followed China's pattern. The Communist "monarchy" of the aged Kim Il-Sung, who in 1984 appointed his son, Kim Jong-Il, as his successor, remains one of the world's most closed and Stalinist states. Its only noteworthy product is military power and its primary export is weaponry and advice on war and terrorism to states as far afield as Iran, Zimbabwe, Grenada, and Nicaragua; North Korean military advisers currently serve in 34 countries. Vietnam, after its 1975 conquest of the South, attempted to impose the Stalinist pattern already proven a failure in the North. The result was economic regression (see p. 1046). A younger generation of leaders came to power in 1986 and announced a sort of NEP (see p. 909): a grudging latitude for private enterprise "within the socialist system."

Why Maoism?

Lu Xun (Lu Hsün, 1881–1936), China's greatest twentieth century short-story writer and social critic, wrote bitter pages in the 1920s that suggest some of the ingredients of Mao's success.

It has never been granted to the Chinese people that they are human beings; at best, they have been raised to the level of slaves, and this is still the case today. In the past, they were often lower than slaves. The Chinese masses are neutral; in time of war they do not know what faction they belong to, and in fact they belong to any faction. Come the rebels: considering the people as being the government's, they loot and murder. Comes the regular army: instead of recognizing its own, it loots and murders too, as if the people belonged to the rebels. At this point, the only wish of the population is to find a Master, a Master who would deign to accept them as his people—no, not even that—who would deign to accept them as his cattle. The people would be ready to eat grass if necessary; all they ask is that the Master point out in what direction they must trot. . . .

As a rule, after each period of anarchy, when chaos reaches its climax, some personality appears—more powerful, more clever, more cunning (sometimes a foreigner)—to unify the empire and grant it some measure of order. . . .

In the end, the simplest and most adequate way of describing the history of China would be to distinguish between two types of periods: (1) the periods when the people wish in vain to enjoy a stable slave condition; and (2) the periods when the people manage to enjoy a stable slave condition. The alternation of these two states is what our old scholars called "the cycle of chaos and order."

From Simon Leys (Pierre Ryckmans), *Chinese Shadows* (New York: Penguin Books, 1978), pp. 200–201.

In contrast, the non-Communist states of Chinese-influenced East and Southeast Asia have prospered mightily. Malaysia, politically Malay but with an economy under the control of its large overseas Chinese minority, has grown at a per capita rate of over 4 percent. Thailand, the one South or Southeast Asian state to avoid colonial occupation, has grown at a comparable rate, thanks to its Chinese minority and relatively literate population. It benefited both from an infusion of dollars during

The Red Guards, vanguard of Mao's revolution against his own party.

the Vietnam War and a subsequent boom in Pacific trade. In Korea, Japanese colonialism (1905–45) and the patronage of the United States helped provide South Korea with an industrial infrastructure and a Western-educated and technologically expert elite capable of swiftly emulating Japan. Politically, South Korea enjoyed enforced stability. The harsh domination after 1948 of a Harvard-educated politician, Syngman Rhee, gave way in 1960–61 to 25 years of military dictatorship. In 1986–87 the new middle class that Korea's industrialization created began forcefully demanding political rights. The military loosened its grip and permitted an election; the military candidate won but promised an increasing measure of democratization. A similar absence of democracy has attended the spectacular per capita growth rates of culturally Chinese and economically capitalist Taiwan, Hong Kong, and Singapore. They outstripped all other contenders including Japan, and suggest in miniature the world-shaking potential of China itself should its ruling Party irrevocably place "economics in command."

The Islamic Middle East

Major cleavages divide the independent states of the Middle East. The most important are (1) between categories of regime, (2) between states aligned with the West or with the Soviet Union, and (3) between states with oil and states without. In addition, cleavages between tribes and between branches of Islam have both split states from one another and divided them internally.

Three main types of regime exist. First come the traditional monarchies and sheikdoms, based on Bedouin or other tribal loyalties—Saudi Arabia, Morocco, Jordan, and the Gulf states from Kuwait to Oman. Egypt, Iraq, and Libya originally belonged to that category, but their monarchies succumbed to military coups in 1952, 1958, and 1969, respectively. The second category is the secular states—Egypt, Syria, Iraq, Tunisia, Algeria, Libya. The Turkey of Kemal Atatürk—military-dominated and dedicated to introducing Western technology and ideas—provided an initial model. Like Turkey, most such states have attempted to make the state the chief motor of economic development. Most have claimed to embody an "Arab socialism" that in practice meant deadening bureaucratic controls that engendered corruption and black markets. Finally, a third model, a revolutionary "Islamic Republic" based on Shi'ite Islam, arose in Iran after 1979 (see pp. 1051–53). It has so far remained unique.

In their external relations, the Middle Eastern states have tended to profess "non-alignment." In practice, they have tilted toward the United States or the Soviet Union; despite much discussion of cleavages between "North" and "South," it is the East-West conflict that has divided the world most deeply. Status quo states such as the traditional monarchies have normally favored the United States. Roosevelt took over Britain's patronage of Saudi Arabia and its oil in 1944–45, and that relationship has endured. Morocco, under its durable monarch King Hassan II (1961–), has usually maintained ties with Washington, as have moderate secular states such as the Tunisia of Habib Bourguiba (1956–87) and the

Egypt of Anwar Sadat after he broke with Moscow in 1976. Algeria, "nonaligned" in rhetoric but less so in practice, has also tended to tilt toward Western Europe and the United States, its customers for gas and oil. Iran until its 1978–79 revolution posed as a bulwark of Western influence in the Gulf—to mask its monarch's megalomaniacal ambitions.

Iran excepted, the Soviets have tended to draw to themselves the most expansionist of Middle Eastern states—Nasser's Egypt, Libya after the revolution of Colonel Muammar Qaddafi in 1969, the Syria of the merciless Hafiz al-Assad (1970–), the Iraq of his equally remorseless counterpart Saddam Hussein (1979–), and the "People's Democratic Republic of Yemen." Lavish provision of arms, the Soviet Union's only major industrial export, and numerous military and "police" advisers have cemented these ties. Soviet influence has nevertheless sometimes been transient. Moscow's position in the region has yet to recover from its loss of Egypt in 1972–76.

After internal politics and external alignments, the possession of oil likewise divides the Middle Eastern states into two classes. Saudi Arabia, Libya, Algeria, Iran, Iraq, Kuwait, the Gulf sheikdoms, and even Egypt after its recovery of Sinai in 1982 have enjoyed to a greater or lesser extent the bounty of oil. After 1973, when the Arab and other oil-producing states combined into the OPEC cartel and more than doubled the real price of oil in a year, that bounty increased markedly. But the newly rich have yet to convert their oil wealth into modern economies. Saudi Arabia and the sheikdoms have small populations that as yet show insufficient willingness to surrender their desert traditions. Secular states with oil sometimes have too little of it, as in Egypt or Algeria. Others smother initiative beneath layers of bureaucracy or attempt to ban enterprise entirely, as in Qaddafi's Libya.

Religious and ethnic fractures likewise divide the Islamic Middle East. Iran after its 1978–79 revolution emerged as the world's only Shi'ite state; religion and Persian nationalism combined to set it at odds with its Sunni Arab neighbors. Iraq, although Arab in population, is mostly Shi'ite in religion; the cleavage between Shi'ite and Sunni is a major source of internal weakness although Arab nationalism partially offsets it. Turkey, Iraq, and Iran contain sizable and militant minorities of Kurds, a mountain warrior people who boast that "Kurds have no friends." Syria contains large Christian communities and its officer corps and rulers are Alawites, a small Shi'ite sect that ruthlessly dominates a Sunni majority.

In Lebanon, five major communities contend. The last census (1932) showed that 29 percent of the population was Maronite Christian, 22 percent Sunni Moslem, 20 percent Shi'ite Moslem, and 7 percent Druze, a heretical and combative Moslem sect. The French, on their departure in 1946, left Lebanon a parliamentary regime that gave the presidency to the Maronites, the prime ministership to the Sunni, and the office of army chief of staff to the Druzes.

Traditional monarchs and secular rulers: King Faisal of Saudi Arabia (1964–75) and (below, left to right) a 1970 encounter between Gaafar Mohammed Nimeiri of the Sudan (1969–85), Muammar Qaddafi of Libya (1969–   ), and Nasser of Egypt (1954–70).

But the relative weights of the communities soon changed, and a fifth group, the Palestinian refugees, took a hand. By 1984, the Shi'ites made up an estimated 31 percent of the population, the Maronites stood second at 25 percent, the Sunni third at 20 percent, and the Druzes had declined to 6 percent. In 1975 a bid for more power by the rapidly growing Shi'ites helped start a religious-ethnic civil war that still continues.

Finally, nationalism divides the Middle Eastern states, despite the common "Arab" character that all except Iran and Turkey share. Efforts at union between states, such as Nasser's attempt to absorb Syria into a "United Arab Republic" (1958–61) or Quaddafi's federations with Egypt (1972–73), Tunisia (1974), and Morocco (1984–86), have all failed. The rulers of Syria had no desire to become a mere province of Egypt. They possessed their own national consciousness and sense of mission, the creation of a "Greater Syria" that includes Lebanon and Palestine. Nasser also failed to subjugate North Yemen between 1962 and 1968 despite massive Egyptian use of Soviet tanks and mustard gas.

The multiple divisions between sects, tribes, and states have tended to stunt the Middle Eastern states both politically and economically. And the state machines and armies of the Islamic secular states have also proved the classic ground for assassinations and coups. In the absence of settled political traditions and long-established legitimacy, as elsewhere in the "Third World," power grows out of the barrel of a gun. Those who have the guns and the smattering of Western technical knowledge needed to use them have seen no reason why they should not command the state and direct the national economy. The resulting one-party regimes range from the merely inefficient (Egypt, Tunisia, Algeria) to the terrifying (Syria, Libya, Iraq); Hafiz al-Assad of Syria and his Soviet advisers chose to deal with Sunni unrest in 1982 by shelling flat much of the town

of Hama and killing perhaps 30,000. The traditional monarchies tend on balance to be less aggressive, less oppressive, and better economic performers than the secular states. But their stability comes from their traditions, the very traditions that economic development undermines. No stable order to replace the defunct Ottoman Empire is in sight, and the rise of Islamic militance has generated new and savage conflicts.

South Asia

The lands of southern Asia are disparate. Four of them, India, Pakistan, Bangladesh (East Pakistan until 1971), and Sri Lanka (Ceylon until 1972) are historically closely linked. They are the ultimate successors, after the British interlude, to the Mughal empire. To the east lies Burma, a borderland between southern Asian and Chinese culture. Indonesia, dominated by Islam, and the Philippines, a compound of Malay, Islamic, Spanish, and U.S. influences, are unique, but their village-based societies are similar in many ways to the pattern of southern Asia. They are Asian but not Confucian.

India and Pakistan have remained locked in struggle since 1947–48. Pakistan, split between the dominant Punjab to the west and East Bengal to the east, failed to consolidate itself. India, under Gandhi's violent successor, Jawaharlal Nehru, quarreled with China over border areas in Tibet in 1961–62; the Chinese army gave the Indians a sharp and persuasive rebuff. Fighting between India and Pakistan erupted once more in 1965–66, and the Soviet Union, seeking favor with India as a counterweight to Mao's increasingly hostile China, brokered a compromise. In 1970–71 the East Bengalis sought autonomy; the generals who ruled West Pakistan answered with massacres. Under Nehru's combative daughter, Indira Gandhi (unrelated to Mohandas Gandhi either by blood or political philosophy), India intervened and swiftly dismembered Pakistan.

East Bengal became independent Bangladesh and soon passed under the rule
of its army. India was now supreme on
the subcontinent, a status confirmed by
its explosion in 1974 of what it whimsi-
cally termed a "peaceful nuclear device." Pakistan countered India's
weapon with clandestine development
of its own "Islamic bomb." The acquisition of Western nuclear fuel technology
through espionage and China's alleged
gift in the early 1980s of a tested bomb
design have perhaps given Pakistan a
temporary edge.

Despite continuing interstate strife
and periodic religious-ethnic massacres
("communal violence") within India
and Pakistan, economic growth has
been steady although slow. In per capita terms, India grew between 1965 and
1985 at a rate of 1.7 percent per year,
Pakistan at 2.6 percent; only Bangladesh, among the world's poorest
states, stagnated at .4 percent. In the
north Indian plain, new strains of rice
and wheat and the entrepreneurship of
India's Sikh minority made an agricultural "Green Revolution" that promised India eventual self-sufficiency in
food. A powerful industrial economy,
although bound with doctrinaire "socialist" red tape, has arisen around cities such as Bombay. A small but growing minority of India's 800 million
people live at "First World" levels.

Pakistan, except for brief interludes
in the 1950s and 1970s, remained a military dictatorship, but India persisted
in the parliamentary traditions derived
from Britain. Indira Gandhi's attempt
at dictatorship in 1975–77 collapsed
amid universal condemnation, although she returned with a majority in
1980 after promising not to repeat the
experiment. Her downfall was the Sikh
minority, whose extremists sought an
independent Sikh state, "Khalistan,"
carved from the Punjab, India's agricultural heart. When heavily armed
Sikh militants seized the Sikh Golden
Temple at Amritsar in 1984, Indira
Gandhi evicted them with the Indian
army and much bloodshed after negotiations failed. Sikhs assassinated Mrs.

Mohandas Gandhi enjoying a joke with his disciple and successor Jawaharlal Nehru (prime minister 1947–64).

Gandhi in retaliation; Hindus then
killed many thousands of Sikhs living
in Hindu areas. Mrs. Gandhi's son and
successor, Rajiv Gandhi, third of the
Congress Party dynasty that Nehru
founded, has as yet failed to pacify either the Sikhs or the numerous other
disaffected communities in India's
patchwork of languages and cultures.

To the south, Sri Lanka showed
great promise. Its peoples were 60 per-

Indira Gandhi (prime minister 1966–77, 1980–84), daughter of Nehru and architect of India's hegemony in South Asia.

cent literate; its agricultural export economy grew rapidly until the 1960s. Then nationalism caught up with it. Alongside the majority Sinhalese, Buddhist in religion and 70 percent of the population, lived a Tamil minority of Hindu religion that had originally immigrated from southern India. Under British rule, the two communities had lived in relative peace, but the creation of an independent sovereign state brought with it a struggle for mastery over that state. Within a decade of independence, Sinhalese politicians had imposed Sinhalese as the official language. Sinhalese ideologues proclaimed their alleged superiority as descendants of conquerors from the north in the sixth century B.C.

The Tamils, an enterprising group that dominated commerce and the professions, responded first with riots and then, after 1983, with guerrilla war and demands for a separate Tamil state around the city of Jaffna in northern Sri Lanka. A cycle of terror and reprisal similar to that in Algeria after 1954 locked Sinhalese and Tamil nationalisms into seemingly irreconcilable conflict over the same territory. Indian army intervention in 1987 to broker a peace goaded the "Tamil Tiger" guerrillas to savage attacks on the Indians and to further massacres of Sinhalese civilians. Despite the war, Sri Lanka maintained a growth rate from 1980 to 1985 of 5.1 percent, but economic growth can scarcely survive further large-scale bloodshed.

Further east, Burma retreated into resentful isolation; in 1962 its most durable leader, General Ne Win, proclaimed a non-aligned "Burmese Road to Socialism" that has led to poverty for all except bureaucrats and black marketeers. Indonesia, further south, enjoyed the massive advantage of oil. Sukarno ruled until 1965–68 and squandered that wealth on palaces, monuments, and mistresses. His successor, General Suharto, took power in the aftermath of the failed Communist coup of 1965 and the immense massacre of Communists that followed. His regime began to realize Indonesia's economic potential, thanks to close economic ties with Japan.

The Philippines suppressed a Communist insurgency after independence in 1947, then succumbed to military dictatorship under General Ferdinand Marcos (1965–86). Marcos's power disintegrated after 1983, when his associates arranged the assassination of a key opponent, Benigno Aquino. With the backing of key army figures, the Catholic Church, U.S. opinion, and the overwhelming majority of articulate Filipinos, the dead man's widow, Corazon Aquino, took power in a largely bloodless "people power" uprising after Marcos sought to steal the 1986 election. Aquino faces economic stagnation and a second and exceedingly bloody Communist insurgency begun during the Marcos years. Despite the restoration of something resembling parliamentary democracy, the prospects for stability appeared poor.

The Three Latin Americas

The "new nations" that arose in Latin America between 1811 and 1839 had few of the advantages of their Dutch and American predecessors. Spain had imposed a centralized bureaucratic pattern that prevented the Creoles, native-born of Spanish descent, from developing experience in self-government—in contrast to the pattern of British "white" colonies from North America to Australia. Narrow landed oligarchies ruled alongside a disproportionately powerful land-owning Church. And Spain had imposed on its colonial economies a pattern similar to that in politics—centralized controls and ruinous taxation that stunted enterprise. Anarchy and despotism, economic stagnation or regression in most cases followed independence (see p. 775).

But not all of the new states suffered the same misfortunes. Latin America is almost as divided as the Islamic Middle East or the "Third World" itself. With the exception of miscellaneous small states such as Guyana and Suriname, the British and Dutch ex-colonies between Venezuela and Brazil, Latin American states fall into three principal categories. First are those with a Creole or European majority: Costa Rica, Argentina, and Uruguay. They began as classic settler economies: Europe transported to the New World. They thrived in the nineteenth century on commodity exports such as coffee, beef, hides, wool, and grain. But as elsewhere, politics intervened.

Costa Rica's parliamentary regime rests on a base of prosperous small landowners, and has maintained an enviable degree of stability and prosperity since the late 1940s. Not so Uruguay. A drop in commodity prices and

Central and South America in 1988

distended bureaucracies and state in-dustries that employed a third of Uruguay's workers brought stagnation and massive inflation by the 1960s. A Marxist urban guerrilla movement, the "Tupamaro National Liberation Front," arose among disaffected children of the upper classes. It sought to destroy parliamentary democracy by provoking the state to violent reprisals that would "unmask" its supposed "true nature" as the organ of repression of domestic "capitalism" and foreign "neocolonialism." The Tupamaros duly brought down the parliamentary regime in 1973–74. The military dictatorship that followed erased the guerrillas with torture and "disappearances." Parliamentary democracy perished, but implacable Rightist dictatorship, not Marxist millennium, replaced it. Civilian government returned hesitantly in 1985.

Argentina traveled a road similar to Uruguay's, but even more savage. Its settler population was overwhelmingly Spanish and Italian, with large German, British, French, and Jewish communities; in 1900 the country had appeared poised to become another Australia. But the Great Depression ended what little political stability it enjoyed. Oligarchic military regimes gave way in 1944–46 to the populist dictatorship of Colonel Juan Perón, admirer of Mussolini and husband of the charismatic Eva (Evita) Duarte, patron saint of Argentina's "shirtless" dispossessed. An army coup destroyed Perón's regime in 1955, but his "Social Justice" [Justicialista] party lived on as Argentina's most powerful political force. Too weak and disunited to overthrow the military, it was strong enough to make Argentina ungovernable until the army wearily permitted Perón to return to power in 1973. Then Perón died in 1974. His third wife, Isabel Martínez Perón, a former cabaret dancer, sought to rule with counsel from the Perónist party and her astrologer. Inflation and a Tupamaro-style Leftist insurgency reduced Argentina to shambles.

In 1976 the military again seized power, and destroyed the guerrillas with torture and mass murder, dumping planeloads of drugged prisoners into the South Atlantic. Between 5,000 and 20,000 suspects "disappeared." The military killed with such abandon that fear of retribution thenceforth locked it into power. Only the inglorious defeat of its 1982 attempt to seize the Falkland Islands from Britain (see p. 1050) led to retreat, and to elections that returned as president a genuine democrat, Raul Alfonsín. Alfonsín had slightly better luck than his predecessors in dominating the Perónists and in spurring an economy crippled by state ownership and bureaucratic sloth. But Argentina's growth rate in GNP per capita from 1965 to 1985 has been .2 percent annually, scarcely better than no growth at all.

The second category of Latin American states, after those with European populations, are the ex-colonies of Spain with an Indian or *mestizo* majority. Of these Chile has the largest Creole population, at 25 percent; there and in most of the remainder, from Bolivia through Central America to Mexico, large *mestizo* or Indian groups remain permanently excluded from a share in power. In Peru and Bolivia, between 30 and 55 percent of the population consists of Indians who speak Quechua or Aymara rather than Spanish; literacy in many of these states is relatively low.

They have nevertheless traveled diverse paths. Mexico and Ecuador, thanks in part to oil, have enjoyed relatively high rates of growth since the 1950s, although the patronage needs and populist rhetoric of Mexico's ruling "Institutional Revolutionary Party" (PRI) have tended to stultify the economy with state-owned industries and unpredictable nationalizations. Colombia has also prospered in relative terms, despite a long-running "*violencia*" or permanent civil war between political parties, Leftist guerrillas, and cocaine lords. Panama, part of Colombia until the United States moved in to build the Canal, has prospered as a banking and shipping center despite the corrupt and oppressive rule of its "National Guard."

Oil did not save Venezuela, nor copper Chile. Venezuela's rulers for much of the twentieth century have been generals, of whom the most conspicuous and brutal were Juan Vincente Gomez (1908–35) and Marcos Peréz Jiménez (1952–58). Thereafter a succession of weak parliamentary regimes nationalized more and more of the economy; the drop in oil prices after 1982 drove Venezuela into negative per capita growth. The government of Chile, the oldest stable parliamentary regime on the continent, collapsed in 1973. Its politics had long been deadlocked between a Marxist Left, a Catholic Christian Democratic center, and a conservative Right. In 1969 the candidate of the Left, Salvador Allende, took power as president on the strength of a plurality of 36.3 percent, less than two points ahead of his closest rival. Despite undertakings to the contrary given to opposition parties that represented a majority of Chileans, Allende attempted to transform in a "socialist" direction an economy largely based on copper mining and inefficient protected industry. He also ostentatiously received Fidel Castro. Both the Nixon administration and the Chilean middle classes objected.

Allende's policies produced 323 percent inflation in 1972–73 and economic paralysis. Politically, he remained intent on a Marxist revolution for which he had no mandate; enthusiasts from all over Latin America and Europe flocked to Chile. In September 1973, with the support of the Right and even of some Christian Democrats, the armed forces rocketed and stormed the presidential palace, and rounded up the Left. Allende apparently killed himself with a treasured machine pistol, a gift of Castro. Allende's supporters accused Kissinger and the CIA of complicity in the coup; Washington had subsidized political opponents of

Argentina, 1973–83: the military, then Perón (above), the military again, and finally Alfonsín (below).

Allende and had attempted in 1970 to provoke the army against him. But no firm evidence of U.S. involvement in 1973 surfaced, despite lengthy congressional investigation. The generals and admirals who overthrew Allende had a domestic mandate.

Their leader, the uncompromising Augusto Pinochet, soon converted that mandate into one of Latin America's most ruthless dictatorships; the military shot between 3,000 and 10,000 Leftists in the months after the coup. Too late, the Christian Democrats and moderate Rightists realized that Pinochet, like Allende, considered himself a man with a mission—the extirpation rather than the establishment of Marxism. Pinochet has endured. The opposition remained too divided and too fearful of the remnants of the Marxist Left to present a credible alternative to dictatorship. Despite the dictatorship's dismantling of protective tariffs, Chile's growth rate has been a mere .5 percent per year from 1965 to 1985.

To the north, in Bolivia and Peru, military regimes predominated until the early 1980s. The Peruvian military ruled from 1968 to 1980 and adopted "Third Worldist" notions of economic development; it nationalized banks and foreign firms. The result was prolonged stagnation. The ensuing civilian government has done little better, and in addition faces an implacable insur-

Two Chilean motorcades:
Allende with Castro (1971)
and Pinochet (1986).

gency of Quechua-speaking Indians and university-educated Maoists that calls itself the *Sendero Luminoso,* the "Shining Path" to revolution. Bolivia too acquired a civilian government in the 1980s, but shows little sign of stability. The Central American states of Honduras, Guatemala, El Salvador, and Nicaragua are among the poorest in Latin America. Revolution and insurgency, explored in the next chapter, are both product and cause of the negative per capita growth rates of Nicaragua and El Salvador.

Finally, the largest of all Latin American states is in a category of its own—

Brazil. Its ethnic mixture, a unique compound of Portuguese, Africans, Italians, Germans, Slavs, East Indians, Japanese, Chinese, and native Indians, defies categorization; blacks remain at the bottom of the social scale, but color lines are less exclusive than in Spanish America. Above all, the New World society that Portugal established left far more room for local and individual initiative than in Spanish America. The result was a society that displays the extremes of wealth and poverty common both in Latin America and in other "new nations." But despite that maldistribution, an ever-growing foreign debt of over $100 billion, and political turmoil that led to army rule between 1964 and 1985, Brazil has prospered. Its per capita growth rate from 1965 to 1985 was 4.3 percent, one of the highest in the "Third World." Its industries have achieved considerable export success. Unfortunately the civilian rule restored in 1985 has yet to take hold convincingly. Galloping inflation, staggering external debt, and political incoherence may yet slow or halt development.

The Sorrows of Africa

No wretchedness in Latin America compares with that found from the fringes of the Sahara southwards. Of the sixteen states of over a million population with negative per capita growth rates between 1965 and 1985, eleven are in Africa south of the Sahara. Of the poorest states in terms of per capita annual GNP, most are African; a few others—Vietnam, Cambodia, Laos, and Afghanistan—probably belong in the same category, but reliable statistics are lacking.

African penury is no accident; Africa's states were poorest at independence. All suffer from a variety of disabilities. Literacy is sometimes below 10 percent. Those who acquire it, either from government or missionary schools, thereby isolate themselves from their society. Traditional animist cults, based on magic, do not prepare

their adherents to function in the cold "disenchanted" world of cause and effect, profit and loss. Islam, Africa's fastest growing religion, carries with it a hostility to the "Christian" West that often extends to Western economic ideas. And the Christian teaching missionaries who remained after independence have often had other priorities than economic development.

States for the most part follow the boundaries drawn by figures such as Bismarck, Lord Salisbury, and Leopold of Belgium, lines that cut across both tribal zones and customary economic units. Black Africa's traditional political units, empires such as those of the Ashanti or the Zulus, tended to expand rapidly for several generations, then crumble from lack of cohesion; they offered little precedent for the creation of nation-states on the European pattern. Economies tend to be subsistence agriculture or export-oriented monoculture. Only Nigeria with its massive oil reserves and the largest population in black Africa, Botswana with its diamonds, and Rhodesia and South Africa with their European economies based on the labor of the black majority ap-

Mengistu Haile Miriam of Ethiopia, exemplar of Lenin's definition of dictatorship: "a power that is not limited by any laws, not bound by any rules, and based directly on force."

The Poorest of the Poor

	Population (millions)	Annual per capita GNP (1985 $)	1965–85 growth in annual per capita GNP	Life expectancy at birth	Literacy (percent) (1982–84)
Ethiopia	42.3	110	.2	45	35
Bangladesh	100.6	150	.4	51	23
Burkina Faso	7.9	150	1.3	45	7
Mali	7.5	150	1.4	46	10
Bhutan	1.2	160		44	5
Mozambique	13.8	160		47	14
Nepal	16.5	160	.1	47	20
Malawi	7.0	170	1.5	45	25
Zaire	30.6	170	−2.1	51	46
Burma	36.9	190	2.4	59	78
Burundi	4.7	230	1.9	48	25
Togo	3.0	230	.3	51	18
Madagascar	10.2	240	1.9	52	53
Niger	6.4	250	2.1	44	10
Benin	4.0	260	.2	49	11
C. African Rep.	2.6	260	−.2	49	20

Source: World Bank, *World Development Report 1987* (New York: Oxford University Press, 1987), pp. 202–203.

Mobutu in 1965, shortly after taking power.

peared sure-fire economic prospects in the 1960s. Most black African states immediately worsened their economic plight by ill-conceived "socialist" measures. Compelling peasants to sell to the state at a fixed price that is sometimes below the cost of production has deprived Africa's farmers of incentives to farm. Much of the continent, self-sufficient in food at independence, now imports it. And food price subsidies for the largely nonproductive urban populations have swelled both their numbers and government debts.

Some states appeared poor prospects from the beginning. Uganda and the Central African Republic succumbed to terrifying dictatorships by former sergeants, Idi Amin Dada and Jean-Bedel Bokassa. Amin killed up to 300,000 between 1971 and 1979. He left the country in a shambles from which it has yet to recover. The states of the Saharan fringe, Mali, Burkina Faso, Niger, Chad, and the Sudan have suffered grievously from a combination of drought and of population pressure on their fragile semi-desert environment.

Ethiopia, east and south of the Sudan, suffered both from drought and from the backward-looking monarchy of Haile Selassie until its overthrow in 1974. His successors, the Marxist-Leninist zealots of the *Derg* ("Provisional Military Administrative Council"), proved far more terrifying than the aged "Lion of Judah." In 1977–78, amid purges and massacres, a Lieutenant Colonel Mengistu Haile Mariam emerged in command of state and army. With Soviet aid he sought implacably to subjugate the Eritreans, the people of the former Italian colony that the United Nations had conceded to Ethiopia on condition that its inhabitants enjoy autonomy. Mengistu also pursued a Stalinist program of collectivization ("villagization") that ruthlessly dispossessed and displaced millions of peasants. Since 1977, war, collectivization, and drought between them have killed more Ethiopians and Eritreans than did Mussolini. The Marxist regimes of Angola and Mo-

Bombed-out remains of a colonial-era house in Nigeria.

zambique, like that of Ethiopia, pressed nationalization and collectivization schemes with similar economic consequences, although less drastic human ones.

Other states adopted forms of "African socialism" less extreme than that of Ethiopia, but with little better results. Ghana achieved independence under Kwame Nkrumah, who styled himself "the Redeemer," established a dictatorship, took on East German and Chinese advisers, and cut a bold figure at "non-aligned" meetings until his removal by Ghana's army in 1966. Economically, Ghana fell steadily further behind its similar but more "capitalist" neighbor, the Ivory Coast; Ghana currently vegetates under the dictatorship of a former air force lieutenant. Tanzania's attempt at a village collectivism that supposedly drew on roots in traditional African culture proved an unmitigated economic disaster, in contrast to the relative success of its "capitalist" northern neighbor, Kenya. Zambia's nationalization of industries and land in the 1970s, along with drought, produced negative per capita growth.

Guinea-Bissau's one-party "socialist" dictatorship and self-inflicted economic failures have exasperated even those most patient of givers of development aid, the Swedes.

Among black Africa's largest and most populous states, Nigeria and Zaire have also proved disappointments. Nigeria's British-style parliamentary regime did not survive the strains of tribalism and of religious conflict between the Arab Moslem north and the black Christian and animist south (a conflict also found in the Sudan). An attempt by the Ibo people of southeast Nigeria to create an independent "Biafra" in 1967–70 met with defeat in a pitiless civil war that left over a million dead. Subsequently, the military ruled until a brief parliamentary interlude in 1979–83 that ended in disorganization and yet another coup. Nigeria's oil wealth prompted ambitious development projects and the building of a new capital—a frequent symbolic gesture of national integration and state power, from St. Petersburg, to Washington, to Brasilia, to Islamabad (Pakistan). But bureaucratic controls and the corruption they generate have slowed growth. As for Zaire, it profited from its great mineral wealth far less than Nigeria has profited from its oil. United Nations and Belgian military intervention helped Mobutu to survive numerous challenges from the provinces. His dictatorship also proved adept at borrowing from Western banks and at spending the money on prestige projects and its own perquisites.

Finally, Rhodesia-Zimbabwe and South Africa, the European economies in Africa, have expanded. Defeat in 1978 did not mean "the suitcase or the coffin" for Zimbabwe's whites. The Marxist victor, Robert Mugabe, pursued a unique course; he encouraged the white minority to remain provisionally and run the economy. But the Boers of South Africa refused to contemplate surrender (see p. 1056). Despite a slowdown produced by international embargoes and sanctions directed against their structure of racial domination, their economy continues to function. It still produces the modern weapons—including possibly nuclear weapons—needed to preserve the supremacy of the "white tribe" of southern Africa.

FUTURES FOR THE "THIRD WORLD"

The history of the "Third World" since 1945 can suggest a variety of conclusions, depending on the observer. The widely differing growth rates of "Third World" states over many years nevertheless make clear that subordination to more powerful economies is hardly a cause of stagnation or regression. The states that sought to *withdraw* from the world market—Burma, Vietnam, Cambodia, Uganda, Ethiopia, and "African socialist" experiments such as Tanzania and Ghana—have done worst. The miseries of those "enslaved by capitalism" are small indeed compared to the miseries of those not "enslaved" by it.

For good or ill development has meant "capitalist development." Private wealth often produces savage contrasts between extremes of luxury and misery. But it is also the only force that has so far powered sustained economic growth. Capitalist development raised the West from poverty; even Marx celebrated it for that. Even the societies over which Stalin and Mao once presided now look to capitalism for economic inspiration (see pp. 1046 and 1063). And sustained capitalist development appears to require guarantees of rights against the state, rights that many "Third World" regimes are reluctant to concede.

The central obstacles to "Third World" development are thus politics and ideology. Most "Third World" single-party elites fiercely distrust private wealth because it is a form of power not under their own control. They have taken easily to forms of Marxism, which provides ready-made legitimation for dictatorship ("their own, naturally," as the anarchist Bakunin once put it; see p. 716). And if rapid development requires the abandonment of arbitrary power and of cherished myths, it also demands political stability. The coup d'état, the dominant form of political change in much of the Middle East, Africa, and Latin America, encourages the unhappy middle classes of those regions to export rather than invest productively what little capital they possess.

Rapid development also requires an economic revolution to end the tariffs and bureaucratic controls that throttle growth from Peru to Tanzania. It requires a relatively free market in agricultural goods to give the peasants incentive for "green revolutions" on the Indian model. It demands and produces both widespread literacy and swift and dislocating cultural change. The "Third World" faces daunting tasks. But the examples of Europe, of Japan, and of much of East Asia show that societies whose rulers give them the opportunity can make the perilous leap from poverty to wealth.

Suggestions for Further Reading

General Works

No adequate survey of the post-1945 "Third World" exists; few reliable or readable works cover even parts of it. G. Chaliand, *Revolution in the Third World* (1978), offers a brief and lively guided tour that is now in some respects dated. It nevertheless provides an interesting critique—from the Left—of "Third Worldist" ideology, and an excellent analysis of the wide cultural differences within the "Third World." See also C. Rangel, *Third World Ideology and Western Reality* (1986). The World Bank's annual *World Development Report* offers comprehensive statistical data with which to test generalizations about the "Third World." E. Luttwak, *Coup d'Etat: A Practical Handbook* (1969, 1979), is a valuable contribution to understanding the "Third World's" dominant method of political change.

Decolonization

No large-scale comparative history of decolonization exists. E. Monroe, *Britain's Moment in the Middle East, 1914–1956* (1963); A. Williams, *Britain and France in the Middle East and North Africa, 1914–1967* (1968); W. R. Louis, *The British Empire in the Middle East, 1945–1951* (1984); and A. Horne, *A Savage War of Peace: Algeria 1954–1962* (1977), are useful on the Middle East and North Africa. B. N. Pandey, *The Break-up of British India* (1969), and *South and Southeast Asia, 1945–1979* (1980), ably covers south and Southeast Asia.

"Third World" Diversity

For the varied cultures of the "Third World" and for post-1945 events there, see—for East Asia—H. C. Hinton, *Three and a Half Powers: The New Balance in Asia* (1975); S. Leys, *Chinese Shadows* (1978), and *The Chairman's New Clothes: Mao and the Cultural Revolution* (1981). On South Asia, see Pandey (listed above) and J. M. Brown, *Modern India: The Origins of an Asian Democracy* (1985). V. S. Naipaul, *India: A Wounded Civilization* (1977), offers pessimistic cultural criticism; N. Maxwell, *India's China War* (1970), is an instructive case study in Indian foreign policy. On the Middle East, D. Pipes, *In the Path of God: Islam and Political Power* (1983), is useful on the force of ideas; P. Mansfield, *The Middle East: A Political and Economic Survey* (1980), imparts basic facts. On Latin America, see especially L. E. Harrison, *Underdevelopment Is a State of Mind: The Latin American Case* (1985); P. Sigmund, *The Overthrow of Allende and the Politics of Chile, 1964–1976* (1977); C. Rangel, *The Latin Americans: Their Love-Hate Relationship with the United States* (1986); and V. S. Naipaul, *The Return of Eva Perón* (1980). On Africa, M. Meredith, *The First Dance of Freedom: Black Africa in the Post-War Era* (1984), provides a sophisticated overview; S. J. Unger, *Africa: People and Politics of an Emerging Continent* (1986), offers an informed popular account; C. Young and T. Turner, *The Rise and Decline of the Zairian State* (1985), provides a depressing case study.

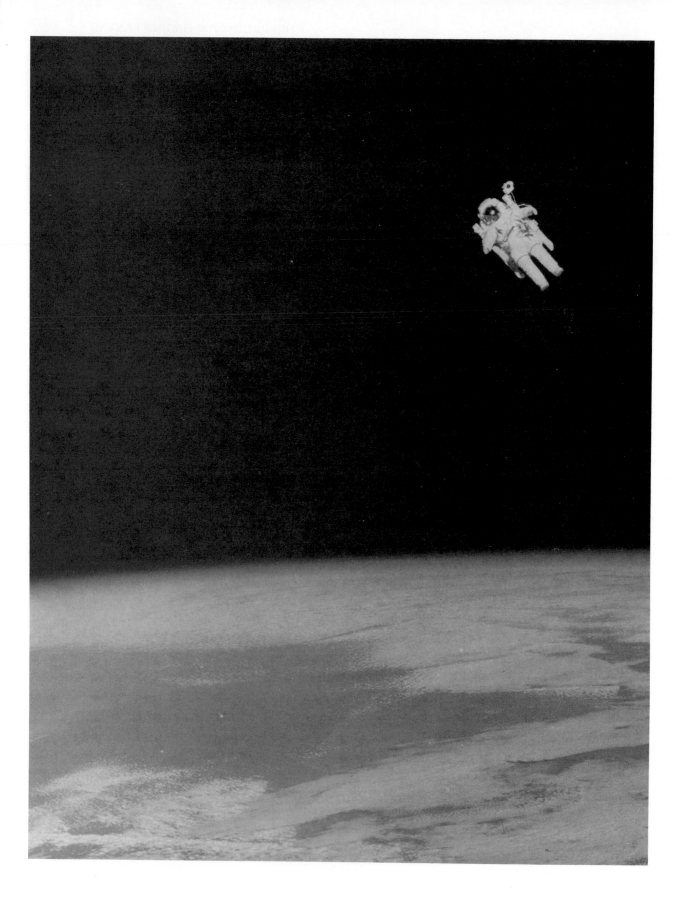

36
The End of the Twentieth Century

The 1975 Helsinki security treaty brought little security. The détente that Nixon and Kissinger had sold to a war-weary Congress as harbinger of a "generation of peace" soon revealed itself as oversold. Soviet military power continued to grow. The Soviet Union acquired a second Soviet empire of "Third World" clients far beyond the "Yalta line" of 1945. In Asia, American withdrawal from Vietnam removed war from U.S. television screens but did not end war; China at last sought to shake off Mao's legacy; Japan's industries stormed the world's markets. Europe suffered stagnation, unemployment, and disorientation reminiscent of the interwar years. In the Middle East, an "Islamic Revolution" swept Iran in 1978–79, generating war and new and potent strains of terrorism. In Lebanon, Israel, southern Africa, and Central America conflicts between or within states exploded or festered. Simultaneous inflation and stagnation battered the world economy. The United States, uncontested world economic leader from 1945 to the 1970s, gradually ceased to lead. And slow economic growth diminished the two superpowers relative to nimbler long-term contenders for superpower status: Japan, Europe, and ultimately China.

In the realm of knowledge, the last half of the century was a period of staggering advance and growing bewilderment about the foundations and purposes of science and scholarship. The geometric expansion of human knowledge brought fragmentation; no single intellect could fully grasp more than a small range of subjects. The gap between high and popular culture inherited from the late nineteenth century further expanded, just as the West's popular culture swept the non-Western world with tides of unprecedented intensity. In this disoriented condition, with world population expanding almost asymptotically, the world prepared to meet the third millennium of the Western era.

THE COLLAPSE OF DÉTENTE, 1975–80

Détente was almost stillborn. Its centerpiece, the SALT I treaty of May 1972, soon attracted criticism as an "unequal treaty" that locked in Soviet nuclear superiority, especially after the Soviet Union developed multiple warhead (MIRV) missiles with unexpected speed. Even nuclear "parity" with the Soviet Union deprived the European

Opposite: Toward the stars? Astronaut Bruce McCandless II maneuvering outside the Space Shuttle *Challenger* in earth orbit (1984).

1039

and Asian allies of the United States of their traditional strategic "umbrella" against Soviet ground superiority. Few in Europe now expected Washington to risk incineration to defend Hamburg or even Bonn against Soviet armor.

Soon after SALT I the "correlation of forces" tipped further in Moscow's favor. The 1973 Yom Kippur War and Arab oil embargo revealed western Europe's pusillanimity; Nixon self-destructed; Congress turned on the "imperial presidency" and sought to reduce the executive branch to impotence; North Vietnam's final victory in April 1975 suggested that the United States was paralyzed. Simultaneously, major opportunities opened for the Soviet Union in both Europe and Africa.

The April 1974 Portuguese military revolution had a strong Marxist flavor. Many in Portugal's officer corps had sought to understand their enemies in Africa through the study of Marxism-Leninism, and had returned converted. They joined with Portugal's small but ruthlessly Stalinist Communist party in turning the revolution toward the creation of a "People's Republic." The Soviet Union supplied money and advice. But in Portugal the "salami tactics" that

had prevailed in eastern Europe ultimately failed, for lack of Red Army backing. Portugal's Socialist party won the 1975 elections with aid from western Europe and the United States. Then it mobilized supporters in the military and consolidated Portugal's first parliamentary democracy.

In Africa, the Soviets entered close relations with newly independent Mozambique. But it was in Angola that they most decisively crossed the "Yalta line." When Portugal departed in November 1975, Soviet aircraft, logistical support, and rubles delivered 12,000 Cuban troops to aid the Marxist-Leninist MPLA ("Popular Movement for the Liberation of Angola") against rivals that enjoyed U.S., Zairean, Chinese, and South African backing. The MPLA established itself as the internationally recognized government of Angola; the U.S. Congress cut off support to the non-Communist guerrillas. But the intervention of the Soviet Union's Cuban "Gurkhas" (as a liberal Democratic Senator described them) did not end the war. The guerrillas of UNITA ("National Union for the Total Independence of Angola") fought on into the 1980s with South African and ultimately U.S. aid. Cuba in response raised its commitment to as many as 50,000 troops and advisers.

Further north, the Soviet Union opened other bridgeheads into the "Third World." It consolidated its foothold at Aden, cemented a close relationship with Somalia by acquiring a base at Berbera, and looked with favor on the approaches of Somalia's rival, Mengistu Haile Mariam of Ethiopia. In 1977–78, Mengistu received over $1 billion in Soviet arms, Soviet and Cuban advisers, and a Cuban armored brigade under the command of the former deputy commander-in-chief of Soviet ground forces. Cubans and Soviets won a war in the Ogaden desert against Mengistu's Somali neighbors, who subsequently gravitated toward the United States. Mengistu failed to crush resistance in Eritrea but at least held Eritrea's cities. After further

On loan to the Soviet Union: Cuban infantry in Angola, 1976.

purges and amid general famine, Mengistu in 1987 proclaimed a Communist "People's Democratic Republic of Ethiopia."

Rapid growth of Brezhnev's navy, which filled out a base network from Cuba to Cam Ranh Bay in Vietnam, complemented disquieting signs of Soviet activism. Most alarming of all was the swift buildup of Soviet conventional and nuclear forces aimed at western Europe. The most important decision of Leonid Brezhnev's long tenure as Soviet leader (1964–82) was to raise the percentage of Soviet GNP spent on the military from roughly 10 percent in 1965 to between 20 and 25 percent by the late 1970s—figures that approximated those of Nazi Germany in 1938–39. On top of its numerical advantage of 2 to 1 or better in deployed divisions, main battle tanks, and artillery, the Soviet Union began to catch up with the West in the sophistication of its armored fighting vehicles, aircraft, and electronics. Détente helped. It allowed the Soviet Union to procure Western high technology openly as well as clandestinely. It encouraged Western bankers and governments to extend lavish credits to the Soviet Union and its satellites. Those credits in essence subsidized Brezhnev's armaments.

In the nuclear arena, the rapid modernization of Soviet strategic forces proceeded within the limits of SALT I. In 1974 Kissinger and Ford signed an agreement with Brezhnev at Vladivostok on the framework for negotiating a SALT II treaty. Then revulsion against Watergate swept the Republicans from office in the 1976 presidential election. Ford's successor, James E. ("Jimmy") Carter, peanut farmer and man of the people, initially shocked the Soviets with a proposal to depart from the Vladivostok framework by *reducing* rather than simply limiting the superpower strategic arsenals. He also irritated the Kremlin mightily by initiating a worldwide crusade for "human rights" that included the rights of Soviet dissidents and Jews. Moscow

Carter and Brezhnev in Vienna for the signing of SALT II, June 1979.

found too late that others took seriously the promises it had made in the 1975 Helsinki treaty. Arms negotiations nevertheless eventually resumed on the old basis; in June 1979 Carter and Brezhnev signed a SALT II Treaty at Vienna. It was apparently less one-sided than SALT I: the SALT II limit of 2,250 intercontinental delivery systems applied equally to both sides. But SALT II still preserved a major Soviet advantage, the 308 massive ten-warhead SS-18 missiles that in theory could by themselves destroy the entire U.S. land-based missile force.

And in theater nuclear forces, which SALT II did not touch, the imbalance was far worse. From 1978 onward the Soviet Union had deployed an entirely new class of intermediate-range ballistic missiles, the three-warhead SS-20. These truck-mounted behemoths were easily hidden, reasonably accurate, and could hit Iceland, Portugal, Japan, and China from deep within the USSR. They also could fire with a minimum of preparation, a valuable quality if Soviet commanders, as their doctrine dictated, should seek to launch a preemptive attack. By 1979 the Soviet Union

The struggle for Afghanistan: the Red Army (above) against the Afghan resistance (below).

dium-range nuclear missiles that would be entirely separate from the U.S. intercontinental arsenal. In theory, the new weapons—464 ground-launched cruise missiles and 108 Pershing II medium-range ballistic missiles—would deter Soviet nuclear or conventional threats. They would also allow Europe to retaliate against SS-20 strikes without necessarily provoking escalation into all-out thermonuclear war. The United States simultaneously offered to negotiate with Moscow a balanced and verifiable agreement limiting all theater nuclear weapons.

That offer did not interest Brezhnev. The Soviets knew that ratification of SALT II was in increasing difficulty in the U.S. Senate, and apparently judged that Carter's embarrassment in Iran after November 1979 (see p. 1052) would paralyze the United States. Washington could thus wield neither carrot nor stick; Moscow saw little reason to resist temptation. On December 27, 1979, KGB commandos and Soviet paratroops descended on Kabul, the capital of Afghanistan, while up to 100,000 Soviet troops rumbled across the Afghan borders.

had deployed 120 SS-20s and no limit appeared in sight; NATO had nothing even remotely similar.

At that point the Europeans reluctantly responded under the leadership of Willy Brandt's successor, the SPD's irascible "Iron Chancellor," Helmut Schmidt. In December 1979 the NATO powers requested the deployment in western Europe of a force of U.S. me-

Afghanistan and the Persian Gulf

That latest and most violent expansion of Soviet power, like its predecessors, was an outgrowth of events not entirely of Moscow's making. In 1978 a Marxist-Leninist Afghan party, the "Democratic People's Party of Afghanistan" (DPPA), had overthrown the five-year-old Afghan republic. That regime had already maintained close relations with the Soviet Union; its DPPA successor invited thousands of additional Soviet advisers and provoked the independent-minded and devoutly Islamic Afghan tribes with talk of secularism and land "reform." By spring 1979 a powerful insurgency was underway; it drew on Afghanistan's proud nineteenth-century tradition of ferocious resistance to both Britain and Russia. A factional struggle within the DPPA replaced its original leader with Hafizullah Amin, a blood-thirsty figure whom Moscow regarded as untrustworthy.

That development and the spreading revolt apparently helped provoke the drastic measures of December 1979: a KGB assassination of Amin and Red Army occupation of Afghanistan. Moscow's new man, Babrak Karmal, had no more luck in dominating the countryside than his predecessors. Unlike the United States in Vietnam, the Soviet Union had to make do with an auxiliary army of a mere 30,000 Afghans, a force so unreliable that it normally fought only with Soviet tanks watching it from the rear. Despite initial disappointments, the Soviets soon revealed that they saw other vistas beyond Afghanistan itself. At Shindand in southwestern Afghanistan they built an immense air base that threatened Iran and the Gulf.

To make good that threat, however, the Soviet Union still had to pacify Afghanistan. Remorseless artillery and air bombardments and numerous deliberate massacres of civilians by ground troops killed over a million Afghans in a few years, and pushed perhaps 5 million of Afghanistan's 16 million inhabitants over the southern borders into Pakistan and Iran. Air-dropped Soviet mines—some camouflaged to resemble toys—maimed guerrillas and civilians alike. But the Afghans, thanks in part to CIA aid through Pakistan that eventually included advanced antiaircraft missiles, gradually whittled down the Soviet advantage.

The West showed less fortitude than the Afghans. Carter indeed reacted. In 1977 he had denounced the foreign policy of his predecessors for its allegedly "inordinate fear of Communism"; he now confessed that the Kabul coup had taught him more about Soviet policy in a few days than he had learned in the previous three years. He withdrew the SALT II Treaty from consideration by the Senate; it now stood no chance of ratification, although in general both powers continued to observe its limits. He slapped an embargo on the grain sales to the Soviet Union that had flourished with détente. He announced a boycott of the 1980 Moscow Summer Olympics. Above all, on January 23, 1980, he sought to deter further Soviet expansion by announcing a "Carter Doctrine"—any attempt "by any outside force to gain control of the Persian Gulf region will be regarded as an assault on the vital interests of the U.S.A., and such assault will be repelled by any means necessary, including military force."

Both Europe and the U.S. farm voter recoiled in horror from Carter. Canada and Argentina supplied the Soviet Union with the grain it required to make good yet another of its thumping crop failures. Europe and especially West Germany sought to preserve their new-found ties to the Soviets and to

ignore the Afghans, inconvenient inhabitants of a far away country. Superpower détente had nevertheless died on the road to Kabul.

WAR AND PEACE IN ASIA

The Third Indochina War

North Vietnam's conquest of the South in March–April 1975 produced predictable results. Hundreds of thousands of Saigon adherents disappeared into "reeducation camps." There many thousands died. Hanoi abolished what was left of the "National Liberation Front" in 1976 and boasted that its world-famous "Front" had been nothing but a front. Northern cadres ruled from "Ho Chi Minh City." Northern bureaucrats sought to stamp the South's economy into the same Stalinist mold as that of the North.

In Cambodia, the Khmer Rouge showed themselves even more implacable than their North Vietnamese patrons. The Khmer Rouge leaders, Pol Pot (born Saloth Sar), Ieng Sary, and Khieu Samphan had imbibed their Maoism at Left Bank cafés while studying in Paris in the 1940s and 1950s. There they acquired a utopian goal of a kind common among uprooted intellectuals: the forging of a unique "Cambodian Road to Socialism" through the eradication of the old society and the severance of all ties between Cambodia and the outside world.

Pol Pot and his associates followed that road with pitiless consistency once they took over Cambodia in the wake of North Vietnam's victory. In a few days in April 1975 they forcibly emptied Phnom Penh, a capital city containing perhaps 3 million inhabitants and refugees; many starved. The teenage peasant zealots of the Khmer Rouge sought out and killed all Cambodians with an education and anyone whose adherence to the collectivized and "ruralized" new order seemed less than total. Cambodia's population had stood in 1970 at perhaps 8 million. By

1980 the population of "Democratic Kampuchea" had fallen to between 5.5 and 6.5 million. Perhaps 750,000 of the 1.5 to 2.5 million missing people had fled across the minefields to Thailand; the rest had died.

World opinion showed its characteristic impotence. Many in the West at first denied the evidence of torture, massacre, and starvation brought by refugees, or blamed the United States—rather than North Vietnam—for having involved Cambodia in war and thus opened the road for Pol Pot. The Khmer Rouge practice of "autogenocide" played no part in their downfall; what destroyed Pol Pot and his associates was their fierce nationalist resentment against their former patrons in Hanoi. In 1977 the Khmer Rouge clashed with Vietnamese troops and shelled Vietnamese villages along the Cambodia-Vietnam border; division-size battles followed. In December 1978 over 100,000 Vietnamese troops with both Soviet and captured U.S. armor and aircraft launched a *Blitzkrieg*

Bones of victims of the Khmer Rouge, Tonle Bati, Takeo Province, Cambodia.

that crushed the Khmer Rouge armies and occupied Cambodia.

That "Third Indochina War" did not remain entirely isolated. China had long looked askance on Hanoi's close ties with Moscow. Hanoi reciprocated. In 1978 it began the expulsion of Vietnam's 900,000 to 1.2 million overseas Chinese. That brutal measure and the

Vietnamese "boat people" after being refused permission to land in Malaysia (1979).

invasion of Cambodia prompted a brief Chinese attack on North Vietnam in February–March 1979. China's inexperienced army did badly and Hanoi's friends in Moscow apparently cautioned Beijing against pressing the attack. Vietnam successfully imposed a colonial regime on Cambodia, complete with hundreds of thousands of Vietnamese settlers. Up to 200,000 Vietnamese troops stayed on indefinitely to fight Khmer Rouge and anti-Communist Cambodian guerrillas. And Moscow fastened on Vietnam itself a semicolonial relationship, with advisers, bases, and 60,000 or more Vietnamese deported to Siberia to do manual labor.

Vietnam itself languished economically except for the black markets of the South; the collectivised North suffered near-famine in 1988. In the decade after 1975, 1 to 1.5 million "boat people" risked death from drowning or Thai pirates rather than remain. At first the refugees were largely ethnic Chinese or Saigon adherents; they soon included disillusioned NLF officials and innumerable ordinary Vietnamese. Hanoi's victory imposed on Indochina endless misery and yet another endless war.

"We can never again undertake . . . radical leftist nonsense": Hu Yaobang (left) and Deng Xiaoping, 1983.

The "De-Maoization" of China

Beijing (Peking) traveled a different road from either Hanoi or Moscow. From 1971 to 1976 the Maoist radicals around Jiang Qing (Chiang Ch'ing), Mao's wife, gradually lost influence. Marshall Lin Biao (Lin Piao), Mao's chief support in the army, mysteriously died in 1971 amid rumors he had attempted a coup. In 1973, Deng Xiaoping (Teng Hsiao-P'ing), the most canny of the Party leaders who had attempted to cage Mao in the early 1960s, achieved rehabilitation. Zhou Enlai (Chou En-lai), who had conducted the delicate negotiations with Kissinger and Nixon, appeared dominant as Mao's health and attention span declined. But in January 1976, Zhou died before Mao. Spontaneous demonstrations of grief by hundreds of thousands of ordinary Chinese provoked Jiang Qing and her radical "Gang of Four" to strike before they lost control. They again disgraced Deng Xiaoping; then Mao died in September 1976 and the radicals lost their principal support. Mao's designated successor was Hua Guofeng (Hua Kuo-feng), a Maoist but no radical. When Hua discredited himself with yet another overambitious program to modernize China, opponents both within the Party and outside it attacked.

With the apparent connivance of Hua's opponents, urban intellectuals posted slogans and essays on a "Democracy Wall" in Beijing. From within the Party, Deng Xiaoping exploited that unrest to oust Hua in 1980–81. In the saddle at last at the age of 76, Deng purged Maoist extremists and suppressed democratic dissidents impartially. He also pressed a radical "de-Maoization" of China's economy. Peasants received the right to sell surpluses from their private plots in free markets. Factory managers gained a measure of freedom from central planning. Opposite Hong Kong, "free enterprise zones" arose to attract foreign investors. The industries of Shanghai prospered mightily. China's GNP growth after 1981 surged to over 10 percent per year.

The Party relaxed its grip on the economy with notable reluctance. It failed to relax politically. Deng's chosen successor, Hu Yaobang (Hu Yaopang), raised expectations among intellectuals. He denounced Mao for having ruled China as a "feudal-monarchist state" and insisted "that from now on we cannot afford to mess things up, we can never again undertake such radical leftist nonsense as 'take class struggle as the key link' and 'better to have socialist weeds than capitalist seedlings.' We can never again afford internal chaos, or we will cause our own collapse and poverty." The Beijing *People's Daily* made the startling announcement that "if we continue to use certain Marxist principles, our historic development will surely be impaired."

In December 1986 the students of China took the new leadership at its word, and demonstrated massively for democratic freedoms. The police gradually contained the demonstrations. Deng sacrificed Hu Yaobang, while Party zealots campaigned against the contagion of "bourgeois liberalism." But Deng nevertheless held to his economic policies, despite inflation and other pains of rapid growth. He also supervised an orderly transfer of power in the middle ranks of the Party and army from the veterans of the "Long March" of the 1930s to a younger and perhaps less dogmatic generation. But whether economic revolution can in the long run coexist with Party autocracy remains to be seen.

Democracy Wall: A Chinese Dissident Speaks   1978

Wei Jingsheng was the most daring of those who wrote on the wall in Beijing; he is rumored to have recently died in prison. His 1978 essay, "Democracy, the Fifth Modernization," shows the bitterness of the generation that suffered the full force of Mao's "Great Proletarian Cultural Revolution."

Today, it is perfectly irrelevant to try to determine the balance account of Mao Zedong's achievements and mistakes. . . . The question which the people should now be asking is this: without Mao Zedong's personal despotism, could China ever have fallen as low as we see her today? Or are we to believe that Chinese people are stupid, or lazy, or devoid of any desire to improve their lot? We know very well that this is not the case. Then what happened? The answer is obvious: the Chinese have taken a path they should never have entered; if they followed it, it is because a despot, who knew how shrewdly to peddle his trash, simply took them for a ride. . . .

German fascism, of stinking memory, was actually called "national socialism." It too was led by a tyrant; it too told the people to tighten their belts; it too deceived the people, assuring them: "You are a great nation!" Above all, it too suppressed basic democracy, because it clearly saw that democracy was for it the greatest danger, the most frightful enemy. Stalin and Hitler could shake hands and sign the famous German-Soviet pact, and on this basis the German and Russian peoples were condemned to suffer slavery and misery. Do we, too, need to continue suffering such slavery and misery? If we wish to break away from it, there is only one way: democracy. In other words, if we want to modernize our economy and science and defense and the like, we must first modernize our people.

From Simon Leys, *The Chairman's New Clothes: Mao and the Cultural Revolution* (London: Allison and Busby Limited, 1981), pp. 260–61.

Japan Triumphant

While the United States floundered in Indochina, Japan became the "workshop of Asia." Its gross national product swelled from roughly 13 percent of that of the United States in 1965 to 34 percent in 1985. Its economic structure, thanks to Japan's narrow, poor, and mountainous land, rested overwhelmingly on industry. With almost no oil, few minerals, and a pampered uncom-petitive agriculture, Japan inevitably concentrated investment in its factories. As in the United States, automobiles and electrical devices led the way. Unlike the industries of the United States, those of Japan immediately targeted export markets from the United States to Southeast Asia to Europe; to import food and oil, Japan had to export. By the mid-1970s Japan had conquered the U.S. market for television sets and was making inroads in automobiles. By the early 1980s even manufacturers of the United States' most innovative product, the computer chip, were complaining of "unfair" Japanese competition; Europe reacted with similar hostility.

Despite such howls of xenophobic protest, Japanese success was not the product of chicanery. It was the result of 30 years of relentless hard work and attention to detail by Japanese management and by Japan's highly educated and dedicated work force. And Japan, despite its transformation in 1983–86 into the world's greatest creditor—displacing the United States from the position it had occupied since 1914–18—had great vulnerabilities. So great was its dependence on foreign trade that a downturn on the scale of 1929 and after could lay its society waste. Thanks to the pacifist constitution that MacArthur had imposed in 1947 Japan also remained virtually disarmed, unable to defend either itself, its oil lines to the Persian Gulf, or the vast East Asian "co-prosperity sphere" it had at last acquired under U.S. protection. Nor did its neighbors want it rearmed. Beijing, which in 1978 signed a "Peace and Friendship Treaty" with Tokyo directed against Moscow's "hegemonism" and military buildup in Northeast Asia, repeatedly reminded its Japanese partner of the immense massacres that had attended Japan's attempt to conquer China in 1937–45.

Under Yasuhiro Nakasone, who discharged the office of Japanese prime minister with more than usual forcefulness from 1982 to 1987, Japan began to take a role in world economic councils befitting its new status. It grudgingly committed itself to opening its domestic markets, although the absurd restrictions that forced the Japanese consumer to pay over five times the world market price for rice remained in place. It pledged to loosen up by consuming and importing more and saving and exporting less. It hesitantly broke the 1 percent of GNP ceiling on military spending to which it had adhered since the 1950s. Japan's new position as the

world's second largest economy, behind the United States but probably ahead of a humiliated Soviet Union, posed the question of how much longer it would or could remain a military-political pygmy.

WESTERN EUROPE IN SEARCH OF ITSELF

Western Europe, although it grew mightily, likewise failed to fill the world role to which its economic power entitled it. The superpower struggle had dwarfed and repressed Europe's nationalisms, but they retained enough vitality to prevent Europe from acting as a unit. Britain attempted to maintain its "special relationship" with its wartime ally, the United States, although it finally joined the European Common Market (EEC) in 1973. France under de Gaulle cemented a "Paris-Bonn axis" designed to keep the West Germans from drifting off eastwards in search of national reunification, and took a high independent line against the United States. As the Soviets achieved nuclear "parity," de Gaulle supplemented the weakened American "umbrella" over western Europe with a French bomber and nuclear missile *force de frappe* under France's sole control. In 1966–67 he withdrew with much fanfare from NATO's combined military command and closed U.S. logistical bases in France. That belated revenge for America's sabotage of the 1956 Suez landing deprived NATO's West German front line of vital lines of communications. France remained in formal terms a NATO member, but its refusal to coordinate war planning and force structure with its allies made it doubtful that French help would reach the battlefield in time if the Soviets attacked. Finally, West Germany under Willy Brandt (1966/69–74) and Helmut Schmidt (1974–82) pursued *Ostpolitik* toward East Germany and the Soviet Union so assiduously that Paris and even Washington began to fear secretly for Bonn's long-term loyalty to the Western alliance.

The EEC rarely rose above indecorous squabbles over budgets and its bloated subsidies to its farmers. It failed even in its initial economic goal, the elimination of trade barriers between member states and the creation of a European market that would give the continent's industries the economies of scale needed to rival the United States. (Bold steps in that direction are scheduled for the 1990s, and transnational satellite television advertising may yet create a true European market where governments have so far failed.)

In the 1973–75 oil crisis, the EEC states acted with astounding disunity. Each nation hastened to make a separate peace with OPEC, whereas a coordinated EEC-USA-Japan policy of joint oil buying and rewards and punishments might have cracked the oil cartel. And détente also opened the coffers of western Europe to the Soviet Union. It precipitated a rush to sell modern industrial plants—some with military uses—to the Soviet bloc and to make western Europe dependent on the lavish supplies of cheap Siberian natural gas that Moscow happily offered.

The end of superpower détente naturally came as a shock. The combination of direct Soviet aggression against Afghanistan and NATO's decision to deploy U.S. missiles to counter Moscow's ever-increasing force of SS-20s led to a wave of trepidation more intense than anything since the Korean War. Much of European opinion by now so feared Moscow that it concentrated its protests against the United States. The American missiles, the protesters announced, were designed to provoke a war that would incinerate Europeans but not Americans.

Protest was strongest in West Germany. There a leftist environmentalist party, the "Greens," offered the children of affluence a vision of an "alternative" anticapitalist future. The other Green appeal was a fierce German nationalism directed primarily against alleged U.S.—rather than Soviet—"colonization" of divided Germany. The protesters proclaimed above all the nobility of fear: *"Ich habe Angst"* ("I am afraid") was a favorite slogan. Protest failed. Elections in 1983 confirmed the British Conservatives in office and in West Germany gave victory to the CDU/CSU, which favored deployment. When the missiles began arriving in 1983–84 the world did not end as the protesters had predicted. Protest largely ended instead. But the Green and left-SPD vision of a magically denuclearized Europe redeemed through German reunification continued to exert a powerful destabilizing pull.

Two additional factors further intensified tension in western Europe after 1979. Carter, crippled by his mishandling of revolutionary Iran (see p. 1052), lost the 1980 presidential election to a former film actor, Ronald Reagan. Most Europeans perceived Reagan as a vague and aging Hollywood "cowboy" with an itch to obliterate both Europe and what Reagan imprudently referred to as Moscow's "Evil Empire." And that empire simultaneously suffered yet another of its periodic crises.

Of all the satellites, Poland had plunged most deeply into debt during détente. Misconceived industrial investments and rising inflation struck at the living standards of Poland's downtrodden workers, whose riots had toppled Gomulka in 1970 as they had toppled his predecessor in 1956. In summer 1980 Polish workers at Gdansk—once known as Danzig—went on strike, a class struggle against a Marxist-Leninist state. Poland's intellectuals and the Catholic Church, the historic vehicle of Polish nationalism, backed the strike. Against all precedent the workers won the right to replace the Party-run sham unions with an independent national trade union, *Solidarnosc* ("Solidarity"). The demoralized Polish Communist Party lost control even of the press, and began to disintegrate. The largest and most strategically vital of all the satellites appeared about to turn against Moscow, with unforeseeable repercussions in East Germany, Czechoslovakia, and Hungary.

Brezhnev and his associates found the answer in a Polish general. Moscow placed the Polish Communist Party in receivership in the hands of Wojciech Jaruzelski, a prim and ruthless military figure with a long record of absolute obedience. In December 1981 Jaruzelski crushed Solidarity with riot police and army, while Soviet tank forces in East Germany, Poland, and European Russia prepared to back him up. Jaruzelski placed the Polish people before a grim choice: acceptance of his dictatorship, or a Soviet intervention that would endanger national survival. Solidarity persisted underground and Polish workers henceforth scarcely even pretended to work, but Jaruzelski and Moscow had won.

Angst and economic interest prevented any concerted Western reaction such as a cutoff of credit to the Soviet bloc. Bonn found the Polish affair an embarrassment to West Germany's increasingly close trading ties to the Soviet Union; many West Germans secretly despised all Poles and saw little reason to suffer for Gdansk. As Jaruzelski's coup unfolded, Helmut Schmidt met happily with Erich Honecker, Ulbricht's successor as leader of East Germany, and sent birthday greetings to Brezhnev. France and Britain took a less benign view of Brezhnev's actions. But no unified Western or even European policy emerged; Reagan's trade sanctions against the Soviet Union and Poland were a solitary gesture.

And Europe's disunity persisted. In April 1982 the Argentine generals, in an act of folly, invaded the British-inhabited Falkland Islands without provocation. The EEC initially balked when Margaret Thatcher, the formidable Conservative prime minister of Britain, requested economic sanctions against Argentina. Europe only swung behind Britain once it became clear that Thatcher—a prime minister from the

mold of Pitt, Disraeli, and Churchill—was determined to reconquer the islands. (That feat the British armed forces swiftly and elegantly accomplished despite severe logistical and operational constraints; Argentine officers normally spent their careers torturing suspects in basements rather than training for war.) In the Middle East, European or Western unity likewise rarely prevailed except in the negative sense that European governments ritually carped at Israel in order to maintain their own flow of oil.

All except Thatcher deplored Reagan's April 1986 air strikes—in response to a particularly bloody series of terrorist attacks (see p. 1055)—against Qaddafi's Libya. France even refused overflight rights for U.S. aircraft. And when in 1987 the United States deployed large naval forces to maintain order along Europe's oil lines in the Persian Gulf, the allies initially held back. Europe's economic power, like that of Japan, far outweighed its ability or will to bring power to bear.

ISLAMIC WORLD REVOLUTION AND ENDLESS WAR

In the Middle East a brief relaxation followed the Yom Kippur War of October 1973. Anwar Sadat of Egypt definitively cast his lot with the United States in 1976. In 1977 he broke with all precedent and flew to Jerusalem in search of peace with Israel; Egypt was war-weary and in dire economic straits. At a 1978 summit meeting at Camp David near Washington, Carter pushed Israel's master of evasion, Menachem Begin, into a peace agreement underwritten with lavish U.S. aid for both Egypt and Israel. In March 1979 Egypt and Israel signed a treaty that ended 30 years of war. The Arab League in reply boycotted Egypt, the largest Arab state. Despite Sadat's assassination by Islamic militants in October 1981, Israel returned the last slice of Sinai to Egypt in 1982. One border in the Middle East was provisionally at peace. Simultaneously a new phase of the "Eastern Question," one in which Moslems fought one another rather than Israel, was opening.

"Death to America": Revolution in Iran

Sadat succumbed to a widespread upsurge of religious militance of which he himself had provided the most trenchant summary: "This is not Islam, this is madness." The source of that "madness" was twofold: the Islamic world's impotence in the face of nineteenth- and twentieth-century Western power, and the failure of the secular states of the Middle East, states such as Egypt, to catch up with the West or even defeat the Jewish state, the West's Middle Eastern outpost. The trigger of that "madness" was the 1978–79 revolution that convulsed Iran.

Shah Mohammad Reza Pahlavi, "King of Kings" and ruler of Iran from 1941 to 1979, was a man of large ambitions. After a CIA-sponsored return in 1953 to the throne from which anti-Western nationalists had briefly displaced him, he sought to use Iran's oil wealth to bring his subjects by forced marches into the twentieth century. Land reform, secular education, and the partial emancipation of women particularly outraged the powerful landowning Shi'ite clergy. In 1963 one of the clergy's most influential figures, the Ayatollah Ruhollah Khomeini of the holy city of Qum, condemned the Shah and all his works. Khomeini went first to jail and then into exile. There he ceaselessly reviled the Shah as an "unclean" tool of the "satanic" West.

The Shah for his part relied increasingly on his secret police, the dreaded SAVAK. He faced the same dilemma as other "modernizing" autocrats. The introduction of Western ideas and economic practices soon created an intelligentsia that rejected the autocracy— just as those same ideas and reforms shrank or alienated the traditional sectors of society on which the autocracy

Sadat, Carter, and Begin clasp hands at the signing of the Israeli-Egyptian peace treaty, March 26, 1979.

rested. The Shah nevertheless pressed on. With Kissinger's encouragement he took over from Britain the role of lord of the Gulf after 1971. That year he also sponsored an immense celebration at Persepolis of the 2,500th anniversary of the Persian empire, which he evidently hoped to recreate. In 1973–74 he led OPEC's assault on the world economy, and used Iran's fabulous oil profits to buy the latest in tanks, ships, and aircraft from the United States and Europe.

Crowds greet the Ayatollah Khomeini upon his return from exile to Tehran, February 1979.

But the Shah failed to spread the profits from the oil boom widely enough to defuse the resentments of his urban lower classes. His apparent sponsorship of the invasion of Iran by European and U.S. goods and customs, from alcohol to "licentious" advertising to women in tailored blue jeans, aroused outrage among the devout. The intelligentsia deplored his refusal to concede parliamentary government. In January 1978 the clergy led riots at Qum against the regime. Disorder spread across all Iran. The Shah, ill with cancer and irresolute, failed to use the army vigorously while his conscript soldiers still remained loyal. In the Teheran riots of September 1978 the army began to crack. Khomeini's unarmed zealots taunted the troops to make them martyrs; the troops deserted or shot sergeants and officers. The Shah's nerve shattered along with a cherished illusion—that his people loved him. In January 1979 he fled.

Khomeini arrived from Paris—a stern medieval figure alighting from a jumbo jet—to sweep a feeble provisional government from office. He soon purged the officer corps and established a form of government never before seen, a theocratic "Islamic Republic" under the rule of Shi'ite clergy. Student militants, revolutionary committees, "Revolutionary Guards," and the shaven-headed zealots of the Hezbollah ("the Party of God") enforced political conformity. They also ruthlessly reimposed Islamic dress on Iran's women. Teheran crowds enthusiastically chanting "Death to America" filled Western television screens. When Carter allowed the dying Shah to visit New York in October 1979 for cancer treatment, Khomeini's "Islamic students" violated the customary niceties observed between states, and seized the U.S. embassy in Teheran and its staff of over 50.

Khomeini may not have originated the embassy coup, but he swiftly exploited it. What better way to mobilize domestic support, dramatize the Islamic Revolution abroad, and humiliate the "Great Satan" America than to hold its diplomats hostage? The Iranians had learned from North Vietnam, which had tied American negotiators in knots over the release of U.S. prisoners. The American television networks rose to the occasion. Soon each evening news broadcast began with an announcement of the number of days the hostages had been imprisoned.

That placed intolerable pressure on Carter in an election year. He warned Iran that harm to the hostages would have serious though unspecified consequences. He also failed to set a deadline for their release. Iran's position between the Soviet Union and the Gulf deterred him from military action, lest Moscow use U.S. intervention as a pretext to expand its Afghan bridgehead toward the warm waters. In April 1980 Carter launched an ineptly planned rescue mission that broke down in the Iranian desert; fierce interservice rivalry and Carter's eccentric insistence on the *minimum* use of force had made failure likely. The hostage crisis decided the 1980 election. Reagan won by

Khomeini: Islamic World Revolution

Holy war means the conquest of all non-Moslem territories. War will perhaps be declared after the formation of an Islamic government worthy of the name. . . . It will then be the duty of all adult ablebodied men to volunteer for this war of conquest whose final goal is to make Koranic law supreme from one end of the earth to the other. But the entire world should know that the universal supremacy of Islam [will] differ considerably from the hegemony of other conquerors. . . .

To ensure the unity of the Moslem nation, to liberate the Moslem homeland from the domination or influence of the imperialists, we have no alternative but to form a truly Islamic government and to take all possible steps to overthrow the other tyrannical pseudo-Islamic governments put in place by the foreigner, and having attained that goal, to install *the* universal Islamic government.

From Ayatollah Khomeini, *Principes politiques, philosophiques, sociaux et religieux* (Paris, Éditions Libres-Hallier, 1979), pp. 22, 28.

a landslide in part because he promised stern action. Iran packed the hostages onto an Air France jet as the new president took the oath of office in January 1981.

The Gulf War

By then Khomeini had other concerns than the "great Satan." After seizing power he repeatedly called for Islamic upheavals throughout the Middle East. Among his preferred targets was Saddam Hussein, Sunni ruler of the Shi'ite majority of neighboring Iraq. The Iraqi regime, apparently thinking that Iran's military power had disintegrated in revolutionary chaos, replied to Khomeini's threats with an armored thrust at Iran's oilfields in September 1980. Iran's 3 to 1 advantage in population soon began to tell. This was no war of maneuver between sophisticated opponents, but a tropical Somme 1916, a demolition derby of military ineptitude.

In early 1982 Iraq lost the oilfields. By 1985–86 it was close to losing Basra, its second city after Baghdad. Iranian "Revolutionary Guards," many of them adolescents with plastic "keys to Paradise" furnished by the clergy in their knapsacks, pressed the attack at immense cost. "Fountains of blood" ran red at Teheran cemeteries in macabre commemoration of the fallen. Endless war, an "Islamic" successor to SAVAK, and mass executions silenced opponents and doubters.

Iraq responded to defeat by appealing to other Arab regimes for aid against the Persian Shi'ite menace. If Iraq foundered, Kuwait and Saudi Arabia might follow. Iran secured clandestine assistance from Israel, which perhaps mistakenly considered Saddam Hussein a worse threat than Khomeini. Israel also struck the only serious blow in history against the proliferation of nuclear weapons when its F-16 fighter-bombers destroyed Iraq's French-built nuclear reactor in June 1981.

As Iran advanced, Iraq in desperation expanded the war by air and sea. It drenched Iranian troops and Kurdish villages with mustard gas, nerve gas, and hydrogen cyanide. Its air force struck at Iranian cities and at the oil exports that financed Iran's war. Iran in reply attacked international shipping bound for the ports of Iraq's Gulf allies and launched heavy missiles at Baghdad in the manner of Hitler's V-2 bombardment of London in 1944. Iraqi missiles in turn flattened entire blocks in Teheran and Qum. In 1987, after an Iraqi air attack gutted a U.S. Navy frigate by mistake, Washington responded to an appeal from Kuwait to escort its tankers. Britain, France, and Italy gradually committed or reinforced flotillas of their own. In April 1988 the Iranians imprudently challenged the U.S. fleet, and lost much of their navy in a flurry of U.S. cruise missiles. The Western flotillas hemmed Iran in, while Iraqi counter-offensives forced a bitterly resentful Khomeini to accept a ceasefire in July–August 1988. The war had cost up to 2.7 million dead and wounded.

The Agony of Lebanon

The Iranian revolution also enlivened events in Lebanon, where as mentioned in Chapter 35 a multicornered civil war had raged in 1975–76 between the private armies of Lebanon's principal communities, the Maronite Christians, the Sunni Moslems, the Shi'ite Moslems, the Druzes, and the Palestinians; Syrian intervention had imposed a troubled ceasefire. In April 1981 the civil war resumed in earnest. In May–June 1982 Palestinian bombardments of northern Israel and the shooting of Israel's ambassador in London furnished Israel the occasion for an attempt to stamp out the PLO in Lebanon. Israel's forces brushed Syria aside, evicted the PLO "state within a state" from Beirut, Lebanon's unhappy capital, and briefly installed a Maronite ally as president of Lebanon. His assassination by car-bomb in September 1982 provoked the Maronite militias, with the apparent approval of some in the Israeli command, to massacre up to 2,000 Palestinian civilians in the Sabra and Chatila refugee camps in West Beirut.

Israel withdrew from the Beirut area in 1983. Even before it left, Reagan sought to prop up the Maronite-dominated Lebanese central government with Marines in the manner of Eisenhower in 1958. The 1,600 Marines landed along with French paratroops and small British and Italian forces. They soon found themselves beleaguered by Syrian and Iranian-backed Shi'ite and Druze militias. Washington ordered naval and air bombardments of the Marines' tormenters, while entertaining a woolly-headed notion that U.S. forces were in Lebanon as "peacekeepers." Sloppy security by the Marines and the French led swiftly to disaster. In October 1983 suicide truck-bombs penetrated the Marine and French perimeters and killed 241 Marines and 58 French paratroopers. Washington fumed impotently, unable to identify the bombers; subsequently it shelled and bombed Shi'ite, Druze, and Syrian positions. Marines and allies withdrew sheepishly in February–March 1984.

That left the mastery of Lebanon to Syria, if it could conquer it. Damascus sought first to destroy all armed Palestinians not loyal to itself. Yasser Arafat, the chief political leader of the Palestinian movement, escaped with his life. Many of his followers perished. Syria then moved into Beirut itself amid all-out struggle between Christian and Moslem militias. While the Syrians mopped up the few remaining armed Palestinians, Shi'ite and Druze militias allied to Syria massacred Palestinian civilians in the refugee camps in the style of the Maronites in 1982.

Syria remained precariously in control of northern and central Lebanon, despite friction with Iranian-backed Shi'ite elements. Israel's forces, under constant car-bomb attack, withdrew in 1985 to a narrow "security zone" along Israel's northern border. The war—now as before largely a war of Arab against Arab—entered a static phase broken only by assassinations, car-

Yasser Arafat, durable leader of the PLO.

bombs, and the taking of Western hostages.

Terrorists on Television

The hostage-taking, which provisionally reached a peak in 1985–86, was only one aspect of a widespread phenomenon of the 1970s and 1980s: terrorism. The term, despite its baggage of emotion, has two commonsense meanings. Its first and oldest form is the assassination by revolutionaries of rulers or key officials. Its exponents have included the *Narodnaya Volya* plotters who killed Tsar Alexander II in 1881, the Bosnian Serb assassins of Archduke Francis Ferdinand at Sarajevo in 1914, and the middle-class urban guerrilla groups of the European student Left of the 1970s. Their purpose was to terrorize those in power, to weaken existing regimes by striking directly at the persons and authority of the rulers. The "propaganda of the deed" spread the gospel of revolution and might perhaps provoke the target regimes to indiscriminate reprisals that would undermine their legitimacy.

But by the late 1960s technology opened other possibilities, especially to groups like the PLO, whose "revolution by exile" was incapable of mounting a sustained guerrilla campaign inside Israel itself. Worldwide jet travel and instantaneous satellite television offered both soft targets and a new order of magnitude of potential publicity. Why attack the rulers or citizens of a target state? They were too well defended, especially if that state was Israel. Why not instead massacre citizens of other states, especially the Americans, whose government funded and supported Israel? The "cause" would thereby receive free worldwide television coverage; as Madison Avenue taught, there was no such thing as *bad* publicity. And in the "struggle for Palestine," Palestinian militants insisted, no bystanders were innocent.

Thus the "new terrorism," *indiscriminate violence for media effect*, was born. By definition, it was effective only against states with free presses and television networks, such as the industrial democracies. And Arafat's PLO and offshoots such as the "Popular Front for the Liberation of Palestine" were its most fervent practitioners. Until 1982 their finishing schools in Beirut and elsewhere trained terrorist cadres from the West German "Red Army Faction," the Japanese "Red Army," the Irish Republican Army, and a bizarre assortment of other groups. Some repaid the Palestinians; in 1972 Japanese Red Army terrorists killed 25 civilians at Lod airport in Israel.

The PLO's eviction from Beirut did not end Lebanon's role as terrorist world capital. The Syrians helped sponsor the Iranian-backed Lebanese Hezbollah ("the Party of God") that probably delivered the car-bombs to the Marines and the French. In 1985 Syria and the Libya of Muammar Qaddafi between them apparently promoted hijackings by Lebanese Shi'ites of a TWA flight and by Palestinians of an Italian cruise ship, the *Achille Lauro*. In both cases the hijackers singled out and killed Americans; the Palestinians pushed a Jewish American invalid overboard in his wheelchair. The U.S. networks, heedless of political consequences and intent only on "scooping" their rivals, provided instant interviews with the hijackers or their bosses. Attacks on U.S. and French civilians in western Europe accompanied the hijackings throughout 1985 and early 1986.

Finally, in April 1986, the Reagan administration bombed Libya in reprisal and barely missed Qaddafi himself. Most Europeans and some Americans disapproved. Many predicted an intensification of terrorist violence in response. Instead, Qaddafi suffered a nervous breakdown, soon reinforced by the inglorious rout of forces he had sent to conquer his southern neighbor, Chad. Syria sought to ingratiate itself with Washington. Washington's new approach produced a lull in Middle Eastern terrorism.

Terrorists on television: a U.S. airliner held hostage at Beirut airport, June 1985.

What it did not do was resolve the hostage issue. After 1983 numerous Americans and Europeans had disappeared in Lebanon and reappeared on videotapes delivered to Western news organizations, reading propaganda from Shi'ite captors and lamenting their governments' refusal to give in to terrorist demands. In 1985–86 Reagan sought with Israeli encouragement to ransom the captured Americans by secretly selling planeloads of anti-tank missiles to the terrorists' Iranian sponsors.

But 2,008 antitank missiles bought only two hostages. Reagan's aides realized too late that the crafty Iranians had "snookered" them (in the words of Reagan's chief of staff). A Lebanese magazine disclosed this "arms-for-hostages" deal in November 1986 and inaugurated a Watergate-style crisis in Washington complete with televised congressional hearings. It soon emerged that profits from the arms sale had gone to the Nicaraguan "*Contra*" rebels (see p. 1058) in apparent violation of a congressional ban. By default Reagan's advisers settled on a sound course: to ignore the hostages and thus deprive terrorists of any leverage over U.S. policy or incentive to take more hostages.

The Struggle for Israel

The turmoil that followed the Iranian Revolution and Lebanese war did not spare Israel itself. Intervention in Lebanon initially appeared a masterstroke that virtually destroyed the PLO. Then the long occupation of hostile southern Lebanon and the consequent attrition began to tell. A weary Menachem Begin retired in 1983. His eventual successors, an ill-assorted coalition of Israel's Right and Center, sought to cut losses by withdrawal. The Gulf War concentrated the energies of Arabs against Persians and of Sunni against Shi'ite; it appeared to give Israel a breathing space. But by 1987 Jerusalem had begun to ponder the possibility that the eventual victor might sweep away the few moderate and pro-Western regimes in the region, possibly including Sadat's successor in Egypt, Hosni Mubarak.

Worse still for Jerusalem, PLO defeat did not mean the end of Palestinian militance. Israel had from the beginning been a demographic time bomb. The several hundred thousand Palestinians who remained within Israel's borders in 1948–49 had a higher birth rate than the Jewish settlers. The subsequent spread under Israeli sponsorship of antibiotics and modern medical techniques further increased Palestinian fertility and decreased infant mortality. By the 1980s, the Arab population of Israel was twice as prolific as the Jewish population. And Israel acquired a further 1 million Arabs on the West Bank of the Jordan and in the Gaza Strip through the great victories of 1967. By the mid-1980s, 3.6 million Jews faced 2.1 million Arabs within the post-1967 borders of "greater Israel." Existing trends, if continued, will give the Arabs close to a majority by 2005. And rapid population growth increases the demographic weight of the young, the most easily aroused and least tolerant segment of any population.

The Palestinians showed little intention of waiting until 2005; they wanted Palestine—*all* of Palestine—now. In

December 1987, the young of the occupied Gaza Strip took on Israel's police and army with rocks and fire bombs. "The Uprising" was a protest against Israel but also against the indifference of the Arab states, preoccupied with the Gulf War. The Israelis, initially badly outnumbered, replied with live ammunition and killed scores of demonstrators. Protest spread from Gaza to the West Bank. The Arabs within Israel's original 1948–49 borders had shown considerable loyalty to a Jewish state that had brought them prosperity; they now joined their fellow Arabs for the first time in political general strikes. Israel's conquest of Palestine had apparently united Palestinians as well as Jews. A no-quarter struggle between the Jewish state and the nationalist aspirations of the Palestinians had apparently begun.

CONFLICTS ON THE PERIPHERY

Besides wars in the Middle East, other struggles between or within small powers punctuated the 1980s. The two most serious, at least potentially, were those in South Africa and Central America.

The Struggle for Mastery in South Africa Resumed

The Boers had long suffered from the same demographic trends that threatened the Jewish state. But the Boer position was far worse than that of the Israelis. In 1951 less than 3 million whites had faced less than 10 million blacks and mixed-race citizens in South Africa. By the late 1980s that gap had widened to 5 million against 30 million. Projections suggest that whites will reach about 7 million in 2050, while blacks and mixed-race will ascend to almost 100 million.

But demography offered only chilling foreboding for the future. In the present, two waves of disturbances in the black townships in 1976 and 1984–

Israel in 1988

LEBANON
SYRIA
Haifa
Mediterranean Sea
Jordan River
Tel Aviv-Yafo
WEST BANK
ISRAEL
Jerusalem
Gaza
Dead Sea
JORDAN
EGYPT

Israeli-administered territory

Gulf of Aqaba
SAUDI ARABIA

87 served notice on the Boers that their adamant refusal to give rights to the black majority had generated ever-growing opposition. The Boer reply was to kill perhaps 3,000 and imprison as many as 25,000, including children. In the face of international pressure, the South African government of Pieter W. Botha also announced a variety of cosmetic changes to its system of racial domination, *Apartheid*. It sought with some success to play off its black opponents, the African National Congress and United Democratic Front, against tribal elements such as the armed Zulu movement *Inkatha*. The result was much bloodshed between blacks.

Pretoria also launched numerous raids into neighboring African "frontline" states, which South Africa dominated economically as well as militarily. Fighting with the Cubans in Angola continued sporadically. Internal unrest and external pressure failed to shake Boer control or cripple the economy, which rested on black labor. The exclusion of Western news cameras from the black townships in 1985–86 won the Boers an external breathing space. But the struggle for mastery between the "white tribe" and its subject populations continued, with potential for full-scale war in southern Africa.

"The Revolution Has No Frontiers": Central America

South of Mexico and north of Panama lie the three unhappy republics of Nicaragua, El Salvador, and Guatemala, along with Costa Rica, Honduras, and Panama. In the 1970s, outside forces combined with indigenous politics, economics, and demography to produce upheaval.

The trigger was Nicaragua. There a dynasty of dictators, the Somoza family, had ruled since 1936 as heir to a series of U.S. Marine interventions that Nicaraguan political factions had invoked to crush their domestic opponents. The first Somoza (Anastasio Somoza García, 1936–56) consolidated his power by presenting himself to Washington as a force for stability. He also assassinated his former ally, Augusto Sandino, a local guerrilla saint of vaguely Leftist leanings who had taken up arms against U.S. Marine intervention in 1927 when it failed to put his own faction in power. The second Somoza dictator (Anastasio Somoza Debayle, 1967–79) carried on the family tradition after a pseudo-constitutional interlude. But youthful opponents from the Nicaraguan moneyed elite sought military and political training in Havana and Moscow. In the 1960s they created a guerrilla movement, the "Sandinista National Liberation Front" (FSLN) with Cuban advice and arms.

The second Somoza began to lose his grip in the mid-1970s. His excessive greed alienated the middle classes. He offended the urban poor by pocketing international relief money sent after a 1972 earthquake partially leveled Managua, the capital. He provoked spontaneous uprisings by assassinating a key opponent in 1978. After his National Guard proved both brutal and ineffectual, Carter urged Somoza to go; he duly fled to Miami in July 1979. Middle-class support and arms shipped from Cuba put the revolution over the top. The Sandinistas promised free elections, political pluralism, non-alignment in foreign policy, and the preservation of a mixed economy. Then they seized control of the victorious revolution through salami tactics.

Elections did not materialize until 1984, after the FSLN had largely suppressed its domestic opponents with arrests and *turbas divinas*, "divine mobs" of youthful fanatics. Nor was the external alignment of the FSLN long in doubt. Within days of Somoza's flight, key Sandinista leaders visited Castro. Within a month the new regime had clinched relations with Moscow, Bulgaria, and Libya. It acquired ties to the PLO and North Korea. Cuban and Soviet-bloc advisers poured into Managua. The FSLN created a propaganda machine that proclaimed America as "the enemy of all humanity." Shipments of Soviet-bloc arms arrived not only for the "Sandinista Armed Forces" (as the new party-army styled itself) but also for insurgencies kindled or rekindled in El Salvador and Guatemala. The revolution, in the slogan of Nicaragua's new ruling class of FSLN *comandantes*, "had no frontiers" ["*la revolución no tiene fronteras*"].

In Guatemala that proved untrue. The Guatemalan army fought back with pacification methods pioneered by the French in Algeria and with home-style massacres of Indian peasants. Washington disapproved and cut off aid, but without effect. At least 12,000 perished; the insurgents shrank from 6,000 in 1980 to 3,000 by 1987. The Guatemalan army handed over power to a civilian government in 1985. The Salvadoran insurgents, with lavish arms supplies from Cuba through Nicaragua, did rather better than their Guatemalan counterparts until 1984, when a Social Democrat, José Napoleón Duarte, won the presidential election. Duarte sought with some success to damp down "death squad" assassinations by the Salvadoran Right; massive U.S. assistance improved the combat performance of the Salvadoran army. The guerrillas dwindled from roughly 10,000 in 1980 to 4,000 in 1987.

The United States also reacted to Sandinista hostility and to the prospect of a Marxist-Leninist state with thousands of Cuban and Soviet-bloc advisers close to Mexico's southern border and to the Panama Canal. In 1981 Reagan halted U.S. economic aid (which amounted to $128 million) to post-revolution Nicaragua; a condition of aid had been that the Sandinistas not supply Marxist insurgents in El Salvador. Reagan soon turned to sterner measures, CIA-organized insurgents known as the *Contras* ("counter-revolutionaries"), recruited from veterans of the Somoza forces, from middle-class opponents of the Sandinistas, and from the Nicaraguan peasantry.

Reagan also struck fear into the Sandinistas by landing troops on the small Caribbean island of Grenada in October 1983, after the leaders of Grenada's Marxist-Leninist "New Jewel Party" (which had seized power in 1979) unexpectedly began shooting one another. Washington found Grenada's close ties to Cuba and the Soviet Union disquieting and feared that U.S. citizens on the island might become hostages. The Grenadans greeted U.S. forces as liberators; Washington soon withdrew in favor of an apparently stable Grenadan parliamentary regime. A Marxist-Leninist dictatorship had fallen—a unique event. The regime's captured archives revealed fierce totalitarian aspirations, an apparently insatiable appetite for weapons, and close ties to the Soviet Union, East Germany, Cuba, Nicaragua, Bulgaria, North Korea, and the PLO.

Along with that apparent portent for Managua came increasing economic strain. *Contra* attacks and military expenditure drained Managua's budget, but Nicaragua's economic regression in the 1980s was above all the result of Stalinist economic experimentation by the FSLN. The regime sought to undermine or expropriate private enterprise in favor of *comandante*-run state businesses and collective farms. Nicaragua's currency-earning exports of coffee and other commodities fell by 50 percent. Living standards dropped to the dirt-poor levels of the 1950s. The regime also created a new form of class division. The Sandinista ruling class had access to special hard currency stores like those serving the Soviet elite. The common people made do with increasingly empty supermarket shelves.

To survive, the Sandinista leaders took the struggle to Washington. To American audiences the *comandantes* gave lavish assurances—assurances contradicted by their words and actions at home and by the frequent ill-timed visits to Moscow of their fatigue-clad supreme leader, Daniel Ortega Saavedra. The Sandinistas protested that only the "*Contra* war" prevented them from fulfilling the promises of political pluralism and non-alignment they had broken in 1979–80, before the *Contras* existed.

Beginning in 1982, Congress sought to leash the *Contras* by rationing or blocking funds and arms. Reagan's National Security Council secretly kept supplies flowing by diverting through Swiss bank accounts the profits from the arms transactions with Iran. The revelation after November 1986 of that clandestine attack on Congress's constitutional power of the purse—and the deep revulsion that most Americans felt against Iran—temporarily made Reagan a "lame duck." That gave the five Central American powers an opening, under the leadership of President Oscar Arias of Costa Rica, to negotiate in July–August 1987 their own "peace plan" to end the region's wars.

The plan's most striking initial success was to win Arias a Nobel Peace Prize. The Salvadoran insurgents broke off talks with Duarte; low-level violence continued in Guatemala. The Sandinistas complied with few of the Arias plan's provisions, which included the restoration of political and press freedoms in Nicaragua. Managua also announced plans to raise the size of the Sandinista armed forces—after the defeat of the *Contras*—to 600,000 regular and reserve troops by 1995. That force would be twice as large as that of Mexico, a country with 24 times Nicaragua's population.

Disclosure of Managua's military plans did not prevent Congress from again cutting off *Contra* aid in February–March 1988. Simultaneously, a Sandinista offensive against *Contra* sanctuaries in Honduras provoked Reagan to dispatch U.S. paratroops to that country for a brief show of force. The *Contras* feared abandonment by Washington, the Sandinistas invasion, continued protracted war, and possible abandonment by Moscow. Both parties therefore compromised on a provisional truce. The Sandinistas apparently hoped that the *Contras* would disintegrate, while the *Contras* looked to

Daniel Ortega (center, in dark glasses) returning to Nicaragua from his trip to Moscow, February 1984.

the United States for renewed aid should Sandinista sabotage wreck the Arias plan. Concurrently, collapse threatened two other pillars of Washington's Central American policy. Duarte of El Salvador contracted a terminal cancer while his party, discredited by corruption, lost control of parliament to the murderous far Right. The brutish ruler of Panama, General Manuel Antonio Noriega, fell afoul of Washington for allegedly renting airfields to U.S.-bound cocaine smugglers. Reagan's subordinates applied economic sanctions that shattered Panama's economy but failed, at least in the short run, to weaken the general's grip on power. Reagan left intractable problems "south of the border" to his successors.

THE WORLD ECONOMY ADRIFT

One backdrop to the crises of the 1970s and 1980s was the steady erosion of the relative economic power and world economic leadership of the United States. In 1945 the United States had commanded perhaps half of world industrial production, for Germany and Japan lay in ruins and the western Soviet Union was devastated. In 1953 the United States share was 44.7 percent; by 1980 it had fallen to 31.5 percent. U.S. production rose steadily in absolute terms, but its relative position—like that of nineteenth-century Britain—inexorably deteriorated.

That deterioration was in a sense an immense U.S. success. The dollar and gold-based Bretton Woods international currency system of 1944, U.S.-sponsored tariff reduction agreements, the Marshall Plan, and the example of the science-based industry of the United States between them propelled the world economy into the greatest spurt in history. The growth of other powers, especially West Germany and Japan, inevitably cut the U.S. share of world production. But economic and foreign policy trends accelerated that relative deterioration and began by the 1970s to compromise the authority of the United States as leader of the world economy inherited from Britain.

Worldwide defense commitments and the overseas investments of U.S. multinational corporations between them generated a persistent balance of payments deficit; from 1950 to 1969 an average of $1.3 billion more left the United States each year than entered. Lyndon Johnson's attempt to fight the Vietnam War painlessly on credit helped provoke a decade of steadily rising inflation. Domestic inflation in turn worsened the balance of payments deficit. Imports, to which the U.S. consumer was becoming pleasantly addicted, cost more dollars than before. And European banks were awash in unwanted "Eurodollars." That oversupply generated unbearable pressure on the Bretton Woods structure of fixed exchange rates based on gold.

In 1971, Nixon briefly clamped wage and price controls on the U.S. economy to check inflation, and devalued the dollar. A second devaluation followed in 1973. By March 1973 the world economy rested on "floating" exchange rates that fluctuated according to demand. The dollar remained the international currency of first and last resort, but "hard" currencies such as West German marks, Swiss francs, and Japanese yen acquired a major role, especially after the EEC created a mark-based European Monetary System in 1979. U.S. leadership was giving way to an oligarchy of the rich.

But western Europe and Japan were ill-equipped to share in world leadership. The more than doubling of the real price of oil in 1973 and again in 1979–80, after Khomeini's revolution and the Gulf War cut Iran's production, helped force the world economy into two recessions (1973–75, 1981–82) more painful than anything since the Great Depression. Unemployment, "stagflation," and oil dependence after 1973 enfeebled the EEC and slowed even Japan.

The United States thus continued to lead by default, through dubious innovations such as the "petrodollar recycling" that piled high the pyramids of international debt. But in the 1980s yet another round of economic irresponsibility in Washington further compromised its leadership position. Reagan came to office apparently convinced that massive tax cuts would so stimulate the economy that federal tax revenues would actually increase and thus balance the budget—a bizarre theory that his vice president, George Bush, had once derided as "voodoo economics." In addition, Reagan inherited a rising military budget from Carter and had pledged to match Brezhnev's buildup.

Unlike Carter, Reagan refused to tell the voters that they must pay for more defense. His first drastic tax cut passed Congress on a wave of bipartisan enthusiasm. The economy expanded steadily after 1982 but tax revenue did not increase as predicted. Reagan therefore loaded the costs of a rebuilt 600-ship navy and numerous new weapons systems onto the national debt, which doubled from $1 trillion in 1981 to $2.1 trillion in 1986. Congress declined to court unpopularity by raising taxes or by cutting into the middle-class social programs that cost even more and grew even faster than the military budget.

"Guns and butter" on credit in the 1980s had effects as dramatic as Johnson's similar attempt to fight in Vietnam while creating a "Great Society" at home. Foreign lenders came to Reagan's rescue by buying Treasury bonds in billion-dollar gulps. Foreign buyers snapped up U.S. corporations. But the inflow of capital was not a free lunch. Foreign buying of dollars to pay for investments in the United States raised the dollar's value sharply against other currencies. That rise in turn increased the price and lessened the competitiveness of U.S. exports. The consequent decline in exports further worsened the balance of payments deficit, as did the ever-increasing interest payments owed to the foreign lenders. The need to continue borrowing to "roll over" an ever-larger debt meant that the United States lost control over its domestic interest rates, which had to remain higher than those abroad to keep foreign investors from taking their money elsewhere. High interest rates in turn made it harder for U.S. industry to invest in the modern plant that it desperately needed to compete in the world market. Finally, the debt binge converted the United States from a net creditor to a debtor for the first time since 1914–18. In 1983–85 Japan took the place of the United States as the world's greatest creditor.

Worse followed. Financial mores had grown loose indeed in the 1970s and 1980s; the shadow of 1929 was far distant. Suspect "financial instruments" proliferated; "junk bonds"—aptly named—financed corporate takeovers and stock manipulation. New financial "products" such as stock index futures—a casino game requiring a 10 to 15 percent down payment and the rest on loan—introduced massive instabilities. Billions in unrepayable "Third World" or eastern European debt undermined U.S. and European banks. Technology opened new frontiers of speed and insecurity. Computers and instantaneous communications welded the world's stock, currency, and commodity exchanges into a seamless 24-hour world market. Instant financial information and fund transfer sent trillions of dollars, marks, yen, and lesser currencies sloshing from market to market, seeking the small exchange rate differences that meant profit. Automatic stock and futures trading driven by computer programs made market hiccups into jagged ascents or hair-raising plunges. The abandonment in the name of free enterprise and efficiency of many post-1929 restrictions on banks and financial institutions further decreased the world economy's margin of safety.

The most dramatic symptom of instability was the giddying rise of the stock market, from a Dow Jones average of below 2,000 in early 1987 to 2,722 by August. In October the Dow broke, and on October 19 it dropped a chilling 508 points. The market lost 36 percent of its August paper value: over half a trillion dollars in assets vaporized. Markets around the world followed;

The crash of '87: Black Monday, October 20, 1987.

only Tokyo stabilized swiftly after a severe drop. The value of the dollar against other currencies followed the markets downward. The jerry-built structures of "Third World," corporate, and consumer debt creaked ominously. But unlike 1929, the U.S. domestic economy remained relatively strong. A cheaper dollar increased U.S. prospects of exporting and thus paying its debts, but also raised the specter of an international devaluation contest of the type that helped deepen the Great Depression (see pp. 885–86). Here too, Reagan left a difficult legacy to his hand-picked successor, George Bush.

THE SUPERPOWERS IN DECLINE

The Soviet Empire

The "Crash of '87" was a visible and outward sign of the relative decline of the United States. The Soviet Union's relative decline was equally if less dramatically demonstrated when its leadership began after 1985 to seek to present a new and softer image to the West. Technological lag, economic stagnation, and the drain of empire apparently dictated a new effort at détente.

Brezhnev's world-spanning navy, his expanding "second Soviet empire" in Africa and Southeast Asia, his intervention in Afghanistan had suggested limitless ambition. But ambition costs. By the mid-1980s, the annual bill for Afghanistan, Cuba, Vietnam and its Cambodian and Laotian empire, Nicaragua, Ethiopia, and other minor dependencies ran into the tens of billions of dollars. Soviet military procurement at last ceased to grow in the early 1980s; the Soviet economy was flagging. Its annual rate of increase fell inexorably from roughly 5 percent in the 1950s to negative growth by the early 1980s. Détente had brought Western loans and technology, but its main consequence was a debt mountain of Brazilian proportions. Central planning,

an uninspired work force ("they pretend to pay us, we pretend to work"), and military expenditure that may have reached 20 percent or more of GNP by 1980 crippled the economy. Rudimentary medical services, a rising industrial accident rate, intense pollution, astounding levels of vodka consumption, and widespread hopelessness made the Soviet Union the only industrialized society in history to experience a long-term *decline* in the life expectancy of its population. Male life expectancy dropped from 65 in 1965 to an estimated 61 or worse in 1981; that of Soviet women from 73 in the early 1970s to 69 in 1985.

And the Soviet Union—Europe's last multinational empire—did not escape the demographic trends that sapped its former rivals. By 1970 only 51 percent of the Soviet population were Great Russians, the ruling nationality. The subject peoples, especially the Moslems of Central Asia, were growing at rates of up to three times that of the peoples of European Russia. Great Russians probably ceased to be a majority in the early 1980s, although they remained the largest single group within the Soviet Union. Nationalist unrest in Soviet Central Asia and the Caucasus accompanied the shift in numbers; demonstrations erupted whenever KGB pressure relaxed. The intervention in Afghanistan apparently provoked resentment and unreliability among Soviet Moslem troops—a portent for the future.

Two transitional figures succeeded Brezhnev upon his death in 1982. Yuri Andropov, long chief of the KGB, came to power at age 68 amid KGB-inspired rumors in the West that he was a "closet liberal" who loved Glenn Miller's music. He reinforced Soviet forces in Afghanistan. After Andropov's death in early 1984 the colorless Konstantin Chernenko briefly held power, then died. In March 1985 the Politburo chose a far younger man, Mikhail Gorbachev. Molotov's pupil and heir at the foreign ministry, Andrei Gromyko, reportedly put Gorbachev over the top

1928	1953	1957	1964	1982	1984	1985
Stalin	Collective Leadership	Khrushchev	Brezhnev			Gorbachev

Andropov

Chernenko

by remarking that he had a nice smile and iron teeth.

Gorbachev proceeded cautiously at first, but in 1986–87 announced a massive program of economic reforms. *"Perestroika"* or *"restructuring"* was to limit central planning, introduce some market mechanisms, and eliminate the technological lag that in the long run imperiled both the Soviet economy and Soviet military power. A Gorbachev speech in late 1987 mentioned favorably Lenin's temporary economic retreat, the NEP (see p. 909) and repeated some of Khrushchev's strictures against Stalin. Subsequently the Party allowed mention of Leon Trotsky and rehabilitated Bukharin, who had dared to question Stalin's crash industrialization and collectivization. In the realm of culture and politics, the ambiguous accompaniment of *"perestroika"* was *"glasnost"*—"publicity"—usually mistranslated in the West as "openness." And in foreign policy, Gorbachev appeared far more willing than his predecessors to give as well as take at the arms control negotiating table; the Soviet Union needed a breathing space. Gorbachev also bid for a rapprochement with China, despite stiff Chinese preconditions that included Vietnamese withdrawal from Cambodia. In May 1988 he also began to withdraw Soviet troops from Afghanistan.

But Gorbachev's attempt to launch a new NEP faced numerous contradictions. Domestically, greater economic freedom meant market discipline: bankruptcies, unemployment, and inflation. It also meant an end to the Party's monopoly over the economy. It might ultimately mean following China's example in questioning collectivization, one crippling Stalin policy that Gorbachev initially defended. Finally, economic restructuring required help

from a Soviet people long accustomed to merely "pretending to work." The appeal by the Communist autocracy for support from its citizens, like the similar appeals of earlier Russian autocrats, was likely to call forth forces ultimately hostile to the autocracy itself. That was precisely the complaint of strong groups within the Party and the state bureaucracy; eastern European satellite leaders also became increasingly distraught.

In foreign policy, Gorbachev faced daunting challenges. On the arms control front, he gained successes in 1986–87. He charmed Western opinion by agreeing to consider Reagan's START ("STrategic Arms Reduction Talks") proposal for a 50 percent cutback in strategic warheads. That sudden Soviet interests in cuts was in part a product of Gorbachev's need to remedy Soviet economic stagnation. But it was even more a result of Reagan's "Strategic Defense Initiative" (SDI or "Star Wars"), a proposed space-based anti-missile shield that might cancel Soviet advantages in heavy missiles and potentially in theater nuclear forces as well. Gorbachev sought to trade Soviet

Nice smiles and iron teeth: Mikhail Gorbachev meets Margaret Thatcher (1985).

missile reductions for restrictions on "Star Wars" that would induce Congress to kill the U.S. program. Reagan held fast. His stubbornness, more that any other factor, brought the Soviets to the bargaining table with realistic proposals.

START did not bear immediate fruit. The two leaders met at Reykjavik in Iceland in November 1986 for an ill-prepared summit that derailed amid utopian discussions of the total elimination of nuclear weapons in ten years. That thoroughly alarmed the NATO allies, for it suggested that Washington sought to leave them naked in the face of Soviet conventional superiority. In a treaty signed in Washington in December 1987, Gorbachev accepted the same U.S. terms for an intermediate-range missile agreement that his predecessors had contemptuously rejected. "Star Wars" and the defeat of the protesters in western Europe had evidently changed Moscow's views. In the December 1987 treaty the United States agreed to scrap its Pershing II and European cruise missiles. The Soviet Union undertook to destroy both SS-20s and medium-range missiles. Both sides accepted "on-site" inspection provisions unprecedented since the Versailles restrictions placed upon Germany. Cynics, especially in Europe, suggested that the agreement made western Europe safer for Soviet armor.

The prospect of theater-force reductions therefore led to renewed NATO demands for a "mutual and balanced" reduction in conventional forces, an issue on which Soviet negotiators had tied the West in knots during the 1970s. Whether agreed "balanced" reductions were possible, given that an ocean divides the United States from Europe whereas the Soviets need only cross a border, was unclear. That Gorbachev, unlike Brezhnev, appeared set on lessening the burden of arms and of the Afghan war on the Soviet economy was a hopeful sign. But any such Soviet retreat would inevitably encourage demands for independence throughout the empire that Stalin and Brezhnev had acquired.

Whether Gorbachev could—or even proposed to—abandon that empire was uncertain. And no Western expert could say whether or how long Gorbachev would remain in power, whether his reforms would succeed, and to what extent they were a genuine attempt to change the Communist autocracy of Lenin and Stalin into something milder. Optimists in the West proclaimed that containment had succeeded, that the "mellowing of Soviet power" that George Kennan had predicted in 1947 was now finally at hand. Skeptics dismissed *glasnost* and *perestroika* as "an improved lie, a new temporary façade," and pointed to the still unshaken structures of the Soviet power-state and to the eastern European empire that Gorbachev could hold only by force. And pessimists foresaw that if Gorbachev indeed prevailed, his reformed and dynamic Soviet Union would bear an ominous resemblance to the Imperial Germany of 1890–1914.

The "Imperial Republic"

That other "weary titan," the United States, also seemed in need of a measure of *perestroika* by the 1980s. Like Great Britain after 1890, its commitments after 1965 appeared to be outrunning its resources. Military expenditure itself was probably not a crushing burden, if paid for by taxation rather than debt. The United States spent considerably more as a percentage of GNP on arms during the prosperous Eisenhower years than under Reagan. In the 1980s its economy also grew faster than those of its European allies, despite the greater proportion of U.S. GNP spent on defense. But military research increasingly diverted too large a proportion of U.S. scientific and engineering talent into extreme "leading edge" military applications, leaving too few good technical minds to translate innovation into consumer products. And cultural and economic trends skewed the civilian economy. The dubious joys of stock manipulation and corporate takeovers injected too much talent into highly paid parasitic occupations such as corporate law and investment banking. Fear of takeovers in turn drove U.S. firms to pursue short-term profits rather than treading the Japanese road of long-term conquest of markets through consumer satisfaction.

Worst of all, the United States—like nineteenth-century Britain—failed to invest in its schools. By the 1980s its inner-city public education systems had virtually collapsed. Its suburban middle-class schools taught curricula whose vacuousness provoked laughter in Europe and Japan, where relentless and advanced instruction in mathematics, chemistry, physics, expository writing, history, geography, and foreign languages was standard fare. Teaching in America had become a low-paying and low-prestige job that demoralized the few talented and learned individuals it still attracted. A work force that contained a rising proportion of functional illiterates threatened U.S. economic growth, just as the United States led the world into the "information age" of computer technology.

In the realms of domestic politics and foreign policy, the United States suffered from numerous maladies. The collapse of education brought with it a loss of "collective memory." U.S. history—much less that of Europe or Asia—went virtually untaught. Generations graduated or failed to graduate with only hazy notions of the principles upon which their government rested, of the workings of its political process, and of the world beyond its borders. Understandably, only a declining proportion of the population bothered to vote.

Simultaneously, television and computerized opinion polling dramatically altered politics. They made "image" all-important and converted all but the strongest leaders into followers. The cycle of presidential politics became a relentless and debilitating four-year grind, thanks to television and to "reforms" that expanded the role of presidential primaries in small unrepresentative states. Presidents rarely survived long in office. Kennedy, Johnson, Nixon, Ford, and Carter all lasted less than six years. That in turn gave U.S. foreign policy a perilous see-saw quality that perplexed and alarmed both allies and adversaries. Europeans sometimes suggested that parliamentary government, in which the executive also led the legislature, produced greater coherence and continuity than the U.S. system, in which the same party rarely controlled the presidency and Congress simultaneously. But many European parliamentary systems failed the test; few European prime ministers rivalled Margaret Thatcher.

A variety of challenges confronted Washington in its weakened condition. America faced further arms-control negotiations with a Gorbachev whose "charm offensive" ultimately aimed at detaching West Germany from NATO. It faced continued turmoil in Central America and dangerous instabilities in the domestic and world economies. It faced a growing clamor at home that it divest itself of at least a few of the immense responsibilities—from the North Cape of Norway to the Persian Gulf to the "demilitarized zone" between the Koreas—shouldered after 1945, when its relative economic strength had been far greater than in the 1980s. Like the Soviet Union, the United States needed a breathing space.

But the informal empire acquired after 1945 was difficult to shed. The United States had paid dearly—at Pearl Harbor and on the hard road to Berlin and Tokyo Bay—for its flight from responsibility after 1919. Almost half a century after 1945, Europe and Japan still appeared unready to shoulder the burdens which the United States had taken on in its own interest, but also in theirs. To maintain the "American empire" unwillingly acquired against Hitler and Stalin appeared increasingly costly and thankless. To give it up was unsafe.

TOWARD THE TWENTY-FIRST CENTURY

Broad and swift scientific and technological advance paralleled the expansion of the world economy under the umbrella of U.S. power after 1945. Simultaneously, the proliferation of knowledge in myriads of highly specialized scientific and scholarly subdisciplines posed a threat already visible

Success and failure: Neil Armstrong walks on the moon, July 1969. Opposite: Space Shuttle *Challenger* explodes after launch, January 1986.

in the nineteenth century—that educated people, each locked in the jargon of their specialties, would cease to speak a common language. Especially in the social sciences and humanities, skepticism about the possibility of establishing truth corroded all established standards. And as the Americanization of the world through television proceeded, high culture retreated into a cloistered existence in the universities.

The Thrust of Science and Technology

"Command science," the systematic government mobilization of scientific knowledge for a specific purpose, came into its own after 1945. The Manhattan Project had shown the way. Its successors were the postwar programs of the great powers that created thermonuclear bombs, or atomic reactors to generate electricity and power submarines and surface ships.

By the 1980s reactor accidents had lessened enthusiasm for nuclear power. A reactor at Three Mile Island in Pennsylvania partially melted in 1979; its containment vessel held and only small amounts of radioactivity reached the atmosphere. The Soviets did not believe in containment vessels or redundant control systems. When their ill-designed reactor at Chernobyl in the Ukraine exploded and burned in 1986, fire and fallout killed at least 31 and contaminated livestock, milk, and crops from Lapland to Portugal. Oil-poor powers such as France and Japan nevertheless pressed on self-confidently with massive nuclear power programs.

Command science was also the instrument of the conquest of space—a dream entertained since the seventeenth century, but now suddenly practical. The Soviet effort that launched *Sputnik* in 1957 put Yuri Gagarin into Earth orbit in 1961. Kennedy responded with a pledge to put an American on the moon by the end of the decade. The National Aeronautics and Space Administration (NASA), which Eisenhower established after *Sputnik,* assembled the largest community of scientific talent ever mobilized for a specific purpose, and spent up to $40 billion. On July 20, 1969, Neil Armstrong of the United States became the first human to walk on the Moon. The Soviet Union stuck closer to Earth; its space program was and remained military in inspiration and priorities.

After its moon triumph NASA bet virtually its entire shrinking budget on one program, the reusable "space shuttle." The explosion after launch of the shuttle *Challenger* in January 1986 therefore paralyzed both civilian and military space programs, including the launch of satellites to monitor Soviet compliance with arms-control agreements or provide early warning of attack. Subsequent investigations of NASA disclosed slovenly engineering and blind mismanagement. A U.S. space station (and perhaps orbiting "Star Wars" installations) may materialize in the 1990s. The Soviet Union already operates a small space station and holds all records for length of stay in space. A Mars landing is technologically feasible but budgetary constraints will probably delay it until after the year 2000.

Command science, despite its magnitude and its many "spin-offs," was only a small part of the continuing scientific and technological revolution. During and after World War II, new materials came into their own. Plastics and glass fiber increasingly replaced steel and other metals. Composites of plastic and boron or carbon fiber, lighter and stronger than steel, became available in the 1970s. Titanium, almost 50 percent lighter than steel and with a higher melting point than aluminum, found innumerable uses in supersonic jet aircraft, nuclear reactors, and submarines.

But the most spectacular advances, a wave of innovation as potentially powerful as the "second industrial revolution" of steel, chemicals and electricity, came in electronics and biology. Semiconductors, materials such as germa-

nium and silicon that conducted current only hesitatingly at room temperature, had been a subject of curiosity since primitive germanium diodes had figured in early radio receivers. In 1947 William Shockley, John Bardeen, and Walter H. Brattain of Bell Laboratories invented the transistor, the first semiconductor amplifying device. By the early 1960s the transistor had evolved into the integrated circuit or "chip," innumerable microscopic transistors, linked in complex patterns, imprinted on silicon wafers.

The arrival of the transistor coincided with the birth, speeded by wartime cryptographic needs, of the new discipline of computing. Its theoretical roots reached back into the nineteenth century; its two leading theoreticians were Alan Turing (1912–54) of Cambridge, who played a leading role in Britain's decipherment of the *Wehrmacht*'s supposedly uncrackable codes, and the Hungarian refugee physicist-mathematician John von Neumann (1903–57) of Princeton. By the 1960s their successors had created theories, computer languages, and machines capable of the unimaginably complex and rapid calculations needed to model thermonuclear explosions, solve engineering problems through simulation, predict the paths of space vehicles, guide missiles and robots, and store and manipulate ever-greater masses of information.

From 1959 to the 1980s, chips and therefore computers doubled in computing power each year. The cost per transistor decreased over 20 years by a factor of over *1 million*. That pace of advance shows no signs of slowing. As chip fabricators have approached the apparent limits that silicon places on computer speed, those limits have receded, while other faster materials such as gallium arsenide have emerged. The discovery in 1986–87 of an entirely new class of ceramics that offer no resistance to electricity at relatively high temperatures may make possible a further qualitative leap in computer speed—as well as loss-free transmission of electrical power, vehicles miraculously levitated with superconducting electromagnets, and innumerable applications as yet unforeseen. The invention in the 1960s of lasers, devices that generated focused light of a single frequency, added to the potential of semiconductors. Lasers offered innumerable applications from surgery to weaponry, and allowed the transmission of information over long distances at densities far exceeding the limits of electrical or microwave circuits.

Potentially even more powerful than semiconductors and lasers were the new techniques of molecular biology. In 1951–53 James D. Watson of the United States and Francis H. C. Crick of Britain jointly deciphered the "double helix," the complex molecular structure of deoxyribonucleic acid or DNA, the material in which cells encode their genetic information. That research led eventually to the beginnings of an understanding of evolution at the molecular level, and to the manipulation of plant and animal genes to make bizarre hybrids that crossed species lines. The mapping of the entire human genetic code—all 100,000 genes, each consisting of 1,500 subunits—appeared a realistic prospect by the end of the century.

Molecular biology opened immense possibilities for good, for the eradication of most diseases and the understanding and possible slowing of aging. It provided the most powerful weapons for fighting the great viral pandemic of the 1980s and 1990s, AIDS ("Acquired Immune Deficiency Syndrome"). The virus, against which conventional medical techniques were almost as powerless as those of the Middle Ages against the Black Death, spread above all through sexual intercourse and the sharing of unsterilized heroin hypodermics. By the late 1980s it threatened millions of victims, especially in Africa, the United States, and Europe.

But together with hope and life, the new biology also appeared to offer death and transfiguration through biological weapons of unprecedented subtlety and power, and through "human perfectibility" in a quite literal sense by the genetic re-engineering of the human species. Nuclear weapons had given humanity a chance to annihilate itself, but also the long European peace after 1945. Molecular biology held out the prospect both of healing and of a new kind of annihilation, the transformation of humanity into something less or more than human.

The Disintegration of Scholarship and High Culture

In the realm of ideas, specialization and the triumph of the relativism that had flourished since the Enlightenment furthered the fragmentation that had already been visible as the twentieth century began. Especially in the Anglo-Saxon countries, philosophers largely abandoned speculation. The new "analytical" philosophers scorned metaphysics—the exploration through imagination of the nature of existence. They sought instead what Bertrand Russell (1872–1970), an early leader of the analytical school, described as the "unattainable ideal of impeccable knowledge." The close examination of language and meaning through logic and mathematics was their method. Their quest led them to narrow increasingly the domain of truth in order to establish certainty.

Ultimately they so narrowed the domain of truth that it vanished. The reclusive Ludwig Wittgenstein (1889–1951), perhaps the greatest of twentieth-century philosophers, abandoned all attempts to describe the world and retreated acerbically into the analysis of language. His taunt that "the belief in the causal nexus is superstition" denigrated all forms of knowledge about nature and human affairs. But as Wittgenstein's eighteenth-century precursor David Hume had pointed out, the philosopher's study was the place for skepticism. Survival in the hard outside world that Wittgenstein shunned still required "superstitions" such as cause and effect.

On the Continent, after Heidegger, traditional forms of philosophy still prospered. The Left Bank sage Jean-Paul Sartre (1905–80) was Heidegger's principal heir. After 1945, Sartre's "existentialism" became a cult phenomenon from Paris to San Francisco that endured until the 1960s. Its basis was Heidegger's call for "authenticity" and his denial of a rational foundation for values. For Sartre, individuals were utterly free to choose their values. Any denial that such freedom existed was inauthentic, was an evasion of responsibility, was "bad faith." But Sartre offered no advice on what values to choose, for advice would constrict freedom and constitute "bad faith." He merely commanded choice, for only

heroic choice was "authentic." Heidegger had chosen Nazism. Sartre, whose only gestures against Nazism had been literary, chose Marxism. He described it as the "unsurpassable philosophy of our time."

French intellectual fashions change as rapidly and wield as powerful an influence throughout the West as the hemlines of Paris designers. After the collapse of the May 1968 student revolt that Sartre's doctrines of heroic commitment helped inspire, new preoccupations became dominant. The most important was an intellectual tendency known as "structuralism." It had originated in linguistics between the world wars and thence spread to anthropology, literary criticism, history, sociology, psychoanalysis, and philosophy. Its lowest common denominator was the claim that the *structure* of a language, myth, or literary or historical "text" was a more fundamental characteristic than other attributes such as origins, history, purpose, or content.

In linguistics, its point of origin, structuralism was largely the product of the insights of the Swiss scholar Ferdinand de Saussure (1857–1913), who suggested that meaning was a product of oppositions or differences between the "signs" that made up language. Meaning was thus entirely relative. "Signs" had meaning only by virtue of their structural relationship to other "signs." An influential American, Noam Chomsky (1928–), added a fruitful conjecture of his own—*all* languages shared a common "deep structure" that grew out of the structure of the human mind itself. Chomsky's apparent biological determinism clashed with his politics; a combative Left-utopian, he rejected the "capitalist" West and implicitly demanded faith in the perfectibility of humanity, a perfectibility doubtful indeed if the human mind was as "hard-wired" as Chomsky the linguist assumed.

Structuralism—though many of its practitioners disclaimed the label—migrated from linguistics through anthropology to a variety of other fields. Its greatest anthropological figure,

The sage of Paris: Jean-Paul Sartre.

Claude Lévi-Strauss (1908–   ) investigated the myths of Brazilian and American Indians as clues to the structures of the "primitive mind." Structure was primary, content far less important; meaning existed only as part of a structure. Critics such as Roland Barthes (1915–80) carried similar notions into literary criticism. The literary "text" became a subject for a decipherment or "deconstruction" that deliberately ignored the "text's" author, historical context, literary excellence or lack of it, and commonsense meaning. For the structuralist critic, the interpreter not the author gave meaning. That doctrine allowed the interpreter to give a "text" any meaning at all. And the implication that all "texts" were of equal value frequently produced bizarre results. Structuralist critics examined with deep seriousness works that few non-structuralists even considered literature.

Historians, beginning in France, took a Lévi-Straussian interest in the "collective mentalities" of past social groups. Analysis of social or intellectual "structures" began to supersede narrative. The study of long-term change—climatic, economic, and demographic—triumphed for a time over short-term "event history" and the history of ideas. Devotees of economics subjected small portions of the past to "cliometric" statistical examination. Historians increasingly though not always wisely borrowed methods from sociology and psychology. Marxism revived. For the first time in history, historians wrote works incomprehensible to the educated public.

Structuralism and the disciplines it influenced mirrored the disorientation of the age. If *all* truths were relative, tolerance even of bizarre claims was the highest virtue. In the humanities and social sciences few dared affirm that some "truths" were less relative than others and that the test of all generalizations was confrontation with empirical evidence. The natural sciences proved more resistant to bewilderment; experimentation imposed discipline and mathematics still offered an unparalleled means of describing nature.

In the arts, disintegration was almost total as the century drew toward its end. In the visual arts the last undisputed master was Pablo Picasso (1881–1973). Creativity nevertheless remained high, although experiments such as the "pop art" of the 1960s that took its images from American advertising sometimes suggested otherwise. In architecture the "international style" persisted although sometimes adorned with "post-modernist" classical flourishes. In music, few composers after Igor Stravinsky (1882–1971) and Sergei Prokofiev (1891–1953) commanded mass audiences. Dissonance and disjointed rhythms bored or repelled all

"Pop art": Andy Warhol, *100 Cans* (1962).

The anonymous crowd: a Tokyo subway in the 1980s.

except specialists. Symphony orchestras and opera companies made do with the time-honored works of nineteenth-century giants such as Beethoven or Wagner. In literature, especially in the United States, poetry and the serious novel fled to academia to be embalmed in "creative writing" courses. Even Paris began to flag as a fountainhead of novelty. Soviet-bloc dissident and emigré writers, along with those of Latin America, showed more life than their European or American counterparts. Western high culture increasingly lacked the vitality and self-confidence of earlier ages.

THE WIDENING AND NARROWING OF THE WEST

As the century drew to a close, Western ideas dominated the globe as never before. In the nineteenth century, the zenith of the West's relative power, its culture had only touched the surface of non-European societies. By the late twentieth century, instant communications relentlessly drove forward the economic and cultural integration of the world. That process generated fierce reactions, above all from Islam. The Western conception of government resting on and limited by the rights of the governed—*democratic government*—found few successful imitators. But the extension of the West's scientific and industrial revolution to all of humanity appeared likely to continue. As James Watt's partner had boasted of the new steam-engines, "I sell, Sir, what all the world desires to have—power." Power over nature and over the conditions of human existence was what the West offered those willing to learn. That temptation has so far proved almost irresistible.

But the West has also narrowed in relative terms. By the 1980s the birth rate of Europe from France to the Urals had fallen to roughly equal the death rate. The United States continued to grow, but at a rate lower than ever before. Not so the other continents. China, despite draconian post-Mao laws against unlicensed births, checked its growth rate only slightly as it passed the 1 billion mark. South Asia continued a relentless rise. Africa's population expanded at a pace faster than that of any other continent, although the AIDS pandemic threatened to slow it in the 1990s. World population was 4 billion in 1975 and will almost certainly surpass 6 billion by the year 2000. Thereafter either economic development will reduce birth rates or natural catastrophes, overcrowding, environmental degradation, epidemics, and wars will increase death rates. Most projections suggest that world population will level off between 8 and 9 billion late in the twenty-first century. Of that 8 to 9 billion, Asia will have 5 billion, Africa and the Americas will have over a billion each, and Europe will have less than a billion. The West's share of the human species is contracting as the West's influence as the "mainstream of civilization" expands to embrace all humanity.

Suggestions for Further Reading

The Superpowers in the 1970s

As the present approaches, perspective vanishes and reliable works become ever more sparse; *The New York Times* and *The Economist* (London) offer a better guide to world events than the innumerable jargon-ridden books by policy gurus. J. Keegan and A. Wheatcroft, *Zones of Conflict: An Atlas of Future Wars* (1986), offers a military and political geography of current antago-nisms. A. Ulam, *Dangerous Relations: The Soviet Union in World Politics, 1970–1982* (1983), remains excellent on superpower relations. On the Carter interlude, see the criticisms of J. Muravchik, *The Uncertain Crusade: Jimmy Carter and the Dilemma of Human Rights Policy* (1982), and the praise of G. Smith, *Morality, Reason, and Power: American Diplomacy in the Carter Years* (1986).

Europe and East Asia

W. Laqueur, *A Continent Astray: Europe, 1970–1978* (1979), and the very pessimistic J. F. Revel, *How Democracies Perish* (1985), survey western European disunity and wishful thinking. Nguyen Van Canh, *Vietnam Under Communism, 1975–1982* (1983), describes the fate of South Vietnam after the departure of the United States. The Khmer Rouge revolution still awaits its his-torian, but see F. Ponchaud, *Cambodia Year Zero* (1978), and W. Shawcross, *The Quality of Mercy: Cambodia, Holocaust, and Modern Conscience* (1984). On China, I. C. Y. Hsü, *China Without Mao: The Search for a New Order* (1983), analyzes post-Mao change; T. Terzani, *Travels in Forbidden China* (1986), suggests its limits.

Conflicts on the Periphery

On the Middle East and Islamic militance, see especially D. Pipes, *In the Path of God: Islam and Political Power* (1983); S. Bakhash, *The Reign of the Ayatollahs* (1984); G. Sick, *All Fall Down: America's Tragic Confrontation with Iran* (1985); and I. Rabinovich, *The War for Lebanon, 1970–1983* (1984). W. Laqueur, *The Age of Terrorism* (1987), places 1970s and 1980s terrorism in perspective. G. Chaliand, *Report from Afghanistan* (1982), provides useful background on the Afghan war. On Central America, S. Christian, *Nicaragua: Revolution in the Family* (1986), gives a *New York Times* eyewitness view. Those curious about the regime the United States overthrew in Grenada should consult its English-language internal documents: P. Seabury and W. McDougall, eds., *The Grenada Papers* (1984).

The View from the 1980s

On the superpowers, see for the Soviet Union H. Carrère d'Encausse, *Decline of an Empire* (1981); and *Confiscated Power: How Soviet Russia Really Works* (1982), as well as D. Holloway, *The Soviet Union and the Arms Race* (1983), and M. Voslensky, *Nomenklatura* (1984). All suggest reasons for caution about the prospects and potential consequences of Gorbachev's reforms. G. Wills, *Reagan's America: Innocents at Home* (1987), comments sardonically on the Reagan phenomenon; D. Ravitch, *What Do Our 17-Year-Olds Know?* (1987), documents America's educational collapse; P. Kennedy's highly readable and informative *The Rise and Fall of the Great Powers: Economic Change and Military Conflict from 1500 to 2000* (1987), offers long-term perspective. For intellectual developments since World War II, see especially J. A. Passmore, *A Hundred Years of Philosophy* (1968), and *Recent Philosphers* (1985); R. N. Stromberg, *After Everything: Western Intellectual History Since 1945* (1975); and the merciless G. Himmelfarb, *The New History and the Old* (1987).

Illustration Credits

853	Imperial War Museum
854	The Bettmann Archive/BBC Hulton
856	(top) The Bettmann Archive; (bottom) Imperial War Museum
857	(top) The Bettmann Archive; (bottom) The Bettmann Archive/BBC Hulton
859	(top) Historical Picture Service; (bottom) The Bettmann Archive
862	Imperial War Museum
863	UPI/Bettmann Newsphotos
865	The Bettmann Archive
866	Keystone Collection
871	Culver Pictures
873	AP/Wide World
874	AP/Wide World

Chapter 31

876	Dr. Erich Salomon/Magnum
878	Culver Pictures, Inc.
879	AP/Wide World
880	AP/Wide World
881	Collection, The Museum of Modern Art, New York
882	(top) AP/Wide World; (bottom) The Bettmann Archive
883	The Bettmann Archive
887	The Bettmann Archive
888	The Bettmann Archive
889	UPI/Bettmann Newsphotos
890	(top) Earl Leaf, Rapho-Guillumette/PRI; (bottom) AP/Wide World
891	AP/Wide World
895	AP/Wide World
896	Bettmann Newsphotos/BBC Hulton
898	The Bettmann Archive
900	UPI/Bettmann Newsphotos
902	Collection, The Museum of Modern Art, New York

Chapter 32

906–7	UPI/Bettmann Newsphotos
909	UPI/Bettmann Newsphotos
912	AP/Wide World
915	AP/Wide World
917	The Bettmann Archive
918	The Bettmann Archive/BBC Hulton
920	The Bettmann Archive

923	Gernsheim Collection, Humanities Research Center, University of Texas, Austin
924	The Bettmann Archive
925	AP/Wide World
931	Gernsheim Collection, Humanities Research Center, University of Texas, Austin
932	AP/Wide World
933	The Bettmann Archive/BBC Hulton
934	UPI/Bettmann Newsphotos
936	Stefan Lorant

Chapter 33

938	The Bettmann Archive/BBC Hulton
940	AP/Wide World
944	(top) The Bettmann Archive/BBC Hulton; (bottom) AP/Wide World
946	Times Newspaper, Ltd.
947	(top) AP/Wide World; (bottom) UPI/Bettmann Newsphotos
950	(top) AP/Wide World; (bottom) The Bettmann Archive
952	Bettmann Newsphotos
956	Sovfoto
960	AP/Wide World
962	Robert Capa/Magnum
963	UPI/Bettmann Newsphotos
964	The Bettmann Archive
965	UPI/Bettmann Newsphotos
966	U.S. Army Photo
968	The Bettmann Archive
971	The Bettmann Archive

Chapter 34

975	AP/Wide World
976	AP/Wide World
978	AP/Wide World
979	UPI/Bettmann Newsphotos
982	(top) AP/Wide World; (bottom) AP/Wide World
984	(top) AP/Wide World; (bottom) Sergio Larrain/Magnum
985	The Bettmann Archive/BBC Hulton
986	AP/Wide World
989	AP/Wide World
990	(top) David Seymour/Magnum; (bottom) Burt Glinn/Magnum
995	AP/Wide World

998	Donald McCullin/Magnum
999	AP/Wide World
1001	AP/Wide World
1003	AP/Wide World
1005	UPI/Bettmann Newsphotos
1006	Charles Gatewood/Magnum

Chapter 35

1009	AP/Wide World
1012	AP/Wide World
1014	(top) Erich Lessing/Magnum; (bottom) AP/Wide World
1016	John Berry/Magnum
1018	UPI/Bettmann Newsphotos
1022	Eastfoto
1024	Rene Burri/Magnum
1025	(top) Guy LeQuerrec/Magnum; (bottom) AP/Wide World
1027	(top) AP/Wide World; (bottom) AP/Wide World
1031	(top) AP/Wide World; (bottom) AP/Wide World
1032	(top) AP/Wide World; (bottom) Reuters/Bettmann Newsphotos
1033	AP/Wide World
1034	AP/Wide World
1035	Bruno Barbey/Magnum

Chapter 36

1038	NASA
1040	AP/Wide World
1041	AP/Wide World
1042	(top) AP/Wide World; (bottom) Reuters/Bettmann Newsphotos
1045	(top) Bob Nicklesburg/Gamma-Liason; (bottom) J. Pavlosky/Sygma
1046	CPA/Magnum
1051	(top) UPI/Bettmann Newsphotos; (bottom) Abbas/Magnum
1054	AP/Wide World
1055	Reuters/Bettmann Newsphotos
1059	UPI/Bettmann Newsphotos
1061	Susan Meiselas/Magnum
1063	Sagansky-Spooner/Gamma-Liason
1066	NASA
1067	UPI/Bettmann Newsphotos; Henri Cartier-Bresson/Magnum
1070	AP/Wide World
1071	© Michael Heron, Woodfin Camp and Associates

Line Art Credits

Figure 24-3   (p. 683)
From Eric Pawson, *The Early Industrial Revolution.* Copyright ©
1979, Harper and Row.

Figure 25-1   (p. 720)
From Theodore S. Hamerow, *The
Birth of a New Europe.* University
of North Carolina, Chapel Hill,
NC. Copyright © 1983.

Figure 31-1   (p. 885)
From Charles P. Kindleberger,
The World in Depression, 1929–39.
Copyright © University of Cali-
fornia Press, Berkeley, 1973.

Index

A

Abbasid dynasty, 219–23
Abelard, Peter, 291–93, 318; *Sic et Non*, 291–92
Abyssinia, 211; *See also* Ethiopia
Act of Supremacy (1534), 462, 463
Actium, battle of, 93
Adenauer, Konrad, 989
Aeneas, 98–99
Afghanistan, 227, 1042–44
Africa: 221; European colonialism in, 761–65, 823–25; First World War, 848; and slave trade, 553, 753–54; and Third World, 1033–36. *See also* individual countries
Agamemnon, 37
agriculture: early, 5–6, 11, 12; and capitalism, 458; medieval, 271–76, 388–89; three-field system, 273, 275. *See also* individual countries
Agrippa, 93
Agrippina, 100
Ahmose, 22
Aix-la-Chapelle (Aachen), 242, 245; treaty of, 629, 630
Akbar, Mughal emperor, 420–22
Akhenaton, 22
Akkadians, 15
Alaric, king of the Visigoths, 124, 125
Alberti, Leon Battista: *On the Family*, 453
Albuquerque, de, Alfonso, 501
Alcuin, 242–43, 260
Alexander I, tsar of Russia, 666–67, 670, 726, 728
Alexander III, tsar of Russia, 754, 820, 821
Alexander II, tsar of Russia, 793, 794
Alexander the Great, 59–61
Alexander Nevsky, 378
Alexandria, 59, 65, 110, 121; Greek culture in, 60, 61, 62
Alexius, Byzantine emperor, 199–200
Alfred the Great, 251, 260
Algeria, 763–64, 988–89, 1015–17
Allende, Salvador, 1031
Allied Powers: First World War, 849, 856, 861–63, 865
alphabets, 25–26, 364. *See also* writing
Ambrose, St., 127

America. *See* Canada; Latin America; New World, United States
American Indians, 503–5
American Revolution, 640–44
Amorites, 16
Anabaptists, 486–87
Anastasius, Byzantine emperor, 181
Angkor Wat, 167
Anglicanism, 487–89
Anglo-Saxons, 132, 133, 260–62; Britain under, 138–40, 153, 260. *See also* Germanic kingdoms; Germanic tribes
Angola, 1040
Anselm, St., 291
Anthony, St., 148
Anti-Comintern Pact, 929–30
Antioch, 62, 110, 121
Anti-Semitism, 792, 797. *See also* Jews, Holocaust, "Final Solution"
Antony, Mark, 92–93
apartheid, 1014, 1057
Apollonius, 63
Aquinas, St. Thomas, 319–21
Aquino, Corazon, 1028
Arab Empire, 212–25; Abbasid dynasty, 219–23; architecture, 217–18; conquests of, 212–14, 216, 221, 224; Fatimid caliphate, 224–25; government, 213–15, 221, 223–25; language and literature, 216–17; military in, 222, 223–24; Ommayyad dynasty, 215–19; religion in, 211–14, 221, 224, 225, 226, 234; science, 233–34; society, 230–33; trade and commerce, 224, 230; Turks in, 222. *See also* Islam; Moslems
Arabic numerals, 233, 259
Arabs: and Byzantine Empire, 186–87, 188, 190, 192, 193; conflicts with Israel, 991–93, 1053–54, 1055. *See also* Arab Empire
archaeology, 3, 9–10; in China, 168; in Greece, 37; in India, 157; in Mesopotamia, 13
Archimedes, 64
architecture: Arabic, 217–18; baroque, 598; Byzantine, 183–84; Gothic, 296, 316, 406; Greek, 42, 53; Hindu, 167; Mesopotamian, 13; nineteenth century, 805–6; Renaissance, 454–55; Romanesque, 294–95; twentieth cen-

tury, 902. *See also* individual countries
Argentina, 1030, 1050
Arias, Oscar, 1059
Aristarchus, 63
Aristarchus of Samos, 64
Aristophanes, 54
Aristotle, 46, 55–56, 64, 233, 317–19, 322
Arkwright, Richard, 684
Arnulf, king of East Franks, 366
art: baroque, 597–98; eighteenth century, 611; medieval, 316, 406–7; nineteenth century, 805–8; prehistoric, 4; twentieth century, 902, 1070. *See also* architecture; painting; sculpture; individual countries
Aryans, 8, 157–60
Ashoka, Mauryan emperor, 161–62
Asquith, Herbert, 801
Assyrian Empire, 26, 27–29
astronomy: in ancient Middle East, 16; Greek, 64, 590; Indian, 165; medieval, 590–91; Renaissance, 524, 594–95; in Scientific Revolution, 594–96
Athanasius, 148
Athens, ancient, 46, 58–59, 65, 66, 79; arts of, 56, 57; empire of, 52–54; government, 45, 49–50, 57; historians and teachers, 54–56; navy, 51–52, 56, 58, 59; Peloponnesian War, 57–58; Persian wars, 49–52; society, 46–47, 49–50. *See also* Greece, ancient
Atlantic Charter, 949
atomic weapons. *See* nuclear weapons
Attila, king of the Huns, 126
Augustine, St., 120–21, 125, 127, 149, 150, 221; *The City of God*, 121; *Confessions*, 120–21
Augustus (Octavian), Roman emperor, 92–93, 94, 96–99
Aurangzeb, Mughal emperor, 422, 630
Australia, 758
Australopithecus, 4
Austria, 868; *Anschluss*, 930; foreign affairs, 629, 631–33, 731, 732, 735, 736, 738, 746–48; government and politics, 625–26, 638–40, 796–97; Napoleonic Wars, 666, 669, 671; post-First World War, 882; and Prussia, 797; rise of, 577–78. *See also* Austria-Hungary

A
B
C
D
E
F
G
H
I
J